OHIO SOCIAL Studies

The United States: Making a New Nation

HOUGHTON MIFFLIN HARCOURT
School Publishers

OHIO SOCIAL Studies

The United States: Making a New Nation

Series Authors

Dr. Michael J. Berson
Professor
Social Science Education
University of South Florida
Tampa, Florida

Dr. Tyrone C. Howard
Associate Professor
UCLA Graduate School of Education &
   Information Studies
University of California at Los Angeles
Los Angeles, California

Dr. Cinthia Salinas
Assistant Professor
Department of Curriculum and
   Instruction
College of Education
The University of Texas at Austin
Austin, Texas

Series Consultants

Dr. Marsha Alibrandi
Assistant Professor
Social Studies Teacher Education
Department of Curriculum and
   Instruction
Graduate School of Education and
   Allied Professions
Fairfield University
Fairfield, Connecticut

Dr. Patricia G. Avery
Professor
College of Education and Human
   Development
University of Minnesota
Minneapolis/St. Paul, Minnesota

Dr. Linda Bennett
Associate Professor
College of Education
University of Missouri–Columbia
Columbia, Missouri

Dr. Walter C. Fleming
Department Head and Professor
Native American Studies
Montana State University
Bozeman, Montana

Dr. S. G. Grant
Dean
School of Education
Binghamton University
Binghamton, New York

C. C. Herbison
Lecturer
African and African-American Studies
University of Kansas
Lawrence, Kansas

Dr. Eric Johnson
Assistant Professor
Director, Urban Education Program
School of Education
Drake University
Des Moines, Iowa

Dr. Bruce E. Larson
Associate Professor
Social Studies Education
Secondary Education
Woodring College of Education
Western Washington University
Bellingham, Washington

Dr. Merry M. Merryfield
Professor
Social Studies and Global Education
College of Education
The Ohio State University
Columbus, Ohio

Dr. Peter Rees
Associate Professor
Department of Geography
University of Delaware
Wilmington, Delaware

Dr. Phillip J. VanFossen
James F. Ackerman Professor of
   Social Studies Education
Director, James F. Ackerman Center
   for Democratic Citizenship
Associate Director, Purdue Center for
   Economic Education
Purdue University
West Lafayette, Indiana

Dr. Myra Zarnowski
Professor
Elementary and Early Childhood
   Education
Queens College
The City University of New York
Flushing, New York

Content Reviewers

Dr. José António Brandão
Associate Professor
Department of History
Western Michigan University
Kalamazoo, Michigan

Dr. Dean Antonio Cantu
Director of Social Studies Education
Associate Professor
Department of History
Ball State University
Muncie, Indiana

Dr. Daniel P. Donaldson
Associate Professor of Geography
University of Central Oklahoma
Edmond, Oklahoma

Dr. Michael B. Dougan
Professor Emeritus
Department of History
Arkansas State University
Jonesboro, Arkansas

Dr. Lorri Glover
Associate Professor
Department of History
University of Tennessee
Knoxville, Tennessee

Dr. Robert P. Green, Jr.
Alumni Distinguished Professor
School of Education
Clemson University
Clemson, South Carolina

Dr. John Kaminski
Director, Center for the Study of
  the American Constitution
University of Wisconsin
Department of History
Madison, Wisconsin

Dr. Constance M. McGovern
Professor Emeritus
Department of History
Frostburg State University
Frostburg, Maryland

Dr. James P. Ronda
Professor
Department of History
University of Tulsa
Tulsa, Oklahoma

Dr. Silvana Siddali
Associate Professor
Department of History
St. Louis University
St. Louis, Missouri

Dr. Regennia N. Williams
Associate Professor
Department of History
Cleveland State University
Cleveland, Ohio

Dr. Fay A. Yarbrough
Assistant Professor
Department of History
University of Kentucky
Lexington, Kentucky

Classroom Reviewers and Contributors

Amy Cody
Teacher
Winds West Elementary School
Oklahoma City, Oklahoma

Tania Farran
Teacher
Rock Creek Elementary School
O'Fallon, Missouri

David Figurski
Teacher
Wilde Elementary School
Warren, Michigan

Pamela Holland
Teacher
Russell Babb Elementary School
Harrah, Oklahoma

Cheryl Maka
Teacher
St. John Bosco Elementary School
Hammond, Indiana

ISBN-13: 978-0-547-29914-3
ISBN-10: 0-547-29914-1

1 2 3 4 5 6 7 8 9 10 0914 16 15 14 13 12 11 10 09

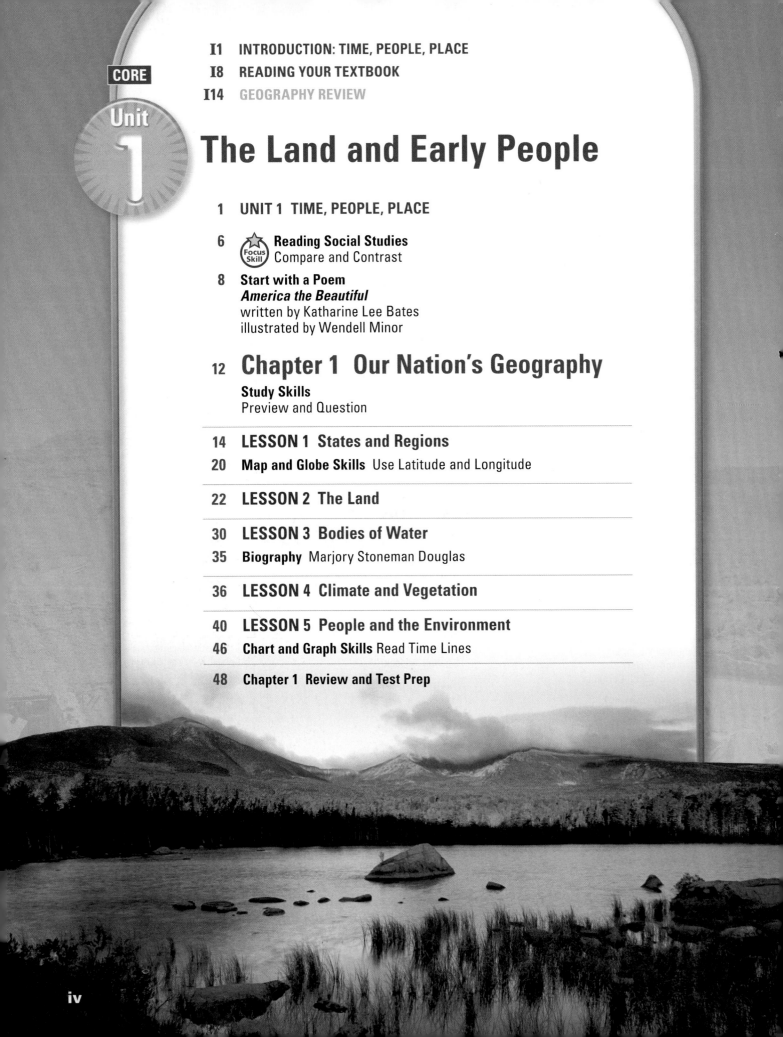

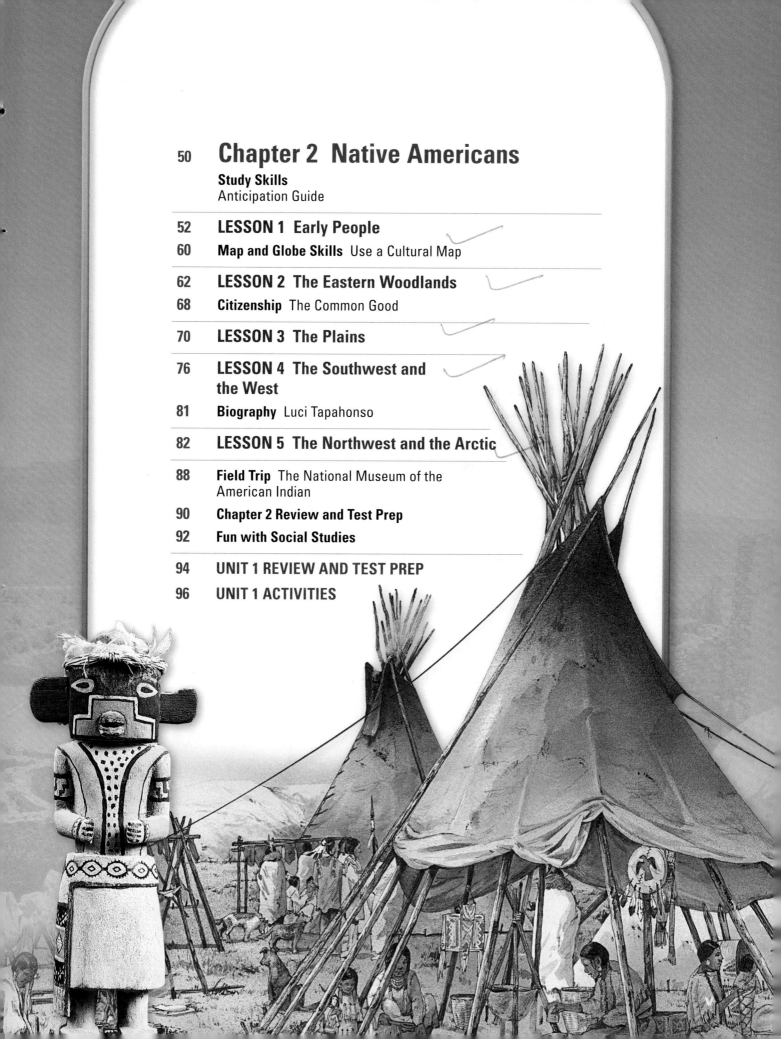

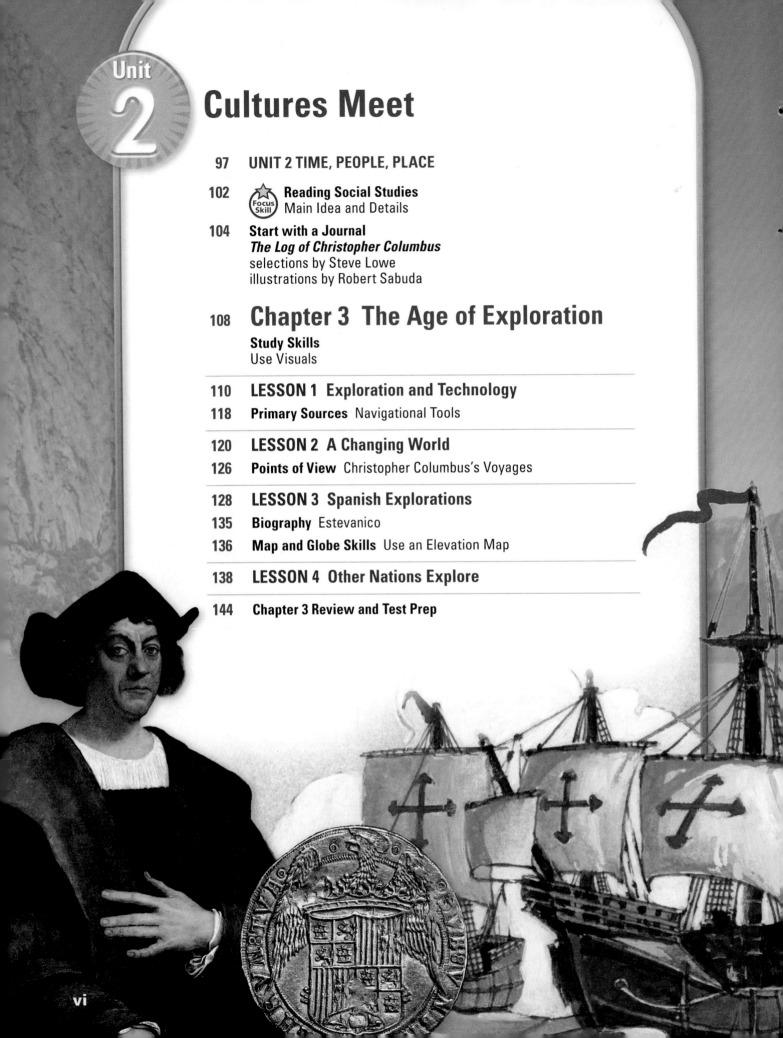

Unit 2

Cultures Meet

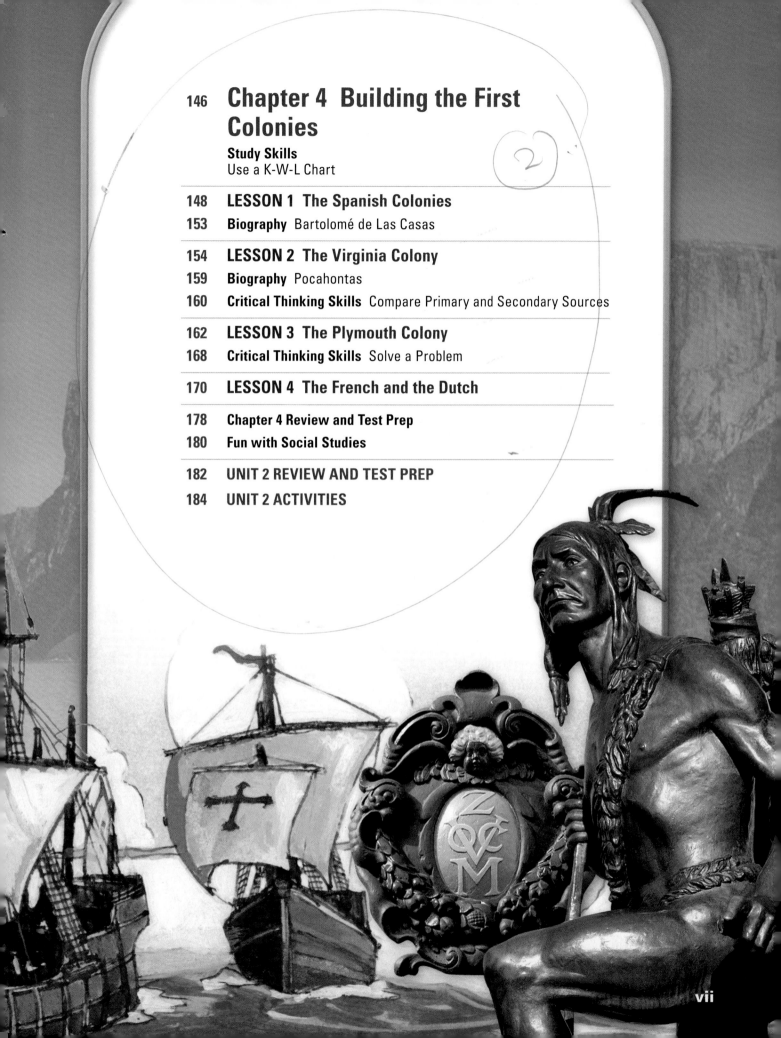

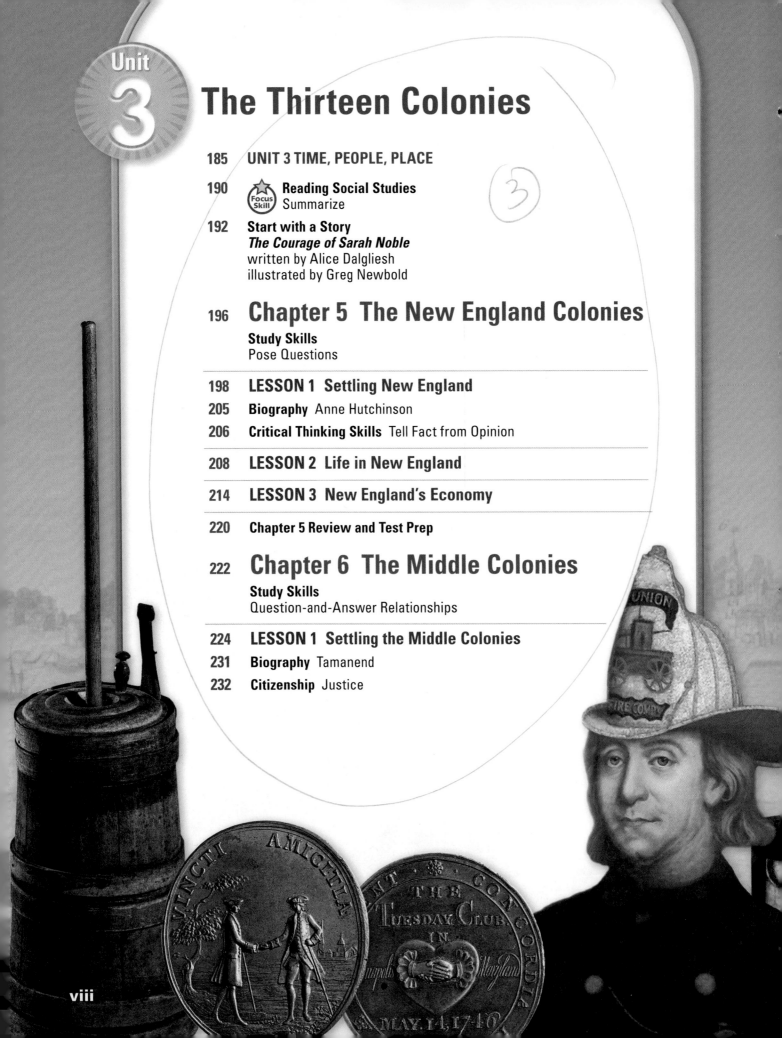

Unit 3

The Thirteen Colonies

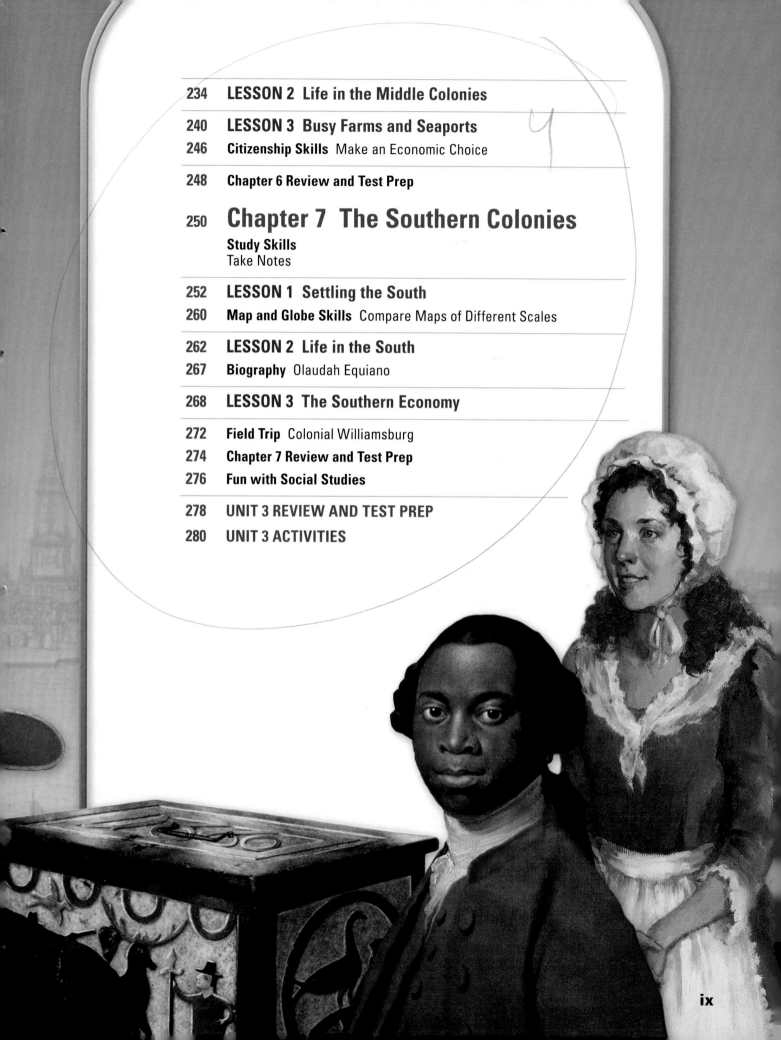

Unit 4

The American Revolution

x

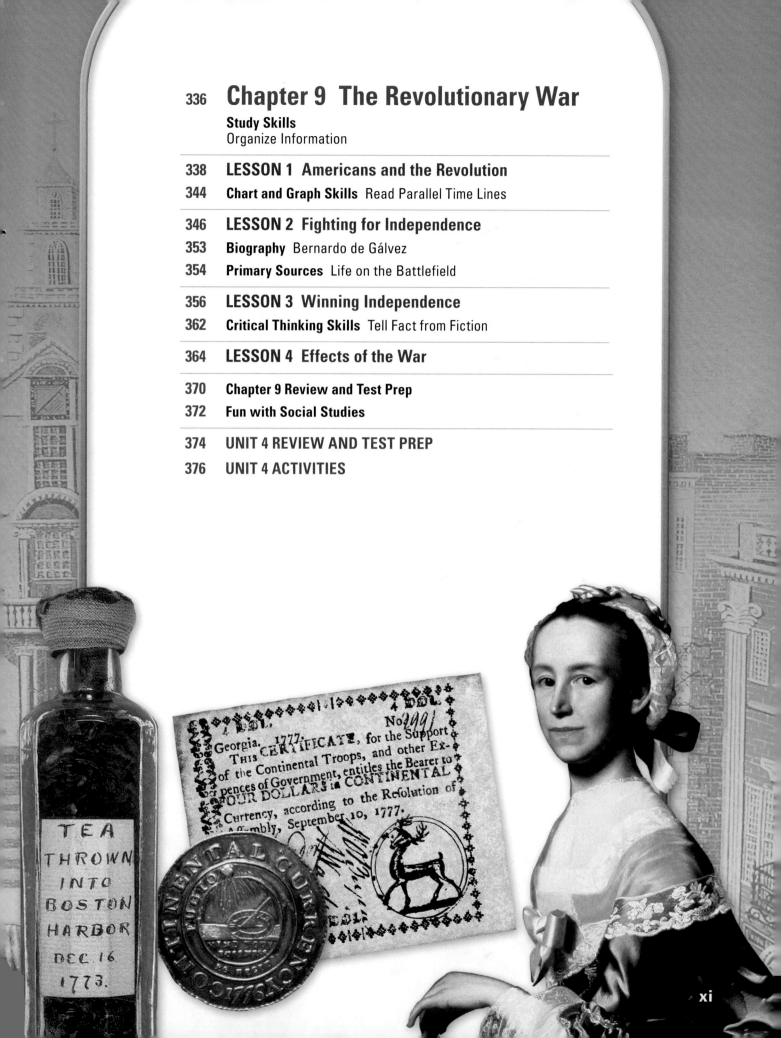

TEA THROWN INTO BOSTON HARBOR DEC. 16. 1773.

Georgia. 1777. THIS CERTIFICATE, for the Support of the Continental Troops, and other Expences of Government, entitles the Bearer to FOUR DOLLARS in CONTINENTAL Currency, according to the Resolution of Assembly, September 10, 1777.

No. 1091

Unit 5

A Growing Nation

Benjamin Banneker

Black Heritage USA 15c

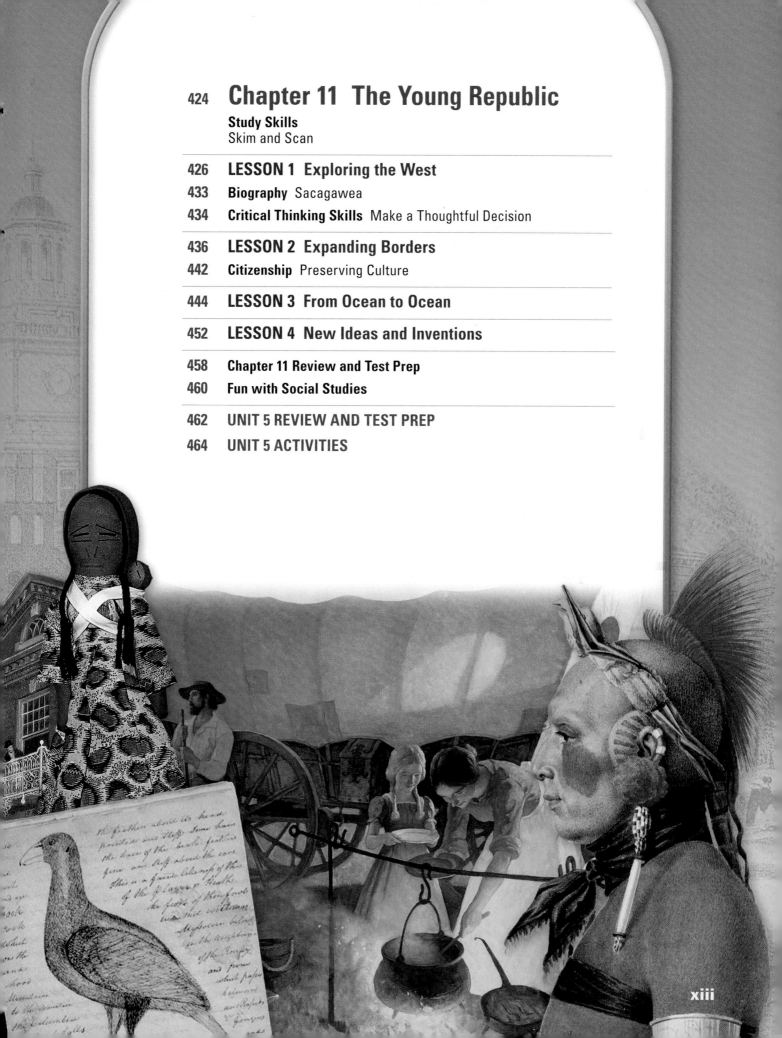

EXTEND

Civil War Times

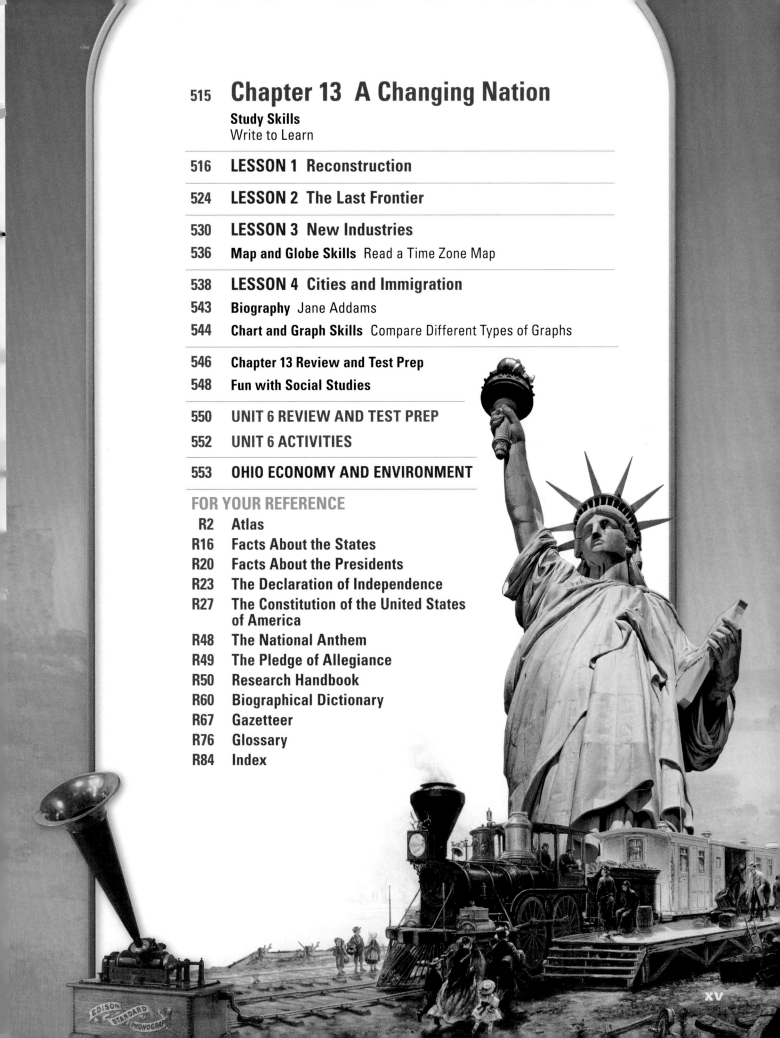

Features

Illustrations

The Story Well Told

"The history of every country begins with the heart of a man or a woman."

Willa Cather, *O Pioneers*

Have you ever wondered how the United States of America came to be and how its past affects you today? This year you will find out. You will read about what it was like to live during the **time** when important events in our nation took place. You will learn about some of the **people** who took part in those events and about the **place** where each event happened. Read now the story of *The United States: Making a New Nation*.

The United States:
MAKING A NEW NATION

The Story of
The United States is about  Time

Studying history helps you see how the present and the past are connected. It helps you see how some things change over time and some things stay the same. As you learn to recognize these links, you will begin to think more like a historian—a person who studies the past.

Historians **research**, or investigate, the time in which events happened. They look for clues in the objects and documents that people left behind. They read diaries, journal entries, letters, newspaper articles, and other writings. They look at photographs, films, and artwork. They also listen to oral histories—stories told aloud by people who lived at the time.

By studying such **evidence**, or proof, historians are better able to understand what the world was like at the time an event took place. It helps them **interpret** the past and explain why events happened as they did.

Historians look closely at how events are connected. One way they do this is by using time lines. A time line shows the **chronology**, or time order, in which events happened. A time line can also suggest how one event may have led to another.

The Story of
The United States is about  People

Historians research the people who lived during different times in the past. They try to imagine what life was like for those people. They try to explain why people did the things they did and how different events affected their feelings and beliefs.

Historians also study people's points of views. A person's **point of view** is how he or she sees things. A point of view is shaped by a person's background and experiences. It can depend on whether a person is old or young, a man or a woman, or rich or poor. People with different points of view may see the same event very differently.

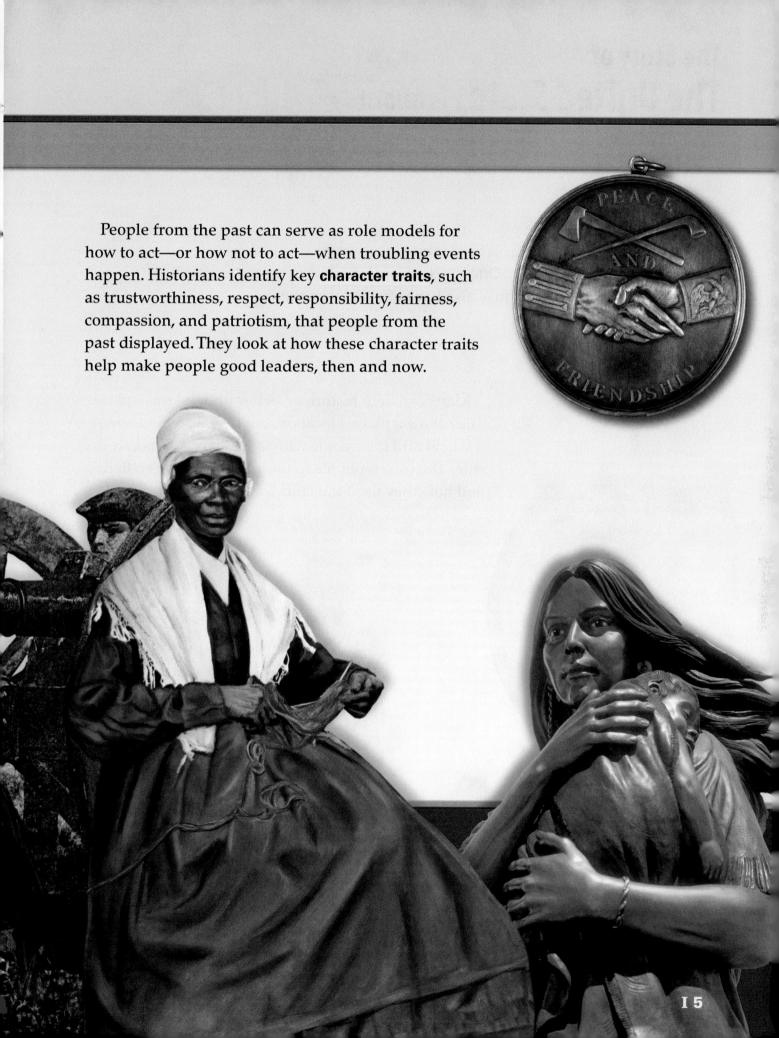

People from the past can serve as role models for how to act—or how not to act—when troubling events happen. Historians identify key **character traits**, such as trustworthiness, respect, responsibility, fairness, compassion, and patriotism, that people from the past displayed. They look at how these character traits help make people good leaders, then and now.

Historians also study the places in which events happened. Every place on Earth has features that set it apart from all other locations. Often those features affected where events occurred. They may also have affected why the events happened as they did.

Maps can help historians better understand a place. They show a place's location, but they also tell about the land and the people who lived there. Maps can show the routes people followed, where they settled, and how they used the land.

Maps, like other kinds of evidence, help historians write the story of the past. They are just one tool that historians use to better understand how time, people, and place are connected.

TRAIL OF TEARS

The New Echota Treaty of 1835 relinquished Cherokee Indian claims to lands east of the Mississippi River. The majority of the Cherokee people considered the treaty fraudulent and refused to leave their homelands in Georgia, Alabama, North Carolina, and Tennessee. 7,000 Federal and State troops were ordered into the Cherokee Nation to forcibly evict the Indians. On May 26, 1838, the roundup began. Over 15,000 Cherokees were forced from their homes at gunpoint and imprisoned in stockades until removal to the west could take place. 2,700 left by boat in June 1838, but, due to many deaths and sickness, removal was suspended until cooler weather. Most of the remaining 13,000 Cherokees left by wagon, horseback, or on foot during October and November, 1838, on an 800 mile route through Tennessee, Kentucky, Illinois, Missouri, and Arkansas. They arrived in what is now eastern Oklahoma during January, February, and March, 1839. Disease, exposure, and starvation may have claimed as many as 4,000 Cherokee lives during the course of capture, imprisonment, and removal. The ordeal has become known as the Trail of Tears.

024-33   GEORGIA HISTORIC MARKER   1988

Reading Your Textbook

GETTING STARTED

Your textbook is divided into six units. Each unit has a title that tells what the unit is about.

The Big Idea tells you the key idea you should understand by the end of the unit.

These questions help you focus on the Big Idea.

LOOKING AT TIME, PEOPLE, AND PLACE

TIME pages tell you when some important events in the unit took place.

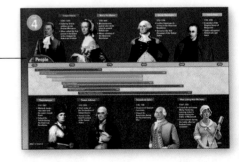

PEOPLE pages introduce you to some of the men and women you will read about in the unit.

PLACE pages show you where some of the events in the unit took place.

READING SOCIAL STUDIES

The Reading Social Studies Focus Skill will help you better understand the events you read about and make connections among them.

This statement explains why this Focus Skill is important.

The Focus Skill is modeled for you, and you will be asked to practice it.

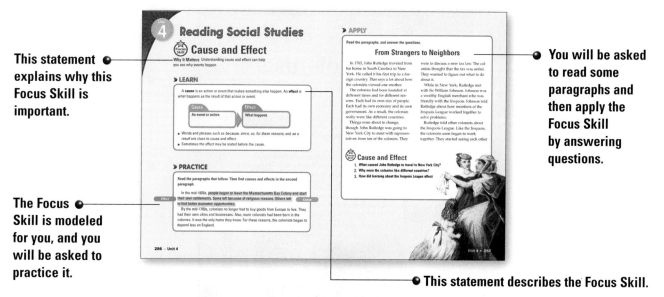

You will be asked to read some paragraphs and then apply the Focus Skill by answering questions.

This statement describes the Focus Skill.

STARTING WITH LITERATURE

Each unit begins with a song, poem, journal, story, or another special reading selection.

Questions let you practice the Reading Focus Skill and relate the literature to your life.

BEGINNING A CHAPTER

Each unit is divided into chapters, and each chapter is divided into lessons.

This Study Skill provides you with a strategy that you can use to remember and organize what you read.

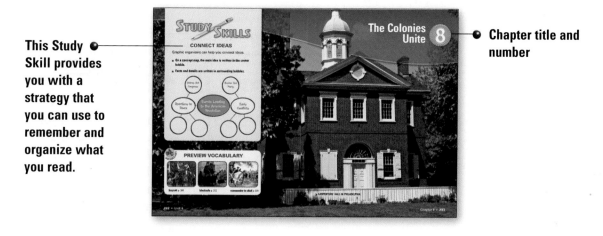

Chapter title and number

READING A LESSON

This question helps you focus on the lesson's main idea.

These are the new vocabulary terms you will learn in the lesson.

Some of the people and places you will read about are listed.

Remember to apply the Reading Social Studies Focus Skill as you read the lesson.

A time line shows when some of the key events in the lesson took place.

Lesson title

You Are There puts you in the time when events in the lesson took place.

Some lessons have special features in which you can read about Children in History or Primary Sources.

Lessons are divided into different sections.

Key people and places are boldfaced.

Vocabulary terms are highlighted in yellow.

Each short section ends with a **READING CHECK** question. It helps you check whether you understand what you have read. Be sure that you can answer this question correctly before you continue reading the lesson.

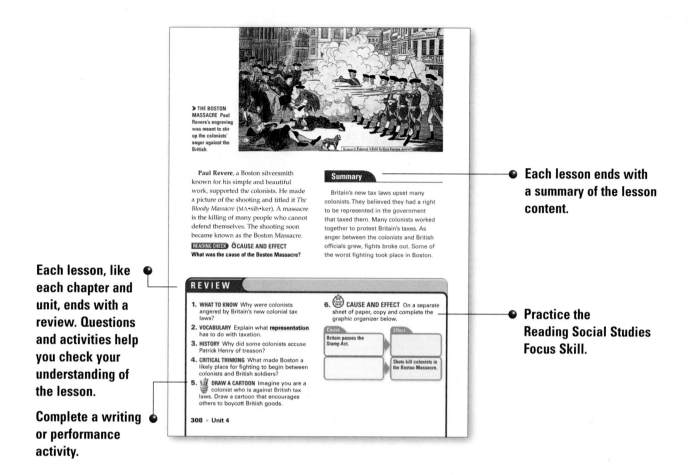

▶ THE BOSTON MASSACRE Paul Revere's engraving was meant to stir up the colonists' anger against the British.

Paul Revere, a Boston silversmith known for his simple and beautiful work, supported the colonists. He made a picture of the shooting and titled it *The Bloody Massacre* (MA•sih•ker). A massacre is the killing of many people who cannot defend themselves. The shooting soon became known as the Boston Massacre.

READING CHECK ŏ̃ **CAUSE AND EFFECT**
What was the cause of the Boston Massacre?

Summary

Britain's new tax laws upset many colonists. They believed they had a right to be represented in the government that taxed them. Many colonists worked together to protest Britain's taxes. As anger between the colonists and British officials grew, fights broke out. Some of the worst fighting took place in Boston.

● Each lesson ends with a summary of the lesson content.

Each lesson, like each chapter and unit, ends with a review. Questions and activities help you check your understanding of the lesson.

Complete a writing or performance activity.

REVIEW

1. **WHAT TO KNOW** Why were colonists angered by Britain's new colonial tax laws?

2. **VOCABULARY** Explain what **representation** has to do with taxation.

3. **HISTORY** Why did some colonists accuse Patrick Henry of treason?

4. **CRITICAL THINKING** What made Boston a likely place for fighting to begin between colonists and British soldiers?

5. 🎨 **DRAW A CARTOON** Imagine you are a colonist who is against British tax laws. Draw a cartoon that encourages others to boycott British goods.

6. **CAUSE AND EFFECT** On a separate sheet of paper, copy and complete the graphic organizer below.

Cause		Effect
Britain passes the Stamp Act.	→	
	→	Shots kill colonists in the Boston Massacre.

● Practice the Reading Social Studies Focus Skill.

308 ▪ Unit 4

LEARNING SOCIAL STUDIES SKILLS

Your textbook has lessons that help you build your Citizenship Skills, Map and Globe Skills, Chart and Graph Skills, and Critical Thinking Skills.

This statement tells you why it is important to learn this skill.

● You will be able to practice and apply the skill.

SPECIAL FEATURES

Biographies give in-depth background about some of the people who lived at the time.

Each biography focuses on a trait that the person showed.

A time line shows when the person was born and died and some key events in his or her life.

The Citizenship feature demonstrates how people today, like people in the past, can be active citizens.

The Field Trip feature lets you "visit" many interesting places.

The Points of View feature lets you examine different points of view people had on certain issues.

The Primary Sources feature shows ways to learn about different kinds of objects and documents.

The Fun with Social Studies feature gives you an interesting way to review the unit.

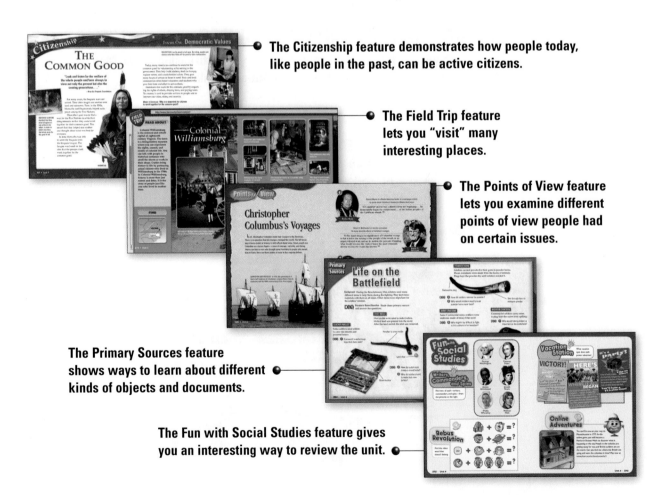

FOR YOUR REFERENCE

At the back of your textbook, you will find different reference tools. You can use these tools to look up words. You can also find information about people, places, and other topics.

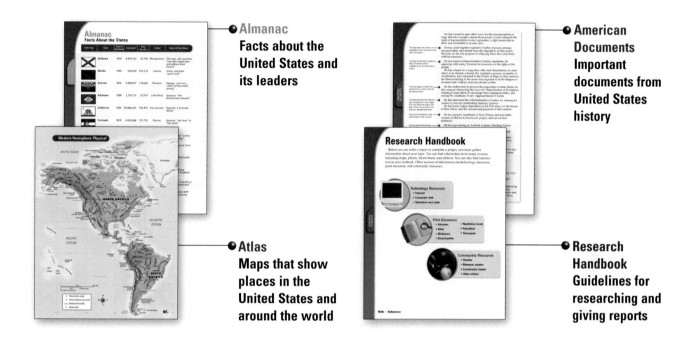

● **Almanac**
Facts about the United States and its leaders

● **Atlas**
Maps that show places in the United States and around the world

● **American Documents**
Important documents from United States history

● **Research Handbook**
Guidelines for researching and giving reports

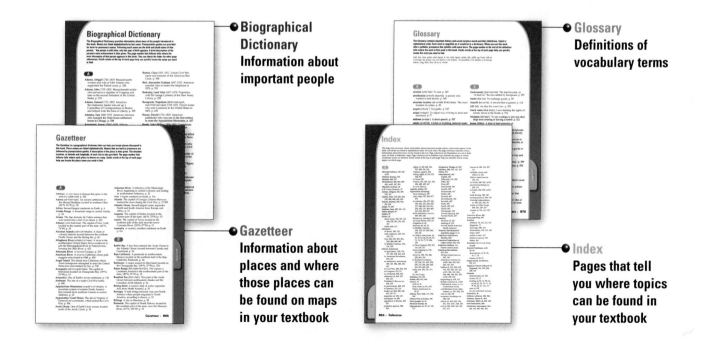

● **Biographical Dictionary**
Information about important people

● **Gazetteer**
Information about places and where those places can be found on maps in your textbook

● **Glossary**
Definitions of vocabulary terms

● **Index**
Pages that tell you where topics can be found in your textbook

The Five Themes of Geography

Learning about places is an important part of history and geography. Geography is the study of Earth's surface and the way people use it. When geographers study Earth and its geography, they often think about five main themes, or topics. Keeping these themes in mind as you read will help you think like a geographer.

GEOGRAPHY

Location

Everything on Earth has its own **location**—the place where it can be found.

Place

Every place has physical and human features that make it different from all other places. **Physical features** are formed by nature. **Human features** are created by people.

Human-Environment Interactions

People and their surroundings interact, or affect each other. People's activities may **modify**, or change, the environment. The environment may affect people, requiring them to **adapt**, or adjust, to their surroundings.

THEMES

Movement

Every day, people in different states and countries exchange products and ideas.

Regions

Areas of Earth with main features that make them different from other areas are called regions. A **region** can be described by its physical features or its human features.

Looking at Earth

A distant view from space shows Earth's round shape. You probably have a globe in your classroom. Like Earth, a globe has the shape of a sphere, or ball. It is a model of Earth that shows Earth's major bodies of water and its seven **continents**, or largest land masses. Earth's continents, from largest to smallest, are Asia, Africa, North America, South America, Antarctica, Europe, and Australia.

Because of its shape, you can see only one-half of Earth at a time when you look at a globe. Halfway between the North Pole and the South Pole on a globe is a line called the **equator**. The equator divides Earth into two equal halves, or

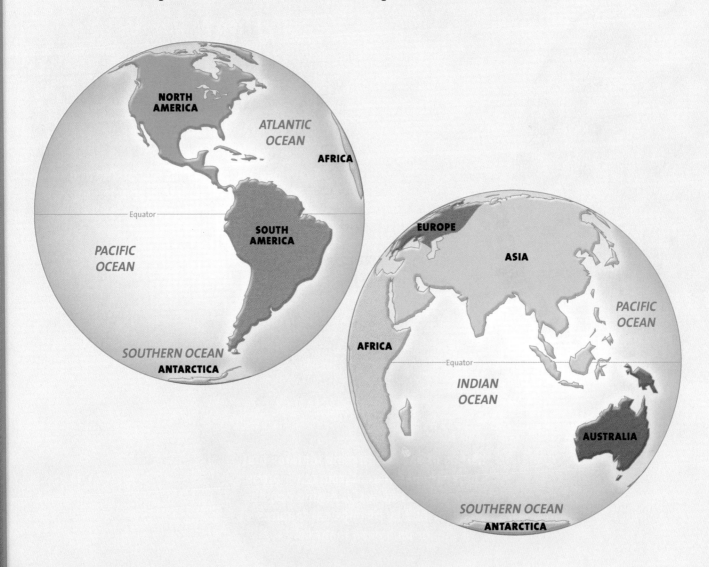

hemispheres. The Northern Hemisphere is north of the equator, and the Southern Hemisphere is south of it. Another line, the **prime meridian**, runs north and south. It is often used to divide Earth into the Western Hemisphere and the Eastern Hemisphere.

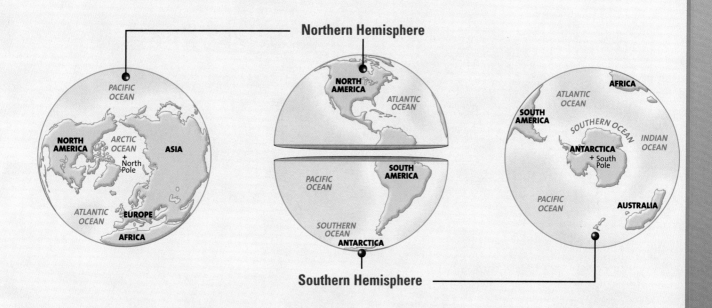

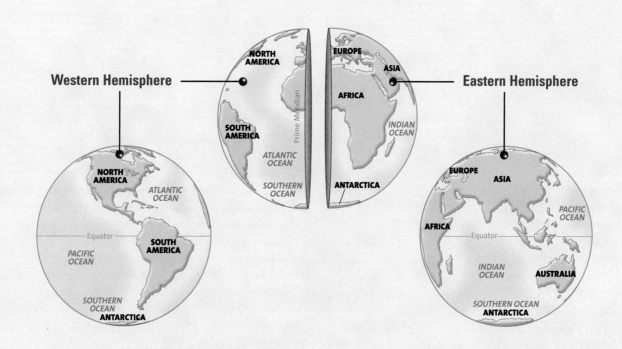

GEOGRAPHY REVIEW

Geography Terms

1. **basin** bowl-shaped area of land surrounded by higher land
2. **bay** inlet of the sea or of some other body of water, usually smaller than a gulf
3. **canyon** deep, narrow valley with steep sides
4. **cape** point of land that extends into water
5. **channel** deepest part of a body of water
6. **coastal plain** area of flat land along a sea or ocean
7. **delta** triangle-shaped area of land at the mouth of a river

8. **fall line** area along which rivers form waterfalls or rapids as the rivers drop to lower land
9. **glacier** large ice mass that moves slowly down a mountain or across land
10. **gulf** part of a sea or ocean extending into the land, usually larger than a bay
11. **inlet** any area of water extending into the land from a larger body of water
12. **isthmus** narrow strip of land connecting two larger areas of land

13 **marsh** lowland with moist soil and tall grasses

14 **mesa** flat-topped mountain with steep sides

15 **mountain pass** gap between mountains

16 **mountain range** chain of mountains

17 **mouth of river** place where a river empties into another body of water

18 **peninsula** land that is almost completely surrounded by water

19 **plain** area of flat or gently rolling low land

20 **plateau** area of high, mostly flat land

21 **savanna** area of grassland and scattered trees

22 **sea level** level of the surface of an ocean or a sea

23 **source of river** place where a river begins

24 **strait** narrow channel of water connecting two larger bodies of water

25 **swamp** area of low, wet land with trees

26 **tributary** stream or river that flows into a larger stream or river

27 **volcano** opening in the earth, often raised, through which lava, rock, ashes, and gases are forced out

Reading Maps

Maps give important information about the world around you. A map is a drawing that shows all or part of Earth on a flat surface. To help you read maps, mapmakers add certain features to most of their maps. These features often include a title, a map key, a compass rose, a locator, and a map scale.

Sometimes mapmakers need to show certain places on a map in greater detail, or they must show places that are located beyond the area shown on the map. Find Alaska and Hawaii on

A **map title** tells the subject of the map. It may also identify the kind of map.
- A **political map** shows cities, states, and countries.
- A **physical map** shows kinds of land and bodies of water.
- A **historical map** shows parts of the world as they were in the past.

A **map key**, or legend, explains the symbols used on a map. Symbols may be colors, patterns, lines, or other special marks.

An **inset map** is a smaller map within a larger one.

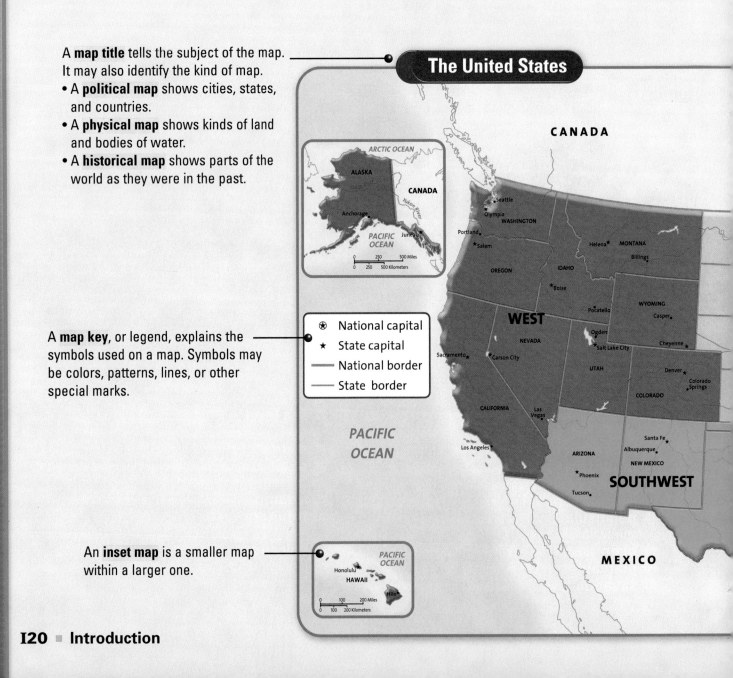

The United States

⊛ National capital
★ State capital
— National border
— State border

the map of the United States on pages R8–R9. The map there shows the location of those two states in relation to the location of the rest of the country.

Now find Alaska and Hawaii on the map below. To show this much detail for these states as well as the rest of the country, the map would have to be much larger. Instead, here Alaska and Hawaii are each shown in a separate inset map, or a smaller map within a larger map.

A **locator** is a small map or globe that shows where the place on the main map is located within a larger area.

A **map scale**, or distance scale, compares a distance on the map to a distance on Earth. It helps you find the real distance between places on a map.

A **compass rose**, or direction marker, shows directions.
- The **cardinal directions** are north, south, east, and west.
- The **intermediate directions**, or directions between the cardinal directions, are northeast, northwest, southeast, and southwest.

GEOGRAPHY REVIEW

Finding Locations

To help people find places on maps, mapmakers sometimes add lines that cross each other. These lines form a pattern of squares called a **grid system**.

Look at the map of the United States below. Around the grid are letters and numbers. The columns, which run up and down, have numbers. The rows, which run from left to right, have letters.

Each square on the map can be identified by its letter and number. For example, the top row of squares on the map includes square A-1, square A-2, square A-3, and so on.

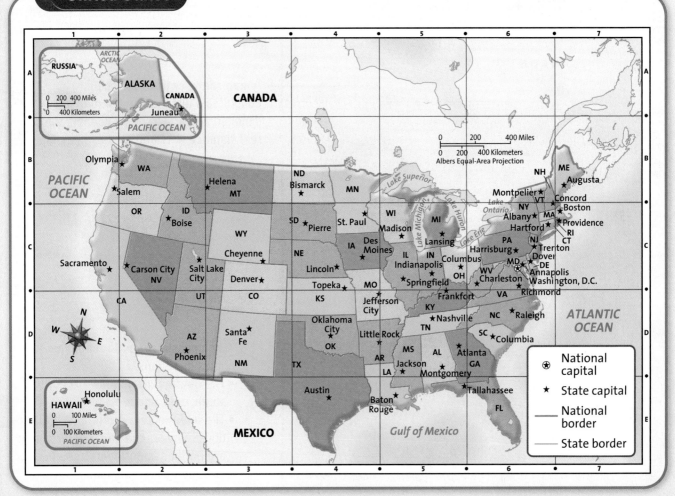

United States

The Land and Early People

CORE

Unit 1

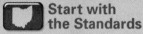
Start with the Standards

OHIO SOCIAL STUDIES CONTENT STANDARDS

History 5.1, 5.2

People in Societies 5.1A, 5.1B, 5.1C, 5.1D, 5.1E, 5.1F, 5.2, 5.4

Geography 5.1, 5.2A, 5.2B, 5.2C, 5.2D, 5.2E, 5.3, 5.4A, 5.4B, 5.4C, 5.5, 5.6A, 5.6B, 5.6C, 5.6D, 5.6E, 5.7B, 5.8, 5.9C, 5.9D

Economics 5.1, 5.2, 5.3, 5.4

Social Studies Skills 5.1A, 5.1B, 5.2, 5.3, 5.8

The Big Idea

Geography

People interact with their environment and are affected by it.

What to Know

✓ How do the geography and the climate of the United States differ from region to region?

✓ What was the impact of early North American civilizations?

✓ How did geography and climate affect Native American groups?

Unit 1 ▪ 1A

NATIVE AMERICAN CULTURES IN OHIO

OHIO CONNECTION

DID YOU KNOW?

The name of Cuyahoga County comes from a Native American word that means "crooked river."

Many Native American tribes in Ohio lived near rivers, such as the Wyandot tribe who settled along the Sandusky and Huron Rivers. They used rivers for fresh water and fishing. They also grew crops and hunted animals, such as beavers, deer, and foxes, for clothing and food.

Even though each tribe had its own culture, the Native Americans in Ohio shared many traits. Many spoke similar languages known as Algonquian. The Algonquian tribes that came to Ohio included the Delaware, Ottawa, Shawnee, and Miami. These tribes, as well as others, decorated pottery with shapes and designs from their surroundings. Women wove baskets and made shoes and clothing. They decorated their clothing with beads, paint, and feathers.

Ceremonies were an important part of Native American culture. Many pieces of Native American art were related to ceremonies. For example, men of the Iroquois tribe made masks of wood to wear during ceremonies. Along with art, singing and dancing were usually part of ceremonies. The Shawnee used dances to welcome the harvest each fall.

Iroquois ceremonial water drum

Native American Groups in Ohio

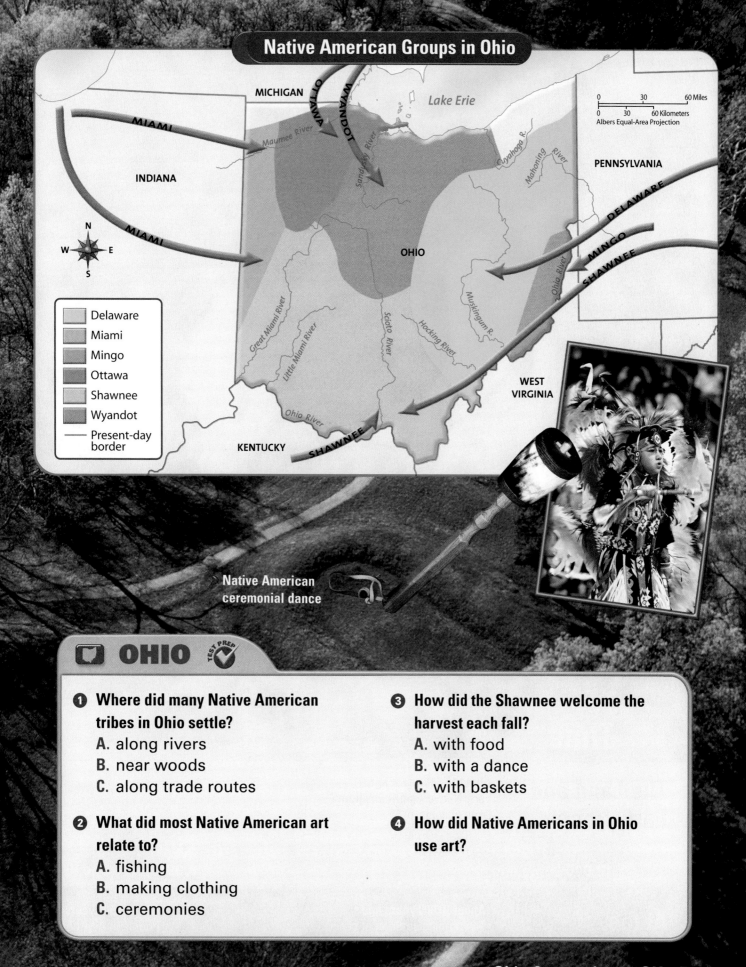

MICHIGAN

OTTAWA

WYANDOT

Lake Erie

MIAMI

INDIANA

Maumee River

Sandusky River

Cuyahoga R.

Mahoning River

PENNSYLVANIA

MIAMI

OHIO

DELAWARE

MINGO

SHAWNEE

Muskingum R.

Ohio River

N
W   E
S

0   30   60 Miles
0   30   60 Kilometers
Albers Equal-Area Projection

Great Miami River

Little Miami River

Scioto River

Hocking River

WEST VIRGINIA

Delaware
Miami
Mingo
Ottawa
Shawnee
Wyandot
Present-day border

Ohio River

KENTUCKY

SHAWNEE

Native American ceremonial dance

OHIO TEST PREP

1 Where did many Native American tribes in Ohio settle?
A. along rivers
B. near woods
C. along trade routes

2 What did most Native American art relate to?
A. fishing
B. making clothing
C. ceremonies

3 How did the Shawnee welcome the harvest each fall?
A. with food
B. with a dance
C. with baskets

4 How did Native Americans in Ohio use art?

Unit

1

Time

The Land and Early People

About 12,000 years ago
Early Native Americans hunt large animals, p. 55

12,000 years ago

8,000 years ago

At the Same Time

 About 10,000 years ago
The farming settlement of Jericho is founded in southwestern Asia.

 About 8,500 years ago
People in Asia begin making pottery

The Land and Early People

About 5,000 years ago
Early Native Americans
begin farming, p. 55

About 1,000 years ago
The Navajo move to the
desert Southwest, p. 77

About 800 years ago
More than 30,000
people live in Cahokia,
p. 58

4,000 years ago

PRESENT

About 4,500 years ago
People in Asia begin
training horses

A Navajo Family

People

People of the Southwest and the West

- Lived in a vast area between the Rocky Mountains and the Pacific Ocean
- Included diverse groups of both hunters and farmers
- Used a variety of natural resources to build their homes

Eastern Woodlands People

- Lived mostly in areas east of the Mississippi River in what is now the United States
- Used wood to make canoes, tools, and shelters
- Main crops were corn, beans, and squash

An Iroquois Family

A Makah Hunter

A Cheyenne Couple

Northwest Coast People

- Lived in what is now Canada, Washington, and Oregon
- Skilled whalers and fishers
- Traveled long distances to trade

Plains People

- Lived in a wide area from what is now Texas to Canada
- Main food source was buffalo

Arctic and Sub-Arctic People

- Lived in an area that covered much of what is now Canada and Alaska
- Used kayaks for fishing
- Skilled seal hunters

An Arctic Family

ARCTIC
OCEAN

INUIT

Brooks Range

Yukon River

INUIT

*Bering
Sea*

INUIT

*Great Bear
Lake*

INUIT

Mt. McKinley
20,320 ft.
(6,194 m)

Alaska △

ATHAPASCAN

HAN

Range

ALEUT

*Gulf of
Alaska*

KASKA

TLINGIT

COAST MOUNTAINS

R O C K Y

G R E A T

HAIDA

**BELLA
COOLA**

KWAKIUTL

KOOTENAI

BLACKFOOT

NOOTKA

M O U N T A I N S

MAKAH

CHINOOK

RANGE

CASCADE

YAKAMA

**NEZ
PERCÉ**

CROW

PACIFIC
OCEAN

HOPI Name of Native
American tribe

△ Highest point

▼ Lowest point

*Great Salt
Lake*

PAIUTE

SHOSHONE

POMO

COAST

SIERRA NEVADA

**GREAT
BASIN**

UTE

PAIUTE

0   500   1,000 Miles

0   500   1,000 Kilometers
Modified Azimuthal Equal-Area Projection

YOKUTS

RANGES

*Grand
Canyon*

Colorado River

HOPI

CHUMASH

▼

*Death Valley
282 ft. (86m)
below sea level*

*Mojave
Desert*

NAVAJO

ZUNI

*Sonoran
Desert*

SIERRA MADRE OCCIDENTAL

Baja California

COCHIMI

*Gulf
of
California*

YAQUI

HUICHOL

N
W   E
S

Pueblo Bonito, in what is
now New Mexico

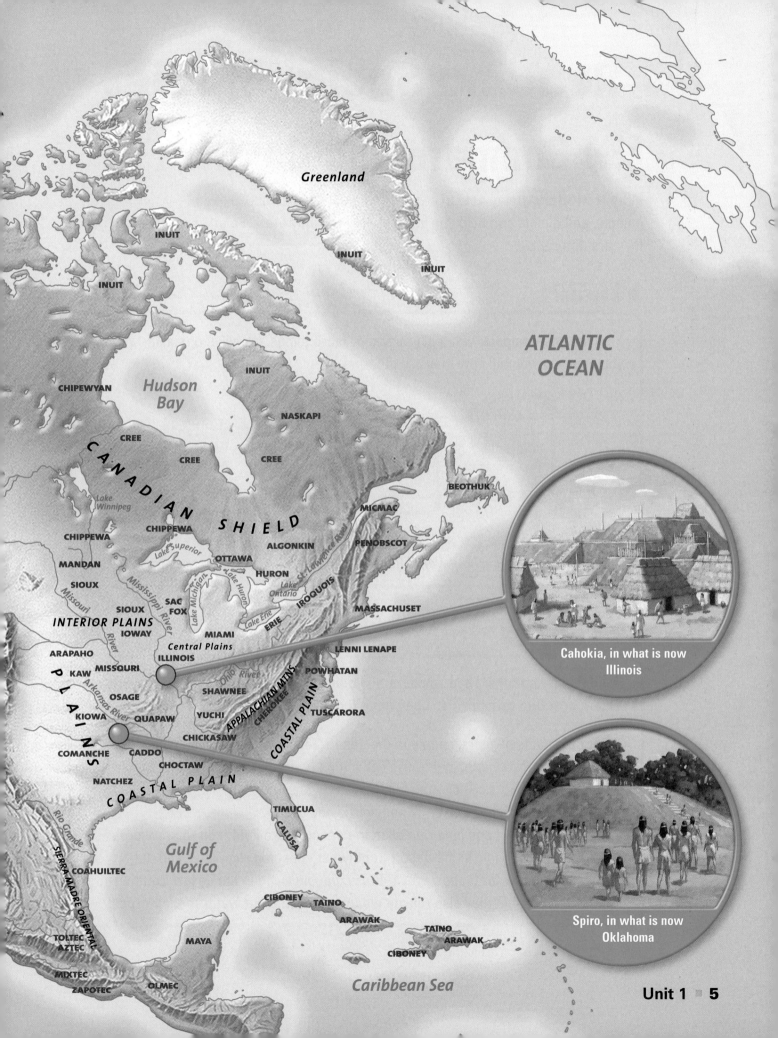

Greenland

INUIT
INUIT
INUIT

ATLANTIC
OCEAN

INUIT

INUIT

CHIPEWYAN

Hudson
Bay

INUIT

NASKAPI

CREE
CREE
CREE

BEOTHUK

Lake Winnipeg

C A N A D I A N   S H I E L D

MICMAC

CHIPPEWA
CHIPPEWA

Lake Superior

ALGONKIN

PENOBSCOT

MANDAN

Mississippi River

OTTAWA

Lake Michigan

HURON

Lake Huron

Lake Ontario

St. Lawrence River

SIOUX

SAC
FOX

IROQUOIS

Lake Erie

ERIE

MASSACHUSET

Missouri River

INTERIOR PLAINS

IOWAY

MIAMI

Central Plains

ILLINOIS

LENNI LENAPE

ARAPAHO

Ohio River

POWHATAN

KAW

MISSOURI

Arkansas River

SHAWNEE

APPALACHIAN MTNS.

OSAGE

YUCHI

CHEROKEE

TUSCARORA

KIOWA

QUAPAW

COASTAL PLAIN

CHICKASAW

P L A I N S

COMANCHE

CADDO

CHOCTAW

NATCHEZ

COASTAL PLAIN

TIMUCUA

Rio Grande

CALUSA

SIERRA MADRE ORIENTAL

COAHUILTEC

Gulf of
Mexico

CIBONEY
TAINO

TOLTEC
AZTEC

ARAWAK

TAINO

MAYA

ARAWAK

MIXTEC

CIBONEY

ZAPOTEC

OLMEC

Caribbean Sea

Cahokia, in what is now
Illinois

Spiro, in what is now
Oklahoma

Reading Social Studies

⭐ Focus Skill Compare and Contrast

Why It Matters Being able to compare and contrast people, places, objects, and events can help you understand how they are alike and how they are different.

❯ LEARN

When you **compare**, you tell how two or more things are alike, or similar. When you **contrast**, you tell how they are different.

- *Like, both, all, also, too, similar,* and *same* are words that compare.
- *But, instead, unlike, however, different,* and *differ* are words that contrast.

❯ PRACTICE

Read the paragraphs. Then compare and contrast early Americans and modern Americans. One example has been done for you.

For thousands of years, people in the desert Southwest have lived with extreme heat. Early people built homes with thick adobe walls to help stay cool. Many modern homes in the region are built the same way. However, people today have air-conditioning, while early people did not.

Similar / Different

The extreme heat and little rainfall in the desert make it difficult to grow crops there. The early people in the desert Southwest collected rainwater and dug ditches to bring water to their crops. Today, people living in the desert Southwest still use ditches, but they also rely on electric pumps to get water to their crops.

► APPLY

Read the paragraphs, and answer the questions.

Living History

It is amazing to think that Americans today have some things in common with early Americans. Much has changed in the thousands of years since people first settled the Americas. Yet in some ways, history lives on.

Long ago, beans and corn were important foods in many parts of the Americas. They are important foods today, too. In fact, they have been on dinner tables for thousands of years. Many early Americans also enjoyed popcorn, just as many people do today.

Many early Americans used canoes and kayaks to travel down rivers and across lakes. In fact, *canoe* and *kayak* both come from Native American words. Many people still use these same boats. Today, however, most people use them for enjoyment, not for transportation.

Some early American groups built large cities with hundreds of buildings. Before building a city, they planned ahead and set aside places for shops, homes, and religious buildings. Today, city planners organize cities and neighborhoods in much the same way.

 Compare and Contrast

1. **How are foods today similar to the foods of early Americans?**
2. **How are the ways in which early Americans used kayaks and canoes different from the ways people use them today?**
3. **How is the way Americans today plan cities similar to the way early Americans planned cities?**

► An early sculpture from what is now southern Mexico

AMERICA

the Beautiful

WRITTEN BY KATHARINE LEE BATES
ILLUSTRATED BY WENDELL MINOR

In 1893, Katharine Lee Bates and some of her fellow teachers decided to climb Pikes Peak, in Colorado. They hired a wagon to help them reach the top of the 14,000-foot-high mountain. When they neared the top, they left the wagon and traveled the rest of the way on mules. The view Bates saw from the top of the mountain inspired her to write a poem about the country. In 1904, music written by Samuel Ward was paired with Bates's poem. The song is still an American favorite.

O beautiful for spacious skies,
For amber waves of grain,
For purple mountain majesties
Above the fruited plain!
America! America!
God shed his grace on thee
And crown thy good with brotherhood
From sea to shining sea!

O beautiful for pilgrim feet
Whose stern, impassioned stress
A thoroughfare for freedom beat
Across the wilderness!
America! America!
God mend thine every flaw,
Confirm thy soul in self-control,
Thy liberty in law!

impassioned feeling strongly

thoroughfare road

O beautiful for heroes proved
In liberating <u>strife</u>,
Who more than self the country loved,
And mercy more than life!
America! America!
May God thy gold <u>refine</u>
Till all success be nobleness
And every gain divine!

O beautiful for patriot dream
That sees beyond the years
Thine alabaster cities gleam
Undimmed by human tears!
America! America!
God shed His grace on thee
And crown thy good with brotherhood
From sea to shining sea!

strife struggle

refine improve

Response Corner

1 (Focus Skill) **Compare and Contrast** What are the different types of geography described in the poem?

2 **Make It Relevant** How would you describe the landscape where you live?

STUDY SKILLS

PREVIEW AND QUESTION

Previewing a lesson to identify main ideas, and asking yourself questions about those ideas, can help you read to find important information.

- **To preview a lesson, read the lesson title and the section titles. Look at the pictures, and read their captions. Try to get an idea of the main topic and think of questions you have.**

- **Read to find the answers to your questions. Then recite, or say, the answers aloud. Finally, review what you have read.**

Our Nation's Geography

Preview	Questions	Read	Recite	Review
Lesson 1 The United States can be divided into regions. Canada and Mexico are our neighbors.	What are the regions of the United States?	✓	✓	✓
Lesson 2				

PREVIEW VOCABULARY

landform region p. 23   **environment** p. 26   **gulf** p. 31

Our Nation's Geography

CHAPTER

1

> GRAND TETON NATIONAL PARK,
WYOMING

Lesson 1

States and Regions

WHAT TO KNOW
How are the 50 states alike, and how are they different?

VOCABULARY
contiguous p. 15
region p. 15
relative location p. 15
continent p. 18
population p. 18

PLACES
United States
Canada
Mexico

COMPARE AND CONTRAST

YOU ARE THERE

You are in the library in the town of Derby Line, Vermont. It looks like any other town library, but it is not. This library is located in two different countries, the **United States** and **Canada**.

If you stand in one part of the library, you are in the state of Vermont. If you walk to another part of the library, you are in the province of Quebec. You enter the library in the United States, but you check out books in Canada!

▶ **DERBY LINE LIBRARY** The black line on the library floor shows where the border between the United States and Canada lies.

The United States

MAP SKILL PLACE What is the capital of your state?

A Nation of 50 States

The United States is a nation made up of 50 states. Forty-eight of them share at least one border with another state. They are **contiguous** (kuhn•TIH•gyuh•wuhs), or next to each other.

Two states, Alaska and Hawaii, are separated from the other states. Alaska, our northernmost state, shares a border with the country of Canada. Hawaii is a group of islands in the Pacific Ocean. It is more than 2,000 miles from the 48 contiguous states.

Regions of the United States

To make it easier to talk about different areas of the country, people often group the 50 states into five large regions.

A **region** is an area in which many features are similar.

The five regions of the United States are the West, the Southwest, the Midwest, the Southeast, and the Northeast. Each region is based on its relative location in the United States. The **relative location** of a place is where it is compared to other places. For example, the Midwest region is between the Northeast and the West.

The states within each region are alike in many ways. The states often have similar kinds of land, and the people who live there often earn their living in similar ways. The states in each region may also share a history and culture.

READING CHECK ⊘ COMPARE AND CONTRAST
How are the states in a region similar?

PACIFIC OCEAN

AK

WA

Bighorn Sheep

OR

ID

MT

Buffalo

NV

CA

Condor

Black Bear

WY

SD

UT

Corn

NE

AZ

CO

KS

Antelope

NM

OK

Cactus

Rattlesnake

TX

Angus Cow

MEXICO

HI

WEST

- Population: 60,423,446
- Area: 1,628,762 square miles
- Climate: Many different climate regions

REGIONS
OF THE UNITED STATES

ILLUSTRATION What are the five regions of the United States? Which region is the largest in area?

SOUTHWEST

- Population: 34,275,528
- Area: 574,103 square miles
- Climate: Eastern half can be hot and rainy in the summer, western half can be hot and dry

MIDWEST
- Population: 65,971,974
- Area: 821,872 square miles
- Climate: Hot summer, cold winter

NORTHEAST
- Population: 55,485,419
- Area: 183,206 square miles
- Climate: Hot summer, cold winter

SOUTHEAST
- Population: 79,703,516
- Area: 578,873 square miles
- Climate: Hot rainy summer, mild winter

ND

CANADA

MN

Lake Superior

WI

Holstein Cow

IA

Pike

Lake Huron

Lake
Michigan

MI

Lake Ontario

VT

ME

IL

Hog

NY

NH

IN

OH

PA

MA

Harbor
Seal

MO

WV

CT

RI

AR

KY

VA

NJ

DE

Lobster

Magnolia Blossom

TN

MD

LA

MS

AL

Deer

NC

GA

SC

Alligator

FL

GULF OF
MEXICO

Flamingo

Dolphin

ATLANTIC
OCEAN

▶ **OTTAWA** Many government buildings are located in Ottawa, Canada's capital.

A Country in North America

If someone asked you to describe the location of the United States, what would you say? You could say that the United States is in North America. North America is one of Earth's seven largest landmasses, or **continents**. From largest to smallest, the continents are Asia, Africa, North America, South America, Antarctica, Europe, and Australia.

The United States is also one of the largest nations in North America. There are two ways to measure the size of a nation. One is to measure its land area. The other is to measure its **population**, or number of people. In land area, Canada is the largest country in North America. The United States ranks second. In population, the United States is the largest country. **Mexico** is second.

Canada, Our Northern Neighbor

Canada is our northern neighbor. It lies north of the contiguous 48 states and east of Alaska. Canada and the United States share similar histories. Both were explored by the French and the British and were once under British rule.

Fewer people live in Canada than in either Mexico or the United States. Much of northern Canada is very cold for

▶ **MEXICO CITY** is one of the oldest cities in North America.

The Three Largest Countries in North America

COUNTRY	AREA (square miles)	POPULATION
Canada	3,855,100	33,212,696
United States	3,718,700	303,824,646
Mexico	761,600	109,955,400

TABLE What is the largest country in area? in population?

most of the year. Few people live there. Instead, most Canadians live near the country's southern border.

Mexico, Our Southern Neighbor

In land area, Mexico is smaller than either Canada or the United States. However, Mexico has more people than Canada. Its population is also more spread out than Canada's. Mexico's

capital, Mexico City, is one of the world's largest cities.

Mexico and the United States also share a history. Long ago, Spain sent settlers to live in what is now Mexico and the southwestern United States.

READING CHECK ☼ COMPARE AND CONTRAST
How are Canada, the United States, and Mexico similar?

Summary

The United States has 50 states. They are often grouped into five regions. North America's three largest countries are Canada, the United States, and Mexico.

REVIEW

1. **WHAT TO KNOW** How are the 50 states alike, and how are they different?

2. **VOCABULARY** Write a sentence that uses the word **region**.

3. **GEOGRAPHY** What are the three largest countries in North America?

4. **CRITICAL THINKING** How would you describe the relative location of each of the five regions in the United States?

5. 🖊 **DRAW A MAP** Draw a map of North America. Label the United States and its neighbors.

6. (Focus Skill) **COMPARE AND CONTRAST** On a separate sheet of paper, copy and complete the graphic organizer below.

Topic 1
Northeast

Similar

Topic 2
Southeast

Use Latitude and Longitude

Why It Matters Maps and globes can help you find the location of a place.

❯ LEARN

Mapmakers use a system of imaginary lines to form a grid system on maps and globes. You can use this grid system to find the **absolute location**, or exact location, of a place.

The lines that run east and west are called **lines of latitude**, or **parallels** (PAIR•uh•lelz). They are measured in degrees north and south of the equator. The equator is labeled 0°, or zero degrees. Lines north of the equator are marked *N* for *north latitude*. Lines south of it are marked *S* for *south latitude*.

The lines that run north and south from the poles are called **lines of longitude**, or **meridians**. They are measured in degrees east and west of the prime meridian. The prime meridian is labeled 0°. Lines west of the prime meridian are marked *W* for *west longitude*. Lines east of it are marked *E* for *east longitude*.

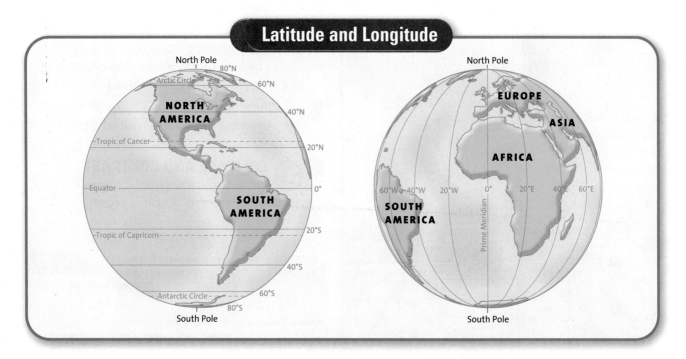

Latitude and Longitude

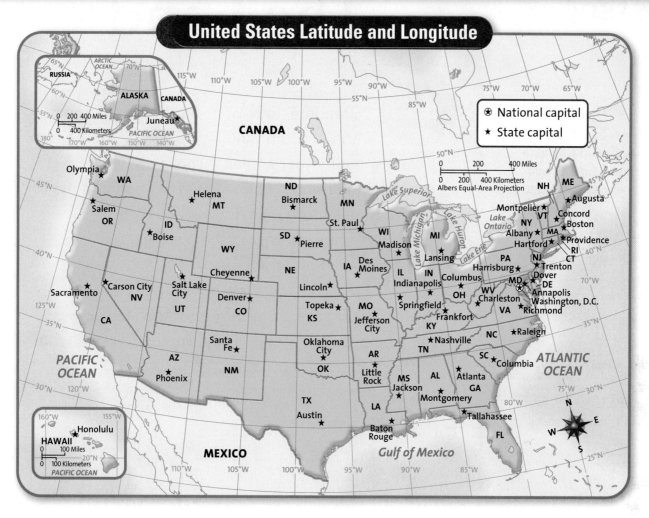

United States Latitude and Longitude

⊛ National capital
★ State capital

Map and Globe Skills

❱ PRACTICE

The map above shows state capitals. You give the absolute location of a place by first naming the line of latitude and then the line of longitude closest to it.

1 Which state capital is nearest to 40°N, 75°W?

2 Which state capital is nearest to 30°N, 85°W?

3 What is the location of Denver, Colorado?

❱ APPLY

Make It Relevant Use lines of latitude and longitude on the map above to describe the location of your state's capital city. Then, use the map on pages R10–R11 to describe the location of different landforms and bodies of water.

Lesson

The Land

WHAT TO KNOW
How does the nation's geography differ as you travel across the 50 states?

VOCABULARY
landform region p. 23

climate p. 23

mountain range p. 25

erosion p. 25

prairie p. 26

environment p. 26

PEOPLE
Robert Louis Stevenson

PLACES
Coastal Plain
Appalachian Mountains
Piedmont
Interior Plains
Rocky Mountains
Great Basin
Sierra Nevada

COMPARE AND CONTRAST

YOU ARE THERE

"Grandma, look what I just found!" You run into the room holding up an old photograph.

Your grandmother smiles. "Those are your great-great-grandparents," she says. "They came to the United States more than 100 years ago."

You look more closely at the picture. "Are they in front of the Statue of Liberty?"

"Yes, they arrived in New York City," your grandmother says. "But they later traveled across the whole United States. They wanted to see all the different parts of our nation."

Landform Regions

The United States is a land of many different kinds of places. To better study the land, geographers often divide it into landform regions. A **landform region** is a region that has similar landforms throughout. Landforms are physical features such as plains, mountains, plateaus, hills, and valleys.

Each landform region is unique, or unlike the others, because of the shape of its landforms and the way they came to be. Dividing the country into landform regions makes it easier to compare and contrast different parts of the country. There are many different landform regions in the United States.

A Long Journey

In the late 1800s, a well-known writer named **Robert Louis Stevenson** traveled across the United States. Stevenson was living in Scotland when he received word that Fanny Osbourne, his sweetheart, was ill. Osbourne lived in the United States, and Stevenson decided to go there.

He did not realize how much his trip across the United States would teach him about the nation's landforms and climate. **Climate** is the kind of weather a place has over a long time.

READING CHECK ○ COMPARE AND CONTRAST
What makes landform regions in the United States different?

▶ **NEW YORK HARBOR** This photograph shows New York Harbor in the 1890s. Robert Louis Stevenson (right) arrived in New York City.

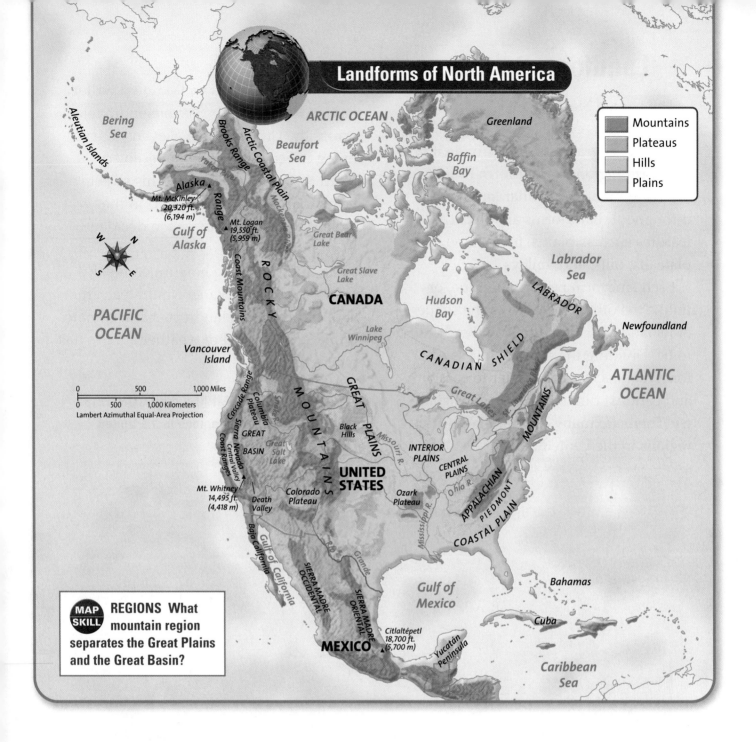

Landforms of North America

Mountains
Plateaus
Hills
Plains

ARCTIC OCEAN
Greenland
Aleutian Islands
Bering Sea
Beaufort Sea
Baffin Bay
Brooks Range
Arctic Coastal Plain
Yukon River
Alaska
Mt. McKinley 20,320 ft. (6,194 m)
Mt. Logan 19,550 ft. (5,959 m)
Range
Gulf of Alaska
Great Bear Lake
Mackenzie R.
Great Slave Lake
Labrador Sea
Coast Mountains
CANADA
Hudson Bay
LABRADOR
Newfoundland
PACIFIC OCEAN
R O C K Y
Lake Winnipeg
CANADIAN SHIELD
ATLANTIC OCEAN
Vancouver Island
GREAT PLAINS
Great Lakes
St. Lawrence River
MOUNTAINS
Cascade Range
Columbia Plateau
Snake R.
GREAT
Black Hills
Missouri R.
INTERIOR PLAINS
Sierra Nevada
BASIN
Great Salt Lake
M O U N T A I N S
CENTRAL PLAINS
Coast Ranges
Central Valley
Mt. Whitney 14,495 ft. (4,418 m)
Death Valley
Colorado Plateau
UNITED STATES
Ozark Plateau
Ohio R.
APPALACHIAN
PIEDMONT
COASTAL PLAIN
Mississippi R.
Baja California
Gulf of California
SIERRA MADRE OCCIDENTAL
Rio Grande
SIERRA MADRE ORIENTAL
Gulf of Mexico
Bahamas
Cuba
MEXICO
Citlaltépetl 18,700 ft. (5,700 m)
Yucatán Peninsula
Caribbean Sea

500   1,000 Miles
500   1,000 Kilometers
Lambert Azimuthal Equal-Area Projection

MAP SKILL **REGIONS** What mountain region separates the Great Plains and the Great Basin?

The Coastal Plain

On August 7, 1879, Stevenson left Scotland. He boarded a ship and spent ten stormy days crossing the Atlantic Ocean. As the ship neared New York City, Stevenson looked out on a broad, tree-lined plain. This flat, low land along the Atlantic Ocean is part of a much larger region called the **Coastal Plain**.

The Coastal Plain begins along the coast of Massachusetts as a strip of land no more than 10 miles wide. It gets much wider farther south, near Florida. From Florida, the Coastal Plain extends west into Texas and the country of Mexico.

READING CHECK ⚙ **COMPARE AND CONTRAST**
What is the difference between the Coastal Plain in Massachusetts and in Florida?

The Appalachians

Stevenson did not stay in New York City long. Osbourne lived on the other side of the United States—in San Francisco, California. To reach California, on the Pacific Coast, Stevenson boarded a train for the long journey west. He was about to travel across many different landform regions.

When Stevenson's train reached Pennsylvania, the land began to change. Instead of being flat, the land was now filled with wide valleys and hills. This region of valleys and hills on the eastern side of the **Appalachian** (a•puh•LAY•chuhn) **Mountains** is called the **Piedmont** (PEED•mahnt). *Piedmont* means "at the base of a mountain." The Piedmont begins in New Jersey and extends to Alabama.

A Long Range

The Appalachians rise above the Piedmont. This **mountain range**, or group of connected mountains, runs from southern Canada to central Alabama.

The tree-covered Appalachians are the oldest mountains in the United States. Their peaks were worn down by glaciers and then by rain and wind. This gradual wearing away of Earth's surface is called **erosion**. Today, the highest peaks in the Appalachians are only about 7,000 feet.

The Appalachians are made up of many smaller mountain ranges that run next to each other. They include the Great Smoky, Blue Ridge, Catskill, and White Mountains.

READING CHECK 🖰 **COMPARE AND CONTRAST**
How are the Appalachian Mountains different from the Coastal Plain?

▶ THE APPALACHIAN MOUNTAINS separate the Coastal Plain from the Interior Plains.

The Interior Plains

West of the Appalachians, the land gets flat again. Here, in the center of the country, Stevenson saw other plains, called the Interior Plains. The **Interior Plains** stretch across the middle of the country, from the Appalachians in the east to the Rocky Mountains in the west.

In the eastern part of the Interior Plains, often called the Central Plains, the land is mostly flat or rolling. There are many streams and rivers. This area is sometimes called a tall-grass prairie. A **prairie** is an area of flat or rolling land covered mostly by grasses. During his journey across the Central Plains, Stevenson wrote that "the country was flat . . . but far from being dull. All through Ohio, Indiana, Illinois, and Iowa, . . . it was rich and various."

The Great Plains

When Stevenson's train stopped in the middle of Nebraska, he saw that the **environment**, or the surroundings in which people, plants, and animals live, was yet again different. This western part of the Interior Plains is called the Great Plains and includes parts of ten states. The Great Plains stretch from southern Texas into Canada.

In the Great Plains, the land becomes much flatter. There are few rivers and almost no trees. To Stevenson, the land seemed to look the same for mile after mile. He wrote that a person "may walk five miles and see nothing; ten, and it is as though he had not moved."

READING CHECK ○ **COMPARE AND CONTRAST**
How is the environment of the Central Plains different from that of the Great Plains?

▶ **THE ROCKY MOUNTAINS** rise sharply above the land around them.

The Rocky Mountains and Beyond

As Stevenson's train moved west, the flat Interior Plains gave way to the towering **Rocky Mountains**. The Rockies cover much of the western United States. They are the country's largest and longest mountain range. The Rockies stretch from Mexico through Canada and into Alaska. Like the Appalachians, the Rocky Mountains are made up of smaller mountain ranges.

The Rocky Mountains are much younger than the Appalachians. The peaks of the Rockies appear sharp and jagged because they have not been eroded for as long a time. Because the Rocky Mountains are so high, many of the peaks are always covered with snow.

Stevenson's train moved slowly, taking two days to cross the Rocky Mountains.

Then the environment changed once again. Now Stevenson looked out the window and saw only "desert scenes, fiery hot and deadly weary."

The Intermountain Region

Between the Rocky Mountains on the east and other mountains farther west is a large area of mostly dry land. It is often called the Intermountain Region.

Part of this land is the **Great Basin**, which includes Nevada and parts of five neighboring states. A basin is low, bowl-shaped land with higher land all around it. At the edge of the Great Basin lies Death Valley, California. This is the lowest land in North America. Part of Death Valley is more than 250 feet below sea level.

READING CHECK ⚛**COMPARE AND CONTRAST**
How do the Rocky Mountains differ from the Intermountain Region?

⚡FAST FACT

The tallest peak in the Rocky Mountains is Mount Elbert in Colorado. It is more than 14,400 feet above sea level, which is equal to the length of about 48 football fields.

More Mountains and Valleys

Stevenson's train left the dry lands, canyons, and plateaus of the Great Basin and the Intermountain Region. It headed west toward even more mountains. Tall trees covered the mountainsides. Between many of the mountain ranges were wide, fertile valleys with thick grasses and rushing streams.

Mountain Ranges to the West

Lying just inside California is the **Sierra Nevada** (see•AIR•uh nuh•VA•duh). *Sierra Nevada* is Spanish for "snowy mountain range." The eastern slope of the mountains is so steep that riders on Stevenson's train were pinned to their seats as the train climbed!

Other mountains lie north of the Sierra Nevada, in Washington and Oregon. These mountains make up the Cascade Range. West of the Sierra Nevada and the Cascade Range are three large, fertile valleys. The largest is the more than 400-mile-long Central Valley in California. The others are the Puget Sound Lowland in Washington and the Willamette (wuh•LA•muht) Valley in Oregon.

Along the Pacific Ocean in California, Oregon, and Washington are the Coast Ranges. These low mountains give the Pacific a rocky, rugged look. At many places, these mountains drop sharply into the ocean. Unlike the Atlantic Coast, the Pacific Coast has very little flat land.

▶ **THE CENTRAL VALLEY,** in California, is a leading farming area of the United States.

▶ **THE PACIFIC COAST** has many rocky cliffs that drop sharply into the ocean.

The Journey Ends

Stevenson arrived in San Francisco on August 31. That was 24 days after he had left home. At long last, he met up with Osbourne, who had regained her health. Stevenson had traveled from one coast of the United States to the other. During his trip, he had seen much of the country and many of its major landform regions. By taking a train across the United States, Stevenson had learned much about the country's landforms and climate. He now understood that the United States was a very diverse country with many different kinds of regions in which to live.

READING CHECK ☼ **COMPARE AND CONTRAST**
How is the Pacific Coast different from the Atlantic Coast?

Summary

Geographers sometimes divide the United States into different landform regions. Each region is unique because of its landforms and climate.

REVIEW

1. **WHAT TO KNOW** How does the nation's geography differ as you travel across the 50 states?

2. **VOCABULARY** Write a sentence that includes the terms **landform region** and **environment**.

3. **GEOGRAPHY** Where are the Appalachian Mountains located?

4. **CRITICAL THINKING** Why do you think Robert Louis Stevenson wrote about the geography of the United States during his trip?

5. 〽 **MAKE FLASH CARDS** Use notecards to make flash cards. On one side of each card, write the name of a landform region. On the other side, write a description of the region.

6. ⭐ **COMPARE AND CONTRAST**
   On a separate sheet of paper, copy and complete this graphic organizer.

Topic 1

Appalachian Mountains   Similar   Rocky Mountains   Topic 2

Lesson

Bodies of Water

 WHAT TO KNOW
What are some of the different bodies of water in the United States?

VOCABULARY

inlet p. 31
gulf p. 31
sound p. 31
tributary p. 32
river system p. 32
drainage basin p. 32
fall line p. 33

PLACES
Gulf of Mexico
Great Lakes
Great Salt Lake
Mississippi River

 **COMPARE AND CONTRAST**

YOU ARE THERE
"Watch out!" You duck as the sail swings over your head. The wind is very strong on Lake Michigan today.

"Sorry," your dad says. "But we're going so fast now that we should be at the dock in Chicago before the sun goes down."

You lean over the side of the boat and look out at the tall buildings of the city ahead.

Inlets and Lakes

Hundreds of inlets along the Atlantic and Pacific coasts help define the shape of the United States. An **inlet** is any area of water extending into the land from a larger body of water.

Gulfs and Inlets

The largest inlets are called **gulfs**. The largest gulf bordering the United States is the **Gulf of Mexico**. Another large gulf, the Gulf of Alaska, lies south of Alaska along the Pacific Coast.

Hundreds of bays and sounds also shape the coastline. A **sound** is a long inlet that separates offshore islands from the mainland. The largest bays and sounds provide harbors where ships can safely dock. Most of the country's largest bays and inlets are found along the Atlantic and Gulf coasts.

Our Largest Lakes

The largest lakes in the United States and in all of North America are together known as the **Great Lakes**. They are located along the border between the United States and Canada. These five lakes—Superior, Michigan, Huron, Erie, and Ontario—are among the world's largest freshwater lakes.

The Great Lakes and the rivers connected to them form an important inland waterway. This waterway links the Midwest and the Atlantic Ocean.

Most lakes in the United States are made up of fresh water, but the **Great Salt Lake** in Utah is as salty as any ocean. Some people even consider it to be a sea—an inland body of salt water.

READING CHECK ö**COMPARE AND CONTRAST**
How do the Great Lakes and the Great Salt Lake differ?

⟩LAKE MICHIGAN The city of Chicago lies on the shore of Lake Michigan.

FAST FACT

People in the United States use more than 40 billion gallons of water from the Great Lakes every day.

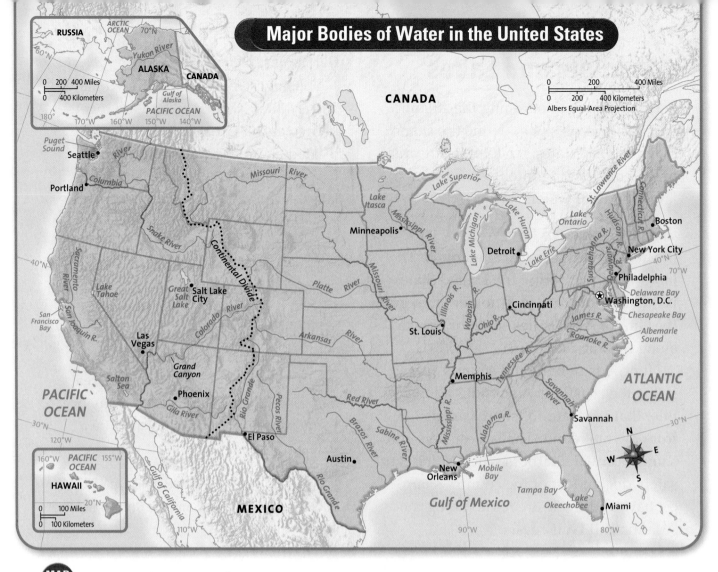

Major Bodies of Water in the United States

RUSSIA
ARCTIC OCEAN
70°N
60°N
Yukon River
ALASKA
CANADA
0 200 400 Miles
0 400 Kilometers
Gulf of Alaska
PACIFIC OCEAN
180° 170°W 160°W 150°W 140°W

CANADA

0 200 400 Miles
0 200 400 Kilometers
Albers Equal-Area Projection

Puget Sound
Seattle
Columbia River
Portland
Columbia
Snake River
Missouri River
Lake Itasca
Lake Superior
St. Lawrence River
Minneapolis
Mississippi River
Lake Michigan
Lake Huron
Lake Ontario
Hudson R.
Connecticut R.
Boston
New York City
Detroit
Lake Erie
Philadelphia
Delaware Bay
Washington, D.C.
Chesapeake Bay
40°N
70°W
Sacramento River
Lake Tahoe
Great Salt Lake
Salt Lake City
Continental Divide
Platte River
Missouri River
Illinois R.
Wabash R.
Ohio R.
Cincinnati
St. Louis
James R.
Roanoke R.
Albemarle Sound
San Francisco Bay
San Joaquin R.
Las Vegas
Colorado River
Arkansas River
Salton Sea
Grand Canyon
Phoenix
Gila River
PACIFIC OCEAN
Rio Grande
Pecos River
Red River
Memphis
Tennessee R.
Savannah River
ATLANTIC OCEAN
Savannah
30°N
30°N
120°W
El Paso
Brazos River
Sabine River
Mississippi R.
Alabama R.
N
W   E
S
160°W PACIFIC 155°W
OCEAN
HAWAII
20°N
0 100 Miles
0 100 Kilometers
Gulf of California
Austin
Rio Grande
MEXICO
New Orleans
Mobile Bay
Tampa Bay
Lake Okeechobee
Miami
Gulf of Mexico
110°W
90°W
80°W

MAP SKILL **LOCATION** Which city on the map borders the Ohio River?

Rivers

Rivers are bodies of fresh, moving water. Every river begins at a source and ends at a mouth, where it empties into a larger body of water.

River Systems

All rivers flow from higher to lower ground. They may be joined by other streams or rivers. A stream or river that flows into a larger stream or river is called a **tributary**.

Together, a river and its tributaries make up a **river system**. A river system drains, or carries water away from, the land around it. The land drained by a river system is its **drainage basin**.

The **Mississippi River** and its tributaries create the largest river system in the United States. It drains most of the land between the Rocky and Appalachian Mountains. It forms an important transportation route through the nation's interior.

The Mississippi River flows from Minnesota to the Gulf of Mexico. Its largest tributaries include the Missouri, Ohio, and Arkansas Rivers.

READING CHECK ⚙ **COMPARE AND CONTRAST**
What is the difference between a river and a river system?

Rivers in the East

Many rivers cross the Coastal Plain and flow into the Atlantic Ocean. Most of these rivers and their tributaries begin in the Appalachian Mountains.

Rivers and Population

Many cities have been built where rivers flow into oceans. For example, New York City was built where the Hudson River flows into the Atlantic Ocean. Living near a river made it easier to travel and to transport goods.

Other cities lie inland along the Fall Line, which divides the Piedmont and the Coastal Plain. A **fall line** is a place where the land drops sharply, causing rivers to form waterfalls or rapids. People once used fast-moving water to power factory machines. They now use it to make electricity.

READING CHECK **SUMMARIZE**
Why were some early cities built near rivers?

Rivers in the West

An imaginary line runs north and south along the highest points of the Rocky Mountains. This line is called the Continental Divide. It divides the major river systems of North America into those that flow into rivers leading to the Gulf of Mexico and the Atlantic Ocean and those that flow into the Pacific or Arctic Oceans.

Children IN HISTORY

Mark Twain

When Samuel Langhorne Clemens, better known as Mark Twain, was four years old, his family moved to Hannibal, Missouri. Hannibal is on the banks of the Mississippi River. As a boy, Twain watched steamboats on the river and dreamed of becoming a steamboat pilot.

After Twain grew up, he earned his pilot's license. When the Civil War shut down steamboat traffic on the Mississippi River, Twain traveled the country and began writing the stories that made him a famous author.

Make It Relevant How does where people live affect the kinds of work they do?

▶ **THE CONTINENTAL DIVIDE** runs through Yellowstone National Park.

Rivers and the Continental Divide

Rivers that begin east of the Continental Divide eventually reach the Atlantic Ocean. Most rivers that begin west of the line empty into the Pacific Ocean.

Rivers that flow from sources east of the Continental Divide include the Missouri River and the Rio Grande. The rivers to the west of the Continental Divide include the Sacramento, Columbia, and Colorado.

READING CHECK ◌**COMPARE AND CONTRAST**
How do rivers east and west of the Continental Divide differ?

Summary

The United States has different bodies of water. Its largest lakes are the Great Lakes. Rivers drain land and are often used for transportation. The Continental Divide separates rivers that flow into the Atlantic from rivers that flow into the Pacific.

REVIEW

1. **WHAT TO KNOW** What are some of the different bodies of water in the United States?

2. **VOCABULARY** Write a sentence that explains how the terms **tributary** and **drainage basin** are related.

3. **GEOGRAPHY** Which countries do the Great Lakes border?

4. **CRITICAL THINKING** Why do you think it is important to have a waterway that connects the Midwest and the Atlantic Ocean?

5. 🖌 **DRAW A POSTER** Find out what river is located nearest to where you live. Make a poster showing the river and its surrounding landforms. Label nearby cities and any tributaries the river may have.

6. ⭐ **GENERALIZE** On a separate sheet of paper, copy and complete the graphic organizer below.

Marjory Stoneman Douglas

Biography

Trustworthiness
Respect
Responsibility
Fairness
Caring
Patriotism

"There are no other Everglades in all the world."

Marjory Stoneman Douglas defended the environment at a time when many people did not think about conserving Earth's natural resources. Her books and volunteer work showed people the importance of protecting the environment, mainly Florida's Everglades.

Douglas was born in Minneapolis, Minnesota, in 1890. When she was 25, she moved to Miami, Florida, to work as a reporter for the *Miami Herald*. In 1942, she began working on a project about American rivers. She published *The Everglades: River of Grass* in 1947. That same year, the Everglades became a national park.

Douglas's book showed people that the Everglades was home to many rare plants and animals that were worth protecting. In 1970, she formed a volunteer group called "Friends of the Everglades." Douglas continued to travel and give speeches about the Everglades until her death at the age of 108.

Why Character Counts

How did Marjory Stoneman Douglas help protect the environment?

Time

1890		1998
Born		Died

1947 *The Everglades: River of Grass* is published

1970 Forms the volunteer group "Friends of the Everglades"

GO ONLINE For more resources, go to www.harcourtschool.com/ss1

Lesson 4

Climate and Vegetation

WHAT TO KNOW
How do climate and vegetation differ across the United States?

VOCABULARY
elevation p. 37

natural vegetation p. 38

arid p. 39

tundra p. 39

PLACES
Rocky Mountains

COMPARE AND CONTRAST

YOU ARE THERE As your horse moves forward to catch up with the group, you feel a rush of cold air. It's cool outside, even though the sun is shining bright. The Rocky Mountains look huge in the distance. It's your first visit to Colorado and your first time horseback riding. There is snow on the mountains ahead, but the land around you is perfectly green.

▶ **THE ROCKY MOUNTAINS** Many people participate in outdoor activities, such as horseback riding or snow skiing, in the Rocky Mountains.

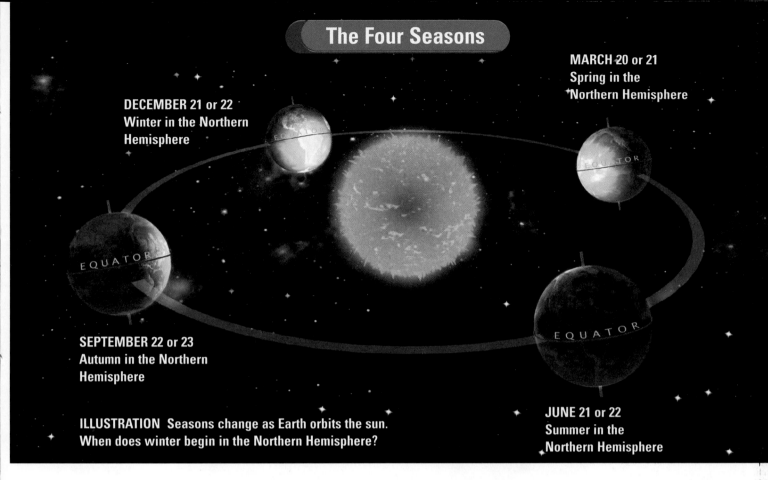

The Four Seasons

DECEMBER 21 or 22
Winter in the Northern Hemisphere

MARCH 20 or 21
Spring in the Northern Hemisphere

SEPTEMBER 22 or 23
Autumn in the Northern Hemisphere

JUNE 21 or 22
Summer in the Northern Hemisphere

ILLUSTRATION Seasons change as Earth orbits the sun. When does winter begin in the Northern Hemisphere?

Climate

The climate of a place can affect what people wear, what kinds of activities they do, and how they earn their living.

Factors Affecting Climate

The climate of a place depends partly on its distance from the equator. Places closer to the equator tend to be warmer than places farther away. That is because the sun shines more directly on Earth at the equator. In the United States, states farther south, such as Florida and Texas, are usually warmer than states farther north, such as Michigan and Montana.

Distance from oceans and other large bodies of water also affects climate. Places are warmed by the water in winter and cooled by it in summer.

Elevation affects climate, too. **Elevation** is the height of the land in relation to sea level. For every 1,000 feet above sea level, the temperature drops about 3° F.

Earth and the Sun

Earth's orbit around the sun causes changes in seasons—summer, autumn, winter, and spring. Because Earth is tilted on its axis as it orbits the sun, places get different amounts of sunlight and heat at different times of the year. These changes are more noticeable in some places than in others. Some places have four distinct seasons. In other places, it is mostly warm all year or mostly cold all year.

READING CHECK ☼ **COMPARE AND CONTRAST**
Why are northern states usually colder than southern states?

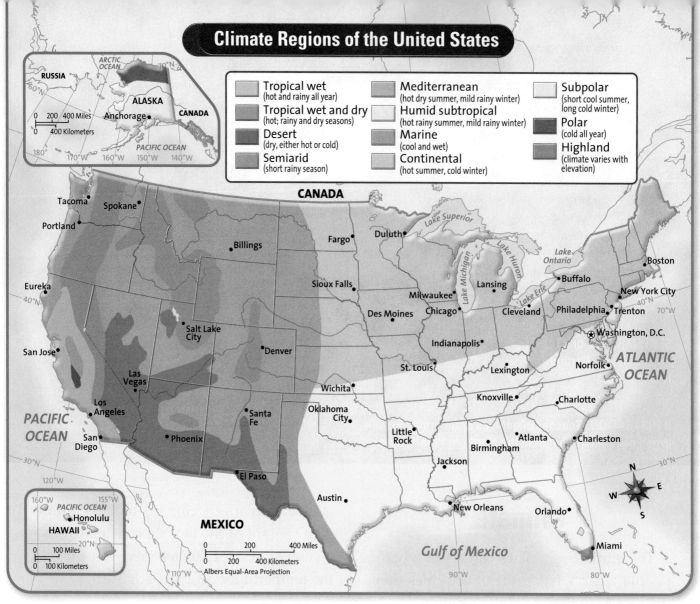

Climate Regions of the United States

Legend:
- Tropical wet (hot and rainy all year)
- Tropical wet and dry (hot; rainy and dry seasons)
- Desert (dry, either hot or cold)
- Semiarid (short rainy season)
- Mediterranean (hot dry summer, mild rainy winter)
- Humid subtropical (hot rainy summer, mild rainy winter)
- Marine (cool and wet)
- Continental (hot summer, cold winter)
- Subpolar (short cool summer, long cold winter)
- Polar (cold all year)
- Highland (climate varies with elevation)

MAP SKILL **REGIONS** What climate region do you live in?

Vegetation

Weather in the 48 contiguous states generally moves from west to east. Mountains block clouds that carry rain. In many places, the western slopes of the mountains receive lots of rain. The eastern slopes are dry.

Earth is covered with different kinds of **natural vegetation**, or plant life that grows naturally in a place. The natural vegetation that grows in a place varies depending on the soil. The vegetation also varies because of temperature and precipitation. In fact, the amount of precipitation in a place is the single most important factor affecting where different kinds of natural vegetation grow.

Vegetation Regions

Most of the United States can be divided into four main vegetation regions. These are forest, grassland, desert, and tundra. Forest regions extend across large areas of both the eastern and western United States.

Trees need lots of water, but grasses can survive in much drier areas. The largest grassland region in the United States stretches across the middle of the country. It includes the western part of the Central Plains and all of the Great Plains.

Only plants that can grow in an **arid**, or dry, climate can grow in deserts. These plants include short grasses, low bushes, and cactuses.

Small hardy plants such as mosses, herbs, and low shrubs grow in tundra regions. A **tundra** is a cold, dry region where trees cannot grow.

▶ **DRY CLIMATES** Only plants that can hold a lot of water can survive in a dry climate like the desert.

Tundra regions are covered by snow more than half the year. Yet there is not enough water for trees to grow because the water in the soil is frozen year-round.

READING CHECK SUMMARIZE
What four main vegetation regions cover the United States?

Summary

Climate can influence the way people live in different parts of the United States. It also affects vegetation. In dry regions, few plants grow. In wet regions, many trees and other plants grow.

REVIEW

1. **WHAT TO KNOW** How do climate and vegetation differ across the United States?

2. **VOCABULARY** Write a sentence using the word **arid**.

3. **GEOGRAPHY** How does the geography of different regions affect climate?

4. **CRITICAL THINKING** How do you think climate affects life in different parts of the United States?

5. ✏ **WRITE A POEM** Write a poem about the climate and vegetation of the region in which you live.

6. ⭐ **COMPARE AND CONTRAST** On a separate sheet of paper, copy and complete this graphic organizer.

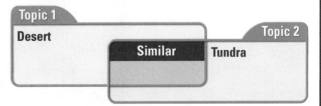

Topic 1
Desert

Similar

Topic 2
Tundra

Lesson 5 People and the Environment

WHAT TO KNOW
How do people adapt to and change the environment?

VOCABULARY
land use p. 42
natural resource p. 42
renewable resource p. 43
nonrenewable resource p. 43
modify p. 44
irrigation p. 44
efficiency p. 45

PLACES
Ohio River
Kentucky
Ohio

COMPARE AND CONTRAST
Focus Skill

YOU ARE THERE
You look out the window of the car as you cross the bridge over the **Ohio River**. "You know, it used to take people much longer to get from **Kentucky** to **Ohio**," your mother says. "Early settlers had to cross the river on rafts. Everyone was glad when the first bridges were built."

You look down at the river below you. You think about how hard it must have been to cross the river long ago.

FAST FACT

The John A. Roebling bridge (right) connects Ohio and Kentucky. When the bridge opened in 1866, it was the longest bridge in the world.

Patterns of Settlement

Today, more than 300 million people live in the United States. However, many areas are not crowded. Thousands of people do live close together in and around large cities. But very few people live in some parts of the country.

Factors Encouraging Settlement

Physical features, such as climate, water, and landforms, can affect where people settle. More than 5,000 years ago, Native Americans began farming. They settled in areas where the soil was rich. Later settlers set up communities where there was farmland and fresh water. People also needed to live near transportation routes, such as rivers.

At first, most people avoided settling in desert, tundra, or mountainous regions. In such areas it can be difficult to build shelters, find food and water, and meet basic human needs. During the 1800s and 1900s, people began to use tools and inventions to live in those areas. As a result of air-conditioning and irrigation, some of the fastest-growing cities in the United States are now in the desert regions of the West.

Today, people live in cities that spread out over large areas. Big cities are often found along transportation routes such as rivers or a coast. No matter where people live, they change the land on which they build.

READING CHECK ○ **COMPARE AND CONTRAST**
How do different climates encourage and discourage settlement?

Using the Land

People use Earth's surface in a variety of ways. They divide land into nations, states, and other government units. They build communities, transportation systems, and businesses. People also get natural resources from the land.

How People Use the Land

Landforms and climate can influence **land use**, or how the land is used. In the United States, about half of the land is used as farmland. Most farming takes place on the Coastal Plain, on the Interior Plains, and in valleys in the West. In those regions, the land is fertile and there is enough water for crops to grow.

Much of the mining in the United States takes place in mountain regions. However, mining may take place wherever there are minerals to gather.

Cities also occupy large areas of the United States. Cities are identified by human features. A human feature is something created by people, such as a building or a road, that alters the land. In cities, most of the land is used for housing, transportation, and businesses. Most manufacturing takes place in or near cities.

Natural Resources

The United States is a land rich in natural resources. A **natural resource** is something found in nature that people can use. Natural resources include soil, plants, water, and minerals.

❯ LAND USE People use the land around them to grow food and to get natural resources.

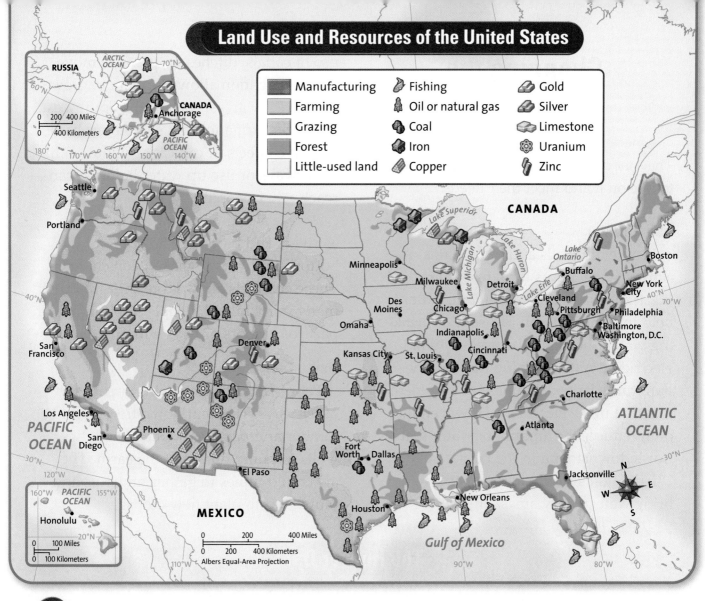

Land Use and Resources of the United States

Legend:
- Manufacturing
- Farming
- Grazing
- Forest
- Little-used land
- Fishing
- Oil or natural gas
- Coal
- Iron
- Copper
- Gold
- Silver
- Limestone
- Uranium
- Zinc

MAP SKILL **REGIONS** What natural resources do people use where you live?

There are two kinds of natural resources. **Renewable resources** are resources that can be made again by people or nature. These include water, trees, and sources of energy such as light and wind.

Nonrenewable resources are resources that cannot be made again by people, or resources that would take thousands of years for nature to replace. These resources include ores, minerals, oil, and gas that people remove from the earth. They were formed by nature over thousands of years. Once gone, it would take just as long for nature to replace them.

People use these types of resources to heat homes and fuel cars. One resource, oil, is the source of every product that is made of plastic.

For many years, Americans did not worry about using up resources. During the last century, people began to realize that the supply of nonrenewable resources is limited. Today, people often make choices to conserve, or save, the resources for future generations.

READING CHECK ☼ **COMPARE AND CONTRAST**
How are renewable resources different from nonrenewable resources?

Changing the Environment

Americans **modify**, or change, the land. They modify the land so that they are able to live on it and meet their needs.

Using Water

People dig wells and build dams across rivers. Dams form reservoirs (REH•zuh•vwarz) behind them. Water held in reservoirs can be used for drinking water. It can also be used to make electricity. Water running through the dam turns large machines called generators that make electricity. However, the dam reduces the amount of water that flows downstream in the river.

Irrigation systems allow people to bring water to dry areas. **Irrigation** is the use of canals, ditches, or pipes to move water. Irrigation allows farmers to grow crops in dry areas, such as the Southwest. However, irrigation can sometimes have negative effects. It can cause pollution in waterways or use up water before it can reach other people.

People also modify waterways such as rivers and harbors. They dig out the bottoms of rivers to make deep channels. These channels allow large ships to travel many miles inland. People also fill in parts of harbors or bays with dirt.

Using the Land

People modify the environment in other ways. They cut down trees to make lumber and paper products. They dig wells to pump oil out of the earth. They also build mines to gather minerals and plow land to plant new crops.

The Hoover Dam

1 Reservoir

2 Power lines

3 Power plant

Balancing the Changes

Many people today understand that they need to use natural resources carefully so the resources do not run out. Engineers have learned much about energy **efficiency**, or using less energy to do the same tasks. Many of the cars people drive today use less gas than cars made years ago. Some appliances, such as refrigerators, use less electricity.

READING CHECK ☼ **COMPARE AND CONTRAST**
How has the way people use natural resources changed?

Summary

People use natural resources. Many resources are nonrenewable and cannot be replaced. People have to think carefully about how they use available resources.

REVIEW

1. **WHAT TO KNOW** How do people adapt to and change the environment?

2. **VOCABULARY** Write a sentence that uses the word **modify**.

3. **GEOGRAPHY** Why do people use pipes to move water to dry places?

4. **CRITICAL THINKING** How has the physical environment influenced the settlement of the United States?

5. ✏ **WRITE A PARAGRAPH** Write a short paragraph about what you can do to conserve natural resources.

6. 🌟 **COMPARE AND CONTRAST**
   On a separate sheet of paper, copy and complete this graphic organizer.

Topic 1		Topic 2
Renewable resources	Similar	Nonrenewable resources

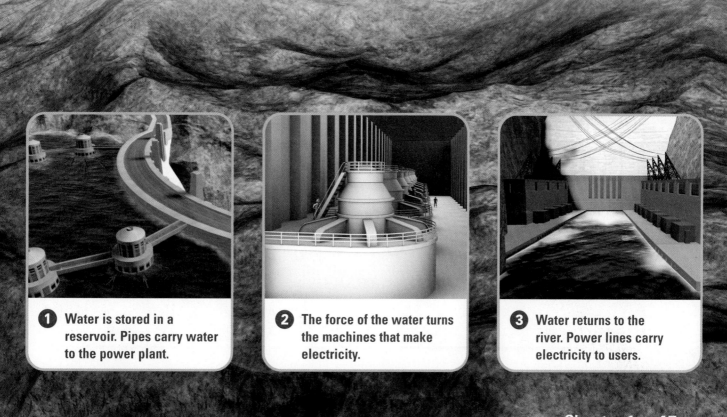

1 Water is stored in a reservoir. Pipes carry water to the power plant.

2 The force of the water turns the machines that make electricity.

3 Water returns to the river. Power lines carry electricity to users.

Read Time Lines

Why It Matters A time line allows you to compare when different events happened.

❯ LEARN

A time line looks like a ruler. It is marked with dates instead of inches. The dates are evenly spaced on the time line.

Horizontal time lines, like the one below, are read from left to right. The earliest date is on the left. The most recent date is on the right. The time line on page 47 is a vertical time line. The earliest date is at the top. The most recent date is at the bottom.

Time lines can show any period of time. Some time lines show events that took place over a decade. A **decade** is a period of ten years. Other time lines may cover a **century**, or a period of 100 years. A decade and a century are labeled on the time line below. Many cities in the United States grew during the period shown.

Some time lines show events that took place over a millennium. A **millennium** is a period of 1,000 years. A millennium is labeled on the vertical time line on page 47.

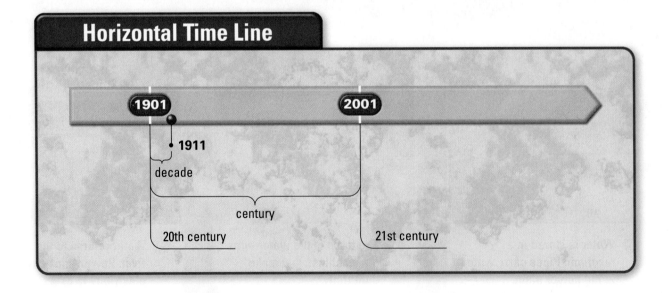

Horizontal Time Line

The time line begins in the ancient past. It ends at nearly the present day. Notice the letters *B.C.* and *A.D.* Many people today use the birth of Jesus Christ to date events. The years before Christ's birth are labeled *B.C.* The years that fall after Christ's birth are labeled *A.D.* An event that took place in 100 *B.C.* took place 100 years before the birth of Christ. An event that happened in *A.D.* 100 took place 100 years after the birth of Christ.

Sometimes, people use the letters *B.C.E.* and *C.E.* instead of *B.C.* and *A.D.* *B.C.E.* means "before the Common Era." It is used in place of *B.C.* *C.E.* stands for "Common Era" and is used in place of *A.D.*

▶ PRACTICE

Use the time lines to answer the following questions.

1 How many centuries are shown on the horizontal time line?

2 What was the first year of the twentieth century?

3 Look at the vertical time line. Which year came earlier, 1001 *B.C.* or 501 *B.C.*?

▶ APPLY

Make It Relevant Make a time line that shows the last 20 years in five-year periods. Then mark important events that have taken place in your life. Share your time line with classmates.

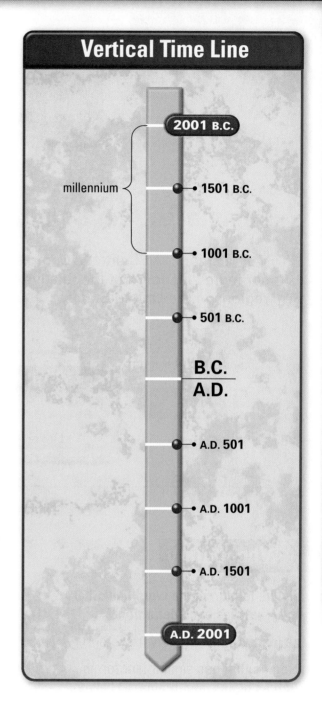

Vertical Time Line

2001 B.C.

millennium { 1501 B.C.

1001 B.C.

501 B.C.

B.C.
A.D.

A.D. 501

A.D. 1001

A.D. 1501

A.D. 2001

Chart and Graph Skills

Mexico City

The Atlantic Coastline

Visual Summary

Summarize the Chapter

Focus Skill **Compare and Contrast** Complete this graphic organizer to compare and contrast the relative locations of two geographic regions in the United States.

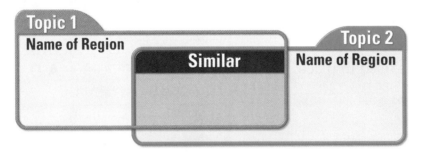

Topic 1
Name of Region

Similar

Topic 2
Name of Region

Vocabulary

Identify the term from the word bank that correctly matches each definition.

1. the land drained by a river system

2. a region that has similar landforms, such as plains, mountains, or valleys

3. the position of one place compared to other places

4. something found in nature that people can use

5. the wearing down of Earth's surface, usually by wind or water

6. the use of canals, ditches, or pipes to move water to dry areas

7. to change

8. the surroundings in which people, plants, and animals live

Word Bank

relative location p. 15   drainage basin p. 32

landform region p. 23   natural resource p. 42

erosion p. 25   modify p. 44

environment p. 26   irrigation p. 44

Yellowstone National Park, Wyoming

Seguaro cactus in the southwestern United States.

 Facts and Main Ideas

Answer these questions.

9. How does dividing land into regions help make geography easier to study?

10. What natural process has worn down the Appalachian Mountains?

11. What landform includes Nevada and parts of five neighboring states?

12. Why is the climate near the equator warmer than the climate of most other places?

13. Why did people modify rivers and streams?

Write the letter of the best choice.

14. What relationship between Earth and the sun causes the seasons?
   A the change in Earth's tilt toward the sun
   B the distance of Earth from the sun
   C the speed of Earth around the sun
   D the change in the sun's heat during the year

15. How is the climate of the Southwest different from the climate of Northeast?
   A It is cooler.
   B It is hotter and drier.
   C It is milder.
   D It is wetter.

16. How do people change the land to improve the movement of goods and people?
   A by drawing maps
   B by building monuments
   C by digging channels
   D by digging wells

 Critical Thinking

17. **Make It Relevant** How have people in your state used tools to modify the land?

18. What do you think are some ways Americans can use natural resources more wisely?

 **Skills**

Use Latitude and Longitude

19. Look at the map on page 21. What state capital is located nearest 40°N and 90°W?

Read a Time Line

20. Look at the time line on page 47. How many millennia occurred between 1001 B.C. and A.D. 1001?

21. How many centuries occurred between A.D. 1501 and A.D. 501?

writing

Write a Narrative Imagine that you are traveling through the five regions of the United States. Write a narrative describing one major landform in each region.

Write a Report Write a report that describes how people in your community can work together to share limited resources.

Chapter 1 ▪ 49

STUDY SKILLS

ANTICIPATION GUIDE

An anticipation guide can help you anticipate, or predict, what you will learn as you read.

- **Read the lesson titles and section titles for clues.**

- **Read the Reading Check question at the end of each section.**

- **Predict what you will learn as you read.**

The Plains

Life on the Plains

Reading Check	Prediction	Correct?
What different ways was buffalo meat prepared?	In this lesson, we will learn how the Plains people prepared buffalo meat.	✓

Farmers and Hunters

Reading Check	Prediction	Correct?

PREVIEW VOCABULARY

longhouse p. 64

council p. 74

barter p. 85

NATIVE AMERICAN FESTIVAL IN CHARLOTTE, NORTH CAROLINA

Lesson 1

Time

14,000 B.C.   **PRESENT**

3000 B.C.
People in the Americas
begin farming

A.D. 300
The Mayan
civilization
begins to grow

A.D. 1200
More than 30,000
people live in Cahokia

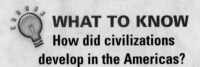 **WHAT TO KNOW**
How did civilizations
develop in the Americas?

VOCABULARY
ancestor p. 53
theory p. 53
migration p. 53
artifact p. 55
civilization p. 56
tradition p. 57
class p. 57

PLACES
Beringia
San Lorenzo
Tikal
Copán
Spiro
Cahokia

 **COMPARE AND
CONTRAST**

Early People

YOU ARE THERE
The time is 10,000 years ago. You are helping your family settle into a new campsite. For many days, your group has been tracking a herd of mammoths. The group's adults are hopeful that the hunting will be good here.

You work as fast as you can, gathering wild plants to help feed your group. The air is bitterly cold, but you keep warm by working quickly. Tomorrow, your group will join in the first hunt. You hope that it will be a great success.

The Land Bridge Story

The history of the United States begins with the first people in North America thousands of years ago. They are the ancestors of present-day Native Americans, or American Indians. An **ancestor** is an early family member.

A Cold World

How did these first people arrive in North America? After many years of study, scientists are still not sure of the answer. However, they do have several theories, or possible explanations. A **theory** is an idea based on study and research.

One theory is that there was once a "bridge" of land between Asia and North America. Scientists call this land bridge **Beringia** (buh•RIN•jee•uh). It was named for the Bering Strait, the body of water that now separates Russia from Alaska.

Many scientists believe that thousands of years ago, there were several Ice Ages. During these long periods of freezing cold, slow-moving sheets of ice called glaciers (GLAY•sherz) covered large parts of Earth.

Scientists think that so much of Earth's water was trapped in these huge glaciers

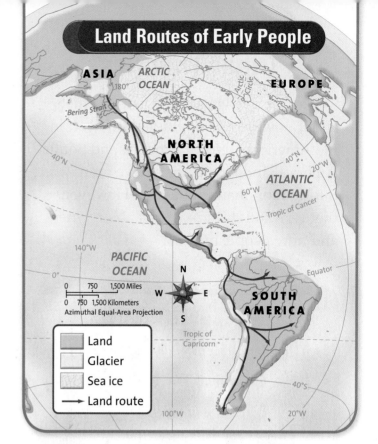

Land Routes of Early People

MAP SKILL

MOVEMENT About how many miles is it from Asia to the tip of South America?

that the level of the oceans fell by as much as 350 feet. Because of this, Earth had more dry land than it does now.

A Long Journey

Many scientists believe that about 12,000 years ago, groups of hunters and their families crossed the land bridge from Asia to North America. This **migration**, or movement of people, probably took place very slowly. Groups may have moved only a few miles in an entire lifetime. At that rate, it would have taken hundreds of years just to reach Alaska!

READING CHECK ᗝ **COMPARE AND CONTRAST** How did the climate of the Ice Ages differ from today's climate?

Other Theories

The land bridge story is just one theory about how people might have arrived in the Americas—North America and South America. Today, scientists have more information than in the past. However, there are still disagreements about when and how people arrived.

Recent discoveries suggest that people may have been in the Americas much longer than was thought. Other discoveries hint that some early peoples may have traveled to the Americas by boat.

Native American Origin Stories

Ideas about the presence of early people in the Americas also come from their descendants. In ancient times, most people passed on their history by retelling stories. They told stories to their children and their grandchildren.

Native American groups have all used stories to tell about their past or how the world was made. The stories about their origins, or beginnings, are called origin stories. Many Native Americans believe their people have always lived in the Americas.

READING CHECK SUMMARIZE

How did Native American groups pass on their history?

HOW THE ROBIN GOT HIS RED BREAST

This story was told by the Miwok people who lived in what is now California. It explains how people got fire and why the feathers on a robin's breast are red.

"A long time ago the world was dark and cold, and the people had no fire. *Wit'-tab-bah* the Robin learned where the fire was, and went on a far journey to get it. After he had traveled a great distance, he came to the place and stole it and carried it back to the people. Every night on the way, he lay with his breast over it to keep it from getting cold; this turned his breast red. Finally he reached home with it and gave it to the people. Then he made the Sun out of it, but before doing this he put some into the *oo'-noo* tree (the buckeye) so the people could get it when they needed it. From that day to this, all the people have known that when they want fire, they can get it by rubbing an oo'-noo stick against a piece of dry wood; this makes the flame come out."

▶ **EARLY PEOPLE** worked together to hunt large animals, such as this woolly mammoth.

Early Ways of Life

Early people most likely led a nomadic way of life. They moved from place to place, living in caves or in tents made of animal skins. They kept moving, following animals they hunted. Scientists know this because they have found spear points and other artifacts near the bones of ancient animals. **Artifacts** are objects made by people.

A Changing Way of Life

Giant animals, such as mastodons and woolly mammoths, once roamed North America. Early people hunted these animals. They ate the meat and used the fur, skins, and bones to make clothing and tools. They also gathered wild foods, such as nuts, plants, and roots. For this reason, scientists refer to these people as hunters and gatherers.

Slowly, the climate changed, becoming warmer and drier. About 8000 B.C., the giant animals became extinct, or died out. People had to find new sources of food. They began to fish and to hunt smaller animals. Over time, they made new hunting tools, such as the bow and arrow.

About 3000 B.C., some people in the Americas began planting seeds and growing crops such as corn and beans. Agriculture, or farming, gave people a reason to settle in one place. As groups raised more food, the population grew.

Some early people formed what are now called tribes, groups who shared the same language, land, and leaders. Each tribe developed its own culture, which made it different from other tribes.

READING CHECK ▶ SUMMARIZE
How did farming change life for people?

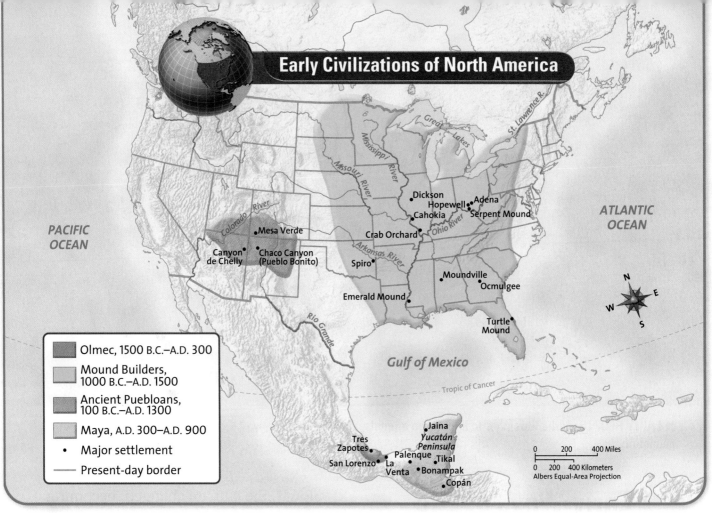

Early Civilizations of North America

PACIFIC OCEAN

ATLANTIC OCEAN

Dickson
Hopewell
Adena
Cahokia
Serpent Mound
Crab Orchard
Mesa Verde
Canyon de Chelly
Chaco Canyon (Pueblo Bonito)
Spiro
Moundville
Ocmulgee
Emerald Mound
Turtle Mound

Gulf of Mexico

Tropic of Cancer

Rio Grande

Tres Zapotes
San Lorenzo
La Venta
Palenque
Bonampak
Tikal
Jaina
Yucatán Peninsula
Copán

Olmec, 1500 B.C.–A.D. 300
Mound Builders, 1000 B.C.–A.D. 1500
Ancient Puebloans, 100 B.C.–A.D. 1300
Maya, A.D. 300–A.D. 900
• Major settlement
— Present-day border

0   200   400 Miles
0   200   400 Kilometers
Albers Equal-Area Projection

MAP SKILL **LOCATION** Which civilization was located farthest south?

The Olmec and the Maya

Over time, groups began to form civilizations. A **civilization** is a group of people with ways of life, religion, and learning. With a more settled way of life, some civilizations built large cities that became centers of learning, religion, and government.

The Olmec Civilization

The Olmec civilization was one of the earliest in the Americas. From about 1500 B.C. to A.D. 300, the Olmec ruled most of what is now southern Mexico.

The oldest Olmec city that scientists have discovered is **San Lorenzo**. Like

many Olmec cities, it is located near a river. The Olmec used rivers to travel between cities and build a trade system. Olmec artifacts have been found across Mexico.

A strong trade system was just one achievement of the Olmec. They also created systems of writing and counting. These systems helped the Olmec develop a 365-day calendar.

No one is sure why the Olmec fell from power, but we know that they influenced other cultures. Today, some historians call the Olmec the "mother culture" of the Americas. That is because many Olmec customs, or ways of doing things, were continued in later civilizations.

The Mayan Civilization

The Mayan civilization was influenced by Olmec traditions. A **tradition** is a way of life or an idea that has been handed down from the past. Between A.D. 300 and A.D. 900, the Maya ruled much of what is now southern Mexico, Guatemala, and northern Belize.

Like the Olmec, the Maya developed their own writing system. This allowed them to record their history. Their writing system was based on hieroglyphs (HY•ruh•glifs), or picture symbols. The Maya also developed a counting system that included the number zero.

The Maya were divided into social classes. A **class** is a group of people in a society who have something in common. At the top of Mayan society were the religious leaders. Then came important families, traders, and farmers.

Mayan civilization had no central government. Instead, powerful kings ruled cities and controlled the surrounding areas. The Maya built more than 100 stone cities. The largest was **Tikal** (tih•KAHL), which had as many as 100,000 people. The city of **Copán** (koh•PAHN) was a center of learning and art.

Scientists are not sure why the Mayan civilization fell. Some scientists blame a series of droughts, or long periods with little or no rain. However, even after the Maya fell from power, their cultural influence continued.

READING CHECK ♻ **COMPARE AND CONTRAST** How were the Mayan and Olmec civilizations alike?

❯ **MAYAN RUINS** are visited by thousands of people every year. Some places allow visitors to climb to the top of stone pyramids.

Other Civilizations

The Olmec and the Maya were two of the largest early civilizations in the Americas. Other civilizations also grew in what is now the United States.

The Mound Builders

Scientists use the name *Mound Builders* to group together many Native American societies. These societies all built large earth mounds. However, their cultures, their locations, and even their reasons for building mounds differed.

The earliest Mound Builders were the Adena (uh•DEE•nuh). Their civilization was located in the Ohio River valley. It lasted from about 1000 B.C. to A.D. 200.

The Adena mounds were used for burials. As more people were buried at these sites, the mounds got bigger and bigger. Some of the mounds reached heights of 90 feet!

The largest of the mound-building civilizations was the Mississippian. It began in the Mississippi River valley in about A.D. 700. Two of the largest Mississippian cities were **Spiro**, in what is now Oklahoma, and **Cahokia**, near present-day East St. Louis, Illinois. By A.D. 1200, more than 30,000 people lived in Cahokia. Cities like Cahokia helped support a strong trade system.

The Ancient Puebloans

Look at the United States map on page 15. Find the place in the Southwest where Utah, Colorado, Arizona, and New Mexico meet. This area is called the Four Corners. Some of the first people to

> **THE MOUND BUILDERS** This painting shows what Cahokia may have looked like.

▶ **AN ANCIENT PUEBLOAN VILLAGE** At the area that is known today as Mesa Verde National Park in Colorado, Ancient Puebloans built stone villages into the canyon walls.

settle this area are known as the Ancient Puebloans (PWEH•bloh•uhnz).

The Ancient Puebloans lived in houses that had many levels. These houses were often built against canyon walls or in caves. When the Spanish arrived in the Southwest many years later, they called this kind of home a pueblo, the Spanish word for "village."

READING CHECK **GENERALIZE**
How were the homes of the Ancient Puebloans built?

Summary

There are several theories about how early people arrived in the Americas. Early people most likely led a nomadic way of life. They kept moving, following animals they hunted. Over time, people began to farm and to build settlements. The Olmec and the Maya lived in what is now Mexico. The Mound Builders and the Ancient Puebloans lived in what is now the United States.

REVIEW

1. **WHAT TO KNOW** How did civilizations develop in the Americas?

2. **VOCABULARY** Use the term **migration** in a sentence about early people.

3. **GEOGRAPHY** What natural feature was important to the Olmec people of San Lorenzo?

4. **CULTURE** How did the Maya preserve their history?

5. **CRITICAL THINKING** Why do you think the Olmec used rivers as trade routes?

6. **WRITE A PARAGRAPH** Describe the different theories about how people arrived in the Americas.

7. **COMPARE AND CONTRAST** On a separate sheet of paper, copy and complete the graphic organizer below.

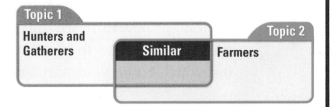

Topic 1
Hunters and Gatherers
Similar
Topic 2
Farmers

Use a Cultural Map

Why It Matters A cultural map shows the different groups who live in a place and what they have in common.

❯ LEARN

A cultural map uses colors and symbols to show cultural regions. A **cultural region** is an area in which people share some ways of life. The map on page 61 has 11 colors. Each one represents a different cultural region in early North America.

Each cultural region was home to several Native American groups. Each group was different. Yet the lifeways and traditions of all groups in a region were alike. All the groups were affected by the same climate and landforms and by the same animals and vegetation.

❯ PRACTICE

Use the map on the next page to answer these questions.

1. Which cultural region includes most of the eastern United States?

2. What is the northernmost cultural region in North America?

3. Which cultural region includes most of the central United States?

❯ APPLY

Partner with a classmate to play a guessing game. You and your partner should each choose a Native American group shown on the cultural map. Take turns asking questions about regions to try to figure out which group your partner chose.

❯ **WOODEN FINGER MASKS** were worn during some Native American ceremonies.

Early Cultures of North America

ARCTIC OCEAN

Greenland

Arctic Circle

INUIT

ALEUT
INUIT
ATHAPASCAN
HAN
INUIT
INUIT
INUIT
INUIT
INUIT
INUIT

TLINGIT
KASKA
INUIT

HAIDA
CHIPEWYAN
Hudson Bay
NASKAPI

BELLA COOLA
CREE
BEOTHUK

NOOTKA
KWAKIUTL
CREE
CREE
CREE

PACIFIC OCEAN
KOOTENAI
CREE
MICMAC

MAKAH
CHINOOK
BLACKFOOT
ASSINIBOINE
CHIPPEWA
CHIPPEWA
ALGONKIN
PENOBSCOT

YAKAMA
NEZ PERCÉ
CROW
MANDAN
CHIPPEWA
OTTAWA
HURON
MASSACHUSET

PAIUTE
SHOSHONE
CHEYENNE
SIOUX
SIOUX
SAC FOX
ERIE
IROQUOIS
IROQUOIS LEAGUE
CAYUGA
MOHAWK

POMO
PAWNEE
IOWAY
MIAMI
LENNI LENAPE
ONEIDA
ONONDAGA
SENECA

SHOSHONE
UTE
ARAPAHO
MISSOURI
ILLINOIS
POWHATAN

YOKUTS
PAIUTE
KAW
SHAWNEE

CHUMASH
HOPI
NAVAJO
APACHE
KIOWA
OSAGE
YUCHI
CHEROKEE
TUSCARORA
ATLANTIC OCEAN

PUEBLO
ACOMA
ZUNI
QUAPAW
CHICKASAW

TOHONO O'ODHAM
APACHE
COMANCHE
CADDO
CHOCTAW
NATCHEZ

YAQUI
TIMUCUA
CALUSA

Gulf of Mexico
Tropic of Cancer

COAHUILTEC
CIBONEY
ARAWAK
ARAWAK

HUICHOL
CIBONEY

TOLTEC
AZTEC
MAYA
Caribbean Sea

MIXTEC
ZAPOTEC

MOSQUITO

SOUTH AMERICA

Legend	
	Arctic
	Subarctic
	Northwest Coast
	Plateau
	California
	Great Basin
	Southwest
	Plains
	Eastern Woodlands
	Middle America
	Caribbean
—	Present-day border

0   300   600 Miles
0   300   600 Kilometers
Azimuthal Equal-Area Projection

Map and Globe Skills

Lesson 2

The Eastern Woodlands

WHAT TO KNOW

How did the geography and climate of the Eastern Woodlands affect the Native Americans there?

VOCABULARY

division of labor p. 63
palisade p. 64
longhouse p. 64
wampum p. 65
confederation p. 65
wigwam p. 66

PEOPLE

Hiawatha
Deganawida

PLACES

Great Lakes

COMPARE AND CONTRAST

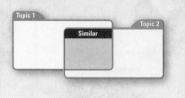

YOU ARE THERE Imagine playing a ball game with other Iroquois children. You scoop up the ball in the small leather basket at the end of your stick and run toward the other team's goal. Darting past the other children, you make your way down the long playing field. As you fling the ball toward the goal, your heart races with excitement. Your skillful play will bring honor to you and your family. Score!

FAST FACT

Lacrosse as it is played today is much like the game played by the Iroquois. Lacrosse players use sticks with nets on one end so that teammates can pass a ball to each other.

▶ **THE EASTERN WOODLANDS** The many forests of this region provided people with wood that was used to make homes and tools.

Life in the Eastern Woodlands

The Eastern Woodlands cultural region stretched east of the Mississippi River. The region's name came from the thick forests that once covered this land. The Eastern Woodlands people built their villages along the banks of the many rivers and streams flowing through the forests.

A Common Resource

Different groups of Native Americans lived in the Eastern Woodlands. However, they all shared an important natural resource—trees. They used trees to make canoes and shelters, and they carved tools and weapons from wood. Trees also gave the people food, such as cherries and plums.

The Eastern Woodlands people were farmers as well as hunters and gatherers.

In the northeastern part of the Woodlands, where the soil was rocky, people did more hunting and gathering than farming.

Jobs were divided between men and women. The men hunted animals for food and used antlers and bones to make tools. Using spears and nets, they fished in the region's many lakes and rivers. The women prepared the food and used animal skins to make clothing and moccasins. This **division of labor** made it possible for people to produce more goods.

In the southern areas of the Eastern Woodlands the soil and climate were better for farming. The people in this area grew corn, beans, squash, and other plants. Usually, the men cleared the land for planting, and the women and children did the planting and harvesting of crops.

READING CHECK ⊙ **COMPARE AND CONTRAST** How were men's jobs and women's jobs divided?

The Iroquois

The Native Americans of the Eastern Woodlands cultural region included two main language groups, the Algonquian (al•GAHN•kwee•uhn) and the Iroquoian (ir•uh•KWOY•uhn). Most of the people who spoke Algonquian languages lived on the Coastal Plain. Most Iroquoian-speaking people lived farther inland.

Among the Iroquoian groups were the Mohawk, the Oneida (oh•NY•duh), the Onondaga (ah•nuhn•DAW•guh), the Cayuga (kay•YOO•guh), and the Seneca. Together, they are known as the Iroquois, or the Five Nations. They lived near the **Great Lakes**, in what is now Pennsylvania and New York and the Lake Ontario region of Canada.

Iroquois Villages

Like other Eastern Woodlands groups, the Iroquois farmed and lived in villages. They built their villages on top of steep hills. To protect against enemies, many Iroquois built **palisades**, or walls of tall wooden poles, around their villages.

The Iroquois lived in shelters called **longhouses**. These long wooden buildings could hold up to 50 people. Their frames were made by cutting poles from small trees, bending the poles, and then covering them with bark. Each longhouse was divided into sections, and each section was home to one or two families.

Near their villages, the Iroquois grew three main crops—corn, beans, and squash. The Iroquois called these the Three Sisters because all three were

An Iroquois Village

ILLUSTRATION The palisades around Iroquois villages protected people from attacks by enemies. What resource was used to build palisades?

Corn, beans, and squash were grown.

The Iroquois were skilled hunters.

planted in the same field. After a field was farmed for a few years, the soil became less fertile. The Iroquois would then clear a field in another location and begin farming there.

Like many other Native Americans, the Iroquois used **wampum**—beads cut from seashells—to make beaded designs that showed important decisions, events, or stories. Wampum was also traded and exchanged for goods.

The Iroquois League

The Five Nations often battled each other over control of hunting areas. A story about one argument tells of an Iroquois warrior named **Hiawatha**. Hiawatha, it was said, saw his family killed by members of another group. By tradition, he was expected to kill those who had killed his family. However, he wanted the fighting to stop.

Hiawatha left his village and met another Iroquois, named **Deganawida** (deh•gahn•uh•WEE•duh), who became known as the Peacemaker. In time, the two men persuaded the Five Nations to unite and work together as a group.

The group that formed about A.D. 1570 was called the Iroquois League. It acted as a **confederation**, a loose group of governments working together. Members from each of the five tribes were sent to speak for their group. They joined the Grand Council, which the league set up to settle disputes among the people peacefully.

READING CHECK **MAIN IDEA AND DETAILS**
What was the Iroquois League?

Baskets were woven from reeds.

Animal hides were used to make clothing.

▶ **THE ALGONQUIAN** This engraving was made by Theodor De Bry in A.D. 1590 from a watercolor made by the English settler John White.

The Algonquian

Among the Algonquian groups were the Delaware, the Wampanoag (wahm•puh•NOH•ag), and the Powhatan (pow•uh•TAN). All three of these tribes lived on the Coastal Plain. Other Algonquian-speaking groups lived farther inland, around the Great Lakes. These people included the Ottawa (AH•tuh•wuh), the Chippewa (CHIH•puh•waw), and the Miami.

Villages and Lifeways

Most Algonquian groups had anywhere from 1 to 20 villages. Some groups built longhouses similar to those of the Iroquois. Others built round, bark-covered shelters called **wigwams**. Apart from their shape, wigwams were made in much the same way as longhouses. The trunks of small trees were bent, tied together into a dome shape, and then covered with bark.

Algonquian Lifeways

The Algonquian who lived near the coast did not rely on their crops for food as much as their Iroquois neighbors. Fish was an important food source. The Algonquian built canoes to fish in the rivers and along the coast. They used animal bones and wood to make hooks and fishing traps.

The Algonquian made clothing mostly from deerskin, which kept them warm during the cold winters. Men wore shirts, leggings, and moccasins. Women usually wore dresses.

Government and Customs

Many Algonquian groups had leaders who governed more than one village. Some groups had two chiefs, one to rule on matters of peace and the other to rule on matters of war.

Among Algonquian groups, marriage ceremonies were very much alike. If a man wanted to marry a woman, he had to show her he was a good hunter. If the woman wanted to marry him, she would show him that she was a good homemaker. When the couple married, they usually exchanged gifts and invited their families to a feast.

READING CHECK ⚙ **COMPARE AND CONTRAST**
How did the diet of the Algonquian differ from that of the Iroquois?

▶ **ALGONQUIAN BOWL** Many Algonquian household items were carved from wood.

Summary

The people of the Eastern Woodlands used trees for food, shelter, and transportation. The two main language groups of the Eastern Woodlands were the Iroquoian and the Algonquian.

REVIEW

1. **WHAT TO KNOW** How did the geography and climate of the Eastern Woodlands affect the Native Americans there?

2. **VOCABULARY** How is the term **confederation** related to the Iroquois League?

3. **GEOGRAPHY** Why was living near the Atlantic Ocean important for the Algonquian peoples?

4. **CRITICAL THINKING** Why did the Iroquois groups choose to come together to form the Iroquois League?

5. 📝 **GIVE A SPEECH** Write and deliver a speech to try to persuade Iroquois leaders to join the Iroquois League. Be sure to include good reasons for working together.

6. ⭐ **COMPARE AND CONTRAST** On a separate sheet of paper, copy and complete the graphic organizer below.

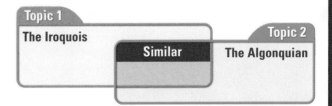

THE COMMON GOOD

"Look and listen for the welfare of the whole people and have always in view not only the present but also the coming generations. . . ."

—from the Iroquois Constitution

IROQUOIS LEADERS decided that they must all agree on any action to be taken, in order to make sure their decisions were for the good of all.

For many years, the Iroquois were not united. They often fought one another over land and resources. Then, in the 1500s, Hiawatha and Deganawida helped make peace among the Five Nations.

Hiawatha's goal was to find a way for the Five Nations to settle their disagreements so that they could work together for their common good. This meant that they helped one another and thought about what was best for everyone.

In time Hiawatha was able to unite the Iroquois with the Iroquois League. The League was based on the idea that the groups could work together for the common good.

HIAWATHA

Focus On: Democratic Values

VOLUNTEERS can be people of all ages. By voting, people can choose what they think will be good for their communities.

Today, many Americans continue to work for the common good by volunteering or by serving in the government. They help build shelters, feed the hungry, register voters, and count election ballots. They give many hours of service to those in need. State and local communities often honor volunteers and teachers who give their time and effort to serve others.

Americans also work for the common good by respecting the rights of others, obeying laws, and paying taxes. Tax money is used to provide services to people and to improve our cities, states, and country.

Make It Relevant Why is it important for citizens to work together for the common good?

VOLUNTEERING to help feed the hungry is one way to work for the common good.

Lesson  3

The Plains

 WHAT TO KNOW
How did the geography and climate of the Plains affect the Native Americans there?

VOCABULARY
lodge p. 72
sod p. 72
scarce p. 73
tepee p. 73
travois p. 73
council p. 74
ceremony p. 74

PEOPLE
Iowa
Missouri
Sioux
Cheyenne
Kiowa
Blackfoot

PLACES
Central Plains
Missouri River
Platte River
Great Plains

 **COMPARE AND CONTRAST**

YOU ARE THERE The sound of thunder wakes you, and you quickly sit up. But this isn't really thunder! You feel the ground rumbling beneath you. Only then do you know that the sound you are hearing is the pounding hooves of thousands of buffalo running from your tribe's hunters.

You listen as your mother and your grandmother talk about the hunt. Soon there will be fresh meat to cook and dry. Grandmother has even promised to make you a new pair of moccasins from part of a buffalo hide.

FAST FACT

Hundreds of years ago, the buffalo herds on the Plains were so large that they sometimes blackened the horizon.

Life on the Plains

The Plains people lived on the Interior Plains between the Mississippi River and the Rocky Mountains. On fields of grass, they hunted buffalo, or American bison. After water, buffalo were the Plains' most important natural resource. Millions of these animals once roamed this large region of dry prairie land in North America.

Hunting the Buffalo

Imagine hunters coming upon a herd of buffalo. Wearing animal skins, they sneak up on the buffalo. A signal is given, all the hunters yell, and the frightened buffalo begin to run. The hunters drive the herd toward a steep cliff. Unable to stop, the animals fall over the side and are killed.

Buffalo were the main source of food for all the Native American groups who lived on the Plains. The meat could be eaten raw or cooked. It could also be mixed with fat and berries to make pemmican, a dried meat that could be stored.

The buffalo gave Plains groups what they needed to make clothing, tools, utensils, and shelters. The people used almost every part of the buffalo. They made clothing and moccasins from the skins. They carried water in bags made from the stomachs. They twisted the hair into cord, and they made tools from the bones and horns. Even the hooves of the buffalo were used to make glue. Nothing was wasted.

READING CHECK ☼COMPARE AND CONTRAST
What different ways was buffalo meat prepared?

DIAGRAM This chart shows only a few of the many uses the Plains people had for the buffalo. How did Plains people use the buffalo to become better hunters?

Native American Uses of the Buffalo

Horns cups, spoons

Skin clothing, shelter, shields, drums

Bones tools, arrowheads, pipes

Farmers and Hunters

While they all needed the buffalo and shared many customs, there were differences among the Plains people. Their ways of life depended in part on where they lived.

People of the Central Plains

Some Plains groups lived in the eastern part of the Plains, or the **Central Plains**. The **Iowa** and the **Missouri** lived there, as did smaller groups of the **Sioux** (SOO), such as the Nakota. These groups were both hunters and gatherers and farmers. They gathered plants and hunted deer, elk, and buffalo. They farmed in the fertile valleys of the **Missouri River** and the **Platte River**. They grew beans, corn, and sunflowers. At times, groups traded some of their crops for other goods.

These Central Plains people lived in villages made up of large round earthen houses called **lodges**. Each lodge was home to several families. One lodge usually held 20 to 40 people.

Each lodge was built of earth over a small pit. In the center was a fireplace under a hole in the roof for letting out smoke. On the northern prairies, the lodges were covered by **sod**, a layer of soil held together by the roots of grasses.

About twice a year, Central Plains tribes took part in a great buffalo hunt. To reach the distant plains where the buffalo lived, the people had to walk from their villages in the river valleys.

READING CHECK Ö **COMPARE AND CONTRAST**
How were the Central Plains Indians both farmers and hunters?

Great Plains Life

ILLUSTRATION The people of the Great Plains used their environment to get food and to make clothing and shelter. What activities do you see in this illustration?

Tepee poles were valuable because wood was scarce.

A travois

A Nomadic Society

Smoke rises from an early morning fire as a **Cheyenne** (shy•AN) woman makes food. Wood is **scarce**, or in short supply. The scarcity of wood means other sources of fuel must be used. So the woman burns dried buffalo droppings, called chips.

People of the Great Plains

The Cheyenne lived in the western part of the Interior Plains, called the **Great Plains**. They and other groups who lived there, such as the **Kiowa** (ky•uh•wah) and the Crow, moved from place to place following herds of buffalo. They did not farm the dry grasslands where they lived. Their digging sticks could not break up the soil.

The Great Plains people built shelters that were easy to move. One such shelter was a cone-shaped tent called a **tepee** (TEE•pee). To build a tepee, wooden poles were set in a circle and tied together at the top. Then the poles were covered with buffalo skins. A hole at the top of the tepee let out the smoke from fires.

The people also used their wooden poles to make a carrier called a **travois** (truh•VOY). A travois was made of two poles tied together at one end and then fastened to a harness on a dog. Goods were carried on a buffalo skin tied between the poles.

READING CHECK **CAUSE AND EFFECT**
Why did people on the Great Plains have a nomadic way of life?

In hot weather, tepee flaps were opened to let air in.

Animal hides were softened by using ashes and fat.

Plains Cultures

Like all Native Americans, the Plains people had different customs and kinds of government.

Government

The Lakota people, another branch of the Sioux, were made up of seven nomadic groups. Each group made its own choices. However, belonging to the larger Lakota group required the smaller groups to respect each other's hunting areas and live in peace.

The Cheyenne governed differently. They were ten groups that were independent of each other in many ways. However, each group sent its leaders to meet in a **council** of chiefs. All the Cheyenne groups had to follow the council's decisions.

Among the Plains people, every person in the group was equal. No one person was born more important than anyone else. Any man could become chief if he was a good warrior and a good leader.

Traditions and Religious Beliefs

Even though they had different ways of governing, many of the Plains groups shared certain traditions and religious beliefs. Each group had a story that told how they came to be. The **Blackfoot**, for example, believed that they were made by a spirit called Old Man.

Among the Plains groups who farmed, corn was very important. Every year, they held ceremonies to celebrate and give thanks for the corn harvest. A **ceremony** is a celebration to honor a cultural or religious event. Other ceremonies marked the beginning and end of buffalo hunts,

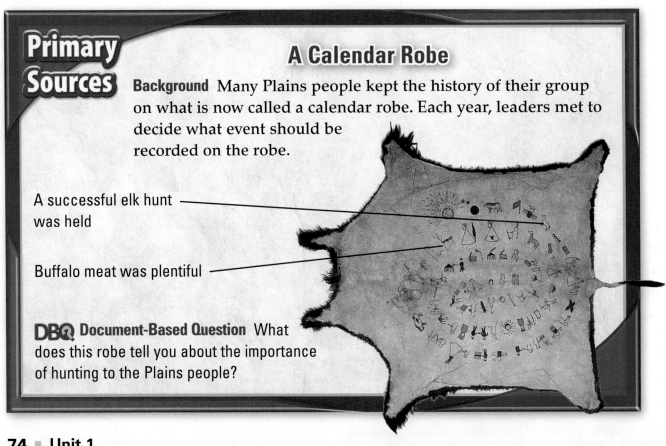

Primary Sources

A Calendar Robe

Background Many Plains people kept the history of their group on what is now called a calendar robe. Each year, leaders met to decide what event should be recorded on the robe.

A successful elk hunt was held

Buffalo meat was plentiful

DBQ Document-Based Question What does this robe tell you about the importance of hunting to the Plains people?

the naming of a child, or the beginning of a marriage.

The Sioux held a ceremony called the Sun Dance. They believed that it helped keep the buffalo strong. Many Plains people held Sun Dances or similar ceremonies before the summer buffalo hunt. Ceremonies such as the Sun Dance showed the Plains people's respect for nature, and helped build a sense of unity.

READING CHECK ☼ **COMPARE AND CONTRAST**
How were the governments of the Lakota and the Cheyenne different?

Summary

The Plains people lived in a large region that stretched across the middle of North America. The Plains people were made up of many different groups. However, different groups lived in similar types of shelters, depended on the same sources of food, and shared certain religious beliefs.

❯ **TRIBAL LEADERS were an important part of Blackfoot religious ceremonies.**

REVIEW

1. **WHAT TO KNOW** How did the geography and climate of the Plains affect the Native Americans there?

2. **VOCABULARY** Explain how **sod** is related to a **lodge**.

3. **CULTURE** What was the purpose of a travois?

4. **CRITICAL THINKING** How did the Plains people use dogs? How are dogs used today?

5. 🖌 **DRAW A BUILDING PLAN** Give step-by-step instructions to build a tepee. Illustrate each step and include a list of materials, using what you know about Plains people's tepees.

6. (Focus Skill) **COMPARE AND CONTRAST** On a separate sheet of paper, copy and complete the graphic organizer below.

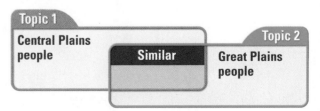

Topic 1
Central Plains people
Similar
Topic 2
Great Plains people

The Southwest and the West

WHAT TO KNOW
How did the geography and climate of the Southwest and the West affect the Native Americans there?

VOCABULARY
adapt p. 77
staple p. 77
surplus p. 77
adobe p. 78
hogan p. 78
trade network p. 80

PEOPLE
Ancient Puebloans
Hopi
Zuni
Navajo
Shoshone
Nez Perce
Chumash

PLACES
Arizona
New Mexico
Great Basin
Columbia Plateau

COMPARE AND CONTRAST

YOU ARE THERE

Today, you worked in the hot sun, digging a path that will bring water to your tribe's crops. Water is so precious in this dry land, you are glad that it will not be wasted.

As you stand on the top of your pueblo, you can see the fine crops below. They lie at the base of the flat-topped mesas and deep cliffs where your people have lived for hundreds of years. Even though you're tired from the day's work, you're excited. Tonight, a storyteller will tell the tale of your ancestors—the **Ancient Puebloans**.

FAST FACT

Ladders were used to enter pueblos. In the event of an attack, the villagers pulled up the ladders.

Clay ovens

A kiva was a room used for ceremonies.

The Southwest

The desert Southwest, with its mesas, canyons, cliffs, and mountains, was a hard place to live. Intense summer heat is usually followed by bitter winter cold. Weeks can go by without a drop of rain or snow.

Adapting to the Southwest

Among the Native Americans who were able to **adapt**, or adjust, their ways of life to this land were the **Hopi** (HOH•pee) and the **Zuni** (ZOO•nee). The Hopi lived in what is today the state of **Arizona**. The Zuni lived farther east, in present-day **New Mexico**. They and most other groups in the region became known as the Pueblo peoples. Like their Ancient Puebloan ancestors, they lived in pueblos built on mesas or on the sides of steep canyons.

Even in the dry environment, the Pueblo people were able to grow their **staple**, or main, foods of corn, beans, and squash. They found ways to collect water and to store **surplus**, or extra amounts, of food. The Pueblo also grew cotton, which they used to weave blankets and clothing.

Not all of the people who lived in the Southwest were Pueblo. The **Navajo** (NA•vuh•hoh) moved into the Southwest in about A.D. 1025, settling in the Four Corners area. The Navajo had led mainly nomadic lives before, but they learned to adapt to the harsh climate.

During a period of drought, some Hopi people went to live with the Navajo. In time, the Navajo began growing food and cotton as the Hopi did.

READING CHECK ŎCOMPARE AND CONTRAST
In what ways were the Pueblo people like the Ancient Puebloans?

A Southwestern Pueblo

ILLUSTRATION Some pueblos had as many as five levels. How does the illustration show that the Pueblo people had a strong sense of unity?

Looms were used for weaving cloth.

An entry

Corn was ground up to make meal.

Clay pottery was used to store food and water.

Children IN HISTORY

Hopi Children

For hundreds of years, Hopi children have received little wooden kachina dolls. These dolls are not toys. Instead, they are learning tools. Each doll is decorated in a special way and represents an important human value, such as kindness, discipline, or respect for elders. Through the kachina dolls, children learn the importance of practicing these values in their own lives.

Make It Relevant Why do you think it might be important for children to learn respect for their elders?

Pueblo Culture

The desert environment shaped how both the Pueblo and the Navajo lived. Little rain fell, so few trees grew. The Hopi and the Zuni used stones and mud to build pueblos. Other groups made houses from **adobe** (uh•DOH•bee), sun-dried bricks made of clay and straw.

The Navajo built homes called **hogans**. These cone-shaped shelters were built by covering a wooden frame with mud or adobe. Navajo hogans were often miles apart, unlike homes in Pueblo villages.

Pueblo and Navajo tribes depended on trade for resources not found nearby. They sometimes traveled far to trade their pottery and baskets with other tribes.

▶ HOPI KACHINA DOLL

Religion and Government

Both the Pueblo and the Navajo people honored their gods in special ceremonies. Navajo ceremonies, for example, were led by religious leaders and healers called medicine people. Medicine people memorized and sang songs or chants believed to have healing powers.

Religion had a strong role in the government of the Pueblo. Usually, a chief who was also a religious leader led the Hopi village. The chief made rules and carried out punishments. The Navajo were organized in groups, each with its own religious leader. The leaders met every few years to make decisions.

READING CHECK ⭕COMPARE AND CONTRAST How were Pueblo and Navajo shelters different?

Groups to the West

Many different groups of Native Americans lived among the mountains, deserts, valleys, forests, and coastal lands that stretch from the Rocky Mountains to the Pacific Ocean. Among the groups living in the western part of what is now the United States were those of the Plateau, Great Basin, and California cultures.

Ways of Life

The **Shoshone** (shoh•SHOH•nee) lived part of the year in the **Great Basin**. They hunted small animals and they built shelters with dry brush. They spent the rest of the year hunting buffalo in the mountains of present-day Wyoming.

The **Nez Perce** (nez•PURS) lived to the northwest on the **Columbia Plateau**.

Its dry hills and flatlands included parts of what is now Idaho, Oregon, and Washington. For food, the Nez Perce relied on the many rivers and streams that drain the high plateau. The Nez Perce made long spears and nets to catch salmon. Salmon was such an important part of their diet that the Nez Perce built movable shelters to use while fishing.

The **Chumash** (CHOO•mash) lived in what is now southern California. The area they lived in was rich with birds, fish, and acorns. Their villages were located near the Pacific Ocean, which was also an important source of food. They built dome-shaped shelters that they covered with thick layers of tule (TOO•lee), a tall, flexible plant with a spongy stem.

❯ **CHUMASH VILLAGES** often had as many as 1,000 people.

Trading for Needed Goods

Native Americans in the Plateau, Great Basin, and California cultural regions depended on nearby natural resources. To get goods they could not make or find themselves, they formed large **trade networks**. These networks allowed them to get goods from faraway places.

Native Americans did not always travel to those faraway places. They traded with people in nearby villages. In turn, the people of those villages traded with villages farther away. In this way, goods and ideas could travel long distances.

READING CHECK **SUMMARIZE**
How did trade networks bring distant goods?

Summary

The people of the Southwest and the West adapted to a variety of environments. They also traded for needed goods by forming trade networks.

▶ **CHUMASH COUPLE** After a Chumash couple was married a husband would travel with his wife to live with her family.

REVIEW

1. **WHAT TO KNOW** How did the geography and climate of the Southwest and the West affect Native Americans there?

2. **VOCABULARY** Write a sentence about the people of the Southwest, using the term **adapt**.

3. **HISTORY** What event caused some Hopi people to live with the Navajo?

4. **CRITICAL THINKING** How did location affect the types of shelters built by people of the Southwest and the West?

5. **DRAW A MAP** Draw a map of the United States. Shade in three cultural areas located in what is now the western part of the United States.

6. **COMPARE AND CONTRAST** (Focus Skill) On a separate sheet of paper, copy and complete the graphic organizer below.

Topic 1
The Hopi

Similar

Topic 2
The Navajo

Luci Tapahonso

Biography

Trustworthiness
Respect
Responsibility
Fairness
Caring
Patriotism

"This is how we were raised. We were raised with care and attention because it has always been this way. It has worked well for centuries."

Luci Tapahonso is a Navajo poet who helps spread Navajo culture through her writing. Tapahonso was born in Shiprock, New Mexico, and grew up in a large Native American community. She started writing poetry at the age of 9 and had her first book published at the age of 28.

Today, Tapahonso is a professor at the University of Arizona. She uses both the Navajo and English languages in her writings, which are often about the land of the Southwest and the history of her people. Tapahonso has read many of her poems on radio and television.

Tapahonso was part of a group that helped plan and organize the National Museum of the American Indian in Washington, D.C. The museum, which covers 10,000 years of history, opened in September 2004.

Why Character Counts

How does Luci Tapahonso work to keep the Navajo community strong?

Time

1953 ———————————————— **PRESENT**

Born

1953 Luci Tapahonso is born

1981 Tapahonso publishes her first collection of poems

GO ONLINE For more resources, go to www.harcourtschool.com/ss1

Lesson 5

The Northwest and the Arctic

WHAT TO KNOW
How did the geography and climate of the Pacific Northwest and the Arctic affect the Native Americans there?

VOCABULARY
harpoon p. 82

clan p. 84

economy p. 84

barter p. 85

potlatch p. 85

kayak p. 86

igloo p. 86

PEOPLE
Kwakiutl
Makah
Chinook
Aleut
Inuit

PLACES
Columbia River
The Dalles
Aleutian Islands

COMPARE AND CONTRAST

YOU ARE THERE

Spring has finally come. For weeks, the village elders have been noting the wind's direction and watching the stars. They have decided that today is a good day to go hunting for a whale.

The whale hunters will take the village's biggest canoes. The hunters carry with them their longest, heaviest **harpoons**—long spears with sharp shell points. If the hunt is a success, there will be singing and dancing to welcome the hunters home!

▶ **WHALEBONE ARTIFACTS** The whalebone artifact at the top is the carved figure of a walrus. The artifact at the bottom may have been an art object or a tool.

▶ **A MAKAH WHALE HUNT** The chief harpooner showed his respect for the whale by singing a special song, promising to give the whale gifts if it allowed itself to be killed.

A Region of Plenty

The Northwest Coast, also known as the Pacific Northwest, stretched between the Pacific Ocean and the mountains to the east. It included parts of what are now Oregon, Washington, and western Canada. Cool ocean winds brought heavy rains to the region, so forests grew tall and thick. These forests and the rivers that ran through them were filled with fish and other animals.

People of the Northwest Coast

Many Native American groups, such as the **Kwakiutl** (kwah•kee•YOO•tuhl), the **Makah** (mah•KAW), and the **Chinook** (shuh•NUK), lived in this region. Instead of farming, the people of the Northwest

Coast met their needs by fishing and hunting and by gathering plants and nuts. The coastal waters were an important resource, and salmon was a staple food for most groups.

Whales were an important resource, too. Whales supplied not only food but also fat, which could be melted into oil to burn in lamps. Most groups, including the Kwakiutl, captured only whales that had become stranded on the shore. In contrast, the Makah hunted whales at sea in large dugout canoes. These boats— each made from a large, hollowed-out log—carried up to 60 people.

READING CHECK ⟳**COMPARE AND CONTRAST**
How were the whale-hunting methods of the Makah different from those of the Kwakiutl?

Resources and Trade

The giant trees that grow in the forests of the Northwest Coast provided many groups with wood for houses, tools, and boats. Makah villages stood near the Pacific Ocean, a common location for many Native American homes in the Pacific Northwest.

Family Shelters

The shelters of the Makah were like those of the Iroquois, but larger. Makah longhouses had a frame made of wooden poles, which could reach 60 feet in length. The walls and floors were covered with wide boards.

All the members of a **clan**, or extended family, lived in the same longhouse. Grandparents, parents, aunts and uncles, and children lived together. Each person in the clan held a specific rank. Clans made important decisions about village life. Clans also taught younger members songs, stories, and woodcarving skills.

Wood was so useful to the people of the Northwest Coast that they made almost everything from it. Dishes, spoons, and other utensils were made of wood. They also carved totem poles made of wood. These tall posts usually showed one or more characters that were used to tell a story or to welcome visitors or traders.

People traveled long distances on the region's waterways in order to trade. Trading was a large part of the region's economy. An **economy** is the way the people of a state, region, or country use their resources to meet their needs.

The Dalles

The best-known traders among the Northwest Coast Indians were the Chinook. The Chinook lived at the mouth of the **Columbia River**, which they controlled from the coast all the way to **The Dalles**—about 200 miles upriver.

The Dalles was a center of the trade network because many groups gathered

Dugout canoes were used for fishing.

there, but the different languages they spoke made communication difficult. The Chinook were able to profit from trading at The Dalles because they developed a unique language for trade. It was made up of Chinook words as well as words borrowed from other Indian languages. This language allowed them to **barter**, or exchange goods, on behalf of two groups who spoke very different languages.

A Potlatch

Trade and natural resources made many Northwest Coast groups rich.

One way they expressed their good fortune was through a celebration known as a **potlatch**. A potlatch was meant to show wealth and divide property among the people. *Potlatch* means "to give." Historians think that the Kwakiutl, who lived along the coast of what is now Canada, helped develop the potlatch custom. A Kwakiutl potlatch was a celebration, with dancing, food, and speeches.

READING CHECK **GENERALIZE**
Why was wood important to people of the Northwest Coast?

A Northwest Coast Village

ILLUSTRATION It is thought that there were hundreds of people living in the many villages along the Northwest Coast. What important resources of the Northwest Coast are pictured below?

Totem poles stood in front of many homes.

Some clothing was made of cedar bark.

Salmon were dried for food.

Baskets were made with long, thin strips of wood.

Lands of the North

The Arctic is the region near the North Pole. This land is mostly a flat plain where the earth stays frozen year-round. One Arctic group known as the **Aleut** (a•lee•OOT) lived along the coast of the **Aleutian** (uh•LOO•shuhn) **Islands**. One group closely related to the Aleut were the **Inuit** (IH•nu•wuht). These people lived in what is now Alaska and northernmost Canada.

Life in the Arctic

Because of the climate, few plants could grow in this region. The Inuit and the Aleut hunted foxes, caribou, and polar bears. They also used harpoons and **kayaks** (KY•aks) to hunt seals, walruses, and whales. A kayak is a one-person canoe made of waterproof skins stretched over wood or bone.

Resources were limited, so nothing was wasted. The people caught seals not only for their meat but also for their skins, which were made into clothes and tents. Oil was used to light and heat houses. Even the bones were used to make tools.

The Aleut lived together in large houses with beams made of whalebone and walls made of sod. During the winter, some Inuit lived in homes made of ice, called **igloos**. Other Inuit families lived year-round in tents of animal skin or in sod houses.

The extended family was an important part of Inuit and Aleut society. Inuit groups, for example, were usually loosely formed bands of 60 to 300 people, made up of several families. These families came together to make important choices for the good of the group. The people hunted and traveled together, often sharing seal meat in order to survive.

▶ **AN INUIT FAMILY** The Inuit people worked together and learned the skills they needed to survive in an icy land.

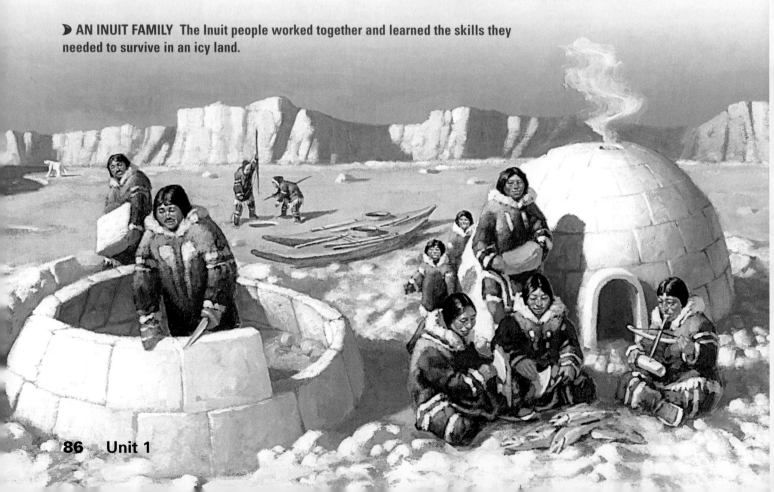

▶ THE INUIT made carvings from whale bone. The artifact (right) shows an Inuit whale hunt.

Life in the Sub-Arctic

South of the Arctic is the sub-Arctic region of North America. It stretches from what is now eastern Canada to what is now Alaska. People of the sub-Arctic region, such as the Cree, relied on hunting and gathering to meet their needs.

The Cree lived over a wide area across what is now Canada. Trees provided the Cree with wood to meet their needs. Since the long winters kept them from being able to get food by farming, they used bows and arrows to hunt for game. Some Cree groups divided the land so the people had an area to hunt as their own. Other groups roamed freely.

READING CHECK ☼**COMPARE AND CONTRAST**
How did the shelters of the Aleut differ from those of the Inuit?

Summary

The rich natural resources of the Northwest helped form a society based on hunting, gathering, and trade. The Arctic and sub-Arctic peoples adapted to life in a land with limited resources.

REVIEW

1. **WHAT TO KNOW** How did the geography and climate of the Pacific Northwest and the Arctic affect the Native Americans there?

2. **VOCABULARY** Write a sentence explaining why trade was important to the economy of the Northwest Coast.

3. **CULTURE** Why do you think Inuit groups had to share food to survive?

4. **CRITICAL THINKING** How might limited resources affect the ways in which people live?

5. ✏️ **WRITE A POEM** Write a poem about the life of a Native American family living in the Northwest or the Arctic.

6. ⭐(Focus Skill) **COMPARE AND CONTRAST** On a separate sheet of paper, copy and complete the graphic organizer below.

Topic 1 — The Makah | Similar | Topic 2 — The Kwakiutl

FIELD TRIP

READ ABOUT

The National Museum of the American Indian is located in Washington, D.C., just south of the United States Capitol Building. The museum chronicles 10,000 years of Native American life in the Americas and has nearly one million artifacts. These artifacts come from more than 1,000 Native American cultures ranging from the Arctic to the tip of South America. Inside the museum, visitors can tour exhibits and watch cultural interpreters demonstrate traditional skills such as weaving, wood-carving, and storytelling.

FIND

MARYLAND

Washington, D.C.

VIRGINIA

The National Museum of the AMERICAN INDIAN

THE NATIONAL MUSEUM OF THE AMERICAN INDIAN in Washington, D.C.

INTERACTIVE EXHIBITS show Native American lifeways.

MAYAN CLAY FIGURE once used as a whistle.

TRADITIONAL NATIVE AMERICAN CLOTHING AND BEADWORK

SCULPTURE from the Northwest Coast

NATIVE AMERICAN METAL WORK AND ART OBJECTS

A VIRTUAL TOUR

GO ONLINE For more resources, go to
www.harcourtschool.com/ss1

Chapter 2 Review

Time 14,000 B.C. | 8,000 B.C.

About 8000 B.C. The large animals that early people hunt begin to die off.

Visual Summary

Summarize the Chapter

Focus Skill — Compare and Contrast Complete this graphic organizer to compare and contrast the Native American groups who lived in different regions of North America.

Topic 1
Some groups relied more on hunting for food.

Similar

Topic 2
Some groups relied more on farming for food.

Vocabulary

Identify the term from the word bank that correctly matches each definition.

1. to adjust ways of living to land and resources

2. a group of people with ways of life, religion, and learning

3. a way of life or an idea that has been handed down from the past

4. a way to divide work

5. the movement of people

6. the way people use their resources to meet their needs

7. a celebration to honor a special event

8. an object made by people

Word Bank

migration p. 53   division of labor p. 63

artifact p. 55   ceremony p. 74

civilization p. 56   adapt p. 77

tradition p. 57   economy p. 84

About 3000 B.C. People in the Americas begin farming.

About 1500 B.C. The Olmec civilization begins.

PRESENT

About A.D. 1200 More than 30,000 people live in Cahokia.

 Time Line

Use the chapter summary time line above to answer these questions.

9. Did people start farming before or after large animals began dying out?

10. About how many people lived in Cahokia in A.D. 1200?

 Facts and Main Ideas

Answer these questions.

11. How does the land bridge theory help scientists explain the movement of people from Asia to North America?

12. How did life change for people once they began farming?

13. What achievement of Mayan culture was unique among early Americans?

Write the letter of the best choice.

14. Which two language groups lived in the Eastern Woodlands region?
    A the Iroquoian and the Algonquian
    B the Shoshone and the Nez Perce
    C the Inuit and the Aleut
    D the Hopi and the Navajo

15. For which two Native American regions was wood one of the most important resources?
    A Southwest and Plains
    B Plains and Eastern Woodlands
    C Eastern Woodlands and Northwest
    D Southwest and Arctic

16. What is one example of a way that Native Americans modified their environment?
    A They traded for things they needed.
    B They irrigated land for farming.
    C They stored food in containers.
    D They traveled long distances for wood.

 Critical Thinking

17. How did changes in climate affect the lives of early people in the Americas?

18. What kinds of things can affect the sources of food, clothing, and shelter available to Native American groups?

 Skills

Use a Culture Map

19. Look at the cultural map on page 61. Near which ocean did the Makah live?

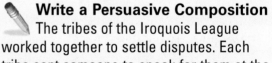

Write a Persuasive Composition The tribes of the Iroquois League worked together to settle disputes. Each tribe sent someone to speak for them at the Grand Council. Write a persuasive composition in favor of this type of government.

Write a Research Report Study a Pueblo historical site. Then write a research report describing the land of the Southwest and how the Pueblo people built their homes.

Chapter 2 ■ 91

Fun with Social Studies

"This city was built and settled by nomadic people."

"This clay pot was made by the Inuit."

"This spear was used to paddle a dugout canoe."

Dig Right In!

Professor Prattle is good at digging up artifacts, but he's not very good at drawing conclusions about them. How do you know his conclusions are wrong?

Family Secrets

The vocabulary words that match the clues are hiding in the family members' names. Can you find the words? The right letters are in order reading from left to right, but there may be other letters in between.

VOCABULARY

A cone-shaped tent

MISTER PEEPERS

UNCLE ANDY

An extended family

Sun-dried bricks of clay and straw

AUNT DORA BELLE

COUSIN LETTY

Water extending into land from a larger body of water

Soil held together by grass roots

SON DAVEY

Very dry

BARKY FIDO

Photo Mix-Up

Match the correct caption to each of Emmy's vacation photos.

It was hot and dry when we were driving through the Southwest.

We camped near here in the Rocky Mountains.

I got some Coastal Plain sand in my shoes here.

Online GO Adventures

In this online game, you'll join Eco on a journey through different times and places to collect artifacts for the Time Museum. Get ready, because it's not as easy as it sounds. If you can solve the puzzles in different early Native American villages, you'll find all the artifacts that the museum curator needs. Play now at **www.harcourtschool.com/ss1**

Review and Test Prep ✔

💡 THE BIG IDEA

Geography People interact with their environment and are affected by it.

Reading Comprehension and Vocabulary

The Land and Early People

The United States is a nation made up of 50 states. It shares some landforms and bodies of water with Canada and Mexico. These three large nations cover most of the land on the <u>continent</u> of North America.

The United States has a variety of landforms and bodies of water, including mountains, hills, plains, valleys, deserts, rivers, and lakes. Geographers often divide the country into five regions—the Northeast, Southeast, Southwest, Midwest, and West. Geographers may also divide land into regions based on relative location, climate, culture, vegetation, or landforms.

People have lived in North and South America for many thousands of years. The land bridge theory is one idea about how people first arrived. About 5,000 years ago, people began farming in the Americas. In Central America, <u>civilizations</u> were forming about 3,500 years ago.

Eastern Woodlands and Northwest Coast peoples found food in the forests and used trees to make homes and tools. Plains Indians relied on buffalo or farming. Arctic people had to adapt to a cold land. They hunted seals and whales. In the Southwest and the West, people hunted and farmed.

Use the summary above to answer these questions.

1. What does the word <u>continent</u> mean in the paragraph above?
   A the land drained by a river
   B a large land mass
   C your surroundings
   D a region

2. Canada, the United States, and Mexico are the three largest nations on this continent. What is this continent?
   A Asia
   B Europe
   C North America
   D South America

3. How did life in the Americas begin to change about 5,000 years ago?
   A An ice age began.
   B Civilizations began to form.
   C Larger animals began to die off.
   D People began to farm.

4. What does the word <u>civilization</u> mean?
   A a group of people who have something in common
   B a group of people with ways of life, religion, and learning
   C a person who studies the past
   D a system for deciding what is best for people

Answer these questions.

5. What large landform region covers most of the area along the Atlantic Ocean?

6. What region covers most of the central United States?

7. Why were the Great Lakes and its rivers important to the Midwest?

8. How did rivers affect human settlement?

9. How can different climate regions affect how people adapt to the environment?

10. Why is the Olmec civilization known as the "mother culture" of the Americas?

Write the letter of the best choice.

11. Which two early American civilizations developed in Mexico?
    A Maya and Olmec
    B Olmec and Mound Builders
    C Mound Builders and Maya
    D Maya and Ancient Puebloans

12. Which early American civilization built its homes in the area now called the Four Corners?
    A the Adena
    B the Ancient Puebloans
    C the Maya
    D the Olmec

13. Which was one of the most important resources to the Plains people?
    A the buffalo
    B the fish
    C the grasses
    D the trees

14. What did Native Americans in the Arctic, the Plains, and the Northwest Coast have in common?
    A They depended on farming.
    B They depended on whales and salmon.
    C They depended on hunting or fishing.
    D They depended on ice to build shelters.

15. How do different landform regions affect how people modify the land?

16. How did Native American economies and resources differ from region to region?

Use Latitude and Longitude

Use the map below to answer the following questions.

17. Which state capital is farther north—Frankfort, Kentucky, or Nashville, Tennessee?

18. Which line of latitude is nearest the state capitals of Illinois, Indiana, and Ohio?

19. Which line of longitude is nearest the state capital of Illinois?

20. Which line of longitude is nearest the state capital of Kentucky?

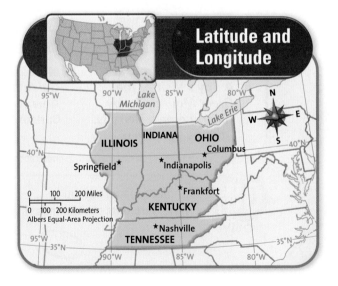

Latitude and Longitude

Activities

Show What You Know

 Unit Writing Activity

Write a Report Focus on two Native American groups in this unit.

- Compare and contrast the environments that affected their ways of life.
- Describe their villages, shelters, and sources of food, clothing, and tools.

 Unit Project

A Native American Book Write and illustrate a book about Native American groups discussed in this unit.

- Include drawings, charts, poems, and maps that describe each group's way of life and their surroundings.
- Include a map of North America with labels for each group and its region.

Read More

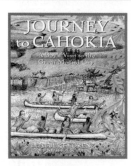

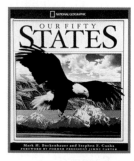

- *Journey to Cahokia: A Boy's Visit to the Great Mound City* by Albert Lorenz. Harry N. Abrams Publishers.

- *More than Moccasins: A Kid's Guide to Traditional North American Indian Life* by Laurie Carlson. Chicago Review Press.

- *National Geographic: Our Fifty States* by Mark H. Bockenhauer. National Geographic Children's Books.

 For more resources, go to
www.harcourtschool.com/ss1

Cultures Meet

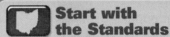

Start with the Standards

OHIO SOCIAL STUDIES CONTENT STANDARDS

History 5.1, 5.2, 5.3, 5.4, 5.6

People in Societies 5.1A, 5.1B, 5.1C, 5.1E, 5.1F, 5.2, 5.3, 5.4, 5.5

Geography 5.3, 5.7A, 5.8, 5.9A, 5.10

Economics 5.1, 5.2, 5.4

Social Studies Skills 5.3, 5.4A, 5.4B, 5.4C, 5.5, 5.8, 5.9A, 5.9B, 5.9C, 5.9D, 5.9E, 5.9F, 5.9G

The Big Idea

Cooperation and Conflict

Cultural differences and competition for land led to conflicts among different groups of people in the Americas.

What to Know

✔ Why did Europeans begin to explore different areas of the world?

✔ What explorers led key expeditions and what routes did they follow?

✔ How did European explorations change the lives of Native Americans?

THE FUR TRADE

DID YOU KNOW?

Although almost hunted to extinction in the nineteenth century, beavers and otters are now protected, and their populations are growing.

A beaver dam

The French explorer René Robert Cavalier, Sieur de La Salle, is the first European known to have entered Ohio. He sailed down the Ohio River in about 1670. La Salle claimed the land he explored for France. His reports about fur-bearing animals in the region brought fur traders to Ohio. Missionaries also came to teach Native Americans about the Christian religion.

Native Americans trapped beavers and other animals for their fur. These furs sold for high prices in Europe, and the fur trade grew quickly. In return for the furs, traders offered Native Americans goods such as tools, knives, guns, blankets, and beads. When the French traders had gathered a large number of furs, they gave them to voyageurs. *Voyageur* is a French word meaning "traveler."

❯ The French set up forts and trading posts throughout the Ohio Valley.

❯ Beavers build dams across rivers using logs, sticks, mud, and grass.

The voyageurs took the furs by canoe to Montreal, in Canada. From there, the furs were loaded onto ships bound for European cities. Then the voyageurs brought back more goods to trade with Native Americans.

The arrival of the French changed the way Native Americans lived. They began to hunt with guns and wear clothing made from woven cloth instead of animal skins. Missionaries worked to change their religious beliefs. Thousands of Native Americans died from the diseases Europeans brought, such as smallpox and measles.

▶ Beaver furs were often used to make men's hats in Europe. The table (right) shows how much the furs were worth.

Value of Some Trade Items

Trade Items	Beaver Furs
4 Knives	🦫
Blanket	🦫🦫🦫🦫🦫🦫
2 Copper Kettles	🦫🦫🦫
4 Buttons	🦫
Pair of Shoes	🦫🦫🦫

🦫 = 1 Beaver Fur

OHIO TEST PREP ✓

1. **Who was the first European to explore Ohio?**
   A. a missionary
   B. Sieur de La Salle
   C. Sieur Voyageur

2. **What did Native Americans get from French traders?**
   A. fresh fruit, gold, and beads
   B. furs, guns, and turquoise
   C. tools, guns, and blankets

3. **What does _voyageur_ mean?**
   A. traveler
   B. trader
   C. explorer

4. **What were some of the effects of contact with the French on Native Americans in Ohio?**

Unit 2

Time

Cultures Meet

1418 Prince Henry opens a navigation school in Portugal, p. 112

1492 Christopher Columbus claims land in the Americas for Spain, p. 116

1400   **1450**   **1500**

At the Same Time

 1450 Johannes Gutenberg develops a new printing press

 1506 The Italian artist Leonardo da Vinci paints the *Mona Lisa*

Cultures Meet

1610 Spain establishes a settlement at Santa Fe, p. 151

1620 English Pilgrims settle the Plymouth Colony, p. 164

1550 | 1600 | 1650

1565 Spain sets up the first European settlement in the Philippines

1632 Work on the Taj Mahal begins in India

Christopher Columbus

1451–1506
- Italian sailor who explored the Americas for Spain
- Made four journeys to the Americas

Bartolomé de Las Casas

1484–1566
- Catholic priest who spoke out against the cruel treatment of Native Americans
- Wrote a book called *Tears of the Indians*

People

1450	1500	1550

1451 • Christopher Columbus — 1506

1484 • Bartolomé de Las Casas — 1566

1503? • Estevanico — 1539

1510 • Francisco Vásquez de Coronado — 1554

John Smith

1580–1631
- English sailor who traveled to many parts of the world
- Served as leader of the Jamestown settlement

Tisquantum (Squanto)

1585?–1622
- Native American who lived near the Plymouth Colony
- Became an interpreter between the colonists and Native Americans

Estevanico

1503?–1539

- Enslaved African who took part in several Spanish explorations
- Learned to speak several Native American languages

Francisco Vásquez de Coronado

1510–1554

- Spanish explorer
- Led an expedition in search of the Seven Cities of Gold

| 1600 | 1650 | 1700 |

1580 • John Smith 1631

1585? • Tisquantum (Squanto) 1622

1590 • William Bradford 1657

1595? • Pocahontas 1617

William Bradford

1590–1657

- English leader who led the Pilgrims to North America
- Served as governor of the Plymouth Colony

Pocahontas

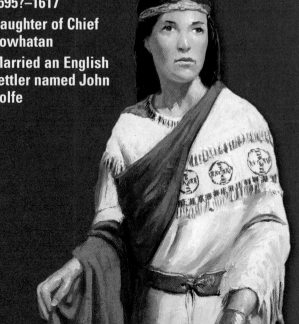

1595?–1617

- Daughter of Chief Powhatan
- Married an English settler named John Rolfe

CHINOOK

YAKIMA

CASCADE RANGE

Columbia River

R O C K Y

Missouri River

NEZ PERCE

MANDAN

CROW

G R E A T

SIOUX

SIOUX

I N T E R I O R
P L A I N S

Snake River

SHOSHONE

CHEYENNE

KLAMATH

MODOC

SHOSHONE

Platte River

PAWNEE

IOWA

PAIUTE

Great Salt Lake

M O U N T A I N S

COAST

POMO

SIERRA

GREAT BASIN

SHOSHONE

ARAPAHO

KANSA

MIWOK

NEVADA

UTE

RANGES

YOKUTS

PAIUTE

Colorado River

Arkansas River

CHUMASH

Mojave Desert

HOPI

NAVAJO

KIOWA

WICHITA

Santa Fe

CAHUILLA

APACHE

APACHE

COMANCHE

PACIFIC OCEAN

PIMA

APACHE

Rio Grande

TONKAWA

CONCHO

Gulf of California

PIMA

At the Same Time

Chumash tribe cultural region

TOBOSO

Monterrey

TEPEHUAN

NEW SPAIN

ZACATECA

0		200		400 Miles
0	200		400 Kilometers	

Albers Equal-Area Projection

Mexico City

CREE

MONTAGNAIS

MICMAC

OJIBWA

Quebec

ABENAKI

OTTAWA

Montreal

NEW FRANCE

ALGONKIN

Lake Superior

Lake Huron

NEW ENGLAND

MASSACHUSET

The *Mayflower* arrives in Massachusetts, 1620

MENOMINEE

POTAWATOMI

Lake Ontario

IROQUOIS

MOHEGAN

Lake Michigan

HURON

NEW NETHERLAND

SAC

ERIE

Lake Erie

New Amsterdam

WINNEBAGO

FOX

DELAWARE

MIAMI

NEW SWEDEN

ILLINOIS

SHAWNEE

River

POWATAN

Central Plains

SAPONI

MISSOURI

Ohio

MONACAN

TUTELO

A P P A L A C H I A N   M O U N T A I N S

Jamestown settlement, in Virginia, 1607

OSAGE

SUGAREE

C O A S T A L   P L A I N

CHEROKEE

CHERAW

CATAWBA

Mississippi River

CHICKASAW

MUSKOGEE

ATLANTIC OCEAN

CADDO

NATCHEZ

CHOCTAW

APALACHI

TIMUCUA

N
W   E
S

ATAKAPA

French land claims

Spanish land claims

English land claims

Dutch land claims

Swedish land claims

HOPI   Name of Native American tribe

CALUSA

Gulf of Mexico

Havana

Mission Nombre de Dios, in Florida, 1565

Reading Social Studies

(Focus Skill) Main Idea and Details

Why It Matters When you identify and understand the main idea and details, you can better understand what you read.

▶ LEARN

The **main idea** is the most important idea of a paragraph or passage. **Details** give more information about the main idea.

Main Idea
The most important idea of a paragraph or passage

↑

Details		
Facts about the main idea	Facts about the main idea	Facts about the main idea

- The main idea is often given at the beginning of a piece of writing.
- In a long article, each paragraph has a main idea and details. The whole article also has a main idea and details.

▶ PRACTICE

Read the paragraphs, and identify details that support the main idea.

Main Idea The Taino (TY•noh) were Native Americans who lived on islands in the Caribbean Sea. They grew crops, fished, and hunted. They were peaceful people. **Details**
Other Native Americans who lived on islands in the Caribbean Sea were the Carib. Like the Taino, the Carib also farmed, hunted, and fished. Unlike the Taino, the Carib were warlike. They were expert navigators who traveled long distances in large canoes.

Read the paragraphs, and answer the questions.

Americans and Europeans Meet

The Taino were among the first Americans to meet European explorers. The Taino were friendly and generous. Christopher Columbus wrote about them: "When you ask for something, they never say no. To the contrary, they offer to share with anyone."

Taino men spent much of their time fishing. They went to sea in canoes and used spears and nets to catch fish. They also hunted small animals.

Taino women grew manioc, a plant used to make flour for bread. They also grew sweet potatoes, corn, and cotton. Women used cotton to make mats, hammocks, ropes, and small sails for fishing boats.

Taino children helped their parents by gathering fruit. In their free time, they played a game that was like soccer. Many children had pet dogs.

The Taino's lives were not completely carefree. They had warlike neighbors, the Carib, who lived on nearby islands. The two groups did not get along and the Carib sometimes attacked Taino villages.

Soon after the arrival of Europeans, life changed for the Taino, the Carib, and many other Native American groups. The Taino lost some of their people because of warfare. Many others died from diseases carried by European explorers.

Main Idea and Details

1. What is the main idea of the first paragraph?
2. What main point does the third paragraph make about how Taino women spent their time?
3. What details explain the idea that although the Taino were peaceful, they faced dangers?

> A Native American statue

The Log of Christopher Columbus

selections by Steve Lowe
illustrated by Robert Sabuda

In 1492, most Europeans thought the world was only as big as the continents of Europe, Asia, and Africa. No one knew what existed beyond the Atlantic Ocean. However, some people wanted to find out.

The Italian explorer Christopher Columbus believed that if he traveled west, he could reach Asia. Facing the unknown, he and his crew set sail in hopes of finding a new trade route and riches. What they found was an entirely different land. During the journey, Columbus kept a logbook that noted daily events and the distance traveled.

Sunday September 9, 1492

This day we completely lost sight of land, and many men sighed and wept for fear they would not see it again for a long time. I comforted them with great promises of land and riches. To sustain their hope and dispel their fears of a long voyage, I decided to reckon fewer leagues than we actually made. I did this that they might not think themselves so great a distance from Spain as they really were.

reckon count

leagues a measure of distance

Thursday October 11, 1492

About 10 o'clock at night, while standing on the <u>sterncastle</u>, I thought I saw a light to the west. It looked like a little wax candle bobbing up and down. . . . I am the first to admit that I was so eager to find land that I did not trust my own senses, so I called for Pedro Gutierrez, the representative of the King's household, and asked him to watch for the light. After a few moments, he too saw it.

Friday October 12, 1492

The moon, in its third quarter, rose in the east shortly before midnight. . . . I hauled in all sails but the mainsail and <u>lay-to</u> till daylight. The land is about 6 miles to the west.

Friday October 12, 1492

At dawn . . . I went ashore in the ship's boat. I unfurled the royal banner. After a prayer of thanksgiving I ordered the captains of the *Pinta* and the *Niña* . . . to bear faith and witness that I was taking possession of this island for the King and Queen. . . . To this island I gave the name *San Salvador*. . . .

No sooner had we concluded the formalities of taking possession of the island than people began to come to the beach. . . . They are very well-built people. . . . Their eyes are large and very pretty. . . . Many of the natives paint their faces. . . . Others paint their whole bodies. . . . They are friendly.

<u>sterncastle</u> a building or structure on a ship, raised above the deck at the rear of the ship

<u>lay-to</u> rested

Tuesday November 27, 1492

As I went along the river it was marvelous to see the forests and greenery, the very clear water, the birds, and the fine situation, and I almost did not want to leave the place. I told the men with me that, in order to make a report to the Sovereigns of the things they saw, a thousand tongues would not be sufficient to tell it, nor my hand to write it, for it looks like an enchanted land.

Sovereigns the king and queen

Response Corner

1. **Focus Skill** **Main Idea and Details** What details in Columbus's logbook show that the goal of his journey was to claim land for Spain?

2. **Make It Relevant** Would you have told the crew how far away from home they really were? Why or why not?

STUDY SKILLS

USE VISUALS

Looking at visuals, such as photographs, charts, and maps, can help you better understand and remember what you read.

- Visuals often show the same information that is in the text but in a different way.

- Many visuals have titles, captions, or labels that help you understand what is shown.

✓	What kind of visual is shown?
✓	What does the visual show?
✓	How does the visual help you better understand the subject that you are reading?

 PREVIEW VOCABULARY

expedition p. 112   **conquistador** p. 129   **missionary** p. 133

The Age of Exploration

REPLICA OF CHRISTOPHER COLUMBUS'S SHIP

Lesson

Time

1400 ———————————————————————————— **1650**

1450s
Johannes Gutenberg
develops a new
printing press

1492
Christopher
Columbus lands
at San Salvador

Exploration and Technology

WHAT TO KNOW

Why did Europeans begin to look for a sea route to Asia?

VOCABULARY

technology p. 111
navigation p. 112
expedition p. 112
empire p. 112
entrepreneur p. 114
cost p. 114
benefit p. 114
Reconquista p. 115

PEOPLE

Marco Polo
Prince Henry
Christopher Columbus
King Ferdinand
Queen Isabella

PLACES

Portugal
Spain
San Salvador

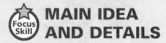

MAIN IDEA AND DETAILS

YOU ARE THERE It is the winter of 1470 in your small village in Spain. The fire crackles as your father reads aloud from a book. The words describe a faraway land in Asia called Cathay. It is a place of amazing cities and great riches.

An explorer named **Marco Polo** wrote the book long ago. Now, thanks to a new kind of printing press, many Europeans are reading Polo's book for the first time. As you listen, you dream of sailing to Asia and finding adventure and riches.

▶ **MARCO POLO** wrote about Asia in *The Travels of Marco Polo.*

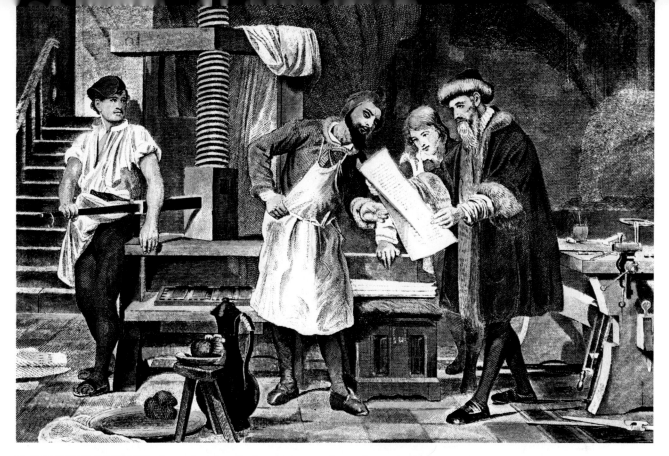

▶ **THE PRINTING PRESS** Gutenberg's printing press used small metal pieces, each with a raised letter or number. Ink was spread over the pieces, and a large screw was turned to press them onto paper.

A Rush of New Ideas

In the 1400s, a new age of learning, science, and art began in Europe. Historians call this time of new ideas the Renaissance (REH•nuh•sahns), which means "rebirth." It began in Italy and then spread across Europe.

Johannes Gutenberg helped with this spread of ideas by developing a printing press in the 1450s. Before this time, most books were hand-written. The new printing press made it faster to print books.

Marco Polo and Trade with Asia

One of the most popular books during the Renaissance was *The Travels of Marco Polo*. Written almost 200 years earlier, it tells of Marco Polo's voyage to Cathay, as China was then called. Europeans were amazed to read about Chinese inventions such as gunpowder and the compass—a tool for finding directions.

European merchants were interested in the riches Marco Polo wrote about. They wanted to buy and then resell Asian goods such as silks and spices. Soon traders from Europe began traveling the long, difficult land routes to Asia. To reach Asia, they had to cross mountains and deserts.

At the time, no Europeans had traveled to Asia by sea. They had no maps that showed the world correctly. Sailors also lacked the **technology**, the scientific knowledge and tools, needed for such a long trip. Sailors and scientists began working to solve these problems.

READING CHECK ᗝ**MAIN IDEA AND DETAILS**
What kept Europeans from sailing to Asia?

The World Awaits

In 1418, **Prince Henry** of **Portugal** helped solve some of these problems by opening a school of navigation. **Navigation** is the science of planning and following a route. The aim of his school was to make better ships, maps, and tools for navigation.

New Technology

At the school, sailors learned how to sail a new kind of ship called a caravel. This long, narrow ship could carry more goods than earlier ships. It could also sail quickly over long distances.

Mapmakers at Prince Henry's school read the journals of early explorers. They read about bodies of water and land shapes. Using these details, they drew better maps.

To keep their ships going in the right direction, sailors needed navigational tools. Prince Henry hired scientists to improve two of these tools—the compass and the astrolabe. Sailors used the compass to help them find their longitude, or distance east or west of the prime meridian. They used the astrolabe to figure out the positions of the sun, moon, and stars.

This tool helped sailors try to find their latitude, or distance north or south of the equator.

These and other developments made ocean exploration possible. Portuguese ships began making expeditions in search of a sea route to Asia. An **expedition** is a trip taken with the goal of exploring. Prince Henry believed that the most direct sea route to Asia from Europe would be to sail south around Africa and then east across the Indian Ocean. In time, the Portuguese found this route.

A New View of the World

Europeans knew about Asia because of Marco Polo's book and because of trade. Traders had long been using the Silk Road—an ancient land route between China and Italy. At this time, Europeans knew all of Asia as "the Indies."

Europeans also traveled to Africa. They traded with merchants in North African cities such as Gao (GOW), Timbuktu (tim•buhk•TOO), and Jenné (jeh•NAY). These cities were the centers of rich empires. An **empire** is made up of lands ruled by the nation that won control of them.

Few Europeans had any idea that there were other continents beyond Europe, Africa, and Asia. Most did not know that some Europeans had already reached North America. In about A.D. 1000, Leif Erickson led a group known as the Vikings from what is today the country of Norway. They sailed west across the Atlantic Ocean, stopping in Greenland. In time, they sailed to Canada and landed in present-day Newfoundland.

While hunting and fishing in the area, the Vikings fought with Native Americans. As the fighting grew worse, they chose to leave. The Vikings wrote about their voyage, but not many people knew about these records or read them. For years, most Europeans did not even consider sailing west across the Atlantic as a way to reach Asia.

READING CHECK ☼ **MAIN IDEA AND DETAILS**
What were the aims of Prince Henry's school of navigation?

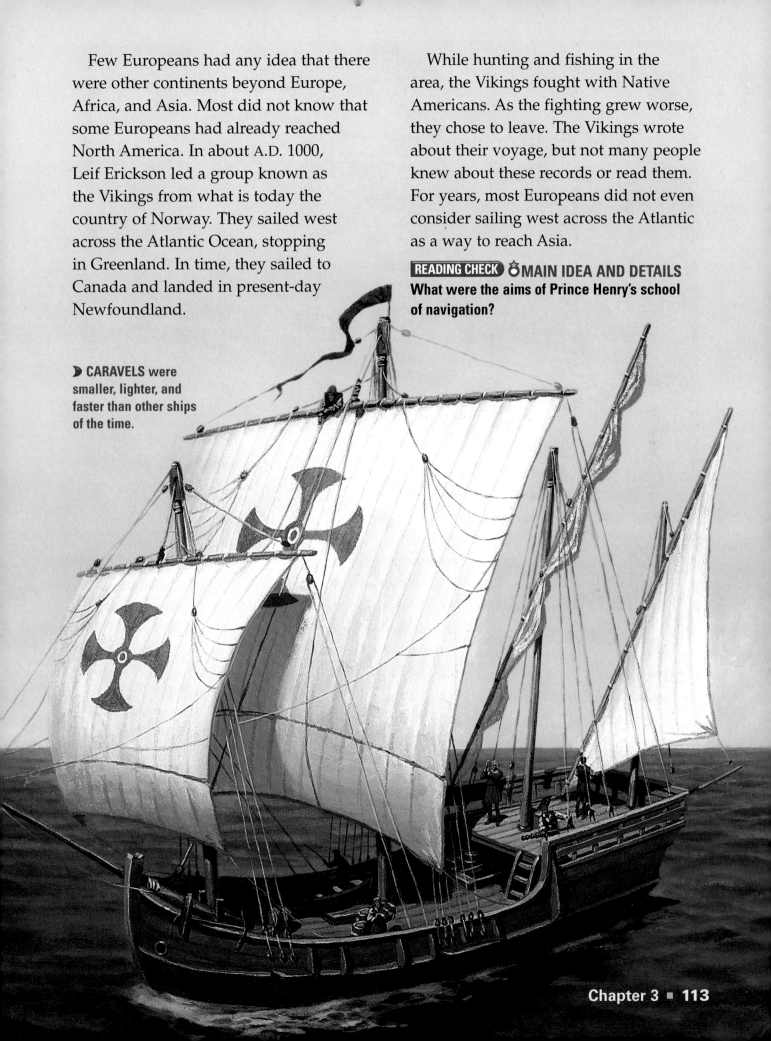

▶ **CARAVELS** were smaller, lighter, and faster than other ships of the time.

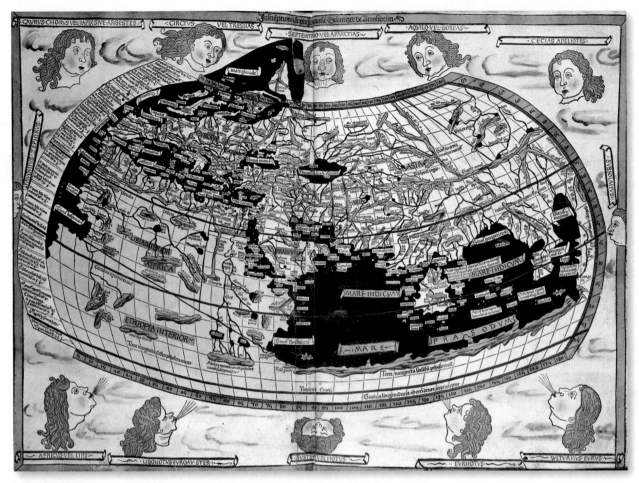

▶ **AN EARLY MAP** This map was made in 1482, using information from ancient times. It shows only Europe, Africa, and Asia.

The Business of Exploring

Most sailors thought the only way to reach Asia was to go east. Not everyone agreed. One such sailor was **Christopher Columbus**.

Christopher Columbus

Columbus was fascinated by the stories he had heard of the wealth in Asia. He had already sailed along the coasts of Europe and Africa. Columbus believed he could reach Asia by sailing west across the Ocean Sea, as the Atlantic Ocean was then known. He thought this would be a more direct route to Asia than sailing around Africa. However, Columbus could not prove this until he had money for a ship, crew, and supplies.

Risks and Rewards

Explorers had to be **entrepreneurs** (ahn•truh•pruh•NERZ). They set up and ran their expeditions just as an entrepreneur sets up and runs a business. Often, explorers had to persuade others that the **cost**, or effort made to achieve or gain something, was worth the risk of an expedition. Ships and supplies cost a great deal. There were many risks, too. For example, a ship could sink, or an explorer might not find any valuable goods.

However, the **benefit**, or reward gained, was the chance of finding riches worth many times the cost. These riches would more than repay the money paid by the trip's supporters.

Columbus Wins Support

Finding a ruler to pay for his trip was not easy for Columbus. His idea of sailing west seemed risky. No one knew how far west you had to sail to reach Asia. First, Columbus asked the king of Portugal for money, but the king turned him down. By sailing around Africa, the Portuguese had already found a sea route to Asia from Europe.

Three years later, in 1485, Columbus asked **King Ferdinand** and **Queen Isabella** of **Spain** to support his plan. Ferdinand and Isabella were Catholic, and at the time, they were fighting a war to push all Muslim people out of Spain. They said no to Columbus.

This movement to make Spain all Catholic was called the **Reconquista** (ray•kohn•KEES•tah). Under the Reconquista, Muslims had to give up their Islamic religion. They had to either become Catholic or leave Spain. By 1492, Ferdinand and Isabella had claimed all of the land the Muslims once held in Spain. They had also forced many thousands of Jews to leave Spain.

When Spain was united under Catholic beliefs, Columbus again asked Ferdinand and Isabella to pay for his voyage. He promised them great riches and new lands. Columbus also said that he would take Catholic beliefs to Asia. This time, the king and queen agreed to help him.

READING CHECK ☼MAIN IDEA AND DETAILS
How did Columbus persuade the king and queen of Spia to support his expedition?

❯ **SUPPORTING EXPLORATION** This painting shows Christopher Columbus asking King Ferdinand and Queen Isabella of Spain to support his expedition.

Two Worlds Meet

On August 3, 1492, Columbus and a crew of nearly 90 sailed from Spain on three ships. The ships were called the *Niña* (NEEN•yuh), the *Pinta* (PEEN•tuh), and the *Santa María*. Two months later, Columbus and his crew were still at sea. They faced many problems. Often, storms damaged their ships. When there was no wind to fill the sails, the ships drifted for days. The sailors grew restless.

Then the sailors began to notice a change in the weather. They saw birds flying south. Columbus changed direction, hoping to follow the birds to land.

The night of October 11, 1492, was a good night for sailing. A strong wind pushed the ships from behind. The moon was shining on the sea in front of them. In the early morning hours of October 12, the sailors finally saw their goal—land! Today, we know that Columbus and his crew had traveled about 4,100 miles across the Atlantic Ocean to an island in the Caribbean Sea.

A Historic Meeting

All three ships anchored off an island that Columbus named **San Salvador**. He claimed this island for Spain. Columbus believed he had reached Asia and was now in the Indies. This belief explains why he called the people he met on the island *Indians*.

The people Columbus met were part of the Taino (TY•noh) tribe. They welcomed Columbus and his men. Although the Europeans were upset not to find any silk or spices, Columbus collected a few gold items and some of the islands' animals and plants. He also captured several Taino and took them to Spain.

Children IN HISTORY

Diego Bermúdez

Some of the sailors on Columbus's expedition were as young as 12. That was the age of Diego Bermúdez when he sailed on the *Santa María* in 1492. Diego was a page, which was the lowest rank on a ship. Pages did the jobs that most sailors did not want to do, like cooking, cleaning, and keeping track of the time. Diego kept track of the time by using a half-hour glass. Every 30 minutes, when all the sand had fallen to the bottom of the glass, Diego rang a bell and called out a short prayer. His actions let everyone know what time it was.

Make It Relevant What jobs do you have to do at home or at school?

Columbus Returns to Spain

When Columbus and his crew got back to Spain, they were treated like heroes. They had crossed the Atlantic Ocean and then returned home. When King Ferdinand and Queen Isabella saw the gold, animals, plants, and people from the Indies, they paid for another expedition. The Spanish rulers made the reasons for this second expedition clear. Columbus was expected to find more riches, start settlements, and convert the people he met to the Catholic religion.

READING CHECK ☼**MAIN IDEA AND DETAILS**
What problems did Columbus and his crew face?

Summary

In the 1400s, stories of riches in Asia made sailors want to explore. Faster ships and new tools made exploration possible. While most explorers looked to the east for a route to Asia, Columbus sailed west and reached land across the Atlantic Ocean.

REVIEW

1. **WHAT TO KNOW** Why did Europeans begin to look for a sea route to Asia?

2. **VOCABULARY** Explain how **technology** helped improve **navigation**.

3. **HISTORY** What did Columbus find on his 1492 voyage?

4. **CRITICAL THINKING** What were the advantages and disadvantages of sailing west from Europe to Asia?

5. ✏️ **WRITE A CONVERSATION** Write a short conversation between a Spanish sailor and a Taino leader. Have the speakers ask one another questions about each other's culture.

6. 🟡 **MAIN IDEA AND DETAILS**
   Focus Skill On a separate sheet of paper, copy and complete this graphic organizer.

Main Idea

Europeans faced problems finding a sea route to Asia.

Details

Navigational Tools

Background Navigational tools helped sailors explore faraway lands and return home. With most of these tools, sailors used the sun, moon, and stars to determine location. In the 1400s, European navigators used the astrolabe and the compass. By the 1700s, more accurate tools were made, including the chronometer.

DBQ **Document-Based Question** Study these primary sources and answer the questions.

COMPASS

A compass tells sailors if they are going north, south, east, or west.

DBQ **1** How did the compass help sailors?

ASTROLABE

Sailors used an astrolabe to find their latitude based on the height of the sun or the North Star.

DBQ **2** How might the weather affect the use of the astrolabe?

Abraham Ortelius created this map of the world in 1574. Navigational instruments helped people make more accurate maps.

DBQ ❸ Why would explorers need more accurate maps?

CHRONOMETER

A chronometer kept very accurate time and was used by sailors to find their longitude.

WRITE ABOUT IT

Write a paragraph that explains the problems sailors might have if they did not have navigational tools.

GO ONLINE For more resources, go to www.harcourtschool.com/ss1

DBQ ❹ Why would sailors need to keep track of the time?

Time

1400   1650

1497
Cabot reaches Newfoundland and Labrador

1513
Balboa reaches the Pacific Ocean

1522
The Magellan expedition completes a voyage around the world

WHAT TO KNOW
Why did Europeans explore the Americas, and what did they find?

VOCABULARY
isthmus p. 123

treaty p. 125

PEOPLE
John Cabot
Amerigo Vespucci
Vasco Núñez de Balboa
Ferdinand Magellan

PLACES
England
Newfoundland and Labrador
Philippine Islands

MAIN IDEA AND DETAILS

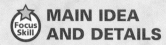

A Changing World

YOU ARE THERE
It is June 1497, and you have been at sea for more than a month. Back in England, you signed up for this journey after hearing about Columbus's expeditions. However, now you are starting to have second thoughts. Fog is all around your ship. Almost everyone on board looks worried. "This cold air chills me to the bone," says a crew member. You squint to try to see through the fog, but it is no use. Whatever is out there remains a mystery.

▶ JOHN CABOT places the English flag on what is now Canada.

▶ **A NORTHERN VOYAGE** Cabot sailed to present-day Newfoundland and Labrador.

England Explores

Columbus returned three times to what he thought was the Indies. He never found great riches, but he did show that it was possible to sail across the Atlantic. Columbus's trips inspired several European rulers to send ships west to claim lands. In time, Europeans created a new culture in the Americas.

John Cabot Sets Sail

In **England**, King Henry VII heard of Columbus's success for Spain. The king paid an Italian sailor, Giovanni Caboto, to lead an expedition sailing west across the Atlantic. The English called him **John Cabot**. King Henry's aim was to help England compete with other European nations for land and wealth.

In May 1497, Cabot and a crew of 18 sailed west on a course far north of Columbus's first route. After a long, slow journey, they reached land on June 24. Once on shore, Cabot claimed the land for England. He then sailed south along the coast before returning to England. Cabot's son Sebastian joined him on this voyage. Years later, Sebastian described the place as "a very sterile [lonely] land."

When Cabot returned to England, he said he had found the Indies. Cabot, like Columbus, thought he had reached Asia. Many people today believe Cabot had actually reached the coast of present-day **Newfoundland and Labrador**, now a part of Canada. This was the same place that the Vikings had visited almost 500 years earlier.

READING CHECK ⏱ **MAIN IDEA AND DETAILS**
What was the aim of King Henry VII when he paid for Cabot's expedition?

▶ **MAPMAKERS** In the 1500s, mapmakers made new maps of the world based on information from early explorations of the Americas.

A New Map of the World

Not everyone believed that Columbus and Cabot had found Asia. **Amerigo Vespucci** (veh•SPOO•chee) of Italy aimed to find out for himself. In 1499, he sailed to a place just south of where Columbus had landed. Two years later, Vespucci sailed down the coast of South America.

Amerigo Vespucci's New Idea

Vespucci looked for signs that he had reached Asia, but he found none. The places he saw did not fit Marco Polo's descriptions of Asia. Vespucci began to think that maybe Earth was larger than most people thought. If so, that would mean Asia was farther away from Europe than Columbus believed.

The Naming of America

Over time, Vespucci came to realize that he, Columbus, and Cabot had found lands not yet known to Europeans. In 1507, a German mapmaker named Martin Waldseemüller (VAHLT•zay•mool•er) published a world map that included these newly found lands. He named the new lands in honor of Amerigo Vespucci.

The land on this new map stood for the present-day continent of South America. Later, the word *America* was also used for the land known today as the continent of North America.

READING CHECK 🔄 **MAIN IDEA AND DETAILS**
How did Vespucci's voyage change how the world was seen?

Reaching the Pacific

After Vespucci's voyages, other explorers sailed around the mysterious "new" lands. Not one of them found China. Still, Europeans wondered what these lands could be if they were not a part of Asia.

Vasco Núñez de Balboa

The Spanish explorer **Vasco Núñez de Balboa** (NOON•yays day bahl•BOH•uh) was one of the first Europeans to settle in the Americas. He had set up a farm on the island of Hispaniola (ees•pah•NYOH•lah), but he was not a good farmer. Soon he owed money to many people. Instead of paying them, he escaped from Hispaniola by hiding on a ship bound for what is now Colombia.

After Balboa arrived, he met the survivors of a failed Spanish settlement. Later, he helped them take land from Native American groups and start a settlement in what is now the country of Panama.

Balboa heard about a huge ocean to the west. In 1513, Balboa and other explorers made their way west across the Isthmus of Panama, which connects North America and South America. An **isthmus** is a narrow strip of land that connects two large land areas. In time, Balboa's group reached the Pacific Ocean. They proved that Amerigo Vespucci was right about an unknown continent.

READING CHECK **CAUSE AND EFFECT**
What caused Balboa to travel across the Isthmus of Panama?

▶ **BALBOA REACHES THE PACIFIC** Balboa was 38 years old when he first saw the Pacific Ocean.

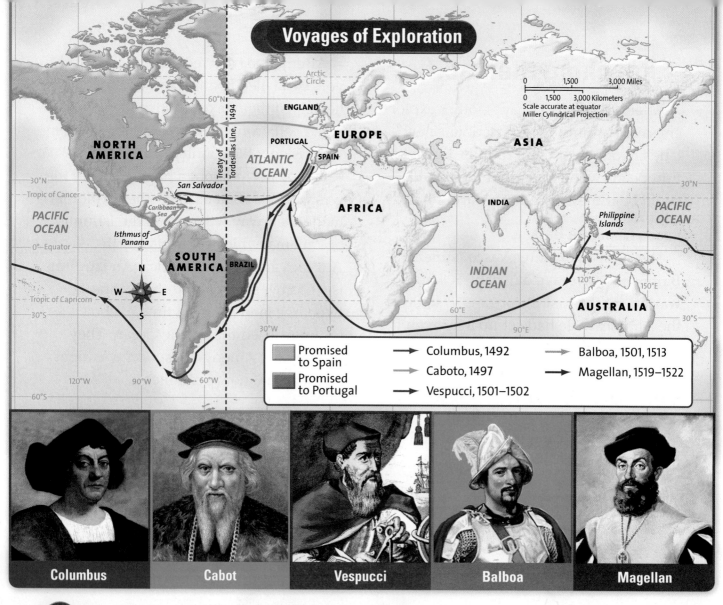

Voyages of Exploration

0   1,500   3,000 Miles
0   1,500   3,000 Kilometers
Scale accurate at equator
Miller Cylindrical Projection

ENGLAND

PORTUGAL   EUROPE

SPAIN

ATLANTIC OCEAN

NORTH AMERICA

Arctic Circle

60°N

Treaty of Tordesillas Line, 1494

30°N   30°N

Tropic of Cancer

San Salvador

PACIFIC OCEAN

Caribbean Sea

Isthmus of Panama

0°—Equator   0°

SOUTH AMERICA   BRAZIL

AFRICA

ASIA

INDIA

Philippine Islands

PACIFIC OCEAN

INDIAN OCEAN

120°E   150°E

AUSTRALIA

Tropic of Capricorn

30°S   30°W   0°   60°E   90°E   30°S

120°W   90°W   60°W

60°S

	Promised to Spain	→ Columbus, 1492	→ Balboa, 1501, 1513
	Promised to Portugal	→ Caboto, 1497	→ Magellan, 1519–1522
		→ Vespucci, 1501–1502	

Columbus   Cabot   Vespucci   Balboa   Magellan

 MAP SKILL   **MOVEMENT** Which explorer sailed across the Pacific Ocean?

A New View of the World

With the aim of finding a western route to Asia, the Portuguese explorer **Ferdinand Magellan** (muh•JEH•luhn) also proved that Vespucci was right. In 1519, Magellan left Spain with five ships and about 250 sailors. They passed through a waterway at the tip of South America. Then the sailors found themselves in the same ocean that Balboa had seen. Magellan named it the *Pacific*, which means "peaceful." To him, its waters seemed calm compared with those of the Atlantic.

Magellan's Long Voyage

Magellan thought he could cross the Pacific in a few days. It took more than three months. Many sailors died of hunger and illness. Magellan himself was killed in a battle in the **Philippine Islands**, 500 miles off the coast of southeastern Asia. One ship finally made it back to Spain in 1522. Its sailors were the first Europeans to travel around the world.

The Treaty of Tordesillas

As more expeditions were organized, more lands were claimed. Often, more than one country claimed the same land. The Catholic rulers of Spain and Portugal asked Catholic Church leaders to settle such a case. In 1493, Church leaders drew a line on a map through the Atlantic Ocean. Portugal was promised the land to the east of the line. Spain was promised the land to the west.

In 1494, Spain and Portugal signed the Treaty of Tordesillas. A **treaty** is an agreement between countries. In this treaty, Spain and Portugal agreed to move the dividing line farther west. This change gave Portugal the land that would become part of the country of Brazil.

READING CHECK ⚙ **MAIN IDEA AND DETAILS**
What did Magellan's expedition accomplish?

Summary

After Columbus's voyages, rulers were eager to pay for trips across the Atlantic. Explorers such as Cabot, Vespucci, Balboa, and Magellan explored many different areas. Spain and Portugal divided the Americas between themselves.

▶ **SPANISH COINS** One side of this gold coin (left) shows King Ferdinand and Queen Isabella.

REVIEW

1. **WHAT TO KNOW** Why did Europeans explore the Americas, and what did they find?

2. **VOCABULARY** Use the term **treaty** to explain how Spain and Portugal divided lands in the Americas.

3. **GEOGRAPHY** What two oceans did explorers cross when they sailed west from Europe to Asia?

4. **CRITICAL THINKING Make It Relevant** How do you think new maps of the world affected explorers? How do people use maps today?

5. **MAKE A TABLE OF EXPLORERS** Make a table that lists the name of each explorer in this lesson and the area that person explored. Then use your table and the map on page 124 to trace their routes and describe the distances they traveled.

6. **MAIN IDEA AND DETAILS** (Focus Skill) On a separate sheet of paper, copy and complete this graphic organizer.

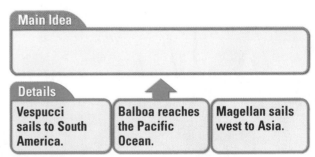

Main Idea

Details

| Vespucci sails to South America. | Balboa reaches the Pacific Ocean. | Magellan sails west to Asia. |

Christopher Columbus's Voyages

In all, Christopher Columbus made four voyages to the Americas. There is no question that his voyages changed the world. The full meaning of these events in history is still talked about today. Some people see Columbus as a heroic figure—a man of courage, curiosity, and daring. Others see him as one who brought great hardship to people who meant him no harm. Here are three points of view in this ongoing debate.

▶ **MODERN DAY REPLICAS** In 1992, the government of Spain built replicas of Columbus's original three ships to commemorate the 500th anniversary of his first voyage.

RUSSELL MEANS

Russell Means is a Native American leader. In a newspaper article, he wrote about Columbus's treatment of Native Americans.

" Columbus' arrival was a disaster from the beginning . . . he immediately began the enslavement . . . of the Indian peoples of the Caribbean islands. "

Robert S. McElvaine is a teacher and author. He wrote about the effects of Columbus's voyages.

" The major long-term significance of Columbus' voyage is that it led to the mixing of the people of the world on an unprecedented scale and set in motion the process of making what would become the United States the most ethnically diverse society the world has known. "

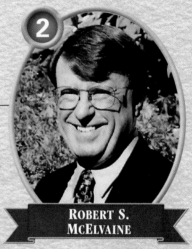

ROBERT S. MCELVAINE

KATHLEEN DEAGAN

Kathleen Deagan is a teacher and author. Her book also describes the effect of Columbus's voyages on the Native Americans.

" Regardless of how many Taínos were living in Hispaniola when Columbus arrived, the stunning reduction in their numbers was the most shocking immediate repercussion [effect] of European contact. "

It's Your Turn

Summarize Points of View Work with a classmate to summarize the point of view held by each writer. Decide how each writer views Columbus's voyages.

Make It Relevant Why might you and a classmate have different points of view about an event or idea?

Time

1400 ———————————————————————— **1650**

1513
Ponce de León
reaches Florida

1521
Cortés destroys
the Aztec capital

1539
De Soto begins his
exploration of Florida

WHAT TO KNOW
Why did the Spanish explore and conquer large areas of the Americas?

VOCABULARY
grant p. 129
conquistador p. 129
reform p. 133
Reformation p. 133
Counter-Reformation p. 133
missionary p. 133

PEOPLE
Juan Ponce de León
Hernando Cortés
Estevanico
Francisco Vásquez
   de Coronado
Francisco Pizarro
Atahuallpa
Hernando de Soto
Martin Luther

PLACES
Florida
Mexico City
New Spain

MAIN IDEA AND DETAILS
Focus Skill

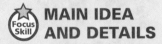

Spanish Explorations

YOU ARE THERE

You make your way through the thick forest, waving the flies away from your face. The air is hot and sticky. Your armor seems to be getting heavier with each step.

Your commander has made it known that he is seeking a "fountain of youth." The idea seems foolish to you, but you know it would be unwise to say so. Near an opening in the forest, a soldier in front orders everyone to stop. Your group has just come face to face with a group of Native Americans.

▷ **FIRST MEETINGS** This painting of Spanish explorers meeting Native Americans was made more than 350 years after the event.

▶ **LA FLORIDA** Ponce de León explored the Florida coast while searching for the Fountain of Youth.

The Spanish Explore Florida

After Spain had claimed land in the Americas, more Spanish explorers and soldiers soon sailed there. Some wanted to find adventure and riches. Some dreamed of becoming rich through trade, by selling things in Europe they had found in the Americas. Others wanted to win national glory and to convert Native Americans to Christianity.

Juan Ponce de León

The king of Spain encouraged the explorers. He offered large sums of money, called **grants**, to those who led expeditions. These Spanish explorers and soldiers became known as **conquistadors** (kahn•KEES•tah•dawrz), or "conquerors."

One of these conquistadors was **Juan Ponce de León** (POHN•say day lay•OHN). He had sailed with Columbus on his second voyage. Later, he helped conquer Puerto Rico. While in Puerto Rico, Ponce de León heard about an island to the north called Bimini (BIH•muh•nee). He also may have heard that the island had a so-called Fountain of Youth. Its water supposedly made old people young again.

In 1513, Ponce de León set out to find Bimini. Instead, he landed in what is now the state of **Florida**. He named the land *La Florida*, Spanish for "flowery," and claimed it for Spain.

In 1521, Ponce de León returned to Florida to start a settlement. The Calusa tribe defended their land against the Spanish. Ponce de León was wounded and later died. He never found the Fountain of Youth. Instead, he became the first Spanish explorer to set foot on land that became part of the United States.

READING CHECK ☼MAIN IDEA AND DETAILS
What was Ponce de León the first Spanish explorer to do?

Early Conquistadors

In 1519, Spain sent **Hernando Cortés** to find gold in the land of the Aztecs. Cortés landed in what is now Mexico with about 650 soldiers. He and his soldiers marched west from the coast toward the Aztec capital, Tenochtitlán (tay•nohch•teet•LAHN). The Aztec Empire covered 80,000 square miles. As many as 5 million people lived in the empire, but some disliked the Aztecs' harsh rule, so they helped the Spanish.

The Fall of the Aztecs

Cortés was also helped by the Aztecs' belief that a light-skinned god would one day return to rule them. Motecuhzoma (moh•tay•kwah•SOH•mah), the Aztec emperor, thought that Cortés might be this god. He welcomed Cortés, but this peace did not last very long.

Cortés took Motecuhzoma prisoner, and fighting broke out between the Spanish and the Aztecs. The Aztecs were strong fighters, but they did not have horses or guns like the Spanish. Many Aztecs died in battles, but most died from diseases carried by the soldiers. By 1521, Cortés had conquered the Aztecs. On the ruins of Tenochtitlán, the Spanish built **Mexico City**. The city became the capital of Spain's new empire in the Americas.

The Seven Cities of Gold

After Cortés found gold among the Aztecs, the Spanish went on looking for more riches. Spanish leaders in Mexico City heard a Native American story about seven cities of gold. They sent a priest named Marcos de Niza (day NEE•sah) on an expedition. De Niza took along an enslaved African named **Estevanico** (es•tay•vahn•EE•koh), who knew about

Spanish Conquistador and Aztec Warrior

ILLUSTRATION A Spanish conquistador (left) had stronger weapons than an Aztec warrior had (right). How might conquistadors on horses have had advantages over Aztec warriors on foot?

Horse

Armor made of steel

Harquebus, a gun invented in the 1400s

Armor made of quilted leather

Wood shield with feather fringe

Wooden club

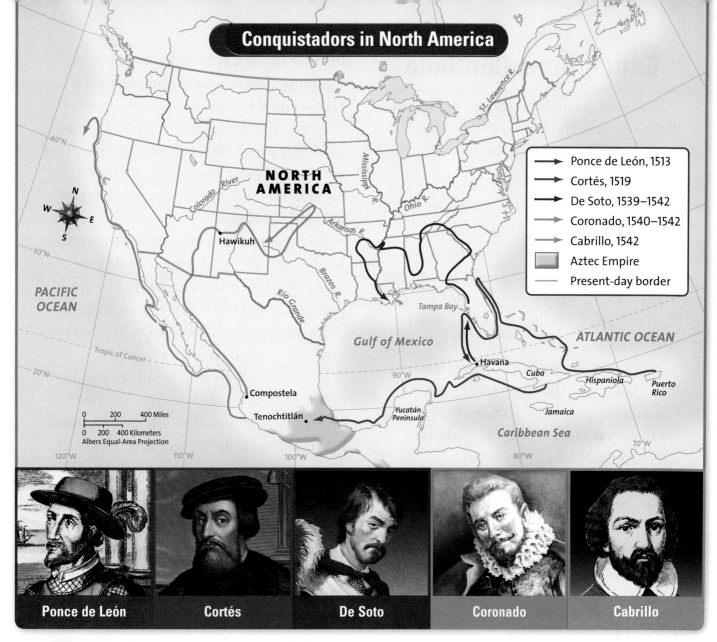

Conquistadors in North America

Ponce de León, 1513
Cortés, 1519
De Soto, 1539–1542
Coronado, 1540–1542
Cabrillo, 1542
Aztec Empire
Present-day border

NORTH AMERICA

PACIFIC OCEAN

ATLANTIC OCEAN

Gulf of Mexico

Caribbean Sea

Hawikuh
Tampa Bay
Havana
Cuba
Hispaniola
Puerto Rico
Jamaica
Compostela
Tenochtitlán
Yucatán Peninsula

Tropic of Cancer

0   200   400 Miles
0   200   400 Kilometers
Albers Equal-Area Projection

Ponce de León   Cortés   De Soto   Coronado   Cabrillo

 MAP SKILL **MOVEMENT** Which conquistador crossed the Mississippi River?

the region. During the expedition, Estevanico was killed. De Niza, however, returned and said he had seen a golden city.

Coronado in the Southwest

Francisco Vásquez de Coronado (kawr•oh•NAH•doh) heard Marcos de Niza's story. In 1540, he set out with about 300 soldiers, several enslaved Africans, and more than 1,000 enslaved Native Americans to find the golden cities. Coronado explored lands in what is now the southwestern United States. In all his travels, he never found any gold. Coronado brought no riches back to Mexico City, but he had claimed lands for Spain. The Spanish lands that included what are today Mexico, the southwestern United States, and Florida became known as **New Spain**.

READING CHECK ✪**MAIN IDEA AND DETAILS** What was the aim of Coronado's expedition?

Expeditions Continue

More conquistadors wanted to explore the Americas. They came to the Americas to claim land and find gold.

Pizarro and the Incas

Francisco Pizarro was a Spanish conquistador. In 1531, he led 180 soldiers on an expedition into the western coast of South America. There, he and his soldiers met with people from the Inca Empire, which was led by **Atahuallpa** (ah•tah•WAHL•pah).

A priest traveling with Pizarro told the Inca leader that the Incas had to accept Christianity and Spanish rule. Atahuallpa said no, and Pizarro and his soldiers attacked the Incas.

The Spanish took Atahuallpa prisoner, so the Inca were left without a leader. After Atahuallpa's death, Pizarro traveled to Cuzco, the capital of the Inca Empire, and took control of the region.

De Soto in the Southeast

Another conquistador named **Hernando de Soto** (day SOH•toh) explored the southeastern United States. In 1539, he and 600 men sailed from Cuba and landed near Tampa Bay. Later, they became the first Europeans to see the Mississippi River.

De Soto and his soldiers met many Native Americans during this expedition. These meetings often ended in bloody battles. One of the worst battles took place against the Mobile tribe in what is now the state of Alabama.

In 1542, de Soto died of a fever. Of the 600 men who started the journey, only about 300 survived. De Soto and his men claimed the land they explored. Spanish claims now covered much of the southern half of what is now the United States.

READING CHECK ☼**MAIN IDEA AND DETAILS**
What part of the present-day United States did de Soto explore and claim?

> **DE SOTO'S EXPEDITION** In addition to soldiers, de Soto's expedition included priests, farmers, and Native American scouts.

Missionaries to America

While the conquistadors were exploring the Americas, many changes were taking place in Europe. Some people began to question the power of the Catholic Church. At the time, the Church forced people to follow its rules and to pay taxes. It even had its own courts. The courts could punish people for disagreeing with Church laws.

Religious Reforms

In 1517, a German priest named **Martin Luther** began to call openly for **reforms**, or changes, in the Catholic Church. This period of reforms is called the **Reformation**. Luther was forced out of the Church, but he gained many supporters. Those who protested the actions of Catholic leaders became known as Protestants. They began new churches, including the Lutheran Church.

As a result, the Catholic Church made some changes. It also tried to keep its power through efforts now called the **Counter-Reformation**. The Church banned books that went against its teachings. People who protested Catholic laws were punished in Church courts.

During the Counter-Reformation, the Catholic Church worked on spreading its power to the Americas. Church leaders wanted to gain new followers. They also wanted to share in the wealth of the lands claimed by European countries. To do this, the Church sent religious teachers, or **missionaries**, to convert Native Americans to the Catholic Church.

Soon after coming to the Americas, missionaries held ceremonies to make Native Americans they met Catholic.

> **MISSIONARIES** Saint Ignatius founded the Jesuits, a Catholic group that did missionary work.

It was not until later that the missionaries actually started teaching them about Catholic beliefs. Some missionaries forced Native Americans to become Catholic and also enslaved them. Many Native Americans fought to hold on to their beliefs, but others were forced to change how they lived and worshipped.

READING CHECK ☼ **MAIN IDEA AND DETAILS**
What was the main result of the Counter-Reformation in the Americas?

Summary

Spanish conquistadors such as Juan Ponce de León, Hernando Cortés, Francisco Coronado, Francisco Pizarro, and Hernando de Soto explored and claimed large areas of the Americas for Spain. Missionaries brought Catholic beliefs to Native Americans.

REVIEW

1. **WHAT TO KNOW** Why did the Spanish explore and conquer large areas of the Americas?

2. **VOCABULARY** Describe the effects of the **Counter-Reformation** on the Americas.

3. **GEOGRAPHY** What lands in the Americas made up the Spanish empire known as New Spain?

4. **CRITICAL THINKING** What were some effects of Spanish exploration of the Americas?

5. ✏ **WRITE A JOURNAL** Imagine that you are traveling with one of the explorers discussed in this lesson. Write a journal entry describing the places you have been.

6. ⭐ (Focus Skill) **MAIN IDEA AND DETAILS** On a separate sheet of paper, copy and complete this graphic organizer.

Main Idea
The Spanish explored and built settlements in the Americas.

Details

Biography

Trustworthiness

Respect
Responsibility
Fairness
Caring
Patriotism

Estevanico

Estevanico was not a Spaniard. He was an African who had been sold into slavery. He never led an expedition, but he may have walked across more of North America than any other explorer of his time.

Estevanico and his owner first joined an expedition to Florida. Later, they made their way to Mexico City. In Mexico City, a Spanish commander chose Estevanico to look for the Seven Cities of Gold. The commander must have trusted that Estevanico had the ability to survive in the wilderness. He also trusted Estevanico to return and to give a true report.

Estevanico was not an explorer by choice. As an enslaved person, he had to go where his owner sent him. But he had much freedom in the wilderness. He had learned how to use plants to cure some illnesses. Many Native Americans thought of him as a medicine man.

Estevanico did not survive his journey to find the Seven Cities of Gold. Still, his name is remembered today, along with those of other explorers who traveled through North America.

Why Character Counts

How did Estevanico's actions show that he was trustworthy?

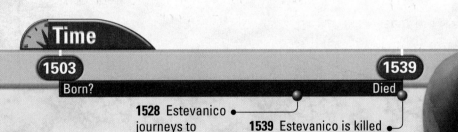

Time

1503 — Born?

1539 — Died

1528 Estevanico journeys to Florida

1539 Estevanico is killed on an expedition to find the Seven Cities of Gold

GO ONLINE For more resources, go to www.harcourtschool.com/ss1

Use an Elevation Map

Why It Matters An elevation map can help you understand what a place looks like—whether it has mountains or is lowland.

▶ LEARN

The **elevation** (eh•luh•VAY•shuhn), or height, of the land is measured from sea level. The elevation of land at sea level is 0 feet. Find sea level on Drawing A. The lines on this drawing of a mountain are contour lines. A **contour line** connects all points of equal elevation. The contour line labeled 1,640 feet connects all points on the mountain that are 1,640 feet above sea level.

Drawing B shows the mountain as you would see it from above. The contour lines are closer together on the steeper side.

On Drawing C, color is added between the contour lines. The key shows the range of elevation that each color stands for. For example, the key shows that the elevation of every place in green is between sea level and 330 feet.

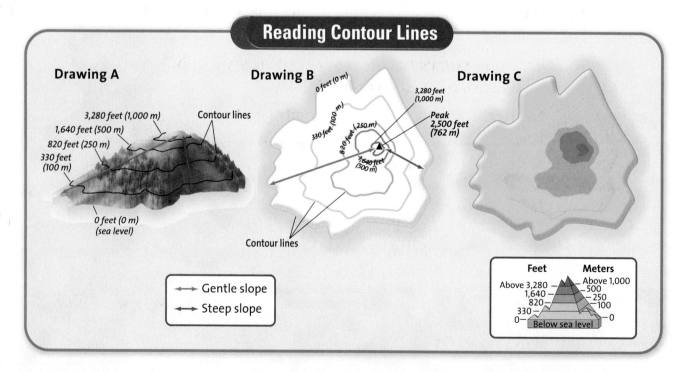

Reading Contour Lines

Drawing A

3,280 feet (1,000 m)
1,640 feet (500 m)
820 feet (250 m)
330 feet (100 m)

Contour lines

0 feet (0 m) (sea level)

Drawing B

0 feet (0 m)
330 feet (100 m)
820 feet (250 m)
1,640 feet (500 m)

Contour lines

3,280 feet (1,000 m)

Peak 2,500 feet (762 m)

←——→ Gentle slope
←—→ Steep slope

Drawing C

Feet	Meters
Above 3,280	Above 1,000
1,640	500
820	250
330	100
0	0
Below sea level	

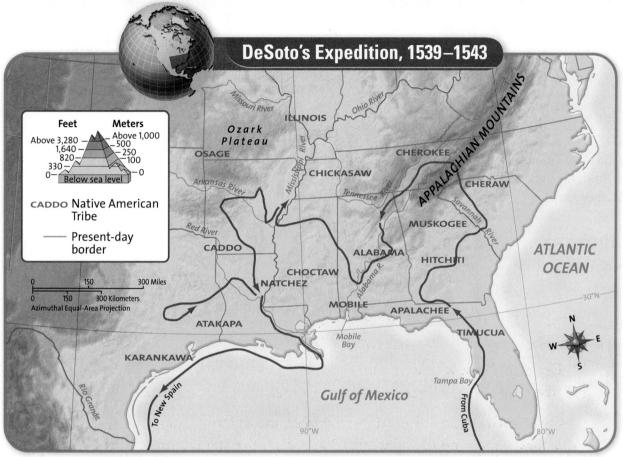

DeSoto's Expedition, 1539–1543

Feet	Meters
Above 3,280	Above 1,000
1,640	500
820	250
330	100
0	0
Below sea level	

CADDO Native American Tribe

Present-day border

0   150   300 Miles
0   150   300 Kilometers
Azimuthal Equal-Area Projection

❱ PRACTICE

The map above also uses color to show elevation. The map key tells you what elevation each color represents. Use the map and the map key to answer the questions below.

1 What is the elevation of the land de Soto reached as he passed through the Appalachian Mountains?

2 What is the elevation where the Mobile lived?

3 What is the elevation of the land that de Soto passed through after crossing the Arkansas River?

❱ APPLY

Use the map to plan a route for de Soto that might have taken him along an easier way through the areas he explored.

Map and Globe Skills

Time

1400 ———————————————————————————— 1650

1524
Verrazano
searches for the
Northwest Passage

1534
Cartier begins
to explore the
St. Lawrence River

1610
Hudson explores
Hudson Bay

💡 **WHAT TO KNOW**
Why did other Europeans
explore North America, and
what did they find?

VOCABULARY
Northwest Passage p. 139
mutiny p. 143

PEOPLE
Giovanni da Verrazano
Jacques Cartier
Henry Hudson

PLACES
St. Lawrence River
the Netherlands
Hudson Bay

⭐ **MAIN IDEA
AND DETAILS**

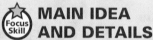

Other Nations Explore

YOU ARE THERE The year is 1609. You are a member of the Lenni Lenape (LEH•nee LEH•nuh•pee) tribe living on the island your people call Mannahatta. Your father tells you that a few days earlier, scouts from your village saw a huge boat on the river. The scouts reported that the men on the boat wore strange coverings. Some people in your village seem eager to talk with the newcomers. You hope they are peaceful.

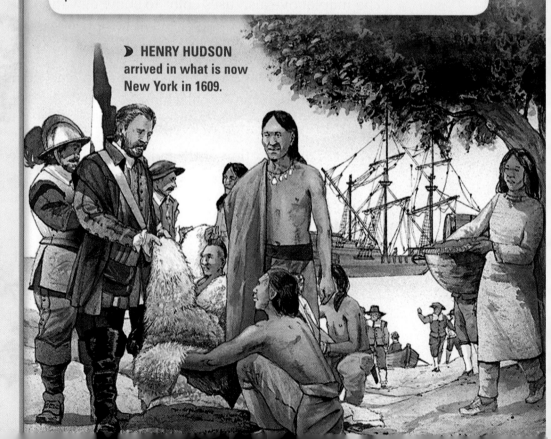

▶ **HENRY HUDSON**
arrived in what is now
New York in 1609.

▶ **THE NORTHWEST PASSAGE** For hundreds of years, European explorers searched for the Northwest Passage.

The Northwest Passage

By the early 1500s, Spain ruled over a large and very rich empire. Spanish ships returned from the Americas with treasure chests full of gold and silver. New expeditions also added to Spain's growing land claims. The rulers of other European countries still wanted to find a shortcut to Asia so that they too could gain wealth and power.

Searching for a New Route

The route followed by Magellan's expedition around South America to Asia was long and dangerous. Many people thought that Asia might be reached more easily by sailing through or around North America. This belief led explorers to search for a route they called the **Northwest Passage**.

The first country to find this waterway would control an important new trade route between Europe and Asia and gain great riches. Some European countries sent explorers to look for the Northwest Passage. The search began in the 1500s and lasted for hundreds of years.

READING CHECK ☉**MAIN IDEA AND DETAILS**
Why did European explorers want to find the Northwest Passage?

Verrazano and Cartier

The French king, Francis I, was one of the many European rulers who wanted to find the Northwest Passage through North America. In 1524, he sent an Italian sailor, **Giovanni da Verrazano**, to find it.

The French in North America

Verrazano set sail in January 1524. He landed on the coast of what is now North Carolina in early March. Verrazano then sailed farther north along the Atlantic coast. He sailed into several bays and rivers, searching for a waterway that led to Asia. Along his route, Verrazano met different Native American tribes. He could not speak their languages. He wrote that some tribes were friendly, but others were not.

Verrazano did not sail any farther north than Newfoundland. He wrote:

"My intention [aim] on this voyage was to reach Cathay and the extreme eastern coast of Asia, but I did not expect to find such an obstacle of new land as I have found.**"**

Verrazano made two more voyages to the Americas to try to find a water route to Asia. On these trips, he searched the coastlines of North America and South America but still found no passage.

In 1534, King Francis sent the French navigator **Jacques Cartier** (ZHAHK kar•TYAY) to look for the Northwest Passage. The king also told Cartier to search for gold. Between 1534 and 1541, Cartier made three trips to North America. On his first trip, he reached the mouth of the **St. Lawrence River**. Cartier claimed all the land around it for France.

▶ **JACQUES CARTIER reported seeing many beavers and otters along the St. Lawrence River. This interested traders in Europe, where they could sell furs for high prices.**

Cartier traveled up the St. Lawrence River on his second voyage. During the trip, he wrote that he saw "fish in appearance like horses." These were not really fish, but walruses. The expedition inland went as far as what is now Montreal. Instead of reaching the Pacific, however, Cartier reached a barrier—river rapids. His boat could not pass the fast-moving water, and he had to turn back.

In 1541, Cartier visited the St. Lawrence River again but was never able to find the Northwest Passage. In search of gold, he sailed up the river past what is now Quebec. Finding nothing, he returned to France. However, Europeans knew more about North America because of Cartier's voyages.

READING CHECK ⚫ **MAIN IDEA AND DETAILS**
What were the aims of Cartier's expeditions?

⚡ *FAST FACT*

When Cartier left North America to return to France, he took a supply of corn that the Iroquoian people had given him. Many Europeans had never seen corn before.

Exploring North America

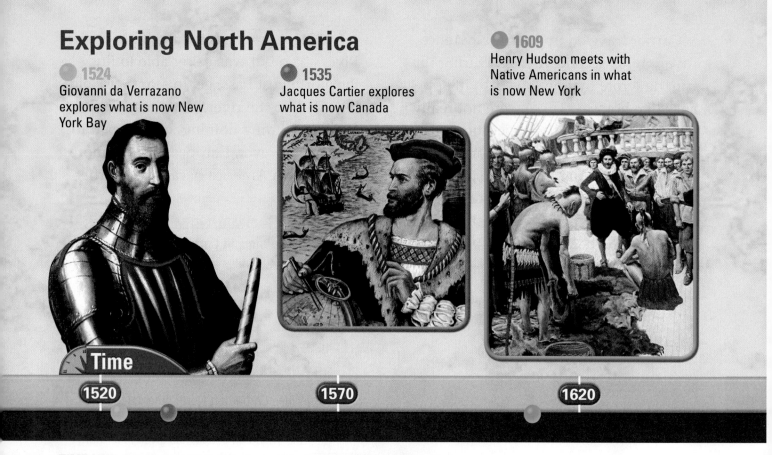

1524
Giovanni da Verrazano explores what is now New York Bay

1535
Jacques Cartier explores what is now Canada

1609
Henry Hudson meets with Native Americans in what is now New York

Time

1520   1570   1620

TIME LINE It took several hundred years for Europeans to explore all of North America. Did Cartier explore what is now Canada before or after Hudson explored New York?

Hudson's Voyages

By the 1600s, exploration was big business. Kings and queens were no longer the only ones paying for expeditions. European trading companies also began sending explorers to look for the Northwest Passage. Their goal was to set up trade routes.

An English explorer named **Henry Hudson** made four voyages in search of the Northwest Passage. A company in England paid for his first two expeditions. In 1608, on his first voyage, Hudson reached an island east of Greenland. He then sailed farther north through the Arctic Ocean but failed to find the Northwest Passage.

The Dutch East India Company paid for Hudson's third voyage. The company was located in Holland, also called **the Netherlands**. The people of this country are known as the Dutch. On this voyage, Hudson spent a month exploring a river in what is now New York. He named the river after himself and claimed the entire Hudson River valley for the Dutch rulers.

A Voyage Ends in Mutiny

In 1610, an English company paid for Hudson's last voyage. He sailed along the northern coast of North America to the bay that also carries his name, **Hudson Bay**. Hudson claimed the land around it for England. He spent three months exploring the huge bay, located in east-central Canada, north of present-day Ontario and west of Quebec.

By November, Hudson's ship was frozen in the ice. After a cold winter and much suffering, his crew **mutinied**, or rebelled. They set Hudson and eight others adrift in a small boat. Hudson and the men were never seen again.

READING CHECK Ŏ**MAIN IDEA AND DETAILS**
For what two countries did Hudson claim land?

Summary

Explorers of North America hoped to find both riches and the Northwest Passage to Asia. Cartier and Hudson claimed lands for the countries that sent them. However, none of the explorers found the Northwest Passage.

▶ **HENRY HUDSON** lands on the coast of North America.

REVIEW

1. **WHAT TO KNOW** Why did other Europeans explore North America, and what did they find?

2. **VOCABULARY** Use the word **mutiny** to describe the last voyage of Henry Hudson.

3. **HISTORY** Why did some trading companies send explorers to North America?

4. **CRITICAL THINKING** What were the costs and benefits of Hudson's expeditions?

5. ✏ **WRITE A SCENE** Pick a European explorer and write a scene about their contact with Native Americans.

6. ⭐(Focus Skill) **MAIN IDEA AND DETAILS** On a separate sheet of paper, copy and complete this graphic organizer.

Main Idea

Details

| Verrazano could not speak Native American languages. | Cartier's boat could not pass rapids. | Hudson's crew mutinied. |

Visual Summary

1492
Columbus lands
at San Salvador

1513
Balboa
sights the
Pacific
Ocean

Summarize the Chapter

Main Idea and Details Complete this graphic organizer to show that you understand the main idea and some supporting details about European explorations of the Americas.

Main Idea

Europeans explored and claimed lands in the Americas.

Details

 Vocabulary

Identify the term from the word bank that correctly matches each definition.

1. a sum of money given for a specific purpose

2. a trip taken with the goal of exploring

3. an agreement between two or more countries

4. to rebel against the leader of one's group

5. a person who sets up and runs a business

6. the scientific knowledge or tools to make or do something

7. a change

8. a Spanish conqueror in the Americas

Word Bank

technology, p. 111   grant, p. 129

expedition, p. 112   conquistador, p. 129

entrepreneur, p. 114   reform, p. 133

treaty, p. 125   mutiny, p. 143

1600

1700

1539
De Soto begins exploring the Southeast

1610
Hudson explores the Atlantic coast

 Time Line

Use the chapter summary time line above to answer these questions.

9. How many years after Columbus reached San Salvador did Balboa see the Pacific?

10. Did Hudson's expedition take place before or after de Soto's?

 Facts and Main Ideas

Answer these questions.

11. What group of Europeans explored North America about A.D. 1000?

12. How was Columbus mistaken about the lands he claimed for Spain?

13. What problems did Magellan's crew face on their trip around the world?

14. Which Spanish explorer conquered the Aztec Empire in Mexico? the Inca Empire in Peru?

Write the letter of the best choice.

15. Who was the first European explorer to explore land that became part of the United States?
    A Christopher Columbus
    B Juan Ponce de León
    C Giovanni da Verrazano
    D Amerigo Vespucci

16. What was Coronado searching for?
    A the Northwest Passage
    B the Seven Cities of Gold
    C the Fountain of Youth
    D the Indies

 Critical Thinking

17. How did the Spanish Reconquista affect Columbus's expedition?

18. What were some of the costs and benefits of expeditions for explorers and sponsors?

19. How did trade and technology play an important role in the growth of exploration?

 Skills

Use an Elevation Map

20. Look at the map on page 137. What is the elevation of the land where de Soto turned toward the Gulf of Mexico?

21. What is the elevation where the Timucua people lived?

22. What is the elevation at the Ozark Plateau?

Write a Persuasive Letter Imagine that you are an explorer. Write a letter to persuade a king or queen to pay for your expedition. Be sure to describe the benefits your expedition will deliver and the obstacles you will face.

Write a Report Write a report about the Northwest Passage. Explain what it was and why Europeans hoped to find it. Also describe Henry Hudson and some of the other explorers who searched for it.

STUDY SKILLS

USE A K-W-L CHART

A K-W-L chart helps you focus on what you already know about a topic and what you want to learn.

- Use the K column to list what you know about a topic.

- Use the W column to list what you want to learn.

- Use the L column to list what you have learned about the topic from your reading.

Building the First Colonies

K—What I Know	W—What I Want to Learn	L—What I Learned
• People from Spain built settlements. • _____	• How did they build settlements? • _____	• _____ • _____

PREVIEW VOCABULARY

plantation p. 150

presidio p. 151

mission p. 151

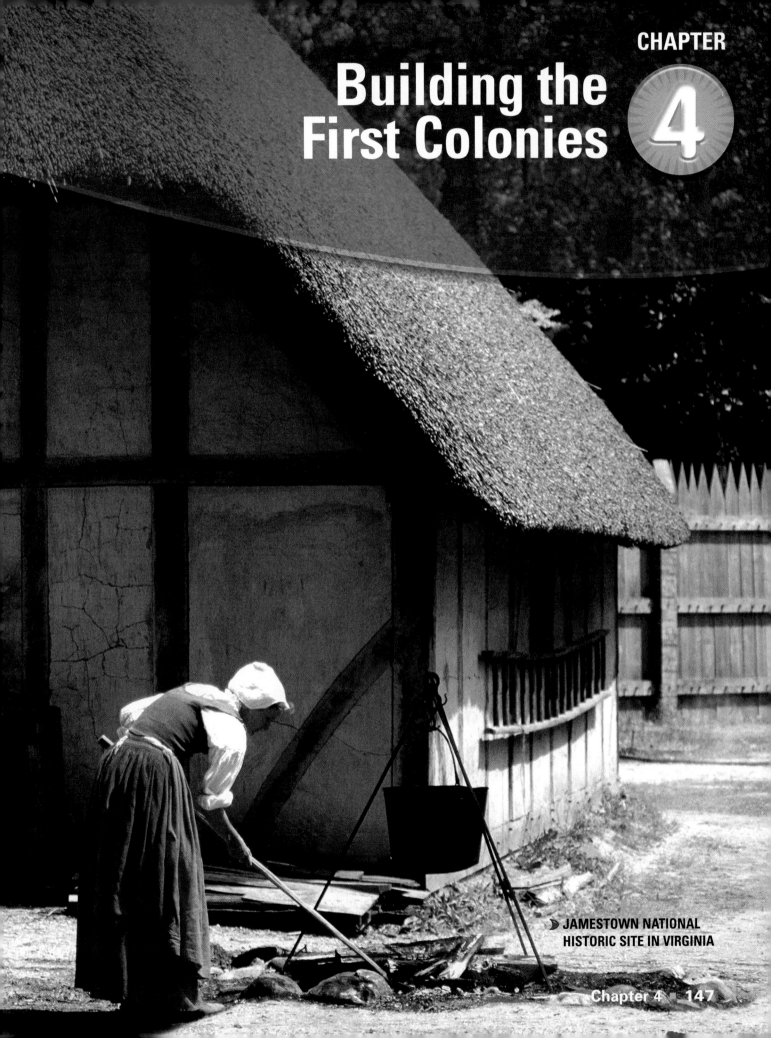

Building the First Colonies

> JAMESTOWN NATIONAL
HISTORIC SITE IN VIRGINIA

Time

1400 — 1650

1535
New Spain
is formed

1565
St. Augustine
is built

WHAT TO KNOW
Why did Spain set up colonies in North America?

VOCABULARY
colony p. 149
plantation p. 150
slavery p. 150
borderlands p. 151
presidio p. 151
mission p. 151
hacienda p. 152

PEOPLE
Bartolomé de Las Casas
Pedro Menéndez de Avilés

PLACES
New Spain
Mexico City
St. Augustine
Santa Fe

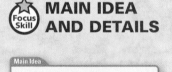

MAIN IDEA AND DETAILS

Main Idea

Details

The Spanish Colonies

YOU ARE THERE

For many days now, warriors from your Hopi village have been watching the actions of the newcomers. You have heard stories about how they ride animals much larger than wolves. You have also heard that sometimes when they arrive in a new place a sickness sweeps across the land.

You see one of the warriors making an arrowhead. "Are we going to war?" you ask. "We shall see," he says. "But we must be prepared."

New Spain

By the 1500s, several European nations, including Spain, had sent explorers to claim land in the Americas. Most explorers stepped onto a beach and claimed the land for hundreds of miles around. They knew little about the lands they were claiming. After claiming the lands, these explorers moved on. No one stayed behind to protect the claims.

Competing Claims

The European countries were competing with each other to win control of as much of the Americas as possible. Often more than one country claimed the same land. Native Americans already lived in most places the explorers claimed. Usually, no one paid attention to anyone else's rights or claims.

Spain had already claimed large parts of the Americas. However, Spain learned that claiming land was not the same as controlling it. Spain came to understand that it needed to protect its lands in the Americas from other European nations. Spain also tried to overpower Native American tribes and take their lands.

Spain formed colonies to protect its lands and to govern the people there. A **colony** is a land ruled by another country. The colony of **New Spain** was formed in 1535, with most of its land in Mexico and its capital in **Mexico City**. New Spain also included many islands in the Caribbean Sea and the Spanish lands north of what is now Panama.

READING CHECK ☼**MAIN IDEA AND DETAILS**
How did Spain protect its claims in the Americas?

▶ **SPANISH FORTS** Spain built forts to protect its claims to land in North America.

Slavery in the Americas

At first, very few Europeans settled in the Americas. After more gold and silver were found, many more colonists came. They hoped to get rich. Others came to start large farms, called **plantations**. By 1550, there were about 100,000 Spanish colonists spread across the Americas. To the south of New Spain, Portugal formed the colony of Brazil.

The Growth of Slavery

Both Spain and Portugal needed many workers to grow crops and to mine gold and silver. They forced the Native Americans they had conquered into slavery. **Slavery** is the practice of holding people against their will and making them work without pay. Many thousands of Native Americans died from hunger and the work they did. Thousands more died from diseases that settlers brought with them from Europe. Diseases such as measles, smallpox, and influenza sometimes killed whole tribes.

Some colonists became concerned about how the Native Americans were being treated. One such colonist was **Bartolomé de Las Casas** (bar•toh•loh•MAY day lahs KAH•sahs). Las Casas was a landowner who later became a priest. He freed his enslaved workers and spoke out in favor of better treatment of Native Americans.

As more Native Americans died, the colonists began to capture Africans to be enslaved workers. Most of these Africans were taken to Brazil or the Caribbean Islands. Soon enslaved Africans were also working under terrible conditions.

READING CHECK Ö**MAIN IDEA AND DETAILS**
How did slavery develop in the Americas?

❱ SUGAR MILLS Enslaved Africans were forced to work in sugar mills in the Portuguese colony of Brazil.

Settlements of New Spain, 1650

NORTH AMERICA

PACIFIC OCEAN

ATLANTIC OCEAN

Colorado River

Santa Fe

El Paso del Norte

Rio Grande

Saltillo • Monterrey

Guadalajara •

Mexico City

Veracruz

Gulf of Mexico

St. Augustine

Mississippi River

Havana • CUBA

Santiago de Cuba •

Santo Domingo

Caribbean Sea

Guatemala City •

Granada •

0 300 600 Miles
0 300 600 Kilometers
Azimuthal Equal-Area Projection

Legend:
- New Spain
- El Camino Real
- 🏠 Mission
- • Settlement

MAP SKILL LOCATION Over time, New Spain's missions and borders spread northward. El Camino Real (el kah•MEE•noh ray•AHL), or "The Royal Road," connected many settlements to Mexico City. Which settlement was farthest north?

Settling the Borderlands

Spain also wanted to protect its lands north of Mexico City. These lands on the edge of Spain's claims were called **borderlands**. The borderlands included parts of what are today northern Mexico and the southern United States, from Florida to California.

St. Augustine and Santa Fe

Spanish soldiers led the way, building **presidios** (pray•SEE•dee•ohz), or forts, in the borderlands. In 1565, **Pedro Menéndez de Avilés** (may•NAYN•days day ah•vee•LAYS) and 1,500 soldiers, sailors, and settlers sailed from Spain. The same year they reached the area that is now **St. Augustine**, Florida. There they built the first permanent, or long-lasting, European settlement in what is now the United States.

Spain's main goal in settling the borderlands was to protect its empire. The Spanish king chose leaders to govern each new settlement. Settlers in the new colonies did not have the right to elect their own leaders. The king also sent missionaries to convert Native Americans to Christianity.

The missionaries built religious settlements called **missions** in many areas of the southern half of North America. In 1610, Spanish missionaries helped settle **Santa Fe**, the capital of the New Mexico Colony. In such places, missionaries and Native Americans lived very near each other.

Europeans in the Western Hemisphere, 1550–1750

YEAR	POPULATION
1550	👤👤👤👤
1650	👤👤👤👤👤👤👤👤👤
1750	👤👤👤👤👤👤👤👤👤👤👤👤👤👤👤👤👤

👤 = 500,000 people   👤 = 250,000 people

GRAPH About how many Europeans lived in the Western Hemisphere in 1550?

Life in the Borderlands

At first, some Native Americans chose to stay at the missions. There they learned new ways of living and working. However, many Native Americans were forced to work on mission farms and ranches. Some fought back, tearing down churches and other mission buildings.

Some settlers in the borderlands held much land. Some built large homes or estates called **haciendas** (ah•see•EN•dahs), where they often raised cattle and sheep. The Spanish—and the animals they brought with them—changed life for many Native Americans. Horses, long extinct in the Americas, once again roamed the land. Some Native American tribes learned to tame horses for use in hunting and in war. Some learned to raise sheep and to use their wool to make clothing.

READING CHECK ŎMAIN IDEA AND DETAILS
How did new animals change Native American life?

Summary

In the 1500s, explorers often paid no attention to other countries' claims to lands. Spain tried to hold on to its claims by setting up colonies. The Spanish needed workers, so they enslaved Native Americans and Africans.

REVIEW

1. **WHAT TO KNOW** Why did Spain set up colonies in North America?

2. **VOCABULARY** Write a sentence using the terms **hacienda** and **mission** to describe life on the borderlands.

3. **HISTORY** What role did religion play in Spanish settlements?

4. **CRITICAL THINKING** Why would it be important to Spain to build different kinds of settlements in the borderlands?

5. **WRITE A REPORT** Research and write a short report about why Spain set up missions.

6. **MAIN IDEA AND DETAILS** On a separate sheet of paper, copy and complete this graphic organizer.

Main Idea
The Spanish built different kinds of settlements for different reasons.

Details

Bartolomé de Las Casas

Biography

Trustworthiness

Respect

Responsibility

Fairness

Caring

Patriotism

"For all the peoples of the world are . . . rational beings. All possess understanding. . . ."

Bartolomé de Las Casas was one of the first Europeans to try to better the lives of Native Americans. He arrived from Spain on the island of Hispaniola in 1502, and started a plantation. At first, he used enslaved Native Americans as workers. He soon came to understand that slavery and the harsh treatment of Native Americans were wrong.

In 1509, Las Casas freed the Native Americans he had enslaved and began to work for better treatment of Native Americans. In 1512, he became a Catholic priest. Later, he wrote letters and essays that questioned the enslavement of Native Americans. He also served as a missionary to the Taino people of Cuba.

Las Casas spoke out so strongly for Native Americans that in 1550, King Charles I of Spain ruled that the Spanish could no longer enslave Native Americans. But this order was not always followed. Las Casas kept working to better the lives of Native Americans until his death in Madrid, Spain, in 1566.

Why Character Counts

In what ways did Bartolomé de Las Casas take responsibility for the treatment of Native Americans?

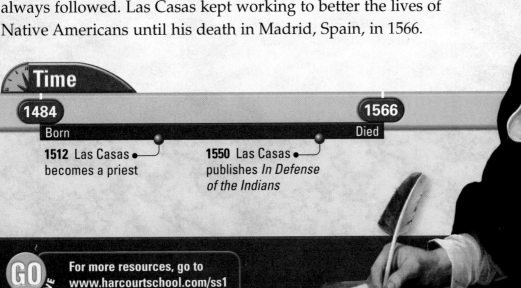

Time

1484			1566
Born			Died

1512 Las Casas becomes a priest

1550 Las Casas publishes *In Defense of the Indians*

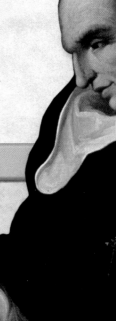

GO ONLINE For more resources, go to www.harcourtschool.com/ss1

Time

1400 — 1650

1585
The first colonists
arrive at Roanoke

1607
The Jamestown
settlement is started

1619
The first Africans
arrive in Virginia

💡 **WHAT TO KNOW**
Why did English settlers
come to North America, and
where did they settle first?

VOCABULARY
raw material p. 155
stock p. 155
cash crop p. 157
profit p. 157
indentured servant p. 157
legislature p. 157
represent p. 158
royal colony p. 158

PEOPLE
Queen Elizabeth I
Walter Raleigh
John White
John Smith
Pocahontas
John Rolfe

PLACES
Roanoke Island
Jamestown

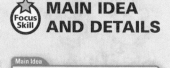
**MAIN IDEA
AND DETAILS**

Main Idea

Details		

The Virginia Colony

YOU ARE THERE
"We're getting off here!" your friend shouts.
The year is 1587. You and 116 other settlers
are on ships off the coast of **Roanoke Island**, in
present-day North Carolina.

Earlier settlers had built homes and a fort on
Roanoke, but they didn't like the island. They all
went home to England. "Maybe we'll be able to use
the houses they left behind," you say. Still, you do
not have a very good feeling
about this place.

▶ QUEEN ELIZABETH I wanted an
English colony in North America.

▶ THE LOST COLONY When John White returned to Roanoke Island, he found that the word *Croatoan*, the name of a local Native American tribe, had been carved into a post.

England Attempts a Colony

England saw that Spain had grown rich from its colonies. England's rulers now wanted their own colonies in the Americas. They knew they would benefit from the lumber and other raw materials the colonies would provide. A **raw material** is a resource that can be used to make a product.

The Lost Colony

In 1584, England's **Queen Elizabeth I** chose **Walter Raleigh** (RAW•lee) to set up a colony in North America. A year later, Raleigh sent **John White** and about 100 colonists to Roanoke Island, in an area Raleigh named Virginia. These colonists did not stay long. They ran low on food and returned to England.

John White led another group of settlers to Roanoke Island in 1587. After a time, White sailed back to England to get more supplies. When he returned—three years later—all the settlers were gone! What happened there is still a mystery. Roanoke is known as the Lost Colony.

The Virginia Company

In the early 1600s, a group of English merchants wanted to try again to start a colony in Virginia. With the approval of King James I, they set up the Virginia Company. In return for money that the merchants had given to set up the company, each owner received stock in the company. **Stock** is part ownership in a business.

READING CHECK ⟳MAIN IDEA AND DETAILS

Why did England's rulers want to start colonies in North America?

▶ **JAMESTOWN** For one year, John Smith (left) served as the leader of Jamestown. Today, a reconstruction of Jamestown (above) stands near the original site.

Jamestown

In 1607, three ships sent by the Virginia Company sailed into the deep bay now called the Chesapeake. The 105 colonists aboard sailed up a river they named the James, in honor of their king. Along the shore, they built the settlement of **Jamestown**.

England's First Permanent Colony

Jamestown was a poor choice for a settlement. The swampy land was not good for farming. The colonists had no interest in farming anyway. Most came to Virginia to find gold and get rich. No one bothered to plant or gather food. More than half the colonists died the first year.

Jamestown might have failed without Captain **John Smith**. As the leader of Jamestown, Smith made an important rule—anyone who did not work did not eat. The colonists were soon busy planting crops and building a fort.

The Powhatan Confederacy

Most of the Native Americans living in Virginia at this time belonged to the Powhatan (POW•uh•tan) Confederacy. Its tribes were united under one main chief. Colonists gave the name *Powhatan* to all the tribes as well as to the chief.

From the start, there was trouble between the Powhatan and the colonists, as hungry colonists often stole the tribes' crops. Chief Powhatan's daughter **Pocahontas** (poh•kuh•HAHN•tuhs) helped bring about a short time of peace between the groups. During this time, both groups cooperated by trading goods.

READING CHECK ⏾ **MAIN IDEA AND DETAILS**
How did John Smith help save Jamestown?

Growth and Government

For all of its troubles, Jamestown grew. A leader named **John Rolfe** brought tobacco plants from the West Indies to the colony. The colonists were soon growing tobacco as a **cash crop**—a crop that people grow to sell. The Virginia Company sold tobacco all over Europe and made huge profits. A **profit** is the money left over after all costs have been paid.

Newcomers Arrive

Growing tobacco required many workers. The Virginia Company paid for people's passages, or trips, to Virginia. In return, the people agreed to work without pay for a length of time. These workers were called **indentured servants**. They usually worked from four to seven years. After that time, they were freed.

In 1619, the first Africans were brought to Jamestown. No one knows whether they were treated as indentured servants or as enslaved people. Over time, more Africans were brought to the colony. They came as enslaved workers. Unlike indentured servants, they were rarely freed. Their hard work helped Virginia prosper.

The House of Burgesses

By 1619, the Virginia Colony had more than 1,000 people. Laws were needed to keep order. The Virginia Company said the colonists could have the same rights as people living in England. So colonists chose to set up a **legislature**, or lawmaking branch of the government.

Virginia's legislature, the House of Burgesses (BER•juhs•iz), met in 1619.

▶ AFRICANS ARRIVE IN JAMESTOWN Dutch traders sold Africans as enslaved workers.

It was the first representative assembly in the English colonies. Now some colonists could elect members to **represent**, or speak for, them in the government.

Only men who owned property could become members and vote in the House of Burgesses. Women, indentured servants, and enslaved people were not allowed to hold office or to vote.

The Powhatan Wars

As more colonists came to Virginia, they took over more Powhatan land. In 1622, the Powhatan fought back. This started years of fighting. The Powhatan Wars led King James I to make Virginia a **royal colony** in 1624. This meant that the king owned the colony. To help run the colony, the king picked a governor, who shared power with the House of Burgesses.

READING CHECK Ŏ MAIN IDEA AND DETAILS
What cash crop helped Virginia grow?

▶ **POWHATAN WARS** The Powhatan tried to defend their lands against colonists.

Summary

Starting in the 1580s, England set up colonies in North America. The Virginia Colony developed slowly. As the colony grew, slavery was introduced and the Powhatan Wars were fought.

REVIEW

1. **WHAT TO KNOW** Why did English settlers come to North America, and where did they settle first?

2. **VOCABULARY** Use the term **royal colony** in a sentence about Virginia.

3. **GOVERNMENT** What was the job of the House of Burgesses?

4. **CRITICAL THINKING** How did enslaved workers help the Virginia Colony succeed?

5. **CONSTRUCT A TIME LINE** Make a time line showing the important events in Jamestown's history and how they are related.

6. **MAIN IDEA AND DETAILS** (Focus Skill) On a separate sheet of paper, copy and complete this graphic organizer.

Main Idea

Details

| The population of Virginia grew. | People wanted laws to keep order. | The Virginia Company gave some colonists rights. |

Pocahontas

Biography

Trustworthiness
Respect
Responsibility
Fairness
Caring
Patriotism

The name *Pocahontas* means "Playful One" in the Algonquian language. Pocahontas was the daughter of the powerful Chief Powhatan. She was about 12 years old when the first English settlers arrived at Jamestown.

In 1607, members of the Powhatan tribe captured John Smith and took him to Chief Powhatan. Smith believed that he was going to be killed, but Pocahontas kept him from being harmed. This famous event was probably just acted out as a ceremony, but no one is sure.

Pocahontas's friendship with the settlers helped bring about a peace between her people and the English. She convinced the English to release Powhatan prisoners and stopped Powhatan warriors from attacking the English. This time of cooperation did not last long, however. In 1613, an English settler kidnapped Pocahontas, hoping her father would pay for her freedom.

While she was held by the English, Pocahontas met John Rolfe. They were married in 1614. In 1616, Pocahontas, Rolfe, and their baby son, Thomas, went to England. Later, on the way home to Virginia, Pocahontas died. She was only about 22 years old when she died, but the story of her life is still told in books and art.

Why Character Counts

How did Pocahontas's actions show she cared for others?

Time

1595 — Born?

1617 — Died

1607 Pocahontas meets English settlers

1614 Pocahontas marries John Rolfe

GO ONLINE For more resources, go to www.harcourtschool.com/ss1

Chapter 4   159

Compare Primary and Secondary Sources

Why It Matters To know what really happened in the past, you need to find evidence. You can do this by studying and comparing primary and secondary sources.

▶ LEARN

Primary sources are the records and artifacts made by people who saw or took part in an event. These people may have written down their thoughts in a journal, letter, or poem. They may have taken a photograph or painted a picture. A primary source gives people of today a direct link to a past event.

A **secondary source** is a record of an event made by someone who was not there at the time. It is not a direct link to an event. If someone who only heard or read about an event writes a newspaper story or a book, that is a secondary source.

Sometimes a source can be either primary or secondary. A newspaper story written by a reporter who saw an event is a primary source. A newspaper story written by a reporter who heard about the event from an eyewitness is a secondary source.

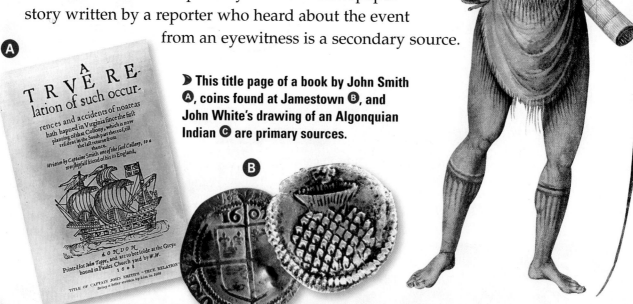

▶ This title page of a book by John Smith **Ⓐ**, coins found at Jamestown **Ⓑ**, and John White's drawing of an Algonquian Indian **Ⓒ** are primary sources.

❱ PRACTICE

Look at the photographs on pages 160 and 161 of objects and printed materials that give information about the Virginia Colony. Use them to answer these questions.

1 How are items C and E alike and different?

2 What kind of information might be found in item A but not in item F?

3 How might secondary sources such as D and F also be primary sources?

❱ APPLY

Look through your textbook for examples of primary and secondary sources. Explain to a classmate what makes each source a primary source or a secondary source.

❱ This Jamestown website **D**, the photograph of reenactors making a dugout canoe **E**, and this recent book about Jamestown **F** are secondary sources.

*(within image F)* Jamestown REDISCOVERY 1994-2004 — William M. Kelso with Beverly Straube

(within image D) Jamestown Rediscovery — Jamestown REDISCOVERY — Home — Findings, Exhibits, History, Visiting, Publications, Resources, Contact, Donations — Welcome to the Association for the Preservation of Virginia Antiquities' *Jamestown Rediscovery* archaeological project. *Jamestown Rediscovery* is investigating the remains of 1607–1698 Jamestown on the APVA property on Jamestown Island, Virginia. — APVA — NEWS FROM THE DIG — Where are We Digging Now? — News on the Latest Discoveries — • What have we found? • History of Jamestown • Visiting Jamestown • Publications • Our new Ukrop's cereal box! — • Our Exhibits • Research Resources • Contact • 2004 Fieldschool • Donations — Copyright 2003 Association for the Preservation of Virginia Antiquities

1620
The *Mayflower*
lands at Plymouth

1630
About 300 colonists
live in Plymouth

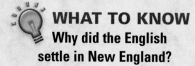

WHAT TO KNOW
Why did the English
settle in New England?

VOCABULARY
pilgrim p. 163
compact p. 164
self-government p. 164
majority rule p. 164

PEOPLE
King Henry VIII
William Bradford
Samoset
Tisquantum

PLACES
Plymouth

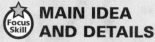
**MAIN IDEA
AND DETAILS**

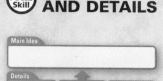

The Plymouth Colony

YOU ARE THERE

You are sitting below deck on a ship called
the *Mayflower*. You have barely enough light
to see. The air is so stale that you wish you didn't
have to breathe. The ship is rising and falling with the
waves, but you're getting used to that. Your mother
brings your dinner—dry bread, cold dried meat, and
an onion.

You've been living like this for two months.
America will have to be a
wonderful place, you think, to
make up for this awful trip.

The Pilgrims' Journey

John Smith left Jamestown and in 1614 explored north along the Atlantic coast. He made a map of the northern area he visited. He also named the region New England and wrote a book called *A Description of New England*. Today, the region includes six states—Connecticut, Rhode Island, Massachusetts, Vermont, New Hampshire, and Maine.

Seeking Religious Freedom

Many people in England read Smith's book. It made them think about building new communities in the region he described. Some people wanted to move there to make money. Others wanted to move there for religious reasons.

Years earlier, **King Henry VIII** had banned the Catholic Church in England and replaced it with the Church of England. Everyone in England had to belong to the Church of England, and those who chose not to were punished.

Hoping to follow their own religious beliefs, one group of English people had moved to the Netherlands. They came to be known as Pilgrims. A **pilgrim** is a person who makes a journey for religious reasons.

The Pilgrims had religious freedom in the Netherlands, but they did not like the Dutch way of life. They wanted to build a society where everyone shared the same religious beliefs. In North America, they would get their chance.

The Virginia Company agreed to pay the Pilgrims' passage to North America. In return, the Pilgrims would repay the company with lumber and furs from their new land. On a cold day in September 1620, they left from England on a ship called the *Mayflower*.

READING CHECK ⊙**MAIN IDEA AND DETAILS** Why did the Pilgrims want to go to North America?

▶ BOARDING THE *MAYFLOWER* In this painting, Pilgrims board rowboats to make their way toward the *Mayflower*.

▶ **PILGRIMS' RIGHTS** Women were not allowed to sign the Mayflower Compact because at this time in history, women had fewer rights than men had.

The Mayflower Compact

The *Mayflower* was headed for Virginia, but storms blew the ship off course. Instead, the *Mayflower* landed at Cape Cod, in what is now Massachusetts.

Self-Government

The settlers arrived in a place with no government. To keep order, all the men aboard the *Mayflower* signed a **compact**, or agreement. This document became known as the Mayflower Compact. The signers agreed that fair laws would be made for the good of the colony. They promised to obey these laws.

The Mayflower Compact gave those who signed it the right to govern themselves. At a time when monarchs ruled, **self-government** was a very new idea.

The Mayflower Compact also included the idea of **majority rule**. If more than half the people agreed to a law or a decision, everyone had to follow it.

The settlers took several weeks to find a place for their colony. They chose a site on a harbor. Fresh water and good land for growing crops were nearby. John Smith had named the place **Plymouth**.

William Bradford, one of Plymouth's early governors, wrote,

> 66 Being thus arrived in a good harbor and brought safe to land, they fell upon their knees and blessed the God of heaven. 99

READING CHECK ⚙️**MAIN IDEA AND DETAILS**
Why was the Mayflower Compact important?

Building a Colony

Although the Plymouth settlers tried to make wise decisions, the first winter was very hard. It was cold and long. By spring, 50 of the 102 settlers had died.

Help from Native Americans

In the spring, the survivors got a very welcome surprise when an Abenaki Native American named **Samoset** arrived, saying, "Welcome, Englishmen." Samoset had learned English from sailors who fished along the Atlantic coast.

Several days later, Samoset returned to Plymouth with **Tisquantum**, or Squanto, as the English called him. He was a member of the Wampanoag (wahm•puh•NOH•ag) tribe and also spoke English. Years before, Tisquantum had been taken and sold as an enslaved worker in Spain. After he escaped, he spent several years in England before returning home.

Tisquantum showed the Pilgrims where to fish and how to plant squash, corn, and pumpkins. Because food was scarce, the Pilgrims were glad to live in peace with the Wampanoag. Both groups benefited from their cooperation. The colonists and the Native Americans both had valuable items that the other group wanted.

Tisquantum helped the colonists trade for furs from neighboring tribes. The Native Americans were able to trade furs for items such as metal goods and cloth. Metal goods were very useful to them because the metal could be reshaped and used to make tools or jewelry.

READING CHECK ⚙MAIN IDEA AND DETAILS
How did Tisquantum help the Pilgrims?

FAST FACT

How did people share news in earlier times? If there was important news to announce in Plymouth, a drummer would call the colonists to gather.

▶ **THE PILGRIMS' THANKSGIVING** This painting was made nearly 300 years after the original event. How do you think this artist viewed the event?

Plymouth Grows

When the Plymouth colonists first arrived, there was very little food to be had. To help, the colony's leaders divided the harvest equally among the families. Then, in 1623, the leaders decided to divide the land among the colonists. The result was that the people worked harder.

Growing Prosperity

The Plymouth colonists began to prosper from their farming, as well as from fishing and fur trading. As new colonists came, earlier colonists had extra goods ready to trade. However, the number of people living in Plymouth stayed low in its first ten years. By 1630, there were only about 300 colonists.

Trouble Starts

After 1630, other English colonists began to settle in different areas of New England. Life there began to change. Many of the new colonists were not friendly toward the Native Americans and settled on more of their lands. Some colonists did not see a need to cooperate with the Native Americans. As fights broke out between the two groups, trade between them came to an end.

This made life harder for the colonists and the Native Americans. William Bradford had once helped make peace with local tribes. He later supported a war to push many Native Americans out of New England. Such actions also caused problems among the tribes. As their homelands grew smaller, tribes fought with each other for control of hunting grounds.

READING CHECK **CAUSE AND EFFECT**
Why did the relationship between the Native Americans and the colonists change?

Summary

The Pilgrims left Europe to establish a society based on their religious beliefs. When they arrived in Plymouth, the settlers wrote the Mayflower Compact to set up self-government. Early on, Native Americans helped the colonists, but when colonists moved onto their land, fighting broke out.

▶ **PLYMOUTH PLANTATION HISTORICAL SITE** This woman shows Native American skills to visitors.

REVIEW

1. **WHAT TO KNOW** Why did the English settle in New England?

2. **VOCABULARY** Write a sentence about the Plymouth Colony using the terms **compact** and **self-government**.

3. **HISTORY** How did growing troubles between English colonists and Native Americans change life in New England?

4. **CRITICAL THINKING** Make It Relevant Do you think the ideas of the Mayflower Compact are still important to people today? Why or why not?

5. **WRITE A SPEECH** Write a speech that gives reasons why Pilgrims should or should not sign the Mayflower Compact.

6. **MAIN IDEA AND DETAILS** On a separate sheet of paper, copy and complete this graphic organizer.

Main Idea
The Virginia Company agreed to pay for the Pilgrims' passage to North America.

Details

Solve a Problem

Why It Matters Knowing how to solve problems is a skill that will help you all your life.

❱ LEARN

Here are some steps that you can use to help you solve a problem.

Step 1 Identify the problem.

Step 2 Gather information.

Step 3 List possible solutions, and consider the advantages and disadvantages of each solution.

Step 4 Choose and try the best solution.

Step 5 Determine how to judge if your solution worked. Think about how well your solution helped solve the problem.

❱ PRACTICE

The Pilgrims were far from home, in a new land with no government. There was no one to make laws or keep order.

1. What problem did the Pilgrims have?

2. How might this problem have affected them?

3. What were some possible solutions to their problem?

4. How did the Pilgrims solve their problem?

5. How well did their solution work? What advantages do you think self-government had over a distant ruler in making laws?

❱ **PILGRIM HAT** This beaver-fur hat was worn by a settler on the *Mayflower.*

Mayflower Compact

IN THE NAME OF GOD, AMEN. We, whose names are underwritten, the Loyal Subjects of our dread Sovereign Lord King James, by the Grace of God, of Great Britain, France, and Ireland, King, Defender of the Faith, &c. Having undertaken for the Glory of God, and Advancement of the Christian Faith, and the Honour of our King and Country, a Voyage to plant the first Colony in the northern Parts of Virginia; Do by these Presents, solemnly and mutually, in the Presence of God and one another, covenant and combine ourselves together into a civil Body Politick, for our better Ordering and Preservation, and Furtherance of the Ends aforesaid: And by Virtue hereof do enact, constitute, and frame, such just and equal Laws, Ordinances, Acts, Constitutions, and Officers, from time to time, as shall be thought most meet and convenient for the general Good of the Colony; unto which we promise all due Submission and Obedience.

IN WITNESS whereof we have hereunto subscribed our names at Cape-Cod the eleventh of November, in the Reign of our Sovereign Lord King James, of England, France, and Ireland, the eighteenth, and of Scotland the fifty-fourth, Anno Domini; 1620.

❯ APPLY

Make It Relevant Identify a problem in your community or school. Use the steps shown to write a plan for solving the problem. What solution did you choose? Why do you think that your solution will help solve that problem?

Lesson 4

Time
1400 — 1650

1608
Champlain founds Quebec

1626
The Dutch set up New Amsterdam

WHAT TO KNOW
Why did the French and the Dutch set up colonies?

VOCABULARY
demand p. 172
supply p. 172
ally p. 174
proprietary colony p. 176

PEOPLE
Samuel de Champlain
Peter Minuit
Jacques Marquette
Louis Joliet
Sieur de la Salle

PLACES
Quebec
New Netherland
New Amsterdam
New Sweden
New Orleans

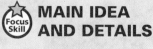
MAIN IDEA AND DETAILS

The French and the Dutch

YOU ARE THERE
The year is 1608, and you're traveling with your father on a trading mission. Your people, the Huron, have started trading furs with the French.

When you arrive at the trading place, you sit quietly and watch. The men use hand signals to communicate. When a trade is agreed on, they nod their heads. Your father has brought several furs to trade, so you expect to take many new things back home. You just hope you'll be able to carry them all!

New France

While Spain and England were building colonies in North America, France was also claiming land in what are today Canada and the northeastern United States. French claims to this region, which became known as New France, began with Jacques Cartier. He explored the St. Lawrence River in the early 1500s. He also started a trading partnership with the Huron people.

French merchants wanted the wealth that came from the fur trade. The French king wanted to add to his country's power. He pushed merchants to start colonies in North America.

Champlain Founds Quebec

In time, a group of merchants hired **Samuel de Champlain** (sham•PLAYN) to find a place to build a settlement. In 1608, Champlain founded **Quebec** along the St. Lawrence River. Quebec was the first French settlement in North America.

In the 1630s, French Catholic missionaries began arriving in New France. These missionaries often lived with Native Americans and learned their languages. The aim of the missionaries was to convert the Native Americans to the Catholic religion.

Some French fur traders also lived with the Native Americans.

> **SAMUEL DE CHAMPLAIN** This statue of Champlain stands in Canada.

Routes of Champlain 1603–1615

MAP SKILL **MOVEMENT** About how far did Champlain travel to reach Lake Huron from Montreal?

They learned their languages and ways of life. Since these traders spent much of their time trapping and hunting, they did not build many long-lasting settlements.

Unlike the Spanish and English colonies, New France grew slowly. Most French people were not interested in moving to North America. In the 1600s, the French built only two main settlements in all of North America—Quebec and Montreal. By 1625, the population of Quebec had grown to only about 60 people.

READING CHECK ⭕**MAIN IDEA AND DETAILS** Why did New France grow slowly?

New Netherland

Not long after the English started colonies in North America, the Dutch began to settle their own colony. They called it **New Netherland**. They built settlements along the Hudson River, in parts of what are now New York and New Jersey.

The Dutch Fur Trade

The Dutch set up a colony in order to profit from the fur trade. The **demand**, or desire, for furs was high. The Dutch traded with Native Americans, adding to their supply of fur. **Supply** is the amount of a good that is offered for sale. When the demand for a good is high, and the supply of a good is low, the price of the good usually goes up.

By 1626, **Peter Minuit** (MIN•yuh•wuht) was governor of New Netherland. During this time, the Dutch believed they had bought Manhattan Island from the Native Americans who were living there. As in other places, the Native Americans' ideas about land were different from those of the new settlers. They believed that the land was for all people to use, and that nobody could own the land. They thought the Dutch were paying them only for the use of what was on the land.

In 1626, the Dutch began laying out a town on the south end of Manhattan Island. They called the settlement **New Amsterdam**, after the city of Amsterdam in the Netherlands. New Amsterdam was built next to a harbor where the Hudson River flows into the Atlantic Ocean.

New Amsterdam, 1640s

ILLUSTRATION New Amsterdam continued to grow. By 1643, more than 400 people lived there. What were the advantages and disadvantages of New Amsterdam's location?

The center of New Amsterdam grew up around the fort. The marketplace, the church, and the windmill were there.

Ships arrived at the public dock on the East River.

This was a good place for trade. Ships could sail down the Hudson to New Amsterdam to drop off their furs and to get supplies. Ships waited in the harbor to carry the furs to Europe.

By the 1630s, New Amsterdam had about 200 people and 30 houses. There were warehouses for storing food and furs. For protection, the Dutch built a fort with high walls made of stone.

New Sweden and More Conflicts

In 1638, Swedish settlers founded the colony of **New Sweden** to the south of New Netherland. New Sweden included parts of present-day Pennsylvania, New Jersey, and Delaware. When the Swedes began building homes, the Dutch worried that these new settlers would enter the fur trade. Dutch colonists and the Algonquian who lived nearby had a strong fur-trading relationship. This relationship would soon face trouble.

By the late 1630s, conflicts with the Native Americans had grown because the settlers had cleared more land for farms. The colonists and the Native Americans attacked each other's farms and villages. The colonists then sent out an army that destroyed Native American villages all over New Netherland.

In 1645, after many colonists and Native Americans had been killed, the two sides signed a peace treaty. By then, the Algonquian of New Netherland had almost been wiped out.

READING CHECK **CAUSE AND EFFECT**
How did conflicts with the Dutch affect Native Americans in New Netherland?

FAST FACT

In the 1630s, there were only about 200 people living in New Amsterdam. Today, the population of the island of Manhattan is over one and a half million people.

Streets were made from paths that farmers used to travel to and from the town center.

Exploring New France

As English and Dutch colonists moved into parts of New France, fighting over the fur trade began among the settlers. Native American groups also fought with each other. Both the Huron and Iroquois wanted to control lands in present-day Canada. The Huron were **allies**, or partners, with the French. The Iroquois were partners with the Dutch and the English. Fighting between these groups nearly destroyed the Huron population and the French fur trade.

Marquette and Joliet

The new French king, Louis XIV, did not want to lose France's North American lands. To protect them, he made New France a royal colony. Then he sent out more explorers to find a river west of Quebec called the *Mississippi*, meaning "Father of Waters." He hoped the Mississippi would prove to be the Northwest Passage.

In 1673, a small group, led by Catholic missionary **Jacques Marquette** (mahr•KET) and fur trader **Louis Joliet** (zhohl•YAY), set out to find the Mississippi. With help from Native Americans, they found the Mississippi. However, because the river kept taking them south, they knew it was not the Northwest Passage. They floated down the river to the present-day state of Mississippi. There, they met some Native Americans who told them that Europeans lived farther south. Fearing the Europeans might be Spanish soldiers, the French turned back.

Founding Louisiana

Later, French explorer René-Robert Cavelier (ka•vuhl•YAY), known as **Sieur de la Salle**, set out to find the mouth of the Mississippi River. In 1682, La Salle led an expedition that traveled south from the Illinois River. During the difficult trip, a member of the expedition wrote that, after running out of food, they were "living only on potatoes and alligators."

After two months, the explorers reached the mouth of the Mississippi, at the Gulf of Mexico. La Salle claimed all of the Mississippi River valley for France. He named the region Louisiana in honor of King Louis XIV.

In 1684, La Salle returned to the Gulf coast. He failed to find the mouth of the Mississippi River and instead landed in Texas. Hardships there led to disagreements, and La Salle was later killed by his men.

READING CHECK ○ **MAIN IDEA AND DETAILS** How did French explorers try to reach the king's goals?

❯ **HURON STATUE**

EXPLORING
THE MISSISSIPPI

Native Americans and the French often cooperated at trading posts. French traders exchanged blankets and cooking pots for furs and animal skins.

Lake Superior

Quebec

Lake Huron

Lake Michigan

Lake Ontario

Lake Erie

Marquette and Joliet on the banks of the Mississippi, 1673

Mississippi River

Champlain settles Quebec, 1608.

ATLANTIC OCEAN

La Salle claims the valley of the Mississippi in 1682.

GULF OF MEXICO

← Marquette and Joliet's route
← La Salle's route

Louisiana

The French king then sent another expedition to Louisiana. Pierre Le Moyne (luh•MWAHN) and his brother Jean-Baptiste (ZHAHN ba•TEEST) reached the northern coast of the Gulf of Mexico in 1699. Soon after, they found the mouth of the Mississippi River. The members of the expedition built a settlement along the river. In time, more settlers came, but they experienced many of the same hardships that La Salle had faced.

New Orleans

In 1712, the French king made Louisiana a **proprietary colony** (pruh•PRY•uh•ter•ee). This meant that he gave the whole colony to one person, who would own it. In 1717, John Law, a Scottish banker, became Louisiana's owner. Law started a company to build plantations and towns. He also brought in thousands of new settlers. In 1722, **New Orleans**, one of the colony's first towns, became Louisiana's capital. Settlers built levees, or earthen walls, to protect the low-lying town from floodwater.

Despite Law's efforts, the colony still needed more workers. Many plantation owners brought in enslaved Africans to do the work. The French government soon passed laws that limited where Africans in Louisiana could live and what kinds of work they could do.

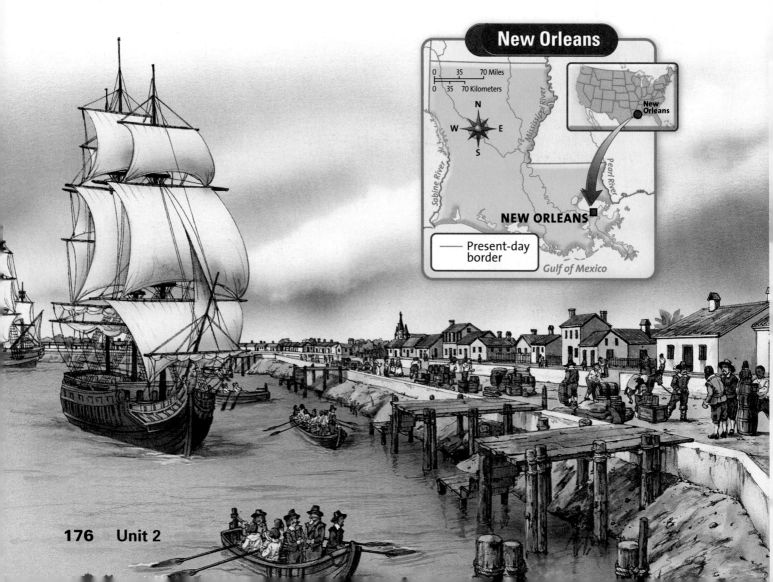

New Orleans

0   35   70 Miles
0   35   70 Kilometers

N
W   E
S

Sabine River

Mississippi River

NEW ORLEANS

Pearl River

—— Present-day border

Gulf of Mexico

New Orleans

Like the rest of New France, Louisiana failed to attract many people. This made it difficult for France to control its lands in North America. By 1763, there were only 80,000 French colonists living in North America. By the same year, there were more than 1,500,000 English colonists in North America.

READING CHECK ☼ **MAIN IDEA AND DETAILS**
Why was it hard for the French to control land in North America?

Summary

The French and the Dutch both began building settlements in North America in the 1600s. Both groups wanted to control the fur trade. This often led to fighting between the settlers and their Native American allies. The French and the Dutch had trouble bringing settlers to North America, so the population of their colonies remained low.

European Colonies in North America

	SPANISH COLONIES	ENGLISH COLONIES	FRENCH COLONIES
Location	Central America and southern North America	Atlantic Coast of North America	Northeastern North America and Mississippi River valley
Government	Ruled by leaders loyal to the Spanish monarch	Ruled by leaders loyal to the English monarch and colonial assemblies	Ruled by leaders loyal to the French monarch
Religion	Only Catholics allowed to settle	Most early settlers were Protestant	Most settlers were Catholic
Economy	Mostly gold and silver mining	Farming, fishing, and trading	Mostly fur trading

CHART How was English colonial government different from that of Spain and France?

REVIEW

1. **WHAT TO KNOW** Why did the French and the Dutch set up colonies?

2. **VOCABULARY** Write definitions of the terms **ally** and **proprietary colony**.

3. **GEOGRAPHY** How was New Amsterdam's location an advantage?

4. **CRITICAL THINKING** Why do you think some Native American tribes made partnerships with settlers?

5. **DRAW A MAP** Create a map showing European land claims in North America. Label each region's main religion and language.

6. **MAIN IDEA AND DETAILS**
(Focus Skill) On a separate sheet of paper, copy and complete this graphic organizer.

Main Idea

Details

The Dutch bought Manhattan Island in 1626.	The Dutch founded New Amsterdam in 1626.	By the 1630s, New Amsterdam had about 200 people.

Visual Summary

Summarize the Chapter

(Focus Skill) **Main Idea and Details** Complete this graphic organizer to show that you understand the main idea and some supporting details about the first European colonies in the Americas.

Main Idea

Europeans started colonies in North America.

Details

 Vocabulary

Write a sentence to explain how each pair of terms is related.

1. **plantation** (p. 150), **slavery** (p. 150)

2. **raw material** (p. 155), **cash crop** (p. 157)

3. **legislature** (p. 157), **represent** (p. 158)

4. **royal colony** (p. 158), **proprietary colony** (p. 176)

5. **supply** (p. 172), **demand** (p. 172)

 Time Line

Use the chapter summary time line above to answer these questions.

6. When was New Spain formed?

7. How many years after the English founded Jamestown did the *Mayflower* sail to Plymouth?

8. When did La Salle found Louisiana for France?

1600

1607
The settlement of Jamestown is founded

1620
The *Mayflower* sails to Plymouth

1700

1682
La Salle claims Louisiana for France

 Facts and Main Ideas

Answer these questions.

9. Why did Spain build missions in the borderlands of New Spain?

10. What was England's first permanent settlement in North America?

11. Who settled the Plymouth Colony, and what was their reason for doing so?

12. Why did some colonists enslave Native Americans and Africans?

Write the letter of the best choice.

13. Which cash crop required many workers but helped the Virginia Colony grow?
    A cotton
    B rice
    C sugarcane
    D tobacco

14. How did traders with the Plymouth Colony benefit Native Americans in the area?
    A They traded for tobacco.
    B They traded for horses.
    C They traded for metal goods and cloth.
    D They traded for corn and beans.

15. Which was the main reason French and Dutch settlers started colonies in North America?
    A They wanted religious freedom.
    B They wanted to gain profits from the sale of furs to Europe.
    C They wanted to set up plantations.
    D They wanted to govern themselves.

 Critical Thinking

16. What are two examples of cooperation and two examples of conflict between early European colonists and Native Americans?

17. How were the Mayflower Compact and the House of Burgesses important to self-government?

18. Compare the settlement of Jamestown to the settlement of St. Augustine.

19. Compare the French settlement of Quebec to the Dutch settlement of New Amsterdam.

 Skills

Compare Primary and Secondary Sources

20. Look at page 168. Identify the object as a primary or a secondary source.

writing

✎ **Write an Informational Report** Write a report that gives information about the Virginia Colony and the Plymouth Colony. Describe at least two events that helped the settlements prosper.

✎ **Write a Narrative** Imagine that you are a reporter in colonial St. Augustine, New Amsterdam, or New Orleans. Write a short story that describes your chosen city, including its location and why it was founded.

Fun with Social Studies

Not Exactly Best-sellers

Who might have written these books?

Pilgrim

Hernando Cortés

John Smith

Got a Consonant?

VOCABULARY

Borrow some consonants from the word *consonant* to complete the vocabulary words that fit the clues.

MI··IO·

·REA·Y

·O·QUI··ADOR

·OMPA··

··O·K

Vacation Station

What vacation spot is each postcard from?

Greetings from the Capital of **New Netherland**

Greetings from the Capital of **New Mexico Colony**

Online Adventures

GO ONLINE

Now Eco is sailing away on the Time Ship. In this online game, you will travel to North America during the Age of Exploration. Eco's expedition is especially exciting because you have found an old treasure map to follow. Use your knowledge of the unit to explore St. Augustine and Jamestown in search of the secret treasure. Play now at **www.harcourtschool.com/ss1**

Review and Test Prep

:̣Q: THE BIG IDEA

Cooperation and Conflict Cultural differences and
competition for land led to conflicts among different
groups of people in the Americas.

Reading Comprehension and Vocabulary

Cultures Meet

In the late 1400s, new technology allowed Europeans to begin exploring the world. Many hoped to find a sea route to Asia for trade. The explorations led people to the Americas. European countries soon sent more explorers to claim and settle the new lands.

As a result of these expeditions, Spain formed New Spain from lands claimed in North America, including what is now Mexico and much of the southwestern United States. England claimed much of the Atlantic Coast and built settlements in present-day Virginia and Massachusetts. The Dutch founded the colony of New Netherland in present-day New York and New Jersey. France claimed much of what is now Canada and the entire Mississippi River valley to form New France.

By 1700, much of North America was divided among these European nations, even though Native Americans already lived there. Some colonists and Native Americans lived in peace and exchanged goods and ideas, but many more fought over the land and resources.

Use the summary above to answer these questions.

1. What is an expedition?
   A a ship designed for long voyages
   B a trip taken with the goal of exploring
   C a method of finding and following a route
   D an agreement between two nations

2. What were Europeans searching for when they first reached the Americas?
   A more land for farming and ranching
   B furs and lumber to sell in Europe
   C a sea route to Asia for trade
   D religious freedom

3. What is a colony?
   A a group of people who make laws
   B a person who conquers other people
   C a share in the ownership of something
   D a land that is ruled by another country

4. Which European country explored and claimed much of what is now Canada?
   A England
   B France
   C the Netherlands
   D Spain

Facts and Main Ideas

Answer these questions.

5. Who was the first explorer sent by Spain to find a western route to Asia?

6. How did Spain's success in finding gold and land in the Americas affect other nations?

7. What were Verrazano, Cartier, and Hudson searching for in the Americas?

8. Why did Dutch and English companies pay Henry Hudson to explore?

9. How did the Spanish protect settlers and claims in the borderlands of New Spain?

10. What was the Mayflower Compact?

11. Who claimed for France all of the Mississippi River valley?

12. Put the following settlements in order from earliest to latest: Jamestown, Quebec, New Amsterdam, St. Augustine, Plymouth.

Write the letter of the best choice.

13. With which settlers did Native Americans mainly fight in the Powhatan Wars?
    A the Dutch
    B the English
    C the French
    D the Spanish

14. Which leader became the governor of the Plymouth Colony?
    A Pedro Menéndez de Avilés
    B William Bradford
    C John Law
    D Peter Minuit

15. When do the supply and the demand for a good usually raise the good's price?
    A when supply is low and demand is low
    B when supply is low and demand is high
    C when supply is high and demand is low
    D when supply is high and demand is high

 Critical Thinking

16. What were some of the costs and possible benefits of expeditions?

17. What role did the Reformation and the Reconquista play in the exploration and settlement of North America?

18. Why do you think enslaved people were not allowed to take part in the government of the Virginia Colony?

 **Skills**

Use Elevation Maps

Use the elevation map below to answer the question.

19. What range of elevations is shown by the color green?

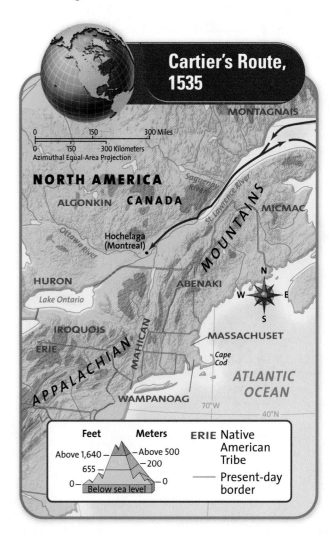

Cartier's Route, 1535

Unit

2 Activities

Show What You Know

 Unit Writing Activity

Write a Persuasive Advertisement
Write an advertisement to persuade settlers to come to a new colony in North America. Support your position with evidence.

- Describe the location of the colony.
- Tell why the colony was founded.
- Describe life in the colony.

Unit Project

A Museum of Exploration Build a museum exhibit about the exploration and early colonization of North America.

- Decide which people, places, and events to include in your museum.
- Prepare brief reports, journal entries, drawings, maps, and models for your museum.

Read More

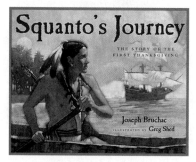

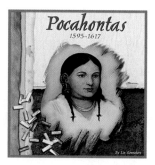

- *Squanto's Journey: The Story of the First Thanksgiving* by Joseph Bruchac. Silver Whistle.

- *Pocahontas 1595–1617* by Liz Sonneborn. Blue Earth Books.

- *Miracle: The True Story of the Wreck of the Sea Venture* by Gail Langer Karwoski. Darby Creek Publishing.

 GO ONLINE

For more resources, go to
www.harcourtschool.com/ss1

The Thirteen Colonies

The Big Idea

Commonality and Diversity

The 13 English colonies were founded in different regions of North America and for different reasons.

What to Know

✓ Why did different people come to the English colonies and where did they settle?

✓ How did new colonies impact Native American groups?

✓ What kinds of governments, economies, and new ideas developed in the colonies?

SETTLING OHIO

DID YOU KNOW?

Christopher Gist was a friend of George Washington, whose life he saved twice.

In the early 1600s, England started colonies along the Atlantic coast of North America. France claimed and settled lands in present-day Canada. In 1750, Christopher Gist explored what is now Ohio for Britain and the colonies. Both Britain and France claimed lands in the Ohio Valley. Each country wanted to control the growing fur trade in the region.

▶ Christopher Gist and George Washington meet with the Delaware Indians.

In 1754, conflicts between the French and the British led to the French and Indian War. Britain won the war in 1763 and gained control of the Ohio Country. After the American Revolution, control passed to the American states and settlers began moving to the region. The first town in Ohio was Marietta. About 50 settlers, led by Rufus Putnam, founded the town in 1788.

Native Americans in Ohio did not want to give up their lands to settlers. They decided to unite to fight the settlers. One of their leaders was Michikinikwa (mih•chih•kin•EE•kwah), also known as Little Turtle. Michikinikwa belonged to the Miami tribe. He led several successful attacks against American soldiers. However, General Anthony Wayne defeated the Native Americans. Most Native Americans were forced out of Ohio to live on reservations.

❱ Rufus Putnam

Michikinikwa (right) and other Native Americans signed the Treaty of Greenville (far right), giving much of their lands to the Americans.

OHIO TEST PREP

1 Who explored Ohio for Britain and the colonies?
A. Christopher Gist
B. Rufus Putnam
C. Michikinikwa

2 When did people begin to settle in Ohio?
A. in about 1670
B. after the American Revolution
C. after the Native Americans were defeated

3 What did Michikinikwa do?
A. founded Marietta
B. explored Ohio
C. led attacks on American soldiers

4 What was the cause of the fighting between Native Americans and settlers in Ohio?

Unit 3

Time

The Thirteen Colonies

1630 The Massachusetts Bay Colony is founded, p. 199

1632 Lord Baltimore founds the Maryland Colony, p. 253

1600

1650

At the Same Time

 **1636** The Dutch set up trading posts on the coast of Taiwan

The Thirteen Colonies

1681 William Penn founds the Pennsylvania Colony, p. 229

1733 James Oglethorpe founds the Georgia Colony, p. 256

1700

1750

 1707 The Act of Union unites England and Scotland as Great Britain

 1742 Native Americans fight against Spanish rule in Peru

John Winthrop

1588–1649
- English Puritan leader
- Served as governor of the Massachusetts Bay Colony

Anne Hutchinson

1591–1643
- Puritan settler who began preaching in her home
- Forced to leave Massachusetts because of her beliefs

People

1550	1600	1650

1588 • John Winthrop   1649

1591 • Anne Hutchinson   1643

1638? • Metacomet

1644 • William Penn

Benjamin Franklin

1706–1790
- Pennsylvania leader and famous inventor
- Published *Poor Richard's Almanack*

George Whitefield

1714–1770
- English minister who helped lead the Great Awakening
- Popular throughout England and the 13 colonies

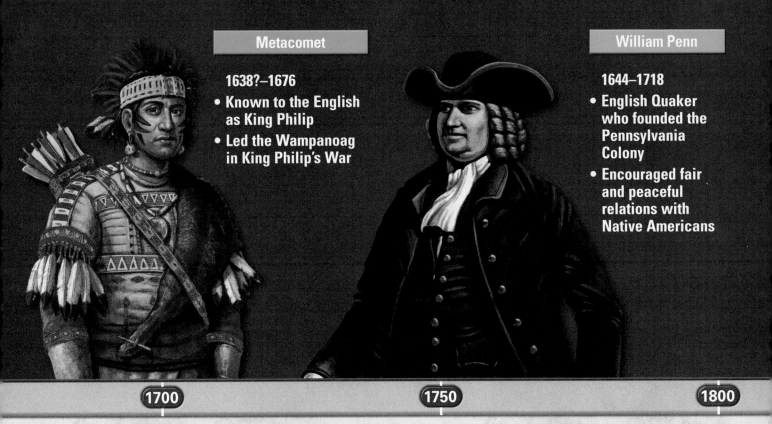

Metacomet

1638?–1676
- Known to the English as King Philip
- Led the Wampanoag in King Philip's War

William Penn

1644–1718
- English Quaker who founded the Pennsylvania Colony
- Encouraged fair and peaceful relations with Native Americans

1700   **1750**   **1800**

1676

1718

1706 • Benjamin Franklin   1790

1714 • George Whitefield   1770

1722 • Eliza Lucas Pinckney   1793

1745? • Olaudah Equiano   1797

Eliza Lucas Pinckney

1722–1793
- Daughter of a South Carolina plantation owner
- Experimented with crops such as indigo

Olaudah Equiano

1745?–1797
- Enslaved African who later purchased his freedom
- Spoke out against slavery in his writings and speeches

RANGE

YAKIMA

CHINOOK

CASCADE

Columbia River

NEZ PERCE

ROCKY

Missouri River

KIOWA

CROW

MANDAN

SIOUX

G R E A T

INTERIOR PLAINS

COAST

MODOC

PAIUTE

Snake River

CHEYENNE

SIOUX

Platte River

IOWA

POMO

SIERRA

MIWOK

NEVADA

YOKUTS

RANGES

Great Salt Lake

M O U N T A I N S

UTE

PAWNEE

ARAPAHO

KAW

PAIUTE

Colorado River

P L A I N S

Arkansas

Mojave Desert

HOPI

NAVAJO

CAHUILLA

PACIFIC OCEAN

Tucson

PIMA

APACHE

COMANCHE

WICHITA

Rio Grande

Gulf of California

At the Same Time

Palace of the Governors, in New Mexico

Monterrey

0   200   400 Miles

0   200   400 Kilometers
Albers Equal-Area Projection

Mexico City

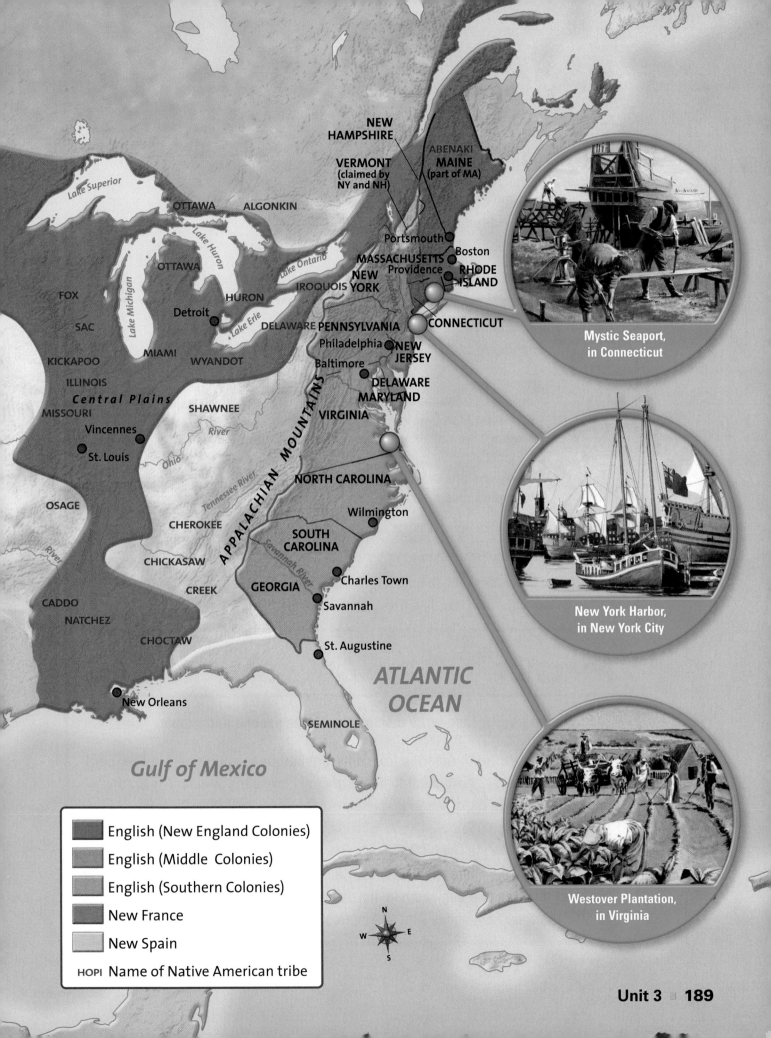

Lake Superior

OTTAWA   ALGONKIN

Lake Huron

OTTAWA

FOX

Lake Michigan

Lake Ontario

HURON

Detroit

Lake Erie

SAC

MIAMI

WYANDOT

KICKAPOO

ILLINOIS

Central Plains

SHAWNEE

MISSOURI

River

Vincennes

St. Louis

Ohio

Tennessee River

OSAGE

CHEROKEE

River

CHICKASAW

CADDO

CREEK

NATCHEZ

CHOCTAW

New Orleans

Gulf of Mexico

NEW HAMPSHIRE

ABENAKI

VERMONT (claimed by NY and NH)

MAINE (part of MA)

Portsmouth

Boston

MASSACHUSETTS

Providence

RHODE ISLAND

NEW YORK

IROQUOIS

CONNECTICUT

DELAWARE   PENNSYLVANIA

Philadelphia

NEW JERSEY

Baltimore

DELAWARE

MARYLAND

VIRGINIA

NORTH CAROLINA

Wilmington

SOUTH CAROLINA

Savannah River

GEORGIA

Charles Town

Savannah

St. Augustine

SEMINOLE

APPALACHIAN MOUNTAINS

Hudson

Mystic Seaport, in Connecticut

New York Harbor, in New York City

Westover Plantation, in Virginia

ATLANTIC OCEAN

N
W   E
S

English (New England Colonies)

English (Middle Colonies)

English (Southern Colonies)

New France

New Spain

HOPI   Name of Native American tribe

Reading Social Studies

Focus Skill Summarize

Why It Matters Summarizing can help you understand and remember the most important information in a paragraph or passage.

❯ LEARN

When you **summarize,** you state in your own words a shortened version of what you read.

Key Facts	Summary
Important idea from the reading	**A shortened version of what you read**
Important idea from the reading	

- A summary includes only the most important ideas from what you have read.
- Always use your own words when you summarize.

❯ PRACTICE

Read the paragraphs. Then write a summary for the second paragraph.

Facts

Settlers came to North America from different European countries, but Spain set up the first permanent settlement to be started by Europeans in what is now the United States. Spanish colonists founded this settlement in 1565 in St. Augustine, Florida. (In 1565, Spain founded St. Augustine, the first permanent European settlement in what is now the United States.)

Summary

Most settlers who came to North America in the 1600s were English. One reason for this was that England had more people than it could feed. Poor people and orphans were sometimes sent to America—sometimes against their will.

Read the paragraphs, and answer the questions.

Young Colonists

Many children came to North America from England without their families. Some of them were orphans. Others came from poor families. In England, many parents did not earn enough money to feed their children.

In the Virginia Colony, tobacco plantations needed lots of workers. The owners of the Virginia Company wanted to put English children to work. They asked English leaders to allow the company to take children to the Virginia Colony as indentured servants. The children would work for a period of time, usually about seven years.

After they completed their service, they would receive some basic supplies, some food, and their freedom.

Many children, however, did not survive long enough to be granted their freedom. The climate and living conditions in North America were very different from those in England. Many indentured servants died from illness within two years.

Indentured service, though, was often the only choice for many poor children and adults. If they could survive their period of service, they would have a fresh start in a new land.

(Focus Skill) Summarize

1. **Why did many orphans and poor children become indentured servants?**
2. **Why did the Virginia Company want to take children to the Virginia Colony?**
3. **How would you describe life for young indentured servants in North America?**

▶ **A reenactor portrays a colonial boy.**

The Courage of Sarah Noble

written by Alice Dalgliesh
illustrated by Greg Newbold

In 1707, eight-year-old Sarah Noble lived in Westfield, Massachusetts, with her mother, father, and seven brothers and sisters. When her father, John, decided to move the family to Connecticut, Sarah went with him. She cooked while he built their family a new home.

At her new home, Sarah became friends with Tall John and his family. They were Native Americans who lived nearby. When Sarah's father traveled back to Massachusetts, Tall John's family cared for Sarah.

October days were warm and sunny. The Indian women spread the corn out to dry. At night Sarah helped them to cover it carefully, so the heavy dew would not wet it.

There were many things to do. Tall John's wife taught Sarah how to weave a basket. And because Sarah's clothes were stiff and heavy, the Indian woman made her clothes of deerskin, such as the Indians wore when the days grew colder. She also made a pair of deerskin moccasins. Sarah's feet felt light and free; she walked softly as the Indian children did.

Often she thought of her family. Were they on the way? Would Hannah and Margaret be afraid of wolves? Stephen would not be. And the baby was too young to know about the danger . . .

There was nothing, she thought, to be afraid of here with Tall John and his family. But there *was*.

The pleasant, quiet days came to an end, and all at once Sarah felt that there was fear and disturbance in the air.

disturbance disorder, trouble

More Indians kept watch on Guarding Hill. The Indians from the North must be coming.

So Sarah scarcely knew whether to sleep at night. Suppose . . . Suppose . . . But tired from long days in the sun she slept at last, always with a fold of her cloak caught in her hand. And before she slept she said to herself: *Keep up your courage, Sarah Noble. Keep up your courage.*

Once in the night she wakened and listened. Tall John had told her, partly in words and partly by signs, that all along the Great River there were hills like Guarding Hill, where men kept watch. If the Indians from the North were coming, the word would be passed from hill to hill by calling—and the villages would be ready.

Sarah listened and listened. Once she seemed to hear a long, low <u>wailing</u>.

Was this the signal? Were the Indians coming down from the North?

wailing a sad cry

She waited for the village to waken, but everything was still. In the darkness she could hear the even sleep-breathing of Tall John and his wife, of Small John and Mary.

"Why, it's nothing but a wolf!" said Sarah. Soon her heart beat quietly and she, too, was breathing evenly in sleep.

In the morning Tall John told her that there had been fear—but the danger had passed. The river villages would not be raided.

So forgetting all her fears of the night before, Sarah played with the other children. It was such a charming game they played in the warm sunshine. Taking off all their moccasins they placed them in a row, then hid a pebble in one. Sarah was pleased when it came her turn to guess— and she guessed right. The pebble was in her own shoe! In the middle of the game she turned suddenly, feeling that someone was watching her.

And it was her father! John Noble stood there, saying not a word. His eyes crinkled up at the corners the way they did when he was amused, and he said, "Sarah! I had thought you were one of the Indian children!"

"Father!" said Sarah, and ran to him. "Has my mother come?"

"We are all here, now," said her father. "I have come to take you home. But, daughter, I think it would be well to put on your own clothes, or your mother will surely not know you!"

So Sarah put on her clothes, piece by stiff piece. She now thought of buttons as tiresome, and as for <u>petticoats</u> . . . The moccasins she kept on, for her feet refused to go into those heavy leather shoes. When she was ready to leave, she saw Tall John looking sadly at her.

"You go . . . Sarah . . ." he said.

"I must," said Sarah. "My mother is here."

<u>petticoat</u> a skirt usually worn under other clothing

Tall John said nothing, but swung Sarah up on his shoulder, as he had done many times before.

Response Corner

1. **(Focus Skill)** **Summarize** Why did Sarah feel she had to be brave?

2. Do you think Sarah liked living in her new environment? Why or why not?

3. **Make It Relevant** What are some of the things you might do to adjust to life in a new place?

STUDY SKILLS

POSE QUESTIONS

Learning to pose, or ask, questions as you read can help improve your understanding.

- **Think of questions that might be answered by reading. For example, you might ask how events are related.**

- **Use the questions to guide your reading. Look for answers as you read.**

Questions	Answers
How were the settlers at Massachusetts Bay like those at Plymouth?	Both groups wanted to live by their religious beliefs.
Why did people settle in Massachusetts?	

PREVIEW VOCABULARY

frontier p. 204

common p. 210

naval stores p. 216

THE TOWN OF WAITS RIVER, IN VERMONT

Time

1600 ———————————————————————————— 1750

1630
The Massachusetts Bay Colony is founded

1636
Roger Williams founds Providence

1675
King Philip's War begins

WHAT TO KNOW
Why did people start colonies in New England?

VOCABULARY
charter p. 199
dissent p. 200
expel p. 200
consent p. 201
sedition p. 201
frontier p. 204

PEOPLE
John Winthrop
Roger Williams
Anne Hutchinson

PLACES
Massachusetts Bay
Rhode Island
Connecticut
New Hampshire

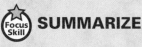 **SUMMARIZE**

Settling New England

YOU ARE THERE
You walk past your small village and look out at the sea. Ten years ago, you and your family traveled here from England. At first, you were sad to leave England, but you have learned to adapt to your new life.

You know that life in this colony requires hard work and a strong spirit. Yesterday, you heard that new settlers from England will soon arrive. You hope that they are ready for all the challenges they will face.

▶ **PLYMOUTH COLONY** Founded in 1620, it was the first colony in New England.

▶ **THE GREAT PURITAN MIGRATION** From 1630 to 1643, more than 20,000 Puritans left Europe to settle in New England.

The Puritans Arrive

In 1628, a small group of settlers arrived in North America. They had a **charter**, or official paper, from the king of England. It gave the settlers permission to start a colony in New England. There, they built a village called Salem.

A New Start

Like the Pilgrims, these settlers came to New England to practice their religious beliefs. They also came to start farms and businesses. Unlike the Pilgrims, the new settlers did not want to break away from the Church of England. They wanted to change some religious practices to make the church more "pure." For this reason, they were called Puritans.

In 1630, **John Winthrop** led a second group of Puritans to settle the **Massachusetts Bay** Colony. Winthrop hoped their settlement would be an example of Christian living. In a sermon, he said, ". . . We shall be as a city upon a hill. The eyes of all people are upon us. . . ."

Winthrop's group chose to build their "city upon a hill" south of Salem, near the mouth of the Charles River. They named their settlement Boston, after a town in England. Most early settlements in New England were built along the Atlantic coast to make it easier for colonists to get supplies from English trading ships.

READING CHECK ☉ **SUMMARIZE**

Why did the Puritans found the Massachusetts Bay Colony?

▶ **JOHN WINTHROP**

New Ideas, New Settlements

In 1630, John Winthrop was elected governor of the Massachusetts Bay Colony. He and the other Puritan leaders kept strict control over life in the colony. They did not welcome people whose beliefs were different from their own. They thought that **dissent**, or disagreement, might hurt their society.

Roger Williams

Some colonists disagreed with the Puritan leaders. One of those colonists was a minister in Salem named **Roger Williams**. Williams often stated his beliefs in his sermons. He and his followers believed that their church should be separate from the colonial government. They also believed that Puritan leaders should not punish people for having different beliefs.

Williams also disagreed with Puritan leaders over their treatment of Native Americans. He said that the settlers ought to live in peace with Native Americans.

Winthrop and the other Puritan leaders decided to punish Williams for his dissent. They held a trial and found him guilty of spreading "new and dangerous opinions." In 1635, the leaders voted to **expel** Williams from Massachusetts, or force him to leave.

▶ ROGER WILLIAMS was expelled from Massachusetts, but the Narragansett tribe gave him shelter.

▶ **ANNE HUTCHINSON** held weekly meetings at her home. They were seen as a challenge to the authority of the men who led the Puritan church.

Williams and his family moved southwest of Boston to what is now Narragansett (nar•uh•GAN•suht) Bay. For a short time, they lived near the coast with the Narragansett tribe. Many of Williams's followers joined him there. In 1636, Williams bought land from the Narragansett and founded a settlement that he called Providence.

Williams organized the settlement based on the **consent**, or agreement, of the people and cooperation with the Native Americans. The settlers could follow almost any religion they chose.

Anne Hutchinson

The leaders of the Massachusetts Bay Colony faced another challenge to their authority, or power, from a colonist named **Anne Hutchinson**. Hutchinson questioned the teachings of the Puritan ministers. At this time in history, women rarely spoke out against men.

Hutchinson's actions angered many Puritan leaders. In 1637, they tried her on charges of **sedition** (sih•DIH•shuhn), or speaking in ways that caused others to work against the government. Hutchinson was found guilty and expelled from the colony.

With her family and several followers, Hutchinson left to start a settlement on an island near Providence. That settlement later joined Williams's settlement under the charter that formed the colony of **Rhode Island** in 1647.

READING CHECK ⭯ **SUMMARIZE**

Why did Roger Williams wish to start a new settlement?

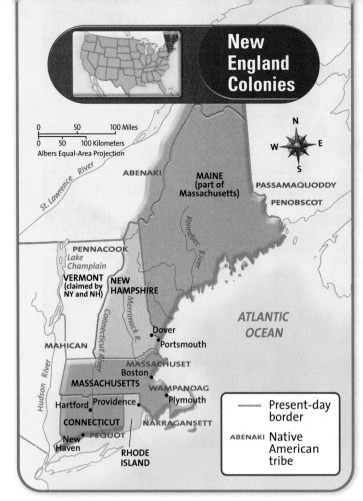

New England Colonies

MAP SKILL **REGIONS** Which of the New England Colonies had the smallest amount of land?

New England Grows

Other settlers moved south from Massachusetts to find better farmland. Some left the poor, rocky soil of coastal New England for the fertile Connecticut (kuh•NEH•tih•kuht) River Valley.

Other Colonies

Most early Connecticut settlers came to find good farmland, but many also came because of their religious beliefs. One of these settlers was a Puritan minister named Thomas Hooker. He left Massachusetts because he disagreed with the way its leaders ruled. Hooker and his followers founded Hartford. In 1636, Hartford and other nearby settlements joined to form the colony of **Connecticut**.

In 1639, the leaders of the Connecticut Colony wrote the Fundamental Orders, a plan of government. These orders let voters elect their own leaders. However, the only people who could vote were white men who owned land.

Other colonists looking for economic opportunities moved north of Massachusetts. In 1623, a Scottish settler named David Thomson set out to start a fishing settlement. In 1679, this settlement, later known as Portsmouth, joined with others to form the colony of **New Hampshire**.

READING CHECK **SUMMARIZE**
Why did farmers settle in the Connecticut River Valley?

Growth Brings Conflict

As the colonists spread across New England, they settled where Native Americans already lived and hunted. In the Connecticut River Valley, fighting broke out between the colonists and the Pequot (PEE•kwaht) tribe. The Pequot wanted to stop the colonists from taking over their lands.

In 1637, the colonists and the Pequot began attacking each other's settlements. The conflict became known as the Pequot War. The colonists defeated the Pequot and the tribe was forced to split up.

Arguments Over Land

The settlers and the Native Americans had different ideas about land ownership. The Mohegan (moh•HEE•guhn), Wampanoag (wahm•puh•NOH•ag), Narragansett, and other tribes believed that no one person could own land. The English, however, believed that if they claimed an area, the land was theirs. The settlers expected Native American tribes to leave the land.

Metacomet, known to the English as King Philip, was the leader of the Wampanoag. When more English settlers moved onto their tribal lands, Metacomet decided that the Native Americans had to unite against the colonists. He said,

> **"I am resolved not to see the day when I have no country."**

King Philip's War

In 1675, arguments over land again led to war between the colonists and the Native Americans. The colonists named the war King Philip's War. It began when Native Americans attacked the town of Swansea in Rhode Island. In return, the settlers destroyed a nearby Native American village.

Over the next year, King Philip's War spread as far north as present-day Maine and as far west as Connecticut. In the end, both sides suffered terrible losses. Among the colonists, 1 of every 16 men died in battle. At least 3,000 Native Americans, including Metacomet, were killed. Some tribes were nearly wiped out, and most were forced to give up their lands.

▶ **THE CONNECTICUT RIVER flows through present-day New Hampshire, Vermont, Massachusetts, and Connecticut.**

Colonists soon moved onto those lands. Some settled in western Connecticut, while others moved to present-day Vermont, northern New Hampshire, and Maine. The **frontier**, or the lands beyond the areas already settled by colonists, was being pushed west, too. By 1700, more than 90,000 colonists lived in New England.

READING CHECK ☼**SUMMARIZE**

What were the two major effects of King Philip's War?

Summary

English settlers came to New England and built colonies along the Atlantic coast. Many lived by their religious beliefs and some founded new colonies. Over time, more settlers arrived, forcing Native Americans to leave their lands.

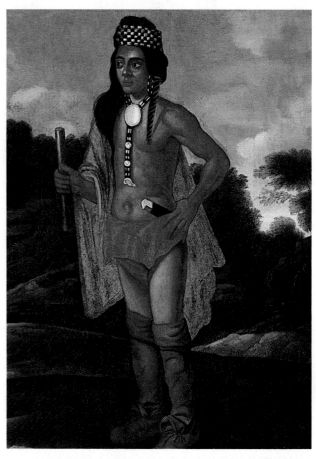

❱ **A NIANTIC WARRIOR** The Niantic and several other tribes did not take part in King Philip's War.

REVIEW

1. **WHAT TO KNOW** Why did people start colonies in New England?

2. **VOCABULARY** Use the term **dissent** in a sentence about Roger Williams.

3. **GEOGRAPHY** How did the physical features of New England affect colonists' decisions about where to settle?

4. **CRITICAL THINKING** In what ways did the actions of John Winthrop, Roger Williams, Anne Hutchinson, and Thomas Hooker show the importance of religious beliefs in early New England government?

5. ⚒ **DRAW A MAP** Make a map that shows the locations of the New England Colonies. Your map should also list the date each colony was founded and who founded it.

6. (Focus Skill) **SUMMARIZE** On a separate sheet of paper, copy and complete this graphic organizer.

Key Facts		Summary
Metacomet asks Native Americans to unite.	❱	
Native Americans and settlers argue over who owns land.	❱	

Anne Hutchinson

Trustworthiness
Respect
Responsibility
Fairness
Caring
Patriotism

"*You condemn me for speaking what in my conscience I know to be truth.*"

Anne Hutchinson spoke those words at her trial in 1637. She stated her right to have her own religious beliefs and challenged the power of the Massachusetts Bay Colony's leaders.

Hutchinson was born in England in 1591. Her father often spoke out against the Church of England. At the age of 21, she married William Hutchinson. Together, they would raise 15 children. In 1634, the Hutchinson family moved to Boston.

In Boston, Hutchinson shared her beliefs at prayer meetings. She said that people did not need to follow church laws to please God. The colony's leaders put her on trial for breaking the law and expelled her from Massachusetts.

In 1638, Hutchinson and her family and followers settled in what became the Rhode Island Colony. She later moved to what is now New York, where she was killed in a Native American raid in 1643. Hutchinson's struggle for religious freedom set an example for others in her time.

Why Character Counts

In what ways did Anne Hutchinson struggle to be treated fairly?

Time

1591		1643
Born		Died

1634 Hutchinson moves to Boston and starts holding religious meetings

1637 Hutchinson is put on trial and expelled from Massachusetts

GO ONLINE For more resources, go to www.harcourtschool.com/ss1

Tell Fact from Opinion

Why It Matters Recognizing fact and opinion helps you better understand what you read.

❯ LEARN

A **fact** is a statement that can be proved or supported by evidence. A fact is true for everyone. An **opinion** is a statement that tells what a person feels or believes. An opinion is held by one person or group.

Writers often combine facts and opinions. Readers must pay attention to notice the difference. Here are some ways in which you can check to see whether a statement is a fact or an opinion.
Fact:
- See whether the statement is true in your own experience or in other people's experiences.
- Check trusted sources of information such as an encyclopedia or an atlas.

Opinion:
- Opinions cannot be proved or supported by evidence.
- Some statements contain clues that they are opinions. Words such as *best, worst, excellent,* and *terrible* are often clues to opinion statements.

❯ PRACTICE

Read the passages on the next page. They are from the diary of Samuel Sewall, an early Massachusetts colonist. Decide whether each passage states a fact, an opinion, or both. If a sentence contains both a fact and an opinion, tell which part is which.

❯ **SAMUEL SEWALL**

▶ **FARMING FAMILIES** were the best workers. Is this a fact or an opinion?

① **April 14, 1685** A ship arrives from New Castle and brings news of the death of Charles the 2nd, and proclamation of James the 2nd, King.

② **May 13, 1685** Mr. Cotton Mather is ordained pastor [of the Second Church] by his father.

③ **January 7, 1686** Mr. Moodey [the minister] preached excellently. A very . . . snowy day [kept] many from going to [church].

④ **July 27, 1686** Mr. Stoughton prays excellently and makes a notable speech at the opening of the Court.

▶ **APPLY**

Write three facts that you have learned so far in this chapter. Then write three opinions about what you have learned.

WHAT TO KNOW
How did the Puritans' religious beliefs affect life and government in the New England Colonies?

VOCABULARY
common p. 210

town meeting p. 210

PLACES
Harvard College

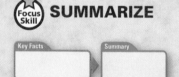

SUMMARIZE

Key Facts		Summary
	▸	
	▸	

Life in New England

YOU ARE THERE

You sit beside your mother on a hard wooden bench in church. Across the aisle, your father and the other Puritan men and boys listen to the minister's sermon. It has already lasted three hours!

You try hard to stay awake. If someone catches you napping, you know that you will be punished. You wish the leaders of your town were not so strict about how people must act in church.

▸ **PURITAN MINISTERS** wrote Sunday sermons that were given at churches like this one in Hingham, Massachusetts.

▶ NEW ENGLAND COLONISTS Colonists in New England often carried their weapons with them wherever they went, including church.

A Religious Life

The Puritans lived their lives based on their religious beliefs. Before making any decision, they thought about the Bible's laws. They also thought about how God and their community might judge them. Their religious beliefs told them how to live, work, and spend their free time.

Church Services

On Sundays, everyone in town had to attend church. Puritan churches had no paintings, statues, or bells. The Puritans believed in simple religious practice. They thought that reading the Bible and praying were the best ways to worship.

A Puritan church service lasted most of the day, with a break for a meal at noon.

People sat on hard wooden benches and could not nap. A person who fell asleep or did not behave was punished harshly.

The Puritans also punished people who missed church or spoke out in dissent. A common punishment was several hours in the town stocks. In the stocks, a person's head, hands, and feet were locked into a wooden frame.

The Puritans lived by strict rules. They did not like stage plays or card games. They believed such activities wasted time. Instead, the Puritans found ways to combine their free time and their work in activities such as fishing and quilt-making.

READING CHECK ☼ SUMMARIZE
How did the religious beliefs of the Puritans affect their daily lives?

Mill

Meeting House

School

Fields

Everyday Life

Most people in colonial New England lived in small towns. They lived, worked, and worshipped close together.

At the center of each town was the **common**. This grassy area was shared by the town's people. It was used for grazing sheep, cattle, and other livestock.

The colonists built their homes and other buildings around the common. Nearly all towns also had a school. Most had a general store, a sawmill, and a blacksmith's shop.

To meet their economic needs, people used a barter system. Instead of using money, people traded with each other.

A blacksmith might make iron tools for the cooper. In turn, the cooper might make barrels for the blacksmith.

The Town Meeting

The meetinghouse, or town church, was a town's most important building. At least once a year, the townspeople gathered there for a **town meeting**. At town meetings, people voted on laws and elected leaders. Anyone could attend, but only free white men who owned property could vote.

Each year, colonists in Massachusetts voted for who would represent them at the General Court, the colony's legislature. The General Court made laws for the whole colony. In 1641, the General

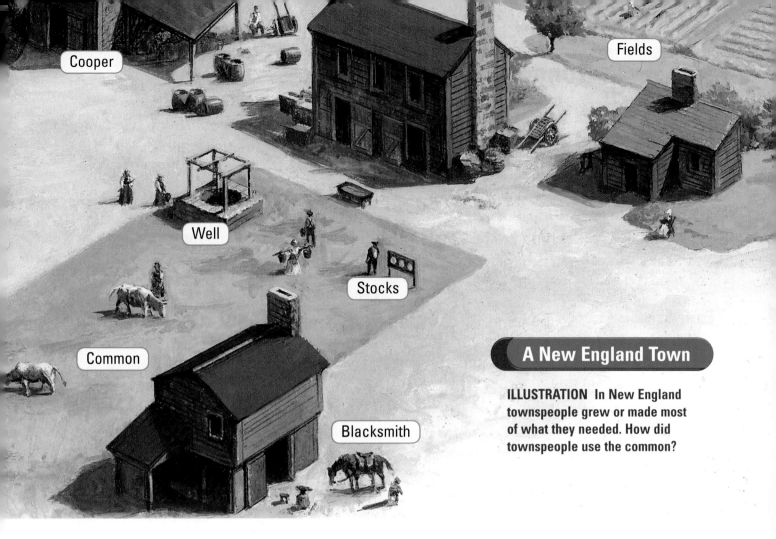

Cooper

Fields

Well

Stocks

Common

A New England Town

ILLUSTRATION In New England townspeople grew or made most of what they needed. How did townspeople use the common?

Blacksmith

Court passed the Massachusetts Body of Liberties. This set of laws listed the rights of all free colonists.

A Puritan Home

The main room of a Puritan home had a large fireplace, where a fire was always burning. All cooking was done there. Most food was roasted over the fire or warmed in large iron kettles. Baking was done in a small oven inside the fireplace.

Women and girls spent hours preparing food. They churned cream to turn it into butter. They dried fruits and vegetables and stored them in jars. This extra food helped feed families during winter.

Women also made other things for their families. They spun thread and made the colonists' clothing. They used animal fat to make soap and candles. They used pig hair to make brushes.

Men and boys spent their days working in the fields and hunting. They cut firewood and made their own tools. They raised cattle for food and leather and sheep for wool. The men also guarded the town.

Every fall, all the colonists helped harvest the crops. They kept part of the crops for themselves and sent some to England to trade for goods such as paper, lead, and paint. They also sent some of the crops to the English colonies in the Caribbean islands to trade for sugar.

READING CHECK ☼SUMMARIZE

How did New England colonists participate in their government?

Childhood in New England

Life was hard for the early Puritans, but children still found time to relax. They had few toys, but they liked playing games and sports. Most families had more than five children, so brothers and sisters always had others to play with when they finished their chores.

Early Schools

Schools were important to the Puritans because they believed everyone should be able to read the Bible. At first, parents taught their children at home.

In 1647, Massachusetts passed a law saying that towns with at least 50 families must have a school. All the other New England Colonies except Rhode Island passed similar laws. As a result, the New England Colonies had more schools than any of the other English colonies.

A typical New England school had one room and one teacher. Most teachers were men, and many were very strict. Some often whipped students for bad behavior or even for a wrong answer!

Learning to Read

The main subject taught in New England schools was reading. In colonial times, paper and ink were very costly, so most students learned to read from a hornbook. This was a piece of paper that was attached to a paddle-shaped frame and that showed the alphabet.

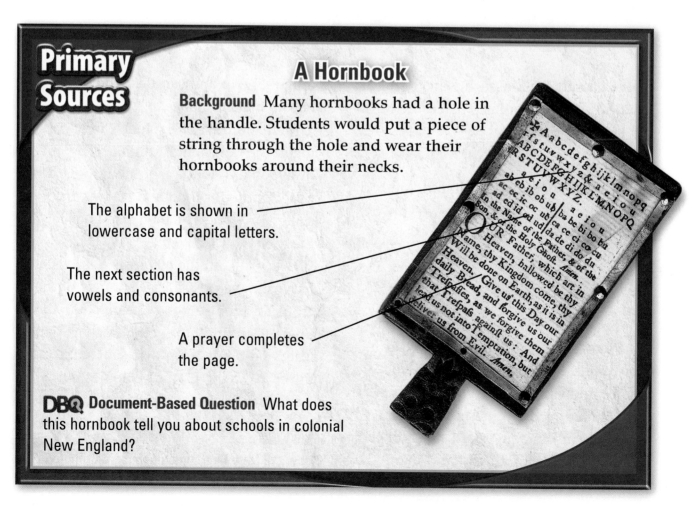

Primary Sources

A Hornbook

Background Many hornbooks had a hole in the handle. Students would put a piece of string through the hole and wear their hornbooks around their necks.

The alphabet is shown in lowercase and capital letters.

The next section has vowels and consonants.

A prayer completes the page.

DBQ Document-Based Question What does this hornbook tell you about schools in colonial New England?

HARVARD COLLEGE This engraving shows Harvard as it would have looked in 1725, nearly 100 years after it was founded.

Children did not go to school for long. They were needed to work at home. However, some boys continued their education and attended college. In 1636, the Puritans founded **Harvard College**, now Harvard University, to train ministers.

READING CHECK ⓈSUMMARIZE
Why was education important to the Puritans?

Summary

The Puritan way of life was based on religion. Religious beliefs influenced life and government in the New England Colonies. New England colonists believed everyone should be able to read, so most towns had schools.

REVIEW

1. **WHAT TO KNOW** How did the Puritans' religious beliefs affect life and government in the New England Colonies?

2. **VOCABULARY** Write a sentence telling what a **town meeting** might have been like.

3. **HISTORY** In what ways did New England colonists practice self-government?

4. **CRITICAL THINKING** Make It Relevant How was an early New England town like your own? How was it different?

5. ✏ **WRITE A NARRATIVE** Write a story about school in the New England Colonies. Your story should tell what school was like, the materials students used, and how teachers taught.

6. (Focus Skill) **SUMMARIZE** On a separate sheet of paper, copy and complete this graphic organizer.

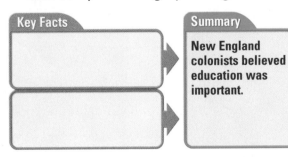

Key Facts		Summary
	➤	New England colonists believed education was important.
	➤	

Lesson 3

Time

1600 ——————————————— 1750

1700s
Triangle trade routes
are established

1750
Boston's population
reaches more than 15,000

WHAT TO KNOW
How did New England's
economy depend on the
region's natural resources?

VOCABULARY
free-market p. 215
industry p. 216
naval stores p. 216
export p. 217
import p. 217
triangular trade route p. 218
Middle Passage p. 218

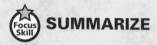

SUMMARIZE

Key Facts | Summary

New England's Economy

YOU ARE THERE You have been digging rows for planting all morning. Your back is aching, but there is still more work to be done. Your mother smiles and says, "In a few weeks, this garden will give us vegetables for you and your brothers and sisters." Your stomach grumbles as you look down at the dirt and wonder why gardens can't grow faster.

▶ **MEETING NEEDS** Most New England families grew their own food.

214 ▪ Unit 3

▶ **FARMS IN NEW ENGLAND** Most New England farms had a variety of animals, such as cows, horses, chickens, hogs, sheep, and goats.

New England Farming

By 1750, many New England towns had become busy cities. Boston, one of the largest cities in the English colonies, had more than 15,000 people. However, most people in New England still lived in small towns surrounded by farmland.

Building an Economy

New England farmers struggled to grow crops. Before they could plant anything, they had to clear rocks and trees from the land. New England's long winters also made it hard to grow crops.

Over time, farmers found other ways to work with their environment. In addition to farming, many began raising dairy cows and sheep. In time, colonists produced surplus farm goods.

Farmers traded or sold their surpluses of livestock, grain, wool, fruit, and firewood in port cities. At the docks, farmers bargained with merchants over prices or items to trade. The merchants then shipped the goods to England or to other colonies. There, the goods were sold for more than the merchants had paid. Many merchants became rich from trade.

This system of trade between farmers and merchants was the beginning of a **free-market** economic system in the colonies. In a free-market economy, people are free to choose which goods to make or buy and which services to offer or use. They are free to compete in business and to set whatever prices they choose for goods and services.

READING CHECK ⏱ **SUMMARIZE**
What did farmers do with their surplus goods?

▶ **CARPENTERS** made many things out of wood. This reenactor is shaving a wooden board using the same kinds of tools colonists used.

Logging and Shipbuilding

The lumber industry made up a large part of the colonists' free-market economy. An **industry** is all the businesses that make one kind of product or offer one kind of service.

New England Forests

In the forests of New England, especially in what are today New Hampshire and Maine, loggers cut down trees. They sent the trees to sawmills to be cut into lumber. Other colonists used their skills and knowledge to build houses, barns, and churches out of the lumber. Much of the lumber was sent to markets in England, which had fewer trees.

New England forests also supplied the natural resources needed to make **naval stores**, the products used to build ships. Two naval stores, turpentine and

tar, were used to make a coating that prevented leaks. Logs cut in the forests were floated down rivers to coastal towns. There, workers used naval stores to build and repair ships. Shipbuilders formed the ships' hulls with oak. To make the masts, they used tall pines.

Europeans valued the strong ships built in New England. By the late 1700s, nearly one-third of all English ships had been built in the region. One reason was the low cost of building ships there. Because wood was not as plentiful in Europe, it cost more to build ships there than it did in New England.

The shipbuilding industry contributed to the growth of coastal towns and cities. Several New England cities—including Boston and Portsmouth—became major shipbuilding centers.

READING CHECK ☼**SUMMARIZE**
In what ways did the colonists use the forests in New England?

Colonial Trade

As a result of the many ships built in New England, trading became the center of the region's economy. The English government set up strict rules for trade. The government said that the colonists could only send their **exports**, or goods leaving a country, to England or to other English colonies. The government also said that colonists could only buy English-made **imports**, or goods brought into a country.

Fishing and Whaling

Many coastal towns did well because of good fishing in the ocean waters. Fishers made a living by catching fish such as cod, herring, and mackerel.

There were so many fish that New Englanders could catch more than they needed. Their surplus fish were dried, packed in barrels, and sent to markets in other English colonies or in Europe.

Thousands of whales swam in the cold Atlantic waters, too. New England whalers hunted for whales along the coast. The whalers then cut up and boiled the whale's blubber, or fat, to get oil, which was used in lamps.

So many whalers hunted close to shore that the number of whales declined. As a result, the whalers began sailing farther out into the ocean. As the years passed, whaling trips became longer and longer. Some whaling ships did not return for months or even years.

READING CHECK ☼ **SUMMARIZE**

Why did fishing and whaling become important industries in colonial New England?

➤ **WHALERS** often had to go on long journeys in dangerous seas to find whales.

Triangular Trade Routes

Trading ships leaving New England carried furs, lumber, grain, whale oil, and dried fish to England. The ships then returned to New England with tea, spices, wine, and English-made goods, such as cloth, shoes, and paper.

Some colonial trading ships made longer ocean voyages. They followed what became known as the **triangular trade routes**. These routes connected England, the English colonies, and Africa. On a map, the routes formed large triangles across the Atlantic Ocean.

The Middle Passage

Trading ships carrying goods and raw materials also carried enslaved people from central and western Africa. These people were kidnapped in Africa and later sold as workers in the English colonies. Millions of enslaved Africans were placed on ships and forced to travel across the Atlantic Ocean from Africa to the West Indies. This journey was called the **Middle Passage**.

The Africans suffered terribly on the ships. Many of them died during the Middle Passage. Their long trip in overcrowded ships was part of a large

 MAP SKILL **MOVEMENT** England, Africa, and the English colonies were connected by trade routes. What goods did the colonies get from England?.

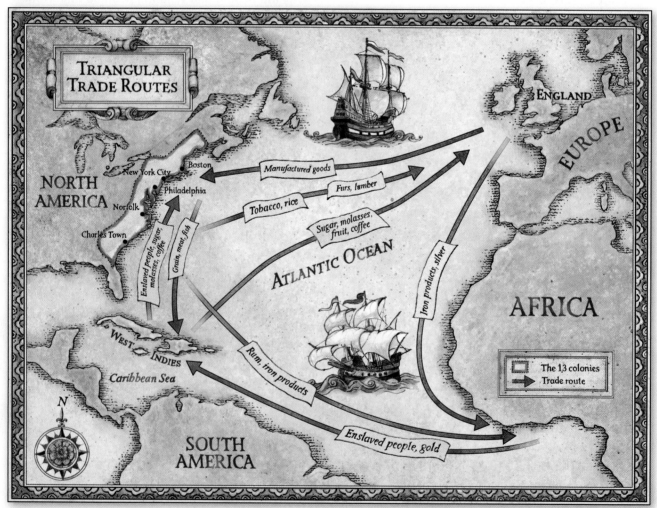

TRIANGULAR TRADE ROUTES

NORTH AMERICA

Boston
New York City
Philadelphia
Norfolk
Charles Town

WEST INDIES

Caribbean Sea

SOUTH AMERICA

ATLANTIC OCEAN

ENGLAND

EUROPE

AFRICA

Manufactured goods
Furs, lumber
Tobacco, rice
Sugar, molasses, fruit, coffee
Enslaved people, sugar, molasses, coffee
Grain, meat, fish
Iron products, silver
Rum, iron products
Enslaved people, gold

The 13 colonies
Trade route

and cruel slave-trade business. During the 1700s, some people in the colonies grew angry about the cruelty of the slave-trade. Over time, some New England colonists formed groups that tried to end slavery.

READING CHECK ⏱ **SUMMARIZE**

What were the triangular trade routes?

Summary

By the 1700s, many industries made up New England's free-market economy. Some colonists grew crops, cut lumber, or caught fish. Merchants made their living by trading. Trade routes connected the English colonies, England, and Africa.

REVIEW

1. **WHAT TO KNOW** How did New England's economy depend on the region's natural resources?

2. **VOCABULARY** Use the terms **import** and **export** in a sentence about trade.

3. **GEOGRAPHY** What was the Middle Passage?

4. **CRITICAL THINKING** How did the free-market economic system affect life in New England?

5. ✏️ **WRITE A LIST OF QUESTIONS** Imagine that you are a colonist deciding what type of work to do. Write a list of questions you might ask a farmer, merchant, shipbuilder, and whaler.

6. ⭐(Focus Skill) **SUMMARIZE** Copy and complete this graphic organizer on a separate sheet of paper.

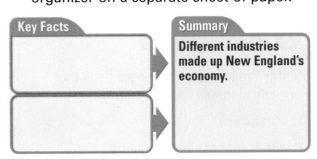

Key Facts

Summary

Different industries made up New England's economy.

Chapter 5 ■ 219

Visual Summary

1628
English Puritans sail to Massachusetts

1635
Roger Williams is expelled from Massachusetts

Summarize the Chapter

(Focus Skill) **Summarize** Complete this graphic organizer to show that you can summarize how the New England Colonies grew.

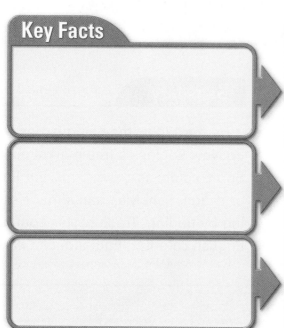

Key Facts

Summary

The New England Colonies grew during the 1600s.

Vocabulary

Identify the term from the word bank that correctly matches each definition.

1. agreement

2. goods brought into a country

3. all the businesses that make one kind of product or offer one kind of service

4. a grassy area shared by the town's people

5. products used to build ships

6. an economic system where people are free to choose which goods to make or buy and which services to offer or use

> **Word Bank**
>
> **consent** p. 201   **industry** p. 216
>
> **common** p. 210   **naval stores** p. 216
>
> **free-market** p. 215   **imports** p. 217

1700　　　　　　　　　　　　　　　1750

1675
King Philip's
War begins

1750
Boston's
population
reaches 15,000

 Time Line

Use the chapter summary time line above to answer these questions.

7. When did King Philip's War begin?

8. How many years after Puritans sailed to Massachusetts was Roger Williams expelled?

 Facts and Main Ideas

Answer these questions.

9. What early colonists came to New England to practice their religious beliefs?

10. What were four important industries in the New England Colonies?

Write the letter of the best choice.

11. How did New England colonists practice self-government?
    A They attended town meetings and elected their own leaders.
    B They let the English government rule.
    C They allowed Spain to rule them.
    D They banned slavery.

12. Who founded Hartford, which became part of the Connecticut Colony?
    A Anne Hutchinson
    B Roger Williams
    C Thomas Hooker
    D David Thomson

 Critical Thinking

13. Why did some settlers leave the Massachusetts Bay Colony to found their own settlements, and how did they affect the areas they settled?

14. What were the triangular trade routes? What effect did they have on the people of Africa? On the English colonies?

 **Skills**

Tell Fact from Opinion

15. Choose an early leader of New England that you read about in this chapter. Write two statements to express your opinions about this leader. Then write two facts to support each opinion.

writing

Write a Narrative Imagine that you have settled in New England with your parents. Write a story that tells how you feel about leaving your home. Describe your new life in New England as a child growing up.

Write a Persuasive Letter Imagine that it is 1650 and you are part of a group that wants to start a colony in North America. Write a letter to a company, explaining why it should pay for ships and supplies to start the colony.

STUDY SKILLS

QUESTION-AND-ANSWER RELATIONSHIPS

Different questions need different kinds of answers. Knowing this can help you write better answers.

- Questions with the words *who, what, when,* and *where* often ask you to give details.

- Questions with the words *how* and *why* often ask you to compare topics or give causes and effects. They require you to make connections.

Questions About Details	Questions About Connections
Question: Who was William Penn?	Question: How was William Penn's colony different from Massachusetts?
Answer: William Penn was the founder of Pennsylvania.	Answer: Pennsylvania had people of different religions. Most of the people in Massachusetts shared the same religion.

PREVIEW VOCABULARY

trial by jury p. 229

immigrant p. 235

artisan p. 244

The Middle Colonies

PENNSBURY MANOR IN
MORRISVILLE, PENNSYLVANIA

Lesson 1

1647
Peter Stuyvesant arrives in New Netherland

1664
England takes over New Netherland and renames it New York

1681
William Penn founds the colony of Pennsylvania

WHAT TO KNOW
Why did people from different places and backgrounds settle in the Middle Colonies?

VOCABULARY
refuge p. 228
proprietor p. 229
trial by jury p. 229
justice p. 229

PEOPLE
King Charles II
Peter Stuyvesant
William Penn
Tamanend

PLACES
New York
New Jersey
New York City
Pennsylvania
Delaware

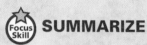

SUMMARIZE

Settling the Middle Colonies

YOU ARE THERE

The year is 1660. **King Charles II** is pleased with his American colonies. In the north, New England produces large amounts of lumber. In the south, Virginia's tobacco plantations are bringing him great wealth.

The king points to a map. "The problem lies here, right in the middle," he tells you. "That Dutch colony is in the way!"

❯ KING CHARLES II

▶ **FORT ORANGE** Built near where Albany, New York, now stands, the fort was right beside the Hudson River.

The Breadbasket Colonies

While the Puritans were settling New England, other groups were setting up colonies directly to the south. This region included what are today the states of New York, New Jersey, Delaware, and Pennsylvania. These colonies became known as the Middle Colonies. The region got its name because of its location between the New England Colonies and the Southern Colonies.

Geography and Climate

When Europeans arrived in the Middle Colonies, they saw flat plains and rolling hills. There were also grassy meadows and thick forests. Settlers found that when this land was cleared, it was much better for farming than the land in New England. Settlers also learned that the climate was good for growing crops. The summers were long, and the amount of rain each year was good for crops such as wheat, corn, and rye. The Middle Colonies grew so many crops used in making bread that they came to be called the "breadbasket" colonies.

In addition to rich land, the region had several large harbors along the Atlantic Ocean. Settlers found that these harbors were connected to many of the region's rivers, such as the Hudson and Delaware Rivers. These rivers stretched far inland. Settlers knew that these deep waterways would let large ships travel inland, making trade with other colonists easier. All of these special features attracted many different settlers to the region.

READING CHECK ☼**SUMMARIZE**
What attracted settlers to the Middle Colonies?

New Netherland Grows

The Dutch still controlled New Netherland, which included the Hudson Valley. However, few Dutch people came to the colony. Their country, the Netherlands, was prosperous. It gave its citizens many freedoms, and people saw no reason to leave. By 1640, only about 2,000 people lived in the colony. These settlers had problems with both Native Americans and nearby English colonists.

▶ **SLAVE AUCTION** The first slave auction in New Amsterdam was held in 1655.

A New Leader

The Dutch West India Company controlled New Netherland. It decided that a new leader was needed to raise the colony's profits and bring order. In 1647, the company sent **Peter Stuyvesant** (STY•vuh•suhnt) to govern the colony.

In the 1650s, Stuyvesant expanded New Netherland into what is now New Jersey. Then he pushed south into what is now Delaware, taking over the small colony of New Sweden in 1655. New Netherland now controlled more land, but it still needed more colonists. It did not have enough people to be successful.

New Colonists

To increase New Netherland's population, the Dutch West India Company let people from Belgium, Denmark, France, Italy, Spain, and Brazil settle in the colony. The new settlers included one of the first groups of Jewish people to move to North America.

Africans also lived in New Netherland. Most had been captured and brought to the colony as enslaved workers, beginning in 1626. Yet not all Africans in New Netherland were enslaved. Some had been able to buy their freedom. However, they were not completely free. Each year, they had to pay their employers in money or goods to remain free.

In 1660, Stuyvesant gave land on Manhattan to about 40 formerly enslaved people. This land became New Netherland's first community of free Africans.

READING CHECK ☼SUMMARIZE

Why did few people from the Netherlands settle in New Netherland?

> PETER STUYVESANT left New Netherland after the English took over the colony, but he later returned and lived in New York.

The English Take Over

King Charles II wanted England to control the Atlantic coast of North America. He wanted more settlements, more lands rich in natural resources, and control of the fur trade. One thing prevented the king from meeting this goal—the colony of New Netherland.

Conflicts over Land

Both the English and the Dutch claimed lands in the Connecticut Valley and on Long Island. King Charles II gave his brother James, the Duke of York, the land between Maine and the Delaware River, including New Netherland.

In 1664, the Duke of York sent four warships to take New Netherland. When the ships arrived off the coast of the colony, the English told Stuyvesant to give up. They said that if he did not, they would attack.

Stuyvesant wanted to fight the English and keep New Netherland. He tried to get the colonists to fight, but they would not. They knew they were outnumbered. New Netherland had fewer than 150 soldiers. Stuyvesant surrendered, and the English took control of New Netherland without firing a shot.

READING CHECK ⓈSUMMARIZE

Why did England want to control New Netherland?

Founding the Middle Colonies

● **1664**
The New Jersey Colony is established

1664
The New York Colony is established

Time

● **1681**
The Pennsylvania Colony is founded by William Penn

1650   1675   1700

TIME LINE All of the Middle Colonies were founded in the 1600s. In what century were they founded?

New York and New Jersey

James, the Duke of York, split the Dutch colony into two parts. He named them **New York** and **New Jersey**. James kept New York for himself, and the city of New Amsterdam became **New York City**. James gave New Jersey to two of his friends, John Berkeley and George Carteret.

The English treated the Dutch settlers fairly. They promised to protect their rights, religious freedom, and property. They also let the colonists elect some of their own leaders. Most Dutch settlers chose to stay.

At first, nearly all of the colonists lived in New York. To attract more settlers to New Jersey, Berkeley and Carteret offered to sell land at low prices. Many of the early settlers arriving in New Jersey were members of the Society of Friends, a religious group also known as the Quakers.

The Quakers

Quakers believed that all people were equal. They refused to fight in wars or to swear loyalty to any king or country. People with different beliefs were often cruel to the Quakers. Thousands of Quakers were forced to leave England.

The Quakers hoped to find a **refuge**, or safe place, to live and worship. In 1674, a group of Quakers bought Berkeley's share of New Jersey and founded Salem, New Jersey, the first Quaker settlement in North America.

READING CHECK ☼**SUMMARIZE**
Why did many Quakers settle in New Jersey?

Pennsylvania and Delaware

In 1681, King Charles II gave a charter to **William Penn**, an English Quaker. The charter made Penn the **proprietor**, or owner, of what is now **Pennsylvania**.

A New Plan of Government

Penn was given the land because the king owed money to Penn's father. The new colony was named Pennsylvania, which means "Penn's woods." Penn wanted all the people living in Pennsylvania—Quakers and non-Quakers—to live together peacefully.

In 1682, Penn wrote the Frame of Government of Pennsylvania. This plan of government set up a legislature called the General Assembly. It also gave citizens freedom of speech, freedom of religion, and the right to a fair trial by jury. In a **trial by jury**, a group of citizens decides if a person is guilty or innocent of committing a crime. Penn later wrote the Pennsylvania Charter of Privileges, which allowed white male colonists to elect representatives to the Assembly.

The Duke of York gave Penn control of the land that now makes up **Delaware** in 1682. Penn gave the colony its own assembly in 1704.

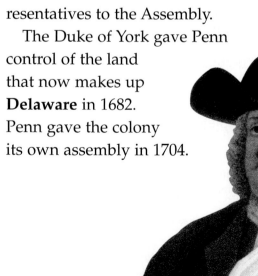

> **WILLIAM PENN**

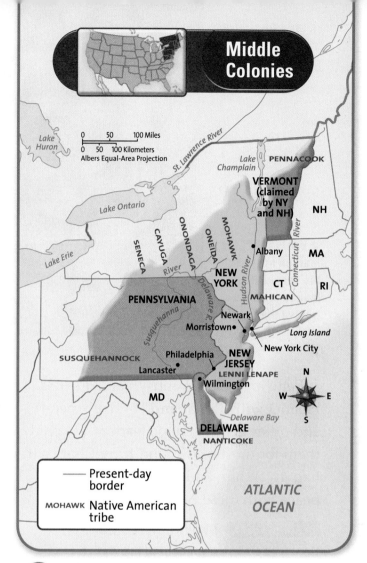

Middle Colonies

Present-day border

MOHAWK Native American tribe

MAP SKILL **LOCATION** What Pennsylvania city was on the Delaware River?

Relations with Native Americans

Penn also wanted Native Americans to be treated with **justice**, or fairness. In a letter, he told the local Lenni Lenape (LEH•nee LEH•nuh•pee) people:

> **❝I desire to enjoy it with your love and consent, that we may always live together as neighbors and friends.❞**

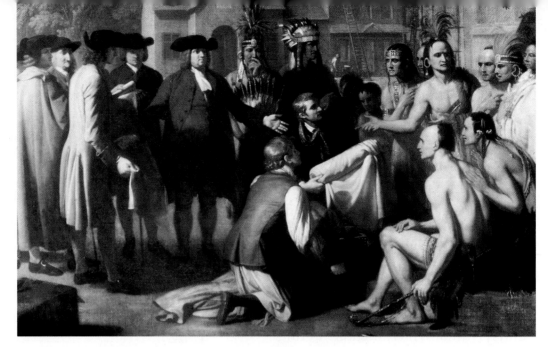

> **WILLIAM PENN** learned to speak the Lenni Lenape language and treated the people fairly.

Penn arrived in Pennsylvania in 1682. He met with **Tamanend** (TAM•uh•nend) and other Lenni Lenape leaders. He paid them for most of the land King Charles II had given him and built a long-lasting peace with these Native Americans.

READING CHECK **DRAW CONCLUSIONS**
How was Penn's treatment of the Native Americans related to Quaker beliefs?

Summary

The Middle Colonies were New York, New Jersey, Pennsylvania, and Delaware. People from many different places and backgrounds settled in the Middle Colonies. Some settlers came because of the good land. Others came to freely practice their religion.

REVIEW

1. **WHAT TO KNOW** Why did people from different places and backgrounds settle in the Middle Colonies?

2. **VOCABULARY** Use the term **trial by jury** in a sentence about the Pennsylvania Colony.

3. **GEOGRAPHY** How does location explain why New York, New Jersey, Pennsylvania, and Delaware were called the Middle Colonies?

4. **CRITICAL THINKING** Why do you think William Penn wanted religious freedom in Pennsylvania?

5. ✏ **WRITE A CONVERSATION** Write a conversation between William Penn and Tamanend. Have each leader describe their hopes for the future.

6. ⭐ **Focus Skill** **SUMMARIZE** On a separate sheet of paper, copy and complete this graphic organizer.

Key Facts		Summary
The Dutch controlled New Netherland.	▶	
England wanted to expand its colonies.	▶	

Tamanend

Biography

Trustworthiness
Respect
Responsibility
Fairness
Caring
Patriotism

"We will live in love with William Penn and his children as long as the creeks and rivers run."

No one was surprised to hear Tamanend speak these kind words. He was a kind leader and was respected by all who knew him. Tamanend grew up along the Neshaminy Creek in the forests of what is now southeastern Pennsylvania. He belonged to the Lenni Lenape tribe, which the English called the Delaware.

In Tamanend's language, his name meant "affable," or friendly and easy to talk to. The name fit him well. One minister described Tamanend as having "every good and noble qualification that a human being can possess."

Tamanend met with Pennsylvania's colonial leaders five times over the years. In each meeting, he agreed to sell land. The colonists paid for the land with guns, clothing, tools, blankets, and other items. Tamanend divided these items equally among his tribe members. Not all colonial leaders were as fair as William Penn. Yet Tamanend always worked to honor the peace he made between the Lenni Lenape and the people of Pennsylvania.

Why Character Counts

In what ways did Tamanend earn the respect of his people and of William Penn?

Time

1628	1701
Born?	Died?

1683 Tamanend first meets with William Penn

1697 Tamanend attends his last meeting with Pennsylvania leaders

GO ONLINE For more resources, go to www.harcourtschool.com/ss1

JUSTICE

"Any government is free to the people under it where the laws rule, and the people are a party to [can help make] those laws."

—from the Frame of Government of Pennsylvania

In some colonies, people accused of a crime did not receive a trial by jury.

In his frame of government, William Penn wrote that all citizens of the Pennsylvania Colony were to be treated equally under the law. This is the basic idea of justice in government. The idea of justice also appeared in the Pennsylvania Charter of Privileges of 1701. Penn knew that people are more likely to follow laws when they have a voice in making them. He believed that treating people justly was the key to good government.

The FRAME of the
GOVERNMENT
OF THE
Province of Pennsilvania
IN
AMERICA:
Together with certain
LAWS
Agreed upon in England
BY THE
GOVERNOUR
AND
Divers FREE-MEN of the aforesaid
PROVINCE.
To be further Explained and Confirmed there by the first
Provincial Council and General Assembly that shall
be held, if they see meet.

Lawyers, judges, and juries work to make sure that people receive fair trials.

One of the most important ways Penn promised a fair government was to give citizens the right to a trial by jury. At that time, very few places in the world gave people this right. In a trial by jury, a group of citizens—rather than a single person—decides if someone has broken the law. A trial by jury gives the power to make decisions about guilt and innocence to the people.

Today, equal justice is an important idea in the United States government. The Bill of Rights says that no citizen can "be deprived of life, liberty, or property, without due process of law." This means that all people in the United States have the right to equal treatment under the law.

The figure of Justice wears a blindfold because the law is supposed to treat all people equally, no matter who they are.

Make It Relevant The Constitution, which includes the Bill of Rights, promises United States citizens the right to a fair and public trial by jury. Why do you think it is important for trials to be public?

Lesson 2

Time

1600 — 1750

1682 William Penn arrives in Philadelphia

1720s The Great Awakening begins in the Middle Colonies

Life in the Middle Colonies

WHAT TO KNOW
How did religious toleration help attract people of different cultures to the Middle Colonies?

VOCABULARY
diversity p. 235
immigrant p. 235
Great Awakening p. 236
religious toleration p. 236
militia p. 238

PEOPLE
George Whitefield
Jonathan Edwards
Benjamin Franklin

PLACES
New York City
Philadelphia

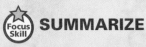

YOU ARE THERE
It's a sunny morning in 1699. You decide to take a walk around **New York City**.

As you walk, you see that the Dutch wall is being torn down to make room for more houses. A new road, Wall Street, is being built where the wall stood. You're not surprised that New York City is the fastest-growing town in the English colonies.

A Mix of People

Settlers in the Middle Colonies came from different places and backgrounds. One church leader described them as a group of people thrown together from many parts of the world. This **diversity** made the Middle Colonies an interesting place to live.

Starting a New Life

Who were the people of the Middle Colonies? At first, most were Dutch, French, Belgian, or Swedish. Then came English Puritans and Quakers, as well as German, Irish, and Scottish settlers. Most Africans arrived in the Middle Colonies as enslaved people, but others lived and worked as free persons.

The variety of people in the Middle Colonies could be seen in the city of Philadelphia. William Penn chose this city's name, which means "brotherly love" in Greek. Like all of Pennsylvania, Philadelphia was founded on the idea that people of different backgrounds could live peacefully together.

Immigrants from different countries came to Philadelphia. An **immigrant** is a person who comes into a country to make a new life. Some immigrants left their home countries to escape war or to find religious freedom. Other immigrants wanted better economic opportunities, including the chance to buy land and start businesses. Many found more freedom in the Middle Colonies than they had ever known.

READING CHECK ☼**SUMMARIZE**

Why did immigrants come to the Middle Colonies?

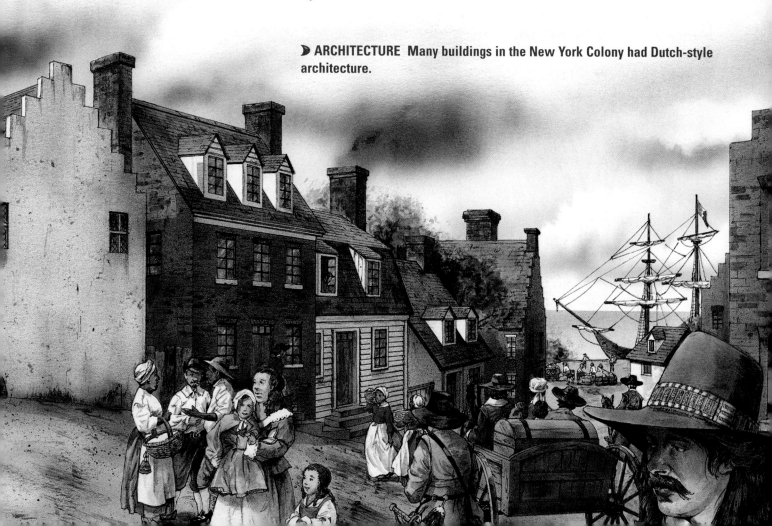

❯ **ARCHITECTURE** Many buildings in the New York Colony had Dutch-style architecture.

The Great Awakening

In the 1720s, a new religious movement began in the Middle Colonies. The movement was known as the **Great Awakening** because it "awakened," or renewed, many peoples' interest in religion. The Great Awakening also changed the way many people practiced their religion.

Religion Expands

Ministers such as **George Whitefield** and **Jonathan Edwards** gave speeches that marked a change in religious ideas and practices. They often talked about people having a direct relationship with God. Not only did these ministers preach new ideas, they practiced religion differently. They would travel long distances to give emotional speeches to people they had never met.

The Great Awakening helped bring people together. This led to greater **religious toleration**, or acceptance of religious differences. At the new revivals, or prayer meetings, everyone was welcomed. Poor people could attend, and women played a large role in the movement. During the Great Awakening, both free and enslaved Africans participated in religious gatherings. Such equal participation was rare at this time in history.

The Great Awakening was not popular with all people, and in time, differences split the movement. This increased the diversity of religious beliefs. The number of church members in the colonies grew, as did the free exercise of religion.

READING CHECK ☼**SUMMARIZE**
What was the Great Awakening?

❱ **GEORGE WHITEFIELD** (right) used a movable field pulpit, such as the one below, for preaching outdoors.

▶ **FARM LIFE** Farmers in the Middle Colonies often hired free African Americans or used enslaved workers on their farms.

Religion and Social Life

Unlike the New England Colonies, the Middle Colonies were home to many different religious groups. Towns often had more than one kind of church. A Presbyterian church, for example, might be only a block away from a Quaker meetinghouse. The first Jewish synagogue in the Middle Colonies was built in New York City in 1730.

Religion was a major part of social life in the Middle Colonies. After religious services, neighbors would talk and exchange news. Religion also changed the ways people viewed one another. Because of their religious beliefs, some colonists thought enslaving Africans was wrong. In 1688, Quakers in Germantown, Pennsylvania, became the first group to protest slavery in the English colonies.

Free Time

The social lives of colonists were as different as their religious beliefs. In cities such as Philadelphia and New York City, people went to dances, plays, concerts, and social clubs. Horse races, sleigh rides, and ice-skating were also common.

In rural areas, a barn raising was a big social event. A farm family would invite their neighbors to help them put in place the frame for a new barn. Afterward, everyone enjoyed a big meal.

READING CHECK ☾**SUMMARIZE**
How did the Middle Colonies differ from the New England Colonies?

Philadelphia Grows

As owner of the Pennsylvania Colony, William Penn planned both its government and its settlements. Penn designed Philadelphia, the colony's most important town, with wide streets and many public parks. He wanted the city to have plenty of space for people to work and to relax.

When Penn first visited Philadelphia in 1682, it had only ten houses. Fifty years later, more than 11,000 people lived there. Over time, Philadelphia became the largest city in the English colonies. By 1770, it had more than 28,000 people—a small number by today's standards but large for that time.

Benjamin Franklin

As Philadelphia grew, it became the home of many famous scientists and artists. The most famous Philadelphian was **Benjamin Franklin**. He helped improve the city in many ways. Franklin set up the first trained firefighting company in the English colonies and raised money to help build the city's first hospital. He set up a **militia**, or volunteer army, to protect the city and the rest of the colony. To educate people, he founded Pennsylvania's first college and first public library.

Benjamin Franklin earned his living as a printer. He printed the *Pennsylvania Gazette* newspaper. He also wrote and published *Poor Richard's Almanack*, a yearly book that had a calendar, weather forecasts, stories, jokes, and wise sayings. It sold many copies and helped make Franklin a rich man.

Philadelphians wondered how Franklin did so much. He was a printer, a writer, a scientist, and an inventor. He also became a leader in the colony's government. It seems that Franklin followed the words of his own almanac: "Early to bed and early to rise, makes a man healthy, wealthy, and wise."

READING CHECK ᛜSUMMARIZE
What were some of the ways Benjamin Franklin improved Philadelphia?

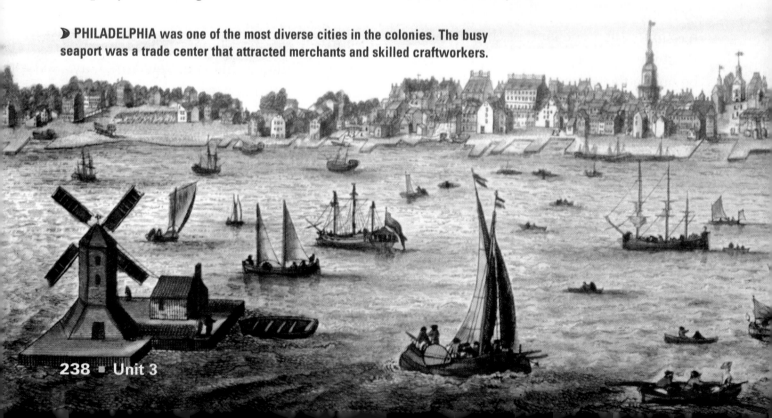

▶ **PHILADELPHIA** was one of the most diverse cities in the colonies. The busy seaport was a trade center that attracted merchants and skilled craftworkers.

▶ **BENJAMIN FRANKLIN** (above left) helped build a hospital (above right) and a firefighting company in Philadelphia.

Summary

The Middle Colonies were home to a mix of people, cultures, and religions. The Great Awakening added to the region's diversity. Philadelphia was a center of culture and the largest city in the English Colonies.

REVIEW

1. **WHAT TO KNOW** How did religious toleration help attract people of different cultures to the Middle Colonies?

2. **VOCABULARY** Write a sentence about **diversity** in the Middle Colonies, using the term **immigrant**.

3. **HISTORY** When did the Great Awakening take place, and who were some of its leaders?

4. **CRITICAL THINKING** If you lived in the Middle Colonies, would you want to live in a farming community or a town? Explain your choice.

5. ✏️ **WRITE A NARRATIVE** Write a story about life in early Philadelphia. Include details about the city's location, people, and businesses.

6. ⭐ Focus Skill **SUMMARIZE** On a separate sheet of paper, copy and complete this graphic organizer.

Key Facts		Summary
	➤	Philadelphia attracted many diverse people.
	➤	

1750
New York City becomes the second-busiest port in the English Colonies

WHAT TO KNOW
How did geography affect the economy of the Middle Colonies?

VOCABULARY
prosperity p. 242
artisan p. 244
apprentice p. 244

PLACES
Philadelphia
Hudson River
Delaware River

SUMMARIZE

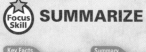

Busy Farms and Seaports

YOU ARE THERE
The year is 1700. You are in a market in **Philadelphia**, surrounded by a busy crowd of farmers and merchants hoping to sell their crops. You are very happy that your family decided to move to the Middle Colonies. The soil is very fertile and your farm produces many crops. You come to the market often to sell and trade. And your family has much more land than they ever did in England!

Farmers grow grain.

Rich Farmlands

When settlers came to the Middle Colonies, they were amazed by the richness of the land and all of its natural resources. Unlike New England, the Middle Colonies had plenty of fertile soil. Since most people made their living by farming, the Middle Colonies attracted many settlers.

Richard Frame used poetry to express his feelings about the rich land in the Middle Colonies. He wrote:

> **The fields, most beautiful, yield such crops of wheat, And other things most excellent to eat.**

Crops, Livestock, and Trade

Wheat fields stretched all across the Middle Colonies. Wheat, corn, and rye were the main crops, but colonists also used the land in other ways. Dairy cows ate the thick grasses. Pigs ran through the forests, eating acorns and berries.

Farmers in the Middle Colonies traveled to market towns to sell or trade their livestock and crops. Every market town had a gristmill, which ground grain into flour. Most towns also had a lumber mill. During visits to market towns, farm families shopped at the general store. They bought things they could not make or grow themselves, such as iron tools, shoes, paint, and buttons.

READING CHECK ☼**SUMMARIZE**
How did geography affect the economy of the Middle Colonies?

A Gristmill

ILLUSTRATION Gristmills ground harvested grain into flour. How did the flour get to market?

Farmers take the grain to the mill.

Millstones grind the grain into flour.

Flour is taken to market.

Port Cities

The merchants who bought livestock and crops from farmers took these goods to port cities. These were major trade centers in the Middle Colonies. The colonies' **prosperity**, or economic success, depended largely on the ports.

New York City

New York City was one of the most important port cities. The **Hudson River** helped make trade easier. Farmers, fur traders, and lumber workers could float their goods down the river to New York City. Also, the port's harbor along the East River was a good place for ships to dock.

Every year, the number of ships sailing into and out of New York City grew. When the English took over in 1664, about 35 ships used the port each year. By 1750, that number had grown to 600. New York City had become the second-busiest port in the English colonies.

Philadelphia

The busiest port was Philadelphia. The city was built along the **Delaware River**.

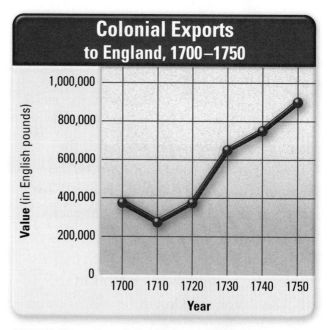

Colonial Exports to England, 1700–1750

GRAPH The value of colonial exports is given in English money, or pounds. In what year did the colonies export the highest value of goods?

Many people moved to Philadelphia because of the port.

Farmers, merchants, and traders in Pennsylvania, New Jersey, and Delaware relied on the Philadelphia port. They sent goods down the Delaware River to the port or took their crops to the merchants in seaports. From Philadelphia, ships sailed down the river into Delaware Bay and then across the Atlantic.

▶ **ENGLISH GOODS** Watches, silver trays, and mugs were shipped from England to the colonies. These goods entered the colonies through port cities, such as New York City (below).

Exports and Imports

Colonial port cities were busy places. The streets were full of sailors and, at times, even pirates. Shopworkers made ropes, sails, and barrels. Shipbuilders hammered ships together. Merchants talked over prices as dockhands moved goods. For many immigrants, their first view of North America was a port city.

As in New England, almost all trade in the Middle Colonies was with England or with other English colonies. New England and the Middle Colonies exported many of the same goods, including furs, salted meat, and lumber. Yet the Middle Colonies exported more wheat and grains. They led the colonies in flour exports.

Most imports to the Middle Colonies came from England. Ships brought furniture, tea, gunpowder, medicines, and metals. Some ships carried enslaved Africans. Most of these people were made to work as craftworkers or servants.

READING CHECK ☼**SUMMARIZE**
Why were New York City and Philadelphia good locations for ports?

Colonial Jobs

Immigrants arriving in the Middle Colonies could choose from many different jobs. In addition to farming and shipping, many colonists worked in skilled trades such as ironworking. Many of these **artisans**, or craftworkers, came to the colonies as indentured servants.

Making Goods

Most artisans used raw materials to make goods. Blacksmiths used iron to form horseshoes and tools. Coopers made barrels out of wood. Carpenters used wood to build houses and ships. Bricklayers worked with stone and clay to pave streets and raise buildings.

Some artisans depended on farm goods. They included bakers, butchers, flour millers, and soap makers. Dressmakers and tailors used wool, linen, and cotton to make clothing. Tanners turned animal skins into leather, which cobblers used to make shoes.

Learning a Trade

A few colonists from rich families went to college to become lawyers, bankers, or ministers. However, the skills needed by artisans, such as carpenters and tanners, were not taught in schools.

Instead, young people learned their skills by becoming apprentices. An **apprentice** lived and worked with an artisan and his family for several years to learn a skill. He could then go on to earn a living as a journeyman and later a master. These professions were practiced by men.

Children IN HISTORY

Benjamin Franklin

Hundreds of colonial boys became apprentices. Benjamin Franklin was one of them. By the age of 10, he was working for his father as a soap maker in Boston. When Franklin's father noticed that he liked to read books more than make soap, he arranged for young Benjamin to work in his brother's print shop.

Franklin helped write pamphlets, set type, and even sell newspapers on the street. When he was 17 years old, Franklin left the shop and moved to Philadelphia to open his own printing business.

Make It Relevant What kind of job would you want if you were an apprentice?

Women and girls had fewer chances to work outside the home. In the 1600s and 1700s, most women were not allowed to own property or businesses. In most cases, when a woman got married, her husband became the owner of everything she had.

Sometimes, if a woman's husband died, she would take over his business. Throughout the colonies, some widows ran taverns, printing businesses, and silversmith shops.

READING CHECK ☼**SUMMARIZE**
How did people learn to be artisans?

Summary

The rich land, wide rivers, and large harbors of the Middle Colonies all led to economic success. The region's economy also depended on its many farmers, artisans, merchants, and sailors.

▶ **CANDLEMAKERS** were called chandlers. Candles were made from tallow, which is animal fat.

REVIEW

1. **WHAT TO KNOW** How did geography affect the economy of the Middle Colonies?

2. **VOCABULARY** How are the terms **artisan** and **apprentice** related?

3. **ECONOMICS** What jobs were most enslaved Africans forced to do in the Middle Colonies?

4. **CRITICAL THINKING** What were the advantages and disadvantages of being an apprentice?

5. **MAKE A CHART** Make a two-column chart that lists colonial jobs and the products made by people who worked at these jobs.

6. **SUMMARIZE**
   Focus Skill   On a separate sheet of paper, copy and complete this graphic organizer.

Key Facts	Summary
The Middle Colonies had rich farmland.	
Many settlers came to the Middle Colonies.	

Make an Economic Choice

Why It Matters Making a good economic choice can help you decide which goods to buy.

▶ LEARN

To pay for what you want, you will have to give up the chance to buy something else. This is called making a **trade-off**. What you give up in order to buy what you want is called an **opportunity cost**. This information and the steps below can help you make a good economic choice.

Step 1 Identify your economic goal and your resources.

Step 2 Identify your choices.

Step 3 Discuss the positive and negative effects of each choice.

Step 4 Identify the opportunity cost of each choice. Then make the choice with the most positive effects.

▶ PRINT SHOPS Running a print shop was not cheap. Printers had to buy a press, type, paper, and ink.

▶ **COOPERS** This historical reenactor shows how coopers made barrels in colonial times.

▶ PRACTICE

Imagine that you are an artisan, and answer the questions below.

1 Which should you buy, a new tool or some new clothes?

2 What would be the result of buying a new tool?

3 What would be the result of buying the new clothes?

4 What will you buy? Explain why.

▶ APPLY

Make It Relevant Imagine that you want to buy either a birthday present for a friend or a computer game for yourself. Explain to a partner the expected result of each of your choices.

1647
Peter Stuyvesant arrives in New Netherland

Visual Summary

Summarize the Chapter

Summarize Complete this graphic organizer to show that you can summarize facts about the Middle Colonies.

Key Facts

People came to the Middle Colonies from many places.

People had different backgrounds and religious beliefs.

There were many ways to make a living in the Middle Colonies.

Summary

Vocabulary

Identify the term from the word bank that correctly matches each definition.

1. a volunteer army

2. an owner

3. a person learning a skill

4. a safe place

5. a craftworker

6. a person who comes into a country to make a new life

Word Bank

refuge p. 228   militia p. 238

proprietor p. 229   artisan p. 244

immigrant p. 235   apprentice p. 244

 1700   1750

1664
England takes
over New
Netherland

1681
William Penn founds
Pennsylvania

1720s
The Great
Awakening
begins in the
Middle Colonies

 Time Line

Use the chapter summary time line above to answer these questions.

7. How long did Peter Stuyvesant govern New Netherland before the English took over?

8. When did William Penn found his colony?

 Facts and Main Ideas

Answer these questions.

9. How did some enslaved people in New Netherland gain more freedom?

10. How did William Penn plan for self-government and religious freedom?

11. What were two effects of the Great Awakening?

Write the letter of the best choice.

12. What religious group found refuge by purchasing land in New Jersey?
    A Puritans
    B Catholics
    C Quakers
    D Anglicans

13. Which of the following was the most widely grown crop in the Middle Colonies?
    A tobacco
    B cotton
    C rice
    D wheat

 Critical Thinking

14. **Make It Relevant** In what ways was the population of the Middle Colonies like the population of the United States today?

15. How did life in the Middle Colonies compare to life in New England?

16. Why did New York City and Philadelphia become important to people who lived outside these cities?

 Skills

Make an Economic Choice

17. Review the information on pages 246–247. Then describe an economic choice you made and the trade-offs and opportunity costs of your choice.

writing

Write a Research Report William Penn built good relations with Tamanend and other Native American leaders. Using facts and details, write a report that tells how Penn did this.

Write a Persuasive Letter Imagine that it is 1700 and you want to be an apprentice. Choose the type of work you want to do. Then write a letter to a business owner and tell the person why he or she should accept you as an apprentice.

STUDY SKILLS

TAKE NOTES

Taking notes can help you remember what you have learned and also help you review for tests.

- **Write down important facts and ideas. You do not have to write complete sentences.**

- **Organize your notes in a chart.**

The Southern Colonies

Reading Notes	Class Notes
Lesson 1 • The first settlers arrived in Maryland in 1633. • _____	• Many Catholics came to Maryland because they could not freely practice their religion in England. • _____

PREVIEW VOCABULARY

constitution p. 255   **backcountry** p. 257   **broker** p. 270

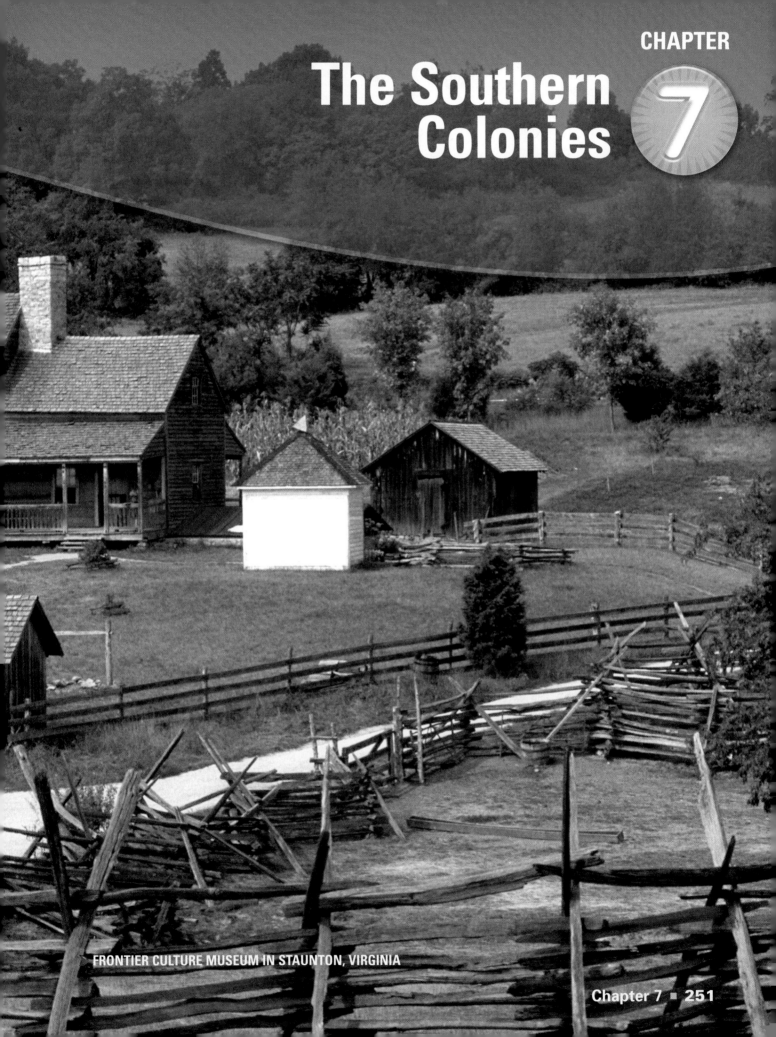

The Southern Colonies

FRONTIER CULTURE MUSEUM IN STAUNTON, VIRGINIA

Lesson 1

Time

1600 ———————————————————————————— 1750

1632
Lord Baltimore receives a charter for the Maryland Colony

1712
The Carolina Colony is split into North Carolina and South Carolina

1733
James Oglethorpe founds the Georgia Colony

WHAT TO KNOW
How did geography affect where people settled in the Southern Colonies?

VOCABULARY
constitution p. 255
debtor p. 256
backcountry p. 257

PEOPLE
George Calvert
Cecilius Calvert
James Oglethorpe

PLACES
Maryland
Virginia
North Carolina
South Carolina
Georgia

 SUMMARIZE

Settling the South

YOU ARE THERE

The year is 1650. You are standing on a hillside looking down at the bay below. Two months ago, you got on a ship in England to come to the **Maryland** Colony. The land looks very different from the busy streets of London. Beyond the bay, fields of crops stretch as far as you can see. You left London because you couldn't find a job there. Here, you'll be working for a rich landowner.

From the looks of things, you'll be working a lot.

FAST FACT

The Chesapeake Bay takes its name from the Native American word *Chesepiooc*, meaning "Great Shellfish Bay."

▶ **FOUNDING MARYLAND** This painting shows an artist's view of the founding of Maryland. Why do you think people are shown carrying a cross?

Maryland

The Maryland Colony was founded by the Calverts, a family of wealthy English landowners. The Calverts, who were Catholic, wanted to build a colony in North America that would make money. They also wanted a refuge for Catholics. Like the Quakers, Catholics in England could not worship as they wished.

The Calverts

George Calvert, also called Lord Baltimore, had invested in the Virginia Company. Calvert asked King Charles I to give him a charter for a new colony along Chesapeake Bay, north of Virginia.

Calvert died before the charter was signed in 1632. His oldest son, **Cecilius Calvert**, became the new Lord Baltimore and the owner of the new colony. He called the colony Maryland.

Cecilius Calvert chose his brother, Leonard, to be Maryland's first governor. The Calvert brothers had learned from the bad experiences at Jamestown, in the Virginia Colony, and they planned their colony carefully. There would be no "starving time" in Maryland.

In 1633, the Calverts sent the first group of colonists to Maryland. Most of these colonists came as indentured servants. Their ships landed near the mouth of the Potomac River. There, the colonists founded their first settlement, now called St. Mary's City.

READING CHECK ☉**SUMMARIZE**

What were the reasons for the founding of the Maryland Colony?

▶ **THE TOLERATION ACT** helped protect the rights of Catholics in Maryland, but by the late 1600s, Protestants ruled the colony.

Life in Maryland and Virginia

The Maryland Colony had much in common with its neighbor, **Virginia**. The two colonies, separated by the Chesapeake Bay and the Potomac River, shared a mild climate. Tobacco grew in the fertile soil along the Coastal Plain.

Farming

Some colonists in Maryland became rich from growing tobacco on large plantations. However, most colonists struggled to make a living on small farms. Many of Maryland's farmers had come to the colony as indentured servants. Maryland's government helped former servants by giving them land, clothes, tools, and barrels of corn.

Government

In the early 1700s, Virginia was the largest English colony in North America. In 1699, Williamsburg became its capital.

Virginia and Maryland had similar governments. Both colonies had governors and elected assemblies. However, the king controlled the royal colony of Virginia, while the Calverts controlled the proprietary colony of Maryland.

In 1649, Maryland passed the Toleration Act, which gave religious freedom to all Christians in the colony. Over time, many members of the Anglican Church settled in Maryland. In 1702, it became the colony's official church.

READING CHECK **COMPARE AND CONTRAST**
What features did Maryland and Virginia share?

The Carolina Colonies

As more people moved to Maryland and Virginia, some colonists moved south to get more land. In 1663, England's new king, Charles II, granted land for another colony, called Carolina.

Lords Proprietors

The charter divided Carolina among eight English leaders called the Lords Proprietors. In 1669, they adopted a **constitution**, or a written plan of government, for Carolina. This let free white male colonists choose some leaders and make some laws. Still, most of the power belonged to the proprietors and the king.

The Carolina Colony soon became hard to govern. It was large, and the colonists often did not follow laws they did not like. In 1712, the Lords Proprietors split the colony into **North Carolina** and **South Carolina**. In hilly North Carolina, farmers grew tobacco and corn. Farmers in South Carolina had trouble making money by growing tobacco. The land was too wet. Things changed when enslaved African workers brought with them the knowledge of how to successfully grow rice. Rice soon became South Carolina's most important crop, and enslaved people became a large part of its population.

READING CHECK ☉**SUMMARIZE**
Why was the Carolina Colony hard to govern?

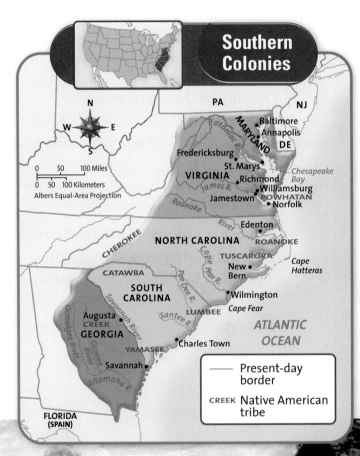

MAP SKILL **HUMAN-ENVIRONMENT INTERACTIONS** Tobacco (below) was mostly grown in the upper South. What city on the map is farthest north?

Southern Colonies

Legend:
— Present-day border
CREEK Native American tribe

Georgia

England, France, and Spain all claimed the area to the south of South Carolina. By 1727, England's new ruler, King George II, knew that to gain control of the area, he had to send colonists there.

A wealthy English leader named **James Oglethorpe** had an idea. Why not send English **debtors**—people who had been put in prison for owing money—to settle a new colony? The settlers would defend the land against other countries. Oglethorpe also hoped to give the debtors a chance to start a new life. He wrote,

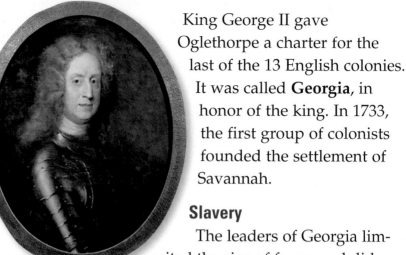

▶ **JAMES OGLETHORPE**

> 66 By such a Colony, many families, who would otherwise starve, will be provided for, and made masters of houses and lands. 99

King George II gave Oglethorpe a charter for the last of the 13 English colonies. It was called **Georgia**, in honor of the king. In 1733, the first group of colonists founded the settlement of Savannah.

Slavery

The leaders of Georgia limited the size of farms and did not allow slavery. As a result, Georgia had no plantations. However, the settlers were divided in their views about slavery. In 1751, Georgia's leaders decided to allow slavery. Over time, Georgia's economy, like that of all the other Southern Colonies, grew as a result of plantations and the labor of enslaved Africans.

READING CHECK **MAIN IDEA AND DETAILS**
Why did James Oglethorpe found the Georgia Colony?

Heading West

In the early 1700s, most towns, farms, and plantations in the English colonies were established near the coast, on the Coastal Plain. At that time, few colonists had settled in the Piedmont—the land between the Coastal Plain and the Appalachian Mountains. Settlers called this land the **backcountry** because it was beyond, or "in back of," the area settled by Europeans.

The Great Wagon Road

The thick forests, steep hills, and few roads made travel to the backcountry hard. However, by the mid-1700s, many settlers were moving west of the Coastal Plain. From Pennsylvania, large numbers of German immigrants began to move into the backcountry of Virginia and the Carolinas. The settlers followed a Native American trail. As more people used the trail, it became wide enough for wagons to use. This trail became known as the Great Wagon Road.

The Great Wagon Road passed through the Shenandoah Valley and along the eastern side of the Blue Ridge Mountains. It was the only way to get wagons loaded with household goods to the backcountry.

READING CHECK ⏿ **SUMMARIZE**

Why was it hard to reach the backcountry?

The Great Wagon Road

Lancaster • Philadelphia
PA • Wilmington
MD • Baltimore
DE
Potomac River
VA
James River • Williamsburg
Jamestown • Norfolk
Roanoke River
NC • New Bern
Pee Dee
Wilmington • 0   50   100 Miles
SC
0 50 100 Kilometers
Santee R.
Azimuthal Equal-Area Projection

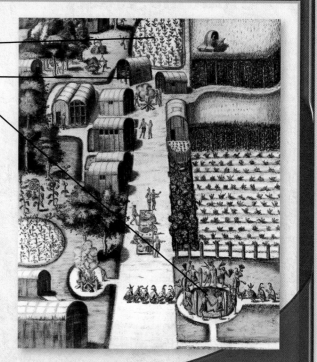

Crops —

Longhouse —

Ceremonial dance circle —

Native American Village

Background This drawing of a Native American village in North Carolina was made by John White, an English colonist, in the 1580s.

DBQ Document-Based Question Why do you think the Native Americans planted crops close to their homes?

Conflicts with Native Americans

Thousands of Cherokee, Creek, Powhatan, and other Native American tribes lived in areas that became the Southern Colonies. As more Europeans arrived, they built their settlements on Native American lands. As in the New England Colonies, conflicts arose between Native Americans and settlers.

The Tuscarora War

In North Carolina, for example, German and Swiss settlers destroyed the Tuscarora village to build a new settlement. Some colonists believed that the remaining Native Americans were not treated justly, either. One settler said that the other colonists had

> " cheated these Indians in trading, and would not allow them to hunt near their plantations. . . . "

In 1711, their land losses caused the Tuscarora to attack several settlements. The Tuscarora hoped to scare off the settlers, but their attacks led to the Tuscarora War. When the war finally ended in 1713, about 950 Tuscarora had been either killed or captured and sold into slavery.

Settlers in the Southern Colonies kept pushing Native Americans off their lands. Some were captured and sent to the West Indies to work on sugarcane plantations. Others died fighting the colonists over land or trade. Even peaceful Native American groups died in large numbers

▶ TOWN CREEK INDIAN MOUND was a center of religion and government for Native Americans in North Carolina.

from European diseases such as smallpox and measles.

As their numbers fell, many Native American groups were forced to move west to lands that European settlers had not yet reached. However, settlers moved west, too.

READING CHECK CAUSE AND EFFECT
What effect did settlers have on Native Americans in the Southern Colonies?

Summary

The Southern Colonies were made up of Virginia, Maryland, North Carolina, South Carolina, and Georgia. Settlers came for land and for religious reasons. Indentured servants and enslaved Africans were brought as workers. Over time, problems between settlers and Native Americans grew.

REVIEW

1. **WHAT TO KNOW** How did geography affect where people settled in the Southern Colonies?

2. **VOCABULARY** Use the term **debtor** in a sentence about the founding of Georgia.

3. **CULTURE** Which Southern Colony was founded as a refuge for Catholics, and who founded it?

4. **CRITICAL THINKING** Why might people have wanted to settle in the backcountry?

5. **MAKE AN ILLUSTRATED TIME LINE** Make a time line from 1600 to 1750. Then label important events in the settlement of the Southern Colonies. Draw pictures near those labels to show what happened.

6. (Focus Skill) **SUMMARIZE**
On a separate sheet of paper, copy and complete this graphic organizer.

Key Facts	Summary
England wanted to protect its land claims.	
Oglethorpe wanted to help debtors.	

Map and Globe Skills

Compare Maps of Different Scales

Why It Matters A map scale shows you the distance between places. Using maps of different scales can help you answer different kinds of questions about an area.

❯ LEARN

The maps on pages 260 and 261 show the Maryland Colony. Map A is drawn using a larger scale. It shows more details of the Maryland Colony. Map B is drawn using a smaller scale. This map also shows land around the colony.

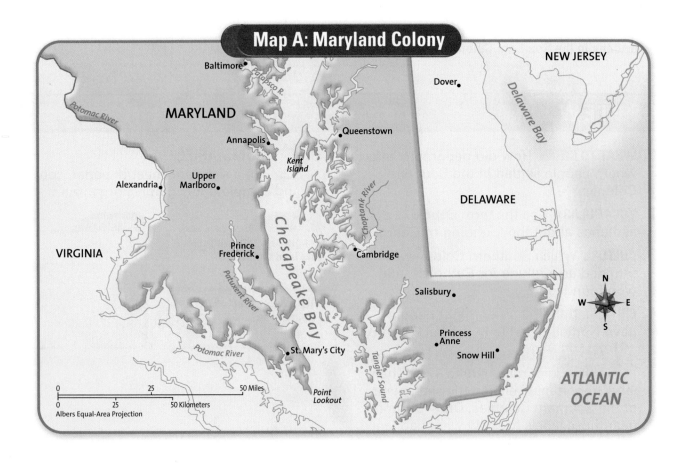

Map A: Maryland Colony

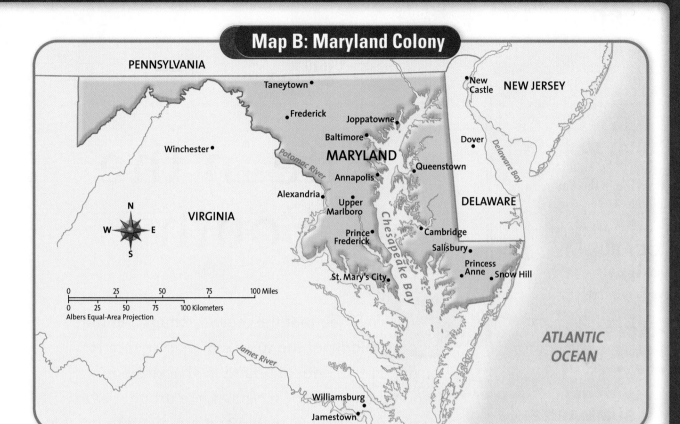

Map B: Maryland Colony

PRACTICE

Use Map A and Map B to answer the questions.

❶ Which map shows the distance between Point Lookout and Annapolis?

❷ Which map could you use to find the distance between Baltimore and Williamsburg?

❸ What is the distance in miles between St. Mary's City and Taneytown? Which map shows both places?

APPLY

Make It Relevant Look at a small-scale map of your state. Imagine that you are taking a trip to one of the cities shown on the map. Use the map to find the distance from your hometown to that city.

Map and Globe Skills

Time
1600   1750

1619
The first Africans
arrive in Virginia

1738
Fort Mose
is founded

WHAT TO KNOW
How did plantations affect life in the Southern Colonies?

VOCABULARY
planter p. 264
overseer p. 264

PLACES
Spanish Florida
Fort Mose

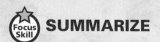

SUMMARIZE

Life in the South

YOU ARE THERE
You see that the crowd gathered in the middle of the town's market square is looking at two people bound in shackles and standing on a platform. They were brought over from Africa on a slave ship and are about to be sold. You try to imagine how scared they must feel after having been taken so far away from their homes and families.

> **SHACKLES** Iron shackles like these (above) were used to bind the hands and feet of enslaved people.

Slavery and Society

For more than 300 years, traders brought millions of Africans to North America, South America, and the Caribbean. These men, women, and children were taken from their homes, chained together in ships, and then sold.

Treatment of Enslaved People

The first Africans in the English colonies most likely arrived in Virginia in 1619. At first, the English colonies used indentured servants as workers. As more workers were needed, colonial governments made slavery legal. By the mid-1700s, slavery was legal in every colony. The laws said that children born to enslaved people were also enslaved. Families were often broken apart and sold to different owners.

In the Southern Colonies, most enslaved Africans worked on plantations. The way enslaved people were treated depended on their owners. Enslaved people were often beaten and abused. It was very difficult to escape, but this did not stop enslaved people from trying.

Enslaved people were not free to speak out against slavery, but they still resisted it. Some rebelled. Others broke tools, pretended to be sick, or worked slowly. Punishment for such acts was often harsh.

Enslaved people tried to deal with their hardships by keeping their culture alive. They told stories and sang songs about Africa. By the late 1700s, the Christian religion also became a source of strength for some enslaved people.

READING CHECK Ŏ SUMMARIZE
How did enslaved people resist slavery?

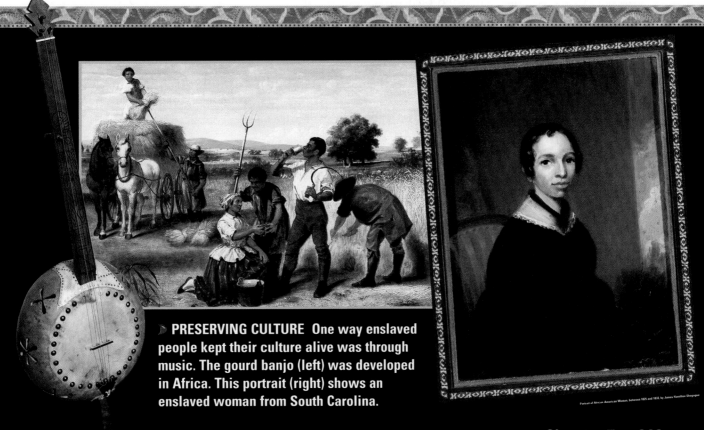

▷ **PRESERVING CULTURE** One way enslaved people kept their culture alive was through music. The gourd banjo (left) was developed in Africa. This portrait (right) shows an enslaved woman from South Carolina.

Portrait of African American Woman, between 1825 and 1833, by James Hamilton Shegogue

Fields

Overseer's house

Hospital

Slave quarters

Workshop

A Farming Economy

The economy of the Southern Colonies was based mostly on plantations, which would not have been possible without the labor of enslaved people. The cash crops produced by enslaved workers made some **planters**, or plantation owners, the richest people in the Southern Colonies.

The Plantation System

The first plantations were built along the Coastal Plain. By 1750, settlers had moved west and started large plantations farther inland. As planters grew richer, the amount of land they owned also grew.

Some plantations looked like small villages. There were many buildings, including workshops where enslaved people made nails, bricks, barrels, and other items used on the plantation.

Plantation owners often hired an **overseer** to watch enslaved people as they worked. The overseer's house was often near the fields. Enslaved workers' houses were usually far away from the planter's house. Near their homes, some enslaved people kept small gardens that they tended after working the planter's land.

Planters ran the plantations, but they did not usually work on them. Enslaved people did the work. Planters sometimes worked for the community as judges or members of the colonial assembly. Many planters hired teachers to educate their children in the home. Enslaved children were not allowed to attend school. In fact, it was illegal for enslaved people to learn to read or write. Those who tried to learn had to do so in secret. They were punished if they were caught.

A Southern Plantation

ILLUSTRATION Many plantations in the Southern Colonies were self-sufficient. Enslaved workers grew food and produced needed goods. Why did large plantations have so many buildings?

Planter's house

Kitchen

Life on Small Farms

The economy of the Southern Colonies depended mostly on the crops from large plantations. However, most colonists lived and worked on small farms.

Former indentured servants often owned small farms. However, few ever became rich. Most owners of small farms did not own enslaved people. Those who did worked alongside their enslaved workers but did not treat them as equals.

Since small farms were often far away from each other, church services became major events. Some families traveled for hours to reach a church. There, they attended services and visited with other farm families.

READING CHECK ⊙**SUMMARIZE**
How did most colonists in the Southern Colonies make their living?

Free Africans

A few Africans were able to buy their freedom and start farms. However, most did not want to be part of the system of slavery. Some free Africans did buy relatives, but only to free them.

To escape slavery, many enslaved people ran away. Those who escaped were often caught and returned to their owners. Some found safety in **Spanish Florida** or were helped by Native American tribes.

The Black Seminoles

The Seminole tribe gave runaways food and shelter. The Seminole also gave them land if they gave back one-third of the crop they raised on it. Many runaways dressed like the Seminole and learned their language. They became known as Black Seminoles.

▶ **SEEKING FREEDOM** Enslaved people who escaped often had to journey hundreds of miles to reach safety.

Fort Mose

Some free Africans in Spanish Florida started small towns, such as **Fort Mose** (moh•SAY). In 1738, it became the first settlement in North America for free Africans. The people of Fort Mose were free to practice African customs.

READING CHECK ☕**SUMMARIZE**
Who were the Black Seminoles?

Summary

Life in the Southern Colonies was full of contrasts. Plantation owners were very rich, but they depended on enslaved Africans. On small farms, many former indentured servants struggled to make a living. Not all Africans were enslaved. Some bought their freedom or escaped.

REVIEW

1. **WHAT TO KNOW** How did plantations affect life in the Southern Colonies?

2. **VOCABULARY** Describe the role of a **planter** and the role of an **overseer**.

3. **CULTURE** How did enslaved people keep their culture alive?

4. **CRITICAL THINKING** Why was the economy of the Southern Colonies dependent on large plantations when most of the colonists worked on small farms?

5. 🖌 **DRAW A SCENE** Choose a scene from daily life in the Southern Colonies that you read about in this lesson. Then draw a picture of that scene, and write a caption describing what it shows about life in a Southern Colony.

6. ⭐(Focus Skill) **SUMMARIZE** On a separate sheet of paper, complete this graphic organizer.

Key Facts	Summary
Plantations were self-sufficient.	
Enslaved people worked on plantations.	

Olaudah Equiano

Biography

Trustworthiness
Respect
Responsibility
Fairness
Caring
Patriotism

> "When I looked around the ship and saw . . . black people of every description chained together, . . . I no longer doubted my own fate."

Olaudah Equiano (OH•luh•dah ek•wee•AH•noh) was one of the first Africans to write and talk about life as an enslaved person. Through his writings and speeches, Equiano helped people understand the harsh realities of slavery.

When he was 12 years old, Equiano was sold to an English sea captain who took him on several journeys. Over time, he was able to earn enough money from trading that he bought his freedom. After earning his freedom, Equiano attended school in London and later worked as a sailor.

In 1789, Equiano published his autobiography. It became popular in England and later influenced many African American writers. His book described life in Africa, his time as an enslaved person, and how he gained his freedom. Equiano spent the rest of his life giving speeches around the world trying to convince people to end slavery.

Why Character Counts

How did Equiano show he cared about enslaved people?

Time

1745
Born?

1797
Died

1756 Equiano is sold into slavery

1789 Equiano's autobiography is published

GO ONLINE
For more resources, go to www.harcourtschool.com/ss1

3

Time

1600   1750

1729
Baltimore,
Maryland,
is founded

1740s
Indigo becomes a major
cash crop

WHAT TO KNOW
How did people in the
Southern Colonies use
natural resources to earn
a living?

VOCABULARY
indigo p. 269
interdependence p. 270
broker p. 270

PEOPLE
Eliza Lucas Pinckney

PLACES
Charles Town
Baltimore
Wilmington

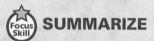 SUMMARIZE

Key Facts   Summary

The Southern Economy

You ARE There It's so hot that your shirt sticks to your back. You are loading hundreds of barrels of rice onto a ship in **Charles Town**, South Carolina. The huge ship arrived from England just two days ago. Its tall mast forms a shadow across the dock. You stop to look up at the ship's folded sails. You wipe the sweat from your forehead and wish you were out at sea, not stuck on this dock working in this heat.

▶ CHARLES TOWN, SOUTH CAROLINA, became the largest city in the Southern Colonies.

Children IN HISTORY

Eliza Lucas Pinckney

Eliza Lucas Pinckney moved to South Carolina with her parents in 1738. When she was 16 years old, her father had to return to the West Indies. Eliza started experimenting with indigo seeds her father had sent her. She worked so hard that she wrote, "I hardly allow myself time to sleep or eat."

After three years, Eliza was able to grow an indigo plant that produced an excellent dye. She gave some of her seeds to neighbors and friends. Within a few years, South Carolina planters were selling one million pounds of indigo a year to clothmakers in Europe.

Make It Relevant **Why is it important to work hard at whatever task you have?**

Cash Crops

Seaports like Charles Town were important to the economy of the Southern Colonies. Plantations produced tons of cash crops each year, and those crops needed to be shipped to markets in England and the West Indies to be sold.

Adapting to the Climate

Plantations in different colonies grew different crops. In Maryland, Virginia, and northern North Carolina, tobacco was the main cash crop. Growing tobacco required many workers and a lot of land. After about seven years, tobacco plants would use up all the nutrients in the soil. As a result, farmers had to clear more land.

In southern North Carolina, South Carolina, and Georgia, the climate was too warm and wet for tobacco to grow well. Many farmers and plantation owners began growing rice. In fact, rice became such a major cash crop in South Carolina that it was often called Carolina gold.

On drier land, rice did not grow well. Here, farmers found they could grow indigo plants. These plants produced a blue dye called **indigo**, which was used in the clothmaking process.

Indigo became an important cash crop after **Eliza Lucas Pinckney** experimented with the plant. By the 1740s, indigo was a major cash crop throughout South Carolina.

READING CHECK ☼SUMMARIZE

What cash crops were grown in the Southern Colonies?

Chapter 7 ▪ 269

The Economy Grows

Plantations were largely self-sufficient, but they depended on merchants and others for some goods and services. Traders and merchants depended on plantations for cash crops and other raw materials. Depending on one another for economic resources is called **interdependence**.

Exporting Goods

As plantations got larger, more cash crops were exported. The owners of large plantations often sold their crops through a broker. A **broker** is a person who is paid to buy and sell for someone else. Brokers took the crops to market to sell and bought the goods the planters wanted.

Location affected how well plantations did. The most successful plantations were on rivers or near ports, which made it easier to ship crops.

Location affected the growth of cities, too. By the mid-1700s, towns along the southern Atlantic coast, such as Norfolk and Savannah, had grown into large cities.

Baltimore, Maryland, was founded in 1729 on the Patapsco River, which flows into Chesapeake Bay. Baltimore exported large amounts of grain and tobacco. As more goods were exported, the demand for new ships grew. Before long, the city of Baltimore became a major center for shipbuilding. Over time, shipbuilders developed the Baltimore clipper. It was one of the world's fastest sailing ships.

Other Industries

Although farming was the most important part of the Southern economy, the region had other industries. Its forests were important natural resources. Forests helped **Wilmington**, North Carolina,

▶ BALTIMORE was founded in 1729. It quickly grew into a busy port city.

▶ **SHIPPING** Large wooden barrels were used to ship everything from tobacco to rice.

become an important shipping center for forest goods. Colonists there built saw-mills and also made naval stores used in building and repairing ships.

READING CHECK ○**SUMMARIZE**
Why were forests an important resource of the Southern Colonies?

Summary

The Southern Colonies had an inter-dependent economy. Enslaved people and other workers produced cash crops and naval stores. Merchants and traders shipped these products to markets.

REVIEW

1. **WHAT TO KNOW** How did people in the Southern Colonies use natural resources to earn a living?

2. **VOCABULARY** What parts of the word **interdependence** help you remember what it means?

3. **GEOGRAPHY** In what colony was Baltimore located?

4. **CRITICAL THINKING** How did a farm's or a plantation's location affect the kind of crops that were grown?

5. **MAKE A TABLE** Make a two-column table. List the Southern Colonies in the first column and the crops grown in each colony in the second column.

6. **SUMMARIZE** On a separate sheet of paper, complete this graphic organizer.

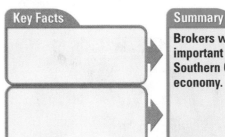

Key Facts		Summary
	→	Brokers were an important part of the Southern Colonies' economy.
	→	

FIELD TRIP

READ ABOUT

Colonial Williamsburg is the restored and rebuilt capital of eighteenth-century Virginia. The town is a living-history museum where you can experience the sights, sounds, and smells of colonial life. You can talk with people in historical costumes who stroll the streets or work in their shops. Guides bring history to life by portraying actual citizens who lived in Williamsburg in the 1700s. In Colonial Williamsburg, history is more than just names and dates. It is the story of people just like you who lived in another time.

FIND

VIRGINIA

Colonial Williamsburg

—Colonial—
Williamsburg

HISTORICAL REENACTORS help create a sense of what life in colonial Williamsburg might have been like.

Reenactors play traditional musical instruments.

Williamsburg has many examples of colonial architecture.

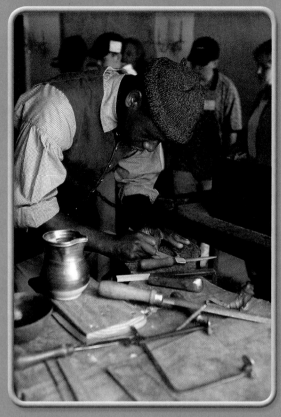

This reenactor works as a carpenter using traditional tools.

This apothecary shop sells medicine.

This shop is used to make barrels, which had many uses in colonial times.

A VIRTUAL TOUR

GO ONLINE For more resources, go to www.harcourtschool.com

1632
Lord Baltimore
founds the
Maryland
Colony

Visual Summary

Summarize the Chapter

(Focus Skill) **Summarize** Complete this graphic organizer to show that
you can summarize facts about the Southern Colonies.

Key Facts

As the South grew, conflicts
arose between settlers and
Native Americans.

Many Africans were brought
to southern plantations as
enslaved workers.

The economy depended on
cash crops grown on
plantations.

Summary

Vocabulary

**Identify the term from the word bank that
correctly matches each definition.**

1. land beyond settled areas

2. a person who buys and sells for
   another person

3. a written plan of government

4. a person who owes money

5. a plant that produces a blue dye

Word Bank

constitution p. 255   indigo p. 269

debtor p. 256   broker p. 270

backcountry p. 257

1700

1712
The Carolina Colony is split into North Carolina and South Carolina

1729
The city of Baltimore, Maryland, is founded

1750

1733
James Oglethorpe establishes Georgia, the last of the 13 colonies

 Time Line

Use the chapter summary time line above to answer these questions.

6. In what year was the Carolina Colony split into two colonies?

7. When was the last of the 13 colonies founded?

 Facts and Main Ideas

Answer these questions.

8. How did the government of the Maryland Colony protect religious freedoms?

9. What led to conflicts between colonists and Native Americans?

10. How did the economy of the Southern Colonies depend on enslaved Africans?

11. Why was Fort Mose important?

Write the letter of the best choice.

12. What was the main cash crop in Virginia, Maryland, and northern North Carolina?
    A rice
    B tobacco
    C indigo
    D wheat

13. Which city was an important shipbuilding center?
    A Jamestown, Virginia
    B Baltimore, Maryland
    C New Bern, North Carolina
    D Savannah, Georgia

 Critical Thinking

14. Why were waterways in the Southern Colonies especially important?

15. How did the location of a farm in the Southern Colonies affect the kind of crops grown there?

16. How did enslaved Africans resist slavery? Why would it be important to come up with creative ways to work against slavery?

 Skills

Compare Maps of Different Scales

17. Look at the maps of the Maryland Colony on pages 260 and 261. Which map would you use to find the distance in miles between Baltimore and Frederick? Explain.

writing

Write a Report Enslaved Africans were able to keep their culture while living under very hard conditions. Write a report with facts and details that tells how they were able to do this.

Write a Narrative Imagine that your family has settled in the backcountry of the Southern Colonies. Write a story about your new life on the frontier. Be sure to describe the land and any challenges you might face.

Chapter 7 ■ 275

Fun with Social Studies

> The winters are cold,
> But that's okay.
> We can worship and
> live in our Puritan
> way.

> Long for peace?
> We can show it.
> We're Quakers
> and proud that
> you know it!

Bound for the Colonies

Can you guess from their songs which colonists are going to Georgia? to Massachusetts? to Pennsylvania?

> Couldn't pay what I owe. Woe is me! Had a chance to get out. Now I'm free! Gonna start a new life 'cross the sea!

It's Only Fair

Crack the code and answer the riddle.

abc VOCABULARY

This is James. He's learning a skill as an **APPR5N8265** to Mr. Toliver.

This is Inky, James's cat. She found a **R5F4G5** under a bed after she turned over a bottle of ink.

Mr. Toliver is angry. He wants to **5XP5L** Inky from the shop.

Mrs. Toliver reminded her husband that he had forgotten to put the cap on the ink bottle. "If Inky were a human, she would be found innocent in a **8R2AL BY 74RY**."

Adopt-a-Pet

Find the perfect pet for each person.

THIS OUTSPOKEN PUP SPEAKS HIS MIND.

OWNER MUST DO THE SAME.

LOVING KITTEN

FREE TO A GOOD HOME.

ENJOYS TRAVELING AND LISTENING TO SPEECHES.

Busy, multi-talented owner a must for this intelligent bird.

Laughs at jokes and wise sayings. Goes to bed early.

Benjamin Franklin

Olaudah Equiano

Anne Hutchinson

Online Adventures

GO ONLINE

Can you succeed at Eco's next challenge? In this online game, you must find, gather, or make everything you need to help a family of English colonists settle in a self-sufficient New England village. Along the way, you will have to solve problems and find clues so you can build a house, make food, and organize games for the kids. Play now at **www.harcourtschool.com/ss1**

Review and Test Prep

💡 THE BIG IDEA

Commonality and Diversity The 13 English colonies were founded in different regions of North America and for different reasons.

Reading Comprehension and Vocabulary

The Thirteen Colonies

Thousands of English Puritans arrived in New England in the 1630s. Their religious beliefs shaped their lives. At town meetings, people voted on laws and elected leaders. These meetings taught the colonists to govern themselves.

The Middle Colonies—New York, New Jersey, Pennsylvania, and Delaware—were south of New England. People from many parts of the world settled there. Fertile land, a mild climate, rivers, and ports helped bring prosperity to the region.

Maryland, Virginia, North Carolina, South Carolina, and Georgia made up the Southern Colonies. Many enslaved Africans lived in this region. Most settlers owned small farms. A few lived on plantations and owned many enslaved workers. Southerners grew cash crops. Like other colonists, they sold these exports to England.

Early settlers often cooperated with Native Americans, but growing settlements led to conflicts. Many Native Americans were killed or moved west.

Use the summary above to answer these questions.

1. What did New England colonists do at town meetings?
   A elected leaders
   B raised barns
   C built schools
   D met with Native Americans

2. What does the word prosperity mean?
   A trade
   B a larger population
   C economic success
   D agriculture

3. Where did most enslaved Africans live in North America?
   A in the New England Colonies
   B in the Middle Colonies
   C in Spanish Florida
   D in the Southern Colonies

4. What is an export?
   A a good only made in New England
   B a good stolen from another country
   C a good that is never sold
   D a good that leaves a country

Answer these questions.

5. What Puritan leader helped found the colony of Massachusetts?

6. Why did the English want to take control of New Amsterdam?

7. Who were the Quakers?

8. What was the largest city in the 13 colonies?

9. In what ways did enslaved Africans respond to their condition?

Write the letter of the best choice.

10. Who founded Providence, which became part of the Rhode Island Colony?
    A Anne Hutchinson
    B Roger Williams
    C Thomas Hooker
    D David Thomson

11. Which region was called the "breadbasket" colonies?
    A New England
    B the Middle Colonies
    C the Southern Colonies
    D the backcountry

12. Who founded the Georgia Colony?
    A William Penn
    B John Winthrop
    C King George II
    D James Oglethorpe

13. In which of the Southern Colonies did Africans most likely arrive first?
    A Georgia
    B North Carolina
    C South Carolina
    D Virginia

14. Why might farming be easier in the Middle Colonies than in New England?

15. What role did religion play in the founding of Maryland and Pennsylvania? How was it different than in New England?

16. **Make It Relevant** How does the founding of the 13 English colonies and their early governments affect Americans today?

Compare Maps of Different Scales

Use the maps below to answer the question.

17. Which map would you use to find the distance between Baltimore and Annapolis? Explain.

Map A: Maryland Colony

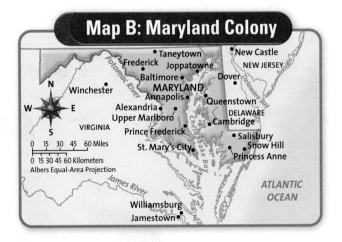

Map B: Maryland Colony

Unit 3 Activities

Show What You Know

Unit Writing Activity

Write a Narrative Imagine that you are a new settler in one of the colonies. Write a story about life in your colony.

- Explain the role of religion and government in your society.
- Explain how colonists earn a living.
- Make sure your narrative has a story.

Unit Project

A Colonial Fair Plan a display for a fair about daily life in one of the New England, Middle, or Southern Colonies.

- Decide how you will show what life was like there.
- Your display should focus on how people lived, governed, worshipped, and worked.

Read More

- *Growing up in a New World* by Brandon Marie Miller. Learner Publications.

- *Colonial Home* by Bobbie Kalman and John Crossingham. Crabtree Publishing Company.

- *American Voices from Colonial Life* by Rebecca Stefoff. Benchmark Books.

 For more resources, go to
www.harcourtschool.com/ss1

The American Revolution

Start with the Standards

OHIO SOCIAL STUDIES CONTENT STANDARDS

History 5.1, 5.5, 5.6

People in Societies 5.1A

Government 5.3

Social Studies Skills 5.1A, 5.1B, 5.2, 5.3, 5.8

The Big Idea

Freedom
Freedom was so important to the colonists that they were willing to suffer terrible hardships and years of war to win it.

What to Know

✓ What disagreements led to the American Revolution?

✓ Which people and groups impacted the American Revolution?

✓ What were the major events and battles of the American Revolution?

✓ How did the American Revolution affect United States history?

Ohio in the American Revolution

OHIO CONNECTION

DID YOU KNOW?

Fort Laurens was named for Henry Laurens, who was president of the Continental Congress.

In the late 1700s, many colonists grew unhappy with British rule. They did not want to pay more taxes. They also wanted to settle where they pleased. Many colonists began to call for independence. The American Revolution began in 1775.

No major Revolutionary War battles were fought in Ohio. However, the British and the Americans both tried to gain the support of the Native Americans in the area. Most tribes sided with Britain. The Native Americans were afraid that an American victory would mean that more settlers would come to Ohio. In 1778, American soldiers built Fort Laurens near what is now Bolivar, Ohio, to defend the area. Native Americans and British soldiers attacked the fort several times without success.

Fort Laurens

OHIO HISTORICAL MARKER

THE 1782 SANDUSKY CAMPAIGN

(Continued from other side)

At the twilight of the American Revolutionary War, British forces hired American Indians to conduct attacks on pioneers living along the Ohio and Pennsylvania border. In response the 13th Virginia Regiment, an over 400-man mounted unit formed by General William Irvine, was led by Colonel William Crawford to destroy the Sandusky towns of the Wyandots and Delawares. This volunteer army departed Mingo Bottom on May 25, 1782, and headed west into the Ohio country. On June 4 they met an Indian force at an area called "Battle Island," located between Carey and Upper Sandusky. The Americans held the field, but withdrew when the British reinforced the Indians with Butler's Rangers and Shawnee Indians. Crawford was ultimately captured, tortured and killed by Delaware Indians.

WYANDOT COUNTY HISTORICAL SOCIETY
PATRIOTIC CITIZENS OF WYANDOT COUNTY
AND
1996   THE OHIO HISTORICAL SOCIETY   I-88

The British urged Native Americans to attack settlers in the Ohio Valley. In 1782, settlers killed about 100 Delaware at Gnadenhutten. In return, members of the Delaware and Wyandot tribes killed Colonel William Crawford at the Battle of the Sandusky. In the same year, George Rogers Clark, hoping to prevent any further attacks, led his soldiers against the Shawnee Indians. Clark won this fight, called the Battle of Piqua.

The United States won the Revolutionary War in 1783. After the war, more settlers began to move to the Ohio Country. Conflicts between the settlers and the Native Americans continued to take place.

➤ Colonel William Crawford

Revolutionary War reenactment at Fort Laurens

OHIO TEST PREP ✓

1 Who did most Native American tribes side with?
A. the British
B. the Americans
C. no one

2 Who won the Battle of Piqua?
A. Native Americans
B. American soldiers
C. British soldiers

3 Why did American soldiers build Fort Laurens?
A. so they could trade with Native Americans
B. so that more people would settle in Ohio
C. to defend Ohio lands

4 What role did Ohio play in the American Revolution?

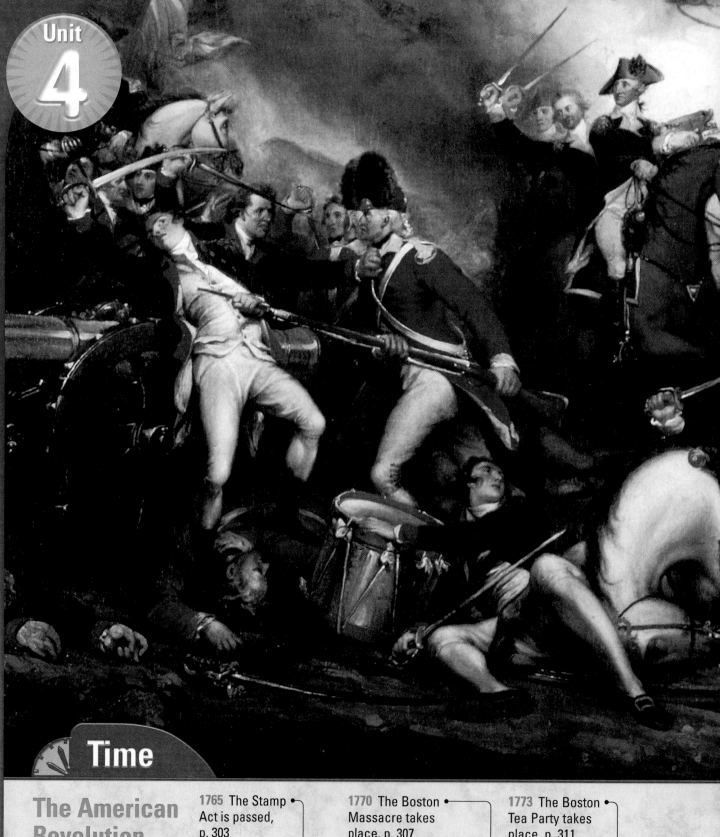

Time

The American Revolution

1765 The Stamp Act is passed, p. 303

1770 The Boston Massacre takes place, p. 307

1773 The Boston Tea Party takes place, p. 311

1760

1770

At the Same Time

 1762 Catherine the Great becomes ruler of Russia

 1769 English inventor James Watt builds a steam engine

 1770 James Cook explores Australia

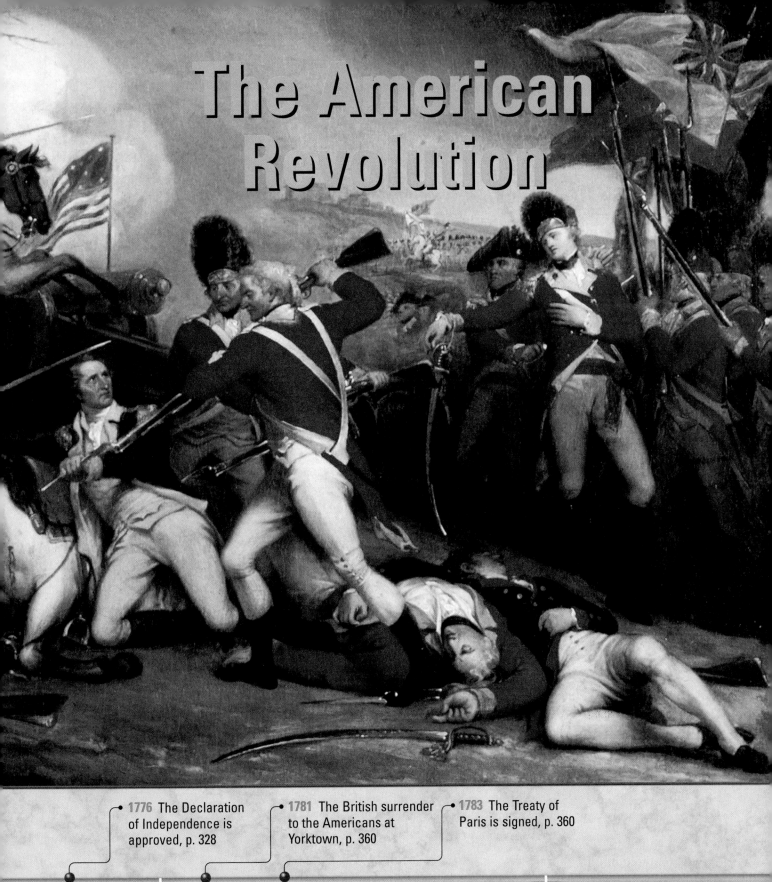

The American Revolution

1776 The Declaration of Independence is approved, p. 328

1781 The British surrender to the Americans at Yorktown, p. 360

1783 The Treaty of Paris is signed, p. 360

1780

1790

 1784 Britain takes control of lands in India

 1789 The French Revolution begins

People

Crispus Attucks
1725?–1770
- Killed by British soldiers at the Boston Massacre
- Often called the first person to be killed in the struggle for American freedom

Mercy Otis Warren
1728–1814
- Massachusetts patriot who wrote plays to protest British rule
- Wrote a history of the American Revolution

1725 ・ **1750** ・ **1775**

1725? • Crispus Attucks — 1770
1728 • Mercy Otis Warren
1732 • George Washington
1736 • Patrick Henry
1742 • Thayendanegea
1743 • Thomas Jefferson
1746 • Bernardo de Gálvez — 1786
1754? • Mary Ludwig Hayes McCauley

Thayendanegea
1742–1807
- Mohawk leader who later took the name Joseph Brant
- Helped the British during the American Revolution

Thomas Jefferson
1743–1826
- Chief writer of the Declaration of Independence
- Served as the third President of the United States

282 ■ Unit 4

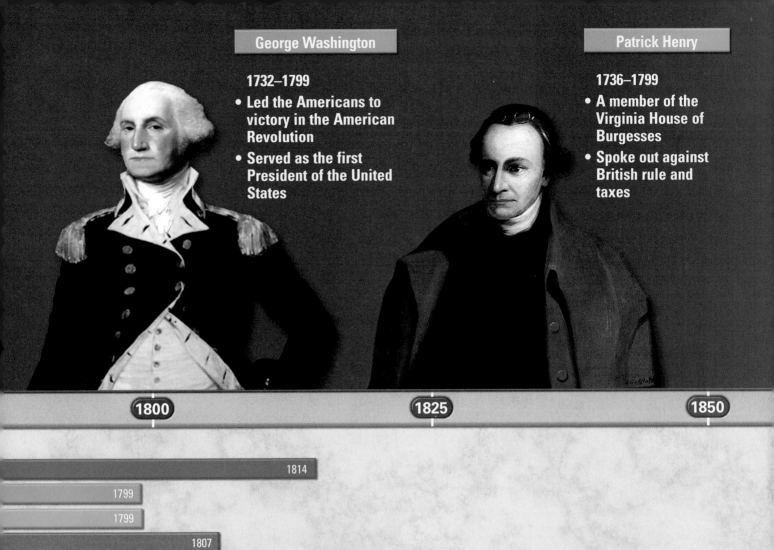

George Washington

1732–1799
- Led the Americans to victory in the American Revolution
- Served as the first President of the United States

Patrick Henry

1736–1799
- A member of the Virginia House of Burgesses
- Spoke out against British rule and taxes

1800   1825   1850

1814

1799

1799

1807

1826

1832

Bernardo de Gálvez

1746–1786
- Governor of Spanish Louisiana
- Helped the Americans during the Revolutionary War

Mary Ludwig Hays McCauley

1754?–1832
- Earned the nickname Molly Pitcher by carrying water to troops during the Battle of Monmouth
- Fired cannons during the battle after her husband was wounded

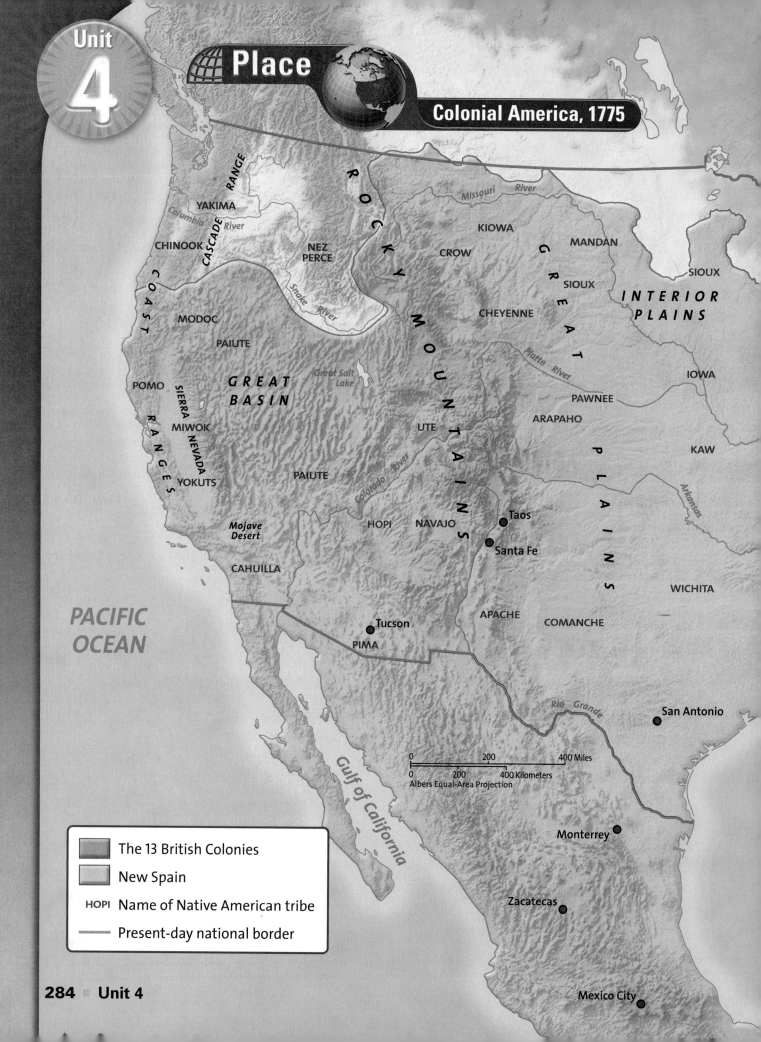

Place

Colonial America, 1775

ROCKY MOUNTAINS

CASCADE RANGE

COAST RANGES

SIERRA NEVADA

GREAT BASIN

GREAT PLAINS

INTERIOR PLAINS

PACIFIC OCEAN

Gulf of California

Columbia River

Snake River

Missouri River

Platte River

Colorado River

Arkansas River

Rio Grande

Great Salt Lake

Mojave Desert

YAKIMA

CHINOOK

MODOC

PAIUTE

POMO

MIWOK

YOKUTS

PAIUTE

CAHUILLA

PIMA

HOPI

NAVAJO

APACHE

NEZ PERCE

CROW

KIOWA

MANDAN

SIOUX

CHEYENNE

SIOUX

UTE

ARAPAHO

PAWNEE

IOWA

KAW

COMANCHE

WICHITA

Taos

Santa Fe

Tucson

San Antonio

Monterrey

Zacatecas

Mexico City

0   200   400 Miles
0   200   400 Kilometers
Albers Equal-Area Projection

The 13 British Colonies

New Spain

HOPI Name of Native American tribe

Present-day national border

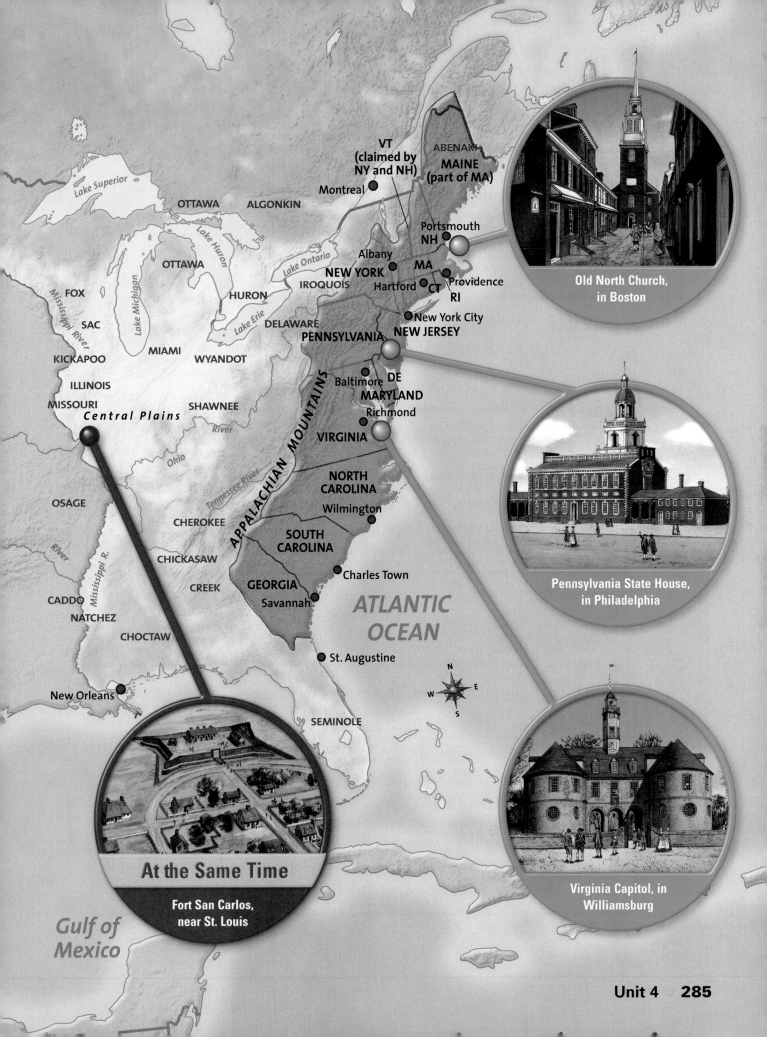

Lake Superior

OTTAWA ALGONKIN

OTTAWA

FOX

Lake Huron

Lake Michigan

SAC

Mississippi River

MIAMI

HURON

Lake Ontario

Lake Erie

KICKAPOO

WYANDOT

IROQUOIS

ILLINOIS

MISSOURI

Central Plains

SHAWNEE

Ohio

River

OSAGE

Tennessee River

River

Mississippi R.

CADDO

NATCHEZ

CHOCTAW

New Orleans

CHEROKEE

CHICKASAW

CREEK

VT
(claimed by
NY and NH)

ABENAKI

MAINE
(part of MA)

Montreal

Portsmouth
NH

Albany

NEW YORK

MA

Hartford

CT

Providence
RI

New York City

DELAWARE

PENNSYLVANIA

NEW JERSEY

Baltimore

DE

MARYLAND

Richmond

APPALACHIAN MOUNTAINS

VIRGINIA

NORTH
CAROLINA

Wilmington

SOUTH
CAROLINA

GEORGIA

Charles Town

Savannah

ATLANTIC
OCEAN

St. Augustine

N
W   E
S

SEMINOLE

Old North Church,
in Boston

Pennsylvania State House,
in Philadelphia

Virginia Capitol, in
Williamsburg

At the Same Time

Fort San Carlos,
near St. Louis

Gulf of
Mexico

Reading Social Studies

Cause and Effect

Why It Matters Understanding cause and effect can help
you see why events happen.

❯ LEARN

A **cause** is an action or event that makes something else happen. An **effect** is
what happens as the result of that action or event.

Cause	Effect
An event or action	What happens

- Words and phrases such as *because, since, so, for these reasons*, and *as a
result* are clues to cause and effect.
- Sometimes the effect may be stated before the cause.

❯ PRACTICE

**Read the paragraphs that follow. Then find causes and effects in the second
paragraph.**

In the mid-1600s, people began to leave the Massachusetts Bay Colony and start
their own settlements. Some left because of religious reasons. Others left
to find better economic opportunities.

Effect

Cause

By the mid-1700s, colonists no longer had to buy goods from Europe to live.
They had their own cities and businesses. Also, more colonists had been born in
the colonies. It was the only home they knew. For these reasons, the colonists
began to depend less on England.

286 ▪ Unit 4

Read the paragraphs, and answer the questions.

From Strangers to Neighbors

In 1765, John Rutledge traveled from his home in South Carolina to New York. He called it his first trip to a foreign country. That says a lot about how the colonists viewed one another.

The colonies had been founded at different times and for different reasons. Each had its own mix of people. Each had its own economy and its own government. As a result, the colonies really were like different countries.

Things were about to change, though. John Rutledge was going to New York City to meet with representatives from ten of the colonies. They were to discuss a new tax law. The colonists thought that the tax was unfair. They wanted to figure out what to do about it.

While in New York, Rutledge met with Sir William Johnson. Johnson was a wealthy English merchant who was friendly with the Iroquois. Johnson told Rutledge about how members of the Iroquois League worked together to solve problems.

Rutledge told other colonists about the Iroquois League. Like the Iroquois, the colonists soon began to work together. They started seeing each other not as foreigners but as neighbors.

Focus Skill Cause and Effect

1. **What caused John Rutledge to travel to New York City?**
2. **Why were the colonies like different countries?**
3. **How did learning about the Iroquois League affect colonists?**

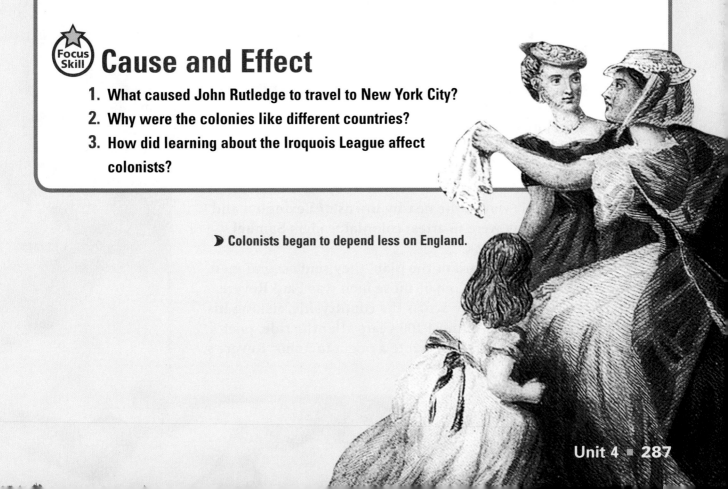

▶ Colonists began to depend less on England.

Paul Revere's Ride

THE LANDLORD'S TALE

BY HENRY WADSWORTH LONGFELLOW
ILLUSTRATED BY CHARLES SANTORE

On the night of April 18, 1775, British troops left Boston. They were on their way to the nearby towns of Lexington and Concord. There they were to arrest colonial leaders Samuel Adams and John Hancock.

When the colonists heard of the plan, they sent several men to warn the townspeople. One of those men was Paul Revere, a Boston silversmith. He rode across the countryside, risking his life to deliver the news. Almost 100 years after the ride, poet Henry Wadsworth Longfellow wrote a poem to honor Revere's brave deed.

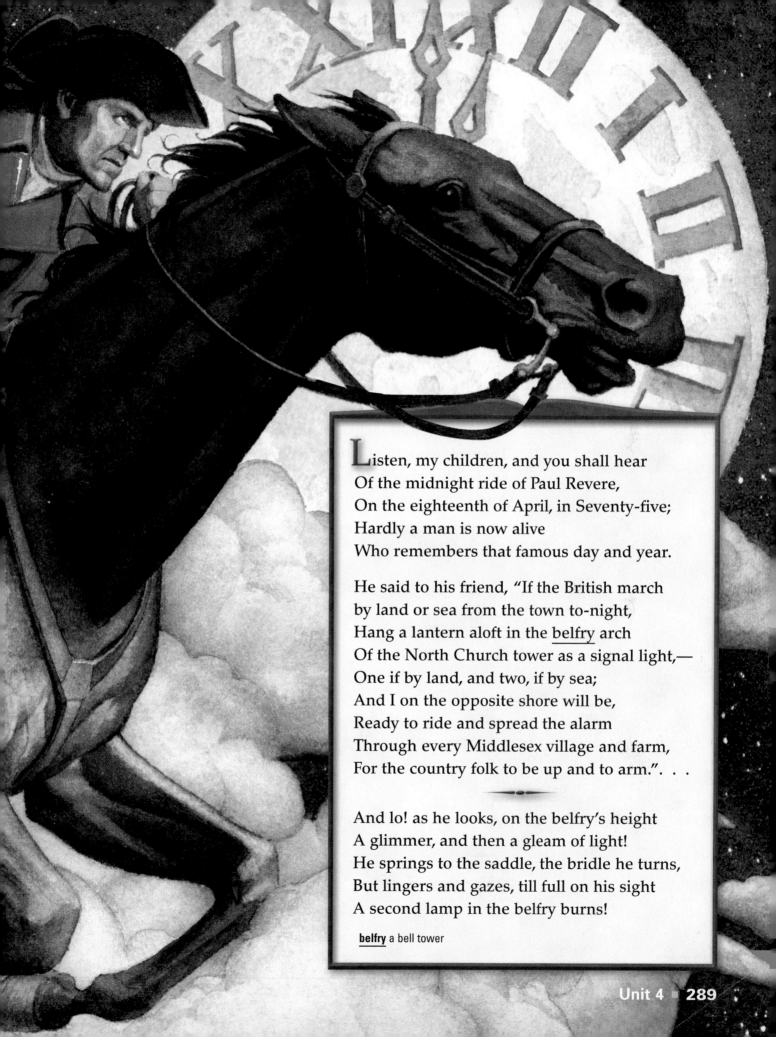

Listen, my children, and you shall hear
Of the midnight ride of Paul Revere,
On the eighteenth of April, in Seventy-five;
Hardly a man is now alive
Who remembers that famous day and year.

He said to his friend, "If the British march
by land or sea from the town to-night,
Hang a lantern aloft in the <u>belfry</u> arch
Of the North Church tower as a signal light,—
One if by land, and two, if by sea;
And I on the opposite shore will be,
Ready to ride and spread the alarm
Through every Middlesex village and farm,
For the country folk to be up and to arm.". . .

And lo! as he looks, on the belfry's height
A glimmer, and then a gleam of light!
He springs to the saddle, the bridle he turns,
But lingers and gazes, till full on his sight
A second lamp in the belfry burns!

belfry a bell tower

A hurry of hoofs in a village street,
A shape in the moonlight, a bulk in the dark,
And beneath, from the pebbles, in passing, a spark
Struck out by a steed flying fearless and fleet;

That was all! And yet, through the gloom and the light,
The fate of a nation was riding that night;
And the spark struck out by that steed, in his flight,
Kindled the land into flame with its heat. . . .

You know the rest. In the books you have read
How the British Regulars fired and fled,—
How the farmers gave them ball for ball,
From behind each fence and farm-yard wall,
Chasing the red-coats down the lane,
Then crossing the fields to emerge again
Under the trees at the turn of the road,
And only pausing to fire and load.

So through the night rode Paul Revere;
And so through the night went his cry of alarm
To every Middlesex village and farm,—
A cry of defiance, and not of fear,
A voice in the darkness, a knock at the door,
And a word that shall echo forevermore!
For, borne on the night-wind of the Past,
Through all our history, to the last,
In the hour of darkness and peril and need,
The people will waken and listen to hear
The hurrying hoof-beats of that steed,
And the midnight message of Paul Revere.

Response Corner

1. **(Focus Skill) Cause And Effect** What signal caused Paul Revere to begin his ride?

2. **Make It Relevant** Think about how people today receive news. Why is it important for people to know about current events?

STUDY SKILLS

CONNECT IDEAS

Graphic organizers can help you connect ideas.

- On a concept map, the main idea is written in the center bubble.

- Facts and details are written in surrounding bubbles.

Stamp Act Congress

Boston Tea Party

Reactions to Taxes

Events Leading to the American Revolution

Early Conflicts

PREVIEW VOCABULARY

boycott p. 304   **blockade** p. 312   **commander in chief** p. 319

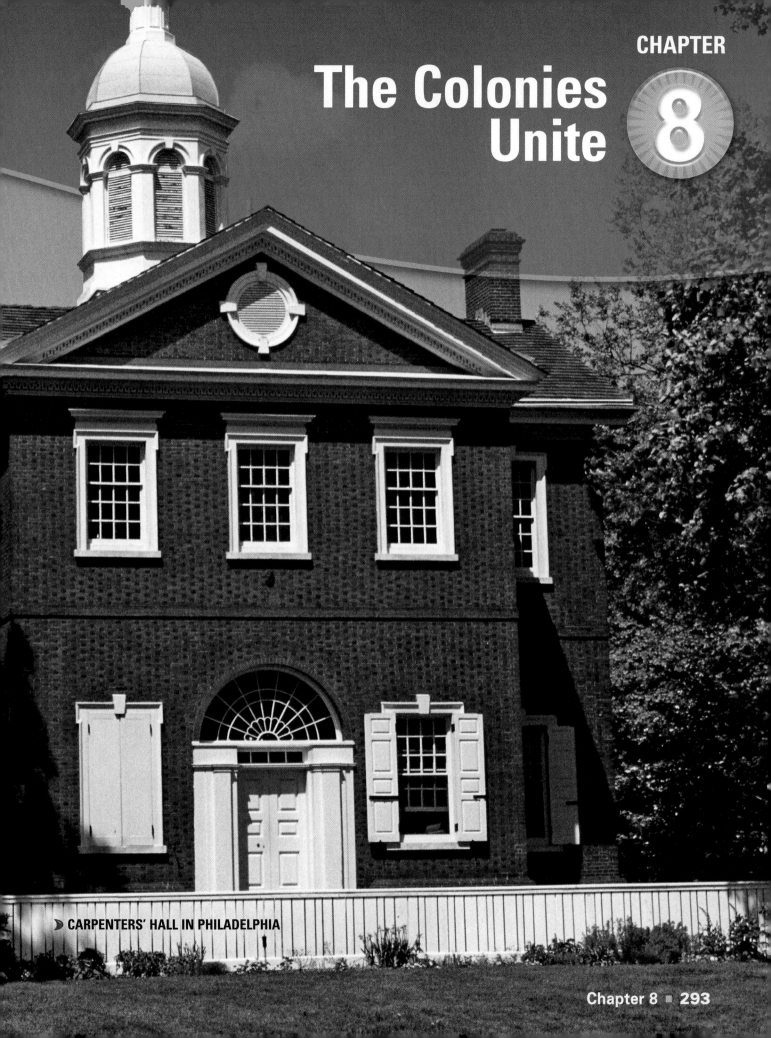

The Colonies Unite

CARPENTERS' HALL IN PHILADELPHIA

Time

1750   1790

1754
The Battle of
Fort Necessity
is fought

1763
The French and
Indian War ends

1764
Britain passes the
Sugar Act

WHAT TO KNOW
How did the French
and Indian War change
relations between the
colonists and Britain?

VOCABULARY
alliance p. 296
delegate p. 296
Parliament p. 297
proclamation p. 298
budget p. 299

PEOPLE
Benjamin Franklin
George Washington
King George III

PLACES
Fort Necessity
Ohio Valley
Albany

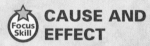

**CAUSE AND
EFFECT**

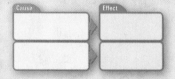

Fighting for Control

YOU ARE THERE It's bright and sunny at **Fort Necessity**, but the Pennsylvania woods around you look dark and dangerous. Any minute now, your small fort may be attacked. You're scared, but you will fight to keep France from getting control of this land.

There is a shout as one of the other soldiers in your group runs into sight. He is out of breath and looks shocked. "It's the French!" he yells. "We're surrounded!"

Conflicting Claims

Spain, France, and Britain, as England became known, were trying to keep control of their lands in North America. Spain claimed mostly the southwestern lands and Florida. France claimed lands to the north and in the middle of what is now the United States. Most of the land that Britain claimed was along the Atlantic coast.

The Ohio Valley

Both Britain and France claimed the **Ohio Valley**. This region stretches along the Ohio River from the Appalachians to the Mississippi River. The British saw the Ohio Valley as an area for trade and growth. To the French, it connected their lands in New France and Louisiana.

By 1750, France sent soldiers to the Ohio Valley to drive out the British. The French also built forts near the eastern end of the valley. The British saw this as an act of war and decided to fight back.

READING CHECK Ŏ **CAUSE AND EFFECT**
What caused the British and the French to compete for the Ohio Valley?

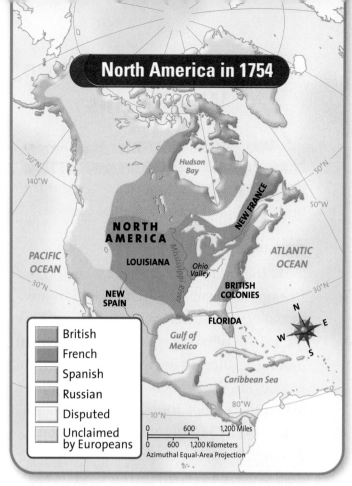

North America in 1754

British
French
Spanish
Russian
Disputed
Unclaimed by Europeans

0   600   1,200 Miles
0   600   1,200 Kilometers
Azimuthal Equal-Area Projection

MAP SKILL **REGIONS** Which two groups of Europeans claimed land east and west of the Ohio Valley?

FAST FACT

During his career as a soldier, George Washington won many battles. The battle fought at Fort Necessity (below) was the only battle in which he ever surrendered.

The French and Indian War Begins

The French and Indian War began in North America in 1754 and later spread to Europe. Native Americans fought for both sides, but mostly for the French.

Alliances and Fighting

By the mid-1700s, both France and Britain had formed alliances with many of the Native American tribes in the Ohio Valley. An **alliance** is a formal agreement among groups or individuals. Once fighting began, the French and the British asked their allies for help.

In June 1754, colonial leaders met at **Albany**, New York, to talk about how to deal with the French forces. Seven colonies sent **delegates**, or representatives, including **Benjamin Franklin**.

Franklin said that the colonies should unite to fight the French. His idea, which became known as the Albany Plan of Union, was not approved. The colonies were not yet willing to fight as one country.

A month earlier, the British governor of Virginia sent 150 soldiers to take the Ohio Valley from the French. **George Washington**, then only 21 years old, led the Virginians. On their way to a French fort, the Virginians fought some French soldiers. Afterward, the Virginians quickly built Fort Necessity. On July 3, 1754, the French and their Native American allies attacked. Outnumbered, the Virginians gave up. This battle turned out to be the start of the French and Indian War.

READING CHECK SUMMARIZE
What became known as the Albany Plan?

> **FIGHTING THE WAR** Red uniform jackets made the British easy targets.

The War Expands

The colonists knew they needed help if they were to win the war. **Parliament**, the lawmaking branch of the British government, sent an army to help fight the French and their Native American allies. General Edward Braddock led the British.

Early Defeats for Britain

In April 1755, Braddock and more than 1,800 troops marched to attack the French at Fort Duquesne. Braddock brought George Washington along as an adviser. Washington later described how the soldiers looked in their bright, colorful uniforms—British red and colonial blue—marching through the deep green forest.

The British soldiers had been trained to fight in open fields. They were surprised to find that the French fought like their Native American allies, from behind trees and large rocks. This made the British soldiers easy targets.

The early battles did not go well for the British, and Braddock was killed in the fighting. In a letter home to his family, Washington wrote,

> **66** I had four bullets through my coat and two horses shot under me, and yet escaped unhurt. **99**

Britain Wins Control

Britain sent more troops and supplies to the colonies, and the war slowly turned in its favor. British soldiers captured Fort Duquesne and several other French forts. They also defeated the French at Quebec and Montreal.

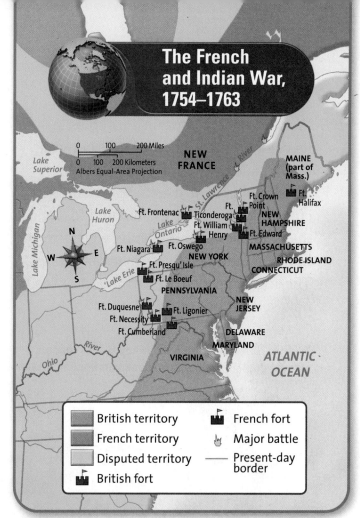

The French and Indian War, 1754–1763

Legend:
- British territory
- French territory
- Disputed territory
- British fort
- French fort
- Major battle
- Present-day border

MAP SKILL **LOCATION** At which French fort in present-day Pennsylvania was a major battle fought?

In 1756, the French and the British started fighting battles in Europe, too. Spain joined France in the fight against Britain. The British had a stronger navy and defeated the Spanish in 1762. To make up for Spain's losses, France gave Spain most of Louisiana.

The Treaty of Paris

The French and Indian War ended in 1763. The Treaty of Paris gave Britain most of Canada, all French lands east of the Mississippi River, and Spanish Florida. France lost nearly all of its lands in North America.

READING CHECK **CAUSE AND EFFECT**
What was the effect of the Treaty of Paris?

More Troubles

The end of the French and Indian War did not end Britain's troubles in its colonies. Because the lands between the Appalachian Mountains and the Mississippi River were now under British control, many colonists wanted to settle there. However, these lands were already home to many Native American groups. These groups were determined to keep new settlers out of their lands.

> ❯ **FRONTIER SETTLEMENTS** Many British leaders blamed Pontiac (below) for attacks on frontier settlers.

In 1763, an Ottawa chief named Pontiac united groups along the Mississippi River. Together, the Native Americans captured some of the British forts. They also attacked the colonists' settlements around those forts.

The Proclamation of 1763

Britain's **King George III** tried to end the fighting. In 1763, the king made a **proclamation**, or public announcement. The Proclamation of 1763 said that all lands west of the Appalachian Mountains belonged to Native Americans. White settlers in those lands were told to leave.

Most colonists ignored the king's proclamation. They believed they had fought

the war to keep the French from blocking their settlement of the western frontier. They did not like the British government telling them to stay out of those lands. As a result, fighting between the Native Americans and the settlers continued.

Paying for the War

Colonists were also angry about new taxes passed by Parliament. After the war ended, British leaders looked at their **budget**, or plan for spending money. They realized that Britain needed more money to pay off the cost of the war. They thought the colonists should help.

In 1764, Parliament passed the Sugar Act to raise money for Britain. This act taxed the sugar and molasses brought into the colonies from the West Indies.

The Sugar Act mostly hurt shipping businesses in the New England Colonies. Many merchants objected to the tax. Still, the British government kept taxing the sugar. Soon it would pass more taxes.

READING CHECK ☼ **CAUSE AND EFFECT**
Why did Parliament pass new taxes for the colonists?

Summary

Conflicting land claims in North America led to the French and Indian War. Britain defeated France in the war. After the war, Britain issued the Proclamation of 1763, but many colonists ignored it and kept moving west.

REVIEW

1. **WHAT TO KNOW** How did the French and Indian War change relations between the colonists and Britain?

2. **VOCABULARY** Use the term **alliance** in a sentence about the French and Indian War.

3. **HISTORY** What events caused the French and Indian War?

4. **CRITICAL THINKING** Why do you think French soldiers chose to fight in the same way as their Native American allies?

5. ✏ **WRITE A NEWSPAPER STORY** Imagine you are a news reporter in 1763. Write a story describing colonists' concerns about the Proclamation of 1763.

6. (Focus Skill) **CAUSE AND EFFECT** On a separate sheet of paper, copy and complete the graphic organizer below.

Cause	Effect
	The French attack troops at Fort Necessity.
The British decide colonists should help pay for the war.	

Compare Historical Maps

Why It Matters A historical map shows a place at a certain time in history. Comparing historical maps can help you learn how a place and its borders changed over time.

❯ LEARN

Follow these steps to compare the historical maps on page 301.

Step 1 Study the map key for each map. The colors show the areas claimed by Britain, France, Spain, and Russia.

Step 2 Look at Map B. It has a pattern of stripes called hatch lines. These hatch lines show areas of British land reserved for Native Americans.

Step 3 Find the thick blue line on Map B. It shows the border created by the Proclamation of 1763.

❯ PRACTICE

Use Maps A and B to answer these questions.

❶ Which country claimed Florida before the French and Indian War? after the war?

❷ Which map shows British lands reserved for Native Americans?

❸ Which country claimed Louisiana after the French and Indian War?

❹ Did Spain gain or lose land as a result of the French and Indian War?

❯ APPLY

Use the maps to write about the changes in land claims caused by the French and Indian War. Share your work with a classmate.

❯ COLONIAL POWDER HORN

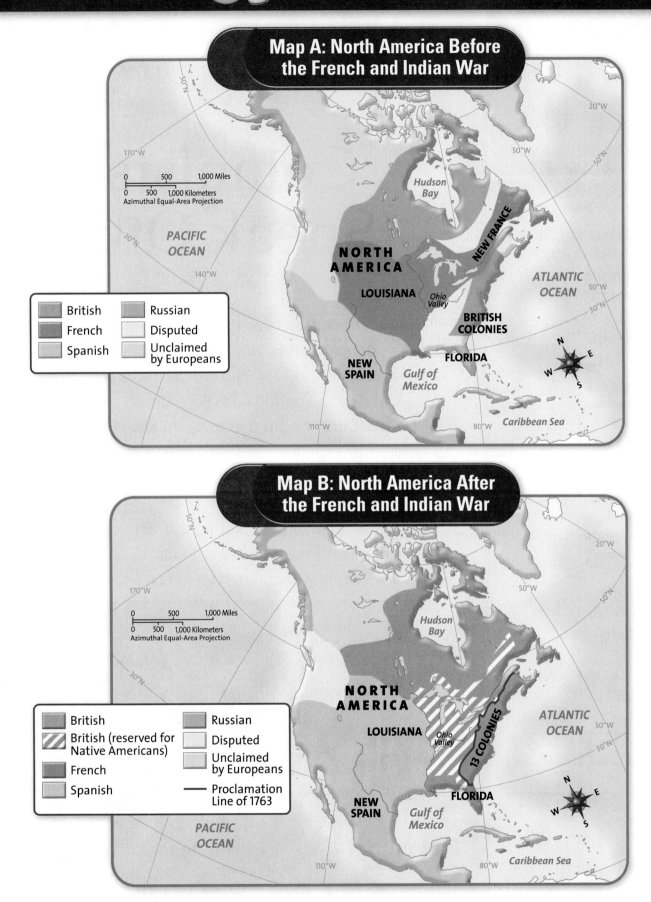

Map A: North America Before the French and Indian War

0   500   1,000 Miles
0   500   1,000 Kilometers
Azimuthal Equal-Area Projection

PACIFIC OCEAN

NORTH AMERICA

Hudson Bay

NEW FRANCE

LOUISIANA

Ohio Valley

BRITISH COLONIES

ATLANTIC OCEAN

NEW SPAIN

FLORIDA

Gulf of Mexico

Caribbean Sea

British
French
Spanish
Russian
Disputed
Unclaimed by Europeans

Map B: North America After the French and Indian War

0   500   1,000 Miles
0   500   1,000 Kilometers
Azimuthal Equal-Area Projection

Hudson Bay

NORTH AMERICA

LOUISIANA

Ohio Valley

13 COLONIES

ATLANTIC OCEAN

NEW SPAIN

FLORIDA

Gulf of Mexico

PACIFIC OCEAN

Caribbean Sea

British
British (reserved for Native Americans)
French
Spanish
Russian
Disputed
Unclaimed by Europeans
Proclamation Line of 1763

Map and Globe Skills

Chapter 8 ■ 301

Time

1750 ———————————————————————— 1790

1765
Britain passes
the Stamp Act

1767
Britain creates
the Townshend Acts

1770
The Boston Massacre
takes place

WHAT TO KNOW
Why were colonists
angered by Britain's new
colonial tax laws?

VOCABULARY
representation p. 303
treason p. 303
congress p. 303
boycott p. 304
repeal p. 304
imperial policy p. 305
protest p. 305

PEOPLE
Benjamin Franklin
Mercy Otis Warren
Patrick Henry
Samuel Adams
Crispus Attucks
Paul Revere

PLACES
New York City
Boston

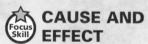

CAUSE AND EFFECT

Colonists Speak Out

YOU ARE THERE A hush falls over the British Parliament. **Benjamin Franklin** is about to speak out against Britain's tax law. The year is 1766, and you have traveled to London with Franklin.

"Do you think it right that the colonies should be protected by Britain and pay no part of the cost?" asks one member of Parliament.

"That is not the case," Franklin says. "The colonies raised, clothed, and paid, during the last year, near 25,000 men, and spent many millions."

Surely, you think, Parliament must take back the law.

▶ **THE BRITISH PARLIAMENT**

Stamp Act Cartoon

Background This 1765 drawing shows colonists in New Hampshire reacting to the Stamp Act.

The straw figure represents a tax collector.

The coffin represents the wish to see the tax die.

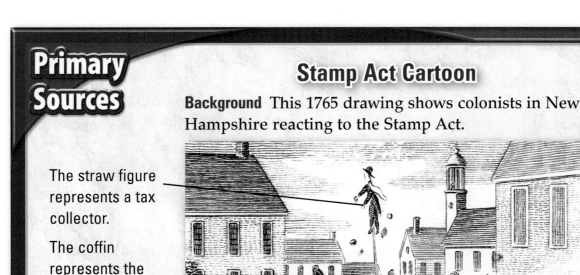

DBQ **Document-Based Question** What does this drawing tell you about how some colonists felt about the Stamp Act?

The Stamp Act

In 1765, Parliament approved another tax law. The Stamp Act put a tax on many paper items in the colonies. Newspapers, legal documents, and even playing cards had to have a special stamp on them to show that the tax had been paid.

No Taxation Without Representation

British leaders felt the tax was fair. Many colonists, however, were angry. They said Britain could not tax them because they had no **representation** in Parliament. No one was speaking or acting for them. **Mercy Otis Warren**, a Massachusetts writer, disagreed with the new tax. She began writing plays that accused British leaders of being greedy.

In Virginia, **Patrick Henry** told other members of the House of Burgesses that Parliament did not represent the colonies. Those who supported Parliament's actions shouted "Treason! Treason!" By accusing Henry of **treason**, they were saying he was guilty of working against his own government.

In October 1765, representatives from nine colonies met in **New York City** in what became known as the Stamp Act Congress. A **congress** is a formal meeting of representatives. There, colonial leaders spoke out against the Stamp Act. Soon people began to repeat these words—"no taxation without representation."

READING CHECK **CAUSE AND EFFECT**
Why were colonists angry about the Stamp Act?

Colonists Work Together

Many colonists tried to force Britain to take back the Stamp Act. Some wrote letters to Parliament. Some chose not to buy taxed goods. Others began to **boycott**, or refuse to buy, all British goods.

The Sons and Daughters of Liberty

Soon after the Stamp Act was passed, a group of colonists called the Sons of Liberty began to work against it. To most colonists, *liberty* meant freedom to make their own laws.

The Sons of Liberty captured several British workers who tried to collect the tax. They covered these tax collectors with sticky tar and dumped feathers on them. The Sons of Liberty also chased tax collectors out of their towns.

Women also took action against the Stamp Act. They formed their own group, known as the Daughters of Liberty. Members of the group spun thread and wove their own cloth instead of buying British cloth. The cloth was so popular that women in Providence, Rhode Island, chose a large place in which to make it—the city courthouse!

The Stamp Act Is Repealed

By 1766, so many colonists opposed the Stamp Act that Parliament voted to **repeal**, or take back, the act. The very next day, however, Parliament passed the Declaratory Act. It said that Britain had the "full power . . . to make laws . . . [for the] people of America . . . in all cases." This new law worried many colonists.

Members of the Committees of Correspondence wrote letters to express their points of view about British laws.

Boston → New York City → Philadelphia →

Journey starts | 1–4 days from Boston | 4–8 days from Boston

Committees of Correspondence

The repeal of the Stamp Act showed that the colonists could work together, but they needed better ways to share information. News traveled slowly because letters were mostly delivered by riders on horseback. It could take many days for people to find out about events in other colonies.

To spread information between colonies more quickly, the colonists formed Committees of Correspondence. Members of these committees wrote letters to one another. In their letters, they told about what was happening in their town and colony.

Samuel Adams organized the first Committee of Correspondence in **Boston** in 1764. Adams had spoken out many times against British **imperial policies**. These were the laws and orders issued by the king and the British Parliament. The next year, colonists in New York formed another committee.

Colonists soon spoke about the need for a Committee of Correspondence in every colony. Virginia formed a committee in 1773. Members of the Virginia committee wrote that all colonists should be "much disturbed by various rumors and reports of proceedings tending to deprive them of their . . . rights."

Committee members then asked other colonies to start their own Committees of Correspondence. Committee members in each colony wrote letters to other cities and towns. They asked people in the other colonies to **protest**, or work against, British policies.

READING CHECK **MAIN IDEA AND DETAILS**
Why were the Committees of Correspondence formed?

Delivering the Mail

DIAGRAM Delivering the mail took much longer than it does today. About how long did it take mail to go from Boston to New York City? from Boston to Williamsburg?

Baltimore
8–12 days from Boston

Williamsburg
12–16 days from Boston

BOSTON 5 MILES 1779

Supporting the Boycott

To support the boycott against British goods, sewing groups sprang up all over the colonies. Much of the spinning, weaving, and sewing was done by girls. Twelve-year-old Anna Green was part of a sewing group at her church in Boston. Each morning, as the minister read from the Bible, Anna worked away at the spinning wheel.

Fifteen-year-old Charity Clark spun wool in her home in New York City. In a letter to her cousin in Britain, she wrote, "Heroines may not distinguish themselves at the head of an Army, but freedom [will] also be won by a fighting army of [women] . . . armed with spinning wheels."

Make It Relevant **What would you have done to support the colonial boycott? Explain.**

The Townshend Acts

In 1767, Parliament passed several new tax laws called the Townshend Acts. The Townshend Acts taxed imports, such as glass, tea, paint, and paper, that were brought into the colonies. The new laws also set up a new group of tax collectors. Even though Parliament had repealed the Stamp Act, the Townshend Acts showed that Parliament believed it still had the right to make laws for the colonists.

More Boycotts

Once again, many colonists joined together in boycotting British goods. The Daughters of Liberty asked people to stop drinking British tea, and merchants in Boston would not import taxed goods. Some colonists would not paint their houses because they did not want to pay the tax on paint.

Like the Stamp Act, the Townshend Acts did not last very long. Sales of British goods in the colonies went down, and tax officers collected little money. In 1770, Parliament repealed all of the Townshend Acts except for the tax on tea. However, many colonists still would not buy British tea.

As the number of people taking part in protests grew, Parliament sent more soldiers to the colonies. By 1770, about 9,000 British soldiers were in the colonies. About 4,000 of them were stationed in the city of Boston.

READING CHECK Ŏ CAUSE AND EFFECT
What were some of the effects of the Townshend Acts?

The Boston Massacre

Having British soldiers in their towns angered many colonists. They made fun of the soldiers' bright red uniform jackets, calling them "lobsters" and "redcoats." Some of the soldiers became so angry that they destroyed colonial property.

Shots Are Fired

As anger between the colonists and the British soldiers grew, fights often broke out. One of the worst fights took place in Boston on March 5, 1770, when a large crowd of angry colonists gathered near several British soldiers. The colonists shouted at the soldiers and threw rocks and snowballs at them.

When the crowd moved forward, they knocked down some of the soldiers. The soldiers opened fire. Three colonists were killed on the spot, and two others died

▶ **CRISPUS ATTUCKS** This painting shows what Crispus Attucks may have looked like.

later. Among the dead was an African American sailor named **Crispus Attucks** (A•tuhks). Many people think of Crispus Attucks as the first person killed in the fight for the colonies' freedom.

▶ **BOSTON** The building in the center of this painting is the Massachusetts State House, which still stands today.

▶ **THE BOSTON MASSACRE** Paul Revere's engraving was meant to stir up the colonists' anger against the British.

Engrav'd Printed & Sold by PAUL REVERE Boston

Paul Revere, a Boston silversmith known for his simple and beautiful work, supported the colonists. He made a picture of the shooting and titled it *The Bloody Massacre* (MA•sih•ker). A massacre is the killing of many people who cannot defend themselves. The shooting soon became known as the Boston Massacre.

READING CHECK ⊙ **CAUSE AND EFFECT**
What was the cause of the Boston Massacre?

Summary

Britain's new tax laws upset many colonists. They believed they had a right to be represented in the government that taxed them. Many colonists worked together to protest Britain's taxes. As anger between the colonists and British officials grew, fights broke out. Some of the worst fighting took place in Boston.

REVIEW

1. **WHAT TO KNOW** Why were colonists angered by Britain's new colonial tax laws?

2. **VOCABULARY** Explain what **representation** has to do with taxation.

3. **HISTORY** Why did some colonists accuse Patrick Henry of treason?

4. **CRITICAL THINKING** What made Boston a likely place for fighting to begin between colonists and British soldiers?

5. 🖌 **DRAW A CARTOON** Imagine you are a colonist who is against British tax laws. Draw a cartoon that encourages others to boycott British goods.

6. (Focus Skill) **CAUSE AND EFFECT** On a separate sheet of paper, copy and complete the graphic organizer below.

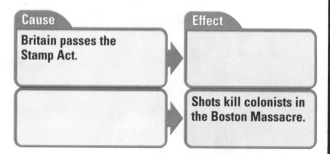

Cause	Effect
Britain passes the Stamp Act.	
	Shots kill colonists in the Boston Massacre.

Patrick Henry

Biography

Trustworthiness
Respect
Responsibility
Fairness
Caring
Patriotism

> "I know not what course others may take: but as for me, give me liberty or give me death!"

These words rang out in the Virginia House of Burgesses on March 23, 1775. The speaker was Patrick Henry. The purpose of his speech was to persuade Virginians to prepare for war against Britain.

Patrick Henry was born in Virginia in 1736. As a young man, Henry worked as a storekeeper and as a farmer. He later became a lawyer.

Over time, Patrick Henry became well known for his skill as a public speaker. In 1765, he was elected to the Virginia House of Burgesses. Henry became an important voice among the colonists who were against British rule. He encouraged them to work together and to think of themselves as Americans.

In 1776, Henry became the governor of Virginia. As governor, he worked hard to get Virginia ready for war. Unlike other leaders, Henry never held a high national office. However, his words and speeches helped unite Americans.

Why Character Counts

How did Patrick Henry's actions and words show his belief in liberty?

Time

1736		1799
Born		Died

1765 Henry is elected to the House of Burgesses

1775 Henry delivers his famous "liberty or death" speech

GO ONLINE For more resources, go to www.harcourtschool.com/ss1

Time
1750 — 1790

1773
The Boston Tea Party takes place

1775
The Battles of Lexington and Concord are fought

 WHAT TO KNOW
What did colonists do to protest British rule?

VOCABULARY
monopoly p. 311
blockade p. 312
quarter p. 312
petition p. 313
Minutemen p. 314
revolution p. 315

PEOPLE
Samuel Adams
Thomas Gage
John Hancock

PLACES
Boston
Philadelphia
Lexington
Concord

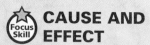 **CAUSE AND EFFECT**

Disagreements Grow

YOU ARE THERE

The year is 1773. It's late at night, and you should be asleep. You hear your father leave the house and quietly close the door. Tonight, he is going to a meeting with **Samuel Adams**. Your father said they plan to teach the British a lesson.

You're worried that your father may be hurt, but he has promised to be careful. Still, you lie wide awake until you hear him come home again.

⚡ **FAST FACT**

After the Boston Tea Party, shown here, colonists sang a new song:
"Rally Mohawks!
Bring out your axes
and tell King George
we'll pay no taxes!"

The Boston Tea Party

In 1773, Parliament passed the Tea Act. It gave Britain's East India Company a monopoly on tea. A legal **monopoly** gives complete control of a good or service in an area to one person or group. This includes control over pricing and competition. Only the East India Company was allowed to sell tea to the colonies.

A Boycott of Tea

The Tea Act meant that colonists had to buy their tea from the East India Company. They could either pay the tax on tea or not drink tea at all. Many colonists decided to boycott tea. Some even made a kind of tea from local sassafras trees.

Ships carrying thousands of pounds of tea set sail for the colonies. In late November 1773, three of the ships reached **Boston**. Against the wishes of many colonists, the Massachusetts governor let the ships dock.

Violence in Boston Harbor

Many people think Samuel Adams planned what happened next. On the night of December 16, 1773, about 150 members of the Sons of Liberty dressed as members of the Mohawk tribe and marched down to Boston Harbor.

At the harbor, hundreds of people were gathered on the docks to watch. When members of the Sons of Liberty arrived, they boarded the ships, broke open more than 300 chests of tea, and threw it all overboard. Their angry protest became known as the Boston Tea Party.

READING CHECK ☼CAUSE **AND EFFECT** What caused colonists to take part in the Boston Tea Party?

▶ **THE BOSTON TEA PARTY** The colonists who took part in the Boston Tea Party refused to pay for the tea they had destroyed.

The Coercive Acts

The Boston Tea Party angered British leaders. In March 1774, Parliament passed a new set of laws to punish the Massachusetts colonists. These laws were called the Coercive Acts because they coerced (koh•ERST), or forced, the colonists to follow laws they felt were unfair.

Punishing the Colonies

One law closed the port of Boston until the colonists paid for the destroyed tea. To enforce this law, Parliament ordered the British navy to **blockade** Boston Harbor. British warships stopped other ships from entering or leaving the harbor.

To punish the colonists further, Britain stopped the Massachusetts legislature from meeting. It put the colony under the control of British General **Thomas Gage**. All town meetings had to be approved by him. Britain also ordered the colonists to **quarter** British soldiers. This order forced colonists to give food and housing to the soldiers.

Many colonists said the new laws were "intolerable," or unacceptable. As a result, the Coercive Acts also became known as the Intolerable Acts. These laws united many colonists against Britain.

Not all British leaders agreed with these laws. In April 1774, Edmund Burke said to Parliament, "You will force them [to buy taxed goods]? Has seven years' struggle yet been able to force them?" However, Parliament did not listen to Burke's call for cooperation.

READING CHECK ŎCAUSE AND EFFECT
What was the effect of the Coercive Acts?

> QUARTERING SOLDIERS The Quartering Act of 1774 was intolerable to many colonists.

The Road To War

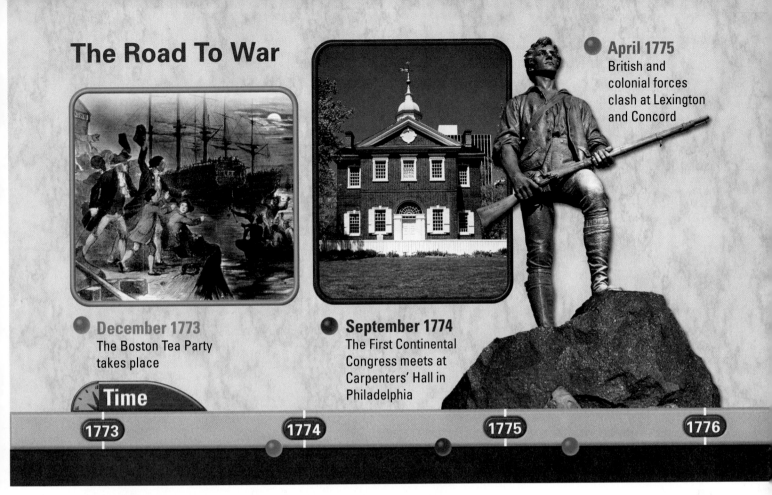

December 1773
The Boston Tea Party takes place

September 1774
The First Continental Congress meets at Carpenters' Hall in Philadelphia

April 1775
British and colonial forces clash at Lexington and Concord

Time

1773   1774   1775   1776

TIME LINE Did the First Continental Congress meet before or after the Boston Tea Party?

The First Continental Congress

Some people in Britain worried about the trouble in the colonies. In June 1774, William Pitt, a member of Parliament, asked British leaders to be patient. He said, "[I] would advise the noble lords in office to adopt [try] a more gentle mode [way] of governing America. . . ."

A Meeting in Philadelphia

Many colonists were afraid that Britain might take stronger action against them. In September 1774, colonial leaders met in **Philadelphia**. Because it was the first meeting of its kind on the North American continent, it was later called the First Continental Congress.

Congress sent a signed request to the king. This **petition** reminded the king of the colonists' basic rights as British citizens. It said that the colonists had the right to life and liberty. It also said that they had the right to assemble, or gather together, and the right to a trial by jury.

Congress set May 10, 1775, as the deadline for Parliament to answer. Congress then voted to stop most trade with Britain. It also asked the colonies to form militias, or armies of citizens.

READING CHECK **SUMMARIZE**
What did the petition sent to King George III by the First Continental Congress ask for?

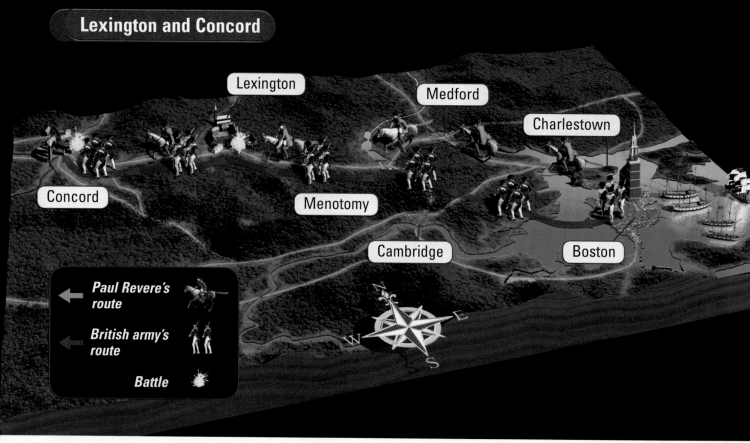

Lexington and Concord

MAP SKILL **PLACE** In which town did Revere's route begin?

Lexington and Concord

Colonists in Massachusetts quickly formed militia units. They were called **Minutemen** because they were said to be ready to fight at a minute's notice.

The British Take Action

In April 1775, General Gage heard that Samuel Adams and **John Hancock** were meeting in **Lexington**. Gage also heard that the Minutemen had weapons in nearby **Concord**. He sent over 700 British soldiers to Lexington and Concord. They planned to arrest the two leaders of the Sons of Liberty and to take the weapons.

The British wanted their march to Lexington to be a secret. However,

Paul Revere, another member of the Sons of Liberty, found out about the plan. He rode to Lexington ahead of the British to warn Adams, Hancock, and the townspeople.

When the British arrived in Lexington, the Minutemen were waiting. The leader of the Minutemen, John Parker, shouted,

> **66** Don't fire unless fired upon, but if they mean to have war, let it begin here. **99**

No one knows which side fired first, but shots rang out. Eight Minutemen were killed, and several others were wounded. The British then marched to Concord to find the weapons stored there, but they had already been moved.

▶ **THE OLD NORTH CHURCH** A statue of Paul Revere stands near the Old North Church in Boston. Two lanterns were hung in the church tower to signal British plans to cross the Charles River by boat.

A Revolution Begins

As the British returned to Boston, the Minutemen fired at them from nearby woods and fields. By the time the British arrived in Boston, 73 soldiers had been killed and 174 wounded. Fewer than 100 colonists had been killed or wounded.

The poet Ralph Waldo Emerson later called the first shot fired at Lexington "the shot heard 'round the world." The fighting that day moved the colonies closer to becoming the United States of America. It was the beginning of a long war called the American Revolution. A **revolution** is a sudden, complete change of government.

READING CHECK ⚫ **CAUSE AND EFFECT**
What were the causes of the fighting at Lexington and Concord?

Summary

After the Boston Tea Party, Parliament passed laws to punish the colonists. The First Continental Congress sent the king a petition reminding him of the rights of colonists. Fighting at Lexington and Concord marked the start of the American Revolution.

REVIEW

1. **WHAT TO KNOW** What did colonists do to protest British rule?

2. **VOCABULARY** Use the term **petition** in a sentence about the First Continental Congress.

3. **ECONOMICS** How did the Coercive Acts affect trade in Boston?

4. **CRITICAL THINKING** William Pitt's advice to Parliament asked for "a more gentle mode [way] of governing America." What might have happened if the king had listened to Pitt?

5. ✏️ **WRITE A POEM** Write a short poem about the events at the Battles of Lexington and Concord. Use details from the lesson to describe the battle scenes.

6. ⭐(Focus Skill) **CAUSE AND EFFECT** On a separate sheet of paper, copy and complete the graphic organizer below.

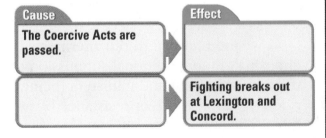

Cause	Effect
The Coercive Acts are passed.	
	Fighting breaks out at Lexington and Concord.

Who Should Govern the Colonies?

King George III and the British Parliament believed that they should govern the 13 colonies. They also believed they had the right to tax the colonies. However, many colonists believed that they should be allowed to make their own laws. The idea of self-government was very important to the colonists.

1

JOHN DICKINSON

John Dickinson was a colonial leader from Pennsylvania. He thought the 13 colonies should resist British rule.

"We are reduced to the alternative of choosing an unconditional submission to the tyranny of irritated ministers [being ruled by Parliament], or resistance by force. The latter is our choice."

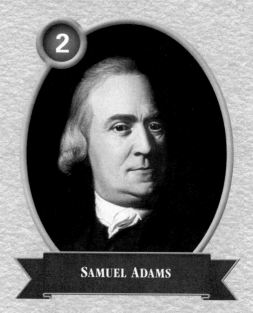

2

SAMUEL ADAMS

Samuel Adams was a leader of the Sons of Liberty in Massachusetts. He thought the colonies had to govern themselves or they would lose all their rights.

"We have no other alternative than [governing ourselves], or the most ignominious [lowly] servitude."

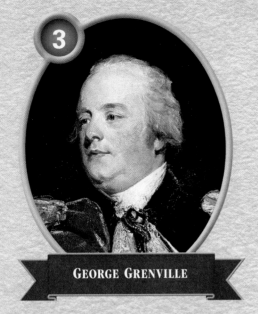

3

GEORGE GRENVILLE

George Grenville was the leader of Parliament. He explained why the colonies should continue to be governed by Britain.

❝ Clearly, the Parliament and the King have authority over the colonies. It is in the name of that authority that we suggest new rules which will make the colonists pay taxes.... ❞

4

DANIEL LEONARD

Daniel Leonard was a Massachusetts colonist who argued that the colonies should obey the king.

❝ Our [people] have been so intent upon building up American rights, that they have overlooked the rights of Great Britain, and our own interest. ❞

It's Your Turn

Compare Points of View
Paraphrase each point of view. Then answer the questions.

1. Who seemed to have the strongest feelings against British rule? What did he compare it to?

2. How were the points of view of Samuel Adams and Daniel Leonard different?

3. Why might leaders living in Britain have a point of view different from that of people living in the colonies?

Make It Relevant Why might people living in different places have different points of view about a topic?

Time

1750   1790

1775
The Second Continental
Congress meets

1775
The Battle of
Bunker Hill

WHAT TO KNOW
How did the colonists
prepare for war with
Britain?

VOCABULARY
commander in chief p. 319

earthwork p. 320

olive branch p. 322

PEOPLE
John Dickinson
John Adams
King George III

PLACES
Breed's Hill

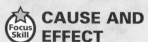

CAUSE AND
EFFECT

The Road to War

YOU ARE THERE

Today, the Second Continental Congress is meeting in Philadelphia. You and others are waiting for news about the meeting. Several men walk by, and a woman nearby grabs your shoulder. "Look! That's George Washington," she whispers. "Some people say he'll lead us against the British."

You try to see what Washington looks like. You wonder what kind of person would lead the fight against the powerful British army.

▶ GEORGE WASHINGTON

▶ **INDEPENDENCE HALL** The Second Continental Congress met in the assembly room of the Pennsylvania State House, now called Independence Hall.

The Second Continental Congress

News of the fighting at Lexington and Concord spread through the colonies. Colonial leaders called for the Second Continental Congress to meet in Philadelphia on May 10, 1775. Its delegates met at the Pennsylvania State House.

The delegates were divided about what the colonies should do. Some called for war against the British. Others, such as **John Dickinson** of Pennsylvania, tried to get the group to avoid fighting. By June, Congress agreed that the colonies should prepare for war.

Preparing for War

The first step was for Congress to form an army. It was called the Continental Army. Unlike the part-time militias that each of the 13 colonies already had, the Continental Army was mostly made up of full-time soldiers.

George Washington was chosen as the army's **commander in chief**, the leader of all the military forces. **John Adams**, a delegate from Massachusetts, suggested Washington. Adams chose Washington partly because he had served in the French and Indian War. Adams believed that Washington both understood soldiers and knew how to fight a war.

To supply the Continental Army, Congress asked each colony to give money to pay for guns, food, and uniforms. Congress also printed its own paper money, which became known as Continental currency. Congress paid the soldiers in bills called Continentals.

READING CHECK ⟳ **CAUSE AND EFFECT**
What caused Congress to form an army?

The Battle of Bunker Hill

By the time George Washington was chosen to lead the new Continental Army, the first major battle of the Revolutionary War had already been fought. The Battle of Bunker Hill took place on June 17, 1775.

The Battle Begins

After sunset on June 16, colonial commanders Israel Putnam and William Prescott arrived at **Breed's Hill**, across the Charles River from Boston. They ordered their soldiers to build **earthworks**, or walls made of earth and stone. These earthworks would help the colonists defend themselves.

When British General Thomas Gage learned of this the next day, he sent General William Howe and 2,400 British soldiers to capture Breed's Hill. When the British drew close, the 1,600 colonists behind the earthworks started shooting. To save bullets, Putnam shouted,

> **"Don't fire until you see the whites of their eyes."**

A Fierce Fight

Fighting on the hill was much tougher than the British had expected. Twice they were forced back toward the river. In Boston, thousands of people climbed on their roofs to view the fighting. They watched in horror as the nearby city of Charlestown was hit and set on fire by cannons shooting from British ships in the harbor.

Back on Breed's Hill, the colonists ran out of ammunition. The British made it over the earthworks, and the colonists had to retreat. By early evening, the British had captured Breed's Hill. The battle at Breed's Hill was wrongly named for nearby Bunker Hill. The British won the battle, but they had suffered heavy losses. More than 1,000 British soldiers had been killed or wounded. About 350 colonists had been killed or wounded.

READING CHECK Ŏ**CAUSE AND EFFECT**
What caused the colonists to retreat from Breed's Hill?

British ship

British forces landed and formed battle lines.

Battle of Bunker Hill

ILLUSTRATION The first major battle of the Revolutionary War, the Battle of Bunker Hill, was fought on June 17, 1775. Why do you think the colonists chose to build earthworks on top of Breed's Hill?

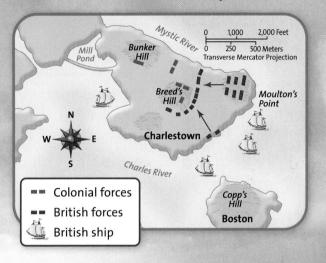

Boston

British forces marched up Breed's Hill to attack the colonists.

Earthworks

Colonists fired on the British from behind earthworks on Breed's Hill.

Trying for Peace

Although the colonists did not win the Battle of Bunker Hill, they had fought bravely. The British learned that fighting the colonists would not be as easy as they had thought.

The Olive Branch Petition

On July 5, 1775, Congress sent another petition to **King George III**. Because it asked for peace, this petition became

known as the Olive Branch Petition. An **olive branch** is an ancient symbol of peace.

By the time the Olive Branch Petition reached London, it could do little good. The Battle of Bunker Hill had further angered British leaders. King George III promised to do whatever was necessary to crush the colonists' rebellion.

READING CHECK ⟲**CAUSE AND EFFECT**
Why did the British leaders ignore the Olive Branch Petition?

Summary

The Second Continental Congress formed the Continental Army and made George Washington the commander in chief. By that time, the Battle of Bunker Hill had been fought. It was the first major battle of the Revolutionary War.

REVIEW

1. **WHAT TO KNOW** How did the colonists prepare for war with Britain?

2. **VOCABULARY** Use the term **earthwork** in a sentence about the Battle of Bunker Hill.

3. **HISTORY** What did King George III do after the Battle of Bunker Hill?

4. **CRITICAL THINKING** Why do you think the colonists were proud of their actions at the Battle of Bunker Hill?

5. **CONDUCT AN INTERVIEW** Imagine you are a reporter who has been asked to interview General Washington. Write a list of questions you would ask and answers Washington might give.

6. **CAUSE AND EFFECT**
On a separate sheet of paper, copy and complete the graphic organizer below.

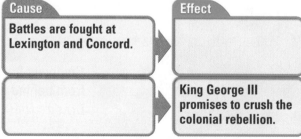

Cause		Effect
Battles are fought at Lexington and Concord.	▶	
	▶	King George III promises to crush the colonial rebellion.

Phillis Wheatley

Biography

Trustworthiness
Respect
Responsibility
Fairness
Caring
Patriotism

*"A crown, a mansion, and a throne that shine,
With gold unfading, WASHINGTON! be thine."*

People are sometimes best able to express their feelings in poems, stories, or songs. Phillis Wheatley was such a person.

Wheatley was one of the best-known poets of her time. She was born in Africa but captured, put on a slave ship, and taken to Massachusetts in 1761. She was about eight years old. During the same year, she was sold to a Boston family named Wheatley. They gave her their name. The family later helped Phillis learn to read and write.

Wheatley began writing poetry as a teenager. Many of her poems are about events in Boston and her life as an enslaved person. Her first book of poetry was published in 1770, and it became well known in the colonies and Britain. She was the first African American woman in the colonies to have her writing published.

In 1775, Wheatley wrote a poem honoring George Washington for being named commander in chief of the Continental Army. The lines above are from that poem.

Why Character Counts

How did **Phillis Wheatley** express her patriotism?

Time

1753			1784
Born?			Died

1761 Wheatley is taken to Boston

1770 Wheatley's first book of poetry is published

GO ONLINE
For more resources, go to
www.harcourtschool.com/ss1

323

Time

1750   1790

1776
Thomas Paine publishes *Common Sense*

1776
The Declaration of Independence is issued

1777
The Articles of Confederation are written

Declaring Independence

WHAT TO KNOW
How did the 13 colonies cut their ties with Britain?

VOCABULARY
independence p. 325
resolution p. 325
declaration p. 325
preamble p. 326
grievance p. 326

PEOPLE
Thomas Paine
Richard Henry Lee
Thomas Jefferson
Abigail Adams

PLACES
Independence Hall

Focus Skill CAUSE AND EFFECT

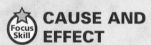

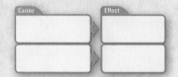

YOU ARE THERE
Your friend waves a pamphlet in your face. "This will change the course of history!" You notice that the short book's title is *Common Sense*. Your friend says, "In here are all the reasons we should be our own country."

The year is 1776, and battles between the colonists and British soldiers have already taken place. Your friend tells you, "*Common Sense* is going to make everyone want to be free of Britain."

▶ **THOMAS PAINE** In *Common Sense*, Thomas Paine argued that the colonies should claim their independence.

COMMON SENSE;
ADDRESSED TO THE
INHABITANTS
OF
AMERICA,
On the following interesting
SUBJECTS.
I. Of the Origin and Design of Government in general, with concise Remarks on the English Constitution.
II. Of Monarchy and Hereditary Succession.
... State of America...

Moving Toward Independence

More colonists were starting to think that their problems with Britain could not be settled. One person who helped shape the colonists' ideas was **Thomas Paine**. In *Common Sense*, Paine wrote that the colonists should rule themselves.

Congress Debates Independence

From Georgia to New Hampshire, people talked about Paine's ideas. Many began to call for **independence**—the freedom to govern themselves.

Delegates at the Second Continental Congress in Philadelphia also started to talk about independence. John Adams of Massachusetts argued strongly for it. He said independence was the only way for the colonists to have liberty. In time, more and more of the delegates came to agree with Adams's point of view.

On June 7, 1776, **Richard Henry Lee** of Virginia slowly rose from his chair at the Second Continental Congress. He told the other delegates that the 13 colonies no longer owed loyalty to the king. Lee then called for a **resolution**, or a formal group statement, of independence:

> 66 Resolved: That these united colonies are, and of right ought to be, free and independent states. 99

A Declaration Is Written

Congress debated Lee's resolution. It also chose a committee to write a **declaration**, or official statement, about independence to be sent to the king.

▶ **THOMAS JEFFERSON** Members of Congress respected Thomas Jefferson's talents as a writer.

The committee asked **Thomas Jefferson** of Virginia to write the first draft. Jefferson was a 33-year-old lawyer who had studied government and law. He used this knowledge to explain his ideas. The other members of the committee also added ideas, but Jefferson was the main author. Every evening for about 17 days, he wrote and rewrote the draft of the Declaration of Independence.

READING CHECK ☼**CAUSE AND EFFECT**
What were some of the reasons why many people in the colonies called for independence?

The Declaration of Independence

Thomas Jefferson carefully planned the Declaration of Independence. In the **preamble**, or first part, Jefferson told why the Declaration was needed. He also explained why the colonies had the right to break away from Britain and form a new nation.

Rights and Grievances

The next part of the Declaration of Independence describes the colonists' main ideas about government. It also states that all people have certain rights that governments cannot take away. Jefferson wrote that people have the right to live, be free, and seek their own happiness. These words have become some of the most famous in United States history:

> **"We hold these truths to be self-evident, that all men are created equal, that they are endowed [provided] by their Creator with certain unalienable Rights, that among these are Life, Liberty, and the pursuit of Happiness."**

The longest part of the Declaration lists the colonists' **grievances**, or complaints, against King George III and Parliament. It also lists the ways the colonists had tried to settle their differences with Britain peacefully. In the last part of the Declaration, Jefferson stated that the colonies were free and independent states.

READING CHECK **SUMMARIZE**
What important ideas did Thomas Jefferson give in the Declaration of Independence?

▶ **PRESENTING THE DECLARATION** This mural shows Thomas Jefferson handing a draft of the Declaration of Independence to John Hancock.

The Declaration of Independence

Background This important document includes the idea that a government gets its power from the consent of the people. You can read the full text of the Declaration on pages R23–R26.

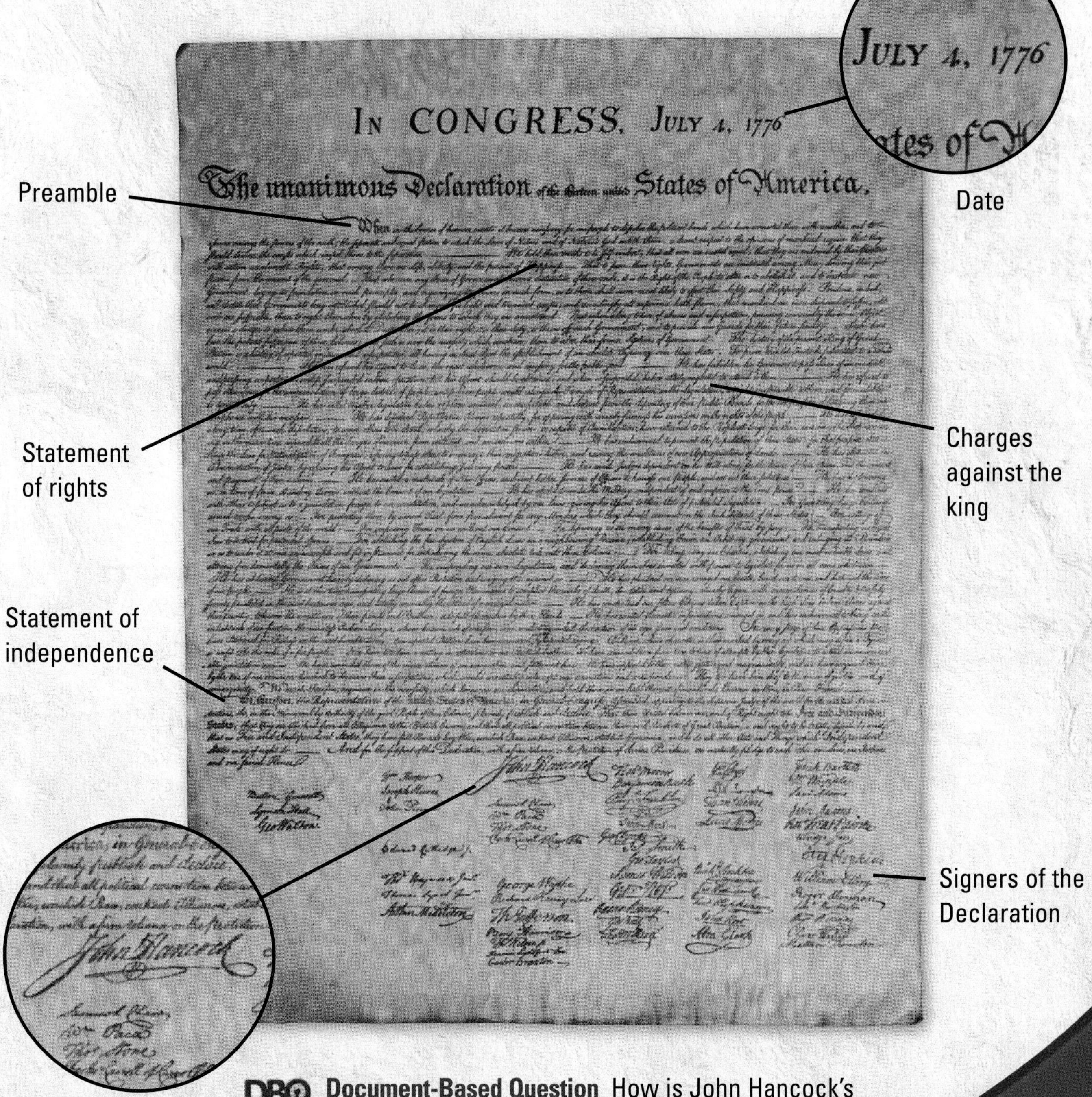

Date

JULY 4, 1776

Preamble

IN CONGRESS. JULY 4, 1776

The unanimous Declaration of the thirteen united States of America,

Statement of rights

Charges against the king

Statement of independence

Signers of the Declaration

DBQ **Document-Based Question** How is John Hancock's signature different from those of the other signers?

FAST FACT

This statue of King George III was melted down, and the metal was used to make bullets for American soldiers.

❯ **NEW YORK CITY** Historical paintings give an artist's view of an event. The women, children, and Native Americans shown in this painting would not have been present at this event.

Congress Approves the Declaration

When he finished writing, Thomas Jefferson gave his draft of the Declaration of Independence to Congress. On June 28, it was read aloud to the delegates. They discussed it for several days and made edits. Then, on July 2, the delegates voted to approve Richard Henry Lee's resolution to cut ties with Britain. The colonies now thought of themselves as independent states. They felt they were free to make their own laws.

A Public Reading

On July 4, 1776, Congress voted to accept the Declaration's final wording. Four days later, on July 8, large crowds gathered outside the Pennsylvania State House, today called **Independence Hall**. Bells rang out, and Colonel John Nixon gave the first public reading of the Declaration of Independence. Members of the Second Continental Congress also listened as Nixon read.

News of the Declaration quickly spread across the former colonies. Many people who supported independence tore down pictures and statues of King George III. They sang songs, rang bells, and fired cannons in celebration.

John Adams was so pleased when he heard of these celebrations that he wrote about them in a letter to **Abigail Adams**, his wife. He said that Independence Day should be celebrated "by succeeding generations . . . from this time forward."

A Dangerous Decision

By August 2, a copy of the Declaration was ready to be signed by the members of the Second Continental Congress. The first to sign it was John Hancock, the president of the Congress. He said that he wrote his name large enough so that King George III could read it without his glasses. The way he signed it became so famous that the term *John Hancock* now means "a person's signature."

Signing the Declaration was dangerous. King George III had promised to do whatever was necessary to end the rebellion. If the Americans lost the war, the British would try the signers for treason, a crime punishable by death. Benjamin Franklin joked about this when it was his turn to sign the Declaration. "We must all hang together," he said, "or . . . we shall all hang separately." He knew the signers had to unite against the British.

The Declaration's Importance

When the Declaration of Independence was approved in 1776, only white men who owned property could vote. Some people believed that was unfair. In a letter to her husband in March 1776, Abigail Adams wrote about her belief that Congress should recognize women's rights. She wrote, "In the new code of law which I suppose it will be necessary for you to make, I desire you would remember the ladies. . . ."

It would take many years for women, African Americans, Native Americans, and other groups of Americans to share fully in the promise of the Declaration of Independence. However, the Declaration has inspired people around the world to work for freedom and equal rights.

READING CHECK ☼**CAUSE AND EFFECT**
Why were the delegates worried about signing the Declaration?

❯ **A HISTORIC ROOM** The Declaration of Independence was first presented in the Assembly Room of the Pennsylvania State House.

Forming a New Government

The Second Continental Congress set up another committee to plan how to unite the 13 states. John Dickinson was chosen to head the committee. It decided that each state would govern itself, but all would work together on national issues. This first plan of government for the United States was called the Articles of Confederation. It was a big change from being governed by a king.

The Articles of Confederation

The Articles of Confederation were approved by Congress in 1777 and later by the states. Under the Articles, each state elected representatives to serve in a national legislature. It was called the Confederation Congress. Each state,

whether large or small, had one vote in Congress.

Until 1789, this Congress made laws for the new nation. It helped keep the states together during the Revolutionary War. However, the Articles had weaknesses that caused problems for the new government.

Weaknesses of the Articles

Americans were fighting a war to win their independence. They feared that a strong national, or central, government might threaten their freedom. As a result, the Articles of Confederation left most power with the states.

Before Congress could pass any law, representatives from at least 9 of the 13 states had to approve it. However, the representatives rarely agreed. No state wanted to be under the control of the other states. Even if the representatives

> **JOHN DICKINSON** helped write the Articles of Confederation.

approved a law, Congress did not have the power to enforce it.

The Articles limited the powers of the national government in other ways, too. For example, Congress had the power to declare war, make treaties, and borrow money. However, it could not control trade or collect taxes. To cover expenses, such as debts from the war, Congress could only ask the states for money. It could not force the states to pay.

The Articles also made Congress depend on the states for the nation's defense. Congress could ask for an army, but the states had to provide the soldiers.

READING CHECK ŏ **CAUSE AND EFFECT**
Why were the new states afraid of a strong national government?

▶ **EARLY MONEY** Most states printed their own money. This money might not be accepted in other states.

Summary

Partly because of Thomas Paine's *Common Sense*, many colonists began to call for independence. Thomas Jefferson wrote the Declaration of Independence. Later, Congress passed the Articles of Confederation, the country's first plan of government.

REVIEW

1. **WHAT TO KNOW** How did the 13 colonies cut their ties with Britain?

2. **VOCABULARY** Use the words **preamble** and **grievance** in a sentence about the Declaration of Independence.

3. **CIVICS/GOVERNMENT** What are some of the ideas described in the Declaration of Independence?

4. **CRITICAL THINKING** Make It Relevant How do the ideas in the Declaration of Independence affect your life?

5. **WRITE A PERSUASIVE LETTER** Imagine it is 1776. Write a letter to the local newspaper. Tell why you do or do not support independence for the 13 colonies. Include evidence that supports your argument.

6. ⭐ (Focus Skill) **CAUSE AND EFFECT** On a separate sheet of paper, copy and complete the graphic organizer below.

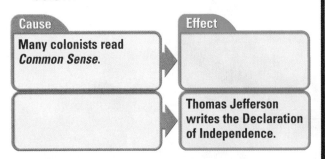

Cause		Effect
Many colonists read *Common Sense*.	▶	
	▶	Thomas Jefferson writes the Declaration of Independence.

Identify Multiple Causes and Effects

Why It Matters To understand why things happen, it is important to identify multiple causes and effects.

❯ LEARN

Sometimes events in history have more than one cause and more than one effect. A **cause** is an event or an action that makes something happen. An **effect** is what happens as a result of that event or action. You can use these steps to help you identify multiple causes and their effects.

Step 1 Look for the effects. Decide whether there is more than one effect.

Step 2 Look for the causes of the effects.

Step 3 Think about the connections between the causes and their effects. An effect of one event can become the cause of another event.

❯ **THE BATTLE OF LEXINGTON** What were some effects of the event shown here?

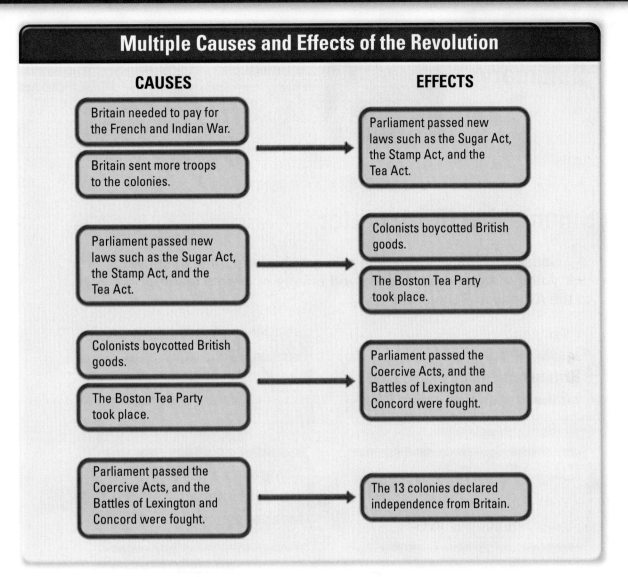

Multiple Causes and Effects of the Revolution

CAUSES

Britain needed to pay for the French and Indian War.

Britain sent more troops to the colonies.

Parliament passed new laws such as the Sugar Act, the Stamp Act, and the Tea Act.

Colonists boycotted British goods.

The Boston Tea Party took place.

Parliament passed the Coercive Acts, and the Battles of Lexington and Concord were fought.

EFFECTS

Parliament passed new laws such as the Sugar Act, the Stamp Act, and the Tea Act.

Colonists boycotted British goods.

The Boston Tea Party took place.

Parliament passed the Coercive Acts, and the Battles of Lexington and Concord were fought.

The 13 colonies declared independence from Britain.

❯ PRACTICE

The chart above lists many of the causes and effects of British actions toward the colonies. Use the chart to answer these questions.

1 What caused new taxes such as the Stamp Act to be passed?

2 What were the effects of new tax laws being passed?

3 What effect did the Coercive Acts and the Battles of Lexington and Concord have?

❯ APPLY

Review this chapter. Find at least one multiple cause-and-effect relationship other than those shown in the chart. Then share your findings with a classmate.

Critical Thinking Skills

Visual Summary

1754
The French
and Indian War
begins

1765
Parliament
passes the
Stamp Act

Summarize the Chapter

Focus Skill **Cause and Effect** Complete this graphic organizer to show that you understand the causes and effects of events leading to the American Revolution.

Cause

Britain needed money to pay for the French and Indian War.

Effect

Congress approves the Declaration of Independence.

TEST PREP Vocabulary

Identify the term from the word bank that correctly matches each definition.

1. to refuse to buy

2. the act of working against one's own government

3. a sudden change of government

4. a plan for spending money

5. the act of speaking or acting for someone else

6. freedom to govern on one's own

7. a formal agreement among groups or individuals

8. a signed request

Word Bank

alliance p. 296   **boycott** p. 304

budget p. 299   **petition** p. 313

representation p. 303   **revolution** p. 315

treason p. 303   **independence** p. 325

1770 — 1780 — 1790

1775
The Battles of Lexington and Concord are fought

1776
Declaration of Independence is signed

 Time Line

Use the chapter summary time line above to answer these questions.

9. In what year did the French and Indian War start?

10. Did the first battles of the Revolutionary War start before or after the Declaration of Independence was signed?

 Facts and Main Ideas

Answer these questions.

11. What was the purpose of the Proclamation of 1763?

12. Why did many colonists boycott British goods?

13. How did the Battle of Bunker Hill change Britain's view of the colonists?

Write the letter of the best choice.

14. Who was chosen to be the commander in chief of the Continental Army?
    A Samuel Adams
    B Thomas Gage
    C Thomas Jefferson
    D George Washington

15. Who headed the committee that wrote the Articles of Confederation?
    A George Washington
    B John Dickinson
    C Thomas Jefferson
    D Richard Henry Lee

 Critical Thinking

16. What effects did the Committees of Correspondence have on the colonies?

17. What were some of the benefits of declaring independence? What were the costs?

 Skills

Compare Historical Maps

18. Study the maps on page 301. Explain how Britain's land claims changed as a result of the French and Indian War.

Identify Multiple Causes and Effects

19. Draw a chart like the one on page 333 to show the causes and effects of the French and Indian War.

writing

🖊 **Write a Persuasive Letter**
Imagine that you are a member of the First Continental Congress. Write a letter to persuade King George III that he ought to respect the colonists' rights.

🖊 **Write a Narrative** Imagine that you are a newspaper reporter assigned to write about the Boston Massacre. Write a narrative describing the events. Use details from your reading and Paul Revere's engraving on page 308 to help you.

STUDY SKILLS

ORGANIZE INFORMATION

Graphic organizers can help you organize information.

- Graphic organizers help you categorize, or group, information.

- Putting people, places, and events into categories makes it easier to find facts and understand what you read.

```
Continental Army          Revolutionary War          British Army
```

- mostly farmers with no military experience
- _____
- _____

- mostly trained and experienced soldiers
- _____
- _____

PREVIEW VOCABULARY

Patriot p. 339

mercenary p. 347

campaign p. 349

The Revolutionary War

MORRISTOWN NATIONAL HISTORICAL PARK IN NEW JERSEY

Time

1760   1790

1776
British soldiers
burn many areas
in New Jersey

1777
Sybil Ludington warns
American soldiers of
a British attack

WHAT TO KNOW
How did the American
Revolution affect people's
lives?

VOCABULARY
Patriot p. 339
Loyalist p. 339
neutral p. 339
inflation p. 340
profiteering p. 340
veteran p. 341

PEOPLE
Martha Washington
Sybil Ludington
Deborah Sampson
Margaret Corbin
Mercy Otis Warren
Abigail Adams
James Armistead
Peter Salem
Thayendanegea

CAUSE AND EFFECT

Cause	Effect

Americans and the Revolution

YOU ARE THERE

It is 1777. Hundreds of British soldiers are
marching by your house in New Jersey.
The stomping of their boots scares you, and your
mother pulls you and your little brother close. For
three months, your father has been away fighting
in the Continental Army. While he has been gone,
your mother has been running the family's printing
business.

Outside, the last of the British soldiers are passing
by. Their coats make a line of red across the street.
"Don't worry," you whisper to your brother. "We'll
beat them all. You'll see."

FAST FACT

British soldiers spent
three hours preparing their
uniforms for review. They
had to powder their hair,
shine all their buttons, and
polish their boots.

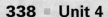

▶ **LOSS OF PROPERTY** Colonists watch as British soldiers burn their home.

Personal Hardships

The Declaration of Independence showed that colonial leaders had united against Britain. But the colonists themselves were deeply divided. Many had to decide whether to support independence or to stay loyal to the British king.

Taking Sides

Colonists who supported independence called themselves **Patriots**. Those who remained loyal to the king were called **Loyalists**. About one-third of the colonists stayed **neutral**, or did not choose sides.

As people took sides, friendships and families were sometimes broken apart. Church groups were also divided. Taking sides was especially hard for members of the Anglican Church, also called the Church of England. The king was the head of their church.

Colonists faced other hardships, too. Often their towns were robbed and destroyed by the British army. In 1776, for example, British soldiers burned many areas of New Jersey. They even stole beds from colonists' houses! In turn, Patriots often took goods from the Loyalists.

In some cases, Patriots destroyed their own belongings to keep them from the British. Others burned their crops so that the British could not get them for food.

READING CHECK ⏱ **CAUSE AND EFFECT**
How did the war affect some colonial families?

American Imports from Britain, 1775–1778

Value (in British Pounds)

200,000

150,000

100,000

50,000

0

1775   1776   1777   1778

Year

GRAPH Imports from Britain decreased during the early years of the war. By about how much did the amount of colonial imports decrease from 1775 to 1776?

Economic Hardships

Along with personal problems, Americans also faced many economic hardships during the Revolutionary War. One problem was a shortage of imported goods. British ships set up blockades so that trading ships could not unload goods at American ports.

Prices Rise

As the shortage of goods grew worse, Americans also faced inflation. **Inflation** is a rise in the price of all goods. Because of inflation, people needed more money to buy the same amounts of goods and services. In just two months, the prices of wheat and beef doubled!

Another cause of inflation was the falling value of colonial paper money, called Continentals. To pay for the war, Congress printed more of the paper money. By printing too many Continentals, however, the government made them less valuable.

Congress also had a difficult time trying to pay for the war. Congress could not force the states to contribute money. It could only ask them. The states could say no if they chose.

Because there was a shortage of goods, some farmers and shopkeepers began **profiteering**, or charging extra-high prices for their crops or goods. Some states passed laws that limited how much farmers could charge for food. These laws also made it illegal for people to hoard, or collect and hide, large amounts of goods. However, these laws were often broken.

READING CHECK ☼ **CAUSE AND EFFECT**

How did inflation affect people during the Revolutionary War?

Women and the War

As men left their homes to fight in the war, women took on new roles. Some women ran family farms or businesses. Others raised money for the war and collected clothing for the soldiers.

In Battle and at Home

Some wives followed their husbands from battle to battle. Every winter when the armies were in their winter quarters, **Martha Washington** traveled to be with her husband, George. In army camps, women cooked food and washed clothes. Some brought water to soldiers during battles.

Some girls and women joined the men in battle. One night in 1777, 16-year-old **Sybil Ludington** rode more than 40 miles to tell Americans of a British attack.

Deborah Sampson pretended to be a man and dressed in men's clothes so that she could fight during the war. **Margaret Corbin** was wounded after taking her husband's place in battle. She became the first woman veteran to be recognized by Congress. A **veteran** is a person who has served in the military.

Other women used their talents to support the Patriot cause. **Mercy Otis Warren** wrote poems and stories about people fighting for freedom. Later, she wrote a history of the American Revolution, the first by a woman. **Abigail Adams** argued for freedom in letters she wrote to her husband, John. She also cared for children who had been made homeless by the war.

READING CHECK **SUMMARIZE**
How did women take part in the Revolutionary War?

❯ SYBIL LUDINGTON

❯ MARTHA WASHINGTON

❯ ABIGAIL ADAMS

▶ **AFRICAN AMERICANS IN THE WAR** The First Rhode Island Regiment fought for the Patriots. James Armistead (right) spied on the British army.

African Americans, Free and Enslaved

At the start of the war, one of every five people in the 13 colonies was of African descent. Some free African Americans had set up communities in northern cities such as Philadelphia. However, the majority of African Americans lived enslaved, mostly in the South.

The Promise of Freedom

Close to 5,000 enslaved African Americans fought for the Continental Army. Many were promised their freedom as a reward for their service. This promise was made to the soldiers of the First Rhode Island Regiment.

James Armistead, an enslaved person from Virginia, was a spy for George Washington. The information that Armistead collected helped the Americans win an important battle at Yorktown, Virginia. After the war was over, the Virginia government gave Armistead his freedom.

The British governor of Virginia promised freedom to all enslaved people who fought for the British. His group of more than 300 African American soldiers wore patches that said *Liberty to Slaves.*

Free African Americans in Battle

Free African Americans also took sides. **Peter Salem** was among at least five African Americans who fought the British at the Battle of Concord. He also fought at Bunker Hill. James Forten, from Philadelphia, was just 14 years old when he joined the Continental Navy.

READING CHECK ⟳ **CAUSE AND EFFECT**
Why did some enslaved African Americans fight in the Revolutionary War?

People in the West

When the war began, many Native Americans remained neutral. Most white settlers in the West, or the lands west of the Appalachian Mountains, also remained neutral.

New Alliances

Native Americans were soon divided by the war. Many groups eventually sided with the British. In 1777, the Mohawk agreed to help the British. The Mohawk leader **Thayendanegea** (thay•en•da•NEG•ah), known as Joseph Brant, hoped to stop settlers from moving west. Groups such as the Oneida and Tuscarora fought for the Americans.

The feelings of many western settlers also changed. Many did not support the Patriot cause, but they wanted to help drive the British out of their lands.

READING CHECK Ŏ **CAUSE AND EFFECT**
What caused Thayendanegea to make alliances with the British?

▶ **THAYENDANEGEA** The Mohawk leader Thayendanegea fought for the British.

Summary

During the Revolutionary War, Americans faced personal and economic hardships. Many women and African Americans contributed to the Patriot cause. At first, Native Americans and settlers in the western lands were neutral, but later they joined the fighting.

REVIEW

1. **WHAT TO KNOW** How did the American Revolution affect people's lives?

2. **VOCABULARY** Explain the difference between a **Loyalist** and a **Patriot**.

3. **ECONOMICS** Why did Congress have problems paying for the war?

4. **CRITICAL THINKING** Make It Relevant Why do you think many people are willing to face hardships during war?

5. ✏ **WRITE A CONVERSATION** Write a conversation between a Patriot and a Loyalist. Make sure each speaker supports his or her position with evidence.

6. ⭐ (Focus Skill) **CAUSE AND EFFECT** On a separate sheet of paper, copy and complete this graphic organizer.

Cause		Effect
	▶	The colonies have a shortage of goods.
Laws are passed against profiteering.	▶	

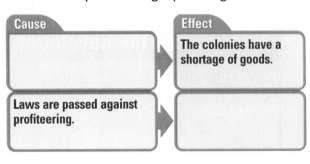

Read Parallel Time Lines

Why It Matters A parallel time line can help you compare events that happen at the same time but in different places.

❱ LEARN

A **parallel time line** is made up of two or more time lines. Each time line shows the same period of time but events that happened in different places.

The parallel time line below shows important events that took place between 1770 and 1776. The top part of the time line shows important events that took place in Britain. The bottom part of the time line shows important events that happened in the colonies.

The American Revolution

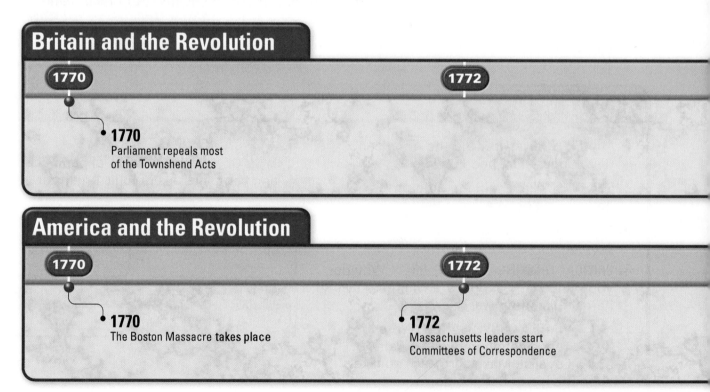

Britain and the Revolution

1770   1772

1770
Parliament repeals most
of the Townshend Acts

America and the Revolution

1770   1772

1770
The Boston Massacre **takes place**

1772
Massachusetts leaders start
Committees of Correspondence

▶ PRACTICE

Use the parallel time line below to answer these questions.

1 Which took place first—the Boston Massacre or the passage of the Coercive Acts?

2 Which time line shows the date the Declaration of Independence was approved?

3 In what year did the First Continental Congress meet?

4 Did the First Continental Congress meet before or after the repeal of the Townshend Acts?

▶ APPLY

Make It Relevant Draw a parallel time line to show events that have happened in your lifetime. Use one part of the time line to show the events that have taken place in your life, beginning with the year you were born and ending with the present year. Use the other part of the time line to show events that have happened in the United States during the same time.

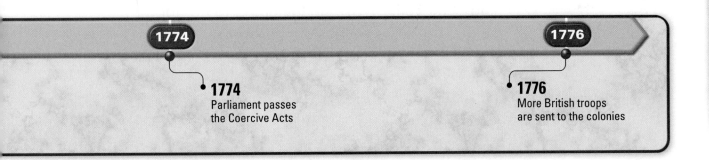

1774
1774
Parliament passes
the Coercive Acts

1776
1776
More British troops
are sent to the colonies

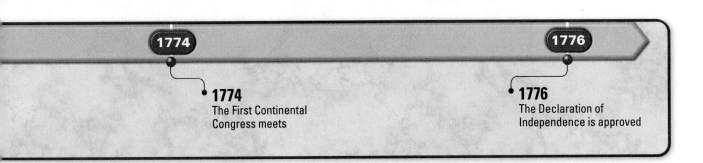

1774
1774
The First Continental
Congress meets

1776
1776
The Declaration of
Independence is approved

Chart and Graph Skills

Time

1750 | 1790

1776
The Battle
of Trenton

1777
The Battle
of Saratoga

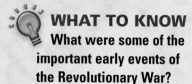

WHAT TO KNOW
What were some of the important early events of the Revolutionary War?

VOCABULARY
enlist p. 347
mercenary p. 347
campaign p. 349
turning point p. 349
negotiate p. 351

PEOPLE
Marquis de Lafayette
Benedict Arnold
Friedrich Wilhelm von
Steuben

PLACES
Trenton
Saratoga
Valley Forge

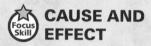

CAUSE AND EFFECT

Cause | Effect

Fighting for Independence

YOU ARE THERE "The soldiers are starving," says the **Marquis de Lafayette** (mar•KEE duh lah•fee•ET). "They eat nothing but firecake made of flour and water." Your stomach growls.

"Since Congress won't send help," General George Washington says, "I'll order the local farmers to sell us their crops."

The air outside is cold, but you don't care. "Let's go," you yell. "We're finally going to get food!"

▷ **MARQUIS DE LAFAYETTE** helped the Continental Army.

An American Soldier and A British Soldier

Tricorn hat

Haversack for food

Musket with bayonet

Cartridge bag with sling

Musket

British redcoat

▶ **SUPPLIES** British soldiers (right) often had better supplies than Continental soldiers (left). What supply item did both types of soldiers carry?

Comparing Armies

In July 1775, George Washington arrived in Massachusetts to take command of the Continental Army. The soldiers had no uniforms—only their everyday clothes. Many had no guns, so they carried spears and axes. Some had fought in the French and Indian War, but most had no military training. Many were farmers who had just **enlisted**, or signed up, to fight. Washington was once so angry that he threw his hat on the ground and shouted, "Are these the men with which I am to defend America?"

Keeping the army fed and clothed took a lot of supplies. Washington told Congress that his army needed 100,000 barrels of flour and 20 million pounds of meat a year! Congress could not raise enough money to pay for everything the army needed.

A Strong Enemy

The Continental Army went to war against one of the most powerful armies in the world. The British army was made up of experienced soldiers. The British had about 50,000 soldiers in the colonies. Washington rarely had more than 15,000 soldiers in his army at any time. The British army also used **mercenaries**, or hired soldiers. Because many of the mercenaries came from a German region called Hesse-Cassel, Americans called them Hessians (HEH•shuhnz).

But the British had problems, too. It was hard to fight a war 3,000 miles from home. Loyalists gave some aid, but the British soldiers still had to wait a long time for supplies and soldiers to replace them.

READING CHECK ⟳ **CAUSE AND EFFECT**
What caused problems for the British army?

▶ **ACROSS THE DELAWARE** This famous painting shows Patriot troops rowing across the Delaware River. It is unlikely that Washington would have been standing up.

Early Battles in the North

By the spring of 1776, Washington and his army had moved south from Massachusetts to New York. They were camped on Long Island when British troops attacked them. The Americans suffered great losses at the Battle of Long Island.

The British army then chased Washington and his army. Many American soldiers had left after the Battle of Long Island, and Washington had to ask the others to stay. He and the soldiers who stayed did their best not to get caught by the British. By winter, they had marched through New Jersey and on to Pennsylvania. British General William Howe and most of the British army were still in New York.

A Surprise Attack

By December 1776, thousands of American soldiers were ready to give up. Washington came up with a plan to attack the Hessian mercenaries in **Trenton**, New Jersey. At this time in history, armies rarely fought battles in winter. Washington knew he could surprise the Hessians.

On Christmas night, 1776, Patriot troops crossed the icy Delaware River in rowboats and marched nine miles to Trenton. There, they found the Hessian troops sleeping. They attacked and the fighting lasted only an hour before the Hessians surrendered. The victory at Trenton gave American soldiers hope for the future.

READING CHECK ♻ **CAUSE AND EFFECT**
What caused Washington to attack Trenton on Christmas night?

An Important Victory

In 1777, the British army planned a new campaign. A **campaign** is a series of military actions carried out for a certain goal. The goal was to separate the New England Colonies from the other colonies. The British thought that if they controlled all of New York, they could cut off communications and supplies to Massachusetts and the rest of New England.

The British campaign called for many groups of soldiers to go to Albany, New York. There, they were supposed to join troops led by British General John Burgoyne coming down from Canada. Together, they would attack the city from the north, south, and west. This plan might have worked, but the British troops never reached Albany. They were slowed by battles along the way.

The Battle of Saratoga

On September 19, 1777, Continental forces circled General Burgoyne's army near the town of **Saratoga**, New York. Burgoyne and his soldiers could not break through the Americans' lines.

The Battle of Saratoga was really two battles that took place over three weeks. During the second battle, the American General **Benedict Arnold** led a group of soldiers in a daring attack.

On October 17, Burgoyne surrendered to the American General Horatio Gates. The British loss at Saratoga was a turning point in the war. A **turning point** is an event that causes an important change. It looked as if the Americans might have a chance to win the war.

READING CHECK ✪ **CAUSE AND EFFECT**
What caused people to believe America could win the war?

▶ **AN AMERICAN VICTORY** Native Americans helped the British at the Battle of Saratoga. This medal (right) shows the British surrendering.

Winter at Valley Forge

In the fall of 1777, the Continental Army faced trouble. While trying to keep the British from taking Philadelphia, the Continental Army lost a battle at Brandywine, Pennsylvania. In September, British soldiers captured Philadelphia, where they got ready to spend the winter in comfort.

Suffering Through Winter

The tired Continental soldiers moved to **Valley Forge**, Pennsylvania. Washington chose this place so that he could keep watch on the British.

The Continental Army at Valley Forge was a ragged group. Congress did not have the money to send supplies. Most soldiers wore clothing brought from home, but it had been torn and burned from battle. Some of the men's shoes were falling apart. Many wrapped their feet in rags. To keep their spirits up, soldiers sang "Yankee Doodle." Even though the song was written during the French and Indian War to make fun of the colonists, the Americans turned it around to make fun of the British.

Since food was also running low, Washington let his soldiers buy food from farmers with money from Congress. New York Governor George Clinton sent barrels of salted pork.

Help from Overseas

More help came from the 20-year-old Marquis de Lafayette, who traveled from France to join the Continental Army. Lafayette later said he had an American heart. Washington liked the young man

▶ **MARCH TO VALLEY FORGE**
Washington (on the white horse) and his army in 1777.

and gave him important jobs. Lafayette spent his own money to buy warm clothes for the soldiers he led. He was so giving that they called him "the soldier's friend."

Life at Valley Forge also got better when **Friedrich Wilhelm von Steuben** (STOO•buhn) arrived. Von Steuben was a German soldier who taught the American troops better ways to march and fight. He showed them how to work together and gave them confidence. By 1778, the Continental Army was much stronger.

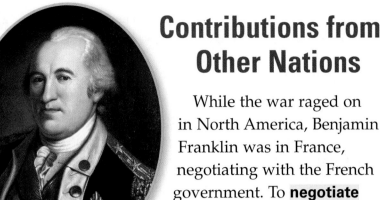

❯ **FRIEDRICH WILHELM VON STEUBEN**

READING CHECK ◯**CAUSE AND EFFECT**
What effect did Friedrich Wilhelm von Steuben have on the Continental Army?

Contributions from Other Nations

While the war raged on in North America, Benjamin Franklin was in France, negotiating with the French government. To **negotiate** is to try to reach an agreement among different people. Franklin asked the French for supplies and soldiers. He said that France would benefit from helping beat its old enemy, Britain.

At first, the French offered only secret help, thinking that Britain would win. When news of the American victory at Saratoga reached France, the French agreed to help the Americans.

Guns, Money, and Food

In 1779, Spain declared war on Britain. Bernardo de Gálvez (GAHL•ves), the governor of Spanish Louisiana, gave guns, food, and money to the Americans. Later, his troops captured many British forts. Jorge Farragut (FAR•uh•guht) came from Spain to fight for the Americans.

Other nations also helped. In 1781, the Netherlands gave a loan to Congress. Russian leaders tried to keep the British from blocking trade with the Americans.

READING CHECK ☼**CAUSE AND EFFECT**
What caused the French to join the war in support of the Americans?

Summary

The Continental Army was less trained than the British army. However, the Americans won important early victories at Trenton and Saratoga. Other nations helped the Patriot cause.

▶ **JORGE FARRAGUT** was 21 years old when he came from Spain to fight for the Americans in 1776. He later became an officer in the United States Navy.

REVIEW

1. **WHAT TO KNOW** What were some of the important early events of the Revolutionary War?

2. **VOCABULARY** Use the word **campaign** in a sentence about the Revolutionary War.

3. **HISTORY** Who led the Americans' negotiations with France?

4. **CRITICAL THINKING** Why was Valley Forge's location important to George Washington?

5. ✎ **WRITE A SPEECH** Imagine that you are camped with the soldiers at Valley Forge. Write a speech to lift the soldiers' spirits.

6. (Focus Skill) **CAUSE AND EFFECT** On a separate sheet of paper, copy and complete this graphic organizer.

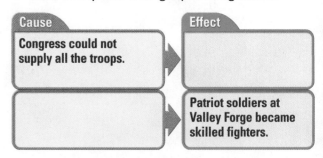

Cause		Effect
Congress could not supply all the troops.	→	
	→	Patriot soldiers at Valley Forge became skilled fighters.

Bernardo de Gálvez

Biography

Trustworthiness

Respect
Responsibility
Fairness
Caring
Patriotism

Bernardo de Gálvez was born in Málaga, Spain, in 1746. Gálvez first came to North America in 1762 with his uncle, who was visiting New Spain. In 1776, he returned to lead a Spanish regiment in Louisiana. One year later, Gálvez became the governor of Spanish Louisiana.

During the Revolutionary War, Gálvez helped American forces. He protected New Orleans against British attack, gaining control of the Mississippi River. Gálvez let American ships use the river to move weapons and food to Patriot forces fighting on the frontier.

In 1779, Spain declared war on Britain. Gálvez captured the British towns of Baton Rouge, Natchez, and Mobile. In 1781, he captured Pensacola. By the time the war ended, Gálvez and his army controlled all of West Florida and East Florida. After the war, the new United States Congress thanked Bernardo de Gálvez for his help during the American Revolution.

Why Character Counts

How did Gálvez prove his trustworthiness to the Americans?

Time

1746		1786
Born		Died

1777 Gálvez becomes governor of Spanish Louisiana

1781 Gálvez captures the town of Pensacola, Florida

GO ONLINE
For more resources, go to
www.harcourtschool.com/ss1

Life on the Battlefield

Background During the Revolutionary War, soldiers used many different items to help them during the fighting. They kept these materials with them at all times. Other items were important for the soldiers' comfort.

DBQ **Document-Based Question** Study these primary sources and answer the questions.

SHOT MOLD

Shot molds were used to make bullets. Melted lead was poured into the mold. After the lead cooled, the shot was removed.

LEATHER WALLET

Some soldiers used wallets to carry documents and personal letters.

DBQ **1** How would a wallet keep important items safe?

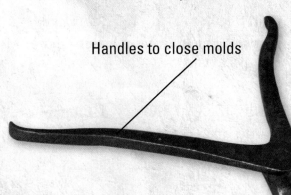

Handles to close molds

Lead shot

Brass buckle

DBQ **2** How did a shot mold create a round bullet?

3 Why did soldiers need to make their own bullets?

POWDER HORN

Soldiers carried powder for their guns in powder horns.
These containers were made from the horns of animals.
Plugs kept the powder dry until soldiers needed it.

Removable plug

DBQ **4** How did soldiers remove the powder?

5 Why would soldiers need to keep
powder horns near them?

See-through horn to
measure powder

ARMY UNIFORM

Some Continental Army soldiers wore
uniforms made of heavy blue wool.

DBQ **6** Why might it be difficult to fight
in this uniform in hot weather?

WOODEN CANTEEN

Canteens let soldiers carry water.
A plug kept the water from spilling.

DBQ **7** Why would having water be
important on the battlefield?

Coat

Undershirt

WRITE ABOUT IT

What do these primary sources tell
you about life on the battlefield? Write
a paragraph that describes the daily
life of a Continental Army soldier.

GO ONLINE For more resources, go to
www.harcourtschool.com/ss1

Lesson 3

Time

1780 — 1790

1781
The Battle of Yorktown

1783
The Treaty of Paris

WHAT TO KNOW
How did the Americans win the Revolutionary War?

VOCABULARY
civilian p. 357
traitor p. 359

PEOPLE
John Paul Jones
Nathan Hale
Mary Ludwig Hays
   McCauley
Tadeusz Kosciuszko
Benedict Arnold
Nathanael Greene
Charles Cornwallis

PLACES
West Point
Savannah
Charles Town
Cowpens
Guilford Courthouse
Yorktown

 **CAUSE AND EFFECT**

Cause	Effect

Winning Independence

YOU ARE THERE The booming sound of cannon fire echoes around you. As you stand on the deck of your ship, you try to see through the smoke. You wonder if the battle is over. Then you see your captain, **John Paul Jones**, walking toward you. "Back to your place, sailor!" he shouts. "This battle is far from over!"

▶ **NAVAL BATTLES** The Continental Navy had about 60 ships while the British navy had 270 ships.

Revolutionary Heroes

During the Revolutionary War, the Continental Army and Navy received help from many **civilians**, or people not in the military.

Nathan Hale was a teacher who served as an American spy in New York City. When he was captured by the British, they hanged him. According to legend, his final words were, "I regret that I have but one life to lose for my country."

Fighting Men and Women

At sea, John Paul Jones, an American navy commander, battled larger British ships. During one battle in the North Sea near Britain, the British asked Jones to give up. He said, "I have not yet begun to fight." Jones kept fighting until the British ship gave up.

▶ MARY McCAULEY

American women also won fame for their bravery during the war. **Mary Ludwig Hays McCauley** earned the name Molly Pitcher by carrying fresh water to American troops during the Battle of Monmouth in New Jersey in 1778. When her husband was wounded, she took his place in battle, loading the cannons. As word of the fight for freedom spread, more volunteers came. **Tadeusz Kosciuszko** (kawsh•CHUSH•koh) left Poland to serve in the Continental Army. He helped design the plans for a fort at **West Point**, New York, that is now part of the United States Military Academy.

READING CHECK ☼**CAUSE AND EFFECT**
What caused Mary McCauley to take part in the Battle of Monmouth?

Major Battles of the American Revolution

MAP SKILL REGIONS In which state was the Battle of Cowpens fought?

The War Moves

When the British learned that the French were helping the Americans, they decided to move the fighting to the South. The British had already captured many important cities in the North. They now hoped to defeat the Americans in the South before French help could arrive.

The British knew that many Loyalists lived in the South. They hoped to get help from these colonists. British leaders also hoped to capture Southern ports so they could receive supplies from British navy ships. Inland, the fighting was much harder. The British lost several battles along the frontier, including the Battle of Vincennes in what is now Indiana.

Battles in the South

Savannah, Georgia, was Britain's first target in the South. On November 25, 1778, about 3,500 British soldiers landed near the town. They quickly attacked the American soldiers who were trying to defend Savannah.

In 1780, the British took **Charles Town**, later known as Charleston, in South Carolina. There, too, the Americans were greatly outnumbered and soon lost.

Early in 1781, **Benedict Arnold**, a former Continental Army officer, led British attacks on Virginia towns. Arnold had become a **traitor**, or someone who acts against his or her country. He betrayed his country because he felt that he had not been treated fairly by the Army.

Americans Fight Back

Although the Americans lost several battles to the British, they kept fighting. General **Nathanael Greene**, who led the Continental Army in the South, told his soldiers not to give up. He wrote, "We fight, get beat, rise, and fight again."

Under Greene's leadership, General Daniel Morgan led the Americans to a major victory at **Cowpens**, South Carolina, in January 1781. The Battle of Cowpens proved that American forces could defeat the British in the South.

The British army then pushed into North Carolina, where they battled American troops at **Guilford Courthouse** in March 1781. The British held the field, but were terribly weakened by the battle. Both sides lost many soldiers in the fierce fighting. However, the British still could not win the war because no one city or town was at the heart of America.

READING CHECK ⊘ **CAUSE AND EFFECT**
Why did the British decide to move the fighting to the South?

❯ **THE BATTLE OF COWPENS, South Carolina, was a major victory for the Americans.**

The War Ends

By the summer of 1781, British General **Charles Cornwallis** had set up his headquarters at **Yorktown**, Virginia. Yorktown was on Chesapeake Bay. The bay made it easy for British ships to bring in supplies. However, Yorktown was also easy to circle around. Knowing this, the French and the Americans made a plan to surround Cornwallis at Yorktown.

Victory at Yorktown

Both French and American soldiers marched south to encircle Yorktown. At the same time, the French navy took control of Chesapeake Bay. General Cornwallis was trapped. He was under attack from both the land and the sea. After being surrounded for weeks, Cornwallis finally gave up on October 19, 1781.

The Treaty of Paris

The Battle of Yorktown was the last major battle of the war. However, some small battles continued to be fought. It was not until April 1782 that the two sides met in Paris, France, to negotiate a peace treaty.

The American negotiators John Jay, Benjamin Franklin, and John Adams wanted Britain to accept American independence. They also wanted all British soldiers removed from American lands. After a year of talks, the British agreed. The Treaty of Paris was signed on September 3, 1783, ending the war.

The Treaty of Paris named the United States of America as a new nation. It also set the new nation's borders.

▶ **YORKTOWN SURRENDER** During the surrender ceremony, a British army band played a song called "The World Turned Upside Down."

▶ **RETIRING** In 1775, when Washington was named commander in chief, he promised to retire when the war was over.

The United States reached from Georgia in the south to the Great Lakes in the north. The Mississippi River formed its western border.

After the War

After British troops left the country, George Washington started for his home in Virginia. In Annapolis, Maryland, he stopped where Congress was meeting. He retired as leader of the army, telling Congress that his work was done.

Congress thanked Washington for his loyal service and wished him well.

READING CHECK ☼**CAUSE AND EFFECT**
What was the effect of the Treaty of Paris?

Summary

American heroes helped the war effort. The Battle of Yorktown was the last major battle. In 1783, the Treaty of Paris declared the United States a new nation.

REVIEW

1. **WHAT TO KNOW** How did the Americans win the Revolutionary War?

2. **VOCABULARY** Use the term **civilian** in a sentence about Mary Ludwig Hays McCauley.

3. **GEOGRAPHY** What were the borders of the new United States?

4. How did the French help the Americans win the Battle of Yorktown?

5. **CRITICAL THINKING** Make It Relevant Why do you think that American heroes risked their lives in the war? Who do you think are heroes today?

6. **DRAW A MEDAL** Draw a medal of honor for one of the Patriot heroes. Be sure that the medal shows the hero's contribution.

7. **CAUSE AND EFFECT**
   Focus Skill On a separate sheet of paper, copy and complete this graphic organizer.

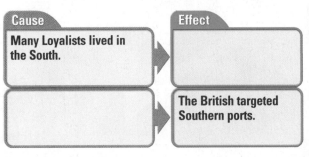

Cause		Effect
Many Loyalists lived in the South.	▶	
	▶	The British targeted Southern ports.

Tell Fact from Fiction

Why It Matters In order to write, research, or talk about history, you need to be able to tell the difference between what is true and what is fiction, or made-up.

❱ LEARN

You can make sure information is factual by finding the same information in a reference source or a nonfiction book. Other sources of facts are **documentary sources**, such as letters and diaries. These sources are written by a person soon after experiencing a historical event. Fiction writers sometimes write stories about events that take place in the past, but they make up details that add to the story.

❱ PRACTICE

On page 363 are two descriptions of the British surrender after the Battle of Yorktown. The first is by François-Joseph-Paul Grasse, a French officer who was there. The second is from *A Message for General Washington*, a fictional book. Read both accounts, and then answer the questions that follow.

❱ **YORKTOWN** Washington worked with French Lieutenant General Rochambeau at the Battle of Yorktown.

▶ YORKTOWN TODAY This photograph shows reenactors at the Yorktown Battlefield, which is part of Colonial National Historical Park in Virginia.

66 In front of each line . . . the commanding officers took their place. . . . At the head of the slowly moving British [line] was General O'Hara. Cornwallis pleaded illness, and O'Hara [carried] his sword. 99

66 A troop of Redcoats marched forward, then halted. . . . 'That isn't Cornwallis. . . . That's Brigadier General Charles O'Hara—an Irish officer!' Muttered protests swept through the crowd. 'Cornwallis is sick,' one woman said . . . 'or so he says. I think he's pretending.' 99

❶ How are the descriptions similar? How are they different?

❷ Tell which source is documentary and which source is fictional, and why.

▶ APPLY

Choose any statement in Lesson 3, and check a reference source or nonfiction book to make sure the statement is a fact.

Time

1760   1790

1783
Slavery is
abolished in
Massachusetts

1787
The Northwest
Ordinance is passed

💡 WHAT TO KNOW
How did the American
Revolution affect life in the
new United States?

VOCABULARY
abolitionist p. 365
abolish p. 365
territory p. 367
ordinance p. 367

PEOPLE
Elizabeth Freeman
Michikinikwa
Segoyewatha

PLACES
Northwest Territory

⭐ CAUSE AND EFFECT
(Focus Skill)

Cause	Effect

Effects of the War

YOU ARE THERE

"Slavery is wrong!" a man shouts to
the crowd. "Just read the Declaration of
Independence. It says everybody should have liberty."
Other members of the group nod their heads. "It's
not right that we should win our freedom but deny
freedom to enslaved people," your mother says.
"We should stop slavery," another person says.
"But that's going to be hard."

▶ **ANTISLAVERY ARTIFACTS**
This medal and sermon
illustrate the antislavery
movement.

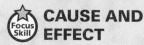

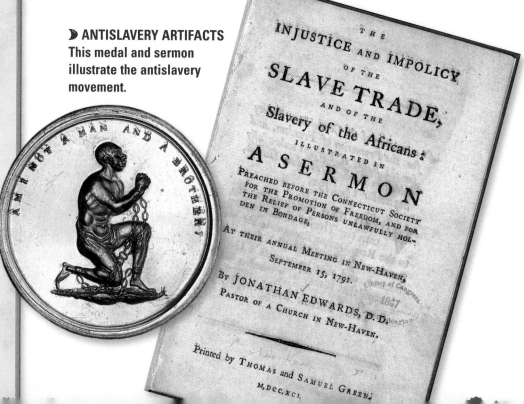

THE
INJUSTICE AND IMPOLICY
OF THE
SLAVE TRADE,
AND OF THE
Slavery of the Africans:
ILLUSTRATED IN
A SERMON
PREACHED BEFORE THE CONNECTICUT SOCIETY
FOR THE PROMOTION OF FREEDOM, AND FOR
THE RELIEF OF PERSONS UNLAWFULLY HOL-
DEN IN BONDAGE,
AT THEIR ANNUAL MEETING IN NEW-HAVEN,
SEPTEMBER 15, 1791.
BY JONATHAN EDWARDS, D. D.
PASTOR OF A CHURCH IN NEW-HAVEN.

Printed by THOMAS and SAMUEL GREEN.
M.DCC.XCI.

▶ **SPEAKING AGAINST SLAVERY** African American ministers were leaders in the effort to end slavery.

New Ideas

By 1776, the states had begun to write their own constitutions. Several of them used Virginia's constitution as a model. It began with a list of basic freedoms, including the right to trial by jury, the freedom to hold elections, and freedom of the press. These and many others were freedoms that people fought for in the American Revolution.

The Declaration of Independence had changed the way some Americans thought about people's rights. It said that each person has the right to life and liberty. However, state constitutions did not give this freedom to all people. Women were not given the same rights as men, such as voting rights, and most African Americans remained enslaved.

Early Attempts to End Slavery

Some people believed that slavery should be ended. In 1775, Quakers in Philadelphia had started the country's first **abolitionist** (a•buh•LIH•shuhn•ist), or antislavery, group. Antislavery feelings grew after the Declaration was approved.

In Massachusetts, an enslaved woman named **Elizabeth Freeman** sued to be free. When asked why she was suing, she said, "I heard that paper [the Declaration] read yesterday that all [people] are born equal." The jury agreed, and she won. In 1783, Massachusetts **abolished**, or ended, slavery. Over time, other northern states also abolished slavery.

READING CHECK ⚙ **CAUSE AND EFFECT**
How did the Declaration of Independence change the way some people viewed slavery?

Western Settlements

When the Revolutionary War ended, the United States did not have enough money to pay all the soldiers who had served. However, the United States had won more land from the British. Instead of paying the soldiers with money, Congress decided to pay some of them with land. Soldiers received different amounts of land based on their rank and how long they had served. Some soldiers were given hundreds of acres of land in areas west of the Appalachians.

Moving West

Many former soldiers moved to these western areas. However, not all of the people who moved west were soldiers. Many families moved west of the Appalachians to start farms. Eager to raise more money, Congress sold large amounts of land to these settlers and to land companies.

The United States now stretched west to the Mississippi River, but British troops were still in some northwestern forts. Spain also claimed lands along the country's western and southern borders. Many Native American groups lived in the lands along the Ohio River.

South of the Ohio River

Some of the fastest growing areas in the country were those lands south of the Ohio River. During the American Revolution, more than 100,000 people moved to the area that later became the state of Kentucky. Others moved to the area that became the state of Tennessee.

READING CHECK ☼ **CAUSE AND EFFECT**
What caused Congress to pay many soldiers with land?

▶ **MOVING WEST** Settlers moved west of the Appalachians to build new lives.

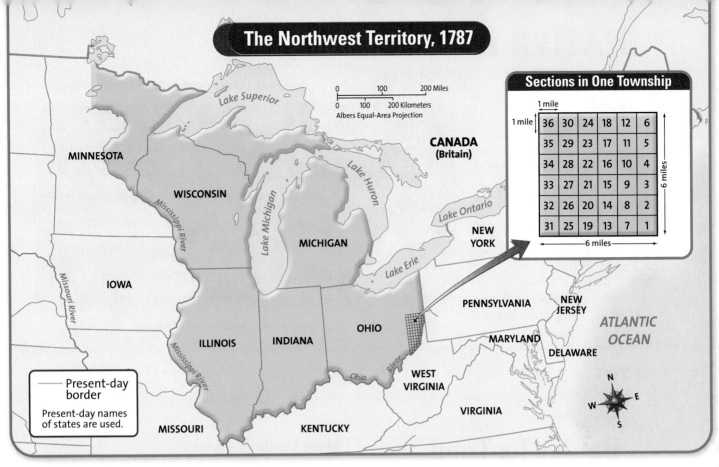

The Northwest Territory, 1787

Sections in One Township

36	30	24	18	12	6
35	29	23	17	11	5
34	28	22	16	10	4
33	27	21	15	9	3
32	26	20	14	8	2
31	25	19	13	7	1

1 mile

6 miles

6 miles

CANADA (Britain)

MINNESOTA

WISCONSIN

Lake Superior

Lake Michigan

Lake Huron

Lake Ontario

Lake Erie

MICHIGAN

NEW YORK

IOWA

Mississippi River

Missouri River

PENNSYLVANIA

NEW JERSEY

ATLANTIC OCEAN

ILLINOIS

INDIANA

OHIO

MARYLAND

DELAWARE

Ohio River

WEST VIRGINIA

VIRGINIA

MISSOURI

KENTUCKY

0   100   200 Miles
0   100   200 Kilometers
Albers Equal-Area Projection

— Present-day border

Present-day names of states are used.

MAP SKILL **LOCATION** The Northwest Territory covered more than 260,000 square miles. What river formed its southern boundary?

The Northwest Territory

Over time, thousands of Americans followed the Ohio River west and settled the lands north of it. That area became known as the **Northwest Territory**. A **territory** is land that belongs to a nation but is not a state and is not represented in the national government.

Governing the Land

At first, there was no plan for how land in the territory should be divided. It was hard to tell where each person's property ended. In 1785, Congress passed a new land **ordinance**, or set of laws. The ordinance explained how land in the

territory would be measured, divided, and sold. Land was first divided into squares called townships. Each township was then divided into 36 smaller squares, or sections.

In 1787, Congress passed another ordinance called the Northwest Ordinance of 1787. It set up a plan for governing the Northwest Territory and for forming new states from its lands. When any region of the Northwest Territory had more than 60,000 people, it could become a state. The ordinance promised settlers freedom of religion. It also said that slavery would not be allowed in states formed from the Northwest Territory.

READING CHECK ⚙ **CAUSE AND EFFECT**
How did the Northwest Ordinance of 1787 affect slavery?

NATIVE AMERICANS
AFTER THE REVOLUTION

▶ Michikinikwa organizes Native Americans

▶ The Battle of Fallen Timbers is fought

1791

1794

Battles for Land

In the months after the Revolutionary War, the British left many of their forts in the West. Without British help, it became harder for Native Americans to stop settlers from moving onto their lands.

New Fighting Breaks Out

Native Americans in the Northwest Territory united to fight against the new settlers. Their leaders included **Michikinikwa** (mih•chih•kin•EE•kwah), also known as Little Turtle, a member of the Miami tribe in what are now Ohio and Indiana.

In the early 1790s, Native American forces soundly defeated United States soldiers in battles in what are now the states of Indiana and Ohio. In 1794, a larger United States force won a major victory at the Battle of Fallen Timbers, near what is now Toledo, Ohio.

More Lands Are Taken

In 1795, Michikinikwa and the leaders of the other tribes agreed to accept the Treaty of Greenville. In this treaty, they gave up most of their land in the Northwest Territory. Many Native Americans were angry that the United States demanded their lands. After the treaty was signed, they stopped trusting in the United States government.

Some Native Americans sold their land to land companies. The Holland Land Company, for example, wanted to buy much of the land in western New York from the Seneca Indians. The Seneca leader **Segoyewatha**, also known as Red Jacket, warned his tribe not to sell its land. However, other leaders ignored his advice and signed the Big Tree Treaty, which let the company buy most of the Seneca's land.

In the years to come, settlers from the United States moved farther and farther

▶ The Treaty of Greenville is signed

▶ Treaty of Greenville peace medal

▶ Red Jacket warns against the Big Tree Treaty

1795   1797

west. They cleared the land for farms and towns. The lives of Native Americans would never be the same.

READING CHECK ○ **CAUSE AND EFFECT**
What was the effect of the Treaty of Greenville?

Summary

After the Revolutionary War, states wrote constitutions. Views on slavery changed. Western settlement led to land policies and fights with Native Americans.

REVIEW

1. **WHAT TO KNOW** How did the American Revolution affect life in the new United States?

2. **VOCABULARY** Describe the difference between a state and a **territory**.

3. **HISTORY** How did Congress pay some soldiers for their service in the Revolutionary War?

4. **CRITICAL THINKING** How do you think Native Americans felt about the Treaty of Greenville?

5. ✎ **WRITE A NEWS ARTICLE** Imagine you are a reporter covering the Elizabeth Freeman court case. Write an article about the jury's decision.

6. ⭐ (Focus Skill) **CAUSE AND EFFECT** On a separate sheet of paper, copy and complete this graphic organizer.

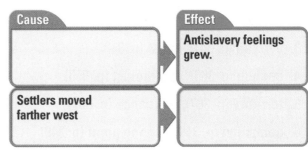

Cause	Effect
	Antislavery feelings grew.
Settlers moved farther west	

Time

1760   1770

• **1776**
The Battle
of Trenton is
fought

1777
The Americans
win the Battle
of Saratoga

Visual Summary

Summarize the Chapter

Cause and Effect Complete this graphic organizer to show
that you understand the causes and effects of some of the key
events of the Revolutionary War.

Cause

Congress printed more
money.

Effect

Cause

Effect

France agreed to help
the Americans.

 Vocabulary

Write a sentence or two to explain how
each pair of terms is related.

1. **Patriot** (p. 339), **Loyalist** (p. 339)

2. **inflation** (p. 340), **profiteering** (p. 340)

3. **veteran** (p. 341), **enlist** (p. 347)

4. **abolish** (p. 365), **abolitionist** (p. 365)

5. **territory** (p. 367), **ordinance** (p. 367)

6. **campaign** (p. 349), **turning point** (p. 349)

 Time Line

Use the chapter summary time line above to
answer these questions.

7. In which year was the Battle of Trenton
fought?

8. Did the Battle of Saratoga happen before or
after the Battle of Trenton?

9. What happened at Yorktown?

10. How many years after the Battle of Yorktown
was the Treaty of Paris signed?

 1780 **1790**

1781
The Americans defeat the British at Yorktown

1783
The Treaty of Paris is signed

Facts and Main Ideas

Answer these questions.

11. How did the British navy cause economic hardship for the colonies?

12. Why did some African Americans decide to fight in the Revolutionary War?

13. How were Native Americans divided by the Revolutionary War?

14. Why did Britain move the fighting to the Southern Colonies?

Write the letter of the best choice.

15. Which country helped the Americans win the Battle of Yorktown?
    A France
    B Germany
    C Spain
    D the Netherlands

16. What was the name of the plan for governing the western lands north of the Ohio River?
    A the Articles of Confederation
    B the Ohio Valley Authority
    C the Northwest Ordinance of 1787
    D the Treaty of Paris

17. What document changed the way many Americans viewed slavery?
    A the Declaration of Independence
    B the Treaty of Paris
    C the Northwest Ordinance
    D the Virginia Constitution

Critical Thinking

18. What do you think might have happened if American soldiers had lost the Battle of Saratoga?

19. How did Yorktown's location help the American forces?

Skills

Read Parallel Time Lines

Use the parallel time line on pages 344–345 to answer these questions.

20. What event happened in Britain in the same year that the Boston Massacre took place?

21. What event happened in Britain in 1774? What happened in the colonies that same year?

writing

Write a Narrative Imagine that you are one of the soldiers camped at Valley Forge in the winter of 1777. Write a story that explains why you are there. Describe the hardships you are facing.

Write a Report Choose one person you read about in this chapter. Then write a report for your class that describes who that person was and what role he or she played in the Revolutionary War.

Fun with Social Studies

Writers, Commanders, and Spies

Find two of each—writers, commanders, and spies—from the pictures at the right.

George Washington

Thomas Paine

James Armistead

Joseph Brant

Phillis Wheatley

Nathan Hale

Rebus Revolution

VOCABULARY

Find the rebus word that doesn't belong.

 + = ?

 + = ?

au + +  = ?

 +   = ?

Vacation Station

What vacation spot does each poster advertise?

VICTORY!

Visit the site of the battle that **decided** the **war!**

See where **General Cornwallis** surrendered to the Americans. Feel the joy of the end of the long fight for **independence.** Today, everyone is welcome!

HERE'S WHERE IT ALL BEGAN

The thump of marching feet . . . shouts of soldiers . . . sounds of musket fire . . . the beginning of war . . . April 1775, on our town square. Come and stroll the green grass where the Minutemen first stood their ground against the British. IT'S PEACEFUL NOW!

It's a party!

Come on board a replica of an East India Company ship. Imagine you're one of the Sons of Liberty, turning this vacation spot into a **giant** teapot! Come see where history was made.

Like no other!

You'll have a TEA-rific time!

Online Adventures

GO ONLINE

Boston Inn

You and Eco are on your way to Massachusetts in 1775. In this online game, you will become a Patriot in Boston. Work to discover what is happening in the city. People in the colonies are getting ready for war, and British soldiers are on the march. Can you find out where the British are going and warn the colonists in time? Play now at **www.harcourtschool.com/ss1**

Review and Test Prep ✓

💡 THE BIG IDEA

Freedom Freedom was so important to the colonists that they were willing to suffer terrible hardships and years of war to win it.

Reading Comprehension and Vocabulary

The American Revolution

In 1764, the British Parliament passed a tax law to help pay the costs of the French and Indian War. This law made many colonists angry. They did not think it was fair to have to pay taxes to a government in which they had no representation.

Anger grew as Parliament passed even more tax laws. Many colonists protested. Some refused to pay taxes, and others began to boycott all British goods.

In 1776, the 13 colonies declared their independence from Britain. They knew this act would cause a war against one of the most powerful nations in the world. The colonies had little money and few trained soldiers. Still, they fought.

George Washington was the leader of the Continental Army. With the help of citizens and other nations, the Patriots began to win battles. After eight difficult years of fighting, the Americans won the war.

The Treaty of Paris officially ended the war in 1783. It also made the United States a new nation. The United States faced many challenges. It had to deal with settlement in the western lands, the problem of slavery, and many other issues.

Use the summary above to answer these questions. Write the letter of the best choice.

1. What does representation mean?
   A freedom to govern on one's own
   B an agreement between two nations
   C the act of speaking for someone else
   D a formal statement

2. Which role did George Washington play in the American Revolution?
   A He raised tax money to pay for the war.
   B He negotiated with France for support.
   C He led the Continental Army.
   D He wrote the Declaration of Independence.

3. What does the word Patriots mean in the sentence above?
   A hired soldiers
   B colonists who supported independence
   C Britain's Native American allies
   D colonists who remained loyal to Britain

4. When did the United States officially become a new nation?
   A 1764
   B 1776
   C 1781
   D 1783

Answer these questions.

5. The French and Indian War began as competition for control of what region?

6. What was the Stamp Act?

7. How did many colonists protest the Townshend Acts?

8. What was Thomas Jefferson's main job at the Second Continental Congress?

9. How did Mercy Otis Warren contribute to the Patriot cause?

10. How did France help the Americans in the Revolutionary War?

Write the letter of the best choice.

11. Which key idea is included in the Declaration of Independence?
   A the right to send grievances to Parliament
   B the right to live, be free, and seek happiness
   C the importance of remaining neutral
   D the abolition of slavery

12. Who was known as "the soldier's friend" at Valley Forge?
   A Friedrich Wilhelm von Steuben
   B George Washington
   C Benedict Arnold
   D Marquis de Lafayette

13. Which was the last major battle of the Revolutionary War?
   A the Battle of Bunker Hill
   B the Battle of Long Island
   C the Battle of Saratoga
   D the Battle of Yorktown

14. How did the United States government pay some Revolutionary War soldiers?
   A with money from the British
   B with positions in the government
   C with land
   D with British goods taken in the war

15. Do you think Britain could have avoided war with the American colonists? Explain.

16. How did Thomas Paine change people's attitudes toward government?

Compare Historical Maps

Use the historical maps below to answer these questions.

17. Why is an area marked in hatch lines on the 1763 map but not on the 1783 map?

18. What areas shown on the maps changed very little between 1763 and 1783? Why?

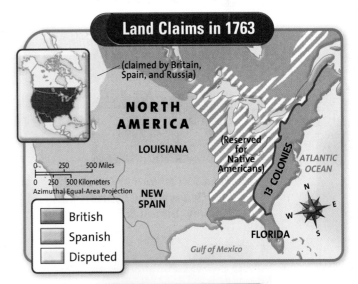

Land Claims in 1763

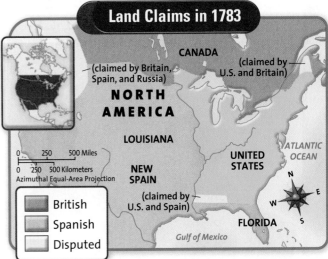

Land Claims in 1783

Unit 4 ▪ 375

Unit 4 Activities

Show What You Know

✏️ Unit Writing Activity

Write a Summary Describe the causes and effects of the American Revolution.

- List three main causes of the war.
- Tell how the colonists won their freedom.
- Explain why the war was important.

Unit Project

A Colonial Newspaper Publish a colonial newspaper that tells about the Revolutionary War.

- Describe events leading up to the war.
- Tell how the colonists won their freedom.
- Decide which people, places, and events to include.

Read More

- *When Washington Crossed the Delaware* by Lynne Cheney. Simon & Schuster.

- *A Voice of Her Own: The Story of Phillis Wheatley, Slave Poet* by Kathryn Lasky. Candlewick Press.

- *Fight for Freedom* by Benson Bobrick. Atheneum.

GO ONLINE For more resources, go to
www.harcourtschool.com/ss1

A Growing Nation

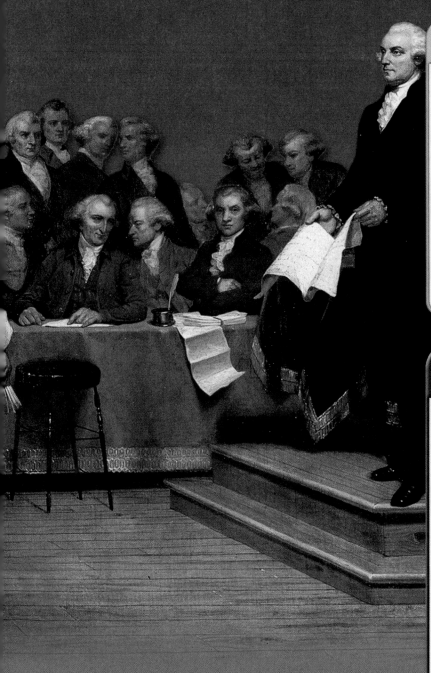

Start with the Standards

OHIO SOCIAL STUDIES CONTENT STANDARDS

History 5.1, 5.4, 5.6

People in Societies 5.4

Geography 5.2B, 5.7A, 5.8

Government 5.1A, 5.1B, 5.1C, 5.2A, 5.2B, 5.2C, 5.2D, 5.2E, 5.3

Citizenship 5.1A, 5.1B, 5.2A, 5.2B, 5.2C, 5.2D, 5.3A, 5.3B, 5.3C, 5.3D

Social Studies Skills 5.4A, 5.4B, 5.4C, 5.5, 5.6, 5.8, 5.9A, 5.9B, 5.9C, 5.9D, 5.9E, 5.9F, 5.9G

The Big Idea

Growth and Change

The United States established a new government and grew larger as more people arrived and lands were acquired.

What to Know

✓ What were some of the major problems faced by the writers of the Constitution?

✓ How does the Constitution secure our liberty?

✓ How did western settlement affect Native Americans?

✓ What kind of changes did the United States face in the early 1800s?

Ohio STATEHOOD

DID YOU KNOW?

Arthur St. Clair, the governor of the Northwest Territory, opposed statehood. He wanted Ohio to become two states.

OHIO

Chillicothe

> Capitol building in Columbus

In 1787, Ohio became part of the Northwest Territory. The United States government set up a procedure for allowing territories to become states by passing the Northwest Ordinance. A territory needed a population of 60,000 and its own constitution to become a state.

Some people living in Ohio wanted Ohio to become a state. In 1800, an official count of the population was made. It showed that 45,000 people lived in the area. Knowing that Ohio would soon have enough people to become a state, settlers gathered in 1802 to write a constitution. They sent the constitution to the United States Congress. Ohio's constitution was approved by Congress. On March 1, 1803, Ohio became the seventeenth state.

Edward Tiffin

Edward Tiffin became Ohio's first governor. Before becoming governor, Tiffin was a doctor and a minister. He served as governor until 1807, when he was elected to the United States Senate. Tiffin also served in the Ohio House of Representatives.

Chillicothe was Ohio's first capital. The state's lawmakers met in a two-story building that served as the statehouse. The capital was moved to Zanesville in 1810 and then to Columbus in 1816.

Ohio's first capitol building in Chillicothe

THE GREAT SEAL OF THE STATE OF OHIO

OHIO TEST PREP

1 How many people did a territory need to become a state?
A. 30,000
B. 45,000
C. 60,000

2 What did Edward Tiffin do?
A. wrote the Northwest Ordinance
B. became Ohio's first governor
C. opposed statehood

3 What city served as Ohio's first capital?
A. Chillicothe
B. Zanesville
C. Columbus

4 How did Ohio become a state?

Time

The New Nation

1787 The United States Constitution is written, p. 405

1789 George Washington becomes President, p. 408

1791 The Bill of Rights is added to the Constitution, p. 407

1780

1800

At the Same Time

1810 The Mexican Revolution begins

A Growing Nation

1803 The United States makes the Louisiana Purchase, p. 429

1825 The Erie Canal opens, p. 453

1846 The Mexican American War begins, p. 448

1848 Gold is discovered in California, p. 450

1820

1840

1860

 1822 Freed African Americans found the colony of Liberia

1834 Slavery is abolished in Britain

 1839 The first photograph system is developed in France

Benjamin Banneker

1731–1806
- Maryland farmer who taught himself mathematics and astronomy
- Helped survey the land for Washington, D.C.

James Madison

1751–1836
- Virginia leader who helped organize the Constitutional Convention
- Served as the fourth President of the United States

People

1700	1750	1800

1731 • Benjamin Banneker 1806

1751 • James Madison

1752 • Gouverneur Morris 1816

1757? • Alexander Hamilton 1804

1774 • Meriwether Lewis 1809

1779 • Francis Scott Key

1786? • Sacagawea 1812?

1790 • John Ross

Meriwether Lewis

1774–1809
- Captain in the United States Army
- Explored the Louisiana Purchase with William Clark

Francis Scott Key

1779–1843
- Worked as a lawyer in Washington, D.C.
- Wrote "The Star-Spangled Banner" after the Battle of Fort McHenry

Gouverneur Morris

1752–1816
- Pennsylvania representative to the Constitutional Convention
- Wrote the Preamble to the United States Constitution

Alexander Hamilton

1757?–1804
- New York leader who worked to help ratify the Constitution
- Served as the first secretary of the treasury

1850   1900   1950

1836

1843

1866

Sacagawea

1786?–1812?
- Daughter of a Shoshone chief
- Served as an interpreter and guide for the Lewis and Clark expedition

John Ross

1790–1866
- Chief of the Cherokee Nation
- Led the Cherokees on the journey known as the "Trail of Tears"

ROCKY

Missouri River

KIOWA

GREAT

CROW

MANDAN

TREATY WITH
BRITAIN
1842

SIOUX

YAKIMA

Oregon City

CHINOOK

NEZ
PERCE

OREGON TERRITORY
1846

MODOC

PAIUTE

SIOUX

CHEYENNE

LOUISIANA PURCHASE
1803

Missouri

River

River

POMO

Lake
Tahoe

GREAT
BASIN

Great
Salt
Lake

Salt Lake
City

Platte River

PAWNEE

IOWA
Omaha

M
O
U
N
T
A
I
N
S

San
Francisco

MIWOK

MEXICAN CESSION
1848

UTE

ARAPAHO

P
L
A
I
N
S

Independence

KAW

YOKUTS

PAIUTE

Arkansas

River

Mojave
Desert

Los Angeles

CAHUILLA

San Diego

Gila River

HOPI

NAVAJO

Santa Fe

Colorado River

Red

River

WICHITA

Lake
Texoma

PACIFIC
OCEAN

GADSDEN
PURCHASE
1853

PIMA

APACHE

COMANCHE

El Paso

Gila River

TEXAS
ANNEXATION
1845

San
Antonio

MEXICO

Gold is discovered at
Sutter's Mill, 1848

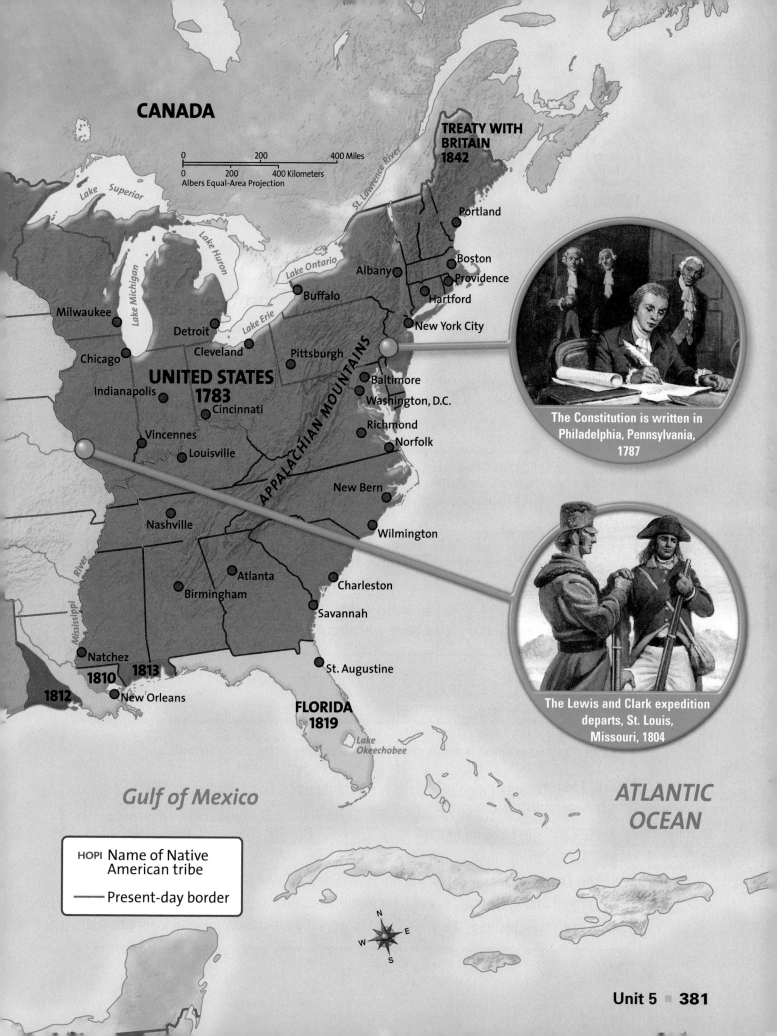

CANADA

0 200 400 Miles
0 200 400 Kilometers
Albers Equal-Area Projection

Lake Superior
Lake Huron
Lake Michigan
Lake Ontario
Lake Erie
St. Lawrence River

TREATY WITH
BRITAIN
1842

Portland

Boston
Providence
Hartford

Albany

Buffalo

New York City

Milwaukee

Detroit

Chicago

Cleveland

Pittsburgh

UNITED STATES
1783

Indianapolis

Cincinnati

APPALACHIAN MOUNTAINS

Baltimore
Washington, D.C.

Vincennes

Louisville

Richmond
Norfolk

New Bern

Nashville

Wilmington

Mississippi River

Atlanta

Birmingham

Charleston

Savannah

Natchez
1810
1813

1812

New Orleans

St. Augustine

FLORIDA
1819

Lake
Okeechobee

Gulf of Mexico

ATLANTIC
OCEAN

The Constitution is written in
Philadelphia, Pennsylvania,
1787

The Lewis and Clark expedition
departs, St. Louis,
Missouri, 1804

HOPI Name of Native
American tribe

Present-day border

N
W E
S

Reading Social Studies

(Focus Skill) Draw Conclusions

Why It Matters Being able to draw a conclusion can help you better understand what you read.

➤ LEARN

A **conclusion** is a broad statement about an idea or event. It is reached by using what you learn from reading, along with what you already know.

Evidence

What you learn

Knowledge

What you already know

Conclusion

A broad statement about an idea or event

- Keep in mind what you already know about the subject and the new facts you learn.
- Look for clues, and try to figure out what they mean.
- Combine new facts with the facts you already know to draw a conclusion.

➤ PRACTICE

Read the paragraphs. Draw a conclusion from the second paragraph.

In 1776, Thomas Paine published a pamphlet titled *Common Sense*. In it, he wrote that people should rule themselves. He also called for a revolution. (The American colonists fought a revolution against Britain. Thomas Paine helped inspire this revolution.)

Evidence
Knowledge
Conclusion

The colonies had united to win the Revolutionary War. After the war, many people hoped that all 13 states could act together as one nation under the Articles of Confederation. Instead, the United States government was weak and disorganized.

Read the paragraphs, and answer the questions.

A Growing Nation

The American colonists had fought hard to win independence from Britain, but the work of making a new country had just begun. The United States government under the Articles of Confederation was very weak. Each state had its own laws, money, and army and navy. This created much confusion. Some Americans doubted that they could ever agree to all be part of the same country.

Someone had to get the United States organized. Strong leaders, such as Benjamin Franklin, James Madison, and Alexander Hamilton, soon stepped forward to propose a new plan of government. In 1789, the Constitution was ratified.

In the years following the American Revolution, the United States grew and many Americans moved west. In 1800, nearly one million settlers lived on the western frontier. Many new states were admitted to the Union. These included Kentucky, Ohio, and Tennessee. Many Americans decided to move west because of the large amounts of cheap land. They saw opportunities to start a new life.

⭐ Focus Skill Draw Conclusions

1. What conclusions can you draw about the United States after the Revolutionary War?
2. Why did the United States need a new form of government?
3. What conclusions can you draw about why settlers would move west and what opportunities they would have?

▶ A soldier in the American Revolution

...If You Were There When They Signed the Constitution

by Elizabeth Levy • illustrated by Peter Siu

In 1787, delegates from 12 states met in Philadelphia, Pennsylvania, to discuss the national government of the young United States. Their debates lasted four months. In that time, they created the plan of government that still guides us today—the Constitution of the United States.

What is the Constitution?

The Constitution of the United States is the basic law of our nation—like the rules for a game, only these rules are for the government, and all citizens must play.

The Constitution sets up the rules for how laws are made, and who will make the laws. Who will decide if we go to war? Who will have power? You? Me? You can find those answers in the Constitution.

The Constitution of the United States was written in 1787. . . . The men who wrote it wanted their new nation to last. They knew how hard it was to create a government that could change with the times. After all, they had just fought and won a war against a government that had refused to change.

When the Convention finally opened, where did the delegates meet?

They met at the Pennsylvania State House or, as people were already beginning to call it, Independence Hall. It was here that Thomas Jefferson had first read his Declaration of Independence to many of the same men who were now gathering to write the Constitution. . . .

The Convention was mostly held in the East Room, a comfortable room about forty feet by forty feet, probably more than twice the size of your classroom, but smaller than your gym. The delegates sat at round tables covered with green cloths, about three or four to a table.

When you visit Independence Hall, you immediately feel that this is a good room for a debate—not too fancy, yet filled with light from the great tall windows on each side.

Response Corner

1. **Focus Skill** **Draw Conclusions** What does the Constitution do?

2. **Make It Relevant** What rules would you include in a constitution for your school? Defend your choices.

STUDY SKILLS

VOCABULARY

Using a dictionary can help you learn new words.

- **A dictionary shows the meanings of a word and tells its origin, or where it came from.**

- **You can use a chart to organize unfamiliar words.**

republic (ri-´pə-blik) *n.* [from the Latin *respublica*, a public thing] **1. a.** a government whose leader is not a monarch and whose citizens elect leaders and representatives **b.** a political unit, such as a nation, having such a form of government **2.** a group of people freely involved in a specific activity

Word	Syllables	Origin	Definition
republic	re•pub•lic	Latin	A country or government where the citizens elect leaders.

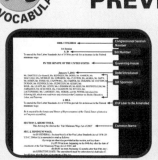

PREVIEW VOCABULARY

bill p. 392   **legislative branch** p. 400   **political party** p. 408

The Constitution

10

INDEPENDENCE HALL IN PHILADELPHIA, PENNSYLVANIA

Chapter 10 387

Time

1780   1820   1860

1787
The Constitutional
Convention begins

1787
The Great Compromise
is approved

WHAT TO KNOW
How was a new plan
of government developed
at the Constitutional
Convention?

VOCABULARY
arsenal p. 389

federal system p. 390

republic p. 390

compromise p. 392

bill p. 392

PEOPLE
Daniel Shays
James Madison
Patrick Henry
George Washington
Edmund Randolph
William Paterson
Gouverneur Morris

PLACES
Philadelphia

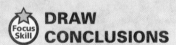

DRAW CONCLUSIONS

The Constitutional Convention

YOU ARE THERE

The year is 1787. The city of **Philadelphia** has hired you to spread dirt over Chestnut Street in front of the Pennsylvania State House. People keep stopping to ask why you are covering up the cobblestones. You explain that a meeting to fix the Articles of Confederation is going on in the State House. The delegates need quiet so they can work. The dirt will soften the clatter of the horses' hooves.

▶ BENJAMIN FRANKLIN, the oldest delegate, arrives at the Pennsylvania State House.

▶ **SHAYS'S REBELLION** During the attack on the arsenal, four of Shays's followers were killed.

Reasons for Change

During the 1780s, many Americans were poor, yet they had to pay high state taxes. People often had to borrow money and go into debt. When they could not repay their debts, state courts took away their farms or sent the people to prison.

In the summer of 1786, poor farmers in Massachusetts protested by refusing to let the courts meet. Armed with pitchforks and guns, they shut down the courthouse and destroyed debt records.

In January 1787, a mob of farmers led by **Daniel Shays** tried to take over a Massachusetts **arsenal**, or weapons store-house. Because there was no national army to defend the arsenal, the governor had to send soldiers to stop Shays. Shays's Rebellion made some people think that the national government could not keep order or protect them.

Ideas for Change

James Madison of Virginia, and other leaders, argued that the country needed a stronger national government. Every state had a governor, but there was no single national leader. To pass any law, nine states had to agree. There was no national court system to settle disputes.

Others did not agree. **Patrick Henry**, of Virginia, was one of many leaders who wanted to keep the Articles as they were. Henry argued that Americans had fought the British because they did not want a powerful government ruling their lives.

In 1787, all of the states except Rhode Island sent delegates to a convention in Philadelphia. The goal of this convention was to fix the Articles.

READING CHECK ⭕ **DRAW CONCLUSIONS**
Why did some people want a stronger national government?

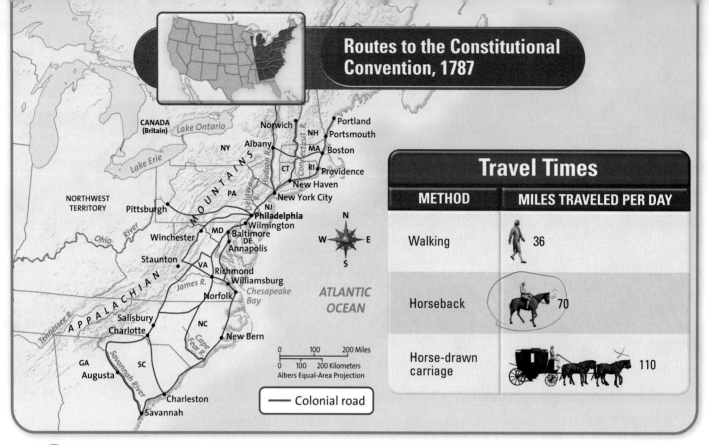

Routes to the Constitutional Convention, 1787

CANADA (Britain)
Lake Ontario
Lake Erie
NORTHWEST TERRITORY
Pittsburgh
Ohio River
Winchester
Staunton
Tennessee R.
Salisbury
Charlotte
Augusta
GA
SC
Savannah River
Charleston
Savannah
APPALACHIAN
MOUNTAINS
Norwich
Albany
NY
PA
NJ
MD
VA
James R.
Richmond
Williamsburg
Norfolk
NC
New Bern
Cape Fear R.
NH
Portland
Portsmouth
MA
Boston
CT
RI
Providence
New Haven
New York City
Philadelphia
Wilmington
Baltimore
DE
Annapolis
Chesapeake Bay
ATLANTIC OCEAN
Hudson R.
Delaware R.
Connecticut R.

N W E S

0   100   200 Miles
0 100 200 Kilometers
Albers Equal-Area Projection

—— Colonial road

Travel Times	
METHOD	**MILES TRAVELED PER DAY**
Walking	36
Horseback	70
Horse-drawn carriage	110

MAP SKILL **LOCATION** About how many miles is it from Pittsburgh, Pennsylvania, to Philadelphia?

The Work Begins

In May 1787, the 55 delegates from 12 states gathered at the Pennsylvania State House. They chose **George Washington** to be president of the Constitutional Convention, as it later came to be known.

Creating the Constitution

When the Constitutional Convention began, the delegates agreed to keep their discussions secret. They felt that talking in private would allow them to speak freely and make good decisions. Windows in the State House were covered, and guards stood at the doors.

Soon after discussions began, **Edmund Randolph** of Virginia asked the delegates to do away with the Articles of Confederation and write a new plan of government. The next day, they agreed.

One issue that the delegates discussed was the relationship between the states and the national government. Some delegates thought there should be a strong national government. Others believed that the states should have more power.

The delegates finally agreed to strengthen the existing **federal system**. The national and state governments would share power. The states would keep some powers, but the federal government would have power over matters that affected the nation as a whole.

When it was finished, the Constitution became the supreme law of the land. It helped found the American republic. In a **republic**, the people choose representatives to run the government.

READING CHECK **DRAW CONCLUSIONS**
How is power shared in a federal system?

A Major Debate

During the convention, the delegates often disagreed with one another. One major disagreement was about how each state would be represented in the new Congress.

The Virginia Plan

Edmund Randolph and the other Virginia delegates introduced a plan for Congress called the Virginia Plan. Under this plan, Congress would have two parts, or houses. The number of representatives that a state would have in both houses of Congress would be based on that state's population. States with more people would have more votes in Congress. This plan would favor the large states, such as Virginia, Massachusetts, and Pennsylvania, which had many people.

The New Jersey Plan

"Not fair!" replied the delegates from the small states. **William Paterson** of New Jersey accused the Virginia Plan of "striking at the existence of the lesser states." Delegates from small states worried that the plan would give large states control of Congress. With more votes, the larger states would be able to pass the laws they wanted.

Paterson offered a different plan, called the New Jersey Plan. Under this plan, the new Congress would have one house, in which each state would be equally represented. This plan would give the small states the same number of representatives as the large states.

READING CHECK ⭕ **DRAW CONCLUSIONS**
How did the delegates disagree about representation in Congress?

❱ **THE PENNSYLVANIA STATE HOUSE IN PHILADELPHIA** is where delegates met for the Constitutional Convention.

Working Together

For weeks, the delegates argued about how the states should be represented in Congress. Finally, they realized that to reach an agreement, each side would have to **compromise**, or give up some of what it wanted.

The Great Compromise

A committee of delegates, led by Roger Sherman of Connecticut and others, presented a new plan. This plan became known as the Connecticut Compromise.

The Connecticut Compromise was based on the idea of a two-house Congress. In one house, representation would be based on the population of each state. In the other house, each state would be equally represented. Either house could present a **bill**, or an idea for a new law. However, both houses had to approve a bill before it became a law.

Delegates from the large states thought the compromise gave too much power to the small states. To gain the support of the large states, the committee added another idea. Only the house in which representation was based on population would be able to propose tax bills.

The committee presented the Great Compromise, as it became known, to the convention. Not all the delegates agreed with it, but most wanted to keep working. On July 16, 1787, they approved the Great Compromise.

READING CHECK ✪ DRAW CONCLUSIONS
How did delegates settle the issue of representation in Congress?

The Constitutional Convention

ILLUSTRATION This painting of the Constitutional Convention was not painted during the convention, but nearly 80 years afterward.

❶ Benjamin Franklin   ❷ Alexander Hamilton   ❸ James Madison
❹ Roger Sherman   ❺ George Read   ❻ George Washington
Why do you think George Washington is seated on a stage?

▶ **AFRICAN AMERICANS** This detail shows an African American woman at work. Before slavery ended, African Americans were not allowed to vote, hold office, or own property.

Compromises on Slavery

Under the Great Compromise, population would affect the representation of each state in Congress. This plan raised an important issue that troubled many people in the young nation—slavery. Delegates argued about whether enslaved African Americans should be counted when figuring each state's population.

Different Points of View

Because the southern states had the largest number of enslaved people, southern delegates wanted to count slaves when figuring out how many representatives a state would have in Congress. That way, the southern states could have more representatives.

Delegates from the northern states did not want slaves to be counted for representation. After all, these delegates argued, slaves were not allowed to vote and did not hold any of the other rights of citizenship. Some delegates hoped that slavery would not continue. However, they knew that ending it would be difficult.

The Three-Fifths Compromise

The delegates finally agreed to count three-fifths of the total number of slaves in each state towards the number of representatives. After this issue was dealt with, some delegates still spoke out against slavery. **Gouverneur** (guh•ver•NIR) **Morris** of Pennsylvania called slavery "the curse of heaven on the states where it prevailed [existed]."

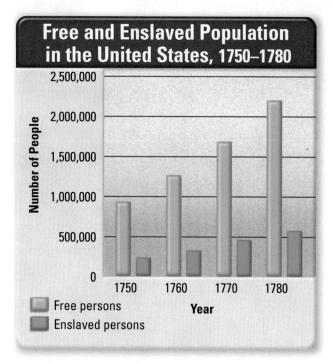

Free and Enslaved Population in the United States, 1750–1780

Number of People

- 2,500,000
- 2,000,000
- 1,500,000
- 1,000,000
- 500,000
- 0

1750   1760   1770   1780

Year

- Free persons
- Enslaved persons

GRAPH How many enslaved people lived in the United States in 1780?

A Continuing Issue

Some delegates were afraid that if the Constitution outlawed slavery or stopped states from importing slaves, the southern states would not approve it. To reach a compromise, the delegates agreed that Congress could not stop states from importing enslaved people from other countries before 1808.

After 1808, Congress banned the slave trade with other countries. However, enslaved people could still be bought and sold within the United States. As a result, many enslaved people continued to be separated from their families.

READING CHECK ☼DRAW CONCLUSIONS

What issue was settled when delegates agreed to the Three-Fifths Compromise?

Summary

Instead of just fixing the Articles of Confederation, the delegates at the Constitutional Convention decided to write a new constitution. The Great Compromise resolved conflicts over representation in the government.

REVIEW

1. WHAT TO KNOW How was a new plan of government developed at the Constitutional Convention?

2. VOCABULARY Explain how the terms **federal system** and **republic** are related.

3. HISTORY Who were some of the people associated with the development of the United States Constitution?

4. CRITICAL THINKING How did the makers of the Constitution try to fix some of the problems that existed under the Articles of Confederation?

5. ✎ **WRITE A PERSUASIVE LETTER** Imagine you are a delegate. Write a letter to your family explaining the role of compromise at the Constitutional Convention.

6. (Focus Skill) **DRAW CONCLUSIONS** On a separate sheet of paper, copy and complete this graphic organizer.

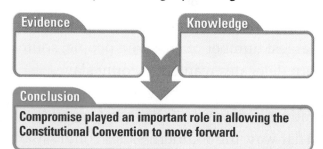

Evidence

Knowledge

Conclusion

Compromise played an important role in allowing the Constitutional Convention to move forward.

Gouverneur Morris

Biography

Trustworthiness
Respect
Responsibility
Fairness
Caring
Patriotism

"In every society the members have a right to the utmost liberty."

The ideas in the United States Constitution were the work of all the Constitutional Convention delegates. However, the one delegate who expressed those ideas in the written Constitution was Gouverneur Morris.

During the American Revolution, Morris served in the Continental Congress. In 1780, Morris hurt his leg, and it later had to be removed. For the rest of his life, he wore a wooden leg. However, this did not stop him from traveling widely and serving his country.

Morris was strongly against slavery, and he argued that the Constitution should outlaw it. Other delegates disagreed. Slavery would not be stopped for another 80 years.

Even after his retirement, Morris continued to be involved in politics. He persuaded the nation's early leaders to compromise for the good of the country. By serving his country, Morris showed his patriotism and loyalty to the government he helped create.

Why Character Counts

How did Gouverneur Morris help create the new nation?

Time

1752 — Born
1816 — Died

1780 Morris is injured and loses his leg

1786 Morris is elected to the Constitutional Convention

GO ONLINE
For more resources, go to
www.harcourtschool.com/ss1

Resolve Conflict

Why It Matters Knowing how to compromise is an important skill for resolving conflicts.

❱ LEARN

The delegates at the Constitutional Convention had many different ideas about a new government. They had to compromise in order to create the Constitution. By compromising, both sides gave up something they wanted in order to resolve their conflicts.

If you need to resolve a conflict, you can follow these steps in order to reach a compromise.

Step 1 Identify the problem.

Step 2 Have both sides explain what they want to happen. Talk about the differences.

Step 3 Think of possible compromises. Choose one that both sides agree on.

Step 4 Try the compromise. Plan to make sure that the compromise works.

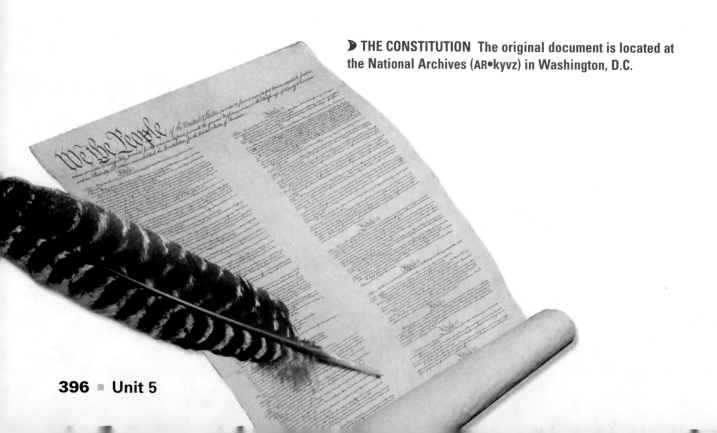

❱ **THE CONSTITUTION** The original document is located at the National Archives (AR•kyvz) in Washington, D.C.

▶ **RESOLVING CONFLICT** Throughout the nation's history, leaders have reached compromises in order to resolve conflicts and make laws.

▶ PRACTICE

Think of a conflict you recently faced. What was the problem? What did you give up to reach a compromise? What did you gain from the compromise? Did the compromise resolve the conflict? Can you think of another compromise that might have solved the problem?

▶ APPLY

Make It Relevant Choose a conflict facing your class or your school. Form two groups, with each group taking a different position. Then follow the steps to reach a compromise.

Lesson 2 — Three Branches of Government

WHAT TO KNOW

What are the powers of each of the three branches of government?

VOCABULARY

separation of powers p. 400
legislative branch p. 400
executive branch p. 401
electoral college p. 401
veto p. 401
impeach p. 401
judicial branch p. 402
justice p. 402
rule of law p. 403
amendment p. 403

PEOPLE

Gouverneur Morris

PLACES

Philadelphia

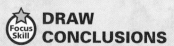

DRAW CONCLUSIONS

YOU ARE THERE

"Fresh berries here!" your father calls out to people passing by your fruit cart. It is the summer of 1787, and the weather in **Philadelphia** is hot and muggy.

You sigh as you arrange the berry boxes. After a moment, you notice a well-dressed man beside the cart. He pays for some berries and walks away. "Who was that?" you ask. "That was **Gouverneur Morris**, one of the wisest minds in our country."

> **DELEGATES** at the Constitutional Convention worked long hours debating and writing the Constitution.

▶ **THE NATIONAL ARCHIVES** The original Constitution is kept at the National Archives Building in Washington, D.C.

The Preamble

The convention delegates planned the new Constitution with great care. Gouverneur Morris was chosen to write the final version.

In the Preamble, or introduction, Morris began with:

> **66 We the People of the United States . . . 99**

He had first written "We the people of the States of New Hampshire, Massachusetts, . . ." and so on, listing the states. He changed the words to show that Americans were citizens of the nation first and of the states second. His words also link the Constitution to the Declaration of Independence, which says that a government gets its "just powers from the consent of the governed."

The Purpose of the Constitution

The Preamble goes on to explain the basic functions of the United States government. According to the Preamble, the government is to establish justice, or fairness, and to ensure domestic tranquility, or peace within the country. The government is to provide for the common defense, or defend the nation against its enemies. The government must also promote the general welfare, or work for the common good of the nation. It must secure liberty, or freedom, for the nation's people and its future generations.

Under the Constitution, the powers of government are limited. The Constitution gives the federal government power to govern the nation, but it also protects the states and citizens from that power.

READING CHECK ⚙ **DRAW CONCLUSIONS**
Why does the Preamble to the Constitution mention liberty and justice?

The Legislative Branch

The Constitution divides the powers of the federal government among three branches—the legislative branch, the executive branch, and the judicial branch. The Constitution's framers, or writers, created this **separation of powers** to keep any one branch from controlling the government. They felt it was important to create a government with limited powers.

Article I of the Constitution explains the **legislative branch**, or lawmaking branch. Powers given to Congress include raising an army and a navy, declaring war, and coining and printing money. Congress also makes laws that control commerce, or trade.

Congress became two houses—the House of Representatives and the Senate. For a bill to become law, a majority in each house has to vote for it.

Citizens Elect Representatives

Citizens were given the power to vote for members of the House of Representatives. Senators would be chosen by their state legislatures. Today, citizens vote directly for members of both houses of Congress.

The number of representatives would depend on the state's population. Today, the total number of representatives in the House is limited to 435. That number is divided among the states based on each state's population. In the Senate, each state has two senators.

Article I outlines other rules for Congress. For example, members of the House of Representatives are elected to two-year terms, while members of the Senate serve six-year terms.

READING CHECK **SUMMARIZE**
What are the main powers of Congress?

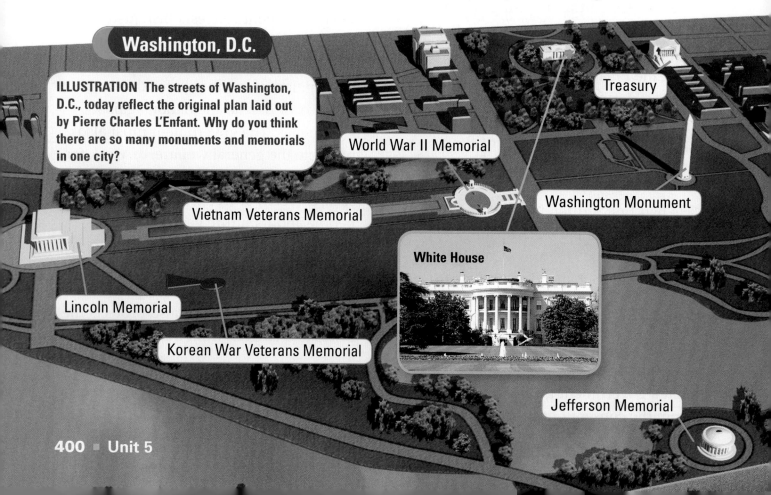

Washington, D.C.

ILLUSTRATION The streets of Washington, D.C., today reflect the original plan laid out by Pierre Charles L'Enfant. Why do you think there are so many monuments and memorials in one city?

Treasury

World War II Memorial

Vietnam Veterans Memorial

Washington Monument

White House

Lincoln Memorial

Korean War Veterans Memorial

Jefferson Memorial

The Executive Branch

In Article II, the Constitution says the power to enforce laws is given to the **executive branch**. Some delegates believed that one person should be the chief executive. Others felt a single executive would be too much like a king.

The delegates decided to have a President. Citizens vote for electors, who vote for the President. This group of electors is called the **electoral college**.

The Role of President

To be elected President, a person must be at least 35 years old and have been born in the United States. The President must also have lived in the United States for 14 years. The President is elected to a four-year term.

Once again, the delegates were careful to maintain the separation of powers. They decided that the President could **veto**, or reject, bills passed by Congress. However, Congress could then override the President's veto with a two-thirds vote.

The delegates also made the President commander in chief of the military. The President's main power, however, would be to "take care that the laws be faithfully executed." If this duty was not met, Congress could **impeach** the President, or accuse the President of crimes. If found guilty, the President could be removed from office.

READING CHECK ○DRAW CONCLUSIONS
Why were the delegates careful to preserve the separation of powers?

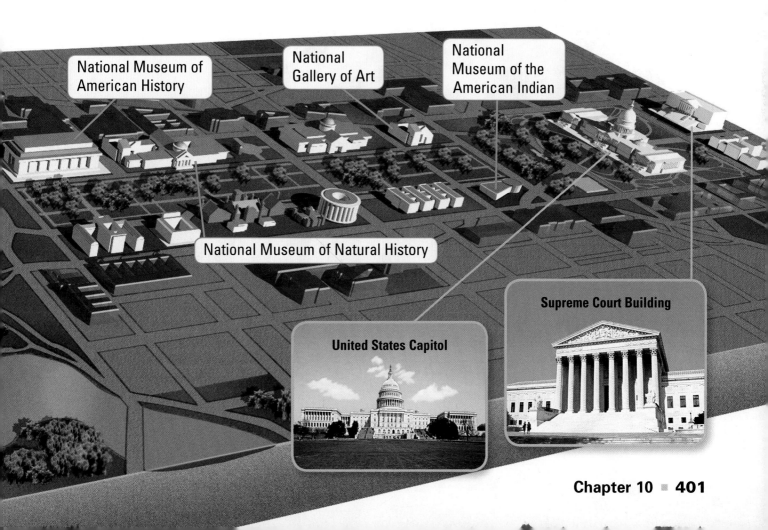

National Museum of American History

National Gallery of Art

National Museum of the American Indian

National Museum of Natural History

Supreme Court Building

United States Capitol

The Judicial Branch

According to Article III, the judicial branch must decide whether laws are working fairly. The **judicial branch** is the court system.

Although the states already had their own courts, the delegates created a federal court system, too. These courts would decide cases that dealt with the Constitution, treaties, and national laws. They would also decide cases between states and between citizens of different states.

The Supreme Court

The delegates did not organize the judicial branch in as much detail as the other branches. Most of their decisions applied only to the Supreme Court, the highest court in the United States. It would head the judicial branch.

The delegates decided that the President would nominate the Supreme Court **justices**, or judges. The Senate would vote whether to approve them. The delegates decided that Supreme Court justices could stay in office for life. This would allow justices to make decisions without worrying about losing their jobs. At first, there were six Supreme Court justices. Today, there are nine.

The Supreme Court has the power to strike down any law that goes against the Constitution. Only by changing the

❯ **THE SUPREME COURT BUILDING** Housed in this building since 1935, the Supreme Court is the highest court in the United States.

Constitution can Congress restore a law struck down by the Supreme Court. The government must also apply laws equally to every person. This is called **rule of law**.

Changing the Constitution

The delegates understood that as time passed the Constitution might need to be changed. The delegates agreed on how citizens could add **amendments**, or changes, to the Constitution.

Amendments may be proposed by a two-thirds vote in Congress or by a national convention called for by two-thirds of the states and approved by Congress. For an amendment to pass, three-fourths of all the states must approve it. This system was set up to give representatives the time they need to study an amendment.

READING CHECK ☼ **DRAW CONCLUSIONS**
How does the Supreme Court limit the power of Congress?

▶ **LAW** This statue, which represents the authority of law, sits at the entrance to the Supreme Court.

Summary

The Constitution divides power among three branches of government—the legislative, the executive, and the judicial.

REVIEW

1. WHAT TO KNOW What are the powers of each of the three branches of government?

2. VOCABULARY Use the terms **legislative branch**, **executive branch**, and **judicial branch** to explain the **separation of powers**.

3. CIVICS/GOVERNMENT What powers do citizens have in selecting the President and members of Congress?

4. CRITICAL THINKING Make It Relevant How are the purposes of government as defined in the Preamble to the United States Constitution still important to people? Explain your answer.

5. ✏ **WRITE A SET OF RULES** Write a set of classroom rules that illustrates the ideas in the Constitution.

6. (Focus Skill) **DRAW CONCLUSIONS** On a separate sheet of paper, copy and complete this graphic organizer.

Evidence	Knowledge
	Leaders work together.

Conclusion
The Constitution divides the powers among the three branches.

Time

1780   1820   1860

1788
The Constitution
is ratified

1791
The Bill of Rights
is added to the
Constitution

The Bill of Rights

WHAT TO KNOW
What is the Bill of Rights,
and why was it added to the
Constitution?

VOCABULARY
ratify p. 405
Federalists p. 406
Anti-Federalists p. 406
due process of law p. 407
reserved powers p. 407
Cabinet p. 408
political party p. 408

PEOPLE
John Adams
Alexander Hamilton
Thomas Jefferson
Benjamin Banneker

PLACES
Washington, D.C.

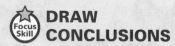
DRAW
CONCLUSIONS

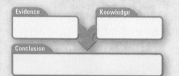

**You
ARE
THERE**
It's September 1787, and you're a carpenter's
apprentice in Philadelphia. For the last
four months, you've heard people talking about an
important meeting at the State House. You decide to
walk downtown in hopes of hearing some news.

When you arrive, you see Benjamin Franklin
leaving. He looks tired but happy. "What's the good
news, Mr. Franklin?" you ask as he steps into his
sedan chair. "It is finally finished," he says.

▶ RATIFICATION Delegates to the Constitutional Convention knew that the
struggle to ratify the Constitution would not be an easy one.

The Struggle to Ratify

On September 17, 1787, work on the Constitution was complete. Thirty-nine delegates were present at the Convention. All but three—Elbridge Gerry, George Mason, and Edmund Randolph—signed the Constitution. In 2004, Congress passed a law declaring every September 17 as Constitution Day. On this day, students in schools across the country learn about the Constitution.

The Call for Basic Rights

The Constitution was not yet the law of the land. According to Article VII, 9 of the 13 states had to **ratify**, or approve, the Constitution. In each state, voters elected delegates to a state convention. These delegates would vote for or against the Constitution.

At the state conventions, arguments began again. Some delegates were against the Constitution. They wanted to limit the power of the federal government and protect people's individual rights. Other delegates said they would be more willing to approve the Constitution if a bill, or list, of rights were added to it. Supporters of the Constitution promised to propose a bill of rights after the Constitution was ratified.

 **READING CHECK** ☼DRAW CONCLUSIONS
What would adding a bill of rights to the Constitution do?

⚡FAST FACT

The Constitution of the United States is the oldest written national constitution. It is also the shortest.

The Vote of Approval

In December 1787, all of the Delaware delegates voted to ratify the Constitution. Later that month, delegates from New Jersey and Pennsylvania approved the Constitution. In January 1788, delegates in Georgia and Connecticut also ratified it.

Those in favor of the Constitution and those against it competed for the support of the remaining eight states. Those citizens who favored the Constitution were called **Federalists**. Federalists wanted a strong national government. Those who disagreed with the Federalists became known as **Anti-Federalists**.

Because there was no bill of rights in the Constitution, the Anti-Federalists feared that the national government would have too much power. The promise of a bill of rights, helped change many people's minds.

The Final Votes

In February 1788, Massachusetts ratified the Constitution. In the spring, Maryland and South Carolina did the same. Then, on June 21, 1788, New Hampshire became the ninth state to ratify the Constitution—the last state needed to put it into effect. Virginia and New York followed later that summer. By the spring of 1789, the new government was at work. Later that year, North Carolina approved the Constitution. Rhode Island gave its approval in 1790.

READING CHECK ⚙DRAW CONCLUSIONS
Why do you think some Anti-Federalists changed their minds about the Constitution?

Constitution Ratification Vote

STATE	DATE	VOTES FOR	VOTES AGAINST
Delaware	Dec. 7, 1787	30	0
Pennsylvania	Dec. 12, 1787	46	23
New Jersey	Dec. 18, 1787	30	0
Georgia	Jan. 2, 1788	26	0
Connecticut	Jan. 9, 1788	128	40
Massachusetts	Feb. 6, 1788	187	168
Maryland	Apr. 28, 1788	63	11
South Carolina	May 23, 1788	149	73
New Hampshire	June 21, 1788	57	47
Virginia	June 25, 1788	89	79
New York	July 26, 1788	30	27
North Carolina	Nov. 21, 1789	194	77
Rhode Island	May 29, 1790	34	32

TABLE Alexander Hamilton (below) worked to convince others of the need for a strong federal government. In which state was the vote closest to being a tie?

▶ **NEWSPAPERS printed the Bill of Rights so that people could read it.**

The Bill of Rights

As promised, ten amendments were added to the Constitution to protect the rights of the people. These amendments, called the Bill of Rights, became part of the Constitution in 1791.

The First Ten Amendments

The First Amendment gives people the freedom to follow any religion or none at all. It says that the government cannot establish or support any religion. It also protects freedom of speech, freedom of the press, freedom to petition the government, and the right to assemble, or gather together.

The Second Amendment protects people's right to have weapons. The Third Amendment says the government cannot make people house soldiers in peacetime. The Fourth Amendment protects people against unfair searches.

The Fifth through Eighth Amendments deal with **due process of law**. This means that people have the right to a fair trial. They have the right to a lawyer and do not have to speak against themselves.

The Ninth Amendment says that people have other rights not listed in the Constitution. The Tenth Amendment says that the government can only do the things listed in the Constitution. This means that all other authority, called the **reserved powers**, belongs to the states or to the people.

The Bill of Rights protects the rights of people in the minority. The majority cannot take their rights away.

READING CHECK 🖎 **DRAW CONCLUSIONS**
Why is the Bill of Rights important?

The New Government

In 1789, George Washington became the nation's first President. **John Adams** became the first Vice President. Working with Congress, Washington set up a State Department, a Treasury Department, and a War Department. Together, the heads of these departments and others would come to be known as the **Cabinet**. Cabinet members advise the President.

Traditions Begin

Two members of Washington's Cabinet began to argue about what was best for the United States. **Alexander Hamilton** wanted a stronger central government. **Thomas Jefferson** wanted less central government. This argument led to the rise of political parties. A **political party** is a group that tries to elect officials who will support its policies.

In Congress, members of both parties agreed to build a national capital on land beside the Potomac River. George Washington chose the location for the city that came to carry his name. **Benjamin Banneker**, a free African American, helped the architect Pierre Charles L'Enfant plan the nation's capital. In 1800, the federal government moved from Philadelphia to **Washington, D.C.**

George Washington was re-elected in 1792. He was President for two terms, each of which was four years long. Many people wanted him to run for a third term, but he refused. He did not think a President should hold power for life. His decision set an example for future Presidents.

▶ **BENJAMIN BANNEKER** helped measure the land, known as the District of Columbia (D.C.), where the national capital was built.

Benjamin Banneker

Black Heritage USA 15c

In the election of 1796, the Federalist party, led by Alexander Hamilton, backed John Adams for President. The Jeffersonian Republican, led by Thomas Jefferson, party backed Jefferson. When the votes were counted, Adams had won.

On March 4, 1797, John Adams became the second President. The day he took the oath of office was an important one. It was the first time that the United States had changed leaders. The change was peaceful.

READING CHECK ○ **DRAW CONCLUSIONS**

Why do you think it was necessary for the President to have a Cabinet?

Summary

The Constitution was ratified in 1788. In 1789, George Washington became the first President. The Bill of Rights was added to the Constitution in 1791.

❯ **JOHN ADAMS** He was the first President to live in what is now the White House.

REVIEW

1. **WHAT TO KNOW** What is the Bill of Rights, and why was it added to the Constitution?

2. **VOCABULARY** Explain the meaning of the term **ratify**.

3. **CIVICS/GOVERNMENT** What rights does the Bill of Rights guarantee?

4. **CRITICAL THINKING Make It Relevant** How does the Bill of Rights support the idea of individual liberty?

5. **MAKE A POSTER** Design a poster that honors the Bill of Rights. List some of the amendments, and add pictures of freedoms that you enjoy.

6. **DRAW CONCLUSIONS**
   (Focus Skill) On a separate sheet of paper, copy and complete this graphic organizer.

Evidence	Knowledge
The Bill of Rights includes freedom of speech.	Freedoms are important to people.

   Conclusion

Read a Population Map

Why It Matters Reading a population map can help you see population patterns and find out where most people live.

❯ LEARN

The first census was taken in 1790. It counted the people living in the United States at that time and told where they lived.

The population map on page 411 uses population density to show the results of that census. **Population density** is the average number of people living in an area of a certain size, usually one square mile. You can follow these steps to read a population map.

Step 1 Read the title of the map.

Step 2 Study the key. Compare its colors with those on the map.

Step 3 Put the information on the map into your own words.

❯ PRACTICE

Use the map on page 411 to answer the following questions.

❶ Which state is more densely populated, Massachusetts or Georgia?

❷ What is the population density of New York City?

❸ Find Nashville, Philadelphia, and Richmond. Which city has the highest population density?

❯ APPLY

Choose five cities shown on the map. List the population density of each city. Make a bar graph comparing the population densities of the five cities.

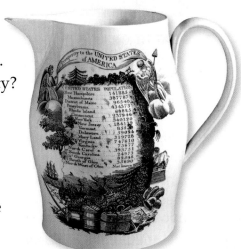

❯ **CENSUS PITCHER** This pitcher lists state populations from the first census.

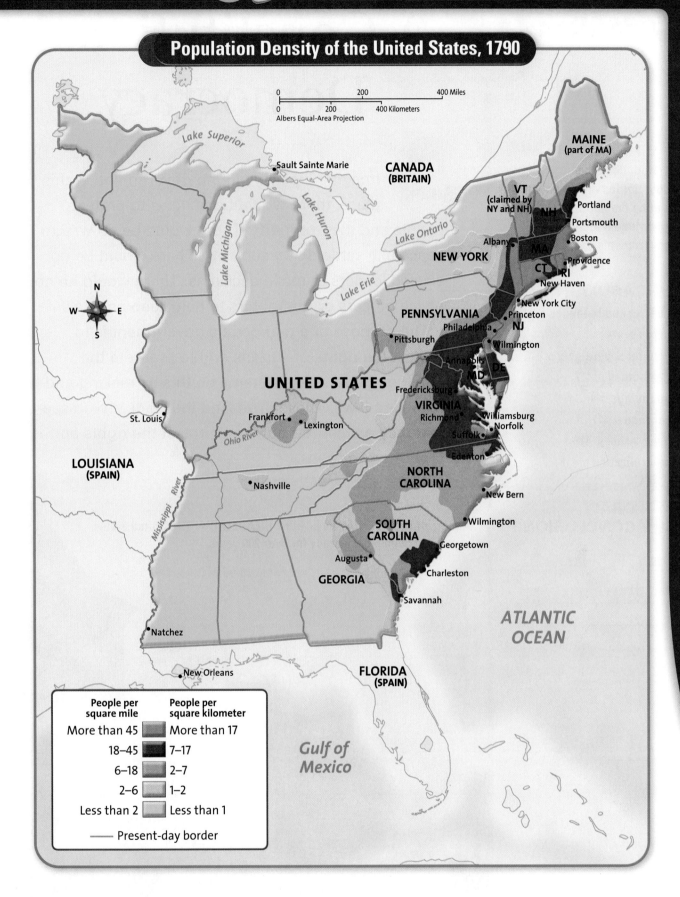

Population Density of the United States, 1790

0   200   400 Miles
0   200   400 Kilometers
Albers Equal-Area Projection

Lake Superior

Sault Sainte Marie

CANADA
(BRITAIN)

MAINE
(part of MA)

Lake Michigan

Lake Huron

VT
(claimed by
NY and NH)   NH

Portland
Portsmouth
Boston

Lake Ontario

Albany   MA

Providence

NEW YORK

CT   RI
New Haven

Lake Erie

New York City

PENNSYLVANIA

Princeton
NJ

Philadelphia

Pittsburgh

Wilmington

Annapolis

DE

MD

UNITED STATES

Fredericksburg

VIRGINIA

St. Louis

Frankfort

Lexington

Richmond

Williamsburg
Norfolk

Ohio River

Suffolk

Edenton

LOUISIANA
(SPAIN)

NORTH
CAROLINA

New Bern

Nashville

Wilmington

SOUTH
CAROLINA

Georgetown

Augusta

Charleston

GEORGIA

Savannah

ATLANTIC
OCEAN

Natchez

FLORIDA
(SPAIN)

New Orleans

Gulf of
Mexico

People per square mile		People per square kilometer
More than 45		More than 17
18–45		7–17
6–18		2–7
2–6		1–2
Less than 2		Less than 1
— Present-day border		

Map and Globe Skills

Lesson 4 A Constitutional Democracy

WHAT TO KNOW
How does the Constitution divide power among the national government and state governments?

VOCABULARY

checks and balances p. 414
union p. 414
popular sovereignty p. 416
democracy p. 417
public agenda p. 417
suffrage p. 417
civic virtue p. 418
naturalization p. 418

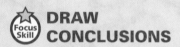

DRAW CONCLUSIONS

YOU ARE THERE Imagine a place with no government. In this place, there would be no laws to protect people and their property. There would be no way to peacefully settle disagreements. There would be no elected leaders to make decisions. There would be no police officers or firefighters to help keep people safe.

The purpose of a democratic government is to protect the rights of citizens and to promote the common good. Governments do this by making and enforcing laws. These laws, and the leaders who see that they are carried out, help protect the rights and property of citizens.

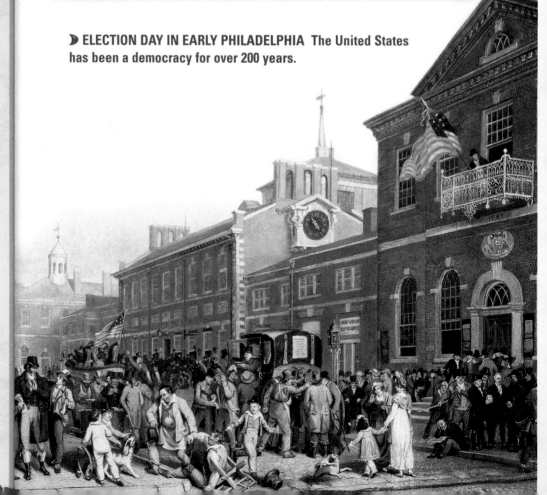

▶ **ELECTION DAY IN EARLY PHILADELPHIA** The United States has been a democracy for over 200 years.

▶ **GOVERNMENT LEADERS** The President, members of Congress, and justices of the Supreme Court often work together across party lines to solve the nation's problems.

Sharing Powers

The Constitution had to empower the federal government, or give it enough power to govern the nation. To do this, the Constitution gives each branch of the government certain powers. The Constitution describes in detail how the federal government's power is shared among the legislative, executive, and judicial branches. This separation of powers keeps the federal government from becoming too powerful. It also protects citizens from the government's power.

The three branches of government must often work together to exercise their powers. If they did not work together, they would not be able to pass laws, make treaties, or use military power to defend the nation.

The federal government takes care of issues that affect the entire country. It makes sure that our military forces are properly trained and equipped. It supports national parks and helps protect and clean up the environment. It also runs programs to help children, people who are ill, and people who are elderly.

READING CHECK ☼DRAW CONCLUSIONS
How does the Constitution both empower and limit the federal government?

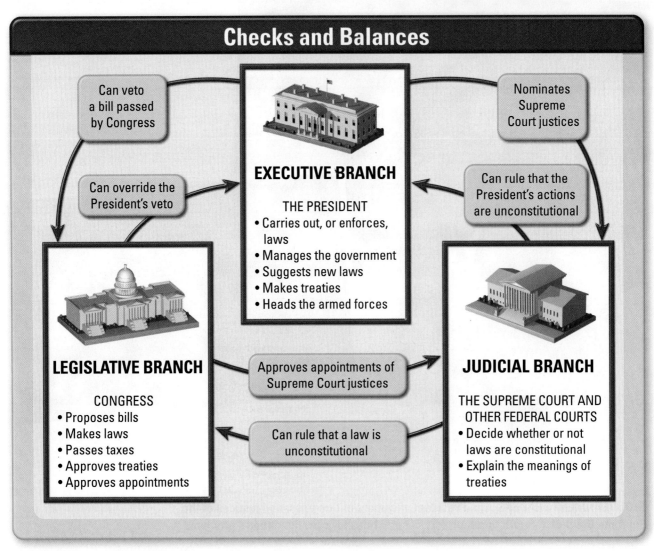

Checks and Balances

	EXECUTIVE BRANCH	
Can veto a bill passed by Congress	**THE PRESIDENT** • Carries out, or enforces, laws • Manages the government • Suggests new laws • Makes treaties • Heads the armed forces	Nominates Supreme Court justices
Can override the President's veto		Can rule that the President's actions are unconstitutional

LEGISLATIVE BRANCH

CONGRESS
• Proposes bills
• Makes laws
• Passes taxes
• Approves treaties
• Approves appointments

Approves appointments of Supreme Court justices

Can rule that a law is unconstitutional

JUDICIAL BRANCH

THE SUPREME COURT AND OTHER FEDERAL COURTS
• Decide whether or not laws are constitutional
• Explain the meanings of treaties

DIAGRAM How can the President check the authority of Congress?

Checks and Balances

Each branch of government is given different powers by the Constitution in a way that allows each branch to watch over the others. This system, called **checks and balances**, keeps any one branch from becoming too powerful or misusing its authority.

Each branch has ways to check, or block, the powers of the others. For example, the President can check the power of Congress by vetoing a bill that Congress has passed. Congress can check

the President's power by voting to override the veto or refusing to give money for programs. The Supreme Court can check the powers of Congress by declaring new laws or government actions unconstitutional.

The system of checks and balances was developed in the hope that it would allow the nation to form "a more perfect union." A **union** is an alliance that works to reach common goals.

READING CHECK ⚙ DRAW CONCLUSIONS
Why does the Constitution provide for a system of checks and balances?

State Powers

The writers of the Constitution were careful to preserve the powers of the states. The Tenth Amendment says that any powers not clearly given to the federal government, or denied to the states, belong to the states or the people. This helps keep the federal government from becoming too powerful.

What State Governments Do

Like the federal government, state governments have many responsibilities. For example, state governments build and manage state highways and state parks. They oversee public schools and state colleges and universities.

State governments also provide many services that help their citizens. They help people in their state who do not have enough money to pay for food, shelter, health care, or other basic needs.

The Constitution keeps the federal government from favoring one state over another. For example, Congress cannot favor one state over another in making trade agreements or in collecting taxes. Congress also cannot tax goods moving from one state to another.

Powers that the states do not have are listed in the Constitution. For example, states cannot print money, raise armies, or make treaties with other countries. Only the federal government can do those things. Also, states cannot set up trade agreements with other states without the approval of Congress.

READING CHECK ☼**DRAW CONCLUSIONS**
What powers do states have under the Constitution?

CHART Why do you think state governments cannot print money?

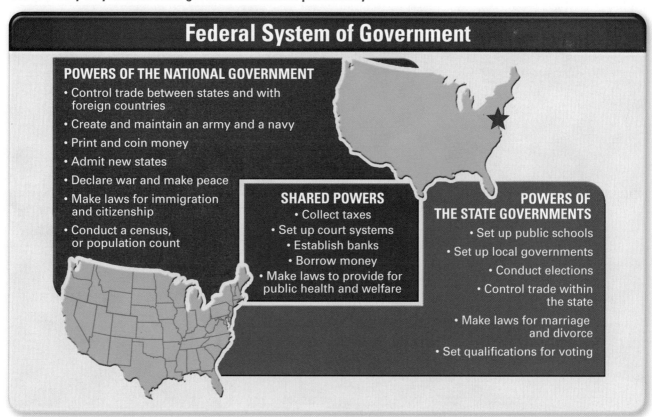

Federal System of Government

POWERS OF THE NATIONAL GOVERNMENT
- Control trade between states and with foreign countries
- Create and maintain an army and a navy
- Print and coin money
- Admit new states
- Declare war and make peace
- Make laws for immigration and citizenship
- Conduct a census, or population count

SHARED POWERS
- Collect taxes
- Set up court systems
- Establish banks
- Borrow money
- Make laws to provide for public health and welfare

POWERS OF THE STATE GOVERNMENTS
- Set up public schools
- Set up local governments
- Conduct elections
- Control trade within the state
- Make laws for marriage and divorce
- Set qualifications for voting

State and Local Governments

In the United States there are three levels of government—federal, state, and local. Local governments include county and municipal, or city, governments. All three levels of government share certain powers. For example, they all collect taxes to pay for government services.

State governments and many local governments have legislative, executive, and judicial branches. The voters in a state elect representatives to their state legislature, which makes state laws. The governor is the head of a state's executive branch.

Many local governments also have an executive, called a mayor. The legislative branch of a local government is often a city council. In a county, it is often a board of commissioners. They help decide on laws for that city or county.

READING CHECK Ŏ**DRAW CONCLUSIONS**
How are the three levels of government alike?

Rights and Responsibilities

Our system of government is based on the basic principles of democracy, which include justice, equality, responsibility, and freedom. The government derives, or gets, its power from the people. This idea is called **popular sovereignty** (SAHV•er•uhn•tee). In a republic, representatives exercise the power given

> **GOVERNORS** are the head of the executive branch in state government.

▶ **VOTING** People vote at polling places such as schools and community centers.

to them by citizens who vote them into office. The people are the sources of the government's authority.

Voting

One responsibility of a good citizen is voting. In a **democracy**, people rule and are free to make choices about their lives and their government. In local, state, and national elections, voters select their representatives and leaders. If the voters do not like certain laws, they can elect leaders who they think will change the laws.

People can also write letters to encourage their leaders to vote a certain way. They can use the Internet to find the addresses of their leaders. Writing one's leaders is an important part of living in a democracy. It helps leaders keep track of a **public agenda**, or what people want from the government.

Citizens can run for office or volunteer to do community service. They can also work on election campaigns. Some citizens go from door to door handing out information on candidates or on issues. Other citizens telephone voters to remind them to go to the polls on election day.

At first, voting rights were not given to all citizens. Women were not given **suffrage**, or the right to vote, in national elections until the Nineteenth Amendment was adopted in 1920. In 1971, the Twenty-Sixth Amendment lowered the voting age from 21 years old to 18 years old. These changes were made to ensure that our constitutional democracy would better represent the people.

READING CHECK ♂ **DRAW CONCLUSIONS**
Why is voting an important responsibility of citizens?

Edna Purtell

By the time she was a teenager, Edna Purtell was already an active member of her community in West Hartford, Connecticut. In 1917, Purtell began working for the National Women's Party, which was trying to get women the right to vote.

The next year she attended a protest for women's rights in Washington, D.C. The women marched in front of the White House and many of them, like Edna, were arrested. They were released after 5 days and immediately held another protest. In 1920, a constitutional amendment was passed that gave women the right to vote. That year, Edna and millions of other women proudly voted for the first time.

Make it Relevant How can you help to make changes in your community?

Being a Citizen

Voting is one responsibility of citizens. Another responsibility is to act with **civic virtue**, or with qualities that add to a healthy democracy. Citizens have to obey laws, serve on juries, and pay taxes. Males must register for the selective service, or military draft, when they turn 18 years old. By doing these things, citizens can reach common goals and help make the country a better place for all people.

Because the government gets its power from the people, citizens are also responsible for helping control the government. Several amendments to the Constitution give the people greater power over their leaders. Originally, state legislatures elected their state senators. In 1913, the Seventeenth Amendment was adopted. It says that the voters of each state can elect their own senators directly.

Term limits are one way to ensure that elected officials regularly change. The Twenty-Second Amendment, which was adopted in 1951, says that a President cannot serve more than two full terms in office.

Citizenship

People who are born in the United States are automatically citizens of the country. Immigrants to the United States can become legal citizens through a process called **naturalization**. A person applying for citizenship must be at least 18 years old and have lived in the United

States for five years, or three years if they are married to a citizen of the United States.

People applying for citizenship must also pass a test on United States government and history. They must be able to write and speak English. Those who pass the tests must take an oath promising their allegiance to the United States.

READING CHECK ☼ **DRAW CONCLUSIONS**
How can people take part in our American constitutional government?

Summary

In a constitutional government, the power to govern comes from the people. The Constitution separates the powers of the federal and state governments. The government operates through checks and balances among the legislative, executive, and judicial branches.

▶ **FREEDOM** This statue representing freedom stands atop the Capitol building in Washington, D.C.

REVIEW

1. **WHAT TO KNOW** How does the Constitution divide power among the national government and state governments?

2. **VOCABULARY** Use the term **checks and balances** to explain how the Constitution keeps any one branch of the federal government from becoming too powerful.

3. **CIVICS AND GOVERNMENT** How can the Supreme Court check the power of Congress?

4. **CRITICAL THINKING** What role do citizens play in selecting the President and members of Congress?

5. **CRITICAL THINKING** How are both rights and responsibilities important for citizens?

6. ✎ **WRITE A PERSUASIVE LETTER** Write a letter to an elected official about an issue that is important to your community.

7. ⭐ **DRAW CONCLUSIONS** On a separate sheet of paper, copy and complete this graphic organizer.

Evidence	Knowledge
The Vice President's vote can break a tie in the Senate.	Congress votes on bills.

Conclusion

Patriotic Artifacts

Background Patriotic artifacts come in many different shapes and forms. One way that Americans have long shown their patriotism is by honoring the United States flag. The first United States flag was designed in 1777. Over the years, the flag has appeared on posters, on clothes, and even on toys.

DBQ **Document-Based Question** Study these primary sources, and answer the questions.

PAINTING

No one is sure who made the first United States flag, but many early flagmakers were women.

DBQ **1** Why did women work together to make early flags?

COIN BANK

This replica of Uncle Sam's hat is a coin bank.

DBQ **2** When might people wear patriotic clothing or accessories?

FLAG DAY POSTER

The first United States flag had 13 stars.

DBQ **3** Why is June 14 an important day for Americans?

AMERICAN EAGLE PIN

The eagle is a patriotic symbol of the United States.

DBQ **4** How might Americans use patriotic symbols in their homes?

PATRIOTIC PIN

Patriotic symbols can be displayed on common objects such as this button.

DBQ **5** Why do you think the colors of the United States flag appear on many items?

WRITE ABOUT IT

What do these primary sources tell you about American patriotism? Write a paragraph describing how Americans can show their patriotism.

GO ONLINE For more resources, go to www.harcourtschool.com/ss1

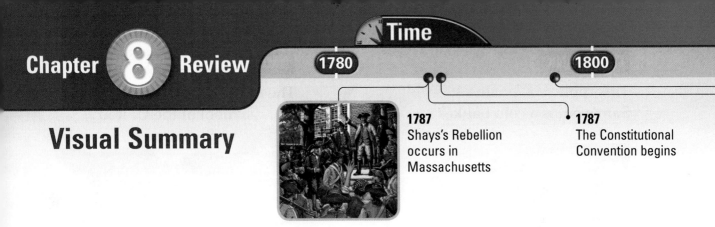

Visual Summary

1787 Shays's Rebellion occurs in Massachusetts

1787 The Constitutional Convention begins

Summarize the Chapter

Draw Conclusions Complete this graphic organizer to show that you can draw conclusions about the Constitution.

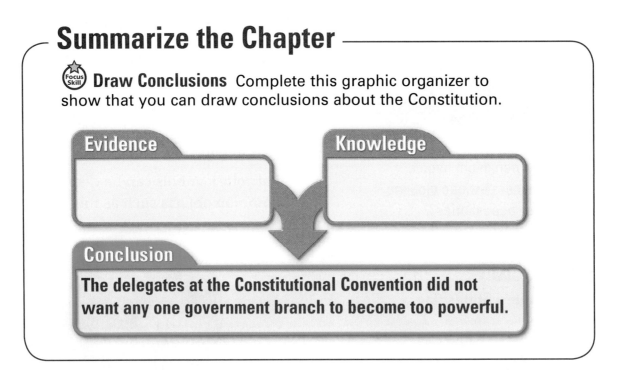

Evidence

Knowledge

Conclusion

The delegates at the Constitutional Convention did not want any one government branch to become too powerful.

Vocabulary

Identify the term from the word bank that correctly matches each definition.

1. a government made up of representatives chosen by the people

2. to accuse the President of crimes

3. to approve

4. a change

5. applying laws equally to every person

6. to give up some of what you want

7. the right to a fair trial

8. the idea that the government gets its power from the people

Word Bank

republic p. 390　　amendment p. 403

compromise p. 392　　ratify p. 405

impeach p. 401　　due process of law p. 407

rule of law p. 403　　popular sovereignty p. 416

1820   1840   1860

1788
The Constitution
is ratified

1791
The Bill of Rights
is added to the
Constitution

Time Line

Use the chapter summary time line above to answer the questions.

9. In what year was the Constitution ratified?

10. How many years after the Constitution was ratified was the Bill of Rights added?

Facts and Main Ideas

Answer these questions.

11. What major debate began when delegates tried to fix the Articles of Confederation?

12. How were powers shared under the federal system?

13. How were powers divided among the three branches of the federal government?

14. Why are checks and balances important?

Write the letter of the best choice.

15. Who wrote the Preamble to the Constitution?
    A George Washington
    B Benjamin Franklin
    C James Madison
    D Gouverneur Morris

16. Which of the following does the First Amendment protect?
    A the right to bear arms
    B the right to a trial by jury
    C the right to privacy
    D the right to free speech

Critical Thinking

17. **Make It Relevant** Why do you think the Bill of Rights is still important today?

18. Why might the delegates to the Constitutional Convention have made the Constitution so hard to change?

Skills

Resolve Conflict

Read the steps on page 396, and answer the questions.

19. What were some of the compromises that the delegates to the Constitutional Convention wanted?

20. What did the delegates gain by agreeing to compromise?

Write a Persuasive letter
Imagine that it is 1788. You have just read the Constitution. Write a letter to the delegates in your state who will decide whether to accept it. Tell them how you want them to vote and why.

Write a Report Choose one of the delegates who attended the Constitutional Convention. Then write a report using facts and details about that delegate's role.

STUDY SKILLS

SKIM AND SCAN

Skimming and scanning are tools that help you quickly learn the main ideas of a lesson.

- **To skim, quickly read the lesson title and the section titles. Look at the visuals, or images, and read the captions. Use this information to identify the main topics.**

- **To scan, look quickly through the text for specific details, such as key words or facts.**

Skim	Scan
Lesson Title: Exploring the West	**Key Words and Facts:**
Main Idea: In the late 1700s and early 1800s, people in the United States began moving west.	• The Wilderness Road went through the Cumberland Gap.
Section Titles: Immigrants and Pioneers, Americans Continue West, The Louisiana Purchase, Lewis and Clark, Pike Explores the Southwest	• More states joined the nation.
Visuals: Map of Wilderness Road, art of pioneers going over mountains, map of the Louisiana Purchase, Lewis and Clark time line	•

PREVIEW VOCABULARY

pioneer p. 427

locomotive p. 454

cotton gin p. 456

The Young Republic

> COVERED WAGONS AT
SCOTTS BLUFF NATIONAL
MONUMENT

1796
Tennessee becomes the sixteenth state

1803
Ohio becomes the seventeenth state

1803
The Louisiana Purchase is made

WHAT TO KNOW
How did the Louisiana Purchase help the United States grow?

VOCABULARY
gap p. 427
pioneer p. 427
consequence p. 431

PEOPLE
Daniel Boone
John Sevier
Thomas Jefferson
Napoleon Bonaparte
Meriwether Lewis
William Clark
York
Sacagawea

PLACES
Cumberland Gap
St. Louis, Missouri
Pikes Peak

DRAW CONCLUSIONS

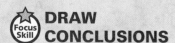

Exploring the West

YOU ARE THERE
The year is 1780. Your family has traveled far to settle here in the Kentucky woods. Few settlers live in this area. Wild animals live all around you.

But you are too excited to be afraid. After a long, hard trip across the Appalachian Mountains, you are in a land that looks like paradise. It has deep woods and meadows full of wild flowers. This beautiful place is going to be your new home.

▶ **FRONTIER LIFE** Many families moved west to settle on the frontier.

▶**PIONEERS** like Daniel Boone traveled across the Appalachians to the frontier.

Immigrants and Pioneers

In the late 1700s and early 1800s, many immigrants came to the United States. Most were from England, Scotland, Ireland, and Germany. Some were escaping hard times. Others wanted a chance to earn money and own land.

European immigrants usually arrived on ships that docked in port cities along the Atlantic coast. Some of them, as well as other Americans, wanted to start farms near the frontier. However, the Appalachians stood in their way.

The Cumberland Gap

One way over the Appalachians was by an old Native American trail that went through the **Cumberland Gap**. A **gap** is a low place between mountains. The Cumberland Gap was at the point where the present-day states of Tennessee, Virginia, and Kentucky meet. One of the best-known pioneers to cross the Appalachians was **Daniel Boone.** A **pioneer** is an early settler of an area.

A private company hired Daniel Boone and about thirty others to widen the trail through the Cumberland Gap. The group built the Wilderness Road, which became the main route to the West. Soon thousands of people were going to Kentucky. By 1792, Kentucky had become the fifteenth state, the first state west of the Appalachians.

READING CHECK ☼**DRAW CONCLUSIONS**
Why was the Wilderness Road important?

Americans Continue West

The trip along the Wilderness Road was challenging. Pioneers had to bring everything they needed with them. There were no places to buy supplies along the way. Settlers brought clothing, furniture, and tools with them in large overland wagons. Although the trip was difficult, more and more people moved west.

New States

Sometimes disputes arose over the forming of new states. During the 1780s, one group of settlers in North Carolina tried to form the "State of Franklin." It was made up of three counties in western North Carolina. **John Sevier**, a former Continental Army general, was elected as governor there in 1785. However, North Carolina soon took back control of the land.

In 1796, John Sevier became the first governor of another place—Tennessee. This time, the area he governed was admitted into the United States as a state. Tennessee was named after Tansai, a Cherokee village.

The addition of new states did not stop with Kentucky and Tennessee. The Northwest Territory was growing fast, too. People used the Ohio River and other rivers in the region for travel. They built towns along many of the rivers. By 1800, more than 45,000 people lived in **Ohio**. In 1803 it became the seventeenth state.

READING CHECK **CAUSE AND EFFECT**
What was an effect of more settlers moving west?

Children IN HISTORY

Daniel Drake

Daniel Drake and his family were pioneers. They moved to Kentucky when it had just become a state. Daniel was a small child, but he worked very hard. He got up before sunrise to feed the horses, cows, and pigs.

Daniel did not go to school, but he studied his lessons at home. When he was fifteen, he became an apprentice to a doctor. He grew up to become a doctor and later moved to Cincinnati, Ohio, where he started a medical school.

Make It Relevant **How were Daniel's chores like or different from your chores?**

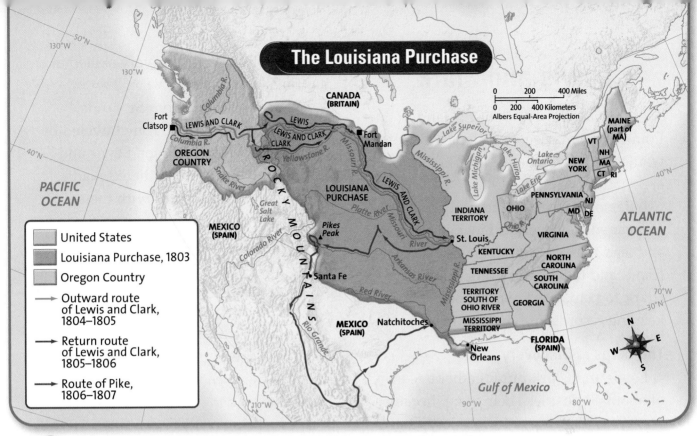

The Louisiana Purchase

MAP SKILL **REGIONS** What river marked the western border of the United States before the Louisiana Purchase?

The Louisiana Purchase

In 1801, **Thomas Jefferson** became the third President of the United States. He wanted to expand the borders of the young nation.

One problem was that the United States had no ports on the Gulf of Mexico. Farmers in western areas had to ship their crops on boats down the Mississippi River to the port of New Orleans, which was controlled by Spain. Farmers wanted an American port where they could ship their goods.

A Very Big Purchase

In 1801, Spain gave New Orleans and the rest of Louisiana back to France. Jefferson feared that France would build more settlements and stop settlers from moving farther west.

Jefferson sent officials to France to ask **Napoleon Bonaparte** (nuh•POH•lee•yuhn BOH•nuh•part), the leader of France, to sell New Orleans. They also asked to buy what is now western Florida. France was preparing for war with Britain, so Napoleon needed money. He offered to sell all of Louisiana—more than 800,000 square miles—for just $15 million.

On April 30, 1803, the deal was made final. The sale, called the Louisiana Purchase, more than doubled the size of the United States. Then, in 1819, the United States gained the rest of Florida. With Florida, the nation had possession of all the land in the Southeast.

READING CHECK ⊘DRAW CONCLUSIONS
Why did France agree to sell Louisiana to the United States?

Lewis and Clark

Little was known about the land in the Louisiana Purchase. President Jefferson wanted to learn what resources the area had.

Jefferson chose a friend and army officer named **Meriwether Lewis** to plan and lead the expedition. Lewis asked his friend and fellow army officer **William Clark** to help. Clark was responsible for keeping records and making maps.

The Corps of Discovery

Lewis and Clark put together a team of about 40 people. Their group became known as the Corps of Discovery. One member of the Corps was **York**, an enslaved African American owned by William Clark. York was very skilled at hunting and fishing.

The group set out from **St. Louis, Missouri**, in May 1804. They traveled by boat up the Missouri River. Lewis and Clark drew maps and gathered plants and animals to take back with them.

In October, the group stopped for the winter in what is today North Dakota. They built a small camp near a Mandan Indian village and named it Fort Mandan. At Fort Mandan, Lewis and Clark hired a French fur trader and his Shoshone wife, **Sacagawea** (sa•kuh•juh•WEE•uh) to guide the expedition through the Shoshone lands.

In the spring of 1805, the Corps of Discovery set out from Fort Mandan. They traveled farther up the Missouri

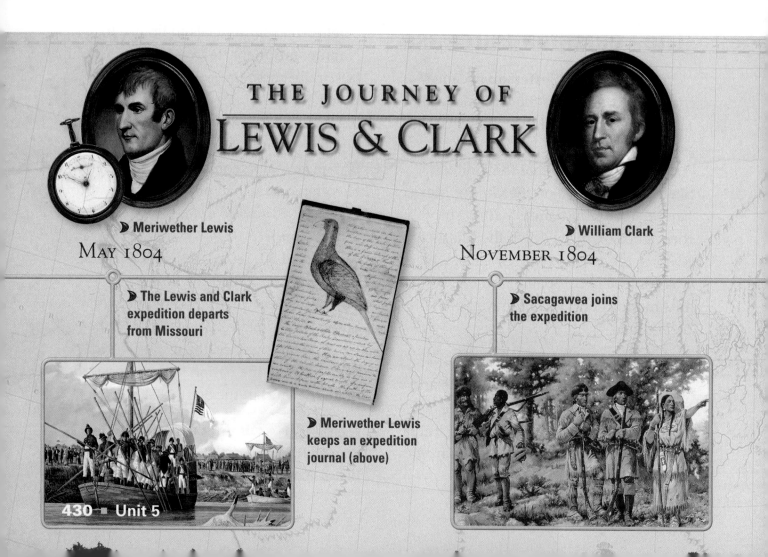

THE JOURNEY OF
LEWIS & CLARK

▶ Meriwether Lewis
MAY 1804

▶ William Clark
NOVEMBER 1804

▶ The Lewis and Clark expedition departs from Missouri

▶ Sacagawea joins the expedition

▶ Meriwether Lewis keeps an expedition journal (above)

River toward the Rocky Mountains. Sacagawea helped the group buy horses from the Shoshone to cross the Rocky Mountains. After the Corps crossed the mountains, they built boats and traveled down the Clearwater, Snake, and Columbia Rivers.

During their journey, Lewis and Clark had to make many hard decisions. These decisions had important consequences for the expedition. A **consequence** is what happens because of an action.

The Expedition Succeeds

In November 1805, the Lewis and Clark expedition finally reached the Pacific Ocean. They had traveled more than 3,000 miles in a year and a half. Clark wrote in his journal: "Ocian [Ocean] in view! O! the joy!"

The expedition spent the winter at Fort Clatsop, in what is now Oregon. In March 1806, the group began the long trip back to St. Louis. They arrived in September. Although there had been many dangers along the way, all but one member of the group returned safely.

Lewis and Clark drew many maps showing mountain passes and major rivers. They brought back seeds, plants, and even animals. President Jefferson was proud of their success. The frontier had been pushed farther west. The work done by the Corps of Discovery added to the knowledge Americans had about the lands that became the West.

READING CHECK SUMMARIZE
What was the goal of the Corps of Discovery?

❱ The expedition reaches the Pacific Ocean

SEPTEMBER 1805

❱ The expedition returns to St. Louis

❱ The expedition reaches present-day Montana

NOVEMBER 1805   SEPTEMBER 1806

❱ Many Native American leaders travel to Washington, D.C., to meet with President Jefferson (shown on the peace medal below)

Pike in the Southwest

In 1806, Captain Zebulon Pike led an expedition to explore the southwestern area of the Louisiana Purchase. In what is now Colorado, he saw a "blue mountain," now known as **Pikes Peak**.

Pike and his men unknowingly entered Spanish territory. They were arrested but released a few months later. When Pike got back, he reported that people in Spanish territories needed manufactured goods. Later more American traders traveled to the Southwest in order to sell goods to Spanish settlers.

READING CHECK ⚙ **DRAW CONCLUSIONS**
What were the results of Pike's expedition?

Summary

In the late 1700s, people began moving west. In 1803, the Louisiana Purchase doubled the size of the United States. Lewis, Clark, and Pike explored the new land.

▶ **PIKES PEAK** Zebulon Pike never made it to the top of the mountain that is named for him.

REVIEW

1. **WHAT TO KNOW** How did the Louisiana Purchase help the United States grow?

2. **VOCABULARY** Write a sentence that gives the meaning of the word **pioneer**.

3. **GEOGRAPHY** What river did Lewis and Clark travel on when they left St. Louis?

4. **CRITICAL THINKING** Why was buying New Orleans important to the growth of the United States?

5. ✎ **WRITE A JOURNAL ENTRY** Imagine you are a member of the Corps of Discovery. Write a journal entry describing the sights and geography of the new lands you are exploring.

6. ⭐ **DRAW CONCLUSIONS** On a separate piece of paper, copy and complete this graphic organizer.

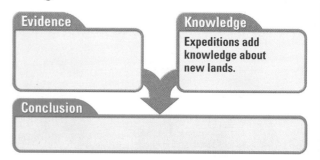

Evidence

Knowledge
Expeditions add knowledge about new lands.

Conclusion

Sacagawea

Biography

Trustworthiness

Respect
Responsibility
Fairness
Caring
Patriotism

Sacagawea, a Shoshone woman, was born in what is now the state of Idaho. In 1800, she was captured by another Native American group and taken away from her people. As a young woman, she married a French trader named Toussaint Charbonneau. When Lewis and Clark hired Charbonneau for their expedition, they asked Sacagawea to come along as a translator.

Sacagawea helped find routes for the explorers to follow. She also carried her baby, Jean Baptiste, along with her for the entire journey. Lewis and Clark both praised Sacagawea's bravery. One day, the boat she was riding in tipped over. Charbonneau panicked, but Sacagawea calmly saved the journals and supplies.

In time, the expedition reached the lands of the Shoshone people. To Sacagawea's surprise, she discovered that her brother, Cameahwait (KAM•ah•wait), had become a Shoshone leader. However, Sacagawea chose to remain with Lewis and Clark.

After the Lewis and Clark expedition ended, Sacagawea and Charbonneau moved to Fort Manuel, in what is now South Dakota. They remained there until her death in about 1812.

Why Character Counts

How did Sacagawea's actions show Lewis and Clark her trustworthiness?

Time

1786	1812
Born ?	Died ?

1800 Sacagawea is captured and taken to North Dakota

1804 Sacagawea joins the Lewis and Clark expedition

GO ONLINE For more resources, www.harcourtschool.com/ss1

Make a Thoughtful Decision

Why It Matters A thoughtful decision is one in which you think about the results before you act. This kind of decision is especially important in situations that involve other people.

❯ LEARN

Here are some steps you can use to help you make a thoughtful decision.

Step 1 Make a list of choices to help you reach your goal.

Step 2 Gather information you will need to make a decision.

Step 3 Predict the possible consequences of each choice, and compare them.

Step 4 Make a choice, and take action.

❯ **THE CORPS OF DISCOVERY** had to make many thoughtful decisions while on their expedition.

➤ MODERN DAY REENACTORS retraced Lewis and Clark's route in 2003.

❯ PRACTICE

Imagine that you are looking for a route to the Pacific coast. As the expedition leader, you must make thoughtful decisions. Your decisions could mean life or death for your group.

Below are two decisions you might face. Think about the consequences of each choice. Then make thoughtful decisions. Explain the steps you followed in making each decision.

1 When getting supplies, should you buy enough food for the entire trip or rely on hunting and gathering food along the way? You must carry all the supplies you bring.

2 At a trading post, you meet two French traders and a Native American. They speak several languages. Should you hire them or save money and keep your group small?

❯ APPLY

Make It Relevant Think about a decision you made at school this week. What steps did you follow? What choices did you have? What were the consequences of each choice? Was your decision a thoughtful one? Explain your answer to a family member.

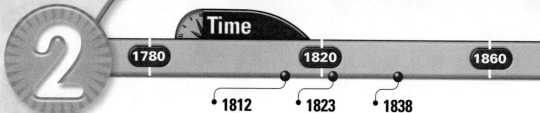

1812
The War of 1812 begins

1823
The Monore Doctrine is issued

1838
The Cherokee are forced to leave their homes

Expanding Borders

WHAT TO KNOW
How did the United States grow in the early 1800s and how were Native Americans affected?

VOCABULARY
impressment p. 437
national anthem p. 438
nationalism p. 439
assimilate p. 440

PEOPLE
Tecumseh
James Madison
Dolley Madison
Francis Scott Key
Andrew Jackson
James Monroe
Sequoyah
John Ross
John Marshall

PLACES
Lake Erie
Washington, D.C.
Baltimore
New Orleans

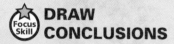

DRAW CONCLUSIONS

YOU ARE THERE   Hundreds of Shawnee have gathered to hear Chief **Tecumseh** (tuh•KUHM•suh) speak. The cold wind chills you as you listen to his words: "Will we let ourselves be destroyed . . . without making an effort worthy of our race?"

The crowd cheers as loud as thunder. "He's right!" your friend shouts. "A hundred years from now, people will still talk of our bravery. We will fight to defend our lands."

❯ **CHIEF TECUMSEH**

▶ **SHIPPING** Many American ships traded with France. This led to problems with Britain.

Troubles Grow

As pioneers moved west, they often settled on lands that belonged to Native Americans. Many times, the United States Army tried to force the Native Americans to leave. Britain, which owned Canada, helped the Native Americans and encouraged them to fight the Americans.

Chief Tecumseh urged his people and other Native Americans to unite. He built a village called Prophetstown, in what is now Indiana. Tecumseh hoped the tribes would come together at Prophetstown to defend their lands from the settlers.

Conflicts With Britain

In the early 1800s, many Americans were angry with Britain. They believed that British actions in both the West and the East threatened the United States.

During this time, Britain was often at war with France. To stop Americans from trading with France and other nations, the British navy captured American trading ships at sea.

After many years at war with France, the British navy needed sailors. British warships stopped American ships at sea. They forced American sailors to work on British navy ships. This action, called **impressment**, angered many Americans. More people began to believe that the United States should go to war.

READING CHECK ⟲ **DRAW CONCLUSIONS**
Why did some Americans want to go to war with Great Britain?

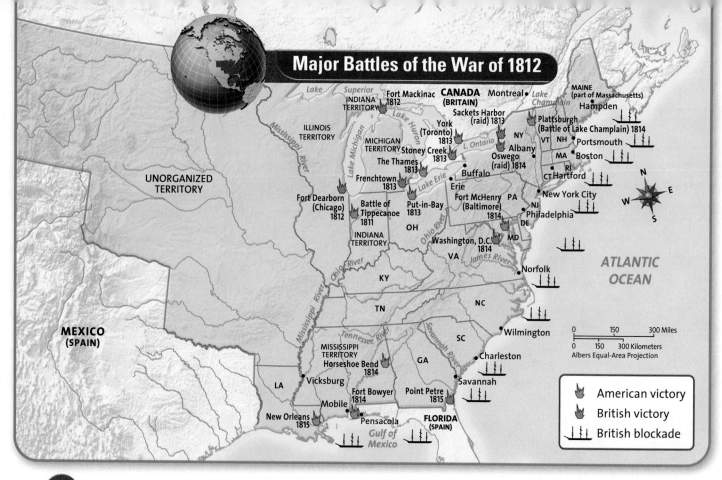

Major Battles of the War of 1812

American victory
British victory
British blockade

MAP SKILL LOCATION Where was the Battle of Tippecanoe fought?

The War of 1812

In June 1812, President **James Madison** asked Congress to declare war on Britain. At the time, Britain had the strongest navy in the world. Britain used its navy to set up a blockade of American ports. Still, the United States won several important naval battles. In September 1813, Captain Oliver Hazard Perry won the Battle of **Lake Erie**. This victory helped the United States keep control of its western lands.

A month later, General William Henry Harrison led 4,500 soldiers into Canada. At the Battle of the Thames (TEMZ) the Americans defeated the British and their Native American allies. Among those killed was Chief Tecumseh. Most tribes then gave up their alliances with Britain.

British Attacks on Cities

In August 1814, the British attacked **Washington, D.C.** First Lady **Dolley Madison** was still at the White House. As she escaped, she saved many important government papers. That evening, the British burned much of the city, including the White House and the Capital.

Next, the British attacked **Baltimore**, Maryland. The city was protected by nearby Fort McHenry. British ships fired for hours on the fort, but the Americans did not give up. After seeing the American flag still waving over the fort, **Francis Scott Key** wrote a poem called "The Star-Spangled Banner." It was later set to music and became the **national anthem**, the official song of the country.

In **New Orleans**, Louisiana, General **Andrew Jackson** led Americans to another victory. Sadly, neither side knew that a treaty ending the war had already been signed two weeks earlier in Europe.

The Growth of Nationalism

After the war ended, many Americans felt a sense of **nationalism**, or pride in one's country. This gave the government confidence to act strongly.

In 1823, President **James Monroe** announced a plan now known as the Monroe Doctrine. It said that "the American continents . . . [are] not to be considered as subjects for future colonization by any European powers. . . ." This meant the United States would try to stop European nations from starting new colonies in the Western Hemisphere.

READING CHECK ⏻ **DRAW CONCLUSIONS**
What were some outcomes of the War of 1812?

Extending Democracy

When the country was founded, only white men who owned property could vote. The new states gave the vote to all white men, and the idea quickly spread.

The election of 1828 was the first time that all white American men could vote. Andrew Jackson of Tennessee was elected President. He was the first President from one of the new states.

The country's new voters felt that Jackson was a "common man" like them. He became a symbol of the country's changing sense of what a democracy should be. These ideas came to be called "Jacksonian Democracy."

READING CHECK ⏻ **DRAW CONCLUSIONS**
How did the country's sense of democracy change?

❯ **FRANCIS SCOTT KEY** wrote "The Star-Spangled Banner" after the British attacked Fort McHenry.

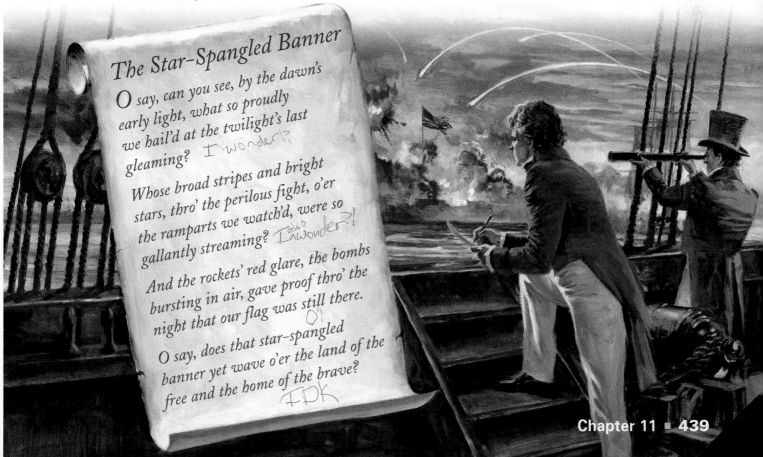

The Star-Spangled Banner

O say, can you see, by the dawn's early light, what so proudly we hail'd at the twilight's last gleaming? *I wonder!?*

Whose broad stripes and bright stars, thro' the perilous fight, o'er the ramparts we watch'd, were so gallantly streaming? *I wonder?!*

And the rockets' red glare, the bombs bursting in air, gave proof thro' the night that our flag was still there.

O say, does that star-spangled banner yet wave o'er the land of the free and the home of the brave?

▶ **TRAIL OF TEARS** This painting shows a group of Cherokee on the Trail of Tears. Many were forced to walk to the Indian Territory.

The Indian Removal Act

The Cherokee lived in the southeastern United States. Unlike most other tribes, the Cherokee **assimilated** to, or adopted, the ways of life of white settlers. However, the Cherokee still wanted to preserve their own culture. A Cherokee named **Sequoyah** (sih•KWOY•uh) created an alphabet for his people's language.

Many settlers began moving onto Cherokee lands. The Cherokee were peaceful people, but they protested the settlers' taking their land. The discovery of gold brought more settlers to the area.

In 1830, President Jackson signed a law called the Indian Removal Act. It forced the Cherokee and other tribes to leave their lands and go to an area called the Indian Territory. It was west of the Mississippi River, in what is now the state of Oklahoma.

The government of Georgia gave land owned by the Cherokee to new settlers looking for land. **John Ross**, the Cherokee chief, went to court to protect the Cherokee's right to their own land.

The United States Supreme Court sided with the Cherokee. Chief Justice **John Marshall** said that Georgia could not take the Cherokee's lands. However, President Jackson decided to ignore the Supreme Court. He would not enforce the ruling.

The Trail of Tears

In 1836, Martin Van Buren was elected President. The Cherokee hoped he would act justly, but he agreed with Andrew Jackson. On March 27, 1838, Van Buren sent the United States Army to force the remaining Cherokee to move west.

In 1838, the Cherokee started their long journey. To get to the Indian Territory, the

Cherokee had to walk about 800 miles through bad weather. Soldiers guarded them, making escape difficult.

One out of every four Cherokee died on their way to Indian Territory. This journey was known as the Trail of Tears.

The United States also forced almost all Native Americans east of the Mississippi River off their lands. They also died by the thousands on the Trail of Tears.

READING CHECK ☼**DRAW CONCLUSIONS**
Why did the journey west by the Cherokee and other tribes become known as the Trail of Tears?

Summary

In the War of 1812, the United States fought Britain. A time of national pride and expanding democracy followed. President Andrew Jackson signed the Indian Removal Act. This act forced the Cherokee to move west.

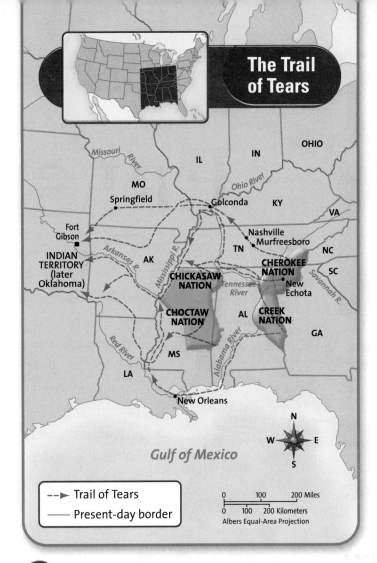

The Trail of Tears

- -▶ Trail of Tears
— Present-day border

0   100   200 Miles
0 100 200 Kilometers
Albers Equal-Area Projection

MAP SKILL **MOVEMENT To where did the Trail of Tears lead?**

REVIEW

1. **WHAT TO KNOW** How did the United States grow in the early 1800s and how were Native Americans affected?

2. **VOCABULARY** Write a sentence that uses the word **assimilate**.

3. **HISTORY** Why did many Americans want to go to war with Britain?

4. **CRITICAL THINKING** Make It Relevant How would you feel if you were forced to move from your home to a new place?

5. ✏️ **WRITE AN ARTICLE** Pretend you are a newspaper reporter who is with Francis Scott Key. Write a newspaper article that describes what happened at Fort McHenry.

6. ⭐ (Focus Skill) **DRAW CONCLUSIONS** On a separate piece of paper, copy and complete this graphic organizer.

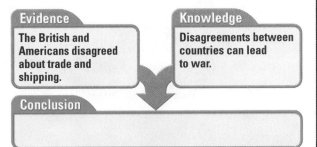

Evidence
The British and Americans disagreed about trade and shipping.

Knowledge
Disagreements between countries can lead to war.

Conclusion

PRESERVING CULTURE

Today, writing is a common way for people to preserve their culture. Before people learned to write, they shared their history through the stories they told.

For centuries, the Cherokee told each other stories. Then Sequoyah created an alphabet for the Cherokee language. His alphabet allowed people to write in Cherokee. In 1821, the Cherokee nation adopted Sequoyah's writing system. Many people learned to read and write in the Cherokee language. Soon there was a Cherokee newspaper and a constitution written in Cherokee.

People celebrate their customs as a way of preserving their heritage. Heritage is something handed down from past generations. Customs such as storytelling, songwriting, art, and cooking allow people to share their culture.

SEQUOYAH developed a Cherokee alphabet that had 85 characters. The *Cherokee Phoenix* (above left) was the first Native American newspaper.

These activities often form a special part of cultural festivals and rituals of worship.

Museums and other organizations also play an important role in preserving cultural history. They display art and crafts that people have made. They often sponsor exhibits and celebrations that help people remember the past.

Make It Relevant Americans preserve their cultures in many ways. How do different groups in your community preserve and share their cultures?

SHARING CULTURE People from all over the world still share their culture through stories and writing.

CEREMONIES Families prepare special dishes and participate in special ceremonies to celebrate and preserve their heritages.

Time

1780 — 1820 — 1860

1845
Texas becomes
a state

1846
The Mexican-American
War begins

1848
Gold is discovered
in California

From Ocean to Ocean

WHAT TO KNOW
How did the United States grow in the 1830s and the 1840s?

VOCABULARY
dictator p. 445
annex p. 446
ford p. 447
manifest destiny p. 448
cession p. 449
gold rush p. 450
forty-niners p. 450

PEOPLE
Davy Crockett
Jim Bowie
Sam Houston
Narcissa Whitman
Brigham Young
James K. Polk
James Marshall
John Sutter

PLACES
Alamo
San Antonio
Oregon Country
Independence

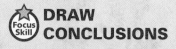

DRAW CONCLUSIONS

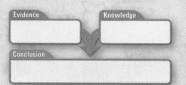

Evidence

Knowledge

Conclusion

YOU ARE THERE
It is March 1, 1836. You and about 100 men are at the **Alamo** in **San Antonio**, in Texas. You are defending the Alamo against the Mexican army.

The cannon fire grows louder. The Mexican army has been attacking for days. You know that you will fight bravely to defend the Alamo. You only hope that you will succeed.

▶ **BATTLE OF THE ALAMO** Defenders of the Alamo fought bravely against Mexican forces.

Texas Independence

In 1821, Mexico won its independence from Spain. Mexico took control of much of the Southwest, including Texas. Because few people lived in Texas, Mexico wanted more settlers to move there. Mexico's leaders offered land in Texas to encourage settlement.

Americans in Texas

Many of these new settlers were Americans. As more and more Americans arrived in Texas, the Mexican government became worried. In 1830, it tried to stop further American settlement. It also raised taxes on Americans already living there. This angered the American settlers.

When General Antonio Lopez de Santa Anna sent troops to Texas to enforce Mexican laws, fighting broke out.

Santa Anna had made himself dictator of Mexico. A **dictator** is a leader who has complete control of the government.

The Alamo

A group of Texans and their supporters turned the **Alamo**, the San Antonio de Valero mission, into a fort. Famous pioneers **Davy Crockett** and **Jim Bowie** were among the Americans at the Alamo. Santa Anna and his army attacked on February 23, 1836. The Alamo defenders held off his army for 13 days. On March 6, the Mexicans won the battle. All but a few of the defenders had died.

While the defenders fought at the Alamo, Texan leaders declared Texas an independent republic. They formed an army led by **Sam Houston**.

READING CHECK ⚙ **DRAW CONCLUSIONS**
What was surprising about the Battle of the Alamo?

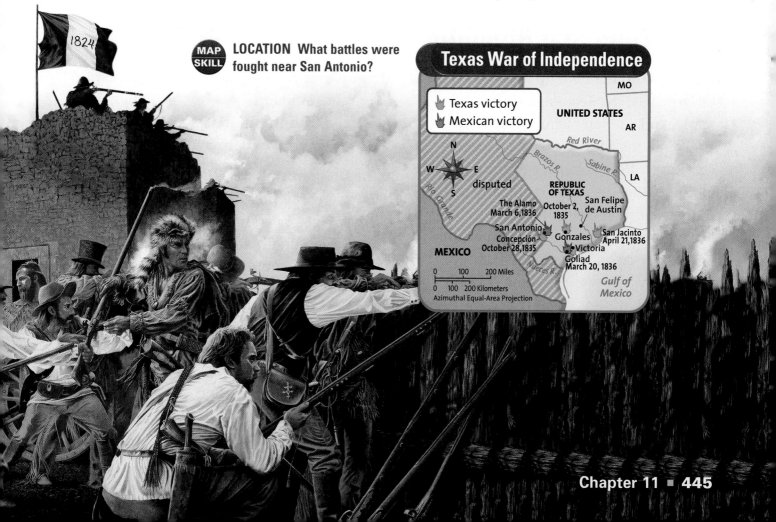

MAP SKILL **LOCATION** What battles were fought near San Antonio?

Texas War of Independence

- 🔥 Texas victory
- 🔥 Mexican victory

MO
UNITED STATES
AR
Red River
LA
Brazos R.
Sabine R.
Rio Grande
disputed
REPUBLIC OF TEXAS
The Alamo March 6, 1836
October 2, 1835
San Felipe de Austin
San Antonio
Gonzales
San Jacinto April 21, 1836
Concepción October 28, 1835
Victoria
MEXICO
Goliad March 20, 1836
Nueces R.
Gulf of Mexico

0 100 200 Miles
0 100 200 Kilometers
Azimuthal Equal-Area Projection

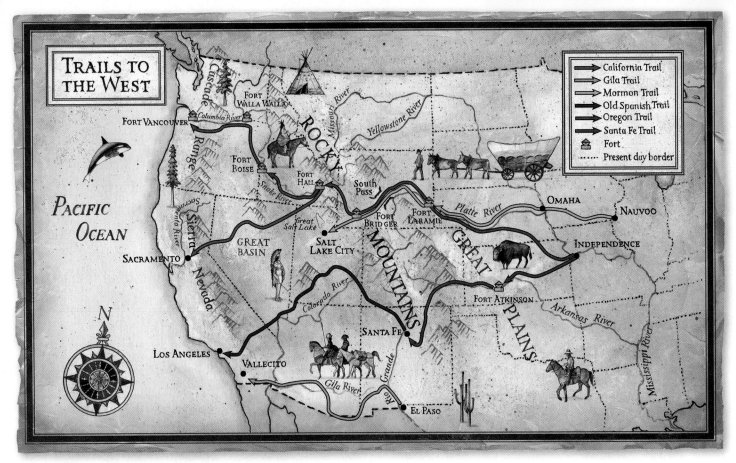

TRAILS TO THE WEST

Legend:
- California Trail
- Gila Trail
- Mormon Trail
- Old Spanish Trail
- Oregon Trail
- Santa Fe Trail
- Fort
- Present day border

MAP SKILL MOVEMENT This map shows the trails that settlers followed to the West. How many trails ended in California?

The Lone Star Republic

Texans did not give up after the Alamo. On April 21, the Texas army attacked Santa Anna at San Jacinto. The Texans surprised the Mexicans and attacked, shouting, "Remember the Alamo!" After a brief battle, they captured many soldiers, including General Santa Anna.

In return for his freedom, Santa Anna granted Texas independence. Sam Houston was elected the new nation's first president. Texas was called the Lone Star Republic because its flag had one star. Texas was an independent republic until it was **annexed**, or added on, by the United States in 1845.

READING CHECK ⊗ **DRAW CONCLUSIONS**
How did the Battle of San Jacinto affect Texas?

Trails West

Americans were always looking west for more land and new opportunities. The **Oregon Country** in the Pacific Northwest was one place that attracted settlers.

The Oregon Trail

Among the first Americans to travel to the Oregon Country were missionaries Marcus and Narcissa Whitman. In letters to her family, **Narcissa Whitman** described the beautiful valleys and rich soil of the Oregon Country. Her letters were later published, and within a few years, thousands of pioneers were following the Oregan Trail west.

The Oregon Trail began in Missouri, at **Independence**. Most pioneers traveled in covered wagons. The wagons were long and shaped like boats, so people called them "prairie schooners."

The pioneers traveled west as part of a group of wagons, called a wagon train. No one wanted to travel in winter, for fear of deadly mountain snowstorms. Since it took about six months to travel to the Oregon Country, wagon trains left in the spring.

The way west was filled with hardships. People walked most of the way, because the wagons were filled with supplies. At night, wagons were pulled into a circle for protection. Wagons faced danger when they had to **ford**, or cross, rivers. If a wagon tipped over, goods could be lost or people could drown.

The Mormon Trail

In the 1840s, the Mormons, or members of the Church of Jesus Christ of Latter-day Saints, were not welcome in many places in the United States. They went west to form their own communities and to find greater religious freedom.

Brigham Young was a Mormon leader. In 1846, he led a group on a 1,000-mile trip from Illinois to the Great Salt Lake valley, in what is now Utah. This route became known as the Mormon Trail.

The Mormons created a city in the valley. The region known as the Utah Territory grew quickly. Brigham Young became the territory's first governor.

READING CHECK **DRAW CONCLUSIONS**
Why did the Mormons move west?

❯ **WAGON TRAINS** Settlers traveled west in covered wagons that carried all the supplies for the journey.

Expanding Borders

In the 1840s, both the United States and Britain claimed the Oregon Country. However, many people in the United States believed that their country had a right to the land. They believed in **manifest destiny**, the idea that the United States was meant to stretch from the Atlantic Ocean to the Pacific Ocean. Many Americans wanted to see the United States expand its borders, even if it meant going to war.

New Conflicts

For a time, it looked like arguments over the Oregon Country might cause another war between Britain and the United States. However, in 1846, the countries settled their differences peacefully and signed a treaty that set region's northern border. Two years later, Congress created the Oregon Territory.

Many Americans also wanted California to be part of the United States. **James K. Polk**, the President of the United States at the time, was a strong supporter of manifest destiny. He offered to buy California and what is now Arizona, and New Mexico for $30 million. Mexico refused to sell the land.

The Mexican-American War

At about the same time, a dispute arose over the border between Texas and Mexico. The United States claimed the border to be the Rio Grande. Mexico said it was the Nueces (nu•AY•says) River, about 100 miles north of the Rio Grande.

When President Polk sent General Zachary Taylor and 3,500 soldiers to the area between the Nueces and the Rio Grande, Mexican troops attacked them at Palo Alto. The United States declared war on Mexico on May 13, 1846.

❯ THE MEXICAN-AMERICAN WAR was fought because of a boundary dispute between the two countries.

The Growth of the United States

RUSSIA

ALASKA PURCHASE 1867

CANADA

0   200   400 Miles
0   400 Kilometers

PACIFIC OCEAN

CANADA

— Present-day border

TREATY WITH BRITAIN 1842

0   200   400 Miles
0   200   400 Kilometers
Albers Equal-Area Projection

TREATY WITH BRITAIN 1818

Missouri River

Columbia River

OREGON TERRITORY 1846

Snake River

Lake Superior

Mississippi River

Lake Michigan

Lake Huron

Lake Ontario

Lake Erie

40°N

LOUISIANA PURCHASE 1803

Platte River

40°N

MEXICAN CESSION 1848

Colorado River

Arkansas River

Ohio R.

UNITED STATES 1783

Tennessee R.

PACIFIC OCEAN

ATLANTIC OCEAN

70°W

30°N

GADSDEN PURCHASE 1853

TEXAS ANNEXATION 1845

1810

30°N

120°W

HAWAII ANNEXATION 1898

PACIFIC OCEAN

0   100 Miles
0   100 Kilometers

1812

1813

FLORIDA 1819

MEXICO

Rio Grande

Gulf of Mexico

N E W S

110°W

90°W

80°W

MAP SKILL REGIONS What lands did the United States take control of in the 1840s?

In 1847, American forces captured the city of Vera Cruz. From there, they marched to Mexico's capital, Mexico City. The Mexican troops fought bravely but were defeated on September 14, 1847. After more than a year of fighting, the Mexican-American War was over.

New Borders

In February 1848, the United States and Mexico signed a treaty that officially ended the war. In the Treaty of Guadalupe Hidalgo (gwah•dah•LOO•pay ee•DAHL•goh), Mexico gave up all of its claims to southern Texas. Later, both governments recognized the Rio Grande as the southern border of Texas.

Mexico also sold the United States a large area known as the Mexican Cession. A **cession**, or concession, is something given up. The Mexican Cession included all of present-day California, Nevada, and Utah, and parts of what are now New Mexico, Arizona, Colorado, and Wyoming. In return, the United States paid Mexico $15 million. In 1853, the United States bought the rest of New Mexico and Arizona from Mexico in what was called the Gadsden Purchase.

READING CHECK ⚙DRAW CONCLUSIONS
Why did the United States and Mexico go to war?

The California Gold Rush

In the 1840s, California was a land of large ranches with a few small towns. However, the discovery of gold in 1848 changed the region forever.

The Forty-Niners

In 1848, **James Marshall** and some other workers were building a sawmill for **John Sutter** along the bank of the South Fork of the American River. On January 24, the workers found a small nugget of gold. No one is sure who found it, but Marshall said that he had.

The workers found more gold, and the news of their discovery spread. It soon caused a **gold rush**, or a sudden rush of people to an area where gold has been found. During the next year, about 90,000 people rushed to California. They were called **forty-niners** because most arrived in 1849. Among the forty-niners were women and as many as 1,000 African Americans, both free and enslaved.

Most of the forty-niners came from other parts of the United States. Some made their way west along the overland trails. Others reached California by sailing around the tip of South America or by crossing the Isthmus of Panama and then sailing up the Pacific coast.

Many of the forty-niners who came to California were from other parts of the world, including Mexico, South America, Europe, and Asia. In fact, about one of every four newcomers was Chinese.

Gold Mining

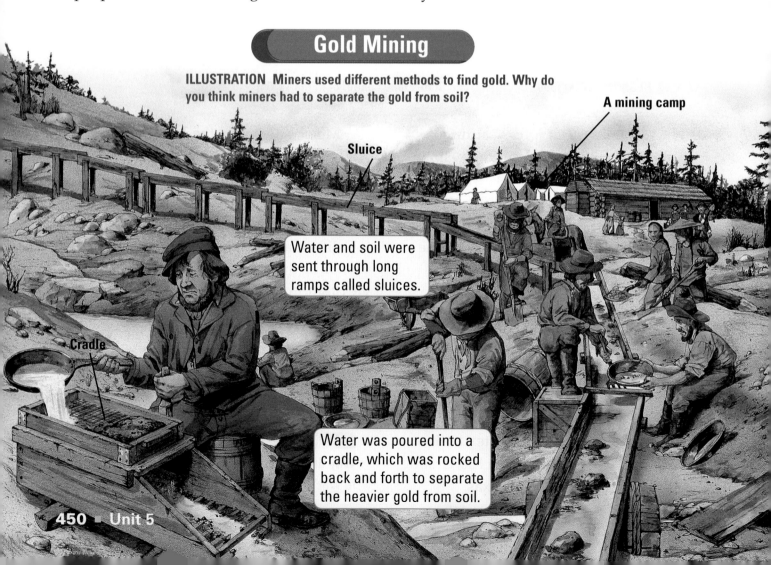

ILLUSTRATION Miners used different methods to find gold. Why do you think miners had to separate the gold from soil?

A mining camp

Sluice

Water and soil were sent through long ramps called sluices.

Cradle

Water was poured into a cradle, which was rocked back and forth to separate the heavier gold from soil.

Changing California

The gold rush brought great changes to California. Those who did not find gold often stayed and turned to ranching or farming. Others started businesses. By the end of 1849, California's population had grown to more than 100,000 people. A group of California leaders decided that California should become a state. After some debate, Congress agreed. In 1850, California became the thirty-first state.

READING CHECK ⊙ **DRAW CONCLUSIONS**
How did the discovery of gold change California?

Summary

Texas gained independence from Mexico and later became a state. Pioneers traveled west on the Oregon and Mormon Trails. The United States gained lands as a result of the Mexican-American War. California grew because of a gold rush.

REVIEW

1. **WHAT TO KNOW** How did the United States grow in the 1830s and 1840s?

2. **VOCABULARY** Use **annex** in a sentence.

3. **GEOGRAPHY** What trails did pioneers use to travel west?

4. **CRITICAL THINKING** Why do you think many Americans believed in manifest destiny?

5. ✏️ **WRITE A JOURNAL ENTRY** Pretend you are a forty-niner traveling to California. Write a diary entry that describes your journey and what you will do when you arrive.

6. ⭐ **DRAW CONCLUSIONS**
   (Focus Skill) On a separate piece of paper, copy and complete this graphic organizer.

Evidence	Knowledge

Conclusion

Disagreements over their shared boundary led the United States and Mexico to go to war.

Some miners were lowered underground to search for gold. This was called coyoting.

Winch

Pans were also used to separate gold from soil.

A Long Tom was a longer version of a cradle.

Long Tom

Time

1780   1820   1860

1790
The first American textile mill is built

1825
The Erie Canal opens

1830
The first American locomotive is built

New Ideas and Inventions

WHAT TO KNOW
How did new inventions change life in the United States?

VOCABULARY
canal p. 453
lock p. 453
locomotive p. 454
Industrial Revolution p. 455
cotton gin p. 456
interchangeable parts p. 456

PEOPLE
Robert Fulton
Peter Cooper
Samuel Slater
Moses Brown
Francis Cabot Lowell
Eli Whitney
Cyrus McCormick
John Deere
Samuel F. B. Morse

PLACES
New York City
Lake Erie
Hudson River
Pawtucket

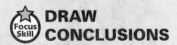

DRAW CONCLUSIONS

Evidence   Knowledge

Conclusion

YOU ARE THERE

It is 1825, and you are at a ceremony in **New York City**. Governor DeWitt Clinton traveled from **Lake Erie** along the Erie Canal to the **Hudson River**. Then his boat sailed down the Hudson to the city.

Governor Clinton pours a bottle of water from Lake Erie into the harbor. The Great Lakes are now linked by water all the way to the Atlantic Ocean.

Transportation

During the first half of the 1800s, new inventions allowed people to travel and transport goods more easily.

Roads and Canals

Settlers living in states west of the Appalachians found it difficult to ship goods east across the mountains. To solve this problem, Congress voted to build the National Road. By 1818, it connected Maryland to present-day West Virginia. Shipping goods over land was still slow and costly, though.

Boats offered faster and cheaper transportation, but many rivers had changes in elevation. In some places, rapids and waterfalls made boat travel impossible.

Canals could avoid such obstacles and extend natural waterways. A **canal** is a human-made waterway that connects bodies of water. In 1817, New York's governor, DeWitt Clinton, decided to begin work on a canal from Lake Erie to the Hudson River.

Irish immigrants and local workers built the Erie Canal in eight years. It was 363 miles long and had 83 locks. In a **lock**, a section of water is held by two gates. When one gate is opened, the water raises or lowers the boat to the level of the water in the next lock.

The Erie Canal linked the Great Lakes to the Atlantic. It cut the time and cost of shipping a ton of goods from Buffalo to New York City from 20 days to 8 days and from about $100 to less than $10. The canal helped make New York City a center of trade.

READING CHECK ☼ **DRAW CONCLUSIONS**
How did the Erie Canal change trade in the nation?

The Erie Canal

1 Water in locks raised or lowered boats to a certain level.

Gate

ILLUSTRATION Canals used locks to safely travel through different elevations. How were boats moved through the canal?

Towing rope

2 Locks let boats travel safely through different elevations.

Canal towpath

3 Horses, mules, and oxen pulled the boats through the locks.

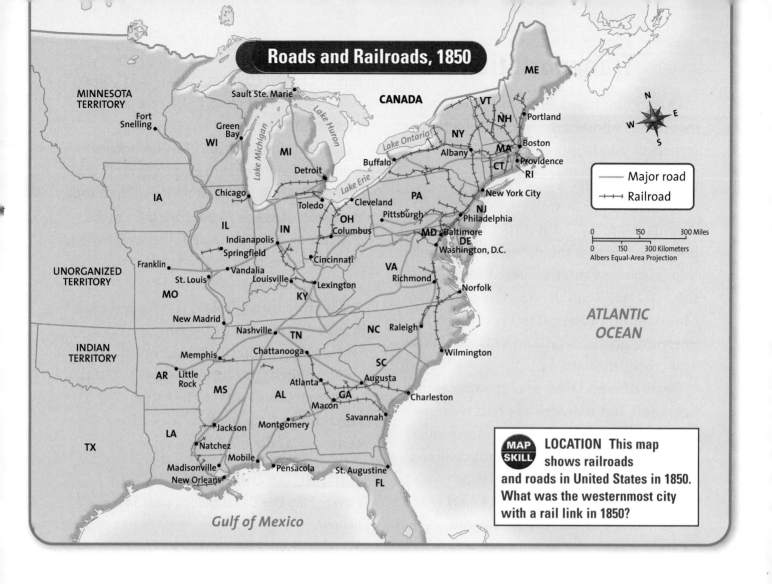

Roads and Railroads, 1850

Major road
Railroad

0   150   300 Miles
0   150   300 Kilometers
Albers Equal-Area Projection

MAP SKILL **LOCATION** This map shows railroads and roads in United States in 1850. What was the westernmost city with a rail link in 1850?

Steamboats and Railroads

After the success of the Erie Canal, many states began building their own canals. However, by the 1840s, canal travel was being replaced by newer and faster ways of moving goods and people.

The steam engine was invented in Britain and had been improved over the years. In 1807, American inventor **Robert Fulton** used a steam engine to power his boat, the *Clermont*. Soon steamboats became the main form of travel on large rivers across the nation. They could easily travel upstream against the current.

Steam engines were also used to build **locomotives**, or railroad engines. In 1830, **Peter Cooper** built the first American locomotive, the *Tom Thumb*. Cooper proved that steam locomotives could pull railroad cars over iron rails.

The number of railroads grew quickly. Tracks soon linked cities in the eastern United States. Rail travel was faster and cheaper than steamboats. By 1850, more than 9,000 miles of railroad track crossed the country. Railroads made it easier for people to travel and ship goods.

READING CHECK **ÖDRAW CONCLUSIONS**
How did the steam engine change travel in the 1800s?

The Industrial Revolution

During the 1800s, new inventions and forms of transportation changed the way people lived and worked. They allowed people to use machines instead of hand tools to make large quantities of goods. Workers could make goods more quickly and at a lower cost. This change in manufacturing came to be called the **Industrial Revolution**.

Mills in the North

The Industrial Revolution began in Britain. People invented machines that spun thread and wove textiles, or cloth. These machines were placed in factories called mills, where many people came to work. Fast-moving water from nearby rivers powered the new machines.

British leaders did not want other countries to learn how to build these machines. Neither the machines nor the workers who used them were allowed to leave Britain. **Samuel Slater**, a British mill worker, memorized every detail about the complicated machines. Then he sneaked aboard a ship for the United States.

In 1793, Slater and **Moses Brown** built the first American textile mill in **Pawtucket**, Rhode Island. It marked the beginning of large-scale manufacturing in the United States. Instead of working at home, more people began to go to work in factories. Many of these workers were women and children.

In 1814, **Francis Cabot Lowell** built a mill in Waltham, Massachusetts. This mill did all the jobs needed to make raw cotton into finished cloth. His workers lived in nearby houses owned by the mill.

READING CHECK ⚙ **DRAW CONCLUSIONS**
Why was Samuel Slater's change important?

➤ GRAPH The number of factories (below) grew from 1849 to 1869. How many factories were in the United States in 1869?

Increase in the Number of Factories in United States from 1849–1869

1849	🏭 🏭
1859	🏭 🏭 🏭
1869	🏭 🏭 🏭 🏭 🏭

🏭 = 50,000 manufacturing businesses

More Inventions

In 1793, **Eli Whitney** visited a cotton plantation. He saw how difficult it was to remove seeds from cotton by hand. Whitney invented the **cotton gin**, a machine that could remove the seeds.

The cotton gin changed plantation farming. Cotton could be prepared for market in less time. This let planters grow more cotton. As a result, they needed more enslaved workers to harvest cotton.

Whitney also invented a system of interchangeable parts for making guns. **Interchangeable parts** are parts that are exactly alike. Guns, like most other goods at that time, were made one at a time by skilled workers. The new parts were made by machine. Almost anyone could learn to put these parts together.

Interchangeable parts made mass production possible. Large amounts of goods could be made at one time. Cheaper machine-made goods replaced many expensive handmade goods.

Other Inventors

New inventions also helped farmers. In 1832, **Cyrus McCormick** invented a mechanical reaper for harvesting grain. With McCormick's reaper, farmers could harvest wheat much faster than they could by hand. In 1837, **John Deere** invented a strong steel plow to cut through the heavy soil in the Midwest.

That same year, **Samuel F. B. Morse** invented a faster way to communicate. His invention, called the telegraph, sent messages from one machine to another

Primary Sources

McCormick Advertisement

Background This advertisement from the mid-1800s shows the McCormick reaper.

A McCormick reaper

Horses pulled the reaper

C.H. & L.J. McCORMICK

MANUFACTURERS OF

HARVESTING MACHINERY.

CHICAGO.

Location of the factory

DBQ How did farmers use the McCormick reaper?

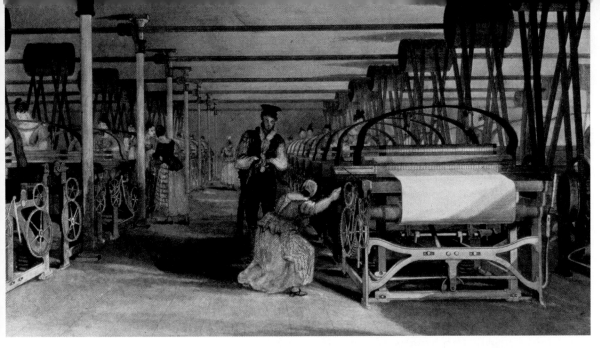

along a wire. To do this, Morse invented a code system in which electronic "dots" and "dashes"—short and long taps on a key—stood for letters of the alphabet.

The Industrial Revolution changed the nation. Some people moved from farms to cities to work in factories. The United States was becoming an industrial power.

READING CHECK ᒣ**DRAW CONCLUSIONS**
How did the reaper help farmers?

Summary

Canals made both travel and the shipping of goods faster and cheaper. Then steamboats and railroads powered by steam improved transportation even more. New inventions, in addition to new kinds of transportation, led to the Industrial Revolution. Life in the United States was changing quickly.

REVIEW

1. **WHAT TO KNOW** How did new inventions change life in the United States?

2. **VOCABULARY** Use the word **canal** in a sentence that gives its meaning.

3. **ECONOMICS** How did the invention of the cotton gin affect plantation owners?

4. **CRITICAL THINKING** How do you think the growth of railroads affected the use of canals?

5. **MAKE AN ADVERTISEMENT** Imagine that you are living during the Industrial Revolution. Make a poster advertising one of the new inventions. Include both words and pictures.

6. (Focus Skill) **DRAW CONCLUSIONS** On a separate sheet of paper, copy and complete this graphic organizer.

Evidence	Knowledge
Railroads became popular after canals.	

Conclusion

Time

1780   1800

1803
The Louisiana
Purchase is
made

1805
Lewis and Clark
reach the Pacific

Visual Summary

Summarize the Chapter

Draw Conclusions Complete this graphic organizer to
draw a conclusion about the westward expansion of the
United States.

Evidence

Today, the United States stretches
from the Atlantic Ocean to the
Pacific Ocean.

Knowledge

The Louisiana Purchase and the
Mexican-American War gave the
United States many new lands.

Conclusion

Vocabulary

**Identify the term from the word bank that
correctly matches each definition.**

1. to cross a deep river

2. a feeling of pride for one's country

3. an early settler of an area

4. a low place between mountains

5. to adopt the customs of another
   culture

6. a human-made waterway that connects
   bodies of water

7. something given up, such as land

Word Bank

gap p. 427	**ford** p. 447
pioneer p. 427	**cession** p. 449
nationalism p. 439	**canal** p. 453
assimilate p. 440	

1820	1840	1860

1825
The Erie
Canal
opens

1830
The Indian
Removal Act
is signed

1846
The Mexican-
American
War begins

 ## Time Line

8. Did Lewis and Clark reach the Pacific Ocean before or after the Erie Canal was opened?

9. When was the Indian Removal Act signed?

 ## Facts and Main Ideas

Answer these questions.

10. What was the Trail of Tears?

11. Where did the Oregon Trail begin?

12. How did the cotton gin affect slavery?

Write the letter of the best choice.

13. Which President was responsible for the Louisiana Purchase?
  A Andrew Jackson
  B James Polk
  C James Monroe
  D Thomas Jefferson

14. Which of the following was the first to become a state?
  A Texas
  B Oregon
  C Kentucky
  D California

15. Who was the first governor of both the states of Franklin and Tennessee?
  A Daniel Boone
  B John Sevier
  C William Clark
  D Zebulon Pike

 ## Critical Thinking

16. What brought the United States into conflict with Native Americans in the 1800s?

17. How did railroads and canals help the United States grow?

18. How were the problems faced by settlers in Texas like those of colonists in the thirteen British colonies?

Skills

Make a Thoughtful Decision

19. Imagine that you are planning to settle in Ohio. Use the steps listed on page 434 to make a thoughtful decision about the supplies you will need for your journey.

 *writing*

Write a Letter Pretend you are part of a pioneer family that has just moved to Kentucky. Write a letter to relatives back in Virginia, telling them about your new home.

Write an Editorial Pretend you are a newspaper editor writing about the Industrial Revolution. Write an editorial that either supports or opposes the building of more factories. Be sure to include reasons for your position.

Fun with Social Studies

What's Going On?

It's the late 1700s, and Philadelphia's papers have big news. What has happened?

Changes Already!
Ten amendments added to document.

Sweaty Delegates Pack State House
New form of government planned in secret talks.

It's Official!
All states finally vote yes.

Crack the Code

Fill in the correct vocabulary words to find the name of a War of 1812 battle.

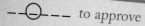

— ◯ — — — to approve

— — — — — — ◯ to charge the President with a crime

◯ — — — — the President's advisors

— ◯ — — — — — an agreement between two groups

— — — ◯ — — — a weapons storehouse

— — ◯ — — — a Supreme Court judge

Lunch Scramble

Match the customers with the lunch they would have ordered.

Customer #1
Dried beans
Crackers
Dried meat
Must not spoil during 6-month trip in covered wagon.

Customer #2
Sandwich
Fresh fruit
Other items to take with me as I survey Washington, D.C.

Customer #3
Nothing
Will find food along the trail with Mr. Lewis and Mr. Clark.

Customer #4
Yellow cheese
Yellow potatoes
Yellow corn
Anything else that's the color of my favorite metal.

Sacagawea

Forty-niner

Benjamin Banneker

Oregon Trail Pioneer

Online Adventures

GO ONLINE

Eco just learned that a thief has stolen pieces of the United States Constitution! Play the online game to recover the missing pieces and save the day. Along with Eco, you'll solve puzzles in different places and times to catch the thief and save the Constitution. Play now at **www.harcourtschool.com/ss1**

Unit 5

Review and Test Prep ✓

🔆 THE BIG IDEA

Growth and Change The United States established a new government and grew larger as more people arrived and lands were acquired.

Reading Comprehension and Vocabulary

The Young Republic

In 1789, American leaders gathered at a convention to improve the Articles of Confederation. Then they decided to replace them instead. This resulted in the Constitution, a new plan of government.

The Constitution established three branches of the federal government— the executive, legislative, and judicial branches. Checks and balances kept any one branch from having too much power. After much debate, all 13 states ratified the Constitution. In 1791, the Bill of Rights was added. These first ten amendments guaranteed certain rights and freedoms for American citizens.

Immigrants poured into the United States during the late 1700s and early 1800s. Many moved west in search of open lands. After the Louisiana Purchase, the nation stretched west to the Rocky Mountains. As the nation grew, many Native Americans lost their lands. Many also suffered during the Trail of Tears.

After the Mexican-American War, the United States gained many western lands from Mexico. By 1850, the United States stretched from sea to sea. Railroads, canals, telegraphs, and other technology helped different regions of the nation connect.

Use the summary above to answer these questions.

1. What is a convention?
   A a plan of government
   B a disagreement
   C an important meeting
   D a change

2. What is the purpose of checks and balances?
   A to keep one branch of the government from having too much power
   B to keep states from printing money
   C to make sure leaders never compromise
   D to stop the states from going to war

3. What does the word amendment mean?
   A change
   B compromise
   C debate
   D decision

4. When did the United States gain land from Mexico?
   A after the Mexican-American War
   B after the American Revolution
   C after the Battle of the Alamo
   D after the War of 1812

Answer these questions.

5. What event made Americans think about the strength of the central government?

6. What explains that the purpose of the Constitution is to create fair government?

7. What is one responsibility that citizens have at the national, state, and local level?

8. Why did immigrants come to the United States in the late 1700s and early 1800s?

9. Why did Tecumseh choose to fight alongside the British during the War of 1812?

10. What period of new inventions and transportation changed life in the 1800s?

Write the letter of the best choice.

11. Which compromise addressed slavery?
    A the Connecticut Compromise
    B the Great Compromise
    C the Three-Fifths Compromise
    D the Virginia Plan

12. Which amendment reserves some rights for the states?
    A the First Amendment
    B the Second Amendment
    C the Fourth Amendment
    D the Tenth Amendment

13. Which of these was one of the earliest pioneers to cross the Cumberland Gap?
    A Davy Crockett
    B Daniel Boone
    C William Clark
    D Meriwether Lewis

14. How did the Industrial Revolution affect the population of cities?
    A The population grew rich.
    B The population grew smaller.
    C The population grew larger.
    D The population stayed the same.

15. What is one way citizens can show their civic virtue?

16. What resources made many settlers want to follow the Oregon Trail?

17. What role did religion have in the settlement of the Utah Territory?

18. How did the invention of the steam engine change transportation?

Read a Population Map

Use the map below to answer the question.

19. Which part of Ohio has the lowest population density?

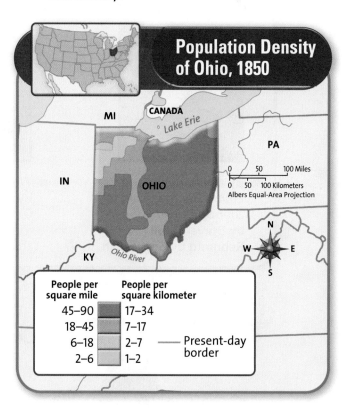

Population Density of Ohio, 1850

People per square mile	People per square kilometer
45–90	17–34
18–45	7–17
6–18	2–7
2–6	1–2

— Present-day border

Unit 5 Activities

Show What You Know

Unit Writing Activity

Write a Persuasive Letter Imagine that you are writing to a student in another country.

- In your letter, convince him or her of the importance of the Constitution.
- Tell why the Constitution is the foundation of the American republic.

Unit Project

Make a Time Line Complete a time line that shows the nation's growth during the late 1700s and early 1800s.

- Choose events in the nation's history that resulted in political, economic, geographic, or population growth.
- Illustrate these events with pictures.

Read More

- *By the Dawn's Early Light: The Story of the Star-Spangled Banner* by Steven Kroll. Rebound by Sagebrush.

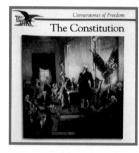

- *The Constitution* by Marilyn Prolman. Children's Press.

- *A Pioneer Sampler* by Barbara Greenwood. Houghton Mifflin.

GO ONLINE For more resources, go to www.harcourtschool.com/ss1

EXTEND

Civil War Times

Start with the Standards

OHIO SOCIAL STUDIES CONTENT STANDARDS

History 5.1, 5.6

People in Societies 5.2, 5.3, 5.4, 5.5

Geography 5.3, 5.7A, 5.7C, 5.8, 5.9B, 5.9D

Economics 5.3, 5.4

Social Studies Skills 5.1A, 5.1B, 5.2, 5.3, 5.4A, 5.4B, 5.4C, 5.5, 5.7, 5.8

The Big Idea

Conflict and Change

Social and economic differences divided the nation and led to war. The nation was reunited, but continued to face many challenges.

What to Know

✓ What caused the Civil War?

✓ How did the Union win the Civil War?

✓ What happened in the South after the Civil War?

✓ How did the United States change after the Civil War?

Unit 6

6

Ohio in the Civil War

DID YOU KNOW?

Ohioan Johnny Clem was nine years old when he joined the Union army and became a famous drummer boy.

During the Civil War, Ohio sided with the Northern states. Many people in Ohio were abolitionists, or people who wanted to end slavery. Ohio senators Samuel P. Chase and Benjamin Wade spoke against slavery before the United States Congress.

Other Ohio abolitionists, such as John Parker, helped enslaved people escape on the Underground Railroad. Ohio author Harriet Beecher Stowe published *Uncle Tom's Cabin*, a fictional book about slavery.

❭ William T. Sherman

❭ Harriet Beecher Stowe

More than 300,000 soldiers from Ohio joined the Union army. Some Ohioans also worked in the war as doctors and nurses. Ohio factories and farms provided supplies to the Union army, such as muskets, uniforms, tents, and food.

Many Union generals came from Ohio, including George McClellan, William T. Sherman, and Ulysses S. Grant. Sherman was involved in many major battles. He won many victories for the North. Grant became the commander of the entire Union army. The war ended in 1865, when Confederate General Robert E. Lee surrendered to Grant at Appomattox Courthouse in Virginia. After the war, Grant was elected President.

▶ Civil War soldiers in Ohio (left) carried gunpowder in flasks (below).

 OHIO TEST PREP

1 **Which Ohioan spoke against slavery before Congress?**
A. John Parker
B. Samuel P. Chase
C. William T. Sherman

2 **How did Ohio factories and farms help the Union army?**
A. They provided supplies.
B. They sent doctors and nurses.
C. They shut down during the war.

3 **Which Ohioan served as a general and as President of the United States?**
A. Harriet Beecher Stowe
B. William T. Sherman
C. Ulysses S. Grant

4 **How did Ohioans help the Union during the Civil War?**

Time

A Divided Nation

1820 The Missouri Compromise is passed

1845 Frederick Douglass publishes his autobiography

1848 The Seneca Falls Convention is held

1861 The Civil War begins

1820

1840

1860

At the Same Time

1825 Britain builds the first steam train

1847 The African nation of Liberia declares its independence

1858 Britain takes control of India

Civil War Times

People

Robert E. Lee

1807–1870
- Born in Virginia and attended the United States Military Academy
- Commanded Confederate forces in the Civil War

Abraham Lincoln

1809–1865
- President of the United States during the Civil War
- Signed the Emancipation Proclamation

1800	1850

1807 • Robert E. Lee   1870

1809 • Abraham Lincoln   1865

1815 • Elizabeth Cady Stanton

1818 • Frederick Douglass

1820 • Harriet Tubman

1821 • Clara Barton

1822 • Ulysses S. Grant

1860 • Jane Addams

Harriet Tubman

1820–1913
- Conductor on the Underground Railroad
- Helped nearly 300 enslaved people escape to freedom

Clara Barton

1821–1912
- Worked as a Union Army nurse during the Civil War
- Founded the American Red Cross in 1881

Elizabeth Cady Stanton

1815–1902
- Women's rights leader who organized the Seneca Falls Convention
- Helped start the National Woman Suffrage Association

Frederick Douglass

1818–1895
- Escaped from slavery when he was 20 years old
- Became a world-famous writer and speaker

1900   **1950**

1902

1895

1913

1912

1885

1935

Ulysses S. Grant

1822–1885
- Commanded Union forces in the Civil War
- Served as the 18th United States President

Jane Addams

1860–1935
- Opened Hull House in Chicago to help immigrants
- The first American woman to win the Nobel Peace Prize

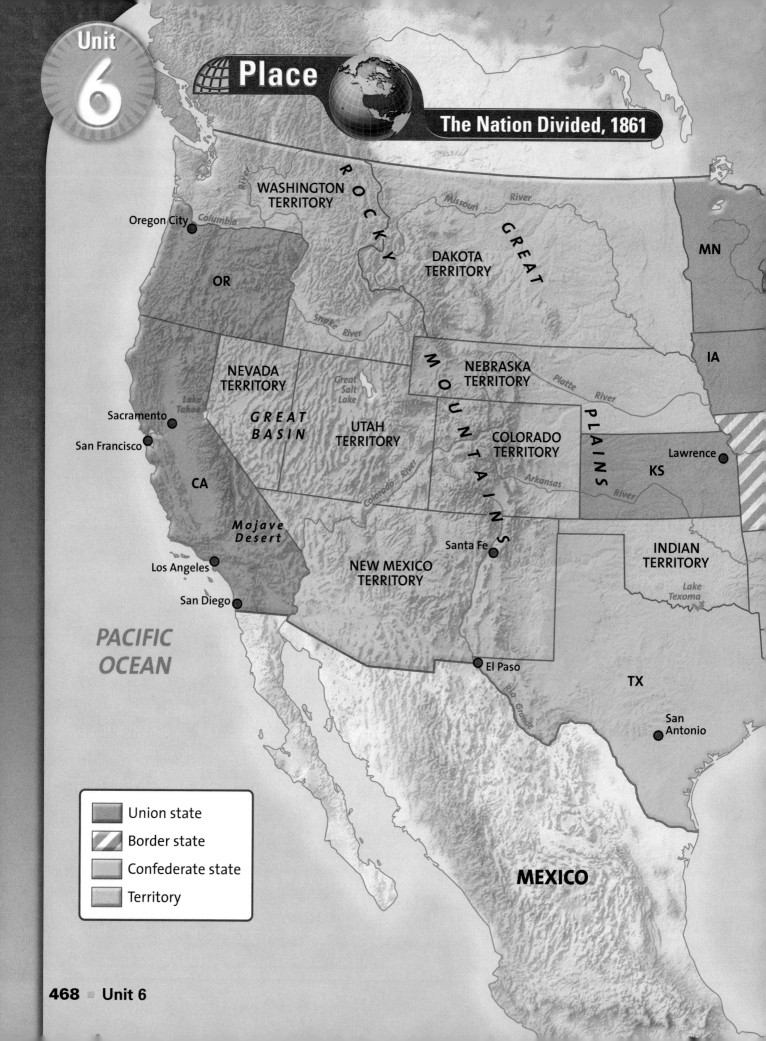

Place

The Nation Divided, 1861

R O C K Y

WASHINGTON
TERRITORY

Oregon City   Columbia   River

OR

Missouri   River

DAKOTA
TERRITORY

G
R
E
A
T

MN

Snake   River

NEVADA
TERRITORY

Great
Salt
Lake

NEBRASKA
TERRITORY

Platte   River

IA

Lake
Tahoe

Sacramento

San Francisco

GREAT
BASIN

UTAH
TERRITORY

M
O
U
N
T
A
I
N
S

COLORADO
TERRITORY

Colorado   River

P
L
A
I
N
S

Arkansas   River

KS

Lawrence

CA

Mojave
Desert

Santa Fe

INDIAN
TERRITORY

Los Angeles

NEW MEXICO
TERRITORY

Lake
Texoma

San Diego

PACIFIC
OCEAN

El Paso

TX

Rio   Grande

San
Antonio

MEXICO

Union state

Border state

Confederate state

Territory

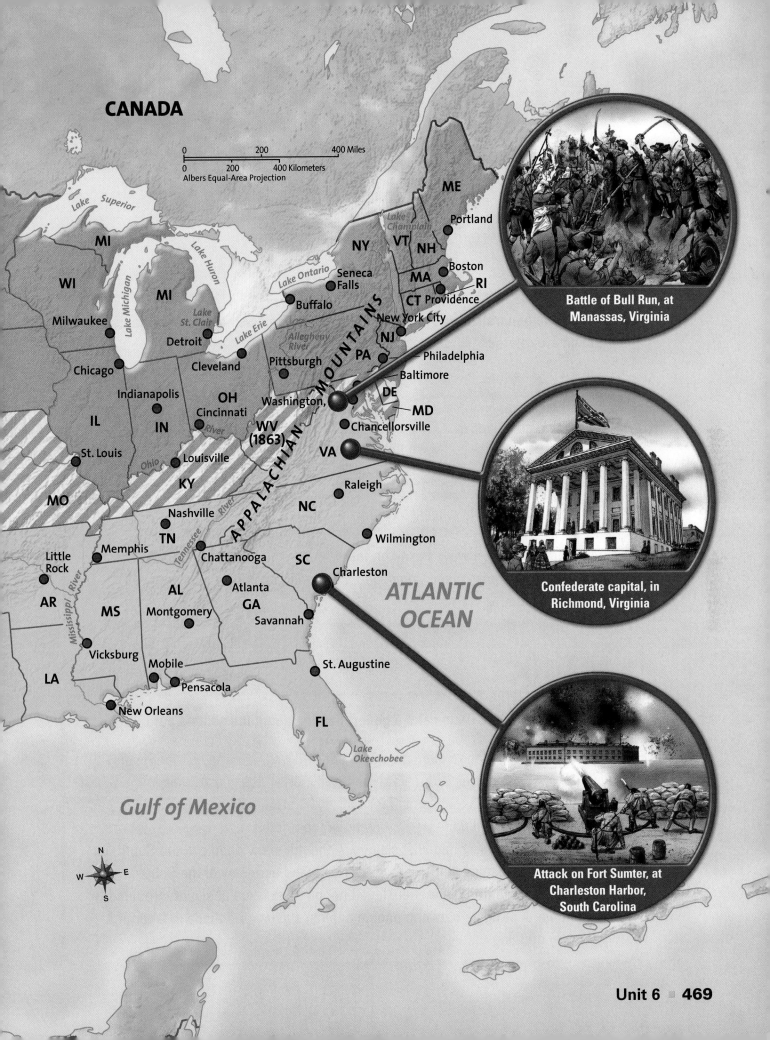

CANADA

Lake Superior

MI

WI

Lake Michigan

Milwaukee

Chicago

IL

St. Louis

MO

Lake Huron

MI

Detroit

Lake St. Clair

Lake Erie

Cleveland

Indianapolis

IN

Cincinnati

OH

Louisville

Ohio River

KY

Nashville

TN

Memphis

Little Rock

AR

MS

Vicksburg

Mobile

LA

Pensacola

New Orleans

0   200   400 Miles

0   200   400 Kilometers

Albers Equal-Area Projection

Lake Ontario

Buffalo

Seneca Falls

Allegheny River

Pittsburgh

PA

Washington,

WV (1863)

APPALACHIAN MOUNTAINS

Tennessee River

Chattanooga

AL

Montgomery

GA

Atlanta

Savannah

ME

Portland

NY

VT

NH

MA

Boston

CT

RI

Providence

New York City

NJ

Philadelphia

Baltimore

DE

MD

Chancellorsville

VA

Raleigh

NC

Wilmington

SC

Charleston

St. Augustine

FL

Lake Okeechobee

Lake Champlain

ATLANTIC OCEAN

Gulf of Mexico

N   E   S   W

Battle of Bull Run, at Manassas, Virginia

Confederate capital, in Richmond, Virginia

Attack on Fort Sumter, at Charleston Harbor, South Carolina

Reading Social Studies

Generalize

Why It Matters Being able to generalize can help you better understand and remember what you read.

▶ LEARN

> When you **generalize**, you make a statement that shows how different facts in a passage are related.

Facts

Information contained in passage	Information contained in passage	Information contained in passage

Generalization

General statement about the information

- A generalization is always based on facts.
- Words such as *most, many, some, generally,* and *usually* are clues to generalizations.

▶ PRACTICE

Read the paragraphs. Then make a generalization about the second paragraph.

Facts → The introduction of the cotton gin in the early 1800s set the Industrial Revolution in motion. While factories in the North churned out textiles, plantations in the South worked to keep up with the demand for cotton. (Factories were growing **Generalization** in the North, and plantations were growing in the South.)

Most Northerners were against slavery. Although many people in the South felt slavery was wrong, they thought it was needed. The economy of the South depended upon the free labor of enslaved people. The issue of slavery troubled many people. A struggle between people against slavery and those in favor of it was slowly growing.

Read the paragraphs, and answer the questions.

A Soldier's Life

Tensions rose as the North and the South faced differences, especially on the issue of slavery. In time, there was talk of a war. Talk became reality when the first shots of the Civil War were fired on April 12, 1861.

No matter which side you were fighting on, life as a soldier was not easy. Most of the soldiers were men, but thousands of young boys fought on both sides. They worked mostly as musicians—buglers and drummers. Some were messengers, flag carriers, and ordinary soldiers.

Soldiers awoke before dawn. On peaceful days, they spent the morning and the evenings practicing drills. For dinner, soldiers sometimes ate pork, beans, rice, and cornbread. However, food often ran out.

Weather could make things difficult. Rainy weather soaked the soldiers' equipment and supplies. Hot weather left soldiers thirsty, dusty, and dirty.

Soldiers earned a paycheck every two months. Privates were paid about $11, and generals were paid about $300. Pay was often late. One soldier complained that he was paid only three times in four years.

 ## Generalize

1. **What generalization can you make about the daily life of a soldier during the Civil War?**
2. **Why do you think young men wanted to take part in the conflict?**
3. **Why do you think soldiers stayed even though they faced hardships?**

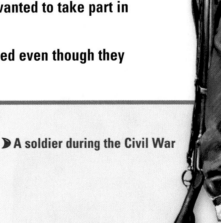

▶ A soldier during the Civil War

A GOOD NIGHT for FREEDOM

Written by Barbara Olenyik Morrow   Illustrated by Leonard Jenkins

Many enslaved people in the United States tried to gain their freedom by escaping. Starting in the 1800s, people who wanted to see slavery end began helping enslaved people escape. That was against the law.

Levi Coffin was a Quaker who lived in Indiana. He gave shelter to escaping slaves. In this story, a girl named Hallie has to decide what to do when slave catchers arrive in her town.

Aunt Katy met me at the door.

"I saw the runaways!" I blurted out. "Susan and Margaret."

For the longest time, the only sounds were the porch boards creaking under my fidgety feet. Finally, Aunt Katy pushed open the door. "Come, Hallie. I'd like thee to meet our guests."

Down we went to the cellar kitchen, the smell of chamomile tea sharp in my nose. The girls were at a table. Their faces clouded when they saw me.

"It's all right, girls," Aunt Katy called to them, while nudging me forward. "Take a seat and visit, Hallie. I'll fetch my knitting and be right back."

"But . . ." I shot a sidelong glance toward the spring room.

"No need for hiding right now," Aunt Katy said, reading my mind. "Only when there's trouble." She disappeared up the steps. . . .

Suddenly footsteps rang out above us, and Mr. Coffin shouted for Aunt Katy. He hurried down the stairs and hustled the girls out of sight.

"Straight home, child," he said to me. "Thy pa will be worried."

The door was barely bolted behind me when I saw the four men, riding fast. A circle of folks gathered across the street. I edged in among them.

Horses snorted, reins jerked. The men jumped from their saddles and started pounding hard on the Coffins' door.

"I saw them." The words spat from my mouth.

"Hallie!" Mr. Coffin threw open the door, pulling it tight behind him. "Child!" he warned.

"I saw two girls headin' up the Winchester Road. This mornin'. They cut across the pasture, then into the woods."

The man came closer. "You saw two of 'em? Headin' north?"

"Yes, sir."

"Him there, did he tell you to say that?"

I gulped. "No, sir. He didn't." I squeezed my eyes shut. . . .

"Up the Winchester Road, right?" He jerked my shoulder.

I raised my arm and pointed. And then he was gone. Really gone.

My knees went soft, and I slumped to the ground. A gentle hand touched my head.

"I meddled," I said, looking up into Mr. Coffin's face.

A long silence passed. Cupping my chin in his hand, Mr. Coffin smiled, then walked slowly toward the house. "Thank thee, child," he called back softly.

Response Corner

1 (Focus Skill) **Generalize** How did Hallie help the runaways?

2 **Make It Relevant** Would you have helped the runaways hide? Why or why not?

STUDY SKILLS

MAKE AN OUTLINE

Making an outline can help you organize main ideas and details.

- Topics in an outline are shown by Roman numerals.

- Main ideas about each topic are shown by capital letters.

- Details about each main idea are shown by numbers.

Civil War

I. The North and the South
  A. Different Regions
    1. New immigrants came to work in factories in the North.
    2. Enslaved Africans worked on plantations in the South.
  B. Different Ideas
    1.
    2.
  C. Division over Slavery
    1.
    2.

PREVIEW VOCABULARY

Underground Railroad p. 485

artillery p. 492

address p. 509

The Civil War

THE BATTLE OF GETTYSBURG
GETTYSBURG, PENNSYLVANIA

Time

1820   1860   1900

1820
The Missouri Compromise is passed

1850
The Compromise of 1850 is passed

1854
The Kansas-Nebraska Act is passed

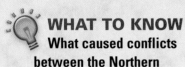

WHAT TO KNOW
What caused conflicts between the Northern states and the Southern states?

VOCABULARY
sectionalism p. 477
diverse economy p. 477
free state p. 478
slave state p. 478
tariff p. 479
states' rights p. 479
fugitive p. 480

PEOPLE
Henry Clay
Andrew Jackson
John C. Calhoun

PLACES
Missouri
Maine
California

GENERALIZE

Facts

Generalization

The North and the South

YOU ARE THERE
The year is 1850. You are boarding a ship to return to your home in Britain. You have just spent two months traveling from New York to Georgia. Along the way, you noticed many differences. In the North, you saw busy cities and lots of small farms. In the South, you saw fewer cities and many large plantations. You wonder what Americans think about these differences.

▶ **SOUTHERN STATES** The economy of the South continued to rely on enslaved workers.

▶ **NORTHERN STATES** Factories and trade were a growing part of the North's economy.

Different Regions

By the mid-1800s, the southern, northern, and western regions of the United States were very different. National leaders often decided issues on what was best for their section, or region, instead of what was best for the whole country. This regional loyalty is called **sectionalism** (SEK•shuhn•uh•lih•zuhm).

Different Ways of Life

The different sections of the United States were different both economically and culturally. In the Northern states there were few plantations. Most farms were small, and they did not require many workers. As a result, all of the Northern states had already abolished slavery.

The Northern states also had a much more diverse economy and more industries than the Southern states. A **diverse economy** is an economy that is based on many industries rather than just a few.

In the 1800s, industries in the Northern states grew. Many people, including immigrants, moved to the Northern states to work in the new industries.

In Southern states, enslaved Africans worked on plantations that grew mainly cotton and tobacco. The cotton gin helped plantations produce more cotton. The money brought in by cash crops such as cotton allowed plantation owners to buy more land and strengthened the system of slavery.

READING CHECK ♻GENERALIZE
How were the Northern and Southern states different?

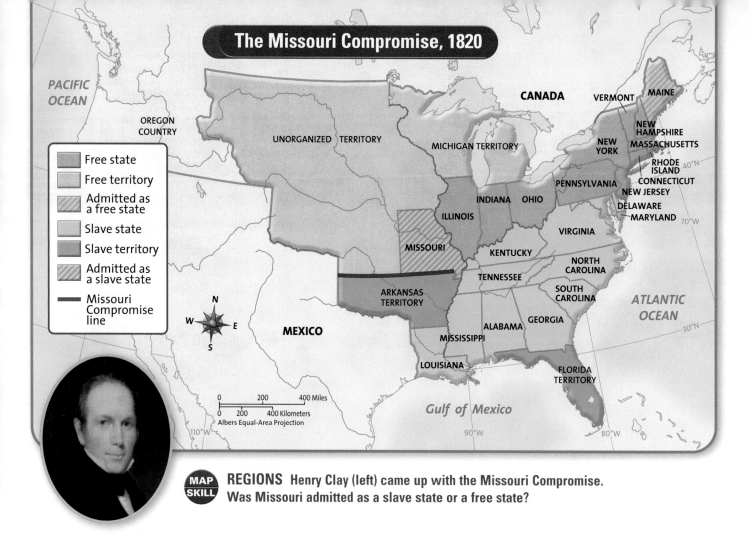

The Missouri Compromise, 1820

Map legend:
- Free state
- Free territory
- Admitted as a free state
- Slave state
- Slave territory
- Admitted as a slave state
- Missouri Compromise line

REGIONS Henry Clay (left) came up with the Missouri Compromise. Was Missouri admitted as a slave state or a free state?

Division Over Slavery

By 1804, all the Northern states had outlawed slavery. The Mason-Dixon line—roughly the border between Pennsylvania and Maryland—was seen as the dividing line between free states and slave states. A **free state** did not allow slavery. A **slave state** did.

For a time there were an equal number of free states and slave states. This kept a balance between the North and South in the Senate.

The Missouri Compromise

Then in 1819, **Missouri** wanted to join the Union as a slave state. That would have upset the balance between free states and slave states. Congress debated the issue for several months. Then **Henry Clay** of Kentucky came up with a compromise. Clay suggested that Missouri be admitted to the Union as a slave state and **Maine** be admitted as a free state.

Clay also suggested that a line should be drawn on a map of all the Louisiana Purchase lands. Slavery would be allowed in the places south of the line. It would not be allowed in places north of the line. This plan became known as the Missouri Compromise. The Missouri Compromise kept the peace for nearly 30 years. The number of free states and slave states remained equal.

READING CHECK ⟳ **GENERALIZE**
What was the purpose of the Missouri Compromise?

Different Ideas

The people in the Northern and the Southern states did not often agree on ideas about trade, slavery, and government. During the 1800s, these disagreements grew.

Arguing Over Trade

In 1828, sectionalism became a serious issue. Congress passed a high **tariff**, or a tax on imports. The tariff helped protect Northern factory owners. It made imported goods more expensive than goods made in the United States.

The tariff also made it easier for factories in the North to sell their products. The tariff hurt wealthy Southerners because they imported many goods from Europe. They blamed the North for supporting the tariff.

Ideas About Government

President **Andrew Jackson** and Vice President **John C. Calhoun** had different views of the national government. Calhoun argued against the tariff. He believed in **states' rights**, or the idea that the states, not the national government, should have the final say on laws that affected them.

President Jackson was known to support states' rights, but he still believed the federal government had the right to set tariffs. Despite the objections of Calhoun and other Southerners, Congress passed a new tariff in 1832. Sectionalism grew stronger, and it further divided the nation.

READING CHECK ⭕ **GENERALIZE**
Why were some Southerners against tariffs?

▶ **ARGUMENTS OVER TARIFFS** Andrew Jackson (right) believed the federal government could set tariffs on trade. Boston (below) was a center of trade in the North.

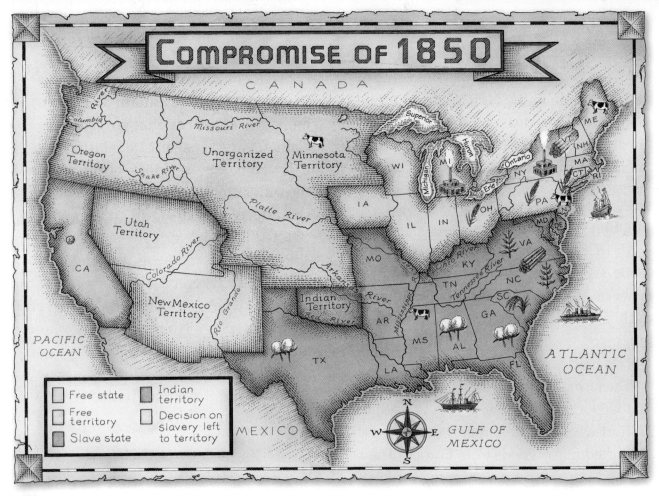

COMPROMISE OF 1850

Legend:
- Free state
- Free territory
- Slave state
- Indian territory
- Decision on slavery left to territory

MAP SKILL REGIONS After 1850, how many free states were there? How many slave states?

More Divisions

In 1848, the United States gained new lands after winning the Mexican-American War. These lands presented a new challenge since the Missouri Compromise did not cover them.

The Compromise of 1850

Settlers in **California**, a part of these new lands, asked to join the Union as a free state. That would give the free states an advantage in the Senate. Southern leaders feared that Congress would pass a law outlawing slavery everywhere.

Henry Clay again worked toward a compromise—the Compromise of 1850. Under this plan, California joined the Union as a free state. The other lands gained from Mexico would be divided into two territories—New Mexico and Utah. The people there would decide for themselves whether to allow slavery.

The Fugitive Slave Act was also part of the compromise. A **fugitive** is someone who escapes from the law. This law required all Americans to turn in people who had escaped slavery. The law was very unpopular in the North.

Henry Clay, who became known as the Great Compromiser, died in 1852. He never gave up hope that the country would find a peaceful way to settle its differences. However, bad feelings between people in the free states and the slave states soon led to violence.

Bleeding Kansas

In 1854, Congress passed the Kansas-Nebraska Act. It gave people living in those territories the right to decide if they wanted slavery. This changed the rules of the Missouri Compromise, which had outlawed slavery in those territories.

The Kansas-Nebraska Act divided the nation even more. People for and against slavery moved into Kansas. Fighting broke out between the two groups. The state became known as "Bleeding Kansas." After an election was held, Kansas joined the Union as a free state.

READING CHECK **CAUSE AND EFFECT**
What was the effect of the Kansas-Nebraska Act?

Summary

Disagreements over trade and slavery divided the states. Compromises kept peace for a time, but the Kansas-Nebraska Act further divided the country.

▶ **BLEEDING KANSAS** People on both sides of the slavery issue held conventions in Kansas.

REVIEW

1. **WHAT TO KNOW** What caused conflicts between the Northern states and the Southern states?

2. **VOCABULARY** Use the term **sectionalism** in a sentence.

3. **ECONOMICS** How did the tariff of 1828 affect people in the South?

4. **CRITICAL THINKING** Why was the Fugitive Slave Act unpopular in the North?

5. 🖌 **MAKE A CHART** Make a two-column chart that shows some of the differences between the Northern states and the Southern states in the 1800s.

6. ⭐ (Focus Skill) **GENERALIZE** On a separate sheet of paper, copy and complete the graphic organizer below.

Facts

Generalization

The Northern states and the Southern states tried to compromise on the slavery issue.

Time

1820   1860   1900

1848
The Seneca Falls
Convention is held

1852
Uncle Tom's Cabin
is published

1857
The Supreme Court
rules on the
Dred Scott case

WHAT TO KNOW
What groups of people resisted slavery?

VOCABULARY
Underground Railroad p. 485

PEOPLE
Dred Scott
Nat Turner
Samuel Cornish
John Russwurm
William Lloyd Garrison
Frederick Douglass
Sojourner Truth
Elizabeth Cady Stanton
Lucretia Mott
Harriet Beecher Stowe
Harriet Tubman

PLACES
Seneca Falls

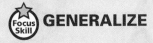
GENERALIZE

Resisting Slavery

YOU ARE THERE   It is late afternoon. As usual, your Quaker family has gathered in the parlor before dinner. Your mother and father are abolitionists and believe that slavery should be outlawed. Your father reads aloud from a newspaper. He is reading about the court ruling regarding the enslaved person named Dred Scott. Dred Scott went to court to fight for his freedom. The Supreme Court refused to grant Scott his freedom. You agree with your parents that slavery should end.

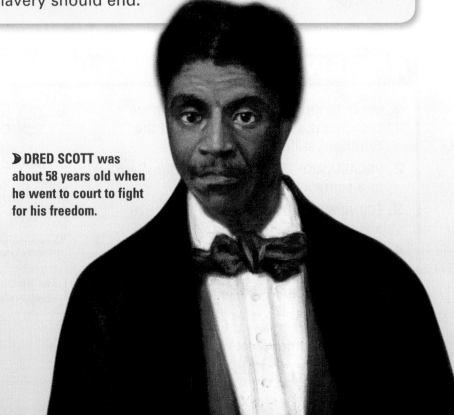

▶ **DRED SCOTT** was about 58 years old when he went to court to fight for his freedom.

An 1857 Newspaper

Background Newspapers across the country carried stories about Dred Scott.

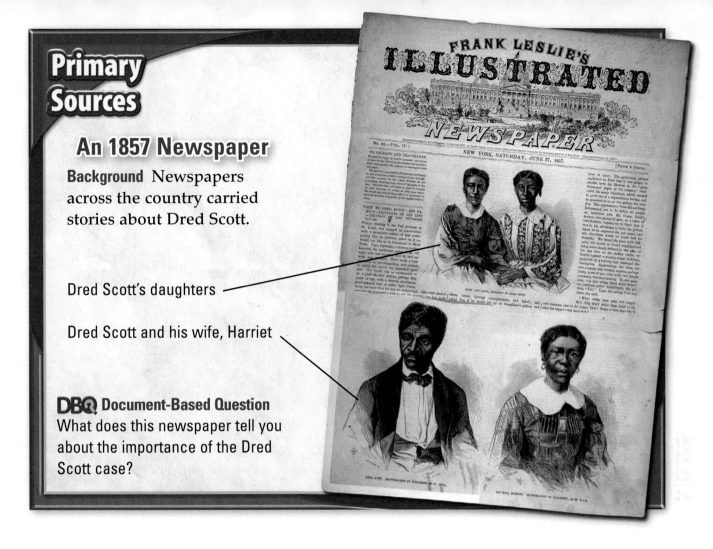

Dred Scott's daughters

Dred Scott and his wife, Harriet

DBQ Document-Based Question
What does this newspaper tell you about the importance of the Dred Scott case?

The Dred Scott Decision

Dred Scott was an enslaved man owned by an army doctor. His owner moved often, and Scott traveled with him. For a time, they lived in Illinois, a free state. Then they lived in Wisconsin, a free territory. After his owner died, Scott went to court to try to win his freedom. He argued that he should be free because he had once lived on free land.

Disagreements Over Scott

Dred Scott's case moved up through the federal court system until it reached the United States Supreme Court. In 1857, the Supreme Court ruled against Scott. Chief Justice Roger B. Taney wrote that since Scott was enslaved, he had "none of the rights and privileges" of an American citizen.

Taney also wrote that enslaved people were property. He said that under the Constitution, Congress could make no laws that took property away from people. This view meant that Congress should not be able to keep slavery out of certain states. This decision went against the Missouri Compromise.

The Supreme Court ruling troubled many people. They had hoped the Dred Scott decision would settle the nation's disagreements over slavery. Instead, this decision only made the problem worse.

READING CHECK ⚙GENERALIZE
Why did Dred Scott go to court?

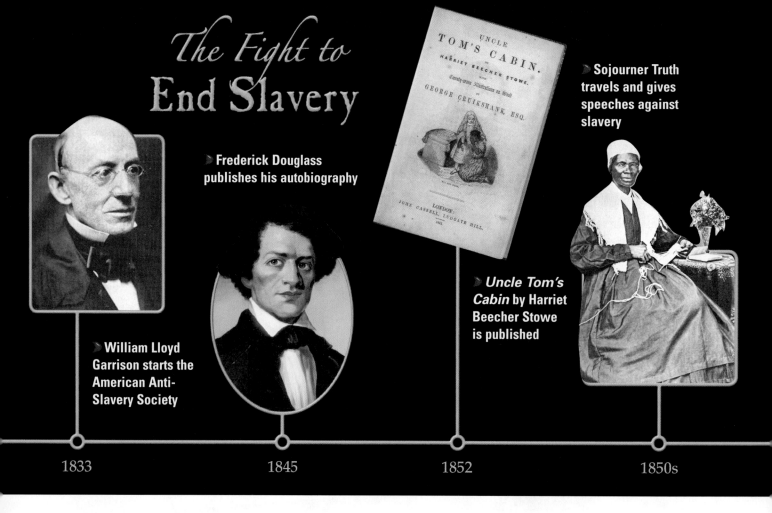

The Fight to End Slavery

Frederick Douglass publishes his autobiography

William Lloyd Garrison starts the American Anti-Slavery Society

Uncle Tom's Cabin by Harriet Beecher Stowe is published

Sojourner Truth travels and gives speeches against slavery

| 1833 | 1845 | 1852 | 1850s |

Challenging Slavery

Enslaved people sometimes rebelled against slavery. In 1831, an enslaved man named **Nat Turner** led an attack that killed many planters. Planters in the area ended the rebellion, but more than 100 enslaved people were killed.

Many white Northerners and free African Americans worked to end slavery. In 1827, two African Americans, **Samuel Cornish** and **John Russwurm**, started the *Freedom's Journal*. It was the first newspaper owned and written by African Americans. In 1833, **William Lloyd Garrison**, a white Northerner, founded the American Anti-Slavery Society.

Frederick Douglass escaped slavery and became famous for his writings and speeches against slavery. He often told his audiences, "I appear this evening as a thief and a robber. I stole this head, these limbs, this body from my master [owner] and ran off with them."

Isabella Van Wagener also traveled the country speaking out against slavery. Van Wagener gained her freedom in 1827. She believed that God had called her to "travel up and down the land" to preach. She changed her name to **Sojourner Truth**. *Sojourner* means "traveler."

Women Fight for Change

Many of the people who worked to end slavery were not entirely free themselves. In the 1800s, women did not have the same rights as men. In 1848, **Elizabeth Cady Stanton** and **Lucretia Mott** organized

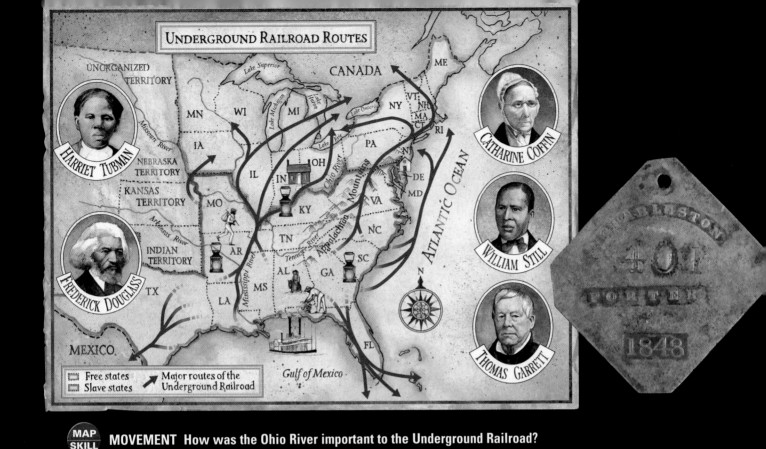

UNDERGROUND RAILROAD ROUTES

HARRIET TUBMAN
FREDERICK DOUGLASS
CATHARINE COFFIN
WILLIAM STILL
THOMAS GARRETT

Free states
Slave states
Major routes of the Underground Railroad

MAP SKILL   **MOVEMENT** How was the Ohio River important to the Underground Railroad?

a women's rights convention in **Seneca Falls**, New York. They wrote a document that called for equality for all Americans.

In 1852, **Harriet Beecher Stowe** wrote a book called *Uncle Tom's Cabin*. It told the story of how enslaved workers were mistreated. Stowe's book helped turn more people in the North against slavery.

The Underground Railroad

By 1860, more than 500,000 free African Americans were living in the United States. Some had been born to parents who were free. Some had bought their freedom, and others had escaped from slavery by running away.

Many runaways had to keep moving for months until they reached a place where slavery was not allowed.

Some found helpers who led the way—the brave men and women of the Underground Railroad.

The **Underground Railroad** was not a railroad, and it was not underground. It was a system of secret escape routes that led enslaved people to free lands. Most routes led from the South to free states or Canada. Some led to Mexico and to islands in the Caribbean Sea.

Conductors, or helpers along the Underground Railroad, worked mostly at night. They led runaways from one hiding place to another. Most conductors were free African Americans or white abolitionists. **Harriet Tubman**, an African American who had escaped from slavery herself, was one of the best-known conductors on the Underground Railroad.

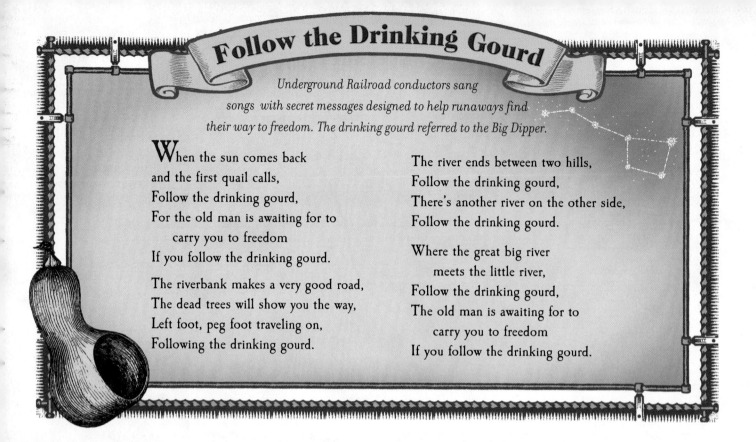

Follow the Drinking Gourd

Underground Railroad conductors sang songs with secret messages designed to help runaways find their way to freedom. The drinking gourd referred to the Big Dipper.

When the sun comes back
and the first quail calls,
Follow the drinking gourd,
For the old man is awaiting for to
   carry you to freedom
If you follow the drinking gourd.

The riverbank makes a very good road,
The dead trees will show you the way,
Left foot, peg foot traveling on,
Following the drinking gourd.

The river ends between two hills,
Follow the drinking gourd,
There's another river on the other side,
Follow the drinking gourd.

Where the great big river
   meets the little river,
Follow the drinking gourd,
The old man is awaiting for to
   carry you to freedom
If you follow the drinking gourd.

Facing Dangers

Escaping on the Underground Railroad was dangerous. Slave catchers were a constant danger. If caught, enslaved people were beaten and sometimes killed. Still, many escaped to freedom.

READING CHECK SUMMARIZE
How did the Underground Railroad work?

Summary

The Dred Scott decision divided the nation. African American and white abolitionists wrote and spoke out against slavery. Enslaved people resisted slavery and thousands escaped on the Underground Railroad.

REVIEW

1. **WHAT TO KNOW** What groups of people resisted slavery?

2. **VOCABULARY** Use the term **Underground Railroad** in a sentence about slavery.

3. **HISTORY** What was the effect of the Dred Scott case?

4. **CRITICAL THINKING** Why do you think enslaved people risked their lives to escape from slavery?

5. **MAKE A POSTER** Make a poster that tells about the work of the Underground Railroad.

6. **GENERALIZE**
   On a separate sheet of paper, copy and complete the graphic organizer below.

Facts		
Enslaved people traveled on the Underground Railroad.	Traveling on the Underground Railroad was dangerous.	

Generalization

Harriet Tubman

Biography

Trustworthiness
Respect
Responsibility
Fairness
Caring
Patriotism

"I never lost a passenger."

Harriet Tubman was born an enslaved person in Bucktown, Maryland. In 1849, when Tubman was about 29 years old, she heard rumors that she was about to be sold. She decided that she would try to escape. Trying to escape was very dangerous, but Tubman made up her mind to attempt it. She was successful and found her way north to Philadelphia, Pennsylvania.

Tubman could have started a new life and forgotten about her past. However, she could not forget that her family and friends were still enslaved. She decided to try to bring as many enslaved people to freedom as she could. In 1850, she made her first trip back to the South. She guided her sister and her sister's children to freedom.

Tubman returned to the South 18 more times. She led more than 300 people to freedom, including her parents. She became the most famous conductor on the Underground Railroad. Southern slave owners offered a $40,000 reward for her capture. Tubman's fame spread across the country. People called her "Moses," like the figure in the Bible, because she helped lead people to freedom.

Why Character Counts

How did Harriet Tubman show she cared about others?

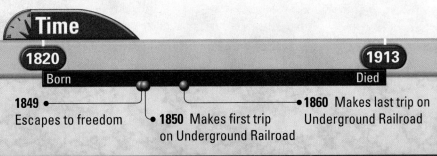

Time

1820		1913
Born		Died

1849 Escapes to freedom

1850 Makes first trip on Underground Railroad

1860 Makes last trip on Underground Railroad

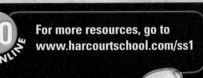

GO ONLINE
For more resources, go to
www.harcourtschool.com/ss1

Chapter 12 ▪ 487

Time

1820   1860   1900

1859
John Brown
raids Harpers Ferry

1860
Abraham Lincoln
is elected President

1861
The Civil
War begins

The Nation Divides

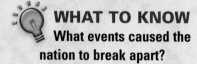

WHAT TO KNOW
What events caused the nation to break apart?

VOCABULARY
secede p. 490
Confederacy p. 491
border state p. 491
artillery p. 492
civil war p. 493

PEOPLE
Abraham Lincoln
Stephen A. Douglas
John Brown
Jefferson Davis
Robert E. Lee

PLACES
Harpers Ferry
Fort Sumter

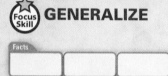

GENERALIZE

Facts

Generalization

YOU ARE THERE
You are in a big crowd in Freeport, Illinois. Excitement is in the air. It is 1858. An important election for the United States Senate will take place soon. Today, the two men running against each other are coming to Freeport.

"There they are!" your father yells, pointing to the stage. Abraham Lincoln and Senator Stephen A. Douglas have taken their places. The crowd quiets. The debate begins.

▶ ABOLITIONISTS Women played a key role in the movement to end slavery.

▶ **DEBATES** were often held outside. This poster was made 100 years after the famous debate.

Abraham Lincoln

Abraham Lincoln was born in Kentucky in 1809, but his family later moved to the Indiana Territory. He spent little time in school, but he learned to read and write. He worked on the family farm and read books in his spare time.

Lincoln's Early Political Life

When he was 21, Lincoln's family moved to Illinois. Lincoln studied law on his own and became a lawyer. In 1834, he was elected to the Illinois legislature. In 1846, he was elected to the United States Congress. After he returned to Illinois, Lincoln became concerned about the spread of slavery to the West. He joined a new political party formed to fight the spread of slavery. This party was called the Republican Party.

The Lincoln-Douglas Debates

In 1858, Lincoln ran for the United States Senate. He was not an abolitionist, but he thought it was wrong for slavery to expand to new states in the West. In a famous speech, Lincoln used words from the Bible to explain his view on slavery:

> 66 A house divided against itself cannot stand. I believe this government cannot endure [last] . . . half slave and half free. 99

Stephen A. Douglas was Lincoln's opponent. He thought that each state should make its own laws about slavery. Douglas won the election, but the public debates made Lincoln well known.

READING CHECK ❂ **GENERALIZE**

What was Abraham Lincoln's view of slavery?

LINCOLN ELECTED!

Let the People Rejoice!

CAPITAL SHALL NOT OWN US!

THE PEOPLE TRUE TO LIBERTY.
ILLINOIS REDEEMED!
SHE VOTES FOR LINCOLN.
She chooses Republican Legislature.
SHE REPUDIATES DOUGLAS.

GOD BLESS THE OLD KEYSTONE!!
GOD BLESS NEW YORK!
Lincoln carries all the Atlantic States but
New Jersey.
AN AVALANCHE OF FREEMEN.
SHOUT BOYS SHOUT, VICTORY IS OURS, FREEDOM IS TRIUMPHANT.

▶ JOHN BROWN (right) hid in this building after his raid on Harpers Ferry. Lincoln's election (left) split the nation.

Events Further Divide the Nation

Many abolitionists hoped for a peaceful end to slavery. Others wanted to stop slavery by force. **John Brown** was one of them.

John Brown's Raid

In 1859, Brown led a group of men in a raid on a government storehouse filled with guns. The storehouse was in **Harpers Ferry**, in what is now West Virginia. Brown planned to give the guns to enslaved people so they could fight for their freedom.

The plan failed. Most of the raiders were either killed or captured. Brown was put on trial and hanged for his actions. His raid divided the nation even more. Some Southerners thought that Brown's raid was a sign that the North was trying to end slavery.

The Election of 1860

Slavery was an important issue in the presidential election of 1860. The Republican Party was against allowing slavery to spread into new places. It nominated Abraham Lincoln. The Democratic Party split into two branches. Northern Democrats, who thought new states should make their own laws about slavery, nominated Stephen A. Douglas. Southern Democrats, who wanted to protect slavery, nominated John Breckinridge of Kentucky.

Some Southerners said they would **secede** from, or leave, the Union if Lincoln was elected. Lincoln did not win a single Southern state. However, Douglas and Breckinridge split the Democratic vote, and Lincoln won the election.

READING CHECK ⚙ **GENERALIZE**
How did the issue of slavery affect the election of 1860?

The Nation Separates

On December 20, 1860, South Carolina voted to secede from the Union. By February 1861, Alabama, Florida, Georgia, Louisiana, Mississippi, and Texas also seceded from the Union.

The states that left the Union formed their own national government. It was called the Confederate States of America, or the **Confederacy**. **Jefferson Davis**, a United States senator from Mississippi, was elected President.

Abraham Lincoln became President on March 4, 1861. As President, he told the Southern states that he opposed secession but that he would not use military force against them. Lincoln said: "We are not enemies but friends. We must not be enemies."

The Border States

Most Northerners supported the Union, while most white Southerners supported the Confederacy. People in the **border states**—Delaware, Maryland, Kentucky, and Missouri—were torn between the two sides. These states, located between the North and the South, permitted slavery but had not seceded.

To keep these states in the Union, Lincoln often stressed that his goal was to save the Union. He wrote to Horace Greeley, a newspaper editor:

> **❝ My [main] object in this struggle is to save the Union, and is not to either save or destroy slavery. ❞**

READING CHECK ⚫ **GENERALIZE**
How were the border states different?

MAP SKILL LOCATION What border state was closest to Kansas?

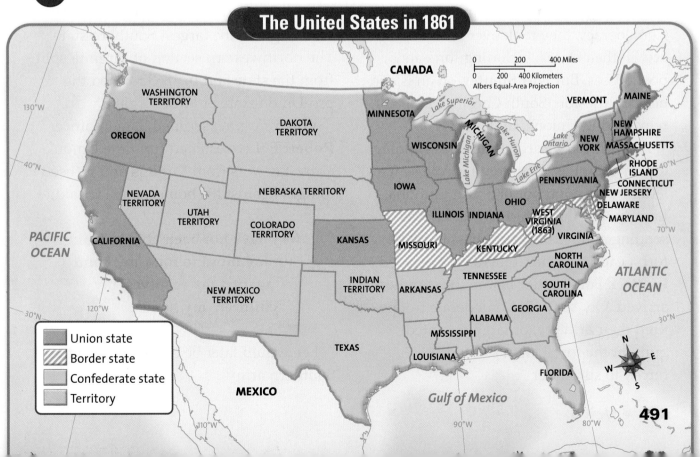

The United States in 1861

- Union state
- Border state
- Confederate state
- Territory

CANADA

0   200   400 Miles
0   200   400 Kilometers
Albers Equal-Area Projection

WASHINGTON TERRITORY — OREGON — DAKOTA TERRITORY — MINNESOTA — VERMONT — MAINE — NEW HAMPSHIRE — WISCONSIN — MICHIGAN — Lake Superior — Lake Huron — Lake Ontario — NEW YORK — MASSACHUSETTS — RHODE ISLAND — CONNECTICUT — NEW JERSEY — NEVADA TERRITORY — UTAH TERRITORY — NEBRASKA TERRITORY — IOWA — Lake Michigan — Lake Erie — PENNSYLVANIA — OHIO — DELAWARE — CALIFORNIA — COLORADO TERRITORY — KANSAS — ILLINOIS — INDIANA — WEST VIRGINIA (1863) — VIRGINIA — MARYLAND — PACIFIC OCEAN — MISSOURI — KENTUCKY — NORTH CAROLINA — ATLANTIC OCEAN — NEW MEXICO TERRITORY — INDIAN TERRITORY — ARKANSAS — TENNESSEE — SOUTH CAROLINA — GEORGIA — ALABAMA — MISSISSIPPI — TEXAS — LOUISIANA — FLORIDA — MEXICO — Gulf of Mexico

130°W   120°W   110°W   90°W   80°W   70°W   40°N   30°N

▶ **FORT SUMTER** was under attack for more than 34 hours before Union soldiers surrendered. This South Carolina state flag (left) was damaged in the battle.

Fort Sumter

After Southern states formed the Confederacy, they took over federal property in their states, including forts and post offices. But **Fort Sumter,** on an island near Charleston, South Carolina, still remained in Union hands.

In April 1861, Fort Sumter was running low on supplies. President Lincoln sent a letter to the governor of South Carolina. Lincoln told the governor that he was sending an unarmed supply ship to the fort. Leaders of the Confederacy decided to attack Fort Sumter before the supplies arrived. On April 12, Confederate troops fired their **artillery**, or large mounted guns, at the fort. Union soldiers were forced to surrender.

President Lincoln called for 75,000 Americans to join the Union army. Four more states seceded. One of the states was Virginia, the largest Southern state. The northwestern section of Virginia split from the state and in 1863 formed the pro-Union state of West Virginia.

When Virginia seceded, Union officer **Robert E. Lee** resigned from the Union army. Lee was from Virginia and refused to fight against his home state. He said,

> **❝I have not been able to make up my mind to raise my hand against my relatives, my children, my home . . .❞**

Lee would later be chosen to lead the Southern army.

The Civil War Begins

President Lincoln had worked for peace and to preserve the Union. With the attack on Fort Sumter, a civil war had started. A **civil war** is a war between people in the same country. The United States Civil War divided the country and divided states. Sometimes even families were divided. In the border states and the Southern states, some family members fought for the Confederacy, while others in a family fought for the Union.

READING CHECK ⭓ **GENERALIZE**
Why did the Confederacy attack Fort Sumter?

Summary

John Brown's raid and the presidential election of 1860 further divided the country. After the election of Abraham Lincoln, Southern states seceded. The Confederacy attacked Fort Sumter, starting the Civil War.

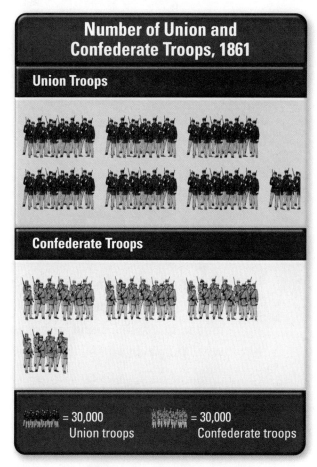

GRAPH At the beginning of the Civil War, the Union army had many more troops than the Confederate army. About how many more troops did the Union army have?

REVIEW

1. **WHAT TO KNOW** What events caused the nation to break apart?

2. **VOCABULARY** What was the **Confederacy**?

3. **HISTORY** How did Abraham Lincoln win the election of 1860?

4. **CRITICAL THINKING** Why do you think Confederate leaders decided to attack Fort Sumter when they did?

5. ✎ **WRITE NEWSPAPER HEADLINES** Write two newspaper headlines, one for a Northern newspaper and one for a Southern newspaper, as they would have appeared the day after the election of 1860.

6. ⭐(Focus Skill) **GENERALIZE** On a separate sheet of paper, copy and complete the graphic organizer below.

Facts

| Many Southern leaders opposed Abraham Lincoln. | Southern leaders formed the Confederacy. | |

Generalization

States' Rights

For nearly 30 years, leaders of the North and the South argued over states' rights, particularly in regard to slavery. Some Southern leaders argued that states could ignore any federal law that they did not agree with. They also argued that states had a right to secede from the Union.

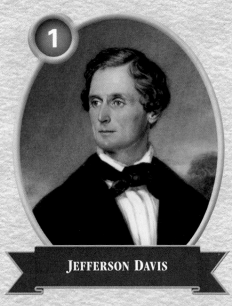

JEFFERSON DAVIS

Senator Jefferson Davis of Mississippi resigned from the United States Senate in 1861. He became President of the Confederate States of America.

❝I have for many years [argued], as a [basic part] of State [power], the right of a State to secede from the Union. . . .❞

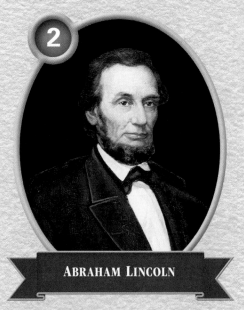

ABRAHAM LINCOLN

Abraham Lincoln became President of the United States in 1861. He did not believe that states had the right to secede from the Union.

❝[I believe] that no State upon its own [wishes] can lawfully get out of the Union; that [declarations it makes] to that effect are [illegal].❞

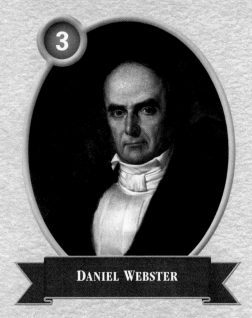

3

DANIEL WEBSTER

Daniel Webster was a United States senator from Massachusetts. He defended the Union in debates about states' rights.

“I wish to speak today, not as a Massachusetts man, nor as a Northern man, but as an American, and a member of the Senate of the United States.”

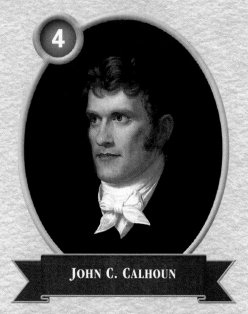

4

JOHN C. CALHOUN

Senator John C. Calhoun of South Carolina was a strong supporter of states' rights.

“What is the cause of this discontent? . . . the belief of the people of the Southern States . . . that they can not remain . . . consistently with honor and safety, in the Union.”

It's Your Turn

Compare Points of View
Summarize each point of view. Then answer the question.

1. How are the views of Davis and Lincoln different?

2. How are the views of Webster and Calhoun different?

3. What might influence the opinion of each of these men?

Make It Relevant Why might you and other people have different points of view about the same topic?

FIELD TRIP

READ ABOUT

Imagine that you could travel back in time to when Abraham Lincoln was President. At the Abraham Lincoln Presidential Library and Museum in Springfield, Illinois, you can do just that! In the library, visitors can see important documents such as the Gettysburg Address and the Emancipation Proclamation up close.

In the museum, visitors can tour exhibits that take them through Lincoln's life. In the Mrs. Lincoln's Attic exhibit, you can try on clothes from the 1800s. The Ask Mr. Lincoln exhibit gives visitors a chance to ask questions that the President himself will answer!

FIND

ILLINOIS

Springfield

THE ABRAHAM LINCOLN *Presidential* Library and Museum

PRESIDENT LINCOLN'S CABINET reacts to his plan to issue the Emancipation Proclamation in this museum reproduction of Lincoln's office.

THE UNION THEATER

FIGURES showing Abraham Lincoln and his wife, Mary Todd

FIGURES of the Lincoln family

VISITORS can see the Battle of Gettysburg up close in this forty-two foot long mural.

IBRARY

A VIRTUAL TOUR

GO ONLINE For more resources, go to www.harcourtshool.com/ss1

Lesson 4

Time
1820   1860   1900

1861
The Battle of Bull Run

1862
The Battle of Antietam

1863
The Emancipation Proclamation is issued

WHAT TO KNOW
What were some of the key events of the war's early years?

VOCABULARY
strategy p. 499
emancipate p. 501
prejudice p. 502

PEOPLE
Robert E. Lee
Dorothea Dix
Clara Barton
Sally Tompkins
Belle Boyd
Robert Gould Shaw

PLACES
Manassas Junction
Antietam Creek
Fort Wagner

GENERALIZE

Facts

Generalization

The War Begins

YOU ARE THERE

Boom! The sound of cannon fire rings in your ears. Your eyes burn from the smoke. In the distance, you can see Union and Confederate soldiers with bayonets, charging toward one another. The war is now in its third year, and thousands of soldiers have already lost their lives. No one seems to know when the fighting will end.

> **CANNONS** Some Civil War cannons could fire cannonballs nearly one mile.

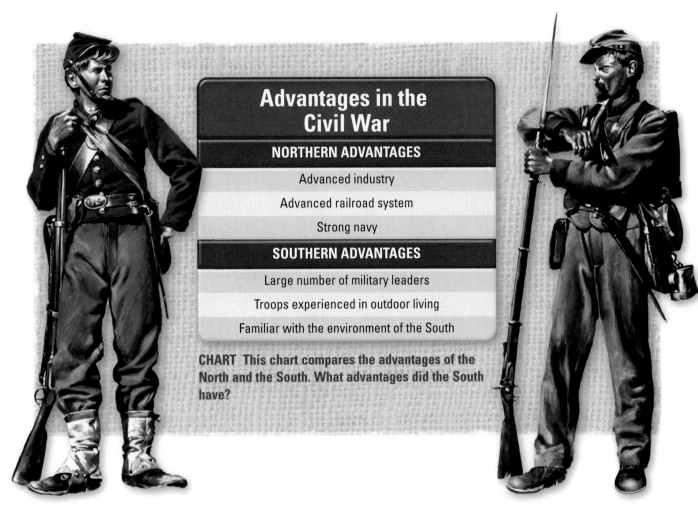

Advantages in the Civil War

NORTHERN ADVANTAGES
Advanced industry
Advanced railroad system
Strong navy

SOUTHERN ADVANTAGES
Large number of military leaders
Troops experienced in outdoor living
Familiar with the environment of the South

CHART This chart compares the advantages of the North and the South. What advantages did the South have?

War Plans

An important part of war is strategy. **Strategy** is a long-range plan made to reach a goal. The Union and the Confederacy both made war strategies.

Union Plans

The Union strategy for winning the war was first to weaken the South and then to invade it. To weaken the South, Lincoln planned to blockade Southern ports. This would stop the South from receiving weapons or supplies from European countries.

This plan was called the Anaconda Plan. An anaconda is a snake that squeezes its prey to death. The Union would squeeze the South by not letting it ship or receive goods. If the South could not sell its cash crops, it would not have money to buy supplies for its army.

Confederate Plans

The Confederate strategy was to defend its lands against Union attack. The South planned to make the war last a long time. Southern leaders saw an advantage in a long war. They thought Northerners would get tired of fighting.

Southern leaders also expected to get help from Britain and France. Both countries depended on Southern cotton to keep their textile mills running. The South was counting on their help.

READING CHECK ⚙GENERALIZE
What were the Union and Confederate strategies?

Early Battles

In the first year of the war, neither side won a major victory. Most of the war's early battles were fought in the South.

The Battle of Bull Run

The first major battle of the Civil War was fought on July 21, 1861. The Battle of Bull Run, also called the Battle of Manassas, was fought on a hot, sunny day near **Manassas Junction**, Virginia.

Both sides arrived at the battlefield with large armies with nearly 30,000 soldiers each. However, most of the soldiers on both sides had not been trained, and it showed when the fighting began.

Thomas Jackson, a general from Virginia, helped keep the Confederate troops together when they tried to fall back. "There is Jackson standing like a stone wall," shouted another general as the Confederates held their ground. From that day on, General Jackson was known as Stonewall Jackson.

It was a confusing battle, but the Confederates eventually won. People soon realized that the war would last far longer than they had first thought.

The Battle of Antietam

In September 1862, General **Robert E. Lee** led the Confederate army into Maryland. Lee hoped to invade the North and end the war. Union forces met his army at **Antietam Creek**, Maryland. Both sides lost many men in the bloody battle. The Confederates retreated to Virginia.

More soldiers died in one day in the Battle of Antietam than on any other day of the war. About 1,550 Confederate soldiers and more than 2,100 Union soldiers were killed. Even though both sides had suffered terrible losses, the battle had an important result. Soon after, President Lincoln announced that he would issue an order freeing all enslaved people in areas still fighting against the Union.

READING CHECK **CAUSE AND EFFECT**

What was an effect of the Battle of Antietam?

▶ **THE BATTLE OF BULL RUN** The Confederate victory at the Battle of Bull Run shocked the Union.

▶ **LINCOLN'S CABINET** This painting shows Abraham Lincoln meeting with his cabinet to discuss the Emancipation Proclamation.

The Emancipation Proclamation

When President Lincoln took office, he was not opposed to slavery in the South. He went to war to keep the nation united. But as the war continued, he believed that it could also help end slavery.

A few days before the Battle of Antietam was fought, Lincoln had shared a secret with his cabinet. He explained that he had decided to **emancipate**, or free, at least some of the South's enslaved people.

On January 1, 1863, Lincoln signed the Emancipation Proclamation. This document declared that all enslaved people in areas still fighting against the Union were free. Enslaved people in the border states and in areas of the South controlled by the Union were not freed.

The Emancipation Proclamation did not actually free many enslaved people. Union forces did not control the Confederacy. However, the document expanded the goals of the war to include freeing all enslaved people.

As the Union troops moved farther into the South, they carried out the Emancipation Proclamation. Many enslaved people, newly freed, joined the Union army or worked as laborers behind the battle lines.

Some people in the South had thought that the Union could win the war, but that slavery could continue. Now they knew that if the Union won the war, slavery would end in the South.

READING CHECK **SUMMARIZE**
What was the Emancipation Proclamation?

Americans At War

During the Civil War, many different groups of people on both sides contributed to the war effort.

Women Help the War Effort

In both the North and the South, only men were allowed to join the army. Women, however, found many ways to help. They took over factory, business, and farm jobs that men left behind.

Women also worked as nurses. **Dorothea Dix** and **Clara Barton** both worked as nurses for the Union army. Barton's kindness earned her the nickname "Angel of the Battlefield." **Sally Tompkins** ran a hospital in Virginia for Confederate soldiers.

Some women even served as spies. **Belle Boyd**, from Virginia, spied for the Confederacy. Her daring missions eventually made her famous.

African American Soldiers

About 180,000 African Americans served in the Union army during the Civil War. These soldiers faced prejudice from people in the North and the South. **Prejudice** is an unfair feeling of dislike for members of a certain group because of their background, race, or religion.

At first, African American soldiers were not paid as much as white soldiers. They were also given poor equipment, and they often ran out of supplies. Despite this, African American soldiers proved themselves in battle. They led raids behind Confederate lines, served as spies and scouts, and fought in almost every major battle of the war.

One of the best-known African American regiments was the Fifty-fourth Massachusetts, led by **Robert Gould Shaw**. In 1863, the Fifty-fourth led an attack on **Fort Wagner**, in South Carolina.

CLARA BARTON

DOROTHEA DIX

SALLY TOMPKINS

FORT WAGNER The attack on Fort Wagner began at dusk on July 18, 1863.

Despite heavy fire, the regiment fought their way into the fort. Confederate forces drove them back. Many soldiers in the regiment, including Shaw, were killed.

READING CHECK ⏾ **GENERALIZE**

How did women on both sides contribute to the war effort?

Summary

The Union and the Confederacy both developed strategies to try to win the war. The Emancipation Proclamation expanded the goal of the war. Women on both sides contributed to the war effort. Thousands of African Americans fought for the Union.

REVIEW

1. **WHAT TO KNOW** What were some of the key events of the war's early years?

2. **VOCABULARY** Use the word **emancipate** in a sentence about Abraham Lincoln.

3. **HISTORY** What was the first major battle of the Civil War?

4. **CRITICAL THINKING** How did the Emancipation Proclamation affect the Union and Confederate armies?

5. ✎ **WRITE A LETTER** Imagine that you are living on a farm in a border state. Your father is off fighting in the Union Army. Write a letter telling him about life on the farm.

6. (Focus Skill) **GENERALIZE** On a separate sheet of paper, copy and complete the graphic organizer below.

Facts

Generalization

The Emancipation Proclamation expanded the goals of the war.

Distinguish Importance of Information

Why It Matters Learning how to distinguish important information from less important information will help you organize your studying.

❱ LEARN

Step 1 Identify relevant and irrelevant information. **Relevant** information relates to the subject you are reading. **Irrelevant** information does not relate to the subject.

Step 2 Tell essential information from incidental information. **Essential** information is needed to understand a subject fully. **Incidental** information does not affect your understanding of a subject.

Step 3 Know the difference between verifiable and unverifiable information. **Verifiable** information can be proved, while **unverifiable** information cannot be proved.

❱**SOLDIERS** Two of Frederick Douglass's sons served in the Fifty-fourth Massachusetts Regiment.

▶MONUMENT This monument to the Fifty-fourth Massachusetts Regiment is located in Boston, Massachusetts.

❱ PRACTICE

The passage below is about the Fifty-fourth Massachusetts Regiment. Read the passage carefully. Then determine which information is important for you to remember.

The Fifty-fourth was mostly made up of free African Americans. Colonel Robert Gould Shaw led the regiment. Shaw's family lived in Boston. Some people in Boston were not aware of the Fifty-fourth. On July 18, 1863, the regiment led an attack on Fort Wagner near Charleston, South Carolina.

❶ The sentence "Colonel Robert Gould Shaw led the regiment" is relevant information. Which sentence is the most irrelevant?

❷ Which of the following sentences contains the most essential piece of information?

  a. The Fifty-fourth was mostly made up of free African Americans.

  b. Shaw's family lived in Boston.

❱ APPLY

Use information in encyclopedias or other sources to determine what information about the Fifty-fourth Massachusetts Regiment in the passage is verifiable or unverifiable.

Time

1820   1860   1900

1863
The Battle of Gettysburg

1864
Sherman's March
to the Sea

1865
The Civil
War Ends

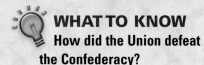

WHAT TO KNOW
How did the Union defeat
the Confederacy?

VOCABULARY
address p. 509
assassinate p. 511

PEOPLE
Ulysses S. Grant
George G. Meade
William Tecumseh Sherman
John Wilkes Booth

PLACES
Vicksburg
Chancellorsville
Gettysburg
Chattanooga
Atlanta
Savannah
Richmond
Appomattox Court House

 **GENERALIZE**

Toward a Union Victory

YOU ARE THERE
It is July 1, 1863, in Gettysburg, Pennsylvania.
Your parents wake you before dawn.
"Be quick," they say. "Get into the wagon."
You are scared but also excited. The Confederate
Army, led by General Robert E. Lee, marched into
Gettysburg yesterday. Your parents say, "The Union
Army will be here shortly. There is going to be a
great battle. It is time for us to get out of town."

▶ VICKSBURG The siege of Vicksburg lasted for about
six weeks.

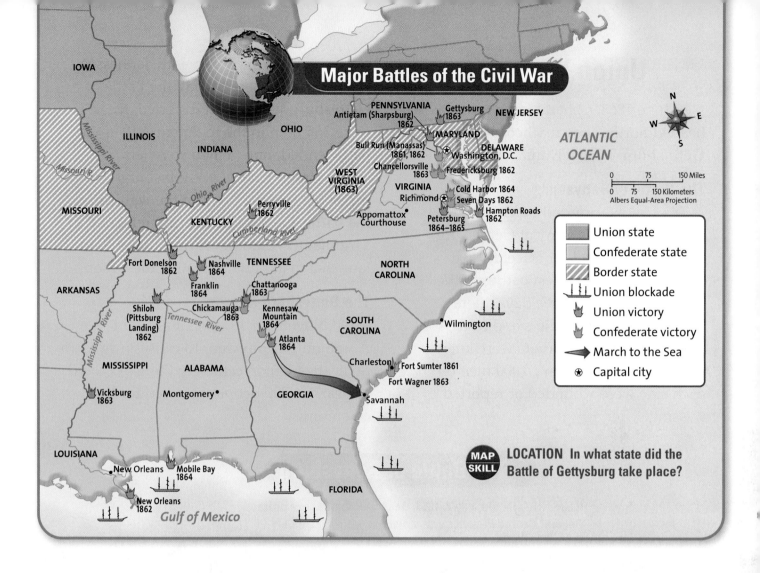

Major Battles of the Civil War

Legend:
- Union state
- Confederate state
- Border state
- Union blockade
- Union victory
- Confederate victory
- March to the Sea
- Capital city

MAP SKILL LOCATION In what state did the Battle of Gettysburg take place?

Two Major Battles

By May 1863, the Union army finally had a general as effective as Confederate General Robert E. Lee. His name was **Ulysses S. Grant**. One of Grant's first important battles began in May at **Vicksburg**, Mississippi.

Vicksburg and Chancellorsville

Grant laid siege to Vicksburg. The Union guns pounded the city, and the Union army cut off all supplies. The people and soldiers in the city ran out of supplies, but they refused to surrender.

Finally, on July 4, two months after the siege began, Vicksburg surrendered to Union troops. This was a major victory for the Union. It gave Union forces control of the Mississippi River. This cut the Confederacy into two parts. States in the Confederacy's western areas could no longer communicate easily with states in its eastern areas.

Shortly before Grant started to lay siege to Vicksburg, General Lee and his army defeated Union troops at **Chancellorsville**, Virginia. This victory gave the Confederacy confidence to try again to invade the North. Southern leaders thought that if they could win a major victory in a Northern state, people in the North would demand an end to the war.

READING CHECK ♻ GENERALIZE
Why was the Battle of Vicksburg important?

Union Victories

In June 1863, General Lee's troops headed north. They reached the town of **Gettysburg**, Pennsylvania, on July 1.

The Battle of Gettysburg

The Union army, led by **George G. Meade**, met Lee's army at Gettysburg. The fighting raged for three days. It was one of the deadliest battles of the war. During those three days, more than 3,000 Union soldiers and nearly 4,000 Confederate soldiers were killed. In addition, more than 20,000 men on each side were wounded or reported missing.

The story of the Fourteenth Tennessee Regiment tells how bloody the Battle of Gettysburg was. When it started, there were 365 men in the regiment. When the battle ended, only 3 men were left.

The Union victory at Gettysburg marked a turning point in the war. After the battle, General Lee's army retreated to Virginia. It would never again be able to launch a major attack against the Union.

The Gettysburg Address

On November 19, 1863, President Abraham Lincoln went to Gettysburg to dedicate a Union cemetery there. A crowd of nearly 6,000 people gathered for the ceremony.

The Battle of Gettysburg

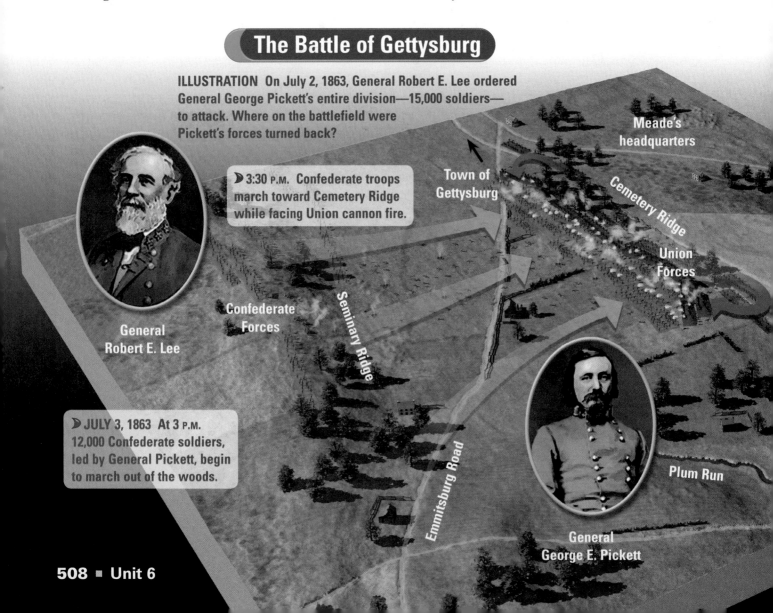

ILLUSTRATION On July 2, 1863, General Robert E. Lee ordered General George Pickett's entire division—15,000 soldiers—to attack. Where on the battlefield were Pickett's forces turned back?

▶ 3:30 P.M. Confederate troops march toward Cemetery Ridge while facing Union cannon fire.

▶ JULY 3, 1863 At 3 P.M. 12,000 Confederate soldiers, led by General Pickett, begin to march out of the woods.

Meade's headquarters

Town of Gettysburg

Cemetery Ridge

Union Forces

Confederate Forces

Seminary Ridge

Emmitsburg Road

Plum Run

General Robert E. Lee

General George E. Pickett

Lincoln gave an **address**, or short speech, that day. He spoke for less than three minutes. Yet, this is one of the most famous speeches in American history.

Lincoln spoke about the ideals of liberty and equality on which the country had been founded. He honored the soldiers who had died defending those ideals. He ended with these words:

> **"** . . . that these dead shall not have died in vain . . . that government of the people, by the people, for the people, shall not perish [disappear] from the earth. **"**

Sherman's March

In 1864, Lincoln appointed Ulysses S. Grant commander of all the Union forces. Grant planned to march to Richmond and capture the Confederate capital. Union General **William Tecumseh Sherman** was ordered to march from **Chattanooga**, Tennessee, to **Atlanta**, Georgia.

In September 1864, Sherman reached Atlanta. From Atlanta, Sherman's army of 62,000 men headed toward **Savannah**, Georgia, in a march that has become known as Sherman's March to the Sea. The army cut a path of destruction 60 miles wide and 300 miles long. Union soldiers burned homes and stores, destroyed crops, and tore up railroad tracks.

READING CHECK SUMMARIZE

Why was the Battle of Gettysburg a turning point in the war?

General George G. Meade

Taneytown Road

▶ **3:45 P.M.** Confederate forces reach Cemetery Ridge and are pushed back. The next day, Lee's army begins its retreat.

▶ **THE SURRENDER**
This painting shows General Lee (seated at left) surrendering to General Grant (seated at right).

The War Ends

In the North, Grant's army was defeating Lee's smaller army. Lee was quickly running out of men and supplies. In April 1865, Confederate troops evacuated **Richmond**, Virginia. As they left, they set the city on fire. Soon after, Union soldiers took control of Richmond.

Appomattox Court House

Lee's army moved west with Grant's army in constant pursuit. Lee's men were starving, and they were now outnumbered by 10 to 1. Lee said, "There is nothing left for me to do but to go and see General Grant, and I would rather die a thousand deaths."

On the afternoon of April 9, 1865, Lee met with Grant in a farmhouse in the Virginia village of **Appomattox** (a•puh•MA•tuhks) **Court House**. Grant wrote out the terms of surrender for Lee's signature. Afterward, Grant said to Lee, "I hope and believe this will be the close of the war."

In the next few weeks, as word of General Lee's surrender reached them, other Confederate generals surrendered. After four years of bloodshed, the Civil War was over. The Union had been preserved, but at a terrible cost.

Bitter Victory

More than 600,000 soldiers died in the Civil War. The South was left in ruins. In the North, there was joy at the victory. However, that joy was short-lived.

On April 14, 1865, just five days after Lee's surrender, President Lincoln went to Ford's Theater in Washington, D.C. There, he was **assassinated**, or murdered, by **John Wilkes Booth**. Booth, an actor, was a Confederate supporter. Lincoln's death shocked the nation. The President who had worked to keep the nation together was dead.

READING CHECK ♻ **GENERALIZE**
How did Lincoln's death affect the country?

Summary

Vicksburg and Gettysburg were turning points in the war. Sherman's March to the Sea caused more damage to the South. Lee's surrender to Grant led to the end of the war.

REVIEW

1. **WHAT TO KNOW** How did the Union defeat the Confederacy?

2. **VOCABULARY** Use the word **address** in a sentence about Abraham Lincoln.

3. **HISTORY** What was General Sherman's March to the Sea?

4. **CRITICAL THINKING** **Make It Relevant** Why do you think people today still find meaning in the Gettysburg Address?

5. ✏ **WRITE A POEM** The Civil War inspired the writing of many patriotic American poems. Write a poem to honor the soldiers who fought in the Civil War.

6. (Focus Skill) **GENERALIZE** On a separate sheet of paper, copy and complete this graphic organizer below.

Facts

Lincoln gave the Gettysburg Address.	The speech is still well known.	

Generalization

▶**RICHMOND IN RUINS, 1865**

1820 The Missouri Compromise is passed

Visual Summary

Summarize the Chapter

 Generalize Complete this graphic organizer to make a generalization about the Civil War.

Facts

| The Northern states and Southern states disagreed about slavery. | After Lincoln's election, many Southern states left the Union. | |

Generalization

 Vocabulary

Write a sentence or two to explain how each pair of terms is related.

1. **sectionalism** (p. 477) **civil war** (p. 493)

2. **free state** (p. 478) **slave state** (p. 478)

3. **tariff** (p. 479) **states' rights** (p. 479)

4. **fugitive** (p. 480) **Underground Railroad** (p. 485)

5. **secede** (p. 490) **Confederacy** (p. 491)

Time Line

6. When was the Missouri Compromise passed?

7. When did the Civil War begin?

8. How long did the Civil War last?

9. What major battle of the Civil War took place in 1863?

1860

1861 The Civil War begins

1863 The Battle of Gettysburg

1865

1865 The Civil War ends

 Facts and Main Ideas

Answer these questions.

10. What did the Missouri Compromise do?

11. What was the Underground Railroad?

12. Why did General Lee order his army north into Maryland?

13. How did General Grant plan to defeat the South?

Write the letter of the best choice.

14. What did the Supreme Court do in its decision in the Dred Scott case?
 A It declared the Fugitive Slave Law unconstitutional.
 B It declared the Missouri Compromise unconstitutional.
 C It gave Dred Scott his freedom.
 D It gave Congress the power to make laws about slavery.

15. What was the first battle of the Civil War?
 A Antietam
 B Gettysburg
 C Fort Sumter
 D Vicksburg

16. Why did General Lee surrender to General Grant?
 A European nations refused to help the South.
 B The issue of slavery had already been resolved.
 C Lee was tired of fighting.
 D Lee's army was starving and outnumbered.

 Critical Thinking

17. What economic advantages did the North have in fighting the Civil War?

18. How do you think people in the border states viewed the Emancipation Proclamation?

19. Why do you think the Confederate Army continued to fight even after it was clear they could not win?

 Skills

Distinguish Importance of Information

20. Tell which of the following facts is more important:

A. It was very hot during the three days of the Battle of Gettysburg.

B. The Union Army allowed Lee to escape back to Virginia after his defeat at Gettysburg.

writing

Write an Editorial You are the editor of a newspaper in Kentucky. Write an editorial that argues why this border state ought to stay in the Union and find a peaceful solution to the slavery issue or why it should secede.

Write an Essay Choose one of the people you read about in this chapter. Write a short essay describing what he or she accomplished.

STUDY SKILLS

WRITE TO LEARN

Writing about what you read can help you better understand and remember information.

- **Write down the information that you learn from each lesson.**
- **Write down your response to the new information you learned.**

Immigration

Information	Responses
Millions of immigrants from Southern and Eastern Europe came to the United States from 1880 to 1920.	Moving to a new country must have been exciting and challenging at the same time.
Immigrants lived in poor neighborhoods in tenements.	

PREVIEW VOCABULARY

freedmen p. 520

skyscraper p. 532

tenement p. 539

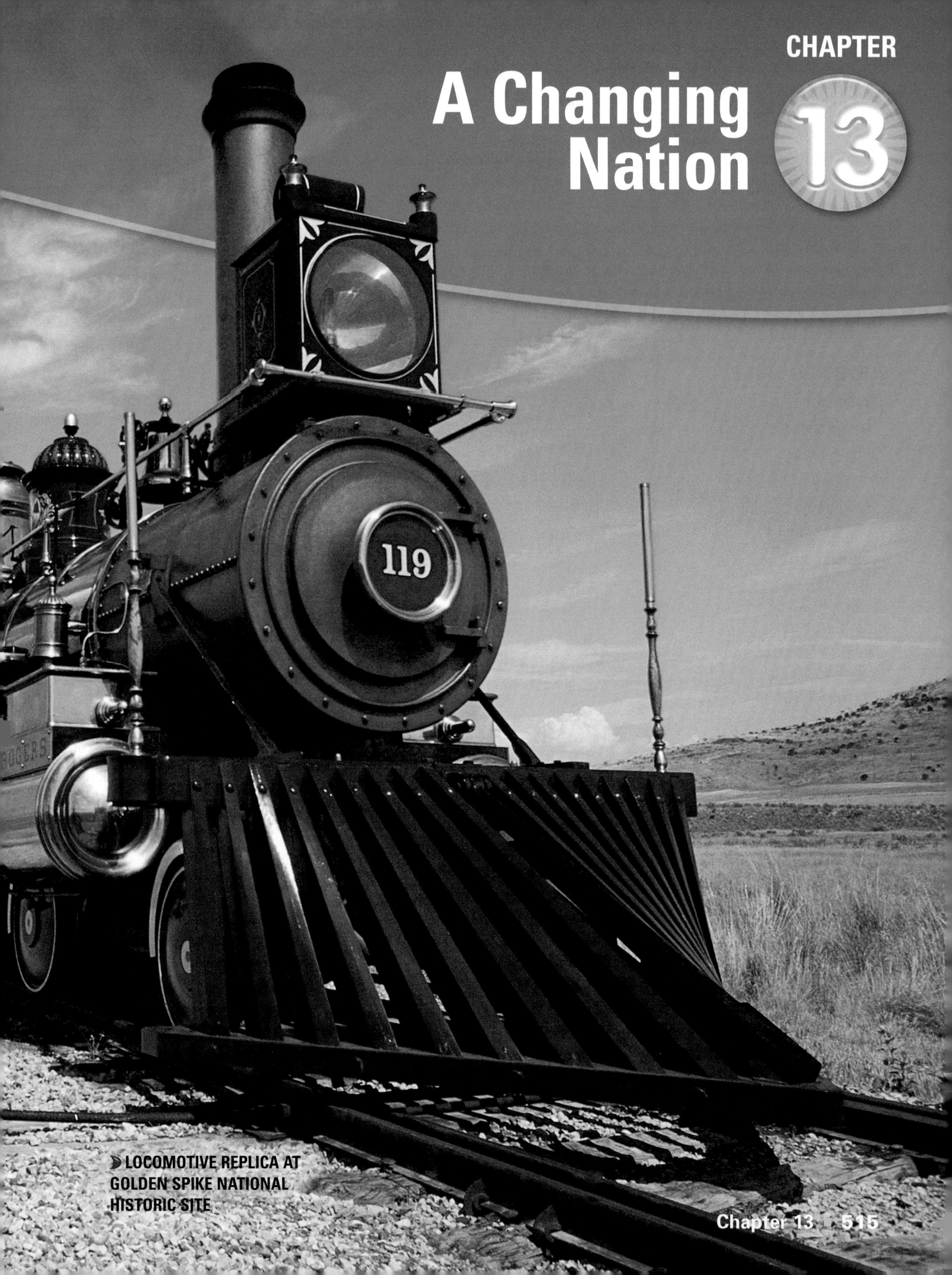

▶ LOCOMOTIVE REPLICA AT
GOLDEN SPIKE NATIONAL
HISTORIC SITE

Lesson 1

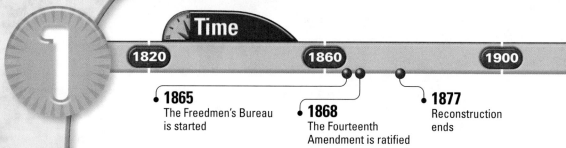

1865 The Freedmen's Bureau is started

1868 The Fourteenth Amendment is ratified

1877 Reconstruction ends

WHAT TO KNOW
What changes to Southern life began during Reconstruction?

VOCABULARY
Reconstruction p. 517
black codes p. 518
acquit p. 519
freedmen p. 520
sharecropping p. 520
secret ballot p. 522
segregation p. 522

PEOPLE
Abraham Lincoln
Andrew Johnson
Hiram R. Revels
Blanche K. Bruce
Booker T. Washington

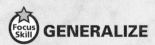

GENERALIZE

Facts

Generalization

Reconstruction

YOU ARE THERE You are in a crowd standing on a street corner in Washington, D.C. Today, you are very sad. You are watching President Lincoln's funeral procession. Men remove their hats, and people bow their heads. You look at all the people around you. Everyone is silent.

▶ **LINCOLN'S FUNERAL PROCESSION** After President Lincoln's death, Vice President Andrew Johnson (right) became President.

Plans for Rebuilding

Before **Abraham Lincoln** was killed, he had started to make plans for the rebuilding, or **Reconstruction**, of the nation.

Lincoln's Plan

Lincoln wanted to bring the nation back together quickly. He believed the South should not be punished. In a speech on March 4, 1865, Lincoln said,

> 66 With malice toward none, with charity for all, . . . let us strive on to finish the work we are in, to bind up the nation's wounds. . . . 99

When Lincoln was killed, the Union lost the man who had led it in winning a bitter war. The South lost a President who had planned to bring it back into the Union quickly and without more suffering.

Johnson's Plan

After Lincoln's death, Vice President **Andrew Johnson** became President. Johnson's plan for Reconstruction was similar to Lincoln's plan. Johnson's plan allowed most Confederates to pledge loyalty to the United States and become full citizens again.

Johnson let the former Confederate states hold elections. State governments went back to work. He said the former Confederate states could rejoin the Union after they abolished slavery. In December 1865, the Thirteenth Amendment to the Constitution was ratified. It ended slavery everywhere in the nation.

READING CHECK ☝ **GENERALIZE**
What did Lincoln and Johnson plan to do during Reconstruction?

Reconstruction Politics

After the Southern state legislatures went back to work, they passed laws to limit the rights of former enslaved people. These laws were called **black codes**. African Americans were treated badly. They could not vote. They could not own certain properties or hold certain jobs.

Many members of Congress were angry at Southern state governments. They felt that President Johnson had made it too easy for Southern states to rejoin the Union.

Congress's Plan

Many members of Congress wanted to make it harder for the Southern states to rejoin the Union. They wanted to punish the South for its part in the Civil War.

Congress put the Southern states under military rule. Union Army officers acted as governors, and soldiers kept order.

Before it could rejoin the Union, each Southern state had to write a new constitution. It had to give African American men the right to vote. Each state also had to approve the Fourteenth Amendment. It says that all people born in the United States, and all who become citizens, are citizens of the nation and their state. This amendment took effect in 1868, but it did not apply to Native Americans.

To further protect the rights of African Americans, Congress also proposed the Fifteenth Amendment to the Constitution. It says that no citizen can be denied the right to vote because of "race, color, or previous condition of servitude." This amendment was ratified in 1870.

CONGRESS DURING RECONSTRUCTION Congress wanted to punish the South for its part in the Civil War.

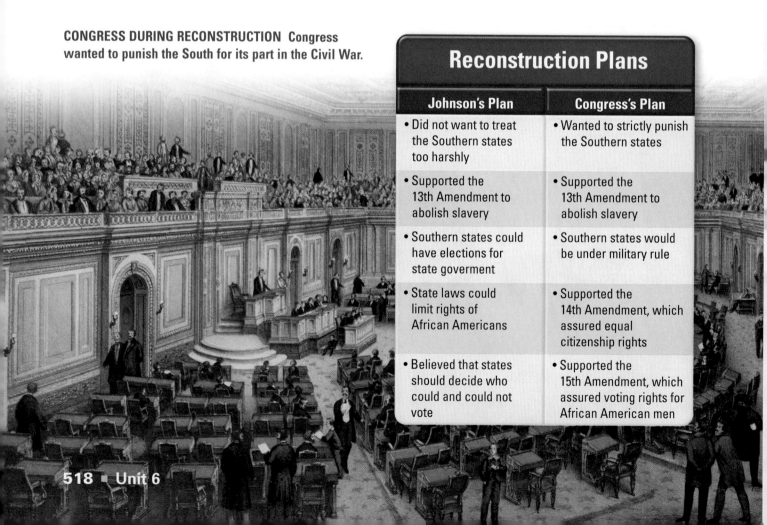

Reconstruction Plans

Johnson's Plan	Congress's Plan
• Did not want to treat the Southern states too harshly	• Wanted to strictly punish the Southern states
• Supported the 13th Amendment to abolish slavery	• Supported the 13th Amendment to abolish slavery
• Southern states could have elections for state goverment	• Southern states would be under military rule
• State laws could limit rights of African Americans	• Supported the 14th Amendment, which assured equal citizenship rights
• Believed that states should decide who could and could not vote	• Supported the 15th Amendment, which assured voting rights for African American men

Reconstruction Cartoon

Background This political cartoon appeared in a magazine in 1867.

African Americans voting

African American soldier protecting the voters

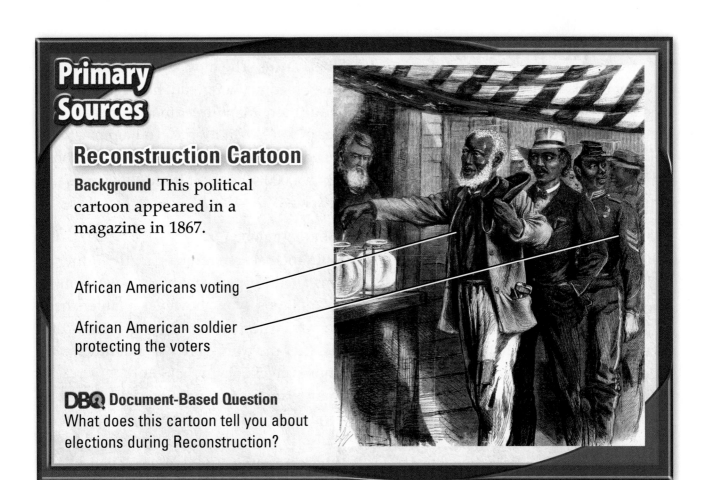

DBQ Document-Based Question
What does this cartoon tell you about elections during Reconstruction?

Impeachment

President Johnson tried to stop parts of Congress's Reconstruction plan. Congress then passed laws to limit the President's powers. One law said that the President could not remove people from office without the Senate's approval.

In spite of this law, President Johnson fired his Secretary of War, Edwin Stanton. The House of Representatives impeached Johnson, or brought charges against him. The Senate put Johnson on trial, but there were not enough votes to remove him from office. Instead, Johnson was **acquitted**, or found not guilty.

President Johnson finished his term. In 1869, Civil War hero Ulysses S. Grant became the next President. He supported Congress's plan for Reconstruction.

New Elections

After Southern states agreed to Congress's plan, they held new elections. Now African Americans in the Southern states could vote. African Americans **Hiram R. Revels** and **Blanche K. Bruce** were elected to the Senate from Mississippi. Overall, twenty African Americans served in Congress during Reconstruction.

African Americans also held offices in the new state and local governments in the South. Joseph C. Corbin served as superintendent of public instruction in Arkansas. He set up the state's first public school system.

READING CHECK ☼GENERALIZE
How did life change for African Americans during Reconstruction?

Hard Times

Many freed African Americans wanted to start new lives. However, after the war, the economy of the South was in ruins. Finding a job was difficult. Both African American and white Southerners struggled to find work.

The Freedmen's Bureau

In March 1865, even before the war ended, the United States Congress set up the Bureau of Refugees, Freedmen, and Abandoned Lands—also known as the Freedmen's Bureau. It helped all needy people in the South, but mainly worked with **freedmen**—men, women, and children who had been enslaved.

The Freedmen's Bureau gave food and supplies to former enslaved people. It also helped some white farmers rebuild their farms. The most important work of the Freedmen's Bureau, however, was education. Many freedmen were eager to learn to read and write. To help meet this need, the Freedmen's Bureau built more than 4,000 schools. It hired thousands of teachers.

Sharecropping

In their search for jobs, many former enslaved people went back to work on plantations. Now, however, planters had to pay African Americans for their work.

After the war, there was not much money available in the South. As a result, many landowners paid workers by letting them keep a share of the crops they harvested. This system was known as **sharecropping**. The worker, called a

> THE FREEDMEN'S BUREAU educated many former enslaved people in the South.

▶ **SHARECROPPING** Many former enslaved people worked as sharecroppers, but they did not earn much money.

sharecropper, farmed land owned by someone else. Each sharecropper was given a cabin, mules, tools, and seed. At harvest time, the landowner took a share of the crops to cover the costs of the worker's housing and supplies. What was left was the worker's share.

This system gave landowners the help they needed to farm. Freedmen got paid for their work. Yet few people got ahead through sharecropping. When crops failed, both landowners and workers suffered. Even when harvests were good, most workers' shares were very small.

Economic Troubles

Most Civil War battles took place in the South. Many bridges, buildings, and railroads were destroyed. To rebuild all these structures, state governments had to raise taxes. In Louisiana, for example, taxes almost doubled. Mississippi's taxes were 14 times higher than they had been.

Some Southerners blamed the higher taxes on African American state legislators and other state government leaders they called carpetbaggers and scalawags. Carpetbaggers were people from the North who moved south to work in Reconstruction governments. A scalawag (SKA•lih•wag) is someone who supports a cause for his or her own gain. Many scalawags were white Southerners who had been against the Confederacy.

Many Southerners believed that their state governments were corrupt, or dishonest. They hoped that if Reconstruction ended, then the corruption would end, too.

READING CHECK ᏧGENERALIZE
What problems did the South face?

Reconstruction Ends

Many white Southerners wanted to return to the way of life they had had before the Civil War. They were angered by heavy taxes and a changing society. They began to organize to regain their authority. One way to do this was to control the way people voted.

In the 1860s, not all states had secret ballots, as they have today. A **secret ballot** is a voting method that does not allow anyone to know how a person has voted. Before the secret ballot was used, the names of voters and how they voted were published in newspapers.

Secret societies formed to keep African Americans from voting or to make sure they only voted in certain ways. Members of some secret societies, such as the Ku Klux Klan, used violence to keep African Americans from voting.

Over time, white Southerners took back control of their state governments. They passed laws to keep African Americans from voting. These laws also established **segregation**, or the practice of keeping people in separate groups based on race. The laws were known as Jim Crow laws.

In time, people in the Northern states grew tired of paying to keep soldiers in the South. Many felt that Reconstruction had not united the country. In 1877, President Rutherford B. Hayes ordered all soldiers to leave the South. Reconstruction ended.

When Reconstruction ended, African Americans lost many of the rights they had gained. However, African American leaders continued to work to help.

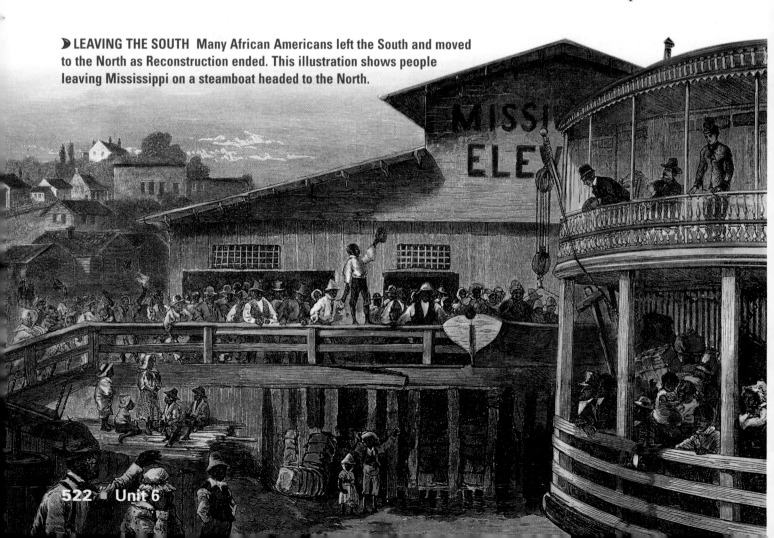

▶ **LEAVING THE SOUTH** Many African Americans left the South and moved to the North as Reconstruction ended. This illustration shows people leaving Mississippi on a steamboat headed to the North.

▶ BOOKER T. WASHINGTON (right) set up a school for African Americans.

Booker T. Washington, a former enslaved person, worked to provide African Americans with more opportunities for education. In 1881, he helped found the Tuskegee Institute, a trade school for African Americans in Alabama.

READING CHECK **CAUSE AND EFFECT**
How did the end of Reconstruction affect African Americans?

Summary

President Johnson and Congress disagreed about a plan for Reconstruction. Congress put the South under military rule. It required Southern states to approve new amendments. In time, white southerners gained control of their states and passed laws that took away African Americans' new rights.

REVIEW

1. **WHAT TO KNOW** What changes to Southern life began during Reconstruction?

2. **VOCABULARY** Use **sharecropping** in a sentence to explain how planters and freedmen farmed after the war.

3. **HISTORY** Why did Congress disagree with President Johnson's Reconstruction plan?

4. **CRITICAL THINKING** How did the Freedmen's Bureau help African Americans? Why was this important?

5. ✏️ **WRITE A SUMMARY** Write a paragraph that summarizes the differences between President Johnson's plan for Reconstruction and Congress's plan.

6. ⭐(Focus Skill) **GENERALIZE** On a separate sheet of paper, copy and complete this graphic organizer.

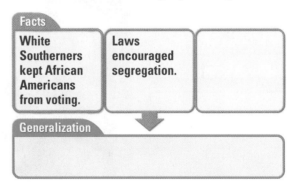

Facts		
White Southerners kept African Americans from voting.	Laws encouraged segregation.	

Generalization

Lesson

Time

1820　　1860　　1900

1862
The Homestead Act
is passed

1876
The Battle of
the Little Bighorn
is fought

1880
Most Native
Americans
live on
reservations

WHAT TO KNOW
Why did many people move west in the late 1800s?

VOCABULARY
prospector p. 525
boom p. 525
bust p. 525
homesteader p. 527
reservation p. 528

PEOPLE
Nat Love
George Armstrong Custer
Sitting Bull
Crazy Horse
Chief Joseph
Geronimo

PLACES
Abilene
Ogallala
Cheyenne
Little Bighorn River

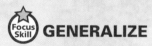

GENERALIZE

Facts

Generalization

The Last Frontier

YOU ARE THERE

One day in 1866, you are walking along a stream in South Dakota. Suddenly you see a gold nugget. You reach for it and put it in your pocket. You remember the stories you heard about the gold rush in California in 1849. You wonder whether to tell anyone about your discovery.

❯ **MINING TOWNS** were built very quickly. Most buildings were made of wood.

524 ■ Unit 6

▶ **MINING FAMILIES** Life was hard for mining families because most mining towns did not have schools or hospitals.

Western Mining

After the California gold rush of 1849, new discoveries of gold and silver brought more people to the West.

More Discoveries

In 1859, news of huge deposits of silver in the area known as the Comstock Lode drew more than 17,000 prospectors to what is now Nevada. A **prospector** is a person searching for gold, silver, or other mineral resources. Between 1860 and 1896, other finds in Idaho, Montana, and Alaska drew even more people.

When gold or silver was discovered in a place, prospectors moved into the area. They quickly set up mining camps. Mining towns usually grew around the camps. The majority of people who lived in these towns were men. Fights often broke out among the prospectors. At first, the towns had no sheriffs. Law and order did not exist. One reporter wrote, "Everyone was on his guard against a random shot."

Business owners set up stores to meet the needs of miners. This caused a **boom**, or a time of fast economic or population growth. As mining towns grew, families began to arrive.

Often, the gold or silver deposits ran out in a few years. Miners then moved on to other places. Once the miners left, a bust often followed. A **bust** is a time of fast economic decline. As a result, entire towns were often abandoned.

READING CHECK ⏀**GENERALIZE**

What made mining towns dangerous places?

▶ **CATTLE DRIVES** Cowhands drove the cattle hard for the first few days of a cattle drive. After they were far from the cattle's territory, the cowhands slowed down.

Life on the Frontier

The vast grasslands in Texas attracted many ranchers to the state. Cattle ranching had begun in Texas in the early 1800s. As cities in the East grew after the Civil War, the demand for beef increased. Ranchers could make more money if they could move their cattle to eastern markets.

Cattle Trails

By the 1870s, railroads had spread rapidly in the western United States. This ̇e ranchers a cheaper, faster way to ̇port their cattle. First, though, they had to get their cattle to the railroads. They had to herd, or drive, their animals hundreds of miles along cattle trails to railroad stations. **Abilene**, Kansas; **Ogallala**, Nebraska; and **Cheyenne**, Wyoming, were towns that grew at the end of the cattle trails.

At each town, the cattle were loaded onto railroad cars and taken to cities to be prepared for market. The meat was then packed in refrigerated railroad cars and taken to cities in the East to be sold.

Ranchers needed skilled cowhands to deliver their herds safely. American cowhands first learned their skills from Mexican vaqueros (vah•KAY•rohs).

About one in three Texas cowhands were Mexican or African American. Many African American cowhands were former enslaved workers.

Nat Love was a well-known African American cowhand. He was born in Tennessee and gained his freedom after the Civil War. Love worked as a cowhand for more than 20 years. He later wrote a book about his life.

Challenges on the Great Plains

In 1862, Congress passed the Homestead Act. This law opened the Great Plains to settlement. It gave 160 acres of land to any head of a family who was over 21 and would live on the land for five years. Thousands of Americans as well as about 100,000 immigrants from Europe rushed to claim these plots of land called homesteads. The people who settled them were known as **homesteaders**.

Living on the Great Plains was very difficult. There were few streams or trees for wood. Droughts and dust storms were common in the summer. In winter, snow and cold temperatures covered the region. Insects were also a problem. In 1874, grasshoppers came by the millions and ate all the crops.

Ranchers and farmers often disagreed over land use. Both groups put up fences. Fences often kept farmers from reaching the water they needed for their crops and kept ranchers from reaching the water they needed for their cattle.

Farmers and ranchers began cutting one another's fences. Sometimes this led to violence. These fights, called range wars, went on through the 1880s.

READING CHECK SUMMARIZE
What were the challenges of settling the Great Plains?

❯ **SOD HOUSES** Many homesteaders used sod to build their houses, but sod houses were difficult to keep clean.

▶ **AT THE BATTLE OF THE LITTLE BIGHORN** many Native American warriors were armed with guns.

Western Conflict

As railroads, ranches, and farms spread farther west, the buffalo began to die out. By 1880, only about 1,000 were left.

Native American Resistance

With fewer buffalo and the loss of more of their lands, many Native Americans had to agree to treaties with the United States. Those treaties set up **reservations**, or areas of land set aside by the government for use only by Native Americans.

Native American groups were often forced onto reservations. In the 1860s, members of the Sioux Nation lived in the Black Hills. After gold was discovered there, the United States sent soldiers to move all the Sioux to reservations.

In June 1876, Lieutenant Colonel **George Armstrong Custer** attacked the Sioux and their allies at the **Little Bighorn River**. Chiefs **Sitting Bull** and **Crazy Horse** led more than 1,500 warriors into battle. All the soldiers were killed. Both chiefs were later defeated, and their people were forced onto reservations.

In 1877, the government tried to force the Nez Perce onto an Idaho reservation. Their leader, **Chief Joseph**, resisted. He later tried to make a new home in Canada with 800 of his people. When the army stopped them, Chief Joseph chose not to fight. He explained,

❝I am tired. My heart is sick and sad. From where the sun now stands, I will fight no more forever.❞

Other Native American groups continued to fight. In the Southwest, an Apache chief named **Geronimo** led attacks against the United States Army. During the 1870s and 1880s, he and his warriors won many battles. In spite of his efforts, he was eventually forced to surrender.

By 1880, almost all Native Americans in the United States lived on reservations. Many Native Americans continue to live on reservations today. They work to keep their customs and traditional ways of life.

READING CHECK ⧖**GENERALIZE**
How did the United States government treat Native Americans?

Summary

Many people moved west in the late 1800s to mine, raise cattle, or set up homesteads. They fought with Native Americans over land. Many Native Americans were forced onto reservations.

▶**CHIEF JOSEPH'S** Nez Perce name means Thunder Rolling in the Mountains.

REVIEW

1. **WHAT TO KNOW** Why did many people move west in the late 1800s?

2. **VOCABULARY** How are the terms **boom** and **bust** related?

3. **ECONOMICS** How did ranchers move cattle to the East during the 1870s?

4. **CRITICAL THINKING** How did the arrival of ranchers and homesteaders affect the lives of Native Americans on the Plains?

5. ✎ **PREPARE A QUESTION LIST** Imagine that you plan to become a homesteader. Write a list of questions that you would want to ask a homesteader already living on the Great Plains.

6. 🟊 (Focus Skill) **GENERALIZE**
   On a separate sheet of paper, copy and complete this graphic organizer.

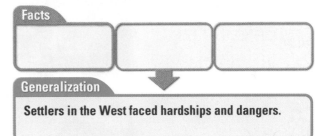

Facts

Generalization

Settlers in the West faced hardships and dangers.

Time

| 1820 | 1860 | 1900 |

1869
The Transcontinental
Railroad is completed

1875
Andrew Carnegie
opens his first
steel mill

1886
The American
Federation of
Labor is founded

WHAT TO KNOW
How did new industries and inventions change people's lives in the late 1800s?

VOCABULARY
transcontinental
  railroad p. 531
skyscraper p. 532
petroleum p. 533
labor union p. 534
strike p. 534
collective bargaining p. 535

PEOPLE
Andrew Carnegie
John D. Rockefeller
Thomas Alva Edison
Lewis Lattimer
Alexander Graham Bell
Samuel Gompers

PLACES
Promontory
Mesabi Range
Cleveland
Chicago

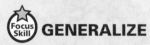

GENERALIZE

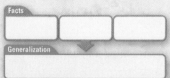

Facts

Generalization

New Industries

YOU ARE THERE

It's been six long years of backbreaking work, but the day you've been waiting for has finally come. Workers at **Promontory**, Utah, are about to join two sets of railroad tracks. One stretches east from Sacramento, California, and the other stretches west from Council Bluffs, Iowa. As the last spike is pounded into the ground, the crowd cheers wildly.

FAST FACT

People gathered at Promontory to celebrate the completion of the Transcontinental Railroad. The last spike used was made of gold and copper.

The Transcontinental Railroad

In 1862, Congress gave two railroad companies—the Union Pacific and the Central Pacific—the right to build a **transcontinental railroad**. This railroad would cross the continent, linking the Atlantic and Pacific coasts.

Building the Railroad

To help build the railroad, the federal government gave the two companies land and loaned them money. Railroads had already been built from the Atlantic coast west to Nebraska. The Union Pacific built its railroad west from Council Bluffs, Iowa. The Central Pacific built east from Sacramento, California.

Thousands of Chinese and Irish immigrants were hired to lay the tracks. Workers also blasted tunnels and cut ledges into the Sierra Nevada and the Rocky Mountains. They built bridges across valleys and rivers.

On May 10, 1869, the two railroads met at Promontory, Utah. For the first time, a person could travel all the way across the country by train.

After 1869, many more railroads were built across the United States. These railroads helped the economy grow. Towns grew up around the railroads. People could now sell their goods in markets in other parts of the country.

READING CHECK ⚙ **GENERALIZE**
How did the Transcontinental Railroad change the nation?

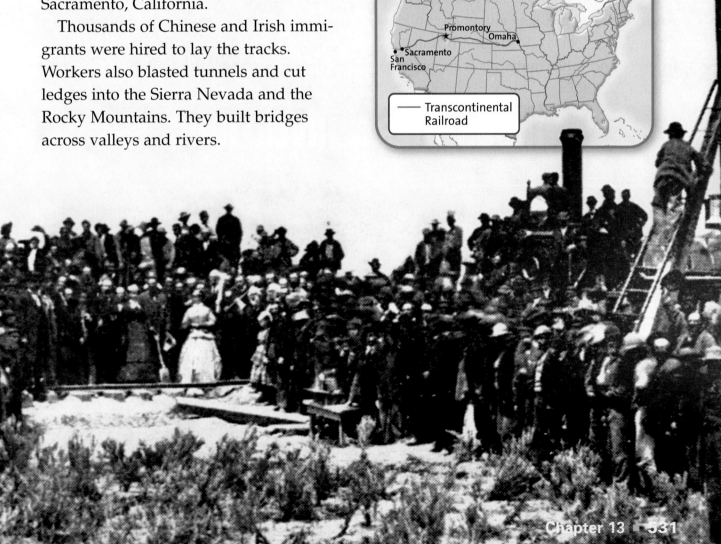

The Trancontinental Railroad

Promontory
Sacramento
San Francisco
Omaha

—— Transcontinental Railroad

Industries and Inventions

After the Civil War, great changes took place in the American economy. Inventors developed new technologies that made it easier for people to travel and communicate. These new inventions also helped the economy grow rapidly.

The Steel Industry

As the economy grew, trains carried more goods and supplies. This meant that trains needed to be bigger and heavier. The iron rails first used for train tracks needed to be replaced with something stronger—steel rails. Steel rails would be stronger and last longer, but they were more expensive to make.

In 1872, a Pennsylvania businessman, **Andrew Carnegie**, saw a new method for making steel while visiting Britain. Iron ore and other materials were melted in a way that made the steel stronger. Carnegie returned to Pennsylvania and found investors to help him build a steel mill. By the early 1870s, Carnegie's steel business was so successful that he built more steel mills. He also bought coal and iron mines to supply them.

Steel was used for many things. In the 1880s, William Jenney used steel frames to build tall buildings, such as the Jenney Building in Chicago. These new kinds of buildings were called **skyscrapers** because they seemed to scrape the sky.

In 1887, iron ore was found in the **Mesabi Range**, west of Lake Superior. This helped the steel industry spread to cities along the Great Lakes, such as **Cleveland**, Ohio, and **Chicago**, Illinois. Ships and railroads carried raw materials and goods to and from steel mills, factories, and cities across the nation. More people moved to cities for jobs.

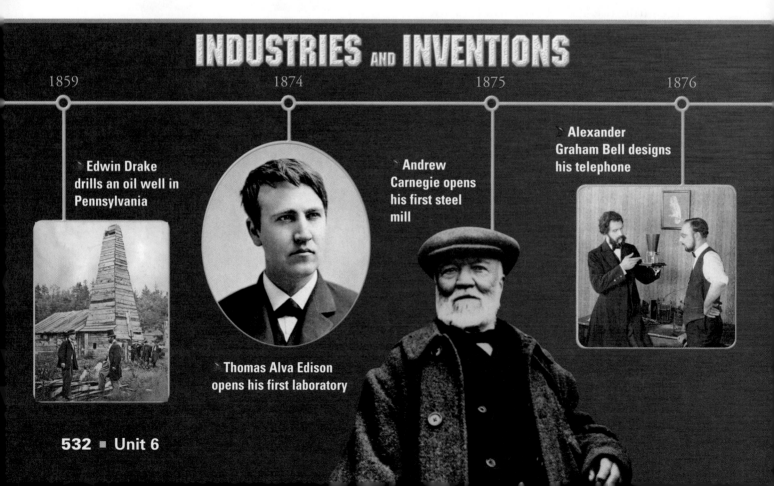

INDUSTRIES AND INVENTIONS

1859

> Edwin Drake drills an oil well in Pennsylvania

1874

> Thomas Alva Edison opens his first laboratory

1875

> Andrew Carnegie opens his first steel mill

1876

> Alexander Graham Bell designs his telephone

The Oil Industry

For years people knew about the **petroleum**, or oil, that gathered in ponds in western Pennsylvania and eastern Ohio. In the 1800s, kerosene, a fuel made from petroleum, became widely used for lighting lamps. The demand for petroleum increased sharply. This caused its price to rise.

In 1863, **John D. Rockefeller** set up an oil refinery near Cleveland. A refinery is a factory where crude, or raw, oil is made into usable products. The first products from Rockefeller's refinery were kerosene for lamps and grease for wheels.

Over time, Rockefeller bought other refineries. In 1867, he combined his refineries into one business. He called it the Standard Oil Company. His company was so successful that other oil companies could not compete. By 1882, Standard Oil controlled the entire industry.

Inventions Change Lives

In 1874, **Thomas Alva Edison** opened a laboratory in New Jersey. His workers were called "Edison's pioneers." Edison and his workers patented about one invention every five days. The best known was the first practical electric lightbulb. In 1882, Edison set up the first central electrical power station in New York City. **Lewis Lattimer**, an African American engineer on Edison's team, directed the building of this first central power station.

In 1876, **Alexander Graham Bell** designed a new telephone. The next year, he started the first telephone company in the United States. For the first time, people could communicate over long distances using their own voices.

READING CHECK ⚆ **GENERALIZE**
Why was steel important to the United States economy?

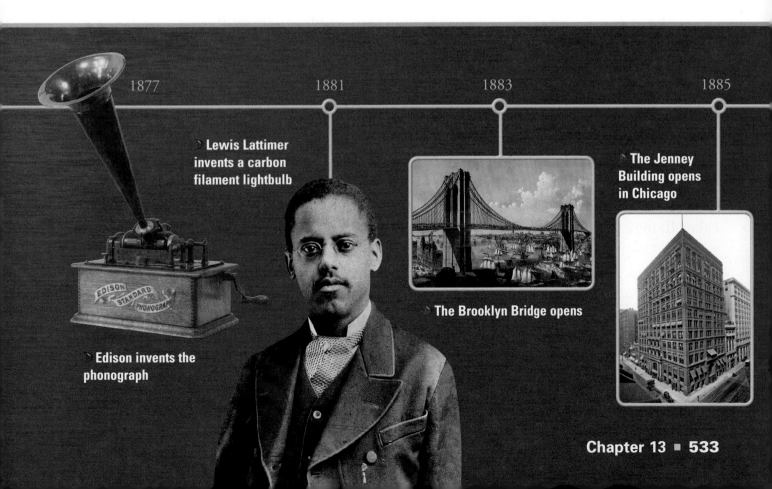

1877
> **Edison invents the phonograph**

1881
> **Lewis Lattimer invents a carbon filament lightbulb**

1883
> **The Brooklyn Bridge opens**

1885
> **The Jenney Building opens in Chicago**

Children IN HISTORY

Rose Cohen

At the age of 12, Rose Cohen came from Russia to New York City. Rose and her father lived in a poor part of the city. Rose got a job sewing coats to earn money to help the rest of her family come to this country.

Rose worked in a dark, crowded place called a sweatshop. Sweatshops were clothing factories where workers made dresses, shirts, and coats. The women and girls worked from before sunrise until long after dark. Rose earned $3 a week.

Rose and her father finally saved enough money to bring their family to the United States. Rose became a union leader and stopped working in sweatshops. Later, she wrote a book about her life.

Make It Relevant Compare and contrast Rose's childhood with yours.

Workers Struggle

The owners of railroads, mills, factories, and mines became rich. However, most workers received low pay for long hours. Jobs were often dangerous. Most mills and factories did not have fresh air. Many people worked 10- or 12-hour days.

Labor Unions

In the late 1800s, workers began to join labor unions. A **labor union** is a workers' group that fights for better working conditions and pay. Employers wanted to stop unions from organizing workers and demanding better working conditions.

Sometimes unions organized strikes. In a **strike**, workers refuse to work until employers meet their demands. Some strikes became violent. In 1892, Pennsylvania steelworkers and private police fought during the Homestead Steel Strike. For many years after this strike, the steel industry had no unions. Workers had long hours and low pay.

A tragedy in 1911 led many New York City garment workers to join unions. The Triangle Shirtwaist Company factory, which made blouses, caught fire. The workers, mostly women and girls, were trapped inside. There was only one fire escape. As a result, 146 workers died.

Samuel Gompers was a labor leader who helped organize the American Federation of Labor, or AFL, in 1886. Under Gompers, the AFL grew and government and business leaders began to listen to its demands. The demands included better wages and an eight-hour workday.

Gompers also encouraged the use of **collective bargaining**. Collective bargaining allows employers and workers to discuss and agree on working conditions. The AFL was able to get better pay and better hours for its members. Today, unions still use collective bargaining to improve working conditions.

READING CHECK Ŏ **GENERALIZE**
How did labor unions help improve workers' lives?

Summary

The railroad, steel, and oil industries grew quickly in the 1800s. Many inventions improved travel and communication. Growing industries made owners wealthy, but workers had long hours and poor pay. They joined labor unions and used strikes to force owners to improve conditions.

▶ **LABOR UNIONS** fought for better wages and an eight-hour workday.

REVIEW

1. **WHAT TO KNOW** How did new industries and inventions change people's lives in the late 1800s?

2. **VOCABULARY** Use the terms **labor union** and **collective bargaining** to explain the labor movement.

3. **HISTORY** What event encouraged garment workers to join unions?

4. **CRITICAL THINKING Make It Relevant** What inventions from the 1800s do people still use today?

5. ⚜ **CREATE A CHART** Make a chart showing the inventors in this lesson and their inventions. Illustrate your chart.

6. 🌟 **GENERALIZE**
   On a separate sheet of paper, copy and complete this graphic organizer.

Facts		

Generalization
New industries developed in the late 1800s.

Read a Time Zone Map

Why It Matters A time zone map can help you know what time it is in different parts of the country and the world.

❯ LEARN

Before clocks, people used the sun to tell time. It was noon when the sun was at it highest point in the sky. Because Earth rotates on its axis, noon is a different time in every place. When railroads tried to schedule trains, people realized that something needed to be done. Sandford Fleming of Canada and Charles Dowd of the United States came up with the idea of time zones.

They divided Earth into 24 different time zones. A **time zone** is a region in which a single time is observed. The time in each time zone is one hour earlier than the time zone just east of it.

The United States has six time zones. Time zones east of you always have a later time than your time zone. Time zones west of you always have an earlier time than your time zone.

❯ PRACTICE

Use the time zone map on page 537 to answer the questions.

1. Which time zone is orange on the map?
2. In which time zone are San Francisco, Los Angeles, and San Diego?
3. If it is 10:00 A.M. in Chicago, what time is it in Portland?
4. Imagine that you are in Cincinnati, Ohio. Is the time earlier than, later than, or the same as in Baltimore?

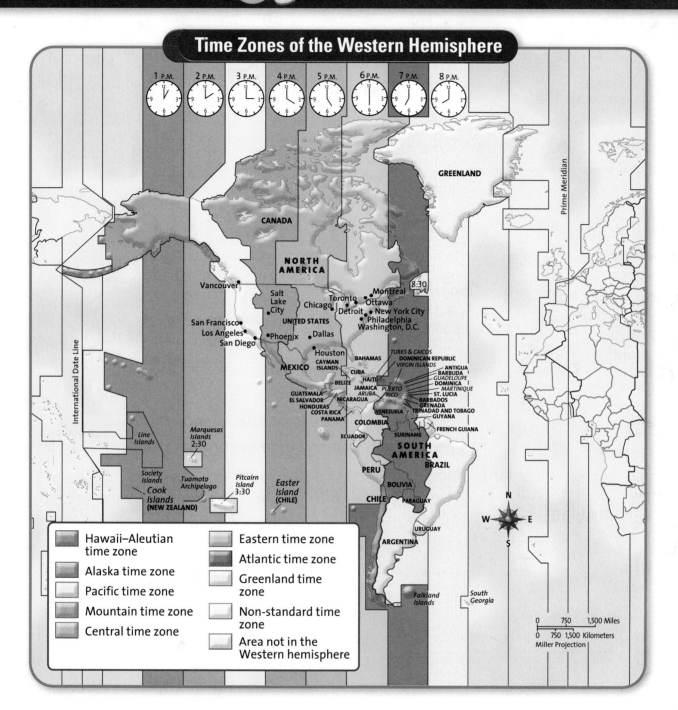

Time Zones of the Western Hemisphere

Map and Globe Skills

> APPLY

Make up two questions about the map on this page. Write your questions on the front of a sheet of paper. Write the answers on the back. Then exchange papers with a classmate. Check each other's answers.

Time

1820	1860	1900

1882
The Chinese Exclusion
Act is passed

1889
Hull House
is founded

1892
Ellis Island
is opened

WHAT TO KNOW
What challenges did new
immigrants face?

VOCABULARY
tenement p. 539
reformer p. 540
settlement house p. 540

PEOPLE
Jane Addams
Lillian Wald

PLACES
Ellis Island
Angel Island
Chicago

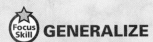

Cities and Immigration

YOU ARE THERE
"There it is!" you yell, pointing
at the Statue of Liberty. You are
on the deck of the ship that has
brought your family to America.

Your mother points out **Ellis Island**.
She tells you that is where everyone
will be checked by officials before you can go into
New York City. Your aunt and uncle and cousins will
meet you at the dock. It's a great day.

> **THE STATUE OF LIBERTY** was placed on
Liberty Island in New York Harbor in 1886.

▶ NEW YORK CITY This photograph from 1909 shows a busy day on Mulberry Street, on the Lower East Side of New York City.

Many Immigrants Arrive

Between 1860 and 1910, about 23 million immigrants arrived in the United States. People often came to escape violence and poverty. They hoped to find freedom, safety, and a better life.

New Immigrants

Before 1890, most immigrants from Europe came from northern and western Europe. After 1890, most immigrants came from countries in southern and eastern Europe, such as Hungary, Italy, Greece, Poland, and Russia.

In 1892, the Ellis Island Immigration Station was opened in New York Harbor. After European immigrants arrived at Ellis Island, they were examined. Those who were not ill were let into the country.

Immigrants were often poor. Many lived in crowded, poorly built apartment buildings called **tenements**. Most immigrants struggled to find jobs and learn English. Often, immigrant children learned English in school. Then they helped their parents use English. Some children had to work full-time to help support their families.

Immigrants also came from Asia. They entered the United States at **Angel Island** in San Francisco Bay. There, they were separated by nationality and made to wait at a processing center while the government decided whether they could enter the country.

READING CHECK ☼GENERALIZE
After 1890, where did most immigrants come from?

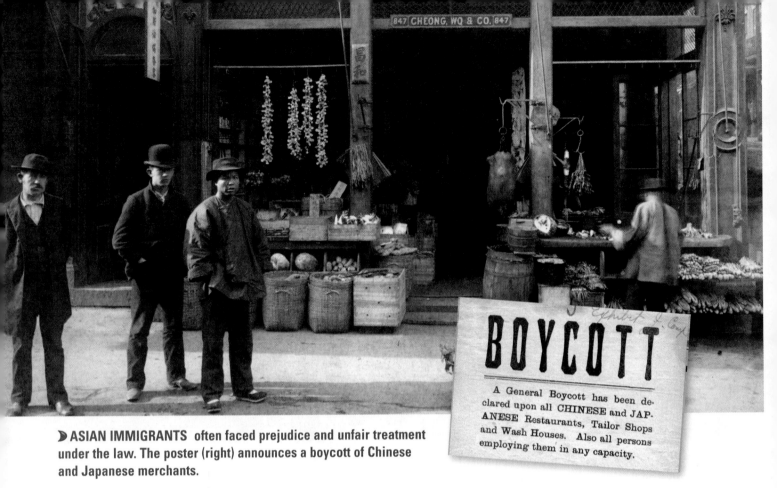

> ▶ **ASIAN IMMIGRANTS** often faced prejudice and unfair treatment under the law. The poster (right) announces a boycott of Chinese and Japanese merchants.

BOYCOTT

A General Boycott has been declared upon all CHINESE and JAPANESE Restaurants, Tailor Shops and Wash Houses. Also all persons employing them in any capacity.

Reactions to Immigration

Many immigrants faced hard times when they arrived in the United States. Finding work and learning to live in a new country was challenging.

Unfair Treatment

Many Americans were opposed to the new immigrants. Some Americans felt that because some immigrants had little education, they were not qualified to take part in a democracy. Others worried that the newcomers would take their jobs.

In the West, there had been opposition to Asian immigrants for a long time. In 1882, Congress passed the Chinese Exclusion Act. This law excluded, or kept out, all Chinese immigrants. It prevented any Chinese immigrants from coming to the United States for ten years.

Help for Immigrants

Immigrants faced other problems. The tenements often did not have clean water. Garbage piled up in the streets. This created health problems.

People called reformers tried to help immigrant families. A **reformer** is someone who tries to change society. **Jane Addams** and **Lillian Wald** were both reformers who started settlement houses. A **settlement house** was a place that provided food, health care, and classes for immigrants.

Jane Addams founded Hull House in **Chicago** in 1889. Lillian Wald started the Henry Street Settlement in New York City. They wanted to help immigrants and give them opportunities.

READING CHECK 🍥 **GENERALIZE**
How did settlement houses help immigrants?

Migration and Immigration

As immigrants moved to the United States, people within the country moved from place to place. Some African Americans moved to the West. Others moved to northern cities.

African Americans Migrate

In the early 1900s, thousands of African Americans began moving to northern cities. This movement of people was so large that it became known as the Great Migration. Many African Americans found jobs in factories in northern cities.

Before the early 1900s, nearly nine of every ten African Americans lived in the South. After the Great Migration, more than half of all African Americans lived in the Northeast and the Midwest.

Immigration Today

Today, immigrants from around the world still come to the United States. After the Civil War, most immigrants came from countries in Europe. Now most immigrants come from countries in Asia and Latin America. In fact, more than half of all foreign-born people in the United States today are from Latin American countries. Almost one-fourth of today's immigrants come from countries in Asia, such as China, Japan, India, Pakistan, and the Philippines.

Many Americans still practice customs and traditions special to their cultures. Differences in American culture can be seen in the foods and music people like and the religious groups they belong to. This all adds to the diversity of American culture. Although Americans are different from one another, they have much in common.

▶ THE GREAT MIGRATION brought thousands of African Americans to northern cities such as Chicago, New York City, and Detroit.

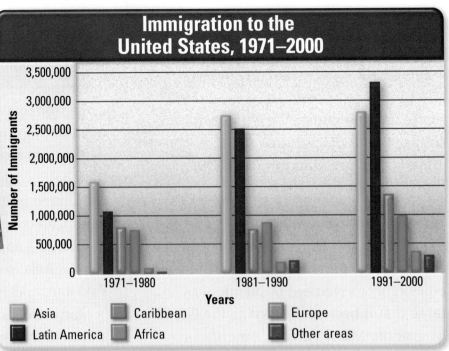

Immigration to the United States, 1971–2000

Number of Immigrants

- 3,500,000
- 3,000,000
- 2,500,000
- 2,000,000
- 1,500,000
- 1,000,000
- 500,000
- 0

Years: 1971–1980, 1981–1990, 1991–2000

Legend: Asia, Latin America, Caribbean, Africa, Europe, Other areas

GRAPH In which decade was immigration from Asia the highest?

They are united by basic American ideals—freedom, opportunity, and a belief in individual rights. Many people come to the United States for those reasons.

READING CHECK ⚙ **GENERALIZE**
Why did many African Americans move to cities in the northern states?

Summary

Millions of immigrants from Europe and Asia came to the United States. They often faced unfair treatment. Many African Americans moved to northern cities. Immigrants continue to come to the United States.

REVIEW

1. **WHAT TO KNOW** What challenges did new immigrants face?

2. **VOCABULARY** Use the word **tenement** in a sentence about immigrants.

3. **HISTORY** What was the Chinese Exclusion Act?

4. **CRITICAL THINKING** How do you think immigration affected the economy of the United States?

5. ✏ **WRITE A DIARY ENTRY** Pretend you are a child in an immigrant family. You are about to land in New York City after your journey across the ocean. Write a diary entry about your hopes and dreams for your new life.

6. ⭐ (Focus Skill) **GENERALIZE** On a separate sheet of paper, copy and complete the graphic organizer.

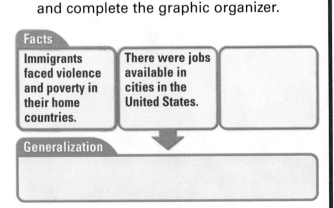

Facts

Immigrants faced violence and poverty in their home countries.

There were jobs available in cities in the United States.

Generalization

Jane Addams

Biography

Trustworthiness

Respect

Responsibility

Fairness

Caring

Patriotism

"Civilization is a method of living and an attitude of equal respect for all people."

Jane Addams was born near Chicago in 1860. When she was a young woman, she took a trip to England. She saw how some people there were helping poor children and families. Addams decided to do that as her life's work.

She returned to Chicago and bought a large house. She named it Hull House. It was the first settlement house in the United States. It provided food, medical care, legal advice, and English classes for thousands of immigrant families.

Hull House grew to include 14 buildings, as well as a summer camp in Wisconsin. Many women came to Hull House to work. They went on to be leaders in an effort to help working families.

Jane Addams realized there was still more work to do. She worked to change laws that hurt immigrants and poor people. She helped start a group that worked for the rights of African Americans. She also worked for world peace. In 1931, she became the first American woman to win the Nobel Peace Prize.

Why Character Counts

How did Jane Addams show responsibility?

Time

1860		1935
Born		Died

1889 Founds Hull House

1931 Wins the Nobel Peace Prize

GO ONLINE

For more resources, go to www.harcourtschool.com/ss1

Compare Different Types of Graphs

Why It Matters Knowing how to read and put together graphs will help you compare a lot of information at once.

❯ LEARN

Graphs show information in different ways. A bar graph uses bars. It is useful for quick comparisons. The bar graph below shows immigration to the United States by decade.

Circle graphs show information in percents. A percent, shown by the symbol %, is one-hundredth of something. For example, if you cut a pie into 100 pieces, those 100 pieces together would equal the whole pie. Fifty pieces would be one-half of the pie, or 50% of it. The circle graph on page 545 shows immigration from Russia, Italy, and Austria-Hungary between 1900 and 1909.

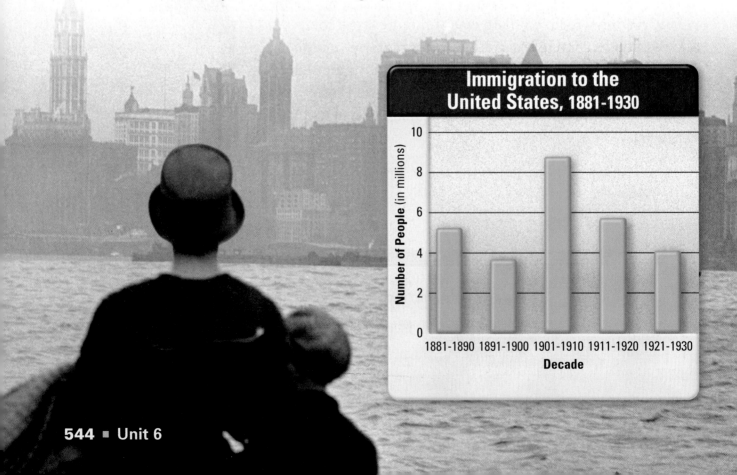

Immigration to the United States, 1881-1930

A line graph shows change over time. The line graph below shows the population of the United States from 1880 to 1920.

❯ PRACTICE

Use the three graphs on this page to answer the questions. Think about the advantages and disadvantages of each kind of graph.

1 About how many millions of immigrants came to the United States between 1881 and 1890?

2 Which decade had more immigrants, 1891–1900 or 1901–1910?

3 In the years 1900–1909, did Italy or Russia have more immigrants entering the United States? In which graph did you find the answer?

4 Look at the line graph. What happened to the population of the United States from 1880 to 1920?

❯ APPLY

Use the information in the bar and line graphs to write a paragraph about immigration and population.

Immigration from Austria-Hungary, Italy, and Russia, 1900-1909

Austria-Hungary 37%
Italy 35%
Russia 28%

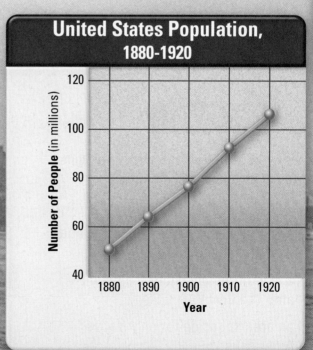

United States Population, 1880-1920

Number of People (in millions)
120
100
80
60
40

Year
1880 1890 1900 1910 1920

Chart and Graph Skills

Time

1860   1865

1862
Congress passes the Homestead Act

Visual Summary

Summarize the Chapter

Generalize Complete this graphic organizer to make a generalization about the United States in the late 1800s and early 1900s.

Facts

Many new imigrants came to the United States.

Generalization

In the late 1800s, the United States changed a great deal because of immigration, migration, and new industries.

TEST PREP

Vocabulary

Identify the term from the word bank that correctly matches each definition.

1. fast economic or population growth

2. a workers' group that fights for better working conditions

3. a time of rebuilding for the nation after the Civil War

4. an area set aside for only Native Americans

5. a crowded, poorly built apartment building

Word Bank

Reconstruction p. 517

boom p. 525

reservation p. 528

labor union p. 534

tenement p. 539

1869
The first transcontinental railroad is completed

1877
Reconstruction ends

1882
The American Federation of Labor is founded

 Time Line

6. Was the first transcontinental railroad completed before or after the Homestead Act was passed?

7. Reconstruction ended how many years after the Homestead Act was passed?

Facts and Main Ideas

Answer these questions.

8. What was the Freedmen's Bureau?

9. What was the Homestead Act? Explain how it affected the settlement of the United States?

10. How did life change for Native Americans as railroads, ranches, and farms spread farther west?

11. Who was Thomas Edison and how did he change life in the United States?

Write the letter of the best choice.

12. What were the workers who farmed land owned by other people called?
    A homesteaders
    B freedmen
    C carpetbaggers
    D sharecroppers

13. Which industry hired thousands of Chinese and Irish immigrants to work in the West?
    A the steel industry
    B the oil industry
    C the railroad industry
    D the telephone industry

 Critical Thinking

14. How did the Reconstruction plans of President Johnson and Congress differ?

15. How did immigrants contribute to the growth of railroads, mining, and ranching?

 Skills

Compare Graphs

16. Look at the graph on page 544. In which of the decades shown did the most immigrants come to the United States?

Read a Time Zone Map

17. Look at the time zone map on page 537. In which time zone are Houston and Chicago?

writing

✏ **Write a Report** Write a report about the sharecropping system. Tell who owned the land, who worked the land, and how they were paid. Explain why it was hard for workers to get ahead under this system.

✏ **Write a Narrative** Imagine that you are an immigrant factory worker. Write a story to explain how you came to the United States and tell about your working conditions.

Fun with Social Studies

Heads and Tails

Match the front of each coin with the correct reverse side.

Rebus Removal

ahc VOCABULARY

All of the following rebus words are vocabulary words, except for one. Find the rebus word that doesn't belong.

Now Showing

What historic events or places do these movie posters describe?

A NATION DIVIDED

CONNECTING THE COUNTRY

A NEW HOME

Online Adventures

GO ONLINE

ECO

It's the dark and difficult time before the Civil War. In this online game, you and Eco will meet Harriet Tubman and help her plan an escape route on the Underground Railroad. You will need to find people who support the fight against slavery. Along the way, be careful not to get captured. If you can solve all the problems, you will be able to help enslaved African Americans escape to freedom! Play now at **www.harcourtschool.com/ss1**

Review and Test Prep ✔

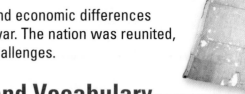

💡 THE BIG IDEA

Conflict and Change Social and economic differences divided the nation and led to war. The nation was reunited, but continued to face many challenges.

Reading Comprehension and Vocabulary

Civil War Times

Sectionalism separated the North and the South as they argued over slavery. Compromises were only temporary solutions. In the North, abolitionists called for the end of slavery. Enslaved people resisted slavery by running away on the Underground Railroad. Harriet Tubman led hundreds of enslaved people to freedom.

The election of President Lincoln caused the South to secede. The Civil War began in 1861. In 1863, Lincoln issued the Emancipation Proclamation. It freed all enslaved people in areas still fighting against the Union. The war ended in 1865, when the Confederate Army surrendered. Lincoln was assassinated five days later.

President Johnson and Congress disagreed about a plan for Reconstruction. Congress passed amendments to the Constitution to protect African Americans. White Southerners gained back control and took away African Americans' new rights.

Many people moved to the West, but Native Americans were forced to move onto reservations. Railroad, steel, and oil industries grew quickly in the 1800s. Many inventions improved travel and communication. Workers struggled to gain their rights. After 1890, millions of immigrants from Southern and Eastern Europe came to the United States.

Use the summary above to answer these questions.

1. What does the term sectionalism mean?
   A a rivalry between nations
   B a rivalry between different parts of a country
   C a disagreement about a tariff
   D a disagreement about how states should come into the Union

2. What caused the South to secede?
   A the Underground Railroad
   B the Seneca Falls Convention
   C the assassination of President Lincoln
   D the election of President Lincoln

3. What is the meaning of the term reservation?
   A an area set aside by the government for use only by Native Americans
   B a place where gold mines are located
   C a law that gives public land to people
   D a place where immigrants first enter

4. Where did most of the immigrants who came to the United States after 1890 come from?
   A Asia
   B Northern and Western Europe
   C Southern and Eastern Europe
   D Latin America and Canada

Answer these questions.

5. What was the Missouri Compromise?

6. How did the Homestead Act help bring settlers to the West?

7. How did Southerners react to John Brown's raid on Harpers Ferry?

8. How did the Fourteenth Amendment help African Americans?

9. What was the Great Migration?

Write the letter of the best choice.

10. Who took part in the Seneca Falls Convention?
    A Harriet Beecher Stowe
    B Harriet Tubman
    C Clara Barton
    D Elizabeth Cady Stanton

11. Which statement best describes Abraham Lincoln's views about slavery in the Lincoln-Douglas Debates?
    A Slavery should not be allowed to expand into the territories.
    B Slavery should be abolished.
    C Congress should outlaw slavery.
    D The people living in the territories should decide whether to allow slavery there.

12. Which person developed the steel industry in the United States?
    A John D. Rockefeller
    B John Wilkes Booth
    C Alexander Graham Bell
    D Andrew Carnegie

13. What was the immediate effect of the Emancipation Proclamation?
    A It freed all enslaved people in all the states.
    B It freed enslaved people in states of the Confederacy.
    C It freed enslaved people in the territories.
    D It freed enslaved people in the border states.

14. How do you think Reconstruction might have been different if Lincoln had not been assassinated?

15. **Make It Relevant** How do you think the growth of the railroads changed America? Do any of these changes still affect your life today?

Read a Time Zone Map

Use the time zone map below to answer the question.

16. When it is 5:00 p.m. in Los Angeles, what time is it in Washington, D.C.?

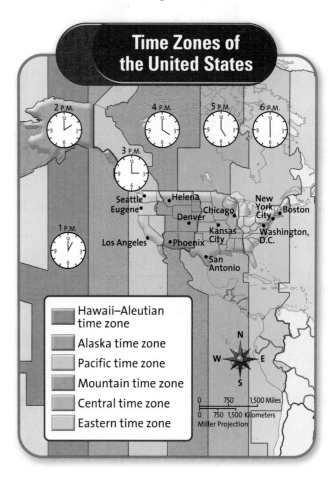

Time Zones of the United States

Unit 6 Activities

Show What You Know

Unit Writing Activity

Write a Summary Explain the causes and effects of the Civil War.

- List two ways leaders tried to solve the problems facing the Union.
- Tell how President Lincoln helped preserve the Union.
- Summarize Reconstruction.

Unit Project

Design a Scrapbook Design a scrapbook about the Civil War.

- Make drawings and paintings of people and events of the Civil War.
- Write captions, stories, and poems to help tell the history of the Civil War.
- Draw maps of places where important events of the Civil War took place.

Read More

- *Life in America's First Cities* by Sally Senzell Isaacs. Heinemann Library.

- *Your Travel Guide to Civil War America* by Nancy Day. Runestone Press.

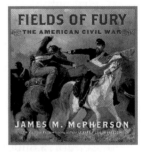

- *Fields of Fury* by James M. McPherson. Atheneum.

GO ONLINE For more resources, go to www.harcourtschool.com/ss1

Ohio Economy and Environment

Start with the Standards

OHIO SOCIAL STUDIES CONTENT STANDARDS

History 5.6

Geography 5.7A, 5.7B, 5.9A, 5.9B, 5.9C, 5.9E

Economics 5.1, 5.2, 5.3, 5.4, 5.5, 5.6, 5.7

Social Studies Skills 5.7, 5.8

OHIO TODAY

DID YOU KNOW?

More than 600,000 Ohioans work in service industries.

After the Civil War, many changes took place in Ohio. Steel, oil, rubber, and glass industries grew rapidly. During this time, many immigrants came to Ohio from Europe. African Americans from southern states also moved to Ohio and other northern states.

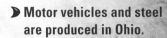
❯ Motor vehicles and steel are produced in Ohio.

When World War I broke out in Europe, more than 200,000 Ohioans served in the military. Camp Sherman, near Chillicothe, was an army training camp. During World War II, about 839,000 men and women from Ohio joined the armed forces. Ohio factories helped supply soldiers in Europe during both wars. They provided items such as weapons, cars, planes, and ships.

During the 1970s and 1980s, many Ohio factories closed. However, manufacturing is still important in the state. Ohio is also a leader in agriculture. In recent years, high-tech industries have grown in Ohio. Scientific laboratories research new and better ways to do things. Today, many Ohioans work in service industries. Health care, education, and tourism are important service industries in the state.

▶ At the Glenn Research Center in Cleveland, scientists are working to improve space travel. Visitors can tour the facility.

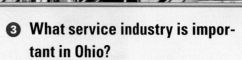

OHIO TEST PREP

1 **When did many immigrants and African Americans move to Ohio?**
A. in the 1980s
B. after World War II
C. after the Civil War

2 **What happened in the 1970s and 1980s?**
A. The Civil War was fought.
B. World War I was fought.
C. Many factories closed.

3 **What service industry is important in Ohio?**
A. health care
B. steel manufacturing
C. agriculture

4 **How has Ohio changed in the last 150 years?**

Our Nation's Economy

WHAT TO KNOW
How does the free enterprise economy of the United States work?

VOCABULARY
free enterprise p. 555
human resources p. 555
capital goods p. 555
scarcity p. 556
command economy p. 556
market economy p. 556
competition p. 557
productivity p. 558
specialization p. 558
interdependent p. 559

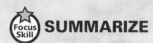 SUMMARIZE

YOU ARE THERE It is lunchtime, and you and your family are at the mall. You stop at the food court to get lunch. Your mother gives you five dollars and says you can get whatever you want to eat.

As you walk around the food court, you think about all the different choices you have. You want to get the food you like the best, but you also want to get the most food for your money. It is not an easy decision!

▶ ECONOMIC DECISIONS People purchase many goods and services at shopping malls.

▶ **FACTORS OF PRODUCTION** What factors of production are shown here?

Free Enterprise

In any economy, individuals and nations must answer three fundamental, or basic, economic questions: *what to produce, how to produce,* and *for whom to produce.* They must decide which goods and services to produce and how much to produce. They must decide the best way in which to produce the goods and services. They must also decide who they want to sell their goods and services to and how much to charge for them.

Providing Goods and Services

In a **free enterprise** economy, such as the United States, these questions are answered by people and businesses. People are free to own and run their own businesses with only limited control by the government. They produce the goods and services that consumers, or buyers, want. In turn, consumers are free to make economic choices about which products and services to buy or not to buy.

To produce any good or provide any service, a business needs different kinds of resources. It must have workers, or **human resources**. It must have natural resources, such as water, minerals, and fuel. It must also have capital, or money, and capital goods. **Capital goods**, also called capital resources, are the land, buildings, machines, and tools needed to produce goods and services. Together, human, natural, and capital resources are called the factors of production.

READING CHECK ⏀**SUMMARIZE**
What are the fundamental economic questions?

555

Using Scarce Resources

The resources needed to produce goods and services are limited. So is the money needed to buy goods and services. There are not enough resources to provide an unlimited supply of goods and services. This **scarcity** means that people can never have everything that they might want. They must make choices about how to use resources, what to produce, and what to buy.

Allocation Resources

Different societies have different allocation methods, or ways of distributing scarce goods and services. In some places, goods and services are shared equally or are divided on a first-come-first-served basis. In some places, they are rationed— only a certain amount is made available. In other places, people barter goods and services among themselves, or they may use a lottery system so that everyone has an equal chance to get them.

Different economic systems have different allocation methods. In countries with a **command economy**, the government controls the factors of production. It tells business owners exactly what to make, how much to make, and what to charge. It tells consumers what and how much they can buy.

In a **market economy**, like the United States, goods and services are allocated largely by prices. Consumers buy goods and services they want and can afford. Producers want to make a profit and see their businesses grow. They produce goods and services that they can sell.

READING CHECK COMPARE AND CONTRAST
How is a market economy different from a command economy?

▶ **A MARKET ECONOMY** In a market economy, consumers decide which goods are most important to purchase.

DIAGRAM Supply and demand affect prices. What factors usually cause prices to rise?

A Market Economy

In a market economy, people base their economic choices in part on prices. They must decide if the benefit of having a good or service is equal to its price.

Prices and Competition

Prices are affected by consumers' demand for a good or service. If the demand increases, prices usually rise. If there are only a few copies of a popular video game, its price is likely to be high. If the demand decreases, prices will fall.

Prices are also affected by the supply of a good or service. If businesses increase the amount of a good they produce, then prices usually fall. If businesses decrease the supply of a good, prices tend to rise.

Competition also affects prices. **Competition** is the contest among businesses to sell the most products. To get people to buy products, businesses may lower prices. If the manufacturer of a video game lowers the price from $100 to $50, more people will be willing to buy the game. Demand will rise, and the business will make more of it. If the demand continues to rise, the supply may go down. Prices may rise again.

When many businesses produce the same goods, they may lower prices so that more people will buy their products. They might also try to make higher-quality products or have better service. Without competition, prices often rise and quality suffers. Competition among consumers for a product may also cause its price to rise.

READING CHECK CAUSE AND EFFECT
How do supply and demand affect prices?

Productivity

In a market economy, producers decide what to produce based on supply and demand. **Productivity** is the measure of how many resources are needed to produce goods and services.

Productive Capacity

Several factors affect the amount of goods and services a business can produce. First among these is an educated workforce. Workers with more skills and knowledge are able to develop better work methods, and they can adapt more easily to new jobs. Workers with more skills are usually able to produce more than workers with fewer skills.

Capital goods also affect productivity. Without the latest and best tools and technologies, companies usually produce fewer goods and services.

Another important factor in productivity is **specialization**, or becoming skilled at one kind of job. When people specialize in a certain job or task, they are usually able to complete it more quickly.

Specialization also allows for division of labor, or dividing work so that each worker does only part of a larger job. Division of labor increases productivity. It allows companies to use assembly lines to make products cheaper and faster.

Interdependence

Each day, people in different states and in different regions of the United States and the world buy and sell goods and services. That is because no one place has all the resources that the people and businesses may want. No one state, region, or nation can produce all the goods and services that people want.

▶ **SKILLED WORKERS** help increase the amount of goods and services that a business can produce.

▶ **INTERDEPENDENCE** Regions have different natural resources and produce different goods.

People in cities such as New York City and Los Angeles depend on farming regions in the Midwest for food. They may also depend on other countries for certain foods. In this way, people in different places are **interdependent**—they depend on one another for natural resources, finished products, and services.

READING CHECK ◌ **SUMMARIZE**
Why are different regions interdependent?

Summary

In the free enterprise economy of the United States, people make decisions about how to use their resources with only limited control by the government. Several factors of production affect the productivity of businesses. Businesses offer goods and services that consumers want and can afford.

REVIEW

1. **WHAT TO KNOW** How does the free enterprise economy of the United States work?

2. **VOCABULARY** Write a sentence or two explaining how **specialization** affects **productivity**.

3. **ECONOMICS** How do people deal with the problem of scarcity?

4. **CRITICAL THINKING** How might productivity levels affect consumers?

5. **MAKE A POSTER** Make a poster explaining the three fundamental economic questions and how producers decide what to produce.

6. **SUMMARIZE** On a separate sheet of paper, copy and complete this graphic organizer.

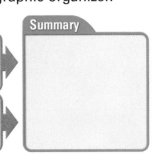

Key Facts	Summary
A rising demand leads to a larger supply. →	
A larger supply leads to lower prices. →	

Lesson

A Global Economy

WHAT TO KNOW

How has the economy of the United States changed in the past 100 years?

VOCABULARY

service industry p. 561
high-tech p. 561
globalization p. 563

SUMMARIZE

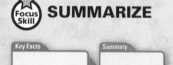

YOU ARE THERE

You are on vacation in New York City. Today, you are visiting your aunt, who works at the New York Stock Exchange on Wall Street. Everyone working there looks extremely busy.

"The New York Stock Exchange is very important," your aunt says to you. "People around the world buy and sell stocks on the New York Stock Exchange."

As you listen to your aunt, you think about how people from all over the world work together to trade stocks.

▶ THE NEW YORK STOCK EXCHANGE

▶ **WORKERS** such as veterinarians work in the service industry.

A Changing Economy

The economy of the United States is changing all the time. Early in its history, the economy was based on agriculture. By the 1900s, the economy was based on manufacturing products like cars or steel.

Service Industries

The United States is still a leading producer of manufactured goods. However, service industries now make up the largest part of the United States economy. **Service industries** are industries that provide services to other people. Today, more Americans work in service jobs than in any other kinds of jobs. They may be doctors, lawyers, or teachers. They may repair cars, cut hair, or work in restaurants.

The Information Age

The 1970s marked the beginning of the Information Age. This period in history has been defined by the growing amount of information available to people.

In recent years, high-tech industries have become more and more important to the American economy. **High-tech** industries are those that invent, build, or use computers and other kinds of electronic equipment. They make it easier for people to communicate, travel, trade goods and services, and organize information. One example of this new technology is the global positioning system, also known as GPS. GPS allows people to find their exact location on Earth.

READING CHECK **MAIN IDEA AND DETAILS**
What industry do most Americans work in today?

561

Free Trade

Just as states and regions are interdependent, the United States also relies on other countries for some resources, goods, and services.

Cooperation and Conflict

The United States and many other countries are interdependent. Modern transportation and communication systems have made it easier for people in one country to trade with people in other countries. Goods from the United States are exported to places all over the world. The United States also imports many goods from other countries.

To increase international trade, many countries have signed free-trade agreements. A free-trade agreement is a treaty in which countries agree not to restrict trade by charging tariffs, or taxes, on goods they buy from and sell to each other. Such an agreement gives industries in each of the trading nations a chance to compete better. In 1994, Mexico, Canada, and the United States put the North American Free Trade Agreement, or NAFTA, into effect.

NAFTA requires the United States and its neighbors to cooperate on issues of trade. Trade has increased, and prices on some goods have fallen. However, NAFTA has also caused conflict. While some new jobs were created in the United

▶ SHIPPING Goods and resources are shipped to ports all over the world.

States, other jobs were lost. Some companies moved jobs to other countries, where workers are paid less. Workers from other countries, especially Mexico, have tried to enter the United States illegally. Illegal immigration has led to conflicts between the nations.

Globalization

International trade adds much to the economy of the United States. The United States also interacts with other countries in other ways. Many companies in the United States have offices and factories in other countries. Many foreign companies also have businesses in the United States.

This means that the nations of the world have experienced **globalization**, or the growth of a global economy. The global economy is the world market in which companies from different countries buy and sell goods and services.

READING CHECK ☝ **SUMMARIZE**
Why are countries more interdependent?

United States Top Export Markets

COUNTRY	DOLLAR AMOUNT
Canada	💵💵💵💵💵 💵💵💵💵💵
Mexico	💵💵💵💵💵💵
China	💵💵💵
Japan	💵💵💵
United Kingdom	💵💵

💵 = 25 billion dollars

GRAPH The United States exports goods to different countries. How much did the U.S. export to Japan?

Summary

Most Americans today work in service industries. Free trade allows countries to easily exchange goods. The United States trades with many other nations, creating interdependent relationships.

REVIEW

1. **WHAT TO KNOW** How has the economy of the United States changed in the past 100 years?

2. **VOCABULARY** Use the word **globalization** in a sentence about trade between nations.

3. **HISTORY** What three countries signed NAFTA?

4. **CRITICAL THINKING** Why do you think high-tech industries have become important in recent years?

5. ✎ **WRITE A LETTER TO THE EDITOR** Write a letter to the editor of a newspaper explaining the advantages or the disadvantages of globalization.

6. (Focus Skill) **SUMMARIZE** On a separate sheet of paper, copy and complete this graphic organizer.

Key Facts		Summary
The United States trades with other nations.	➤	
Other nations gain resources from the United States.	➤	

Lesson

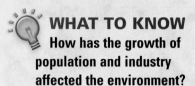

3

WHAT TO KNOW
How has the growth of population and industry affected the environment?

VOCABULARY

urban sprawl p. 565

SUMMARIZE

Growth and the Environment

YOU ARE THERE You and your family are at a city council meeting. Everyone is discussing whether to build a public park in your neighborhood. Some people at the meeting want to build a mall instead.

Some people say that a mall will be good for the economy. Others say that a public park will be better for the environment. At the end of the meeting, the city council members vote to build a public park.

▶ **CITY COUNCILS** Members of city councils meet to find ways to deal with fast growth and changes to the environment.

564

▶ **NEW SUBURBS** As the population continues to grow, more homes are built.

The Effects of Growth

The United States is a growing country. In 1990, the population was about 248 million people. Ten years later it was 281 million. Today, more than 300 million people live in the United States. Most of them live in cities.

Crowded and Open Places

The United States is a huge country. In some places, there are few people or none at all. However, the metropolitan areas in some parts of the United States are among the most densely settled areas in the world.

Population growth causes growth in housing. Since 1980, more than 10 million acres of what was open land and forest have been used for new houses, apartment buildings, roads, and businesses. That is more than twice the size of four of the largest national parks combined. This spread of urban areas is sometimes called **urban sprawl**.

Growth creates jobs. It also affects the environment as people clear land for building. Water, land, and even wildlife have been affected. People's actions sometimes damage natural resources.

Population growth also means that more water and electricity are needed. More people in an area means more cars, traffic, and air pollution. Many communities work hard to balance growth and protect the environment.

READING CHECK ⏻SUMMARIZE
How might population growth affect the environment?

Changing the Environment

People change the environment in many ways. They build bridges and highways. They build dams across rivers and irrigate the land. All these actions help make life easier for people, but they can also affect the environment.

Consequences of Change

The interstate highway system, for example, allows people to travel and transport goods. But highways are sometimes built through forests or other types of natural land. This affects the plants and animals that live there.

Many rivers flow into and out of bodies of water, such as the Great Lakes. Ships can travel all over the world from Great Lakes ports. They can use the St. Lawrence Seaway to reach the Atlantic Ocean or the Illinois Waterway to reach the Mississippi River and the Gulf of Mexico. Navigation through the Great Lakes has improved shipping, but it has also affected the environment there.

People sometimes bring different species of plants and animals to an area. These new species can harm the plants and animals already in the area. For example, ships sailing the Great Lakes have brought zebra mussels to places where they did not exist before. The zebra mussel can damage fish and plants.

Conflict and Cooperation

Today, many farmers rely on the Rio Grande for irrigation. However, people in Colorado and New Mexico used so much of the Rio Grande's water that sometimes people downstream, in Mexico, did not have enough. This caused conflicts.

The Rio Grande supplies water for more than half of all irrigated land in Mexico. To protect Mexico's use of the river, the United States has agreed that a certain amount of water must reach Mexico.

▶ **HIGHWAYS** Land is often cleared to make room for new highways.

▶ **THE RIO GRANDE** is used by people in the Southwest and in Mexico.

The United States and other countries around the world often cooperate to use resources. They also work together to conserve nonrenewable resources. At the same time, engineers and scientists are working to develop affordable energy from renewable resources.

READING CHECK Ð**SUMMARIZE**
How do people change the environment?

Summary

Almost 300 million people live in the United States. Most people live in cities. Americans change the environment in many ways. These changes have positive and negative effects. At times, the United States and other nations must work together to share natural resources and protect the environment.

REVIEW

1. **WHAT TO KNOW** How has the growth of population and industry affect the environment?

2. **VOCABULARY** Use the term **urban sprawl** in a sentence about growing communities.

3. **GEOGRAPHY** How are the Great Lakes connected to the Atlantic Ocean and the Gulf of Mexico?

4. **CRITICAL THINKING** Why do you think it was important for the United States and Mexico to come to an agreement about the use of the Rio Grande?

5. **CREATE A POSTER** Create a poster that shows people how to help protect the environment.

6. **SUMMARIZE**
   On a separate sheet of paper, copy and complete this graphic organizer.

Key Facts	Summary
People have developed land for housing and businesses.	
People can hurt the land when they develop it.	

567

For Your Reference

ATLAS/ALMANAC

AMERICAN DOCUMENTS

RESEARCH HANDBOOK

BIOGRAPHICAL DICTIONARY

GAZETTEER

GLOSSARY

INDEX

The World: Political

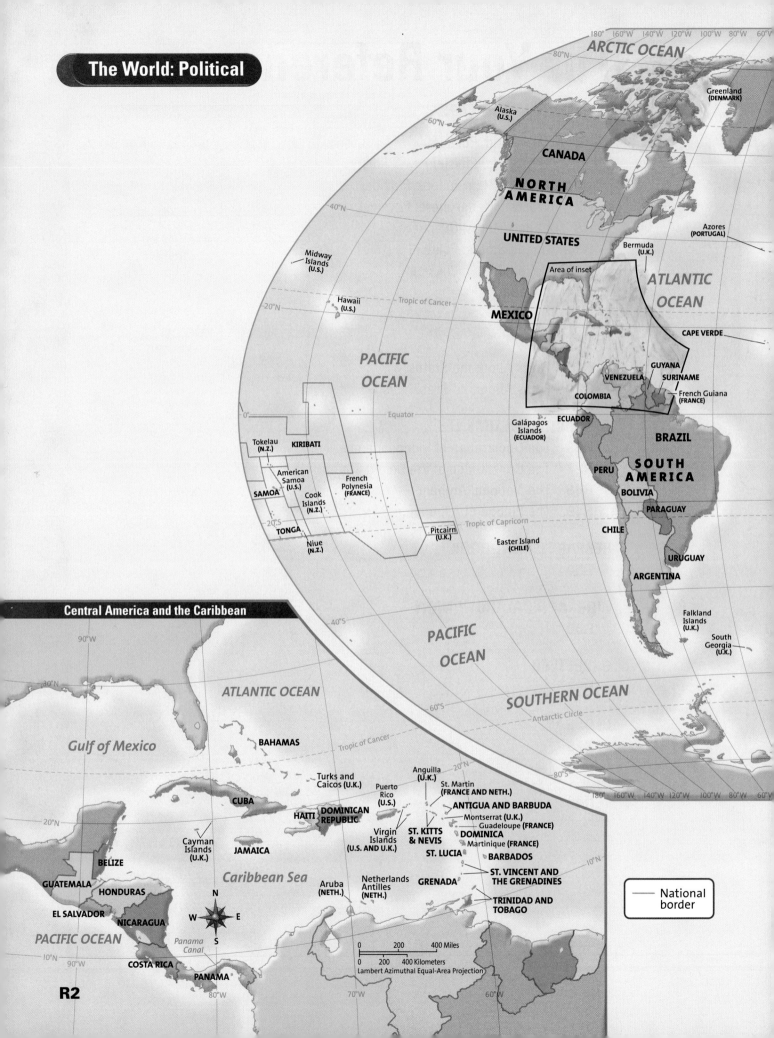

ARCTIC OCEAN

Greenland (DENMARK)

Alaska (U.S.)

CANADA

NORTH AMERICA

UNITED STATES

Azores (PORTUGAL)

Bermuda (U.S.)

Area of inset

ATLANTIC OCEAN

Midway Islands (U.S.)

Tropic of Cancer

Hawaii (U.S.)

MEXICO

CAPE VERDE

PACIFIC OCEAN

GUYANA

VENEZUELA

SURINAME

COLOMBIA

French Guiana (FRANCE)

Equator

Galápagos Islands (ECUADOR)

ECUADOR

BRAZIL

Tokelau (N.Z.)

KIRIBATI

PERU

SOUTH AMERICA

American Samoa (U.S.)

French Polynesia (FRANCE)

BOLIVIA

SAMOA

Cook Islands (N.Z.)

PARAGUAY

TONGA

Pitcairn (U.K.)

CHILE

Tropic of Capricorn

Niue (N.Z.)

Easter Island (CHILE)

URUGUAY

ARGENTINA

PACIFIC OCEAN

Falkland Islands (U.K.)

South Georgia (U.K.)

SOUTHERN OCEAN

Antarctic Circle

Central America and the Caribbean

ATLANTIC OCEAN

Gulf of Mexico

BAHAMAS

Tropic of Cancer

Turks and Caicos (U.K.)

Anguilla (U.K.)

St. Martin (FRANCE AND NETH.)

CUBA

Puerto Rico (U.S.)

ANTIGUA AND BARBUDA

HAITI

DOMINICAN REPUBLIC

Montserrat (U.K.)

Guadeloupe (FRANCE)

Cayman Islands (U.K.)

Virgin Islands (U.S. AND U.K.)

ST. KITTS & NEVIS

DOMINICA

Martinique (FRANCE)

JAMAICA

ST. LUCIA

BELIZE

Caribbean Sea

Aruba (NETH.)

Netherlands Antilles (NETH.)

BARBADOS

GUATEMALA

GRENADA

ST. VINCENT AND THE GRENADINES

HONDURAS

N

EL SALVADOR

W E

PACIFIC OCEAN

NICARAGUA

S

Panama Canal

TRINIDAD AND TOBAGO

COSTA RICA

PANAMA

0 200 400 Miles

0 200 400 Kilometers

Lambert Azimuthal Equal-Area Projection

National border

R2

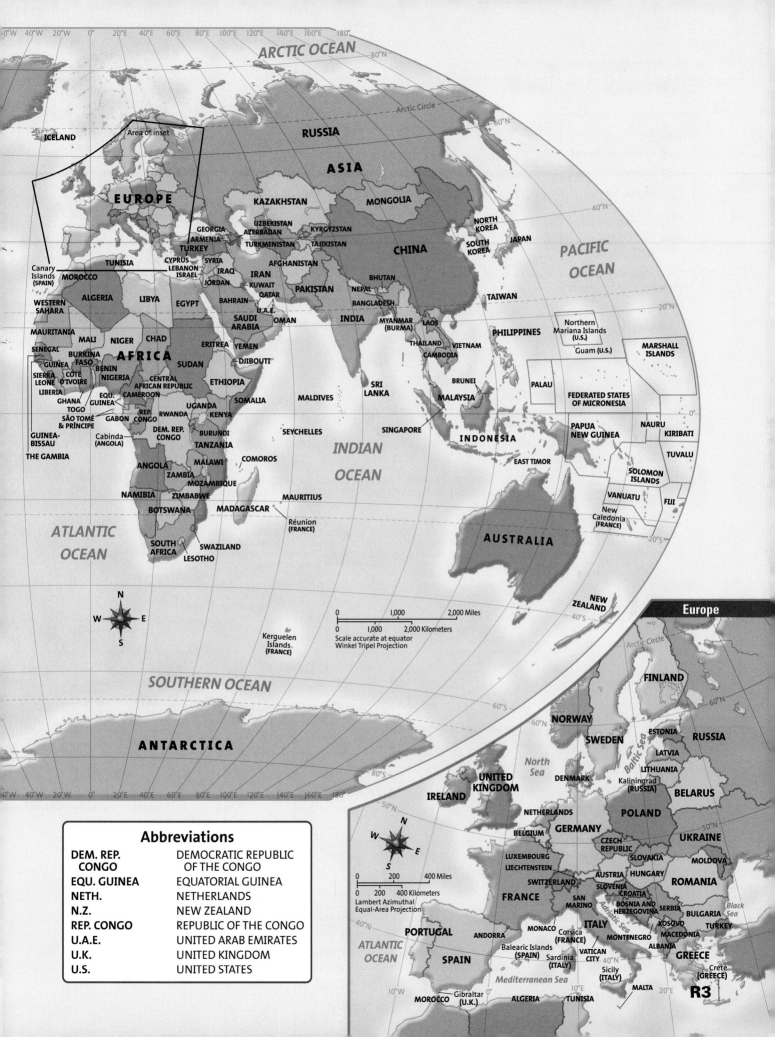

ARCTIC OCEAN

80°N

Arctic Circle

60°N

RUSSIA

ASIA

EUROPE

ICELAND

Area of inset

KAZAKHSTAN

MONGOLIA

40°N

NORTH KOREA

JAPAN

PACIFIC OCEAN

GEORGIA
ARMENIA
AZERBAIJAN
TURKEY
UZBEKISTAN
KYRGYZSTAN
TURKMENISTAN
TAJIKISTAN

CHINA

SOUTH KOREA

TUNISIA

CYPRUS
LEBANON
ISRAEL

SYRIA

AFGHANISTAN

Canary
Islands
(SPAIN)

MOROCCO

IRAQ
JORDAN

IRAN

PAKISTAN

BHUTAN

NEPAL

TAIWAN

20°N

ALGERIA

LIBYA

EGYPT

KUWAIT
BAHRAIN

QATAR

SAUDI
ARABIA

U.A.E.

OMAN

INDIA

BANGLADESH

MYANMAR
(BURMA)

LAOS

PHILIPPINES

Northern
Mariana
Islands
(U.S.)

MARSHALL
ISLANDS

WESTERN
SAHARA

MAURITANIA

MALI

NIGER

CHAD

ERITREA

YEMEN

DJIBOUTI

THAILAND

VIETNAM

CAMBODIA

Guam (U.S.)

SENEGAL

BURKINA
FASO

AFRICA

SUDAN

ETHIOPIA

SRI
LANKA

MALDIVES

BRUNEI

PALAU

FEDERATED STATES
OF MICRONESIA

0°

GUINEA

SIERRA
LEONE

CÔTE
D'IVOIRE

BENIN

NIGERIA

CENTRAL
AFRICAN REPUBLIC

CAMEROON

EQU.
GUINEA

GHANA

LIBERIA

TOGO

SÃO TOMÉ
& PRÍNCIPE

GABON

REP.
CONGO

UGANDA

RWANDA

KENYA

SOMALIA

MALAYSIA

SINGAPORE

INDONESIA

PAPUA
NEW GUINEA

NAURU

KIRIBATI

GUINEA-
BISSAU

Cabinda
(ANGOLA)

DEM. REP.
CONGO

BURUNDI

TANZANIA

SEYCHELLES

INDIAN

OCEAN

EAST TIMOR

TUVALU

THE GAMBIA

ANGOLA

ZAMBIA

MALAWI

COMOROS

SOLOMON
ISLANDS

MOZAMBIQUE

NAMIBIA

ZIMBABWE

MAURITIUS

VANUATU

FIJI

BOTSWANA

MADAGASCAR

Réunion
(FRANCE)

AUSTRALIA

New
Caledonia
(FRANCE)

20°S

ATLANTIC

OCEAN

SOUTH
AFRICA

SWAZILAND

LESOTHO

N
W   E
S

Kerguelen
Islands
(FRANCE)

0   1,000   2,000 Miles

0   1,000   2,000 Kilometers

Scale accurate at equator
Winkel Tripel Projection

NEW
ZEALAND

N.Z.

40°S

SOUTHERN OCEAN

ANTARCTICA

60°S

80°S

Abbreviations

DEM. REP. CONGO	DEMOCRATIC REPUBLIC OF THE CONGO
EQU. GUINEA	EQUATORIAL GUINEA
NETH.	NETHERLANDS
N.Z.	NEW ZEALAND
REP. CONGO	REPUBLIC OF THE CONGO
U.A.E.	UNITED ARAB EMIRATES
U.K.	UNITED KINGDOM
U.S.	UNITED STATES

FINLAND

NORWAY

SWEDEN

ESTONIA

RUSSIA

LATVIA

LITHUANIA

Baltic Sea

Kaliningrad
(RUSSIA)

BELARUS

IRELAND

UNITED
KINGDOM

North
Sea

DENMARK

NETHERLANDS

GERMANY

POLAND

UKRAINE

BELGIUM

LUXEMBOURG

CZECH
REPUBLIC

SLOVAKIA

MOLDOVA

LIECHTENSTEIN

AUSTRIA

HUNGARY

ROMANIA

FRANCE

SWITZERLAND

SAN
MARINO

SLOVENIA

CROATIA

BOSNIA AND
HERZEGOVINA

SERBIA

Adriatic Sea

BULGARIA

Black
Sea

MONACO

Corsica
(FRANCE)

ITALY

MONTENEGRO

KOSOVO

MACEDONIA

TURKEY

PORTUGAL

ANDORRA

Balearic Islands
(SPAIN)

Sardinia
(ITALY)

VATICAN
CITY

ALBANIA

GREECE

ATLANTIC
OCEAN

SPAIN

Mediterranean Sea

Sicily
(ITALY)

MALTA

Crete
(GREECE)

MOROCCO

Gibraltar
(U.K.)

ALGERIA

TUNISIA

N
W   E
S

0   200   400 Miles

0   200   400 Kilometers

Lambert Azimuthal
Equal-Area Projection

R3

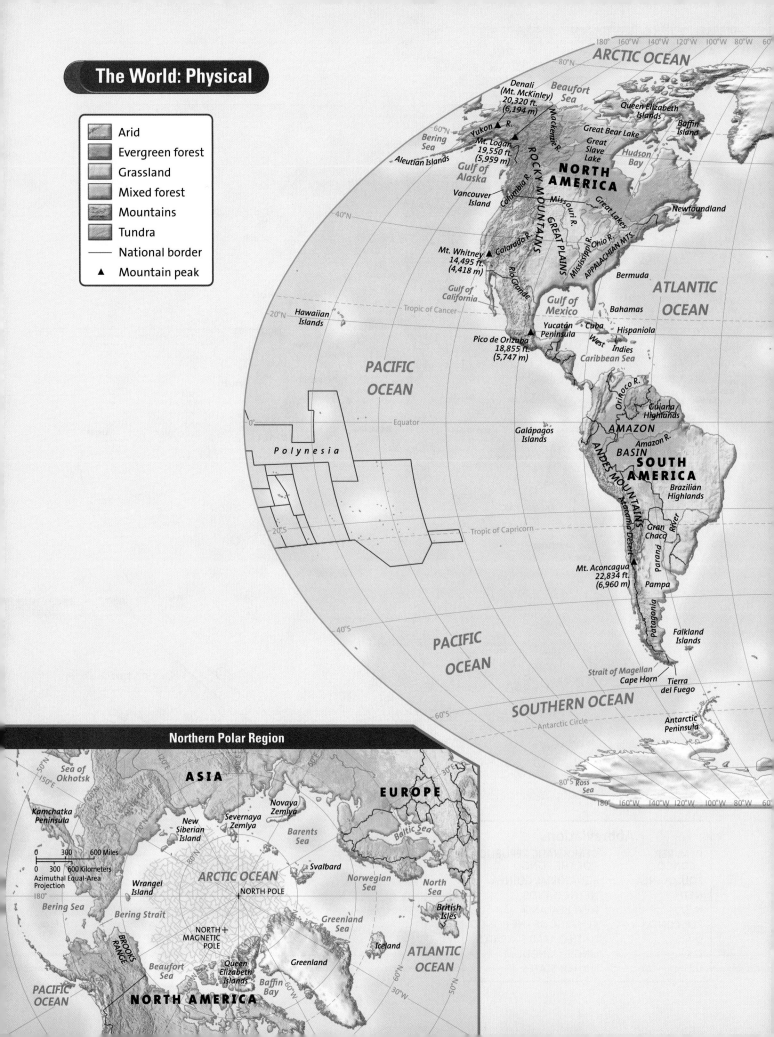

The World: Physical

Legend:
- Arid
- Evergreen forest
- Grassland
- Mixed forest
- Mountains
- Tundra
- National border
- ▲ Mountain peak

ARCTIC OCEAN

Beaufort Sea

Denali (Mt. McKinley) 20,320 ft. (6,194 m)

Queen Elizabeth Islands

Baffin Island

Yukon R.
Bering Sea

Mt. Logan 19,550 ft. (5,959 m)

Great Bear Lake

Great Slave Lake

Hudson Bay

Aleutian Islands

Gulf of Alaska

NORTH AMERICA

Vancouver Island

Columbia R.

ROCKY MOUNTAINS

Missouri R.

Great Lakes

Newfoundland

Mt. Whitney 14,495 ft. (4,418 m)

Colorado R.

GREAT PLAINS

Mississippi R.
Ohio R.
APPALACHIAN MTS.

Rio Grande

Bermuda

Gulf of California

Gulf of Mexico

Bahamas

ATLANTIC OCEAN

Tropic of Cancer

Hawaiian Islands

Pico de Orizaba 18,855 ft. (5,747 m)

Yucatán Peninsula

Cuba

Hispaniola

West Indies

Caribbean Sea

PACIFIC OCEAN

Equator

Galápagos Islands

Orinoco R.

Guiana Highlands

AMAZON

Amazon R.

BASIN

SOUTH AMERICA

Brazilian Highlands

Polynesia

ANDES MOUNTAINS

Atacama Desert

Paraná River

Gran Chaco

Tropic of Capricorn

Mt. Aconcagua 22,834 ft. (6,960 m)

Pampa

PACIFIC OCEAN

Patagonia

Falkland Islands

Strait of Magellan
Cape Horn

Tierra del Fuego

SOUTHERN OCEAN

Antarctic Circle

Antarctic Peninsula

Ross Sea

Northern Polar Region

Sea of Okhotsk

ASIA

Novaya Zemlya

EUROPE

Kamchatka Peninsula

New Siberian Island

Severnaya Zemlya

Barents Sea

Baltic Sea

Wrangel Island

ARCTIC OCEAN

Svalbard

Norwegian Sea

North Sea

British Isles

0   300   600 Miles
0   300   600 Kilometers
Azimuthal Equal-Area Projection

NORTH POLE

Bering Sea

Bering Strait

NORTH + MAGNETIC POLE

Greenland Sea

Iceland

ATLANTIC OCEAN

BROOKS RANGE

Beaufort Sea

Queen Elizabeth Islands

Greenland

Baffin Bay

PACIFIC OCEAN

NORTH AMERICA

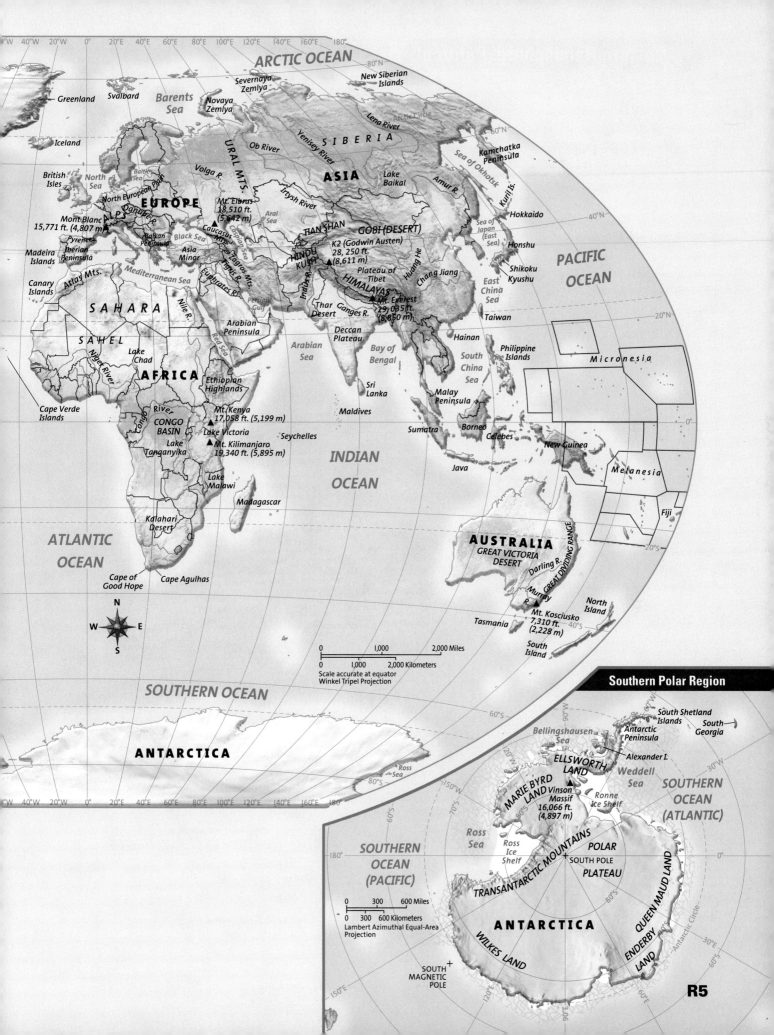

ARCTIC OCEAN

Greenland
Svalbard
Severnaya Zemlya
New Siberian Islands
Barents Sea
Novaya Zemlya
Iceland
URAL MTS.
SIBERIA
Lena River
Kamchatka Peninsula
British Isles
North Sea
Baltic Sea
North European Plain
Ob River
Yenisey River
ASIA
Lake Baikal
Sea of Okhotsk
Kuril Is.
EUROPE
ALPS
Danube R.
Volga R.
Irtysh River
Mt. Elbrus 18,510 ft. (5,642 m)
Aral Sea
TIAN SHAN
GOBI (DESERT)
Amur R.
Sea of Japan (East Sea)
Hokkaido
Mont Blanc 15,771 ft. (4,807 m)
Pyrenees
Balkan Peninsula
Black Sea
Asia Minor
Caucasus Mts.
Zagros Mts.
Caspian Sea
HINDU KUSH
K2 (Godwin Austen) 28,250 ft. (8,611 m)
Plateau of Tibet
Huang He
Chang Jiang
Honshu
Shikoku
Kyushu
PACIFIC OCEAN
Madeira Islands
Iberian Peninsula
Tigris R.
Euphrates R.
HIMALAYAS
Mt. Everest 29,035 ft. (8,850 m)
East China Sea
Canary Islands
Atlas Mts.
Mediterranean Sea
Nile R.
Red Sea
Arabian Peninsula
Persian Gulf
Indus R.
Thar Desert
Ganges R.
Deccan Plateau
Taiwan
Hainan
SAHARA
SAHEL
Lake Chad
Niger River
Arabian Sea
Bay of Bengal
Philippine Islands
South China Sea
Micronesia
Cape Verde Islands
AFRICA
Congo River
CONGO BASIN
Ethiopian Highlands
Mt. Kenya 17,058 ft. (5,199 m)
Lake Victoria
Mt. Kilimanjaro 19,340 ft. (5,895 m)
Sri Lanka
Maldives
Seychelles
INDIAN OCEAN
Malay Peninsula
Sumatra
Borneo
Celebes
New Guinea
Lake Tanganyika
Lake Malawi
Java
Melanesia
Fiji
Madagascar
Kalahari Desert
AUSTRALIA
GREAT VICTORIA DESERT
Darling R.
GREAT DIVIDING RANGE
ATLANTIC OCEAN
Cape of Good Hope
Cape Agulhas
Murray R.
North Island
Mt. Kosciusko 7,310 ft. (2,228 m)
N W E S
Tasmania
South Island

0   1,000   2,000 Miles
0   1,000   2,000 Kilometers
Scale accurate at equator
Winkel Tripel Projection

SOUTHERN OCEAN

ANTARCTICA

Ross Sea

80°S

Southern Polar Region

South Shetland Islands
Bellingshausen Sea
Antarctic Peninsula
South Georgia
Alexander I.
ELLSWORTH LAND
Weddell Sea
SOUTHERN OCEAN (ATLANTIC)
MARIE BYRD LAND
Vinson Massif 16,066 ft. (4,897 m)
Ronne Ice Shelf
Ross Sea
Ross Ice Shelf
TRANSANTARCTIC MOUNTAINS
POLAR PLATEAU
SOUTH POLE
SOUTHERN OCEAN (PACIFIC)
QUEEN MAUD LAND
ANTARCTICA
WILKES LAND
ENDERBY LAND

0   300   600 Miles
0   300   600 Kilometers
Lambert Azimuthal Equal-Area Projection

SOUTH MAGNETIC POLE

R5

Western Hemisphere: Political

ARCTIC OCEAN

Bering Strait

Beaufort Sea

Viscount Melville Sound

Baffin Bay

Greenland
(DENMARK)

ALASKA
(U.S.)

Yukon River

Fairbanks

Anchorage

Whitehorse

Juneau

Gulf of Alaska

Mackenzie River

Liard River

Great Bear Lake

Yellowknife

Great Slave Lake

CANADA

Peace River

Athabasca R.

Lake Athabasca

Edmonton

Calgary

Saskatoon

Regina

Saskatchewan R.

Lake Winnipeg

Winnipeg

Foxe Basin

Hudson Strait

James Bay

Hudson Bay

Davis Strait

Arctic Circle

Labrador Sea

Bering Sea

60°N

Vancouver

Seattle

Portland

Puget Sound

Columbia R.

Boise

Snake R.

Reno

San Francisco

Las Vegas

Los Angeles

San Diego

Great Salt Lake

Salt Lake City

Denver

Colorado R.

Phoenix

Tucson

El Paso

UNITED STATES

Missouri R.

Mississippi R.

St. Louis

Chicago

Indianapolis

Memphis

Dallas

Thunder Bay

Great Lakes

Detroit

St. Lawrence River

Ottawa

Toronto

Cleveland

Albany

Montreal

Quebec

St. John

Halifax

St. John's

Gulf of St. Lawrence

Boston

New York City

Philadelphia

Washington, D.C.

Richmond

Norfolk

Atlanta

Raleigh

Charleston

ATLANTIC OCEAN

Hermosillo

Rio Grande

Houston

San Antonio

New Orleans

Savannah

Jacksonville

Tampa

Orlando

Miami

30°N

HAWAII
(U.S.)

Honolulu

PACIFIC OCEAN

Gulf of California

Chihuahua

MEXICO

Durango

Monterrey

Gulf of Mexico

Havana

CUBA

BAHAMAS

Nassau

HAITI

Port-au-Prince

Santo Domingo

Puerto Rico (U.S.)

DOMINICAN REPUBLIC

Tropic of Cancer

León

Guadalajara

Tampico

Mexico City

Puebla

Veracruz

Acapulco

Guatemala City

GUATEMALA

BELIZE

Belmopan

JAMAICA

Kingston

HONDURAS

San Salvador

Tegucigalpa

EL SALVADOR

Managua

NICARAGUA

San José

Caribbean Sea

Maracaibo

Caracas

VENEZUELA

GUYANA

SURINAME

Georgetown

Paramaribo

Cayenne

FRENCH GUIANA (FRANCE)

COSTA RICA

PANAMA

Panama City

Medellín

Cali

Bogotá

COLOMBIA

Quito

Guayaquil

ECUADOR

Galápagos Islands
(ECUADOR)

Iquitos

Rio Negro

Manaus

Amazon River

Belém

Fortaleza

Recife

Equator

0°

Papeete

French Polynesia
(FRANCE)

Trujillo

PERU

Lima

Cuzco

Lake Titicaca

La Paz

Arequipa

BOLIVIA

Sucre

Tapajós River

Xingu R.

Tocantins R.

BRAZIL

Brasília

São Francisco R.

Salvador

Belo Horizonte

Rio de Janeiro

São Paulo

Goiânia

Campo Grande

Antofagasta

PARAGUAY

Salta

Asunción

Paraguay R.

Curitiba

Tropic of Capricorn

San Miguel de Tucumán

Córdoba

CHILE

Paraná R.

Pôrto Alegre

URUGUAY

Valparaíso

Rosario

Santiago

Buenos Aires

La Plata

Montevideo

Rio de la Plata

Mar del Plata

Concepción

Bahía Blanca

30°S

Valdivia

ARGENTINA

Punta Arenas

Falkland Islands
(U.K.)

South Georgia
(U.K.)

Scale

0 — 1,000 — 2,000 Miles

0 — 1,000 — 2,000 Kilometers

Miller Cylindrical Projection

Legend

— National border

⊛ National capital

• City

N W E S

R6

150°W   120°W   90°W   60°W   30°W

Western Hemisphere: Physical

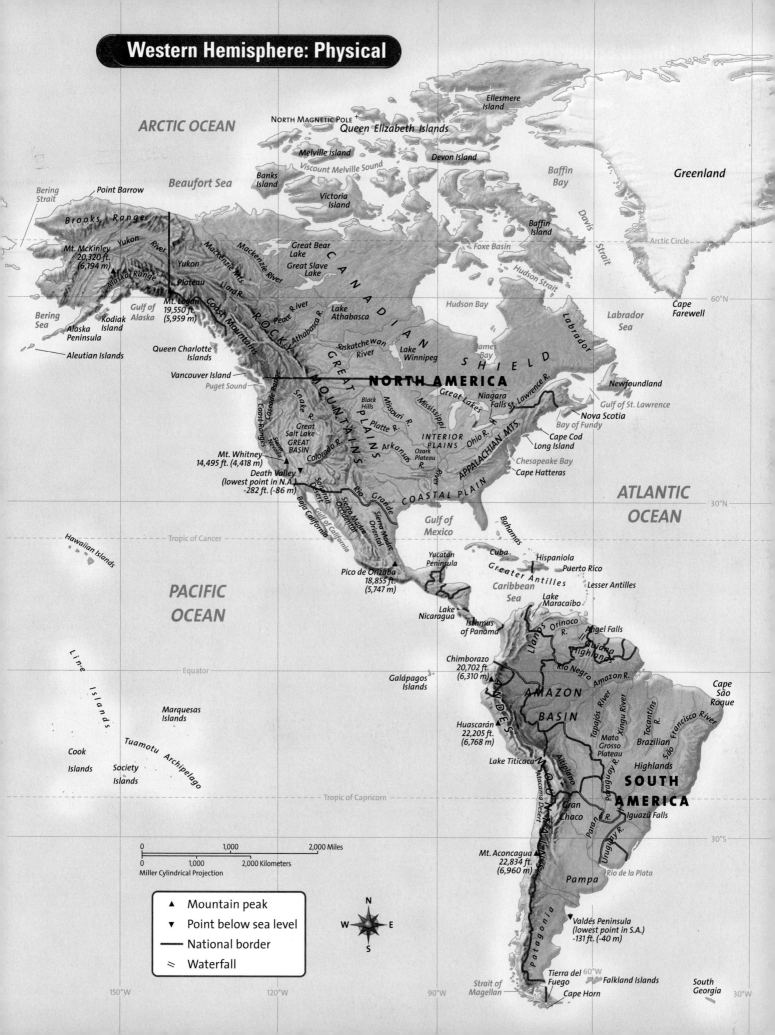

ARCTIC OCEAN

NORTH MAGNETIC POLE

Queen Elizabeth Islands

Ellesmere Island

Melville Island

Devon Island

Viscount Melville Sound

Banks Island

Baffin Bay

Greenland

Beaufort Sea

Victoria Island

Baffin Island

Bering Strait

Point Barrow

Brooks Range

Foxe Basin

Hudson Strait

Davis Strait

Cape Farewell

60°N

Mt. McKinley 20,320 ft. (6,194 m)

Yukon River

Mackenzie Mts.

Great Bear Lake

Great Slave Lake

Hudson Bay

James Bay

Labrador Sea

Alaska Range

Yukon Plateau

Mackenzie River

Labrador

Gulf of Alaska

Mt. Logan 19,550 ft. (5,959 m)

Liard R.

Peace River

Lake Athabasca

CANADIAN SHIELD

Bering Sea

Kodiak Island

Coast Mountains

Athabasca R.

Saskatchewan River

Lake Winnipeg

Newfoundland

Alaska Peninsula

Queen Charlotte Islands

ROCKY

GREAT

Gulf of St. Lawrence

Aleutian Islands

Vancouver Island

Cascade Range

NORTH AMERICA

Great Lakes

Niagara Falls

St. Lawrence R.

Nova Scotia

Puget Sound

Coast Ranges

MOUNTAINS

PLAINS

Black Hills

Missouri R.

Mississippi

Appalachian MTS.

Bay of Fundy

Cape Cod

Long Island

Snake R.

Sierra Nevada

Great Salt Lake GREAT BASIN

Platte R.

INTERIOR PLAINS

Ohio R.

Chesapeake Bay

Mt. Whitney 14,495 ft. (4,418 m)

Colorado R.

Arkansas

Ozark Plateau

Mississippi River

Cape Hatteras

Death Valley (lowest point in N.A.) -282 ft. (-86 m)

Sonoran Desert

Rio Grande

COASTAL PLAIN

ATLANTIC OCEAN

30°N

Sierra Madre Occidental

Sierra Madre Oriental

Gulf of Mexico

Bahamas

Tropic of Cancer

Baja California

Gulf of California

Hawaiian Islands

Yucatán Peninsula

Cuba

Hispaniola

Puerto Rico

Pico de Orizaba 18,855 ft. (5,747 m)

Greater Antilles

Lesser Antilles

Caribbean Sea

Lake Maracaibo

PACIFIC OCEAN

Galápagos Islands

Lake Nicaragua

Isthmus of Panama

Llanos

Orinoco R.

Angel Falls

Guiana Highlands

Chimborazo 20,702 ft. (6,310 m)

Río Negro

Amazon R.

Cape São Roque

Equator

AMAZON BASIN

Line Islands

Marquesas Islands

ANDES

Tapajós River

Xingu River

Tocantins R.

São Francisco River

Huascarán 22,205 ft. (6,768 m)

Mato Grosso Plateau

Brazilian Highlands

Cook Islands

Tuamotu Archipelago

Society Islands

Lake Titicaca

Altiplano

SOUTH AMERICA

Atacama Desert

Paraguay R.

Tropic of Capricorn

ANDES MTS.

Gran Chaco

Paraná R.

Iguazú Falls

Mt. Aconcagua 22,834 ft. (6,960 m)

Uruguay R.

30°S

Pampa

Rio de la Plata

Valdés Peninsula (lowest point in S.A.) -131 ft. (-40 m)

Patagonia

0   1,000   2,000 Miles

0   1,000   2,000 Kilometers

Miller Cylindrical Projection

▲ Mountain peak

▼ Point below sea level

— National border

≈ Waterfall

N W E S

Tierra del Fuego

Strait of Magellan

Cape Horn

60°W

Falkland Islands

South Georgia

150°W   120°W   90°W   60°W   30°W

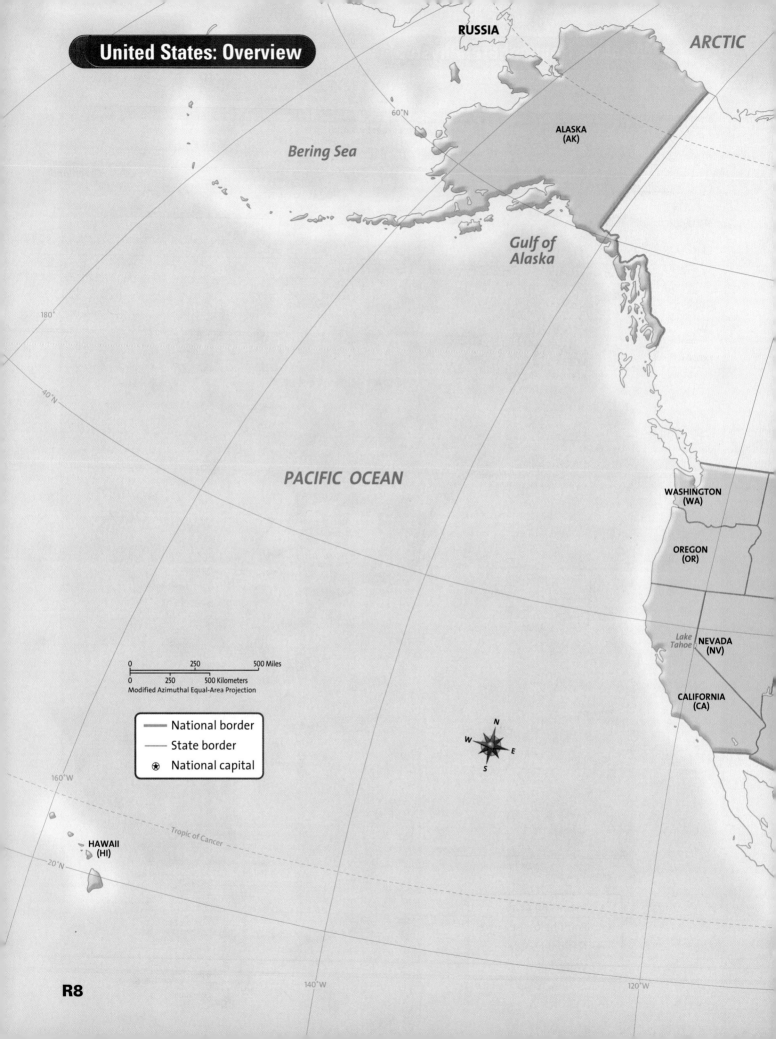

RUSSIA

ARCTIC

60°N

Bering Sea

ALASKA
(AK)

Gulf of
Alaska

180°

40°N

PACIFIC OCEAN

WASHINGTON
(WA)

OREGON
(OR)

Lake
Tahoe

NEVADA
(NV)

CALIFORNIA
(CA)

0   250   500 Miles

0   250   500 Kilometers
Modified Azimuthal Equal-Area Projection

N
W   E
S

——— National border
——— State border
⊛ National capital

160°W

Tropic of Cancer

HAWAII
(HI)

20°N

140°W

120°W

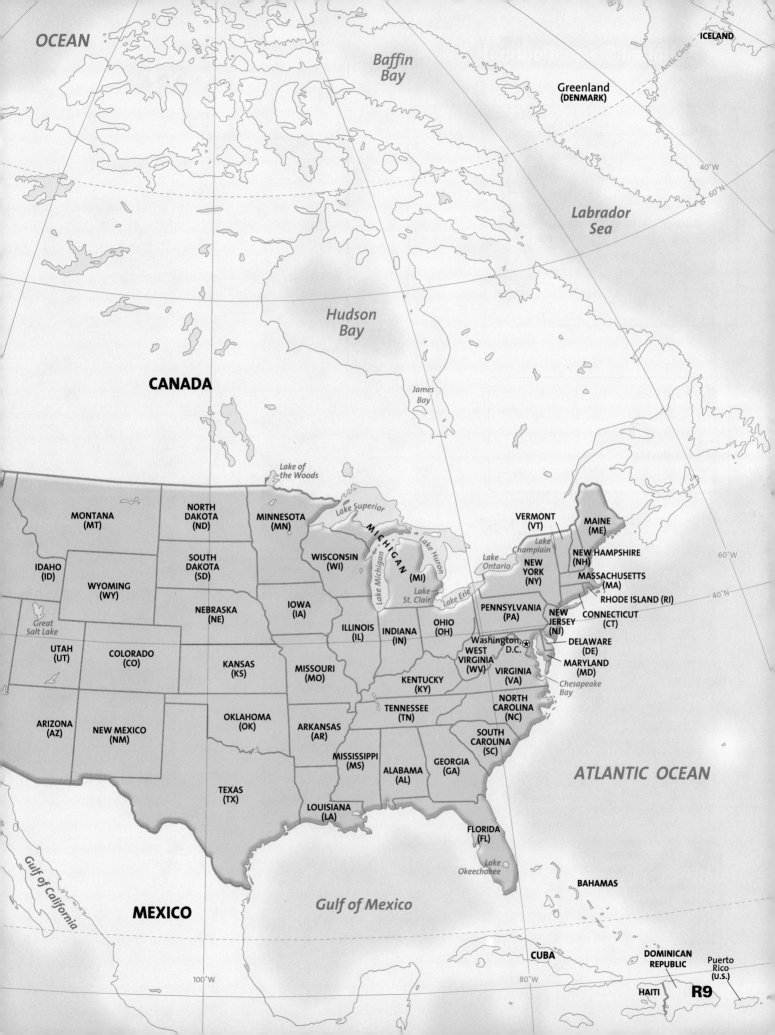

OCEAN

ICELAND

Baffin
Bay

Greenland
(DENMARK)

Labrador
Sea

Hudson
Bay

James
Bay

CANADA

Lake of
the Woods

Lake Superior

MONTANA
(MT)

NORTH
DAKOTA
(ND)

MINNESOTA
(MN)

VERMONT
(VT)

MAINE
(ME)

IDAHO
(ID)

SOUTH
DAKOTA
(SD)

WISCONSIN
(WI)

MICHIGAN

Lake Huron

Lake
Champlain

NEW HAMPSHIRE
(NH)

WYOMING
(WY)

(MI)

Lake
Ontario

NEW
YORK
(NY)

MASSACHUSETTS
(MA)

Great
Salt Lake

NEBRASKA
(NE)

IOWA
(IA)

Lake Michigan

Lake
St. Clair

Lake Erie

RHODE ISLAND (RI)

PENNSYLVANIA
(PA)

CONNECTICUT
(CT)

UTAH
(UT)

COLORADO
(CO)

ILLINOIS
(IL)

INDIANA
(IN)

OHIO
(OH)

Washington,
D.C.

NEW
JERSEY
(NJ)

DELAWARE
(DE)

KANSAS
(KS)

MISSOURI
(MO)

WEST
VIRGINIA
(WV)

VIRGINIA
(VA)

MARYLAND
(MD)

ARIZONA
(AZ)

NEW MEXICO
(NM)

OKLAHOMA
(OK)

ARKANSAS
(AR)

KENTUCKY
(KY)

TENNESSEE
(TN)

NORTH
CAROLINA
(NC)

Chesapeake
Bay

MISSISSIPPI
(MS)

ALABAMA
(AL)

GEORGIA
(GA)

SOUTH
CAROLINA
(SC)

ATLANTIC OCEAN

TEXAS
(TX)

LOUISIANA
(LA)

FLORIDA
(FL)

Gulf of California

MEXICO

Lake
Okeechobee

BAHAMAS

Gulf of Mexico

CUBA

DOMINICAN
REPUBLIC

Puerto
Rico
(U.S.)

HAITI

R9

60°W

40°N

60°N

40°W

60°N

Arctic Circle

100°W

80°W

United States: Political

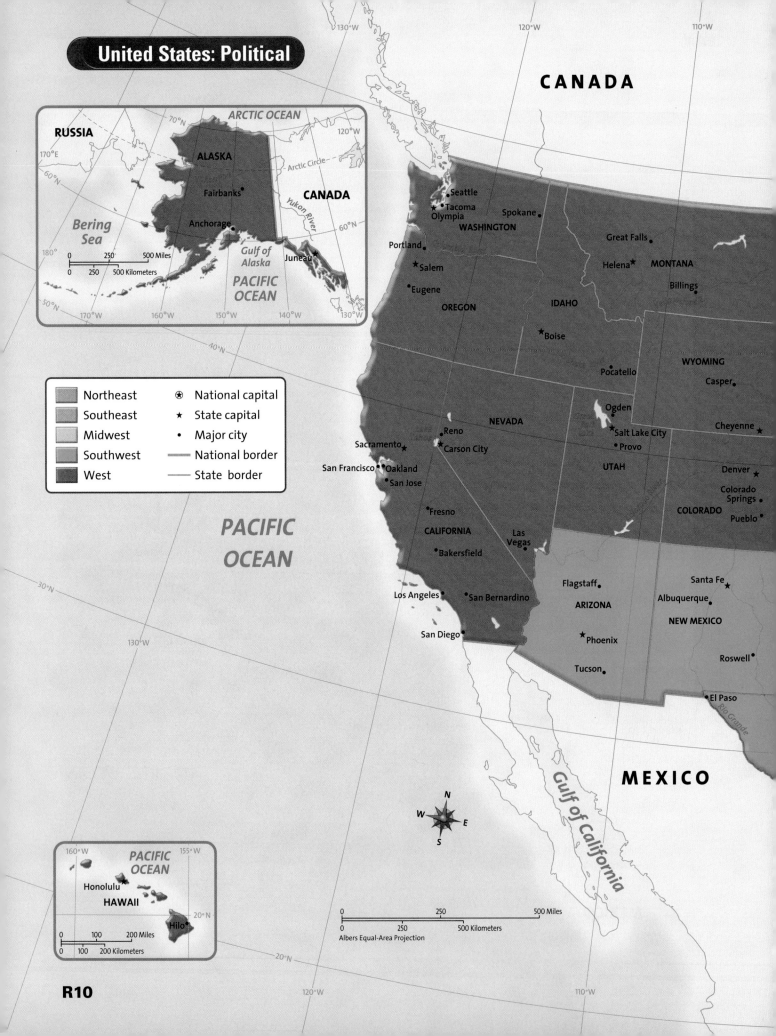

CANADA

Legend
- Northeast
- Southeast
- Midwest
- Southwest
- West
- ⊛ National capital
- ★ State capital
- • Major city
- ▬ National border
- ▬ State border

Alaska Inset
RUSSIA

ARCTIC OCEAN

170°E

ALASKA

CANADA

Arctic Circle

70°N

120°W

60°N

Fairbanks

Bering Sea

Anchorage

Yukon River

Gulf of Alaska

Juneau

PACIFIC OCEAN

180°

170°W   160°W   150°W   140°W   130°W

0   250   500 Miles
0   250   500 Kilometers

50°N

Main map cities

Seattle
Tacoma
Olympia   ★
Spokane
WASHINGTON

Great Falls
Helena ★   MONTANA
Billings

Portland

Salem ★
Eugene

OREGON

IDAHO

Boise ★

Pocatello

WYOMING
Casper

Ogden
Salt Lake City ★

Cheyenne

Reno
Carson City ★
NEVADA

Provo
UTAH

Denver
Colorado Springs
COLORADO
Pueblo

Sacramento ★
San Francisco   Oakland
San Jose

Fresno

CALIFORNIA
Bakersfield

Las Vegas

Los Angeles
San Bernardino

San Diego

Flagstaff

ARIZONA

Phoenix ★

Tucson

Santa Fe ★
Albuquerque
NEW MEXICO

Roswell

El Paso

Rio Grande

PACIFIC OCEAN

40°N
30°N
130°W

MEXICO

Gulf of California

N
W   E
S

0   250   500 Miles
0   250   500 Kilometers
Albers Equal-Area Projection

Hawaii Inset
160°W   155°W
PACIFIC OCEAN

Honolulu
HAWAII

Hilo

20°N

0   100   200 Miles
0   100   200 Kilometers

20°N

United States: Physical

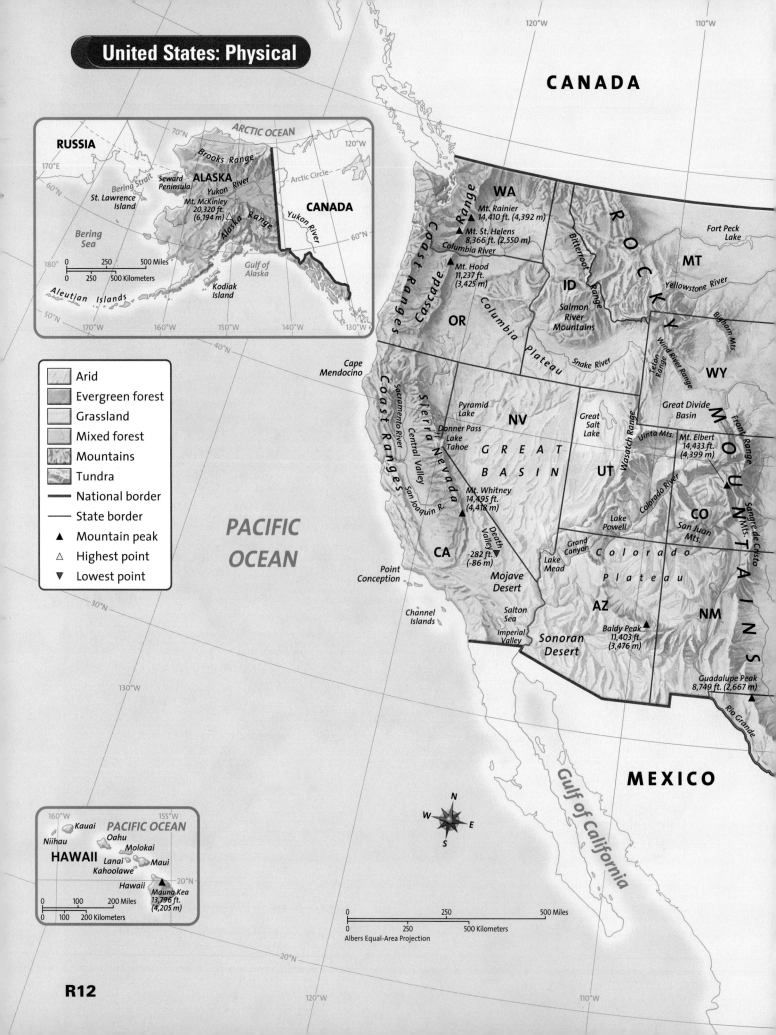

CANADA

Alaska Inset
RUSSIA
ARCTIC OCEAN
170°E
70°N
Brooks Range
Seward Peninsula
ALASKA
Bering Strait
St. Lawrence Island
Yukon River
60°N
Mt. McKinley 20,320 ft. (6,194 m) △
Alaska Range
Bering Sea
Gulf of Alaska
Aleutian Islands
Kodiak Island
50°N
120°W
Arctic Circle
CANADA
Yukon River
60°N
140°W
130°W
0 250 500 Miles
0 250 500 Kilometers
170°W 160°W 150°W

Legend
- Arid
- Evergreen forest
- Grassland
- Mixed forest
- Mountains
- Tundra
- ▬ National border
- ─ State border
- ▲ Mountain peak
- △ Highest point
- ▼ Lowest point

PACIFIC OCEAN

Main map labels
40°N
30°N
120°W
110°W

Coast Range
WA
Mt. Rainier 14,410 ft. (4,392 m) ▲
▲ Mt. St. Helens 8,366 ft. (2,550 m)
Columbia River
Cascade Ranges
Mt. Hood ▲ 11,237 ft. (3,425 m)
OR
Columbia Plateau
Bitterroot Range
ID
Salmon River Mountains
Snake River
ROCKY
Fort Peck Lake
MT
Yellowstone River
Bighorn Mts.
Teton Range
Wind River Range
WY
Great Divide Basin
Front Range
MOUNTAINS

Cape Mendocino
Coast Ranges
Sacramento River
Sierra Nevada
Central Valley
San Joaquin R.
Pyramid Lake
Donner Pass
Lake Tahoe
NV
GREAT BASIN
Great Salt Lake
Wasatch Range
Uinta Mts.
Mt. Elbert 14,433 ft. (4,399 m)
Mt. Whitney 14,495 ft. (4,418 m) ▲
Death Valley -282 ft. (-86 m) ▼
UT
Lake Powell
Colorado River
CO
Sangre de Cristo Mts.
San Juan Mts.

Point Conception
CA
Mojave Desert
Lake Mead
Grand Canyon
Colorado Plateau

Channel Islands
Salton Sea
Imperial Valley
Sonoran Desert
AZ
Baldy Peak 11,403 ft. (3,476 m) ▲
NM
Guadalupe Peak 8,749 ft. (2,667 m) ▼
130°W
Rio Grande

MEXICO

Gulf of California

Compass
N W E S

Scale
0 250 500 Miles
0 250 500 Kilometers
Albers Equal-Area Projection

Hawaii Inset
160°W 155°W
PACIFIC OCEAN
Kauai
Niihau
Oahu
Molokai
Lanai
Maui
Kahoolawe
HAWAII
Hawaii
Mauna Kea 13,796 ft. (4,205 m) ▲
20°N
0 100 200 Miles
0 100 200 Kilometers

20°N
110°W

CANADA

Lake of
the Woods

Isle
Royale

Lake Superior

Upper
Red Lake

Lower
Red Lake

Mesabi
Range

Keweenaw
Peninsula

Upper Peninsula

Lake Huron

St. Lawrence River

Moosehead
Lake

ME

Mt. Katahdin
5,269 ft.
(1,606 m)

Lake Sakakawea

ND

Leech
Lake

Mille
Lacs
Lake

MN

WI

Wisconsin River

Lake
Michigan

Lower Peninsula

MI

Lake
St. Clair

Lake
Champlain

VT

NY

Adirondack
Mountains

Green Mts.

NH

White Mts.

Mt. Washington
6,288 ft.
(1,917 m)

Cape Ann

Cape
Cod

Lake
Oahe

SD

Missouri River

Lake
Winnebago

Lake Michigan

Finger
Lakes

Hudson R.

Connecticut R.

MA

CT

RI

Niagara
Falls

Lake Ontario

Lake Erie

Long
Island

Black
Hills

G
R
E
A
T

IA

Illinois River

Wabash River

OH

PA

NJ

50°N

50°N

40°N

North Platte R.

Sand Hills

NE

Platte River

I N T E R I O R

IL

IN

MD

Allegheny Mts.

DE

Delaware
Bay

Piedmont

Potomac R.

South Platte R.

P
L
A
I
N
S

Missouri River

P L A I N S

CENTRAL PLAINS

Ohio River

WV

VA

James R.

Cape
Charles

Chesapeake
Bay

Smoky Hills

KS

MO

Lake of
the Ozarks

KY

Cumberland
Gap

Roanoke R.

A
P
P
A
L
A
C
H
I
A
N

M
O
U
N
T
A
I
N
S

Albemarle
Sound

Red Hills

Harry S. Truman
Reservoir

Ozark Plateau

Lake Barkley

Mt. Mitchell
6,684 ft.
(2,037 m)

NC

Cape
Hatteras

OK

Arkansas

River

Mississippi River

Cumberland R.

TN

Tennessee R.

Cape Fear River

Llano
Estacado

Canadian River

Ouachita
Mountains

Red River

Lake
Texoma

AR

MS

Tombigbee R.

Stone
Mountain

Clark
Hill Lake

Savannah River

SC

Cape
Fear

ATLANTIC
OCEAN

Edwards
Plateau

Pecos River

Brazos River

TX

Sabine River

Toledo
Bend
Reservoir

LA

Alabama R.

AL

Chattahoochee R.

GA

Ocmulgee R.

Oconee R.

Altamaha R.

C
O
A
S
T
A
L

P
L
A
I
N

30°N

30°N

Colorado River

Sam Rayburn
Reservoir

C
O
A
S
T
A
L
P
L
A
I
N

Lake
Maurepas

Lake
Pontchartrain

Mobile
Bay

Okefenokee
Swamp

St. Johns River

Cape
Canaveral

Rio Grande

Galveston
Bay

Mississippi
Delta

Tampa
Bay

FL

Lake
Okeechobee

BAHAMAS

Gulf of Mexico

Everglades

Cape
Sable

Florida Keys

Straits of Florida

CUBA

100°W

90°W

80°W

70°W

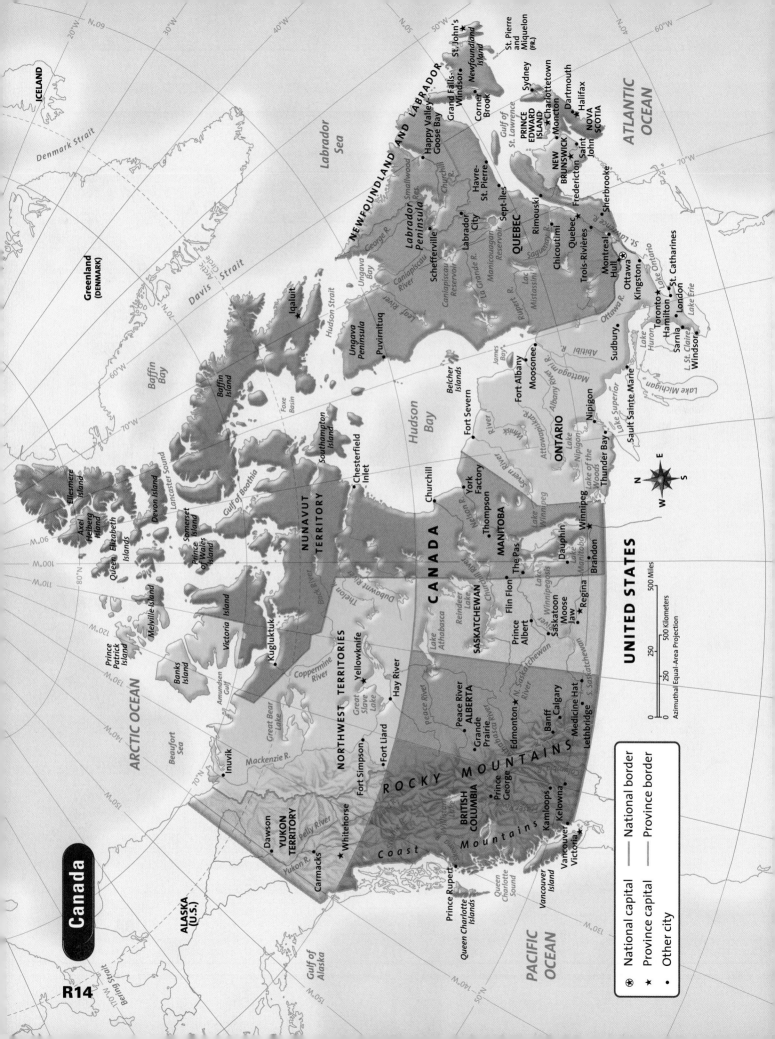

Canada

ICELAND

Greenland (DENMARK)

ALASKA (U.S.)

UNITED STATES

CANADA

NEWFOUNDLAND AND LABRADOR

QUEBEC

ONTARIO

MANITOBA

SASKATCHEWAN

ALBERTA

BRITISH COLUMBIA

YUKON TERRITORY

NORTHWEST TERRITORIES

NUNAVUT TERRITORY

NEW BRUNSWICK

NOVA SCOTIA

PRINCE EDWARD ISLAND

ROCKY MOUNTAINS

Coast Mountains

Oceans and Seas

ARCTIC OCEAN
PACIFIC OCEAN
ATLANTIC OCEAN
Beaufort Sea
Bering Strait
Gulf of Alaska
Denmark Strait
Labrador Sea
Davis Strait
Baffin Bay
Hudson Bay
Hudson Strait
Foxe Basin
Gulf of St. Lawrence
James Bay
Ungava Bay
Queen Charlotte Sound
Amundsen Gulf
Gulf of Boothia
Lancaster Sound

Islands

Ellesmere Island
Axel Heiberg Island
Queen Elizabeth Islands
Devon Island
Baffin Island
Melville Island
Prince Patrick Island
Banks Island
Victoria Island
Prince of Wales Island
Somerset Island
Southampton Island
Belcher Islands
Vancouver Island
Queen Charlotte Islands
Newfoundland Island
St. Pierre and Miquelon (FR.)

Cities

St. John's
St. Pierre
Sydney
Charlottetown
Dartmouth
Halifax
Moncton
Saint John
Fredericton
Sherbrooke
Grand Falls-Windsor
Corner Brook
Happy Valley-Goose Bay
Churchill
Rimouski
Chicoutimi
Quebec
Trois-Rivières
Montreal
Hull
Ottawa
Kingston
Toronto
St. Catharines
London
Hamilton
Sarnia
Windsor
Sudbury
Nipigon
Thunder Bay
Sault Sainte Marie
Moosonee
Fort Albany
Fort Severn
York Factory
Churchill
Thompson
Winnipeg
Brandon
Dauphin
The Pas
Flin Flon
Reindeer
Saskatoon
Prince Albert
Moose Jaw
Regina
Medicine Hat
Lethbridge
Calgary
Banff
Edmonton
Grande Prairie
Peace River
Prince George
Kamloops
Kelowna
Vancouver
Victoria
Prince Rupert
Whitehorse
Dawson
Carmacks
Inuvik
Fort Simpson
Fort Liard
Hay River
Yellowknife
Kugluktuk
Chesterfield Inlet
Iqaluit
Puvirnituq
Schefferville
Labrador City
Sept-Îles
St. Pierre
Havre-St. Pierre

Rivers and Lakes

Mackenzie R.
Coppermine River
Great Bear Lake
Great Slave Lake
Back River
Thelon River
Dubawnt River
Lake Athabasca
Peace River
Athabasca River
N. Saskatchewan River
S. Saskatchewan River
Lake Winnipeg
Lake Winnipegosis
Lake Manitoba
Lake of the Woods
Nelson R.
Churchill R.
Reindeer Lake
Severn River
Attawapiskat R.
Albany River
Moose River
Abitibi R.
Mattagami River
Lake Superior
Lake Huron
Lake Michigan
Lake Ontario
Lake Erie
L. St. Clair
Lake Nipigon
Ottawa R.
St. Lawrence R.
Saguenay R.
Lac Mistassini
Lac St-Jean
Rupert R.
La Grande R.
Manicouagan Reservoir
Caniapiscau Reservoir
Caniapiscau River
Smallwood Res.
Churchill R.
George R.
Leaf River
Whiskf R.
Pelly River
Yukon R.
Peel River
Liard River

Physical Features

Labrador Peninsula
Ungava Peninsula

Legend

⊛ National capital
★ Province capital
• Other city
— National border
— Province border

500 Miles
500 Kilometers
250
Azimuthal Equal-Area Projection

N E S W (compass)

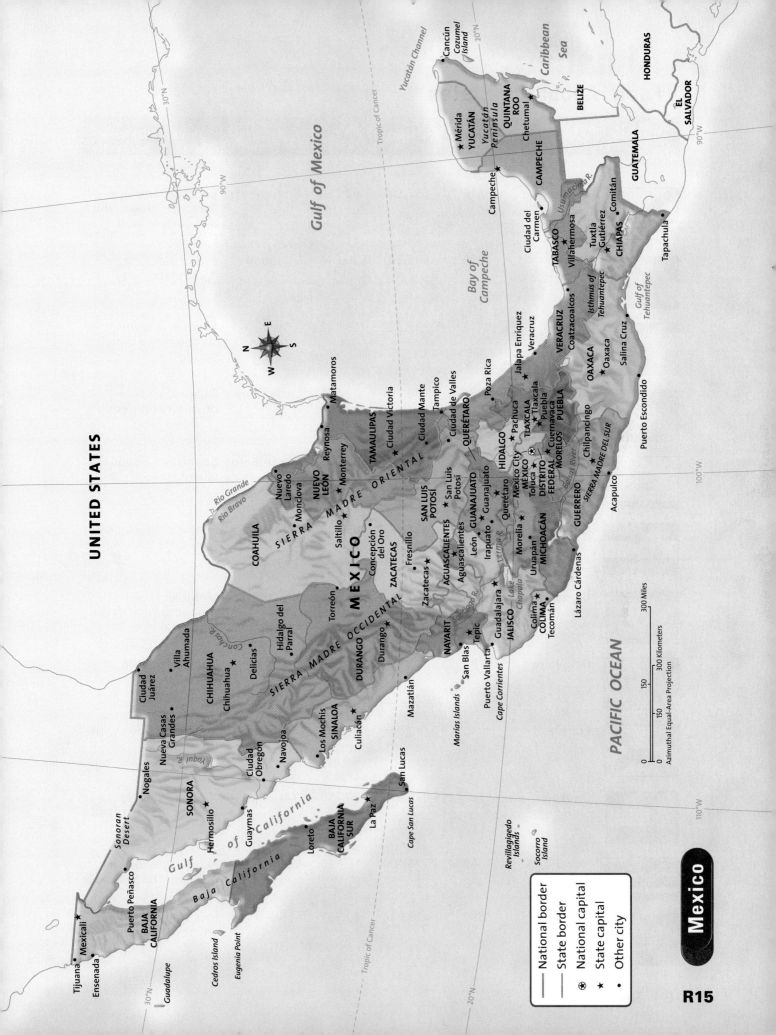

UNITED STATES

Gulf of Mexico

Tropic of Cancer

Caribbean
Sea

HONDURAS

Cancún
Cozumel
Island

QUINTANA
ROO

Mérida
YUCATÁN

Yucatán
Peninsula

Chetumal

BELIZE

EL
SALVADOR

Campeche

CAMPECHE

GUATEMALA

Ciudad del
Carmen

Comitán

Yucatán Channel

Usumacinta R.

TABASCO

Tuxtla
Gutiérrez

Villahermosa

CHIAPAS

Tapachula

Bay of
Campeche

Coatzacoalcos

VERACRUZ

Isthmus of
Tehuantepec

Gulf of
Tehuantepec

Salina Cruz

Jalapa Enríquez

Veracruz

OAXACA

Oaxaca

Puerto Escondido

Matamoros

Ciudad Victoria

Ciudad Mante

Tampico

Poza Rica

Pachuca

Reynosa

TAMAULIPAS

Ciudad de Valles

QUERÉTARO

HIDALGO

Tlaxcala

TLAXCALA

Puebla

PUEBLA

Monterrey

SIERRA MADRE ORIENTAL

Nuevo
Laredo

NUEVO
LEÓN

Monclova

San Luis
Potosí

SAN LUIS
POTOSÍ

Querétaro

MÉXICO

Mexico City

DISTRITO

Cuernavaca

MORELOS

Chilpancingo

SIERRA MADRE DEL SUR

FEDERAL

Toluca

Balsas River

Acapulco

GUERRERO

Saltillo

Concepción
del Oro

COAHUILA

Fresnillo

ZACATECAS

Zacatecas

AGUASCALIENTES

Aguascalientes

León

GUANAJUATO

Guanajuato

Irapuato

Lerma R.

Morelia

MICHOACÁN

Uruapán

Lázaro Cárdenas

MEXICO

Torreón

DURANGO

Durango

Lake
Chapala

Santiago R.

Guadalajara

JALISCO

Colima

COLIMA

Tecomán

Hidalgo del
Parral

SIERRA MADRE OCCIDENTAL

Villa
Ahumada

Delicias

CHIHUAHUA

Chihuahua

Los Mochis

SINALOA

Culiacán

Mazatlán

NAYARIT

Tepic

San Blas

Puerto Vallarta

Cape Corrientes

Marías Islands

Ciudad
Juárez

Conchos R.

Nueva Casas
Grandes

Nogales

SONORA

Navojoa

Ciudad
Obregón

Hermosillo

Yaqui R.

Guaymas

Sonoran
Desert

Rio Grande

Rio Bravo

N
E
W
S

Tijuana

Ensenada

BAJA
CALIFORNIA

Mexicali

Puerto Peñasco

Gulf of California

San Lucas

BAJA
CALIFORNIA
SUR

Loreto

La Paz

Cape San Lucas

Baja California

Cedros Island

Eugenia Point

Guadalupe

Revillagigedo
Islands

Socorro
Island

PACIFIC OCEAN

300 Miles

300 Kilometers

150

150

0

0

Azimuthal Equal-Area Projection

90°W

100°W

110°W

20°N

20°N

30°N

30°N

90°W

Tropic of Cancer

Mexico

National border

State border

⊛ National capital

★ State capital

• Other city

Almanac
Facts About the States

State Flag	State	Year of Statehood	Population*	Area (sq. mi.)	Capital	Origin of State Name
	Alabama	1819	4,557,808	50,750	Montgomery	Choctaw, *alba ayamule*, "one who clears land and gathers food from it"
	Alaska	1959	663,661	570,374	Juneau	Aleut, *alayeska*, "great land"
	Arizona	1912	5,939,292	113,642	Phoenix	Papago, *arizonac*, "place of the small spring"
	Arkansas	1836	2,779,154	52,075	Little Rock	Quapaw, "the downstream people"
	California	1850	36,132,147	155,973	Sacramento	Spanish, a fictional island
	Colorado	1876	4,665,177	103,730	Denver	Spanish, "red land" or "red earth"
	Connecticut	1788	3,510,297	4,845	Hartford	Mohican, *quinnitukqut*, "at the long tidal river"
	Delaware	1787	843,524	1,955	Dover	Named for Lord de la Warr
	Florida	1845	17,789,864	54,153	Tallahassee	Spanish, "filled with flowers"
	Georgia	1788	9,072,576	57,919	Atlanta	Named for King George II of England
	Hawaii	1959	1,275,194	6,450	Honolulu	Polynesian, *hawaiki* or *owykee*, "homeland"
	Idaho	1890	1,429,096	82,751	Boise	Invented name with unknown meaning

State Flag	State	Year of Statehood	Population*	Area (sq. mi.)	Capital	Origin of State Name
	Illinois	1818	12,763,371	55,593	Springfield	Algonquin, *iliniwek*, "men" or "warriors"
	Indiana	1816	6,271,973	35,870	Indianapolis	*Indian + a*, "land of the Indians"
	Iowa	1846	2,966,334	55,875	Des Moines	Dakota, *ayuba*, "beautiful land"
	Kansas	1861	2,744,687	81,823	Topeka	Sioux, "land of the south wind people"
	Kentucky	1792	4,173,405	39,732	Frankfort	Iroquoian, *ken-tah-ten*, "land of tomorrow"
	Louisiana	1812	4,523,628	43,566	Baton Rouge	Named for King Louis XIV of France
	Maine	1820	1,321,505	30,865	Augusta	Named after a French province
	Maryland	1788	5,600,388	9,775	Annapolis	Named for Henrietta Maria, Queen Consort of Charles I of England
	Massachusetts	1788	6,398,743	7,838	Boston	Massachusetts American Indian tribe, "at the big hill" or "place of the big hill"
	Michigan	1837	10,120,860	56,809	Lansing	Ojibwa, "large lake"
	Minnesota	1858	5,132,799	79,617	St. Paul	Dakota Sioux, "sky-blue water"
	Mississippi	1817	2,921,088	46,914	Jackson	Indian word meaning "great waters" or "father of waters"
	Missouri	1821	5,800,310	68,898	Jefferson City	Named after the Missouri Indian tribe. *Missouri* means "town of the large canoes."

* latest available population figures

State Flag	State	Year of Statehood	Population*	Area (sq. mi.)	Capital	Origin of State Name
	Montana	1889	935,670	145,566	Helena	Spanish, "mountainous"
	Nebraska	1867	1,758,787	76,878	Lincoln	From an Oto Indian word meaning "flat water"
	Nevada	1864	2,414,807	109,806	Carson City	Spanish, "snowy" or "snowed upon"
	New Hampshire	1788	1,309,940	8,969	Concord	Named for Hampshire County, England
	New Jersey	1787	8,717,925	7,419	Trenton	Named for the Isle of Jersey
	New Mexico	1912	1,928,384	121,365	Santa Fe	Named by Spanish explorers from Mexico
	New York	1788	19,254,630	47,224	Albany	Named after the Duke of York
	North Carolina	1789	8,683,242	48,718	Raleigh	Named after King Charles II of England
	North Dakota	1889	636,677	70,704	Bismarck	Sioux, *dakota*, "friend" or "ally"
	Ohio	1803	11,464,042	40,953	Columbus	Iroquois, *oheo*, "great water"
	Oklahoma	1907	3,547,884	68,679	Oklahoma City	Choctaw, "red people"
	Oregon	1859	3,641,056	96,003	Salem	Unknown; generally accepted that it was taken from the writings of Maj. Robert Rogers, an English army officer
	Pennsylvania	1787	12,429,616	44,820	Harrisburg	*Penn + sylvania*, meaning "Penn's *woods*"

State Flag	State	Year of Statehood	Population*	Area (sq. mi.)	Capital	Origin of State Name
	Rhode Island	1790	1,076,189	1,045	Providence	From the Greek island of Rhodes
	South Carolina	1788	4,255,083	30,111	Columbia	Named after King Charles II of England
	South Dakota	1889	775,933	75,898	Pierre	Sioux, *dakota*, "friend" or "ally"
	Tennessee	1796	5,962,959	41,220	Nashville	Name of a Cherokee village
	Texas	1845	22,859,968	261,914	Austin	Native American, *tejas*, "friend" or "ally"
	Utah	1896	2,469,585	82,168	Salt Lake City	From the Ute tribe, meaning "people of the mountains"
	Vermont	1791	623,050	9,249	Montpelier	French, *vert*, "green," and *mont*, "mountain"
	Virginia	1788	7,567,465	39,598	Richmond	Named after Queen Elizabeth I of England
	Washington	1889	6,287,759	66,582	Olympia	Named for George Washington
	West Virginia	1863	1,816,856	24,087	Charleston	From the English-named state of Virginia
	Wisconsin	1848	5,536,201	54,314	Madison	Possibly Algonquian, "the place where we live"
	Wyoming	1890	509,294	97,105	Cheyenne	From Delaware Indian word meaning "land of vast plains"
	District of Columbia		550,521	67		Named after Christopher Columbus

* latest available population figures

Almanac
Facts About the Presidents

1 George Washington

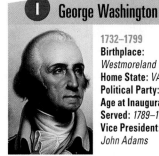

1732–1799
Birthplace:
Westmoreland County, VA
Home State: *VA*
Political Party: *None*
Age at Inauguration: *57*
Served: *1789–1797*
Vice President:
John Adams

2 John Adams

1735–1826
Birthplace: *Braintree, MA*
Home State: *MA*
Political Party: *Federalist*
Age at Inauguration: *61*
Served: *1797–1801*
Vice President: *Thomas Jefferson*

3 Thomas Jefferson

1743–1826
Birthplace: *Albemarle County, VA*
Home State: *VA*
Political Party: *Democratic-Republican*
Age at Inauguration: *57*
Served: *1801–1809*
Vice Presidents: *Aaron Burr, George Clinton*

4 James Madison

1751–1836
Birthplace: *Port Conway, VA*
Home State: *VA*
Political Party: *Democratic-Republican*
Age at Inauguration: *57*
Served: *1809–1817*
Vice Presidents: *George Clinton, Elbridge Gerry*

5 James Monroe

1758–1831
Birthplace: *Westmoreland County, VA*
Home State: *VA*
Political Party: *Democratic-Republican*
Age at Inauguration: *58*
Served: *1817–1825*
Vice President: *Daniel D. Tompkins*

6 John Quincy Adams

1767–1848
Birthplace: *Braintree, MA*
Home State: *MA*
Political Party: *Democratic-Republican*
Age at Inauguration: *57*
Served: *1825–1829*
Vice President: *John C. Calhoun*

7 Andrew Jackson

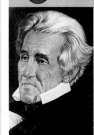

1767–1845
Birthplace: *Waxhaw settlement, SC*
Home State: *TN*
Political Party: *Democratic*
Age at Inauguration: *61*
Served: *1829–1837*
Vice Presidents: *John C. Calhoun, Martin Van Buren*

8 Martin Van Buren

1782–1862
Birthplace: *Kinderhook, NY*
Home State: *NY*
Political Party: *Democratic*
Age at Inauguration: *54*
Served: *1837–1841*
Vice President: *Richard M. Johnson*

9 William H. Harrison

1773–1841
Birthplace: *Berkeley, VA*
Home State: *OH*
Political Party: *Whig*
Age at Inauguration: *68*
Served: *1841*
Vice President: *John Tyler*

10 John Tyler

1790–1862
Birthplace: *Greenway, VA*
Home State: *VA*
Political Party: *Whig*
Age at Inauguration: *51*
Served: *1841–1845*
Vice President: *none*

11 James K. Polk

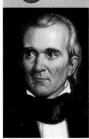

1795–1849
Birthplace: *near Pineville, NC*
Home State: *TN*
Political Party: *Democratic*
Age at Inauguration: *49*
Served: *1845–1849*
Vice President: *George M. Dallas*

12 Zachary Taylor

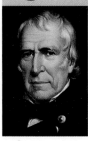

1784–1850
Birthplace: *Orange County, VA*
Home State: *LA*
Political Party: *Whig*
Age at Inauguration: *64*
Served: *1849–1850*
Vice President: *Millard Fillmore*

13 Millard Fillmore

1800–1874
Birthplace: *Locke, NY*
Home State: *NY*
Political Party: *Whig*
Age at Inauguration: *50*
Served: *1850–1853*
Vice President: *none*

14 Franklin Pierce

1804–1869
Birthplace: *Hillsboro, NH*
Home State: *NH*
Political Party: *Democratic*
Age at Inauguration: *48*
Served: *1853–1857*
Vice President: *William R. King*

Home State refers to the state of residence when elected.

15 James Buchanan

1791–1868
Birthplace:
near Mercersburg, PA
Home State: PA
Political Party:
Democratic
Age at Inauguration: 65
Served: 1857–1861
Vice President:
John C. Breckinridge

16 Abraham Lincoln

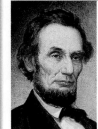

1809–1865
Birthplace:
near Hodgenville, KY
Home State: IL
Political Party:
Republican
Age at Inauguration: 52
Served: 1861–1865
Vice Presidents:
Hannibal Hamlin,
Andrew Johnson

17 Andrew Johnson

1808–1875
Birthplace: Raleigh, NC
Home State: TN
Political Party:
National Union
Age at Inauguration: 56
Served: 1865–1869
Vice President: none

18 Ulysses S. Grant

1822–1885
Birthplace:
Point Pleasant, OH
Home State: IL
Political Party:
Republican
Age at Inauguration: 46
Served: 1869–1877
Vice Presidents:
Schuyler Colfax,
Henry Wilson

19 Rutherford B. Hayes

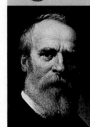

1822–1893
Birthplace:
near Delaware, OH
Home State: OH
Political Party:
Republican
Age at Inauguration: 54
Served: 1877–1881
Vice President:
William A. Wheeler

20 James A. Garfield

1831–1881
Birthplace: Orange, OH
Home State: OH
Political Party:
Republican
Age at Inauguration: 49
Served: 1881
Vice President:
Chester A. Arthur

21 Chester A. Arthur

1829–1886
Birthplace: Fairfield, VT
Home State: NY
Political Party:
Republican
Age at Inauguration: 51
Served: 1881–1885
Vice President: none

22 Grover Cleveland

1837–1908
Birthplace: Caldwell, NJ
Home State: NY
Political Party:
Democratic
Age at Inauguration: 47
Served: 1885–1889
Vice President:
Thomas A. Hendricks

23 Benjamin Harrison

1833–1901
Birthplace: North Bend,
OH
Home State: IN
Political Party:
Republican
Age at Inauguration: 55
Served: 1889–1893
Vice President:
Levi P. Morton

24 Grover Cleveland

1837–1908
Birthplace: Caldwell, NJ
Home State: NY
Political Party:
Democratic
Age at Inauguration: 55
Served: 1893–1897
Vice President:
Adlai E. Stevenson

25 William McKinley

1843–1901
Birthplace: Niles, OH
Home State: OH
Political Party:
Republican
Age at Inauguration: 54
Served: 1897–1901
Vice Presidents:
Garret A. Hobart,
Theodore Roosevelt

26 Theodore Roosevelt

1858–1919
Birthplace: New York, NY
Home State: NY
Political Party:
Republican
Age at Inauguration: 42
Served: 1901–1909
Vice President:
Charles W. Fairbanks

27 William H. Taft

1857–1930
Birthplace: Cincinnati, OH
Home State: OH
Political Party:
Republican
Age at Inauguration: 51
Served: 1909–1913
Vice President:
James S. Sherman

28 Woodrow Wilson

1856–1924
Birthplace: Staunton, VA
Home State: NJ
Political Party:
Democratic
Age at Inauguration: 56
Served: 1913–1921
Vice President:
Thomas R. Marshall

29 Warren G. Harding

1865–1923
Birthplace:
Blooming Grove, OH
Home State: OH
Political Party:
Republican
Age at Inauguration: 55
Served: 1921–1923
Vice President:
Calvin Coolidge

30 Calvin Coolidge

1872–1933
Birthplace:
Plymouth Notch, VT
Home State: *MA*
Political Party:
Republican
Age at Inauguration: *51*
Served: *1923–1929*
Vice President:
Charles G. Dawes

31 Herbert Hoover

1874–1964
Birthplace: *West Branch, IA*
Home State: *CA*
Political Party:
Republican
Age at Inauguration: *54*
Served: *1929–1933*
Vice President:
Charles Curtis

32 Franklin D. Roosevelt

1882–1945
Birthplace: *Hyde Park, NY*
Home State: *NY*
Political Party:
Democratic
Age at Inauguration: *51*
Served: *1933–1945*
Vice Presidents:
John N. Garner,
Henry A. Wallace,
Harry S. Truman

33 Harry S. Truman

1884–1972
Birthplace: *Lamar, MO*
Home State: *MO*
Political Party:
Democratic
Age at Inauguration: *60*
Served: *1945–1953*
Vice President:
Alben W. Barkley

34 Dwight D. Eisenhower

1890–1969
Birthplace: *Denison, TX*
Home State: *NY*
Political Party:
Republican
Age at Inauguration: *62*
Served: *1953–1961*
Vice President:
Richard M. Nixon

35 John F. Kennedy

1917–1963
Birthplace: *Brookline, MA*
Home State: *MA*
Political Party:
Democratic
Age at Inauguration: *43*
Served: *1961–1963*
Vice President:
Lyndon B. Johnson

36 Lyndon B. Johnson

1908–1973
Birthplace:
near Stonewall, TX
Home State: *TX*
Political Party:
Democratic
Age at Inauguration: *55*
Served: *1963–1969*
Vice President:
Hubert H. Humphrey

37 Richard M. Nixon

1913–1994
Birthplace: *Yorba Linda, CA*
Home State: *NY*
Political Party:
Republican
Age at Inauguration: *56*
Served: *1969–1974*
Vice Presidents:
Spiro T. Agnew,
Gerald R. Ford

38 Gerald R. Ford

1913–2006
Birthplace: *Omaha, NE*
Home State: *MI*
Political Party:
Republican
Age at Inauguration: *61*
Served: *1974–1977*
Vice President:
Nelson A. Rockefeller

39 Jimmy Carter

1924–
Birthplace: *Plains, GA*
Home State: *GA*
Political Party:
Democratic
Age at Inauguration: *52*
Served: *1977–1981*
Vice President:
Walter F. Mondale

40 Ronald W. Reagan

1911–2004
Birthplace: *Tampico, IL*
Home State: *CA*
Political Party:
Republican
Age at Inauguration: *69*
Served: *1981–1989*
Vice President:
George Bush

41 George Bush

1924–
Birthplace: *Milton, MA*
Home State: *TX*
Political Party:
Republican
Age at Inauguration: *64*
Served: *1989–1993*
Vice President:
Dan Quayle

42 William Clinton

1946–
Birthplace: *Hope, AR*
Home State: *AR*
Political Party:
Democratic
Age at Inauguration: *46*
Served: *1993–2001*
Vice President:
Albert Gore

43 George W. Bush

1946–
Birthplace: *New Haven, CT*
Home State: *TX*
Political Party:
Republican
Age at Inauguration: *54*
Served: *2001–2009*
Vice President:
Richard Cheney

44 Barack Obama

1961–
Birthplace: *Honolulu, HI*
Home State: *IL*
Political Party:
Democratic
Age at Inauguration: *47*
Served: *2009–*
Vice President:
Joseph Biden, Jr.

ATLAS/ALMANAC

R22 ■ **Reference**

Home State refers to the state of residence when elected.

American Documents

THE DECLARATION OF INDEPENDENCE

In Congress, July 4, 1776.
The unanimous Declaration of the
thirteen United States of America,

When in the Course of human events it becomes necessary
for one people to dissolve the political bands which have connected
them with another, and to assume among the powers of the earth,
the separate and equal station to which the Laws of Nature and
of Nature's God entitle them, a decent respect to the opinions of
mankind requires that they should declare the causes which impel
them to the separation.

We hold these truths to be self-evident, that all men are
created equal, that they are endowed by their Creator with certain
unalienable Rights, that among these are Life, Liberty and the
pursuit of Happiness.

That to secure these rights, Governments are instituted among
Men, deriving their just powers from the consent of the governed,

That whenever any Form of Government becomes destructive
of these ends, it is the Right of the People to alter or to abolish it,
and to institute new Government, laying its foundation on such
principles and organizing its powers in such form, as to them shall
seem most likely to effect their Safety and Happiness. Prudence,
indeed, will dictate that Governments long established should
not be changed for light and transient causes; and accordingly all
experience hath shown, that mankind are more disposed to suffer,
while evils are sufferable, than to right themselves by abolishing
the forms to which they are accustomed. But when a long train
of abuses and usurpations, pursuing invariably the same Object
evinces a design to reduce them under absolute Despotism, it is
their right, it is their duty, to throw off such Government, and to
provide new Guards for their future security.

Such has been the patient sufferance of these Colonies; and
such is now the necessity which constrains them to alter their former
Systems of Government. The history of the present King of Great
Britain is a history of repeated injuries and usurpations, all having
in direct object the establishment of an absolute Tyranny over these
States. To prove this, let Facts be submitted to a candid world.

He has refused his Assent to Laws, the most wholesome and
necessary for the public good.

He has forbidden his Governors to pass Laws of immediate and
pressing importance, unless suspended in their operation till his
Assent should be obtained; and when so suspended, he has utterly
neglected to attend to them.

Preamble
The Preamble tells why the
Declaration was written. It
states that the members of the
Continental Congress believed the
colonies had the right to break
away from Britain and become a
free nation.

A Statement of Rights
The opening part of the
Declaration tells what rights
the members of the Continental
Congress believed that all people
have. All people are equal in
having the rights to life, liberty,
and the pursuit of happiness. The
main purpose of a government is
to protect the rights of the people
who consent to be governed by
it. These rights cannot be taken
away. When a government tries
to take these rights away from
the people, the people have the
right to change the government or
do away with it. The people can
then form a new government that
respects these rights.

Charges Against the King
The Declaration lists more than
25 charges against the king. He
was mistreating the colonists, the
Declaration says, in order to gain
total control over the colonies.

The king rejected many laws
passed by colonial legislatures.

He has refused to pass other Laws for the accommodation of large districts of people, unless those people would relinquish the right of Representation in the Legislature, a right inestimable to them and formidable to tyrants only.

He has called together legislative bodies at places unusual, uncomfortable, and distant from the depository of their public Records, for the sole purpose of fatiguing them into compliance with his measures.

He has dissolved Representative Houses repeatedly, for opposing with manly firmness his invasions on the rights of the people.

He has refused for a long time, after such dissolutions, to cause others to be elected; whereby the Legislative powers, incapable of Annihilation, have returned to the People at large for their exercise; the State remaining in the mean time exposed to all the dangers of invasion from without, and convulsions within.

He has endeavored to prevent the population of these States; for that purpose obstructing the Laws for Naturalization of Foreigners; refusing to pass others to encourage their migrations hither, and raising the conditions of new Appropriations of Lands.

He has obstructed the Administration of Justice, by refusing his Assent to Laws for establishing Judiciary powers.

He has made Judges dependent on his Will alone, for the tenure of their offices, and the amount and payment of their salaries.

He has erected a multitude of New Offices, and sent hither swarms of Officers to harass our people, and eat out their substance.

He has kept among us, in times of peace, Standing Armies without the Consent of our legislatures.

He has affected to render the Military independent of and superior to the Civil power.

He has combined with others to subject us to a jurisdiction foreign to our constitution, and unacknowledged by our laws; giving his Assent to their Acts of pretended Legislation:

For quartering large bodies of armed troops among us:

For protecting them, by a mock Trial, from punishment for any Murders which they should commit on the Inhabitants of these States:

For cutting off our Trade with all parts of the world:

For imposing Taxes on us without our Consent:

For depriving us in many cases, of the benefits of Trial by Jury:

For transporting us beyond Seas to be tried for pretended offenses:

For abolishing the free System of English Laws in a neighboring Province, establishing therein an Arbitrary government, and enlarging its Boundaries so as to render it at once an example and fit instrument for introducing the same absolute rule into these Colonies:

The king made the colonial legislatures meet at inconvenient times and places.

The king and the king's governors often dissolved colonial legislatures for disobeying their orders.

The king stopped people from moving to the colonies and into the western lands.

The king prevented the colonists from choosing their own judges. The king chose the judges, and they served only as long as the king was satisfied with them.

The king hired people to help collect taxes in the colonies.

The king appointed General Thomas Gage, commander of Britain's military forces in the Americas, as governor of Massachusetts.

The king expected the colonists to provide housing and supplies for the British soldiers in the colonies.

The king and Parliament demanded that colonists pay many taxes, even though the colonists did not agree to pay them.

Colonists were tried by British naval courts, which had no juries.

Colonists accused of treason were sent to Britain to be tried.

For taking away our Charters, abolishing our most valuable Laws, and altering fundamentally the Forms of our Governments:

For suspending our own Legislatures, and declaring themselves invested with power to legislate for us in all cases whatsoever.

He has abdicated Government here, by declaring us out of his Protection and waging War against us.

He has plundered our seas, ravaged our Coasts, burnt our towns, and destroyed the lives of our people.

He is at this time transporting large Armies of foreign Mercenaries to complete the works of death, desolation and tyranny, already begun with circumstances of Cruelty & perfidy scarcely paralleled in the most barbarous ages, and totally unworthy the Head of a civilized nation.

He has constrained our fellow Citizens taken Captive on the high Seas to bear Arms against their Country, to become the executioners of their friends and Brethren, or to fall themselves by their Hands.

He has excited domestic insurrections amongst us, and has endeavored to bring on the inhabitants of our frontiers, the merciless Indian Savages, whose known rule of warfare, is an undistinguished destruction of all ages, sexes and conditions.

In every stage of these Oppressions We have Petitioned for Redress in the most humble terms: Our repeated Petitions have been answered only by repeated injury. A Prince, whose character is thus marked by every act which may define a Tyrant, is unfit to be the ruler of a free people.

Nor have We been wanting in attentions to our British brethren. We have warned them from time to time of attempts by their legislature to extend an unwarrantable jurisdiction over us. We have reminded them of the circumstances of our emigration and settlement here. We have appealed to their native justice and magnanimity, and we have conjured them by the ties of our common kindred to disavow these usurpations, which, would inevitably interrupt our connections and correspondence. They too have been deaf to the voice of justice and of consanguinity. We must, therefore, acquiesce in the necessity, which denounces our Separation, and hold them, as we hold the rest of mankind, Enemies in War, in Peace Friends.

We, therefore, the Representatives of the united States of America, in General Congress, Assembled, appealing to the Supreme Judge of the world for the rectitude of our intentions, do, in the Name, and by Authority of the good People of these Colonies, solemnly publish and declare, That these United Colonies are, and of Right ought to be Free and Independent States; that they are Absolved from all Allegiance to the British Crown, and that all political connection between them and the State of Great Britain, is and ought to be totally dissolved; and that as Free and Independent States, they have full Power to levy War, conclude Peace, contract Alliances, establish Commerce, and to do all other Acts and Things which Independent States may of right do.

The king allowed General Gage to take military action to enforce British laws in the colonies.

The king hired Hessian mercenaries and sent them to fight the colonists.

The king's governor in Virginia promised freedom to all enslaved people who joined the British forces. The British also planned to use Indians to fight the colonists.

The Declaration explained the efforts of the colonists to avoid separation from Britain. But the colonists said that the king had ignored their protests. Because of the many charges against the king, the writers of the Declaration concluded that he was not fit to rule free people.

A Statement of Independence
The writers declared that the colonies were now free and independent states. All ties with Britain were broken. As free and independent states, they had the right to make war and peace, to trade, and to do all the things free countries could do.

And for the support of this Declaration, with a firm reliance on the protection of divine Providence, we mutually pledge to each other our Lives, our Fortunes and our sacred Honor.

John Hancock

NEW HAMPSHIRE
Josiah Bartlett
William Whipple
Matthew Thornton

MASSACHUSETTS
John Adams
Samuel Adams
Robert Treat Paine
Elbridge Gerry

NEW YORK
William Floyd
Philip Livingston
Francis Lewis
Lewis Morris

RHODE ISLAND
Stephen Hopkins
William Ellery

NEW JERSEY
Richard Stockton
John Witherspoon
Francis Hopkinson
John Hart
Abraham Clark

PENNSYLVANIA
Robert Morris
Benjamin Rush
Benjamin Franklin
John Morton
George Clymer
James Smith
George Taylor
James Wilson
George Ross

DELAWARE
Caesar Rodney
George Read
Thomas McKean

MARYLAND
Samuel Chase
William Paca
Thomas Stone
Charles Carroll of Carrollton

NORTH CAROLINA
William Hopper
Joseph Hewes
John Penn

VIRGINIA
George Wythe
Richard Henry Lee
Thomas Jefferson
Benjamin Harrison
Thomas Nelson, Jr.
Francis Lightfoot Lee
Carter Braxton

SOUTH CAROLINA
Edward Rutledge
Thomas Heyward, Jr.
Thomas Lynch, Jr.
Arthur Middleton

CONNECTICUT
Roger Sherman
Samuel Huntington
William Williams
Oliver Wolcott

GEORGIA
Button Gwinnett
Lyman Hall
George Walton

Resolved, That copies of the Declaration be sent to the several assemblies, conventions, and committees, or councils of safety, and to the several commanding officers of the continental troops; that it be proclaimed in each of the United States, at the head of the army.

THE CONSTITUTION OF THE UNITED STATES OF AMERICA

Preamble*

We the people of the United States, in order to form a more perfect Union, establish justice, insure domestic tranquillity, provide for the common defense, promote the general welfare, and secure the blessings of liberty to ourselves and our posterity, do ordain and establish this Constitution for the United States of America.

Preamble
The introduction to the Constitution states the purposes for writing it. The writers wanted to set up a fairer form of government and to secure peace and freedom for themselves and for future generations.

ARTICLE I
THE LEGISLATIVE BRANCH
SECTION 1. CONGRESS

All legislative powers herein granted shall be vested in a Congress of the United States, which shall consist of a Senate and House of Representatives.

Congress
Congress has the authority to make laws. Congress is made up of two groups of lawmakers: the Senate and the House of Representatives.

SECTION 2. THE HOUSE OF REPRESENTATIVES

(1) The House of Representatives shall be composed of members chosen every second year by the people of the several states, and the electors in each state shall have the qualifications requisite for electors of the most numerous branch of the state legislature.

(1) Election and Term of Members
Qualified voters are to elect members of the House of Representatives every two years. Anyone whom state law allows to vote for a state's legislators may also vote for its representatives to Congress.

(2) No person shall be a Representative who shall not have attained to the age of twenty-five years, and been seven years a citizen of the United States, and who shall not, when elected, be an inhabitant of that state in which he shall be chosen.

(2) Qualifications
Members of the House of Representatives must be at least 25 years old. They must have been citizens of the United States for at least seven years. They must live in the state that they will represent.

(3) Representatives [*and direct taxes*]** shall be apportioned among the several states which may be included within this Union, according to their respective numbers [*which shall be determined by adding to the whole number of free persons, including those bound to service for a term of years, and excluding Indians not taxed, three-fifths of all other persons*]. The actual enumeration shall be made within three years after the first meeting of the Congress of the United States, and within every subsequent term of ten years, in such manner as they shall by law direct. The number of Representatives shall not exceed one for every 30,000, but each state shall have at least one Representative [; *and until such enumeration shall be made, the State of New Hampshire shall be entitled to choose three; Massachusetts eight; Rhode Island and Providence Plantations one; Connecticut five; New York six; New Jersey four; Pennsylvania eight; Delaware one; Maryland six; Virginia ten; North Carolina five; South Carolina five; and Georgia three*].

(3) Determining Apportionment
The number of representatives a state may have depends on the number of people living in each state. Every ten years the federal government must take a census, or count, of the population in every state. Every state will have at least one representative.

*Titles have been added to make the Constitution easier to read. They did not appear in the original document.

**The parts of the Constitution that no longer apply are printed in italics within brackets [ ]. These portions have been changed or set aside by later amendments.

(4) Filling Vacancies
If there is a vacancy in the House of Representatives, the governor of the state involved must call a special election to fill it.

(5) Special Authority
The House of Representatives chooses a Speaker as its presiding officer. It also chooses other officers as appropriate. The House is the only government branch that may impeach, or charge, an official in the executive branch or a judge of the federal courts for failing to carry out his or her duties. These cases are then tried in the Senate.

(1) Number, Term, and Selection of Members
Each state is represented by two senators. Until Amendment 17 was passed, state legislatures chose the senators for their states. Each senator serves a six-year term and has one vote in Congress.

(2) Overlapping Terms and Filling Vacancies
One-third of the senators are elected every two years for a six-year term. This grouping allows at least two-thirds of the experienced senators to remain in the Senate after each election. Amendment 17 permits state governors to appoint a replacement to fill a vacancy until the next election is held.

(3) Qualifications
Senators must be at least 30 years old. They must have been citizens of the United States for at least nine years. They must live in the state that they will represent.

(4) President of the Senate
The Vice President acts as chief officer of the Senate but does not vote unless there is a tie.

(5) Other Officers
The Senate chooses its other officers and a president pro tempore, who serves if the Vice President is not present or if the Vice President becomes President. *Pro tempore* is a Latin term meaning "for the time being."

(4) When vacancies happen in the representation from any state, the executive authority thereof shall issue writs of election to fill such vacancies.

(5) The House of Representatives shall choose their Speaker and other officers; and shall have the sole power of impeachment.

SECTION 3. THE SENATE

(1) The Senate of the United States shall be composed of two Senators from each state [*chosen by the legislature thereof*], for six years, and each Senator shall have one vote.

(2) [*Immediately after they shall be assembled in consequence of the first election, they shall be divided as equally as may be into three classes. The seats of the Senators of the first class shall be vacated at the expiration of the second year, of the second class at the expiration of the fourth year, and of the third class at the expiration of the sixth year, so that one-third may be chosen every second year; and if vacancies happen by resignation, or otherwise, during the recess of the legislature of any state, the executive thereof may make temporary appointments until the next meeting of the legislature, which shall then fill such vacancies.*]

(3) No person shall be a Senator who shall not have attained to the age of thirty years, and been nine years a citizen of the United States, and who shall not, when elected, be an inhabitant of that state for which he shall be chosen.

(4) The Vice President of the United States shall be President of the Senate, but shall have no vote, unless they be equally divided.

(5) The Senate shall choose their other officers, and also a President *pro tempore*, in the absence of the Vice President, or when he shall exercise the office of the President of the United States.

(6) The Senate shall have the sole power to try all impeachments. When sitting for that purpose, they shall be on oath or affirmation. When the President of the United States is tried, the Chief Justice shall preside; and no person shall be convicted without the concurrence of two-thirds of the members present.

(7) Judgment in cases of impeachment shall not extend further than to removal from office, and disqualification to hold and enjoy any office of honor, trust, or profit under the United States; but the party convicted shall nevertheless be liable and subject to indictment, trial, judgment, and punishment, according to law.

SECTION 4. ELECTIONS AND MEETINGS

(1) The times, places, and manner of holding elections for Senators and Representatives shall be prescribed in each state by the legislature thereof; but the Congress may at any time by law make or alter such regulations, [*except as to the places of choosing Senators*].

(2) The Congress shall assemble at least once in every year, [*and such meeting shall be on the first Monday in December, unless they shall by law appoint a different day*].

SECTION 5. RULES OF PROCEDURE

(1) Each house shall be the judge of the elections, returns and qualifications of its own members, and a majority of each shall constitute a quorum to do business; but a smaller number may adjourn from day to day, and may be authorized to compel the attendance of absent members, in such manner and under such penalties as each house may provide.

(2) Each house may determine the rules of its proceedings, punish its members for disorderly behavior, and, with the concurrence of two-thirds, expel a member.

(3) Each house shall keep a journal of its proceedings, and from time to time publish the same, excepting such parts as may in their judgment require secrecy; and the yeas and nays of the members of either house on any question shall, at the desire of one-fifth of those present, be entered on the journal.

(6) Impeachment Trials
If the House of Representatives votes in favor of impeachment, the Senate holds a trial. A two-thirds vote is required to convict a person who has been impeached.

(7) Penalty for Conviction
If convicted in an impeachment case, an official is removed from office and may also be banned from ever holding office in the United States government again. The convicted person may also be tried in a regular court of law for any crimes.

(1) Holding Elections
Each state makes its own rules about electing senators and representatives. However, Congress may change these rules. Today congressional elections are held on the Tuesday after the first Monday in November, in even-numbered years.

(2) Meetings
The Constitution requires Congress to meet at least once a year. That day is the first Monday in December, unless Congress sets a different day. Amendment 20 changed this date to January 3.

(1) Organization
Each house of Congress may decide if its members have been elected fairly and are entitled to hold office. Each house may do business only when a quorum—a majority of its members—is present. By less than a majority vote, each house may compel absent members to attend.

(2) Rules
Each house may decide its own rules for doing business, punish its members, and expel a member from office if two-thirds of the members agree.

(3) Journal
The Constitution requires each house to keep records of its activities and to publish these records from time to time. The House Journal and the Senate Journal are published at the end of each session. How each member voted must be recorded if one-fifth of the members ask for this to be done.

(4) Adjournment
When Congress is in session, neither house may take a recess for more than three days without the consent of the other.

(1) Pay and Privileges
Members of Congress set their own salaries, which are to be paid by the federal government. Members cannot be arrested or sued for anything they say while Congress is in session. This privilege is called congressional immunity. Members of Congress may be arrested while Congress is in session only if they commit a crime.

(2) Restrictions
Members of Congress may not hold any other federal office while serving in Congress. A member may not resign from office and then take a government position created during that member's term of office or for which the pay has been increased during that member's term of office.

(1) Money-Raising Bills
All money-raising bills must be introduced first in the House of Representatives, but the Senate may suggest changes.

(2) How a Bill Becomes a Law
After a bill has been passed by both the House of Representatives and the Senate, it must be sent to the President. If the President approves and signs the bill, it becomes law. The President can also veto, or refuse to sign, the bill. Congress can override a veto by passing the bill again by a two-thirds majority. If the President does not act within ten days, one of two things will happen. If Congress is still in session, the bill becomes a law. If Congress ends its session within that same ten-day period, the bill does not become a law.

(3) Orders and Resolutions
All attempts by Congress to make law must be submitted to the President for the President's agreement or veto. Congress may decide on its own when to end the session. Other such acts must be signed or vetoed by the President.

---

(4) Neither house, during the session of Congress, shall, without the consent of the other, adjourn for more than three days, nor to any other place than that in which the two houses shall be sitting.

SECTION 6. PRIVILEGES AND RESTRICTIONS

(1) The Senators and Representatives shall receive a compensation for their services, to be ascertained by law and paid out of the Treasury of the United States. They shall in all cases, except treason, felony, and breach of the peace, be privileged from arrest during their attendance at the session of their respective houses, and in going to and returning from the same; and for any speech or debate in either house, they shall not be questioned in any other place.

(2) No Senator or Representative shall, during the time for which he was elected, be appointed to any civil office under the authority of the United States, which shall have been created, or the emoluments whereof shall have been increased, during such time; and no person holding any office under the United States shall be a member of either house during his continuance in office.

SECTION 7. MAKING LAWS

(1) All bills for raising revenue shall originate in the House of Representatives; but the Senate may propose or concur with amendments as on other bills.

(2) Every bill which shall have passed the House of Representatives and the Senate shall, before it become a law, be presented to the President of the United States; if he approve, he shall sign it, but if not, he shall return it, with his objections, to that house in which it shall have originated, who shall enter the objections at large on their journal, and proceed to reconsider it. If after such reconsideration two-thirds of that house shall agree to pass the bill, it shall be sent, together with the objections, to the other house, by which it shall likewise be reconsidered, and, if approved by two-thirds of that house, it shall become a law. But in all such cases the votes of both houses shall be determined by yeas and nays, and the names of the persons voting for and against the bill shall be entered on the journal of each house respectively. If any bill shall not be returned by the President within ten days (Sundays excepted) after it shall have been presented to him, the same bill shall be a law, in like manner as if he had signed it, unless the Congress by their adjournment prevent its return, in which case it shall not be a law.

(3) Every order, resolution, or vote to which the concurrence of the Senate and House of Representatives may be necessary (except on a question of adjournment) shall be presented to the President of the United States; and before the same shall take effect, shall be approved by him, or being disapproved by him, shall be repassed by two-thirds of the Senate and House of Representatives, according to the rules and limitations prescribed in the case of a bill.

SECTION 8. POWERS DELEGATED TO CONGRESS
The Congress shall have power

(1) To lay and collect taxes, duties, imposts and excises, to pay the debts and provide for the common defense and general welfare of the United States; but all duties, imposts and excises shall be uniform throughout the United States;

(1) Taxation
Congress has the authority to raise money to pay debts, defend the United States, and provide services for its people by collecting taxes or tariffs on foreign goods. All taxes must be applied equally in all states.

(2) To borrow money on the credit of the United States;

(2) Borrowing Money
Congress may borrow money for the federal government's use. This is usually done by selling government bonds.

(3) To regulate commerce with foreign nations, and among the several states and with the Indian tribes;

(3) Commerce
Congress can control trade with other countries, with Indian nations, and between states.

(4) To establish an uniform rule of naturalization, and uniform laws on the subject of bankruptcies throughout the United States;

(4) Naturalization and Bankruptcy
Congress decides what requirements people from other countries must meet to become United States citizens. Congress can also pass laws to protect people who are bankrupt, or cannot pay their debts.

(5) To coin money, regulate the value thereof, and of foreign coin, and fix the standard of weights and measures;

(5) Coins, Weights, and Measures
Congress can coin money and decide its value. Congress may also decide on the system of weights and measures to be used throughout the nation.

(6) To provide for the punishment of counterfeiting the securities and current coin of the United States;

(6) Counterfeiting
Congress may pass laws to punish people who make fake money or bonds.

(7) To establish post offices and post roads;

(7) Postal Service
Congress can build post offices and make rules about the postal system and the roads used for mail delivery.

(8) To promote the progress of science and useful arts by securing for limited times to authors and inventors the exclusive right to their respective writings and discoveries;

(8) Copyrights and Patents
Congress can issue patents and copyrights to inventors and authors to protect the ownership of their works.

(9) To constitute tribunals inferior to the Supreme Court;

(9) Federal Courts
Congress can establish a system of federal courts under the Supreme Court.

(10) To define and punish piracies and felonies committed on the high seas and offenses against the law of nations;

(10) Crimes at Sea
Congress can pass laws to punish people for crimes committed at sea. Congress may also punish United States citizens for breaking international law.

(11) Declaring War
Only Congress can declare war.

(11) To declare war, grant letters of marque and reprisal, and make rules concerning captures on land and water;

(12) The Army
Congress can establish an army, but it cannot vote money to support it for more than two years. This part of the Constitution was written to keep the army under Congressional control.

(12) To raise and support armies, but no appropriation of money to that use shall be for a longer term than two years;

(13) The Navy
Congress can establish a navy and vote money to support it for as long as necessary. No time limit was set because people thought the navy was less of a threat to people's liberty than the army was.

(13) To provide and maintain a navy;

(14) Military Regulations
Congress makes the rules that guide and govern all the armed forces.

(14) To make rules for the government and regulation of the land and naval forces;

(15) The Militia
Each state may organize some or all of its citizens into a militia, or military force, capable of fighting to protect the state. The militia can be called into federal service by the President, as authorized by Congress, to enforce laws, to stop uprisings against the government, or to protect the people in case of floods, earthquakes, and other disasters.

(15) To provide for calling forth the militia to execute the laws of the Union, suppress insurrections and repel invasions;

(16) Control of the Militia
Congress may help each state arm, train, and organize its citizens into an armed military force. Each state may appoint its own officers and train this force according to rules set by Congress.

(16) To provide for organizing, arming, and disciplining the militia, and for governing such part of them as may be employed in the service of the United States, reserving to the states, respectively, the appointment of the officers, and the authority of training the militia according to the discipline prescribed by Congress;

(17) National Capital and Other Property
Congress may pass laws to govern the nation's capital (Washington, D.C.) and any land owned by the government.

(17) To exercise exclusive legislation in all cases whatsoever, over such district (not exceeding ten miles square) as may, by cession of particular states, and the acceptance of Congress, become the seat of government of the United States, and to exercise like authority over all places purchased by the consent of the legislature of the state in which the same shall be, for the erection of forts, magazines, arsenals, dock-yards, and other needful buildings; —and

(18) Other Necessary Laws
The Constitution allows Congress to make laws that are necessary to enforce the powers listed in Article I. This clause has two conflicting interpretations. One is that Congress can only do what is absolutely necessary to carry out the powers listed in Article I and in other parts of the Constitution. The other view is that Congress can do whatever is reasonably helpful to carrying out those powers, so its authority becomes very broad though not unlimited.

(18) To make all laws which shall be necessary and proper for carrying into execution the foregoing powers, and all other powers vested by this Constitution in the government of the United States, or in any department or officer thereof.

SECTION 9. POWERS DENIED TO CONGRESS

(1) [*The migration or importation of such persons as any of the states now existing shall think proper to admit shall not be prohibited by the Congress prior to the year 1808; but a tax or duty may be imposed on such importation, not exceeding 10 dollars for each person.*]

(1) Slave Trade
Some authority is not given to Congress. Congress could not prevent the slave trade until 1808, but it could put a tax of ten dollars on each slave brought into the United States. After 1808, this section no longer applied, and Congress banned the slave trade.

(2) The privilege of the writ of habeas corpus shall not be suspended, unless when in cases of rebellion or invasion the public safety may require it.

(2) Habeas Corpus
A writ of habeas corpus entitles a person to a hearing before a judge. The judge must then decide if there is good reason for that person to have been arrested. If not, that person must be released. The government is not allowed to take this privilege away except during a national emergency, such as an invasion or a rebellion.

(3) No bill of attainder or ex post facto law shall be passed.

(3) Special Laws
Congress cannot pass laws that impose punishment on a named individual or group. Congress also cannot pass laws that punish a person for an action that was legal when it was done.

(4) [*No capitation or other direct tax shall be laid, unless in proportion to the census or enumeration herein before directed to be taken.*]

(4) Direct Taxes
Congress cannot set a direct tax on people—as opposed to taxes on transactions, such as on imports into the country, or on sales of certain goods—unless it is in proportion to the total population. Amendment 16, which provides for the income tax, is an exception.

(5) No tax or duty shall be laid on articles exported from any state.

(5) Export Taxes
Congress cannot tax goods sent from one state to another or from a state to another country.

(6) No preference shall be given by any regulation of commerce or revenue to the ports of one state over those of another; nor shall vessels bound to, or from, one state, be obliged to enter, clear, or pay duties in another.

(6) Ports
When making trade laws, Congress cannot favor one state over another. Congress cannot require ships from one state to pay a duty to enter another state.

(7) No money shall be drawn from the Treasury, but in consequence of appropriations made by law; and a regular statement and account of the receipts and expenditures of all public money shall be published from time to time.

(7) Public Money
The government cannot spend money from the treasury unless Congress passes a law allowing it to do so. A written record must be kept of all money spent by the government.

(8) No title of nobility shall be granted by the United States; and no person holding any office of profit or trust under them, shall, without the consent of the Congress, accept of any present, emolument, office, or title, of any kind whatever, from any king, prince, or foreign state.

(8) Titles of Nobility and Gifts
The United States government cannot grant titles of nobility. Government officials cannot accept gifts from other countries without the permission of Congress. This clause was intended to prevent government officials from being bribed by other nations.

SECTION 10. POWERS DENIED TO THE STATES

(1) Complete Restrictions
The Constitution does not allow states to act as if they were individual countries. No state government may make a treaty with other countries. No state can print or coin its own money.

(1) No state shall enter into any treaty, alliance, or confederation; grant letters of marque and reprisal; coin money; emit bills of credit; make anything but gold and silver coin a tender in payment of debts; pass any bill of attainder, ex post facto law, or law impairing the obligation of contracts, or grant any title of nobility.

(2) Partial Restrictions
No state government can tax imported goods or exported goods without the consent of Congress. States may charge a limited fee to inspect these goods, but profits must be given to the United States Treasury.

(2) No state shall, without the consent of the Congress, lay any imposts or duties on imports or exports, except what may be absolutely necessary for executing its inspection laws; and the net produce of all duties and imposts, laid by any state on imports or exports, shall be for the use of the Treasury of the United States; and all such laws shall be subject to the revision and control of the Congress.

(3) Other Restrictions
No state government may tax ships entering its ports unless Congress approves. No state may keep an army or navy during times of peace other than its citizen-soldier militia. No state can enter into agreements, or "compacts," with other states without the consent of Congress.

(3) No state shall, without the consent of Congress, lay any duty of tonnage, keep troops, or ships of war in time of peace, enter into any agreement or compact with another state, or with a foreign power, or engage in war, unless actually invaded, or in such imminent danger as will not admit of delay.

ARTICLE II
THE EXECUTIVE BRANCH
SECTION 1. PRESIDENT AND VICE PRESIDENT

(1) Term of Office
The President has the authority to carry out our nation's laws. The term of office for both the President and the Vice President is four years.

(1) The executive power shall be vested in a President of the United States of America. He shall hold his office during the term of four years, and together with the Vice President, chosen for the same term, be elected as follows:

(2) The Electoral College
This group of people is to be chosen by the voters of each state to elect the President and Vice President. The number of electors in each state is equal to the combined number of senators and representatives that state has in Congress.

(2) Each state shall appoint, in such manner as the legislature thereof may direct, a number of electors, equal to the whole number of Senators and Representatives to which the state may be entitled in the Congress; but no Senator or Representative, or person holding an office of trust or profit under the United States, shall be appointed an elector.

(3) Election Process
This clause describes in detail how the electors were to choose the President and Vice President. In 1804 Amendment 12 changed the process for electing the President and the Vice President.

(3) [*The electors shall meet in their respective states, and vote by ballot for two persons, of whom one at least shall not be an inhabitant of the same state with themselves. And they shall make a list of all the persons voted for, and of the number of votes for each; which list they shall sign and certify, and transmit sealed to the seat of the government of the United States, directed to the president of the Senate. The president of the Senate shall, in the presence of the Senate and House of Representatives, open all the certificates, and the votes shall then be counted. The person having the greatest number of votes shall be the President, if such number be a majority of the whole number of electors appointed; and if there be more than one who have such majority, and have an equal number of votes, then the House of Representatives shall immediately choose by ballot one of them for President; and if no person have a majority, then from the five highest on the list the said House shall in like manner choose the President. But in choosing the President the votes shall be taken by states, the representation from each state having one vote: A quorum for this purpose shall consist*

of a member or members from two-thirds of the states, and a majority of all the states shall be necessary to a choice. In every case, after the choice of the President, the person having the greatest number of votes of the electors shall be the Vice President. But if there should remain two or more who have equal votes, the Senate shall choose from them by ballot the Vice President.]

(4) The Congress may determine the time of choosing the electors, and the day on which they shall give their votes; which day shall be the same throughout the United States.

(4) Time of Elections
Congress decides the day the electors are to be elected and the day they are to vote.

(5) No person except a natural-born citizen [*or a citizen of the United States, at the time of the adoption of this Constitution,*] shall be eligible to the office of the President; neither shall any person be eligible to that office who shall not have attained to the age of thirty-five years, and been fourteen years a resident within the United States.

(5) Qualifications
The President must be at least 35 years old, be a citizen of the United States by birth, and have been living in the United States for 14 years or more.

(6) [*In case of the removal of the President from office, or of his death, resignation, or inability to discharge the powers and duties of the said office, the same shall devolve on the Vice President, and the Congress may by law provide for the case of removal, death, resignation or inability, both of the President and Vice President, declaring what officer shall then act as President, and such officer shall act accordingly, until the disability be removed, or a President shall be elected.*]

(6) Vacancies
If the President dies, resigns, or is removed from office, the Vice President becomes President.

(7) The President shall, at stated times, receive for his services, a compensation, which shall neither be increased nor diminished during the period for which he shall have been elected, and he shall not receive within that period any other emolument from the United States, or any of them.

(7) Salary
The President receives a salary that cannot be raised or lowered during a term of office. The President may not be paid any additional salary by the federal government or any state or local government. Today the President's salary is $400,000 a year, plus expenses for things such as housing, travel, and entertainment.

(8) Before he enter on the execution of his office, he shall take the following oath or affirmation:—"I do solemnly swear (or affirm) that I will faithfully execute the office of President of the United States, and will to the best of my ability, preserve, protect, and defend the Constitution of the United States."

(8) Oath of Office
Before taking office, the President must promise to perform the duties faithfully and to protect the country's form of government. Usually the Chief Justice of the Supreme Court administers the oath of office.

SECTION 2. POWERS OF THE PRESIDENT

(1) The President shall be Commander in Chief of the Army and Navy of the United States, and of the militia of the several states, when called into the actual service of the United States; he may require the opinion, in writing, of the principal officer in each of the executive departments, upon any subject relating to the duties of their respective offices, and he shall have power to grant reprieves and pardons for offenses against the United States, except in cases of impeachment.

(1) The President's Leadership
The President is the commander of the nation's armed forces and of the militia when it is in service of the nation. All heads of government departments must respond to the President's requests for their opinions. The President can pardon people, or excuse them from punishment for crimes they committed.

(2) Treaties and Appointments
The President has the authority to make treaties, but they must be approved by a two-thirds vote of the Senate. The President nominates justices to the Supreme Court, ambassadors to other countries, and other federal officials with the Senate's approval. Congress may allow the President to appoint some officials without Senate confirmation. It may also let courts or heads of federal departments appoint some officials.

(2) He shall have power, by and with the advice and consent of the Senate, to make treaties, provided two-thirds of the senators present concur; and he shall nominate, and by and with the advice and consent of the Senate, shall appoint ambassadors, other public ministers and consuls, judges of the Supreme Court, and all other officers of the United States, whose appointments are not herein otherwise provided for, and which shall be established by law; but the Congress may by law vest the appointment of such inferior officers, as they think proper, in the President alone, in the courts of law, or in the heads of departments.

(3) Filling Vacancies
If a government official's position becomes vacant when the Senate is not in session, the President can make a temporary appointment.

(3) The President shall have power to fill up all vacancies that may happen during the recess of the Senate, by granting commissions which shall expire at the end of their next session.

Duties
The President must report to Congress on the condition of the country. This report is now presented in the annual State of the Union message. The President is also responsible for enforcing federal laws.

SECTION 3. DUTIES OF THE PRESIDENT

He shall from time to time give to the Congress information of the state of the Union, and recommend to their consideration such measures as he shall judge necessary and expedient; he may, on extraordinary occasions, convene both houses, or either of them, and in case of disagreement between them, with respect to the time of adjournment, he may adjourn them to such time as he shall think proper; he shall receive ambassadors and other public ministers; he shall take care that the laws be faithfully executed, and shall commission all the officers of the United States.

Impeachment
The President, the Vice President, or any government official will be removed from office if impeached, or accused, and then found guilty of treason, bribery, or other serious crimes.

SECTION 4. IMPEACHMENT

The President, Vice President and all civil officers of the United States, shall be removed from office on impeachment for, and conviction of, treason, bribery, or other high crimes and misdemeanors.

ARTICLE III
THE JUDICIAL BRANCH
SECTION 1. FEDERAL COURTS

Federal Courts
The authority to decide legal cases is granted to a Supreme Court and to a system of lower courts established by Congress. The Supreme Court is the highest court in the land. Justices and judges are in their offices for life, subject to good behavior.

The judicial power of the United States shall be vested in one Supreme Court, and in such inferior courts as the Congress may from time to time ordain and establish. The judges, both of the supreme and inferior courts, shall hold their offices during good behavior, and shall, at stated times, receive for their services a compensation, which shall not be diminished during their continuance in office.

SECTION 2. AUTHORITY OF THE FEDERAL COURTS

(1) General Authority
Federal courts have the authority to decide cases that arise under the Constitution, laws, and treaties of the United States. They also have the authority to settle disagreements among states and among citizens of different states.

(1) The judicial power shall extend to all cases, in law and equity, arising under this Constitution, the laws of the United States, and treaties made or which shall be made, under their authority; to all cases affecting ambassadors, other public ministers and consuls; to all cases of admiralty and maritime jurisdiction; to controversies to which the United States shall be a party; to controversies between two or more states; [*between a state and citizens of another state;*]

between citizens of different states; —between citizens of the same state claiming lands under grants of different states, [*and between a state or the citizens thereof, and foreign states, citizens, or subjects.*]

(2) In all cases affecting ambassadors, other public ministers and consuls, and those in which a state shall be party, the Supreme Court shall have original jurisdiction. In all the other cases before mentioned, the Supreme Court shall have appellate jurisdiction, both as to law and fact, with such exceptions, and under such regulations as the Congress shall make.

(3) The trial of all crimes, except in cases of impeachment, shall be by jury; and such trial shall be held in the state where the said crimes shall have been committed; but when not committed within any state, the trial shall be at such place or places as the Congress may by law have directed.

SECTION 3. TREASON

(1) Treason against the United States shall consist only in levying war against them, or in adhering to their enemies, giving them aid and comfort. No person shall be convicted of treason unless on the testimony of two witnesses to the same overt act, or on confession in open court.

(2) The Congress shall have power to declare the punishment of treason, but no attainder of treason shall work corruption of blood, or forfeiture except during the life of the person attainted.

ARTICLE IV
RELATIONS AMONG STATES
SECTION 1. OFFICIAL RECORDS

Full faith and credit shall be given in each state to the public acts, records, and judicial proceedings of every other state. And the Congress may by general laws prescribe the manner in which such acts, records, and proceedings shall be proved, and the effect thereof.

SECTION 2. PRIVILEGES OF THE CITIZENS

(1) The citizens of each state shall be entitled to all privileges and immunities of citizens in the several states.

(2) A person charged in any state with treason, felony, or other crime, who shall flee from justice, and be found in another state, shall on demand of the executive authority of the state from which he fled, be delivered up, to be removed to the state having jurisdiction of the crime.

(2) Supreme Court
The Supreme Court can decide certain cases being tried for the first time. It can review cases that have already been tried in a lower court if the decision has been appealed, or questioned, by one side.

(3) Trial by Jury
The Constitution guarantees a trial by jury for every person charged with a federal crime. Amendments 5, 6, and 7 extend and clarify a person's right to a trial by jury.

(1) Definition of Treason
Acts that may be considered treason are making war against the United States or helping its enemies. A person cannot be convicted of attempting to overthrow the government unless there are two witnesses to the act or the person confesses in court to treason.

(2) Punishment for Treason
Congress can decide the punishment for treason, within certain limits.

Official Records
Each state must honor the official records and judicial decisions of other states.

(1) Privileges
A citizen moving from one state to another has the same rights as other citizens living in that person's new state of residence. In some cases, such as voting, people may be required to live in their new state for a certain length of time before obtaining the same privileges as citizens there.

(2) Extradition
At a state governor's request, a person who is charged with a crime in a state and who tries to escape justice by crossing into another state may be returned to the state in which the crime was committed.

(3) Fugitive Slaves
The original Constitution required that runaway slaves be returned to their owners. Amendment 13 abolished slavery, eliminating the need for this clause.

(1) Admission of New States
Congress has the authority to admit new states to the Union. The Supreme Court has held that all new states have the same rights as existing states.

(2) Federal Property
The Constitution allows Congress to make or change laws governing federal property. This applies to territories and federally owned land within states, such as national parks.

Guarantees to the States
The federal government guarantees that every state shall have a republican form of government. The United States must also protect the states against invasion and help the states deal with rebellion or local violence.

Amending the Constitution
Changes to the Constitution may be proposed by a two-thirds vote of both the House of Representatives and the Senate or by a national convention called by Congress when asked by two-thirds of the states. For a proposed amendment to become law, the legislatures or conventions in three-fourths of the states must approve it.

(1) Public Debt
Any debt owed by the United States before the Constitution went into effect was to be honored.

(2) Federal Supremacy
This clause declares that the Constitution, federal laws, and treaties are the highest law in the nation. Whenever a state law and a federal law are found to disagree, the federal law must be obeyed so long as it is constitutional.

---

(3) [*No person held to service or labor in one state, under the laws thereof, escaping into another, shall in consequence of any law or regulation therein, be discharged from such service or labor, but shall be delivered up on claim of the party to whom such service or labor may be due.*]

SECTION 3. NEW STATES AND TERRITORIES

(1) New states may be admitted by the Congress into this Union; but no new state shall be formed or erected within the jurisdiction of any other state; nor any state be formed by the junction of two or more states, or parts of states, without the consent of the legislatures of the states concerned as well as of the Congress.

(2) The Congress shall have power to dispose of and make all needful rules and regulations respecting the territory or other property belonging to the United States; and nothing in this Constitution shall be so construed as to prejudice any claims of the United States, or of any particular state.

SECTION 4. GUARANTEES TO THE STATES

The United States shall guarantee to every state in this Union a republican form of government, and shall protect each of them against invasion; and on application of the legislature, or of the executive (when the legislature cannot be convened) against domestic violence.

ARTICLE V
AMENDING THE CONSTITUTION

The Congress, whenever two-thirds of both houses shall deem it necessary, shall propose amendments to this Constitution, or, on the application of the legislatures of two-thirds of the several states, shall call a convention for proposing amendments, which, in either case, shall be valid to all intents and purposes, as part of this Constitution, when ratified by the legislatures of three-fourths of the several states, or by conventions in three-fourths thereof, as the one or the other mode of ratification may be proposed by the Congress; provided that [*no amendment which may be made prior to the year 1808 shall in any manner affect the first and fourth clauses in the Ninth Section of the First Article; and that*] no state, without its consent, shall be deprived of its equal suffrage in the Senate.

ARTICLE VI
GENERAL PROVISIONS

(1) All debts contracted and engagements entered into, before the adoption of this Constitution, shall be as valid against the United States under this Constitution, as under the Confederation.

(2) This Constitution, and the laws of the United States which shall be made in pursuance thereof, and all treaties made, or which shall be made, under the authority of the United States, shall be the supreme law of the land; and the judges in every state shall be bound thereby, anything in the Constitution or laws of any state to the contrary notwithstanding.

(3) The Senators and Representatives before mentioned, and the members of the several state legislatures, and all executive and judicial officers, both of the United States and of the several states, shall be bound by oath or affirmation, to support this Constitution; but no religious test shall ever be required as a qualification to any office or public trust under the United States.

ARTICLE VII
RATIFICATION

The ratification of the conventions of nine states, shall be sufficient for the establishment of this Constitution between the states so ratifying the same.

Done in convention by the unanimous consent of the states present the seventeenth day of September in the year of our Lord one thousand seven hundred and eighty seven and of the independence of the United States of America the Twelfth. In witness whereof we have hereunto subscribed our names.

George Washington—President and deputy from Virginia

DELAWARE
George Read
Gunning Bedford, Jr.
John Dickinson
Richard Bassett
Jacob Broom

MARYLAND
James McHenry
Daniel of St. Thomas Jenifer
Daniel Carroll

VIRGINIA
John Blair
James Madison, Jr.

NORTH CAROLINA
William Blount
Richard Dobbs Spaight
Hugh Williamson

SOUTH CAROLINA
John Rutledge
Charles Cotesworth Pinckney
Charles Pinckney
Pierce Butler

GEORGIA
William Few
Abraham Baldwin

NEW HAMPSHIRE
John Langdon
Nicholas Gilman

MASSACHUSETTS
Nathaniel Gorham
Rufus King

CONNECTICUT
William Samuel Johnson
Roger Sherman

NEW YORK
Alexander Hamilton

NEW JERSEY
William Livingston
David Brearley
William Paterson
Jonathan Dayton

PENNSYLVANIA
Benjamin Franklin
Thomas Mifflin
Robert Morris
George Clymer
Thomas FitzSimons
Jared Ingersoll
James Wilson
Gouverneur Morris

ATTEST: William Jackson, secretary

(3) Oaths of Office
All federal and state officials must promise to follow and enforce the Constitution. These officials cannot be required to follow a particular religion or satisfy any religious test.

Ratification
In order for the Constitution to become law, 9 of the 13 states had to approve it. Special conventions were held for this purpose. The process took 9 months to complete.

Freedom of Religion, Speech, Press, Assembly, and Petition
The Constitution provides for the freedoms of religion, speech, the press, peaceable assembly, and petition for redress of grievances. It also prohibits Congress from establishing religion.

AMENDMENT 1 (1791)***
FREEDOM OF RELIGION, SPEECH, PRESS, ASSEMBLY, AND PETITION

Congress shall make no law respecting an establishment of religion, or prohibiting the free exercise thereof; or abridging the freedom of speech, or of the press; or the right of the people peaceably to assemble, and to petition the government for a redress of grievances.

Weapons
Amendment 2 protects the right of individuals to own guns.

AMENDMENT 2 (1791)
WEAPONS

A well-regulated militia, being necessary to the security of a free state, the right of the people to keep and bear arms shall not be infringed.

Housing Soldiers
The federal government cannot force people to house soldiers in their homes during peacetime. However, Congress may pass laws allowing this during wartime.

AMENDMENT 3 (1791)
HOUSING SOLDIERS

No soldier shall, in time of peace, be quartered in any house, without the consent of the owner; nor in time of war, but in a manner to be prescribed by law.

Searches and Seizures
This amendment protects people's privacy and safety. Subject to certain exceptions, a law officer cannot search a person or a person's home and belongings unless a judge has issued a valid search warrant. There must be good reason for the search. The warrant must describe the place to be searched and the people or things to be seized, or taken.

AMENDMENT 4 (1791)
SEARCHES AND SEIZURES

The right of the people to be secure in their persons, houses, papers, and effects, against unreasonable searches and seizures, shall not be violated; and no warrants shall issue but upon probable cause, supported by oath or affirmation, and particularly describing the place to be searched, and the persons or things to be seized.

Rights of Accused Persons
If a person is accused of a crime that is punishable by death or of any other serious crime, a grand jury must decide if there is enough evidence to hold a trial. People cannot be tried twice for the same crime, nor can they be forced to testify against themselves. No person shall be fined, jailed, or executed by the government unless the person has been given a fair trial. The government cannot take a person's property for public use unless fair payment is made.

AMENDMENT 5 (1791)
RIGHTS OF ACCUSED PERSONS

No person shall be held to answer for a capital, or otherwise infamous crime, unless on a presentment or indictment of a grand jury, except in cases arising in the land or naval forces, or in the militia, when in actual service in time of war or public danger; nor shall any person be subject for the same offense to be twice put in jeopardy of life or limb; nor shall be compelled in any criminal case to be a witness against himself; nor be deprived of life, liberty, or property, without due process of law; nor shall private property be taken for public use without just compensation.

*** The date beside each amendment is the year that the amendment was ratified and became part of the Constitution.

AMENDMENT 6 (1791)
RIGHTS RELATED TO CRIMINAL TRIALS

In all criminal prosecutions, the accused shall enjoy the right to a speedy and public trial, by an impartial jury of the state and district wherein the crime shall have been committed, which district shall have been previously ascertained by law, and to be informed of the nature and cause of the accusation; to be confronted with the witnesses against him; to have compulsory process for obtaining witnesses in his favor, and to have the assistance of counsel for his defense.

AMENDMENT 7 (1791)
JURY TRIAL IN CIVIL CASES

In suits at common law, where the value in controversy shall exceed 20 dollars, the right of trial by jury shall be preserved, and no fact tried by a jury shall be otherwise re-examined in any court of the United States, than according to the rules of the common law.

AMENDMENT 8 (1791)
BAIL AND PUNISHMENT

Excessive bail shall not be required, nor excessive fines imposed, nor cruel and unusual punishments inflicted.

AMENDMENT 9 (1791)
RIGHTS OF THE PEOPLE

The enumeration in the Constitution, of certain rights, shall not be construed to deny or disparage others retained by the people.

AMENDMENT 10 (1791)
POWERS OF THE STATES AND THE PEOPLE

The powers not delegated to the United States by the Constitution, nor prohibited by it to the states, are reserved to the states respectively, or to the people.

AMENDMENT 11 (1798)
SUITS AGAINST STATES

The judicial power of the United States shall not be construed to extend to any suit in law or equity, commenced or prosecuted against one of the United States or citizens of another state, or by citizens or subjects of any foreign state.

Rights Related to Criminal Trials
A person accused of a crime has the right to a public trial by an impartial jury, locally chosen. The trial must be held within a reasonable amount of time. The accused person must be told of all charges and has the right to see, hear, and question any witnesses and to call his or her own witnesses. The government must allow the accused to have a lawyer. This has also been interpreted as requiring the government to provide a lawyer free of charge to a person who is accused of a serious crime and who is unable to pay for legal services.

Jury Trial in Civil Cases
In most federal civil cases involving more than 20 dollars, a jury trial is guaranteed. Civil cases are those disputes between two or more people over money, property, personal injury, or legal rights. Usually civil cases are not tried in federal courts unless they involve a federal law, rather than just state law, or much larger sums of money are involved.

Bail and Punishment
Courts cannot punish convicted criminals in cruel and unusual ways and cannot impose fines that are too high. Bail is money put up as a guarantee that an accused person will appear for trial. In certain cases bail can be denied altogether.

Rights of the People
People disagree about the meaning of this amendment. Some think it authorizes courts to protect certain individual rights even though those rights are not expressly stated in the Bill of Rights. Others think the amendment recognizes that state laws may protect a wide range of individual rights that are not mentioned in the Bill of Rights but that those unenumerated rights may be defined or repealed by the democratic process in each state.

Powers of the States and the People
Any powers not given to the federal government or denied to the states belong to the states or to the people.

Suits Against States
A citizen of one state or of a foreign country cannot sue another state in federal court.

AMENDMENT 12 (1804)
ELECTION OF PRESIDENT AND VICE PRESIDENT

Election of President and Vice President
This amendment replaces the part of Article II, Section 1, that originally explained the process of electing the President and Vice President. Amendment 12 was an important step in the development of the two-party system. It allows a party to nominate its own candidates for both President and Vice President.

The electors shall meet in their respective states, and vote by ballot for President and Vice President, one of whom, at least, shall not be an inhabitant of the same state with themselves; they shall name in their ballots the person voted for as President, and in distinct ballots the person voted for as Vice President, and they shall make distinct lists of all persons voted for as President, and of all persons voted for as Vice President, and of the number of votes for each, which lists they shall sign and certify, and transmit, sealed, to the seat of government of the United States, directed to the President of the Senate; the President of the Senate shall, in the presence of the Senate and House of Representatives, open all the certificates, and the votes shall then be counted; the person having the greatest number of votes for President shall be the President, if such a number be a majority of the whole number of electors appointed; and if no person have such majority; then from the persons having the highest numbers not exceeding three on the list of those voted for as President, the House of Representatives shall choose immediately, by ballot, the President. But in choosing the President, the votes shall be taken by states, the representation from each state having one vote; a quorum for this purpose shall consist of a member or members from two thirds of the states, and a majority of all the states shall be necessary to a choice. [*And if the House of Representatives shall not choose a President whenever the right of choice shall devolve upon them, before the fourth day of March next following, then the Vice President shall act as President, as in the case of the death or other constitutional disability of the President.*] The person having the greatest number of votes as Vice President, shall be the Vice President, if such number be a majority of the whole number of electors appointed, and if no person have a majority, then, from the two highest numbers on the list the Senate shall choose the Vice President; a quorum for the purpose shall consist of two thirds of the whole number of Senators, and a majority of the whole number shall be necessary to a choice. But no person constitutionally ineligible to the office of President shall be eligible to that of Vice President of the United States.

AMENDMENT 13 (1865)
END OF SLAVERY

End of Slavery
People cannot be forced to work against their will unless they have been tried for and convicted of a crime for which this means of punishment is ordered. However, there are historical exceptions where compulsory work is permitted, such as the military draft and jury duty. Congress may enforce this by law.

SECTION 1. ABOLITION

Neither slavery nor involuntary servitude, except as a punishment for crime whereof the party shall have been duly convicted, shall exist within the United States, or any place subject to their jurisdiction.

SECTION 2. ENFORCEMENT

Congress shall have power to enforce this article by appropriate legislation.

AMENDMENT 14 (1868)
RIGHTS OF CITIZENS

SECTION 1. CITIZENSHIP

Citizenship
All persons born or naturalized in the United States are citizens of the United States and of the state in which they live. State governments may not deny any citizen the full rights of citizenship. This amendment also guarantees that no state may take away a person's life, liberty, or property without following the procedure prescribed by law. All citizens must be protected equally under law.

All persons born or naturalized in the United States and subject to the jurisdiction thereof, are citizens of the United States and of the state wherein they reside. No state shall make or enforce any law which shall abridge the privileges or immunities of citizens of the United States, nor shall any state deprive any person of life, liberty, or property, without due process of law; nor deny to any person within its jurisdiction the equal protection of the laws.

SECTION 2. NUMBER OF REPRESENTATIVES

Representatives shall be apportioned among the several states according to their respective numbers, counting the whole number of persons in each state, [*excluding Indians not taxed*]. But when the right to vote at any election for the choice of electors for President and Vice President of the United States, representatives in Congress, the executive and judicial officers of a state, or the members of the legislature thereof, is denied to any of the [*male*] inhabitants of such state, being [*twenty-one years of age and*] citizens of the United States, or in any way abridged, except for participation in rebellion or other crime, the basis of representation therein shall be reduced in the proportion which the number of such [*male*] citizens shall bear to the whole number of [*male*] citizens [*twenty-one years of age*] in such state.

SECTION 3. PENALTY FOR REBELLION

No person shall be a Senator or Representative in Congress, or elector of President and Vice President, or hold any office, civil or military, under the United States, or under any state, who, having previously taken an oath, as a member of Congress, or as an officer of the United States, or as a member of any state legislature, or as an executive or judicial officer of any state, to support the Constitution of the United States, shall have engaged in insurrection or rebellion against the same, or given aid or comfort to the enemies thereof. But Congress may, by a vote of two thirds of each house, remove such disability.

SECTION 4. GOVERNMENT DEBT

The validity of the public debt of the United States, authorized by law, including debts incurred for payment of pensions and bounties for services in suppressing insurrection or rebellion, shall not be questioned. But neither the United States nor any state shall assume or pay any debt or obligation incurred in aid of insurrection or rebellion against the United States, [*or any claim for the loss or emancipation of any slave;*] but all such debts, obligations, and claims shall be held illegal and void.

SECTION 5. ENFORCEMENT

The Congress shall have power to enforce, by appropriate legislation, the provisions of this article.

AMENDMENT 15 (1870)
VOTING RIGHTS
SECTION 1. RIGHT TO VOTE

The right of citizens of the United States to vote shall not be denied or abridged by the United States or by any state on account of race, color, or previous condition of servitude.

SECTION 2. ENFORCEMENT

The Congress shall have power to enforce this article by appropriate legislation.

AMENDMENT 16 (1913)
INCOME TAX

The Congress shall have power to lay and collect taxes on incomes, from whatever source derived, without apportionment among the several states, and without regard to any census or enumeration.

Number of Representatives
Each state's representation in Congress is based on its total population. Any state denying eligible citizens the right to vote will have its representation in Congress decreased. This clause abolished the Three-fifths Compromise in Article I, Section 2. Later amendments granted women the right to vote and lowered the voting age to 18.

Penalty for Rebellion
No person who has rebelled against the United States may hold federal office. This clause was originally added to punish the leaders of the Confederacy for failing to support the Constitution of the United States.

Government Debt
The federal government is responsible for all federal public debts. It is not responsible, however, for Confederate debts or for debts that result from any rebellion against the United States.

Enforcement
Congress may enforce these provisions by law.

Right to Vote
No state may prevent a citizen from voting because of race or color or condition of previous servitude.

Income Tax
Congress has the power to collect taxes on its citizens, based on their personal incomes, rather than requiring the states to impose and collect such taxes.

AMENDMENT 17 (1913)
DIRECT ELECTION OF SENATORS

Direct Election of Senators
Originally, state legislatures elected senators. This amendment allows the people of each state to elect their own senators directly. The idea is to make senators more responsible to the people they represent.

SECTION 1. METHOD OF ELECTION

The Senate of the United States shall be composed of two Senators from each state, elected by the people thereof, for six years; and each Senator shall have one vote. The electors in each state shall have the qualifications requisite for electors of the most numerous branch of the state legislatures.

SECTION 2. VACANCIES

When vacancies happen in the representation of any state in the Senate, the executive authority of such state shall issue writs of election to fill such vacancies: *Provided*, that the legislature of any state may empower the executive thereof to make temporary appointments until the people fill the vacancies by election as the legislature may direct.

SECTION 3. EXCEPTION

[*This amendment shall not be so construed as to affect the election or term of any Senator chosen before it becomes valid as part of the Constitution.*]

AMENDMENT 18 (1919)
BAN ON ALCOHOLIC DRINKS

Prohibition
This amendment made it illegal to make, sell, or transport liquor within the United States or to transport it out of the United States or its territories. Amendment 18 was the first to include a time limit for approval. If not ratified within seven years, it would be repealed, or canceled. Many later amendments have included similar time limits.

SECTION 1. PROHIBITION

[*After one year from the ratification of this article the manufacture, sale, or transportation of intoxicating liquors within, the importation thereof into, or the exportation thereof from the United States and all territory subject to the jurisdiction thereof for beverage purposes is hereby prohibited.*]

SECTION 2. ENFORCEMENT

[*The Congress and the several states shall have concurrent power to enforce this article by appropriate legislation.*]

SECTION 3. RATIFICATION

[*This article shall be inoperative unless it shall have been ratified as an amendment to the Constitution by the legislatures of the several states as provided in the Constitution, within seven years from the date of the submission hereof to the states by the Congress.*]

AMENDMENT 19 (1920)
WOMEN'S VOTING RIGHTS

Women's Voting Rights
This amendment protected the right of women throughout the United States to vote.

SECTION 1. RIGHT TO VOTE

The right of citizens of the United States to vote shall not be denied or abridged by the United States or by any state on account of sex.

SECTION 2. ENFORCEMENT

Congress shall have power to enforce this article by appropriate legislation.

AMENDMENT 20 (1933)
TERMS OF OFFICE

Terms of Office
The terms of the President and the Vice President begin on January 20, in the year following their election. Members of Congress take office on January 3. Before this amendment newly elected members of Congress did not begin their terms until March 4. This meant that those who had run for reelection and been defeated remained in office for four months.

SECTION 1. BEGINNING OF TERMS

The terms of the President and Vice President shall end at noon on the 20th day of January, and the terms of Senators and Representatives at noon on the 3rd day of January, of the years in which such terms would have ended if this article had not been ratified; and the terms of their successors shall then begin.

SECTION 2. SESSIONS OF CONGRESS

The Congress shall assemble at least once in every year, and such meeting shall begin at noon on the 3rd day of January, unless they shall by law appoint a different day.

SECTION 3. PRESIDENTIAL SUCCESSION

If, at the time fixed for the beginning of the term of the President, the President-elect shall have died, the Vice President-elect shall become President. If a President shall not have been chosen before the time fixed for the beginning of his term, or if the President-elect shall have failed to qualify, then the Vice President-elect shall act as President until a President shall have qualified; and the Congress may by law provide for the case wherein neither a President-elect nor a Vice President-elect shall have qualified, declaring who shall then act as President, or the manner in which one who is to act shall be selected and such person shall act accordingly until a President or Vice President shall be qualified.

SECTION 4. ELECTIONS DECIDED BY CONGRESS

The Congress may by law provide for the case of the death of any of the persons from whom the House of Representatives may choose a President whenever the right of choice shall have devolved upon them, and for the case of the death of any of the persons from whom the Senate may choose a Vice President whenever the right of choice shall have devolved upon them.

SECTION 5. EFFECTIVE DATE

[*Sections 1 and 2 shall take effect on the 15th day of October following the ratification of this article.*]

SECTION 6. RATIFICATION

[*This article shall be inoperative unless it shall have been ratified as an amendment to the Constitution by the legislatures of three fourths of the several states within seven years from the date of its submission.*]

AMENDMENT 21 (1933)
END OF PROHIBITION

SECTION 1. REPEAL OF AMENDMENT 18

The eighteenth article of amendment to the Constitution of the United States is hereby repealed.

SECTION 2. STATE LAWS

The transportation or importation into any state, territory, or possession of the United States for delivery or use therein of intoxicating liquors, in violation of the laws thereof, is hereby prohibited.

SECTION 3. RATIFICATION

[*This article shall be inoperative unless it shall have been ratified as an amendment to the Constitution by conventions in the several states, as provided in the Constitution within seven years from the date of the submission hereof to the states by Congress.*]

Sessions of Congress
Congress meets at least once a year, beginning at noon on January 3. Congress had previously met at least once a year beginning on the first Monday of December.

Presidential Succession
If the newly elected President dies before January 20, the newly elected Vice President becomes President on that date. If a President has not been chosen by January 20 or does not meet the requirements for being President, the newly elected Vice President becomes President. Congress may enact a law that indicates who will temporarily serve as President if neither the newly elected President nor the newly elected Vice President meets the requirements for office.

End of Prohibition
This amendment repealed Amendment 18. This is the only amendment to be ratified by state conventions instead of by state legislatures. Congress felt that this would give people's opinions about prohibition a better chance to be heard.

Two-Term limit for Presidents
A President may not serve more than two full terms in office. Any President who serves less than two years of a previous President's term may be elected for two more terms.

AMENDMENT 22 (1951)
TWO-TERM LIMIT FOR PRESIDENTS
SECTION 1. TWO-TERM LIMIT

No person shall be elected to the office of the President more than twice, and no person who has held the office of President, or acted as President, for more than two years of a term to which some other person was elected President shall be elected to the office of the President more than once. [*But this article shall not apply to any person holding the office of President when this article was proposed by the Congress, and shall not prevent any person who may be holding the office of President, or acting as President, during the term within which this article becomes operative from holding the office of President, or acting as President, during the remainder of such term.*]

SECTION 2. RATIFICATION

[*This article shall be inoperative unless it shall have been ratified as an amendment to the Constitution by the legislatures of three-fourths of the several states within seven years from the date of its submission to the states by the Congress.*]

Presidential Electors for District of Columbia
This amendment grants three electoral votes to the national capital.

AMENDMENT 23 (1961)
PRESIDENTIAL ELECTORS FOR DISTRICT OF COLUMBIA
SECTION 1. NUMBER OF ELECTORS

The District constituting the seat of Government of the United States shall appoint in such manner as Congress may direct:

A number of electors of President and Vice President equal to the whole number of Senators and Representatives in Congress to which the District would be entitled if it were a state, but in no event more than the least populous state; they shall be in addition to those appointed by the states, but they shall be considered, for the purposes of the election of President and Vice President, to be electors appointed by a state, and they shall meet in the District and perform such duties as provided by the twelfth article of amendment.

SECTION 2. ENFORCEMENT

The Congress shall have power to enforce this article by appropriate legislation.

Ban on Poll Taxes
No United States citizen may be prevented from voting in a federal election because of failing to pay a tax to vote. Poll taxes had been used in some states to prevent African Americans from voting.

AMENDMENT 24 (1964)
BAN ON POLL TAXES
SECTION 1. POLL TAX ILLEGAL

The right of citizens of the United States to vote in any primary or other election for President or Vice President, for electors for President or Vice President, or for Senator or Representative in Congress, shall not be denied or abridged by the United States or any state by reason of failure to pay any poll tax or other tax.

SECTION 2. ENFORCEMENT

The Congress shall have power to enforce this article by appropriate legislation.

AMENDMENT 25 (1967)
PRESIDENTIAL SUCCESSION
SECTION 1. PRESIDENTIAL VACANCY

Presidential Vacancy
If the President is removed from office or resigns from or dies while in office, the Vice President becomes President.

In case of the removal of the President from office or of his death or resignation, the Vice President shall become President.

SECTION 2. VICE PRESIDENTIAL VACANCY

Whenever there is a vacancy in the office of the Vice President, the President shall nominate a Vice President who shall take the office upon confirmation by a majority vote of both houses of Congress.

SECTION 3. PRESIDENTIAL DISABILITY

Whenever the President transmits to the President pro tempore of the Senate and the Speaker of the House of Representatives his written declaration that he is unable to discharge the powers and duties of his office, and until he transmits to them a written declaration to the contrary, such powers and duties shall be discharged by the Vice President as Acting President.

SECTION 4. DETERMINING PRESIDENTIAL DISABILITY

Whenever the Vice President and a majority of either the principal officers of the executive departments or of such other body as Congress may by law provide, transmit to the President pro tempore of the Senate and the Speaker of the House of Representatives their written declaration that the President is unable to discharge the powers and duties of his office, the Vice President shall immediately assume the powers and duties of the office as Acting President.

Thereafter, when the President transmits to the President pro tempore of the Senate and the Speaker of the House of Representatives his written declaration that no inability exists, he shall resume the powers and duties of his office unless the Vice President and a majority of either the principal officers of the executive department or of such other body as Congress may by law provide, transmit within four days to the President pro tempore of the Senate and the Speaker of the House of Representatives their written declaration that the President is unable to discharge the powers and duties of his office. Thereupon Congress shall decide the issue, assembling within 48 hours for that purpose if not in session. If the Congress, within 21 days after receipt of the latter written declaration, or, if Congress is not in session, within 21 days after Congress is required to assemble, determines by two-thirds vote of both houses that the President is unable to discharge the powers and duties of his office, the Vice President shall continue to discharge the same as Acting President; otherwise the President shall resume the powers and duties of his office.

AMENDMENT 26 (1971)
VOTING AGE
SECTION 1. RIGHT TO VOTE

The right of citizens of the United States, who are 18 years of age or older, to vote shall not be denied or abridged by the United States or any state on account of age.
SECTION 2. ENFORCEMENT

The Congress shall have the power to enforce this article by appropriate legislation.

AMENDMENT 27 (1992)
CONGRESSIONAL PAY

No law, varying the compensation for the services of the Senators and Representatives, shall take effect, until an election of Representatives shall have intervened.

Vice Presidential Vacancy
If the office of the Vice President becomes open, the President names someone to assume that office and that person becomes Vice President if both houses of Congress approve by a majority vote.

Presidential Disability
This section explains in detail what happens if the President cannot continue in office because of sickness or any other reason. The Vice President takes over as acting President until the President is able to resume office.

Determining Presidential Disability
If the Vice President and a majority of the Cabinet inform the Speaker of the House and the president pro tempore of the Senate that the President cannot carry out his or her duties, the Vice President then serves as acting President. To regain the office, the President has to inform the Speaker and the president pro tempore in writing that he or she is again able to serve. But, if the Vice President and a majority of the Cabinet disagree with the President and inform the Speaker and the president pro tempore that the President is still unable to serve, then Congress decides who will hold the office of President.

Voting Age
All citizens 18 years or older have the right to vote. Formerly, the voting age was 21 in most states.

Congressional Pay
A law raising or lowering the salaries for members of Congress cannot be passed for that session of Congress.

THE NATIONAL ANTHEM

The Star-Spangled Banner

(1)

Oh, say can you see by the dawn's early light
What so proudly we hail'd at the twilight's last gleaming,
Whose broad stripes and bright stars through the perilous fight
O'er the ramparts we watch'd were so gallantly streaming?
And the rockets' red glare, the bombs bursting in air,
Gave proof through the night that our flag was still there.
Oh, say does that star-spangled banner yet wave
O'er the land of the free and the home of the brave?

(2)

On the shore dimly seen through the mists of the deep,
Where the foe's haughty host in dread silence reposes,
What is that which the breeze, o'er the towering steep,
As it fitfully blows, half conceals, half discloses?
Now it catches the gleam of the morning's first beam,
In full glory reflected now shines in the stream.
'Tis the star-spangled banner, oh, long may it wave
O'er the land of the free and the home of the brave!

(3)

And where is that band who so vauntingly swore
That the havoc of war and the battle's confusion
A home and a country should leave us no more?
Their blood has wash'd out their foul footstep's pollution.
No refuge could save the hireling and slave
From the terror of flight or the gloom of the grave,
And the star-spangled banner in triumph doth wave
O'er the land of the free and the home of the brave.

(4)

Oh, thus be it ever when freemen shall stand
Between their lov'd home and the war's desolation!
Blest with vict'ry and peace may the heav'n-rescued land
Praise the power that hath made and preserv'd us a nation!
Then conquer we must, when our cause it is just,
And this be our motto, "In God is our Trust,"
And the star-spangled banner in triumph shall wave
O'er the land of the free and the home of the brave.

THE PLEDGE OF ALLEGIANCE

I pledge allegiance to the Flag

of the United States of America,

and to the Republic

for which it stands,

one Nation under God, indivisible,

with liberty and justice for all.

The flag is a symbol of the United States of America. The Pledge of Allegiance says that the people of the United States promise to stand up for the flag, their country, and the basic beliefs of freedom and fairness upon which the country was established.

Research Handbook

Before you can write a report or complete a project, you must gather information about your topic. You can find information from many sources, including maps, photos, illustrations, and artifacts. You can also find information in your textbook. Other sources of information are technology resources, print resources, and community resources.

RESEARCH HANDBOOK

Technology Resources

- Internet
- Computer disk
- Television and radio

Print Resources

- Almanac
- Atlas
- Dictionary
- Encyclopedia
- Nonfiction book
- Periodical
- Thesaurus

Community Resources

- Teacher
- Museum curator
- Community leader
- Older citizen

Technology Resources

The main technology resources you can use for researching information are the Internet and computer disks. Your school or local library may have CD-ROMs or DVDs that contain information about your topic. Other media, such as television and radio, can also be good sources of current information.

Using the Internet

The Internet contains vast amounts of information. By using a computer to go online, you can read letters and documents, see pictures and artworks, listen to music, take a virtual tour of a place, and read about current events.

Information that you find online is always changing. Keep in mind that some websites might contain mistakes or incorrect information. To get accurate information, be sure to visit only trusted websites, such as museum and government sites. Also, try to find two or more websites that give the same facts.

❱ Plan Your Search
- Identify the topic to be researched.
- Make a list of questions that you want to answer about your topic.
- List key words or groups of words that can be used to write or talk about your topic.
- Look for good online resources to find answers to your questions.
- Decide if the information you find is relevant, reliable, and accurate.

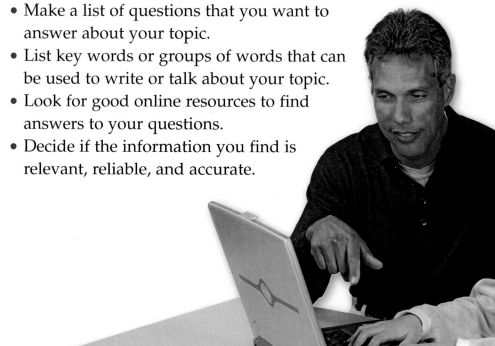

Use a Search Engine

A search engine is an online collection of websites that can be sorted by entering a key word or group of words. There are many different search engines available. You may want to ask a librarian, a teacher, or a parent for suggestions on which search engine to use.

▶ Search by Subject To search by subject, or topic, use a search engine. Choose from the list of key words that you made while planning your search, and enter a key word or group of words in the search engine field on your screen. Then click SEARCH or GO. You will see a list of available websites that have to do with your topic. Click on the site or sites you think will be most helpful. If you do not find enough websites listed, think of other key words or related words, and search again.

▶ Search by Address Each website has its own address, called a Uniform Resource Locator, or URL for short. To get to a website using a URL, simply type the URL in the LOCATION/GO TO box on your screen and hit ENTER or click GO.

▶ Use Bookmarks The bookmark feature is an Internet tool for keeping and organizing URLs. If you find a website that seems especially helpful, you can save the URL so that you can quickly and easily return to it later. Click BOOKMARKS or FAVORITES at the top of your screen, and choose ADD. Your computer makes a copy of the URL and keeps a record of it.

Print Resources

Books in libraries are organized through a system of numbers. Every book has its own title and a number called a call number. The call number tells where in the library the book can be found.

You can locate information in the book by using its table of contents and index. Some reference books, such as encyclopedias, are usually kept in a separate section of a library. Each book has R or RE—for *reference*—on its spine. Most reference books can only be used in the library. Most libraries also have a special section for periodicals, which include magazines and newspapers.

❱ Almanac

An almanac is a book or electronic resource that contains facts about different subjects. The subjects are listed in alphabetical order in an index, and many number-based facts are shown in tables or charts. New almanacs are published each year, so they have the most current information.

❱ Atlas

An atlas is a book of maps that gives information about places. Different kinds of atlases show different places at different times. Your teacher or librarian can help you find the kind of atlas you need for your research.

❱ Dictionary

A dictionary gives the correct spelling of words and their definitions, or meanings. It also gives the words' pronunciations, or how to say the words aloud. In addition, many dictionaries have lists of foreign words, abbreviations, well-known people, and place names.

de•mand\di-´mand*n* **1:** to ask with authority **2:** the desire or need for a product or service
de•pend\di-´pend*vi* **1:** to be undecided **2:** to rely on for help
de•pos•it\di-´pä-zit*vb* **1:** to put money into a bank account **2:** to place for safekeeping or as a pledge

Dictionary entry

Encyclopedia

An encyclopedia is a book or set of books that gives information about many different topics. The topics are arranged alphabetically. An encyclopedia is a good source to use when beginning your research. In addition to words, electronic encyclopedias often have sound and video clips as well.

Nonfiction Books

A nonfiction book gives facts about real people, places, and things. All nonfiction books in a library are arranged in order and by category according to their call numbers. To find a book's call number, you use a library's card file or computer catalog. You can search for a book in the catalog by subject, author, or title.

Periodicals

A periodical is published each day, each week, or each month. Periodicals are good resources for current information on topics not yet found in books. Many libraries have a guide that lists magazine articles by subject. Two such guides are the *Children's Magazine Guide* and the *Readers' Guide to Periodical Literature.* The entries in guides are usually in alphabetical order by subject, author, or title.

Thesaurus

A thesaurus (thih•SAWR•uhs) gives synonyms, or words that mean the same or nearly the same as another word. A thesaurus also gives antonyms, or words that have the opposite meanings. Using a thesaurus can help you find words that better describe your topic and make your writing more interesting.

Encyclopedia article

Capitol, United States, houses the United States legislative branch, or Congress. The Capitol building is in Washington, D.C., on Capitol Hill. The Capitol is a government building and a symbol of the United States. Visitors from different countries visit the Capitol each year. The public can go inside and see where the House of Representatives and the Senate meet.

Community Resources

People in your community can share oral histories or information about your research topic. You can learn facts, opinions, or points of view by asking these people thoughtful questions. Before you talk to any of them, always ask a teacher or a parent for permission.

Listening to Find Information

It is important to plan ahead whenever you talk with people as part of your research. Planning ahead will help you gather the information you need. Follow these tips as you gather information from people in your community.

❱ Before

- Find out more about the topic you want to discuss.
- Think about the kind of information you still need.
- Consider the best way to gather the information you need.
- List the people you want to talk to.
- Make a list of useful questions you want to ask. Make sure your questions are clear and effective.

❱ During

- Speak clearly and loudly enough when asking questions.
- Listen carefully. Make sure you are getting the information you need, and revise your questions based on what you hear. You may also think of new questions to ask.
- Think about the speaker's perspective, tone of voice, and word choice. Use these clues to evaluate whether the speaker is a good source of information about your topic.
- Be polite. Do not interrupt or argue with the person who is speaking.
- Take notes to help you remember important ideas and details.
- Write down the person's exact words if you think you will want to quote them in your report. If possible, use a tape recorder. Be sure to ask the speaker for permission in advance.

❱ After

- Thank the person you spoke with.
- Follow up by writing a thank-you note.

Writing to Get Information

You can also write to people in your community to gather information. You can write an e-mail or a letter. Keep these ideas in mind as you write:

- Write neatly or use a computer.
- Say who you are and why you are writing. Be clear and specific about what you want to know.
- Carefully check your spelling and punctuation.
- If you are writing a letter, provide a self-addressed, stamped envelope for the person to send you a response.
- Thank the person.

222 Central Avenue
Dover, NJ 07801
October 25, 20- -

Regional Tourism Division
Attn: Ms. Stephanie Nguyen
123 Main Street
Cape May, NJ 08204

Dear Ms. Nguyen:

My name is David Thomas, and I am writing this letter to see if you can send me some information about scenic attractions in southern New Jersey. My family is planning a vacation next month, and we would like to visit some of the attractions in the southern part of the state. Please send a brochure listing the scenic attractions and a highway map. I understand this is a service you provide for those planning vacations in the area. I am excited about visiting your part of the state.

Thank you for your help.

Sincerely,

David Thomas

David Thomas
222 Central Avenue
Dover, NJ 07801

Bureau of Tourism
Attn: Stephanie Nguyen
123 Main Street
Cape May, NJ 08204

Reporting

▶ Written Reports

Your teacher may ask you to write a report about the information you find. Knowing how to write a report will help you make good use of the information. The following tips will help you write your report.

▶ Before Writing

- Choose a main idea or topic.
- Think of questions about your topic. Questions should be clear and focus on specific ideas about your topic.
- Gather information from two or more sources. You may use print resources, technology resources, or community resources. Be sure to look for answers to your questions.
- Take notes that paraphrase or summarize the information.
- Review your notes to be sure you have the information you need. Write down ideas and details about your topic to put in your report.
- Use your notes to make an outline of the information you found. Organize your ideas in a way that is easy to understand.

▶ Citing Sources

An important part of research and writing is citing sources. When you cite a source, you keep a written record of where you got your information. The list of sources will be presented as a bibliography. A bibliography is a list of the books, periodicals, and other sources that you used to find the information in your report.

Outline

Little Rock, Arkansas

I. The History of Little Rock, Arkansas

  A. Little Rock is the state capital of Arkansas.

    1. The site was explored and named by a French trapper in 1722.

    2. Little Rock became the capital of the Arkansas Territory in 1820.

  B. During the Civil War, Little Rock was in the Confederacy.

    1. In 1861, the Confederacy took over a Union arsenal in Little Rock.

    2. In 1863, Little Rock was captured by the Union.

  C. Little Rock became an economic center.

    1. Railroads were built to link industries and natural resources around Little Rock in the 1880s.

    2. In 1969, dams and canals were built to link Little Rock with the Mississippi River.

  D. Important events happened in Little Rock during the Civil Rights movement.

    1. In 1957, nine African American children became students at a previously all-white school.

    2. The school later became a national historic site.

Bibliography

Hernandez, Elizabeth. *Little Rock Through the Years*. San Antonio, Texas: Old Alamo Press, 2004

Wyatt, Adam. *The History of Arkansas*. Philadelphia, Pennsylvania: Scenic River Publishing, 2003

Bibliography Card

Wyatt, Adam. *The History of Arkansas*. Philadelphia, Pennsylvania: Scenic River Publishing, 2003, page 25.

San Jose was the first state capital of California. Eventually the state government moved to Sacramento in 1854.

LITTLE ROCK, ARKANSAS

Reading Notes	Class Notes
• Little Rock was named after a nearby rock formation on the Arkansas River	• Little Rock is in Arkansas, a state in the South
• Little Rock is located in the central part of the state of Arkansas	• After the Civil War, many states in the South were still segregated
• Little Rock expanded economically in the 1940s	• Segregation is the practice of keeping people in separate groups based on their race or culture
• Timber and coal are found in Arkansas	• In 1954, the Supreme Court decided that segregation was unconstitutional
• Farmers from all around Arkansas sell their produce in Little Rock	• In 1957, nine African American students, known as the Little Rock Nine, were sent to Central High School, a previously all-white school
• The University of Arkansas is located in Little Rock	• Today, Central High School is a national historic site

Marta Berzina
Social Studies

A History of Little Rock, Arkansas

Little Rock is the capital of the state of Arkansas. The city has a rich history. In 1722, the site were Little Rock is located was explored by a french trapper. He named the area Little Rock after a rock formation that he saw there. About 100 years later, in 1820, Little Rock became the capital of the Arkansas Territory. During the Civil War, Arkansas was one of the states in the Confederacy. In 1861, Confederate troops took over a Union arsenal in Little Rock. The Union captured Little Rock in 1863.

After the Civil War, Little Rock's economy grew. In the 1880s, railroads began to connect the industries in Little Rock with the natural resources around Arkansas. Timber and coal, especially, were important natural resources for Little Rock. Also, farmers from around the state of Arkansas sold their produce in markets in Little Rock. After that In 1969, a network of canals and dams linked Little Rock to the Mississippi River, bringing more trade.

Little Rock is also famous for what happened there during the Civil Rights movement. After the Civil War, Arkansas, like most other states in the South, became segregated. Segregation meant that African Americans and whites were separated. They ate in different restaurants used different restrooms, and attended different schools. In 1954, the Supreme Court decided that segregation was against the Constitution. The Little Rock Nine were nine African American students from Little Rock who, in 1957, were the first to be sent to a school that before had only allowed white students to attend. Central High School, the school where this took place, is now a national historic site.

Write a First Draft

- Use your notes and your outline to write a draft of your report. Keep in mind that your purpose is to share information.
- Write in paragraph form. Develop your topic with facts, details, examples, and explanations. Each paragraph should focus on one new idea.
- Get all your ideas down on paper. You can revise your draft and correct errors in the next step.

Revise

- Read over your draft. Does it make sense? Does your report have a beginning, a middle, and an end? Have you answered all your questions?
- Rewrite sentences that are unclear or poorly worded. Move sentences that seem out of place.
- Add details when needed to support your ideas.
- If too many sentences are alike, make some sentences shorter or longer to keep your report interesting.
- Check any quotations to be sure you have shown someone's exact words and that you have noted the source correctly.

Marta Berzina
Social Studies

A History of Little Rock, Arkansas

Little Rock is the capital of the state of Arkansas. The city has a rich history. In 1722, the site were Little Rock is located was explored by a French trapper. He named the area Little Rock after a rock formation that he saw there. About 100 years later, in 1820, Little Rock became the capital of the Arkansas Territory.

During the Civil War, Arkansas was one of the states in the Confederacy. In 1861, Confederate troops took over a Union arsenal in Little Rock. The Union captured Little Rock in 1863.

After the Civil War, Little Rock's economy grew. In the 1880s, railroads began to connect the industries in Little Rock with the natural resources around Arkansas. Timber and coal, especially, were important natural resources for Little Rock. Also, farmers from around the state of Arkansas sold their produce in markets in Little Rock. In 1969, a network of canals and dams linked Little Rock to the Mississippi River, bringing more trade to the city.

Little Rock is also famous for what happened there during the Civil Rights movement. After the Civil War, Arkansas, like most other states in the South, became segregated. Segregation meant that African Americans and whites were separated. They ate in different restaurants, used different restrooms, and attended different schools. In 1954, the Supreme Court decided that segregation was unconstitutional. The Little Rock Nine were nine African American students from Little Rock who, in 1957, were the first to be sent to a school that before had only allowed white students to attend. Central High School, the school where this took place, is now a national historic site.

Proofread and Edit

- Proofread your report, checking for errors.
- Correct any errors in spelling, capitalization, or punctuation. If you are writing your report on a computer, use the spell-check feature.
- Use a thesaurus to find words that better describe your topic or that make your report more interesting.

Publish

- Make a neat, clean copy of your report.
- Include graphs, tables, maps, or other illustrations to help explain your topic.

Proofreading marks and their meanings	
Mark	**Meaning**
∧	Insert word.
∧,	Insert comma.
¶	Start a new paragraph.
= cap	Use capital letter.
℘	Delete.
lc	Use lowercase letter.

RESEARCH HANDBOOK

Listening to Find Information

Sometimes in class you may be asked to give an oral presentation. Like a written report, the purpose of an oral presentation is to share information. These tips will help you prepare an oral presentation:

- Follow the steps described in Before Writing to gather and organize information.
- Use your notes to plan and organize your presentation. Include an introduction and a conclusion in your report.
- Prepare note cards that you can refer to as you speak.
- Prepare visuals such as illustrations, diagrams, maps, graphs, tables, or other graphics to help listeners better understand your topic.
- Give your audience a controlling idea about your topic. A controlling idea is the main idea that you support with facts and details.
- Practice your presentation.
- Be sure to speak clearly and loudly enough. Keep your listeners interested in your report by using facial expressions and hand movements.

Biographical Dictionary

The Biographical Dictionary provides information about many of the people introduced in this book. Names are listed alphabetically by last name. Pronunciation guides are provided for hard-to-pronounce names. Following each name are the birth and death dates of that person. If the person is still alive, only the year of birth appears. A brief description of the person's main achievement is then given. The page number that follows tells where the main discussion of that person appears in this book. (You can check the Index for other page references.) Guide names at the top of each page help you quickly locate the name you need to find.

A

Adams, Abigail *1744–1818* Massachusetts woman and wife of John Adams who supported the Patriot cause. p. 328

Adams, John *1735–1826* Massachusetts leader who served as a member of Congress and later as the second President of the United States. p. 319

Adams, Samuel *1722–1803* American Revolutionary leader who set up a Committee of Correspondence in Boston and helped form the Sons of Liberty. p. 305

Addams, Jane *1860–1935* American reformer who founded the Hull House settlement house in Chicago. p. 540

Armistead, James *1760?–1830* African American who served as a spy for the Patriots during the Revolutionary War. p. 342

Arnold, Benedict *1741–1801* Continental Army officer who later became a traitor and worked for the British during the Revolutionary War. p. 349

Atahuallpa (ah•tah•WAHL•pah) *1502?–1533* Inca ruler who was killed in the Spanish conquest of the Inca Empire. p. 132

Attucks, Crispus (A•tuhks) *1725?–1770* African American sailor who was killed during the Boston Massacre. p. 307

B

Balboa, Vasco Núñez de (bahl•BOH•ah, NOON•yes day) *1475–1519* Spanish explorer who reached the Pacific Ocean in 1513. p. 123

Banneker, Benjamin *1731–1806* Free African American who helped survey the land for the new capital of the United States. p. 408

Barton, Clara *1821–1912* Union Civil War nurse and founder of the American Red Cross. p. 502

Bell, Alexander Graham *1847–1922* American scientist who built a version of the telephone in 1876. p. 533

Bonaparte, Napoleon (BOH•nuh•part, nuh•POH•lee•uhn) *1769–1821* French leader who sold Louisiana in 1803. p. 429

Boone, Daniel *1734–1820* American pathfinder who was one of the first settlers to cross the Appalachian Mountains. p. 427

Booth, John Wilkes *1838–1865* Confederate supporter who assassinated President Abraham Lincoln. p. 511

Bowie, Jim *1796–1836* American killed while fighting at the Battle of the Alamo during the Texas War for Independence. p. 445

Bradford, William *1590–1657* English Pilgrim settler and governor of the Plymouth Colony. p. 164

Brant, Joseph *See* Thayendanegea.

Brown, John *1800–1859* American abolitionist who led a raid on a government weapons storehouse at Harpers Ferry. p. 490

Bruce, Blanche K. *1841–1898* Former enslaved person who became a United States senator during Reconstruction. p. 519

C

Caboto, Giovanni (kah•BOH•toh) *1450?–1499?* Italian explorer, also known as John Cabot, who explored Newfoundland for the English. p. 121

Calhoun, John *1782–1850* Vice President under John Quincy Adams and Andrew Jackson. He was a strong supporter of states' rights. p. 479

Calvert, Cecilius *1605–1675* Established the Maryland Colony. p. 253

Calvert, George *1580?–1632* Member of the Virginia Company and the first Lord Baltimore; received the original charter for Maryland. p. 253

Carnegie, Andrew *1835–1919* Pennsylvania entrepreneur who helped the steel industry grow in the United States. p. 532

Cartier, Jacques (kar•TYAY, ZHAHK) *1491–1557* French explorer who explored the eastern coast of what is now Canada. p. 140

Cavelier, René-Robert (ka•vuhl•YAY) *See* La Salle.

Champlain, Samuel de (sham•PLAYN) *1567?–1635* French explorer who founded Quebec in what is now Canada. p. 171

Charles II *1630–1685* English king who gained control of the Atlantic coast of North America. p. 224

Clark, William *1770–1838* American explorer who aided Meriwether Lewis during an expedition through the Louisiana Purchase. p. 430

Clay, Henry *1777–1852* Representative from Kentucky who worked for compromises on the slavery issue. p. 478

Columbus, Christopher *1451–1506* Italian explorer who sailed for Spain. He was searching for a western route to Asia but reached islands near the Americas. p. 114

Cooper, Peter *1791–1883* American manufacturer who built *Tom Thumb,* one of the first locomotives in the United States. p. 454

Corbin, Margaret *1751–1800* American Revolutionary hero; the first woman veteran recognized by Congress. p. 341

Cornish, Samuel *1795–1858* One of the founders of the *Freedom's Journal.* p. 484

Cornwallis, Charles *1738–1805* British general who surrendered at the Battle of Yorktown. p. 360

Coronado, Francisco Vásquez de (kawr•oh•NAH•doh) *1510?–1554* Spanish explorer who led an expedition through southwestern North America searching for the Seven Cities of Gold. p. 131

Cortés, Hernando (kawr•TEZ) *1485–1547* Spanish conquistador who led a group that defeated the Aztec in what is now Mexico. p. 130

Crazy Horse *1842?–1877* Sioux leader who fought against Lieutenant Colonel George Armstrong Custer. p. 528

Crockett, Davy *1786–1836* American pioneer who was killed while defending the Alamo. p. 445

Custer, George Armstrong *1839–1876* United States Army lieutenant colonel who led an attack against the Sioux and the Cheyenne. p. 528

D

Davis, Jefferson *1808–1889* United States senator from Mississippi who became president of the Confederacy. p. 491

de Soto, Hernando (day SOH•toh) *1496?–1542* Spanish explorer who led an expedition through southeastern North America. p. 132

Deere, John *1804–1886* American industrialist who created steel plows for use on the Great Plains. p. 457

Deganawida (deh•gahn•uh•WEE•duh) *1500s* Legendary Iroquois leader who, along with Hiawatha, helped start the Iroquois League. p. 65

Dickinson, John *1732–1808* Member of the Continental Congress who helped write the Articles of Confederation, which were adopted in 1781. p. 319

Dix, Dorothea *1802–1887* Nurse for the Union Army during the Civil War. p. 502

Douglas, Stephen A. *1813–1861* Senator from Illinois who wrote the Kansas-Nebraska Act. p. 489

Douglass, Frederick *1817–1895* African American abolitionist who escaped from slavery and became a famous speaker and writer. p. 484

E

Edison, Thomas Alva *1847–1931* American inventor who developed the phonograph, the electric lightbulb, and many other inventions. p. 533

Elizabeth I *1533–1603* Queen of England from 1558 to 1603. p. 155

Equiano, Olaudah (ek•wee•AHN•oh, OHL•uh•dah) *1750?–1797* Former enslaved person who bought his freedom and later wrote a book about his life. p. 267

Eriksson, Leif (AIR•ik•suhn, LAYV) *?–1020?* Viking explorer who sailed from Greenland to North America in the A.D. 1000s. p. 113

Estevanico (es•tay•vahn•EE•koh) *1474?–1539* African enslaved person who went on an expedition in search of the Seven Cities of Gold. p. 135

F

Farragut, Jorge (FAIR•uh•guht, HAWR•hay) *1755–1817* Spanish–born soldier who fought in the Continental Army and Navy. p. 352

Ferdinand II *1452–1516* King of Spain who, with Queen Isabella, funded Christopher Columbus's voyages. He also helped lead the Spanish Reconquista. p. 115

Franklin, Benjamin *1706–1790* American leader and delegate to the Constitutional Convention. He was also a respected scientist and business leader. p. 238

Freeman, Elizabeth *1742?–1829* African American woman from Massachusetts who sued for, and won, her freedom in 1780. p. 365

Fulton, Robert *1765–1815* American engineer and inventor who created the first commercial steamboat. p. 454

G

Gage, Thomas *1721–1787* Governor of Massachusetts and a leader in the British army during the Revolutionary War. p. 312

Gálvez, Bernardo de (GAHL•ves) *1746–1786* Spanish governor of Louisiana who helped the Americans in the Revolutionary War. p. 353

Garrison, William Lloyd *1805–1879* American abolitionist who founded the American Anti-Slavery Society in 1833. p. 484

Gates, Horatio *1728–1806* American general who defeated the British in 1777 at Saratoga, New York. p. 349

George III *1738–1820* King of Britain during the Revolutionary War. p. 298

Gompers, Samuel *1850–1924* Labor leader who helped organize the American Federation of Labor, or AFL, in 1886. p. 534

Grant, Ulysses S. *1822–1885* Commander of the Union army in the Civil War and 18th President of the United States. p. 507

Greene, Nathanael *1742–1786* Continental Army officer who led Americans to a major victory against the British at Cowpens. p. 359

Grenville, George *1712–1770* British prime minister who passed the Stamp Act in 1765. p. 317

Gutenberg, Johannes *1390–1468* German inventor of an improved printing press. p. 111

H

Hale, Nathan *1755–1776* American Revolutionary hero who was hanged by the British for spying for the Patriots. p. 357

Hamilton, Alexander *1755–1804* American leader who helped organize the Constitutional Convention and supported a strong national government. p. 408

Hancock, John *1737–1793* A leader of the Sons of Liberty in Massachusetts. p. 314

Henry *1394–1460* Henry the Navigator, prince of Portugal, who set up the first European school for training sailors in navigation. p. 112

Henry, Patrick *1736–1799* Virginia leader who spoke out against British policies and later opposed the Constitution. p. 309

Hiawatha (hy•uh•WAH•thuh) *1500s* Legendary Onondaga chief who, along with Deganawida, helped start the Iroquois League. p. 65

Hooker, Thomas *1586?–1647* Minister who helped form the Connecticut Colony. p. 202

Houston, Sam *1793–1863* President of the Republic of Texas and, later, governor of the state of Texas. p. 445

Hudson, Henry *1570?–1611* English explorer who claimed a large area of what is now New York for the Dutch. p. 142

BIOGRAPHICAL DICTIONARY

Hutchinson, Anne *1591–1643* English colonist who was expelled from the Massachusetts Bay Colony because of her religious beliefs. p. 205

Isabella I *1451–1504* Queen of Spain who, with King Ferdinand, funded Christopher Columbus's voyages. She also helped lead the Spanish Reconquista. p. 115

Jackson, Andrew *1767–1845* Seventh President of the United States. He ordered the removal of many Native American groups from their lands. p. 438

James I *1566–1625* King of England in the early 1600s. The James River and Jamestown were named for him. p. 155

James, the Duke of York *1633–1701?* English leader who took over New Netherland from the Dutch and set up New York and New Jersey. p. 227

Jay, John *1745–1829* American leader who became the first chief justice of the United States Supreme Court. p. 360

Jefferson, Thomas *1743–1826* Third President of the United States and the main writer of the Declaration of Independence. He was President when the United States purchased Louisiana from France in 1803. p. 325

Johnson, Andrew *1808–1875* Seventeenth United States President. He was impeached during Reconstruction, but he was found not guilty. p. 517

Joliet, Louis (ZHOHL•yay, LOO•ee) *1645–1700* French fur trader who with Jacques Marquette and five others explored North America for France. p. 174

Jones, John Paul *1747–1792* American naval officer during the Revolutionary War. p. 356

Key, Francis Scott *1779–1843* American lawyer and poet who wrote "The Star-Spangled Banner." p. 438

Kosciuszko, Tadeusz (kawsh•CHUSH•koh) *1746–1817* Polish soldier who helped the Americans in the Revolutionary War. p. 357

La Salle, Sieur de (luh•SAL) *1643–1687* French explorer who found the mouth of the Mississippi River and claimed the Mississippi Valley for France. p. 174

Lafayette, Marquis de (lah•fee•ET) *1757–1834* French soldier who fought alongside the Americans in the Revolutionary War. p. 346

Las Casas, Bartolomé de (lahs KAH•sahs, bar•toh•loh•MAY day) *1474–1566* Spanish missionary who spent much of his life trying to help Native Americans. p. 153

Latimer, Lewis *1848–1928* African American engineer who directed the building of Thomas Edison's first central power station. p. 533

Lee, Richard Henry *1732–1794* American Revolutionary leader who believed the colonies should become independent from Britain. p. 325

Lee, Robert E. *1807–1870* United States Army colonel who gave up his post to become commander of the Confederate army in the Civil War. p. 492

L'Enfant, Pierre-Charles *1754–1825* American engineer who designed the original layout of Washington, D.C. p. 408

Lewis, Meriwether *1774–1809* American explorer chosen by Thomas Jefferson to explore the lands of the Louisiana Purchase. p. 430

Lincoln, Abraham *1809–1865* Sixteenth President of the United States, leader of the Union in the Civil War, and signer of the Emancipation Proclamation. p. 489

Lowell, Francis Cabot *1775–1817* American entrepreneur who set up the first textile mill in Massachusetts. p. 455

Ludington, Sybil *1761–1839* Revolutionary War hero who rode to warn American soldiers of a British attack in 1777. p. 341

Luther, Martin *1483–1546* German religious leader who began the Protestant Reformation by protesting the policies of the Catholic Church. p. 133

Madison, Dolley *1768–1849* Wife of James Madison and First Lady during the War of 1812. p. 438

Madison, James *1751–1836* Fourth President of the United States. He helped plan and write the United States Constitution. p. 389

Magellan, Ferdinand (muh•JEH•luhn) *1480?–1521* Portuguese explorer who led an expedition to sail west to Asia in 1519. p. 124

Marquette, Jacques (mar•KET, ZHAHK) *1637–1675* French Catholic missionary who explored North America for France. p. 174

Marshall, James *1810–1885* Carpenter who found gold at John Sutter's sawmill near Sacramento, California, leading to the California gold rush of 1849. p. 450

Marshall, John *1755–1835* Chief justice of the Supreme Court who ruled that the United States should protect the Cherokee tribe and their lands in Georgia. p. 440

McCauley, Mary Ludwig Hayes *1754?–1832* Woman who earned the nickname Molly Pitcher because she carried water to American soldiers during the Battle of Monmouth. p. 357

McCormick, Cyrus *1809–1884* American inventor who developed a machine to harvest wheat better. p. 456

Meade, George C. *1815–1872* Led the Union Army during the Battle of Gettysburg in the Civil War. p. 508

Menéndez de Avilés, Pedro (may•NAYN•days day ah•vee•LAYS) *1519–1574* Spanish leader who helped build the settlement at St. Augustine, Florida. p. 151

Metacomet *1639?–1676* Leader of the Wampanoag tribe. Called King Philip by the English. Led King Philip's War in New England. p. 203

Michikinikwa (mih•chik•kin•EE•kwah) *1752–1812* A leader of the Miami tribe, also known as Little Turtle. He battled American forces in the 1790s. p. 368

Minuit, Peter *1580–1638* Dutch leader of New Netherland who purchased Manhattan Island. p. 172

Morgan, Daniel *1736–1802* American general who defeated the British at Cowpens in the Revolutionary War. p. 359

Morris, Gouverneur (guh•ver•NIR) *1752–1816* American leader who helped write the United States Constitution. p. 395

Morse, Samuel F. B. *1791–1872* The inventor of the telegraph. p. 457

Motecuhzoma (moh•tay•kwah•SOH•mah) *1466–1520* Emperor of the Aztec at the time of the arrival of the Spanish in the Americas. p. 130

Mott, Lucretia *1793–1880* American reformer who helped organize the Seneca Falls Convention. p. 484

Oglethorpe, James *1696–1785* English leader who founded the Georgia Colony. p. 256

P

Paine, Thomas *1737–1809* Writer during the American Revolution. His pamphlet *Common Sense* led many Americans to favor independence. p. 325

Parker, John *1729–1775* Leader of the Minutemen in Massachusetts. p. 314

Paterson, William *1745–1806* New Jersey delegate to the Constitutional Convention who submitted the New Jersey Plan. p. 391

Penn, William *1644–1718* English Quaker who founded the Pennsylvania Colony. p. 229

Pike, Zebulon *1779–1813* American explorer who led an expedition to explore the southwestern part of the Louisiana Purchase. p. 432

Pinckney, Eliza Lucas *1722?–1793* South Carolina colonist who experimented with growing indigo plants. p. 269

Pitt, William *1708–1778* British leader of Parliament during the French and Indian War. p. 313

Pizarro, Francisco (pee•ZAR•oh) *1475?–1541* Spanish conquistador who conquered the Inca Empire. p. 132

Pocahontas (poh•kuh•HAHN•tuhs) *1595–1617* Daughter of Chief Powhatan. She married English settler John Rolfe. p. 159

Polk, James K. *1795–1849* Eleventh President of the United States. Led the United States during the Mexican American War. p. 448

BIOGRAPHICAL DICTIONARY

Polo, Marco *1254–1324* Italian explorer who visited Asia in the late 1200s. He wrote a famous book about his travels. p. 110

Ponce, de León, Juan (POHN•say day lay•OHN) *1460–1520* Spanish explorer who claimed what is now Florida for Spain in 1513. p. 129

Pontiac *1720?–1769* Ottawa chief who led a rebellion against the British to stop the loss of Native American hunting lands. p. 298

Powhatan (pow•uh•TAN) *1550?–1618* Algonquian chief who governed the area that later became the Virginia Colony. He was the father of Pocahontas. p. 156

R

Raleigh, Sir Walter (RAH•lee) *1554–1618* English explorer who helped set up England's first colony in North America, on Roanoke Island. p. 155

Randolph, Edmund *1753–1813* Virginia delegate to the Constitutional Convention who wrote the Virginia Plan. p. 391

Revels, Hiram R. *1827?–1901* Minister from Mississippi who became the first African American elected to the United States Senate. p. 519

Revere, Paul *1735–1818* Massachusetts colonist who warned the Patriots that the British were marching toward Concord. p. 308

Rockefeller, John D. *1839–1937* American oil entrepreneur who joined many refineries into one business, called the Standard Oil Company. p. 533

Rolfe, John *1585–1622* Jamestown settler who introduced a new form of tobacco that led to great profits. p. 157

Ross, John *1790–1866* Cherokee chief who used the legal system to try to prevent the loss of Cherokee lands. Later, he led his people on the Trail of Tears. p. 440

Russwurm, John *1799–1851* One of the founders of the *Freedom's Journal*. p. 412

S

Sacagawea (sah•kuh•juh•WEE•uh) *1786?–1812?* Shoshone woman who was an interpreter for the Lewis and Clark expedition. p. 430

Salem, Peter *1750?–1816* Free African American who fought at the Battle of Concord and at the Battle of Bunker Hill. p. 342

Samoset *1590?–1653?* Native American who spoke English and helped English settlers at Plymouth. p. 165

Sampson, Deborah *1760–1827* Massachusetts woman who disguised herself as a soldier to fight for the Americans in the Revolutionary War. p. 341

Santa Anna, Antonio López de *1794–1876* Mexican general and dictator who led his country during the Mexican American War. p. 445

Scott, Dred *1795?–1858* Enslaved African American who sued for his freedom in 1857. The United States Supreme Court ruled against him. p. 483

Segoyewatha *1756?–1830* Seneca chief, also known as Red Jacket, who urged his tribe not to sell its land. p. 368

Sequoyah (sih•KWOY•uh) *1765–1843* Cherokee leader who created a writing system for the Cherokee language. p. 440

Sevier, John *1745–1815* First governor of Tennessee. p. 428

Shaw, Robert Gould *1837–1863* Union Army officer who led the Fifty–fourth Massachusetts regiment during the Civil War. p. 502

Shays, Daniel *1747?–1825* Leader of a farmers' rebellion in Massachusetts in 1787. p. 389

Sherman, Roger *1721–1793* Connecticut delegate to the Constitutional Convention who worked out a compromise on representation. p. 392

Sherman, William Tecumseh *1820–1891* Union Army general who led the March to the Sea, which destroyed large areas of Georgia. p. 509

Sitting Bull *1831–1890* Sioux leader who fought against General George Custer. p. 528

Slater, Samuel *1768–1835* British mill worker who helped bring the Industrial Revolution to the United States by providing plans for a new textile machine. p. 455

Smith, John *1580–1631* English explorer and leader of the Jamestown settlement. p. 156

BIOGRAPHICAL DICTIONARY

Stanton, Elizabeth Cady *1815–1902* American reformer who helped organize the Seneca Falls Convention. p. 484

Steuben, Friedrich, von (vahn SHTOY•buhn) *1730–1794* German soldier who helped train American troops during the Revolutionary War. p. 351

Stowe, Harriet Beecher *1811–1896* American abolitionist whose novel *Uncle Tom's Cabin*, published in 1852, helped turn more people in the North against slavery. p. 485

Stuyvesant, Peter (STY•vuh•suhnt) *1610?–1672* Dutch governor of New Netherland. p. 226

Tamanend *1776–1857* Lenni Lenape chief who established peaceful relations with William Penn and the Pennsylvania settlers. p. 231

Tapahonso, Luci *1953–* Navajo poet and author. p. 81

Tecumseh (tuh•KUHM•suh) *1768–1813* Shawnee leader of Native Americans in the Northwest Territory. p. 436

Thayendanegea (thay•en•da•NEC•ah) *1742–1807* Mohawk leader who helped the British during the Revolutionary War known as Joseph Brant. p. 343

Thomson, David *1592–1628* Scottish settler and founder of Portsmouth, New Hampshire. p. 202

Tisquantum *1585?–1622* Native American who spoke English and who helped English settlers at Plymouth. p. 165

Tompkins, Sally *1833–1916* Confederate Civil War nurse who ran a hospital in Richmond, Virginia. p. 502

Truth, Sojourner *1797?–1883* Abolitionist and former enslaved person who became a leading spokesperson against slavery. p. 484

Tubman, Harriet *1820–1913* African American abolitionist and former enslaved person who helped lead others to freedom along the Underground Railroad. p. 485

Turner, Nat *1800–1831* An enslaved man who led an attack against slaveholders. p. 412

Verrazano, Giovanni da (ver•uh•zah•noh) *1458?–1528?* Italian explorer who explored what is now New York Bay. p. 140

Vespucci, Amerigo (veh•spoo•chee, uh•mair•ih•goh) *1454–1512* Italian explorer who made several voyages to South America. p. 122

W

Wald, Lillian *1867–1940* Reformer who started the Henry Street Settlement in New York City. p. 540

Warren, Mercy Otis *1728–1814* Massachusetts colonist who wrote poems and plays supporting the Patriot cause. pp. 303, 341

Washington, George *1732–1799* First President of the United States and leader of the Continental Army during the Revolutionary War. p. 296

Washington, Martha *1731–1802* Wife of George Washington. p. 341

Wheatley, Phillis *1753?–1784* Enslaved African woman who became a famous poet and supported the Patriots during the Revolutionary War. p. 323

White, John *1537?–1593?* English settler who led the second group that settled on Roanoke Island. p. 155

Whitefield, George *1714–1770* English minister who helped lead the Great Awakening. p. 236

Whitney, Eli *1765–1825* American inventor who developed the cotton gin and interchangeable parts. p. 456

Williams, Roger *1603?–1683* Founder of Providence in what is now Rhode Island. He was forced to leave the Massachusetts Bay Colony. p. 200

Winthrop, John *1588–1649* Puritan leader who served as governor of the Massachusetts Bay Colony. p. 199

York *1800s* Enslaved African American whose hunting and fishing skills contributed to the Lewis and Clark expedition. p. 430

Gazetteer

The Gazetteer is a geographical dictionary that can help you locate places discussed in this book. Place names are listed alphabetically. Names that are hard to pronounce are followed by pronunciation guides. A description of the place is then given. The absolute location, or latitude and longitude, of each city is also provided. The page number that follows tells where each place is shown on a map. Guide words at the top of each page help you locate the place name you need to find.

Abilene A town in Kansas that grew at the end of a cattle trail. (38°N, 97°W) p. 526

Adena (uh•DEE•nuh) An ancient settlement of the Mound Builders; located in present-day southern Ohio. (40°N, 81°W) p. 58

Adirondack Mountains (a•duh•RAHN•dak) A mountain range in northeastern New York. p. R13

Africa Second-largest continent on Earth. p. 4

Alamo A mission in San Antonio, Texas located in the southeastern part of the state; used as a fort during the Texas War for Independence. (29°N, 98°W) p. 445

Alaska Range A mountain range in central Alaska. p. 24

Albany (AWL•buh•nee) The capital of New York; located in the eastern part of the state. (42°N, 74°W) p. 15

Aleutian Islands (uh•LOO•shuhn) A chain of volcanic islands; located between the northern Pacific Ocean and the Bering Sea. p. 86

Allegheny Mountains (a•luh•GAY•nee) A mountain range in the northeastern United States, part of the Appalachian Mountains. p. R13

Altamaha River A river in Georgia. p. 255

American River A river in California where gold nuggets were found in 1848. p. 450

Annapolis (uh•NA•puh•luhs) The capital of Maryland; located on Chesapeake Bay. (39°N, 76°W) p. 15

Antarctica One of Earth's seven continents. p. 116

Antietam The site of a major Civil War battle in Maryland. p. 500

Appalachian Mountains (a•puh•LAY•chuhn) A mountain system of eastern North America that extends from southern Canada to central Alabama. p. 25

Appomattox Court House The site in Virginia of General Lee's surrender, which ended major fighting in the Civil War. p. 510

Arctic Ocean One of Earth's four oceans; located north of the Arctic Circle. p. 24

Arkansas River A tributary of the Mississippi River; begins in central Colorado and ends in southeastern Arkansas. p. 32

Asia Largest continent on Earth. p. I16

Atlanta The capital of Georgia; General Sherman burned the city during the Civil War. (33°N, 84°W) p. 15

Atlantic Ocean Second-largest ocean; separates North and South America from Europe and Africa. p. 15

Augusta The capital of Maine; located in the eastern part of the state. (44°N, 70°W) p. 15

Austin The capital of Texas; located in the south central part of the state near the lower Colorado River. (30°N, 97°W) p. 15

Australia A country; smallest continent on Earth. p. I16

Baffin Bay A bay that connects the Arctic Ocean to the Atlantic Ocean; located between Canada and Greenland. p. 24

Baja California A peninsula in northwestern Mexico. p. 24

Baltimore A major seaport in Maryland; located on the Chesapeake Bay. (39°N, 77°W) p. 270

Baton Rouge (ba•tuhn•ROOZH) The capital of Louisiana; located in the southeastern part of the state. (30°N, 91°W) p. 15

Beaufort Sea (BOH•fert) That part of the Arctic Ocean between northeastern Alaska and the Canadian Arctic Islands. p. 24

Bering Strait A narrow strip of water; separates Asia from North America. p. 53

Beringia A land bridge between Asia and North America where people migrated to North America, according to theory. p. 53

Billings A city in Montana. (45°N, 108°W) p. 38

Bismarck The capital of North Dakota; located in the southern part of the state, on the Missouri River. (47°N, 101°W) p. 15

Black Hills A group of mountains in western South Dakota and northeastern Wyoming. p. 24

Boise The capital of Idaho; located in the south-western part of the state. (43°N, 116°W) p. 15

Bonampak An ancient settlement of the Mayan civilization; located in present-day southeastern Mexico. (16°N, 91°W) p. 56

Boston The capital of Massachusetts, located in the eastern part of the state; an important city during the American Revolution. (42°N, 71°W) p. 15

Brazos River A river in Texas. p. 131

Brandywine A battlefield on Brandywine Creek in southeastern Pennsylvania; site of a major Revolutionary War battle in 1777. (40°N, 76°W) p. 358

Breed's Hill The site of the first major battle of the Revolutionary War; battle was wrongly named for nearby Bunker Hill. p. 320

Brooks Range A mountain range crossing northern Alaska. p. 24

Cahokia (kuh•HOH•kee•uh) An ancient settlement of the Mound Builders; located in southwestern Illinois. (39°N, 90°W) p. 58

Camden A city in north-central South Carolina; site of a major Revolutionary War battle in 1780. (34°N, 81°W) p. 358

Canada A country in northern North America. p. R14

Canyon de Chelly (SHAY) A settlement of the Ancient Puebloans; located in present-day northeastern Arizona. p. 56

Cape Fear River A river in central and southeastern North Carolina; formed by the Deep and Haw Rivers; flows southeast into the Atlantic Ocean. p. 255

Caribbean Sea A part of the Atlantic Ocean bounded by the West Indies and Central and South America. p. 24

Carson City The capital of Nevada; located in the western part of the state near Lake Tahoe. (39°N, 120°W) p. 15

Cascade Range A mountain range north of the Sierra Nevada; located mostly in Washington and Oregon. p. 28

Central Plains The eastern part of the Interior Plains. p. 72

Chaco Canyon (CHAH•koh) A settlement of the Ancient Puebloans; located in present-day northwestern New Mexico. (37°N, 108°W) p. 56

Chancellorsville The site of a major Civil War battle in Virginia. p. 507

Charleston A city in southeastern South Carolina; a major port on the Atlantic Ocean; once known as Charles Town. (33°N, 80°W) p. 268

Charleston The capital of West Virginia; located in the west-central part of the state. (38°N, 81°W) p. 15

Charlestown A city in Massachusetts; located on Boston Harbor between the mouths of the Charles and Mystic Rivers. (42°N, 71°W) p. 314

Charlotte The largest city in North Carolina; located in the south-central part of the state. (35°N, 81°W) p. 390

Chattanooga A city in southeastern Tennessee; located on the Tennessee River, site of a Civil War battle in 1863. (35°N, 85°W) p. 507

Chesapeake Bay An inlet of the Atlantic Ocean; surrounded by Virginia and Maryland. p. 32

Cheyenne (shy•AN) The capital of Wyoming; located in the southeastern part of the state; grew at the end of a cattle trail. (41°N, 105°W) p. 15

Chicago A city in Illinois; located on Lake Michigan. (41°N, 81°W) p. 540

Cincinnati (sin•suh•NA•tee) A city in south-western Ohio; located on the Ohio River. (39°N, 84°W) p. 469

Cleveland A city in Ohio; located on Lake Erie. (41°N, 81°W) p. 38

Coast Ranges The mountain ranges that stretch along the Pacific coast of North America. p. 24

Coastal Plains Low, flat land along the Atlantic Ocean and the Gulf of Mexico. p. 24

Colorado River A river in the southwestern United States. p. 32

Columbia The capital of South Carolina; located in the central part of the state. (34°N, 81°W) p. 15

Columbia Plateau An area of dry hills and flat lands that includes parts of what are now Idaho, Oregon, and Washington. p. 79

Columbia River A river that begins in the Rocky Mountains in southwestern Canada. p. 84

Columbus The capital of Ohio; located in the central part of the state. (40°N, 83°W) p. 15

Compostela (kahm•poh•STEH•lah) A city in west-central Mexico. (21°N, 105°W) p. 131

Concord The capital of New Hampshire; located in the southern part of the state. (43°N, 71°W) p. 15

Concord A town in northeastern Massachusetts, near Boston; site of a major Revolutionary War battle in 1775. (42°N, 71°W) p. 314

Connecticut River The longest river in New England; begins in New Hampshire and empties into Long Island Sound, New York. p. 229

Continental Divide An imaginary line that runs north and south along the highest points of the Rocky Mountains. p. 33

Copán (koh•PAHN) A Mayan city that was a center of learning and art; located in present-day Honduras, in northern Central America. (15°N, 89°W) p. 57

GAZETTEER

Cowpens A town in northwestern South Carolina, located near the site of a major Revolutionary War battle in 1781. (35°N, 82°W) p. 359

Crab Orchard An ancient settlement of the Mound Builders; located in present-day southern Illinois. (38°N, 89°W) p. 56

Cuba An island country in the Caribbean; the largest island of the West Indies. (22°N, 79°W) p. 131

The Dalles The site of the Northwest Native American trade network along the Columbia River. p. 84

Delaware Bay An inlet of the Atlantic Ocean; located between southern New Jersey and Delaware. p. 32

Delaware River A major river that helped New England colonists trade easier. p. 242

Denver The capital of Colorado; located in the central part of the state. (40°N, 105°W) p. 15

Des Moines (dih•MOYN) The capital of Iowa; located in the southern part of the state. (41°N, 94°W) p. 15

Dickson An ancient settlement of the Mound Builders; located in present-day central Illinois. p. 56

Dover The capital of Delaware located in the central part of the state. (39°N, 76°W) p. 15

Edenton (EE•duhn•tuhn) A town in northeastern North Carolina; located near the Chowan River. (36°N, 77°W) p. 255

Emerald Mound An ancient settlement of the Mound Builders; located in present-day southwestern Mississippi. (32°N, 91°W) p. 56

Europe One of Earth's seven continents. p. I16

Fort Atkinson A fort in what is now southern Kansas; located on the Sante Fe Trail. (43°N, 89°W) p. 446

Fort Boise (BOY•zee) A fort in what is now western Idaho; located on the Snake River and on the Oregon Trail. p. 446

Fort Bridger A present-day village in southwestern Wyoming; once an important station on the Oregon Trail. (41°N, 110°W) p. 446

Fort Clatsop The place in what is now Oregon where members of the Corps of Discovery spent the winter of 1805. p. 429

Fort Crown Point A French fort; located in what is now northeastern New York, on the shore of Lake Champlain. p. 297

Fort Cumberland A British fort located in what is now northeastern West Virginia, on its border with Maryland. p. 297

Fort Duquesne (doo•KAYN) A French fort in present-day Pittsburgh, Pennsylvania; captured by the British, who built a new fort on the same site named Fort Pitt. (40°N, 80°W) p. 297

Fort Edward A British fort in New York, on the Hudson River; a present-day village. (43°N, 74°W) p. 297

Fort Frontenac (FRAHN•tuh•nak) A French fort once located on the site of present-day Kingston, Ontario, in southeastern Canada. (44°N, 76°W) p. 297

Fort Gibson A fort in what is now eastern Oklahoma; end of the Trail of Tears. (36°N, 95°W) p. 441

Fort Halifax A British fort in what is now Maine. p. 297

Fort Hall A fort in what is now southeastern Idaho; located on the Snake River, at a junction on the Oregon Trail. p. 446

Fort Laramie A fort in what is now southeastern Wyoming; located on the Oregon Trail. (42°N, 105°W) p. 446

Fort Le Boeuf A French fort in what is now Pennsylvania. p. 297

Fort Ligonier (lig•uh•NIR) A British fort; located in what is now southern Pennsylvania near the Ohio River. p. 297

Fort Mandan A fort in present-day central North Dakota, on the Missouri River; site of a winter camp for the Lewis and Clark expedition. (48°N, 104°W) p. 429

Fort McHenry The Baltimore fort where a battle inspired the writing of "The Star-Spangled Banner." p. 438

Fort Mose (Moh•SAY) A town in Spanish Florida started by free Africans. (30°N, 81°W) p. 266

Fort Necessity A British fort located in southwestern Pennsylvania; located in present-day Great Meadows. (38°N, 80°W) p. 294

Fort Niagara A fort located in present-day western New York, at the mouth of the Niagara River. (43°N, 79°W) p. 297

Fort Oswego A British fort; located in western New York, on the shore of Lake Ontario. (43°N, 77°W) p. 297

GAZETTEER

Fort Sumter A fort on an island guarding the harbor of Charleston; the site of the first battle in the Civil War. p. 492

Fort Ticonderoga (ty•kahn•der•OH•gah) A historic fort on Lake Champlain, in present-day northeastern New York. (44°N, 73°W) p. 297

Fort Vancouver A fort in present-day southwestern Washington, on the Columbia River; the western end of the Oregon Trail; present-day Vancouver. (45°N, 123°W) p. 446

Fort Wagner The site of a major Civil War battle in South Carolina. (45°N, 87°W) p. 507

Fort Walla Walla A fort in what is now southeastern Washington; located on the Oregon Trail. (46°N, 118°W) p. 446

Fort William Henry A British fort located in what is now eastern New York. (43°N, 74°W) p. 297

Four Corners The place in the Southwest where Utah, Colorado, Arizona, and New Mexico meet. p. 58

Frankfort The capital of Kentucky; located in the northern part of the state. (38°N, 85°W) p. 15

G

Gadsden Purchase The purchase of part of what are now New Mexico and Arizona from Mexico in 1853. p. 449

Germantown Part of present-day Philadelphia; site of a major Revolutionary War battle in 1777. (40°N, 75°W) p. 237

Gettysburg The site in Pennsylvania of one of the deadliest Civil War battles; the turning point of the war. p. 508

Golconda (gahl•KAHN•duh) A city in the southeastern corner of Illinois; a point on the Trail of Tears. (37°N, 88°W) p. 441

Grand Canyon A canyon in northwestern Arizona, formed by the Colorado River. p. 32

Great Basin An area of dry land that includes Nevada and parts of five neighboring states. p. 27

Great Lakes A chain of the largest five lakes in the United States and North America; located along the border between the United States and Canada. p. 31

Great Plains Western part of the Interior Plains. p. 73

Great Salt Lake The saltwater lake in Utah. p. 31

Great Wagon Road A former route used in the mid-1700s by colonists moving to settle in the backcountry. p. 257

Greenland The largest island on Earth; located in the northern Atlantic Ocean, east of Canada. p. 24

Guilford Courthouse (GIL•ferd) A location in north-central North Carolina, near Greensboro; site of a major Revolutionary War battle in 1781. (36°N, 80°W) p. 359

Gulf of Alaska A large gulf that lies south of Alaska along the Pacific coast. p. 24

Gulf of California An inlet of the Pacific Ocean; located between Baja California and the northwestern coast of Mexico. p. 24

Gulf of Mexico The largest gulf bordering the United States. p. 15

H

Harrisburg The capital of Pennsylvania; located in the southern part of the state, near the Susquehanna River. (40°N, 77°W) p. 15

Hartford The capital of Connecticut; located in the center of the state, near the Connecticut River. (42°N, 73°W) p. 15

Havana The capital of Cuba; located on the northwestern coast of the country. (23°N, 82°W) p. 131

Hawikuh (hah•wee•KOO) A former village in southwestern North America; located on the route of the Spanish explorer Coronado in present-day northwestern New Mexico. (35°N, 109°W) p. 131

Helena (HEH•luh•nuh) The capital of Montana; located in the western part of the state. (46°N, 112°W) p. 15

Hispaniola (ees•pah•NYOH•lah) An island in the West Indies made up of Haiti and the Dominican Republic; located in the Caribbean Sea between Cuba and Puerto Rico. p. 131

Honolulu The capital of Hawaii; located on the island of Oahu. (21°N, 158°W) p. 15

Hopewell An ancient settlement of the Mound Builders; located in present-day southern Ohio. (39°N, 83°W) p. 56

Hudson Bay A sea in Canada surrounded by the Northwest Territories, Manitoba, Ontario, and Quebec; named for the explorer Henry Hudson. p. 142

Hudson River A river in the northeastern United States beginning in upper New York and flowing into the Atlantic Ocean; named for the explorer Henry Hudson. p. 32

I

Illinois River A river in Illinois and a tributary of the Mississippi River. p. 32

Independence A city in western Missouri; the starting point of the Oregon and Santa Fe Trails. (39°N, 94°W) p. 446

Indian Ocean One of Earth's four oceans; located east of Africa, south of Asia, west of Australia, and north of Antarctica. p. R19

Indianapolis (in•dee•uh•NA•puh•luhs) The capital of Indiana; located in the center of the state. (40°N, 86°W) p. 15

GAZETTEER

Interior Plains The plains that stretch across the middle of the country, from the Appalachians in the east to the Rocky Mountains in the west. p. 26

Isthmus of Panama A strip of land that connects North America and South America. p. 123

Jackson The capital of Mississippi; located in the southern part of the state. (32°N, 90°W) p. 15

Jamaica (juh•MAY•kuh) An island country in the West Indies; south of Cuba. p. 131

James River A major river in Virginia; settlers used this river to settle Jamestown. p. 32

Jamestown The first permanent English settlement in the Americas. (37°N, 76°W) p. 156

Jefferson City The capital of Missouri; located in the center of the state, near the Missouri River. (38°N, 92°W) p. 15

Juneau (JOO•noh) The capital of Alaska; located in the southeastern part of the state. (55°N, 120°W) p. 15

Kaskaskia (kas•KAS•kee•uh) A village in southwestern Illinois; site of a major Revolutionary War battle in 1778. (38°N, 90°W) p. 358

Kennebec River (KEN•uh•bek) A river in west central and southern Maine; flows south from Moosehead Lake to the Atlantic Ocean. p. 202

Kings Mountain A ridge in northern South Carolina and southern North Carolina; site of a Revolutionary War battle in 1780. p. 358

Knoxville A city in Tennessee. (36°N, 84°W) p. 38

La Venta An ancient settlement of the Olmec; located in present-day southern Mexico, on an island near the Tonalé River. (18°N, 94°W) p. 56

Labrador A peninsula in northeastern North America. p. 24

Labrador Sea Located south of Greenland and northeast of North America. p. 24

Lake Champlain (sham•PLAYN) A lake between New York and Vermont. p. 202

Lake Erie The fourth-largest of the Great Lakes; borders Canada and the United States. p. 32

Lake Huron The second-largest of the Great Lakes; borders Canada and the United States. p. 32

Lake Michigan The third-largest of the Great Lakes; borders Michigan, Illinois, Indiana, and Wisconsin. p. 32

Lake Okeechobee (oh•kuh•CHOH•bee) A large lake in southern Florida. p. 32

Lake Ontario The smallest of the Great Lakes; borders Canada and the United States. p. 32

Lake Superior The largest of the Great Lakes; borders Canada and the United States. p. 32

Lake Tahoe A lake on the California-Nevada border. p. 32

Lancaster A city in southeastern Pennsylvania. (40°N, 76°W) p. 229

Lansing The capital of Michigan; located in the southern part of the state. (43°N, 85°W) p. 15

Las Vegas A major city in Nevada. (36°N, 115°W) p. 38

Lexington A town in northeastern Massachusetts; site of the first battle of the Revolutionary War in 1775. (42°N, 71°W) p. 314

Lincoln The capital of Nebraska; located in the southeastern part of the state. (41°N, 97°W) p. 15

Little Rock The capital of Arkansas; located in the center of the state, near the Arkansas River. (35°N, 92°W) p. 15

Long Island An island located east of New York City and south of Connecticut; lies between Long Island Sound and the Atlantic Ocean. p. 229

Los Angeles The largest city in California; located next to the Pacific Ocean; founded by Spanish settlers in 1781. (34°N, 119°W) p. 380

Louisiana Purchase A region of land that doubled the size of the nation when it was purchased from France in 1803; extended from the Mississippi River to the Rocky Mountains and from the Gulf of Mexico to Canada. p. 429

M

Macon (MAY•kuhn) A city in central Georgia; located on the Ocmulgee River. (33°N, 84°W) p. 454

Madison The capital of Wisconsin; located in the southern part of the state. (43°N, 89°W) p. 15

Manassas Junction A site in Virginia where the Battle of Bull Run was fought. p. 500

Medford A city in northeastern Massachusetts, north of Boston. (42°N, 71°W) p. 314

Mediterranean Sea (meh•duh•tuh•RAY•nee•uhn) An inland sea, enclosed by Europe on the west and north, Asia on the east, and Africa on the south. p. R20

Menotomy Town in northeastern Massachusetts where Minutemen attacked British forces after the Battles of Lexington and Concord. (42°N, 71°W) p. 314

Merrimack River A river in southern New Hampshire and northeastern Massachusetts; empties into the Atlantic Ocean. p. 202

Mesabi Range An area west of Lake Superior where iron ore was found in 1887; helped the steel industry spread to more areas. p. 532

Mexican Cession A region that included all of California, Nevada, Utah, and parts of New Mexico, Arizona, Colorado, and Wyoming acquired by the United States in 1848. p. 449

Mexico City A city built on the ruins of Tenochtitlan; the present-day capital of Mexico. (19°N, 99°W) p. 130

Milwaukee A city in Wisconsin. (43°N, 88°W) p. 38

Mississippi River Along with its tributaries, it is the largest river system in the United States; located through the nation's interior. p. 32

Missouri River A tributary of the Mississippi River; it begins in Montana and ends at St. Louis, Missouri. p. 32

Montgomery The capital of Alabama; located in the southern part of the state. (32°N, 86°W) p. 15

Montpelier (mahnt•PEEL•yer) The capital of Vermont; located in the northern part of the state. (44°N, 72°W) p. 15

Mormon Trail The pathway the Mormons followed to reach the Great Salt Lake Valley in present-day Utah. p. 447

Morristown A town in northern New Jersey; a campsite for the Continental Army during the Revolutionary War. (41°N, 74°W) p. 229

Moundville An ancient settlement of the Mound Builders; located in present-day central Alabama. (33°N, 88°W) p. 56

Murfreesboro A city in central Tennessee; located on the west fork of the Stones River; a site on the Trail of Tears. (36°N, 86°W) p. 441

Narragansett Bay An inlet of the Atlantic Ocean in southeastern Rhode Island. p. 201

Nashville The capital of Tennessee; located in the center of the state near the Cumberland River. (36°N, 87°W) p. 15

Natchitoches (NA•kuh•tahsh) The first settlement in present-day Louisiana; located in the northwest-central part of the state. (32°N, 93°W) p. 429

National Road A road built in 1818 that connected Maryland to present-day West Virginia. p. 453

the Netherlands A country of northwest Europe on the North Sea; also called Holland. p. 142

New Bern A city and port in southeastern North Carolina. (35°N, 77°W) p. 255

New Echota (ih•K•OH•tuh) A Native American town in northwestern Georgia; chosen as the capital of the Cherokee Nation in 1819. (34°N, 85°W) p. 441

New France The possessions of France in North America from 1534 to 1763; included Canada, the Great Lakes region, and Louisiana. p. 295

New Haven A city in southern Connecticut; located on New Haven Harbor. (41°N, 73°W) p. 202

New Netherland The area including the Hudson Valley and the lands around it. p. 226

New Orleans The largest city in Louisiana; a major port located between the Mississippi River and Lake Pontchartrain. (30°N, 90°W) p. 43

New Spain The North American lands once claimed by Spain, which included much of what is now Mexico, the southwestern United States, and Florida. p. 131

New York City The largest city in New York, originally founded by the Dutch and later taken over by the English; a major port city. (40°N, 74°W) p. 242

Newark A city in New Jersey. (40°N, 74°W) p. 229

Newfoundland An island off the eastern coast of Canada. p. 121

Newport A city on the southern end of Rhode Island; located at the mouth of Narragansett Bay. (41°N, 71°W) p. 189

Norfolk (NAWR•fawk) A city in southeastern Virginia; located on the Elizabeth River. (37°N, 76°W) p. 218

North America One of Earth's seven continents. p. I16

North Pole The northernmost point on Earth. p. I17

Northwest Territory Region west of the Ohio River that included what is today Minnesota, Wisconsin, Michigan, Illinois, Indiana, and Ohio. p. 367

Nueces River (Nu•AY•sahs) A river in Texas that Mexico claimed was the Mexican-American border. p. 448

Ocmulgee (ohk•MUHL•gee) An ancient settlement of the Mound Builders; located in present-day central Georgia. p. 56

Ocmulgee River A river in central Georgia; formed by the junction of the Yellow and South Rivers; flows south to join the Altamaha River. p. 255

Oconee River (oh•KOH•nee) A river in central Georgia; flows south and southeast to join the Ocmulgee and form the Allamaha River. p. 255

Ohio River A tributary of the Mississippi River; begins in Pittsburgh, Pennsylvania, and ends at Cairo, Illinois. p. 32

Ohio Valley A region claimed both by Britain and France in the early 1700s; stretched along the Ohio River from the Appalachians to the Mississippi River. p. 295

Oklahoma City The capital of Oklahoma; located in the center of the state, near the Canadian River. (35°N, 98°W) p. 15

Old Spanish Trail Part of the Santa Fe Trail that linked Santa Fe to Los Angeles. p. 446

Olympia (oh•LIM•pee•uh) The capital of Washington; located in the western part of the state near Puget Sound. (47°N, 123°W) p. 15

Omaha (OH•muh•hah) The largest city in Nebraska; the Union Pacific built its railroad west of it. (41°N, 96°W) p. 531

Oregon Territory Land in the Pacific Northwest that drew settlers looking for opportunities. p. 446

Oregon Trail A former route that started at Independence, Missouri, and led to the Oregon Country. p. 446

Ozark Plateau A plateau extending from southeastern Missouri across Arkansas and into eastern Oklahoma. p. 24

Pacific Ocean Largest body of water on Earth; extends from the Arctic Circle to the Antarctic regions, separating North and South America from Australia and Asia. p. 27

Palenque (pah•LENG•kay) An ancient settlement of Mayan civilization; located in present-day southern Mexico. (18°N, 92°W) p. 56

Pawtucket City in which the first American textile mill was built. p. 455

Pee Dee River A river in North Carolina and South Carolina; forms where the Yadkin and Uharie Rivers meet; empties into Winyah Bay. p. 255

Philadelphia A city in southeastern Pennsylvania, named by William Penn; a major United States port. (40°N, 75°W) p. 238

Philippine Islands A group of more than 7,000 islands off the coast of southeastern Asia, making up the country of the Philippines. p. 124

Phoenix The capital of Arizona; located in the southern part of the state. (33°N, 112°W) p. 15

Piedmont Area of high land on the eastern side of the Appalachian Mountains. p. 25

Pierre (PIR) The capital of South Dakota; located in the center of the state, near the Missouri River. (44°N, 100°W) p. 15

Platte River (PLAT) A river in central Nebraska; flows east into the Missouri River below Omaha. p. 32

Plymouth A city on Plymouth Bay in Massachusetts; the site of the first settlement built by the Pilgrims who sailed on the *Mayflower*. (142°N, 71°W) p. 164

Portland A port city in southwestern Maine; located on Casco Bay. (44°N, 70°W) p. 390

Portsmouth (PAWRT•smuhth) A port city in southeastern New Hampshire; located at the mouth of the Piscataqua River. (43°N, 71°W) p. 216

Potomac River (puh•TOH•muhk) A river on the Coastal Plain of the United States; begins in West Virginia and flows into Chesapeake Bay. p. 255

Princeton A township in west-central New Jersey; site of a major Revolutionary War battle. (40°N, 75°W) p. 358

Promontory The site in Utah where the transcontinental railroad was completed in 1869. p. 530

Providence (PRAH•vuh•duhns) The capital of Rhode Island; located in the northern part of the state, near the Providence River. (42°N, 71°W) p. 15

Pueblo Bonito (PWEH•bloh boh•NEE•toh) Largest of the prehistoric pueblo ruins; located in Chaco Canyon. p. 56

Puerto Rico An island of the West Indies; located southeast of Florida; a commonwealth of the United States. p. 131

Quebec (kwih•BEK) The capital of the province of Quebec, Canada; the first successful French settlement in the Americas; established in 1608. (47°N, 71°W) p. 171

Raleigh (RAH•lee) The capital of North Carolina; located in the eastern part of the state. (36°N, 79°W) p. 15

Red River A tributary of the Mississippi River; forms much of the Texas-Oklahoma border. p. 441

Richmond The capital of Virginia; the site of a Civil War battle. (38°N, 77°W) p. 15

Rio Grande A river in southwestern North America; forms the border between Texas and Mexico. p. 32

Roanoke Island An island near Virginia, known as England's lost colony. p. 155

Roanoke River A river in southern Virginia and northeastern North Carolina; flows into Albemarle Sound. p. 32

Rocky Mountains A mountain range that covers much of the western United States and Mexico through Canada and into Alaska. p. 27

S

Sacramento (sa•kruh•MEN•toh) The capital of California; located in the northern part of the state, near the Sacramento River. (39°N, 122°W) p. 15

Sacramento River A river in northern California. p. 32

Salem (SAY•luhm) The capital of Oregon; located in the western part of the state. (45°N, 123°W) p. 15

Salt Lake City The capital of Utah; located in the northern part of the state near the Great Salt Lake. (41°N, 112°W) p. 15

San Diego A large port city in southern California; located on San Diego Bay. (33°N, 117°W) p. 38

San Francisco A city in California; located on San Francisco Bay. (38°N, 123°W) p. 537

San Lorenzo The oldest Olmec city that scientists have discovered; located in what is now southern Mexico. (29°N, 113°W) p. 56

San Salvador An island in the Bahamas; Christopher Columbus landed there in 1492. p. 116

Santa Fe (SAN•tah FAY) The capital of New Mexico, founded by Spanish missionaries. (35°N, 106°W) p. 151

Santa Fe Trail A former commercial route to the western United States; extended from western Missouri to Santa Fe, in central New Mexico. p. 446

Santee River A river in southeast-central South Carolina; formed by the junction of the Congaree and Wateree Rivers; flows southeast into the Atlantic Ocean. p. 255

Saratoga A village in eastern New York; site of a major Revolutionary War battle in 1777. (43°N, 74°W) p. 349

Savannah The oldest city in Georgia; located on the Savannah River; also part of General Sherman's March to the Sea during the Civil War. p. 507

Savannah River A river that forms the border between Georgia and South Carolina; flows into the Atlantic Ocean at Savannah, Georgia. p. 255

Seattle The largest city in Washington; located on Puget Sound. p. 32

Seneca Falls A city in New York where a womens' rights convention was held in 1848. p. 484

Serpent Mound An ancient mound of the Mound Builders; located in present-day southern Ohio. (39°N, 83°W) p. 56

Sierra Madre Occidental (ahk•sih•den•TAHL) A mountain range in western Mexico, running parallel to the Pacific coast. p. 24

Sierra Madre Oriental (awr•ee•en•TAHL) A mountain range in eastern Mexico, running parallel to the coast along the Gulf of Mexico. p. 24

Sierra Nevada A mountain range in eastern California that runs parallel to the Coast Ranges. p. 28

Sioux Falls A city in South Dakota. p. 38

Snake River A river that begins in the Rocky Mountains and flows west into the Pacific Ocean; part of the Oregon Trail ran along the Snake River. p. 429

South America One of Earth's seven continents. p. I16

South Pass A pass in southwestern Wyoming; crosses the Continental Divide; part of the Oregon Trail. p. 446

South Pole The southernmost point on Earth. p. I17

Southern Ocean The Southern Ocean surrounds Antarctica and includes the southern parts of the Atlantic, Pacific, and Indian Ocean south of about latitude 60°S. p. I16

Spiro An ancient settlement of the Mound Builders; located in present-day Oklahoma. (35°N, 95°W) p. 58

Spokane A city in Washington. p. 38

Springfield The capital of Illinois; located in the center of the state. (40°N, 90°W) p. 15

Springfield A city in southwestern Missouri; a point on the Trail of Tears. (37°N, 93°W) p. 440

St. Augustine (AW•guh•steen) A city on the coast of northeastern Florida; the first permanent European settlement in what is now the United States. (30°N, 81°W) p. 151

St. Lawrence River A river in northeastern North America; begins at Lake Ontario and flows into the Atlantic Ocean. p. 140

St. Mary's City Maryland's first settlement, founded in 1633. p. 253

St. Paul The capital of Minnesota; located in the southeastern part of the state on the Mississippi River. (45°N, 93°W) p. 15

Susquehanna River (suhs•kwuh•HA•nuh) A river in Maryland, Pennsylvania, and central New York. p. 358

T

Tacoma A city in Washington. p. 38

Tallahassee (ta•luh•HA•see) The capital of Florida; located in the northwestern part of the state. (300N, 84°W) p. 15

Tampa Bay A bay on the west coast of Florida where Ponce De Leon landed. p. 32

Tennessee River A tributary of the Ohio River. p. 32

Tenochtitlan (tay•nohch•tee•LAHN) The ancient capital of the Aztec Empire, now the site of Mexico City. (19°N, 99°W) p. 130

Tikal (tih•KAHL) The largest Mayan city; located in present day Guatemala, in Central America. (17°N, 89°W) p. 57

GAZETTEER

Topeka The capital of Kansas; located in the northeastern part of the state. (39°N, 96°W) p. 15

Trail of Tears A 800-mile trail into the Indian Territory that was the result of the Indian Removal Act of 1830. p. 440

Trenton The capital of New Jersey, located in the west central part of the state; the site of a major Revolutionary War battle. (40°N, 74°W) p. 348

Tres Zapotes (TRAYS sah•POH•tays) An ancient settlement of the Olmec; located in southern Mexico. (18°N, 95°W) p. 56

Turtle Mound An ancient site of the Mound Builders; located on the present-day east-central coast of Florida. (29°N, 81°W) p. 56

Valley Forge A site in southeastern Pennsylvania, where the Continental Army camped during the winter of 1777. (40°N, 77°W) p. 350

Vicksburg A site in Mississippi of a major Civil War battle; a major turning point in the war. p. 507

Vincennes (vihn SENZ) A town in southwestern Indiana; site of a Revolutionary War battle in 1779. (39°N, 88°W) p. 358

Wabash River (WAW•bash) A river in western Ohio and Indiana; flows west and south to the Ohio River, to form part of the Indiana-Illinois border. p. 358

Washington, D.C. The capital of the United States; located between Maryland and Virginia, a special district that is not part of any state. (39°N, 77°W) p. 408

West Indies The islands enclosing the Caribbean Sea, stretching from Florida in North America to Venezuela in South America. p. R20

West Point A United States military post since the Revolutionary War; located in southeastern New York on the western side of the Hudson River. p. 357

Williamsburg A city in southeastern Virginia; capital of the Virginia Colony. p. 255

Wichita A city in Kansas. p. 38

Wilmington A city in southeastern North Carolina; was an important shipping center for forest goods during the colonial period. p. 270

Yellowstone River A river in northwestern Wyoming, southeastern Montana, and northwestern North Dakota; flows northeast to the Missouri River. p. 429

Yorktown A town in southeastern Virginia; located on Chesapeake Bay; site of the last major Revolutionary War battle in 1781. (37°N, 76°W) p. 360

Yucatan Peninsula A peninsula in southeastern Mexico and northeastern Central America. p. 24

Yukon River A river that flows from Canada through Alaska. p. 32

GAZETTEER

Glossary

The Glossary contains important history and social science words and their definitions, listed in alphabetical order. Each word is respelled as it would be in a dictionary. When you see this mark ′ after a syllable, pronounce that syllable with more force. The page number at the end of the definition tells where the word is first used in this book. Guide words at the top of each page help you quickly locate the word you need to find.

add, āce, câre, pälm; end, ēqual; it, īce; odd, ōpen, ôrder; tŏŏk, pōōl; up, bûrn; yōō
as u in fuse; oil; pout; ə as a in above, e in sicken, i in possible, o in melon, u in
circus; check; ring; thin; this; zh as in vision

A

abolish (ə•bä′lish) To end. p. 365

abolitionist (a•bə•li′shən•ist) A person who wanted to end slavery. p. 365

absolute location (ab′sə•lōōt lō•kā′shən) The exact location of a place. p. 20

acquit (ə•kwit′) Not guilty. p. 519

adapt (ə•dapt′) To adjust way of living to land and resources. p. 77

address (ə•dres′) A short speech. p. 508

adobe (ə•dō′bē) A brick or building material made of sun-dried earth and straw. p. 78

alliance (ə•lī′ənts) A formal agreement among groups or individuals. p. 296

ally (a′lī) A partner. p. 174

amendment (ə•mend′mənt) A change. p. 403

ancestor (an′ses•tər) An early family member. p. 53

annex (ə•neks′) To add to. p. 446

Anti-Federalists (an′tī•fe′də•rə•list) Citizens who were against ratification of the Constitution. p. 406

apprentice (ə•pren′təs) A person who lived and worked with an artisan's family for several years, learning a skill in order to earn a living. p. 244

arid (ar′əd) Dry. p. 39

arsenal (är′sə•nəl) A weapons storehouse. p. 389

artifact (är′tə•fakt) An object made by a person. p. 55

artillery (är•ti′lər•ē) Large mounted guns such as a cannon. p. 492

artisan (är′tə•zən) A craftworker. p. 244

assassinated (ə•sa′sən•āt•əd) Murdered in a sudden or secret attack. p. 511

assimilated (ə•si′mə•lā•təd) Adopted. p. 440

B

backcountry (bak′kən•trē) The land beyond, or "in back of," the area settled by Europeans. p. 257

barter (bär′tər) To exchange goods. p. 85

benefit (be′nə•fit) A reward that is gained. p. 114

bill (bil) An idea for a new law. p. 392

black codes (blak kōdz) Laws limiting the rights of former enslaved people in the South. p. 518

blockade (blä•kād′) To use warships to prevent other ships from entering or leaving a harbor. p. 312

boom (bōōm) A time of fast economic or population growth. p. 525

border states (bôr′dər stāts) States located between the North and the South that permitted slavery but had not seceded. p. 491

borderlands (bôr′dər•landz) Areas of land on or near the borders between countries, colonies, or regions. p. 151

boycott (boi′kät) To refuse to buy or use goods or services. p. 304

broker (brō′kər) A person who is paid to buy and sell for someone else. p. 270

budget (bu′jət) A plan for spending money. p. 299

bust (bust) A time of fast economic decline. p. 525

C

Cabinet (kab′ə•nit) A group of the President's most important advisers. p. 408

campaign (kam•pān′) A series of military actions carried out for a certain goal. p. 349

canal (kə•nal′) A human-made waterway that connects bodies of water. p. 453

cardinal direction (kärd′nəl də•rek′shən) One of the main directions: north, south, east, or west. p. I21

cash crop (kash krop) A crop that people grow to sell. p. 157

cause (kôz) An event or action that makes something else happen. p. 332

century (sen´chə•rē) A period of 100 years. p. 46

ceremony (ser´ə•mō•nē) A celebration to honor a cultural or religious event. p. 74

cession (se´shən) Something that is given up, such as land. p. 449

character traits (kâr´ik•tər trāts) A person's qualities and ways of acting. p. I5

charter (chär´tər) An official paper in which certain rights are given by a government to a person, group, or business. p. 199

checks and balances (cheks and ba´lən•səz) A system that keeps each branch of government from becoming too powerful or misusing its authority. p. 414

chronology (krə•nä´lə•jē) Time order. p. I3

civic virtue (si´vik vər´chōō) Qualities that add to a healthy democracy. p. 418

civil war (si´vəl wôr) A war between people in the same country. p. 493

civilian (sə•vil´yən) A person who is not in the military. p. 357

civilization (si•və•lə•zā´shən) A group of people with ways of life, religion, and learning. p. 56

clan (klan) An extended group of family members. p. 84

class (klas) A group of people in a society who have something in common. p. 57

climate (klī´mət) The kind of weather a place has over a long time. p. 23

collective bargaining (kə•lek´tiv bär´gən•ing) A process that allows employers and workers to discuss and agree on working conditions. p. 535

colony (kä´lə•nē) A land ruled by another country. p. 149

commander in chief (kə•man´dər in chēf´) A person who is in control of all the armed forces of a nation. p. 319

common (kä´mən) A grassy area shared by the town's people, and used for grazing sheep, cattle, and other livestock. p. 210

compact (käm´pakt) An agreement. p. 164

compass rose (kum´pəs rōz) A circular direction marker on a map. p. I21

compromise (käm´prə•mīz) To give up some of what you want in order to reach an agreement. p. 392

Confederacy (kən•fe´də•rə•sē) The states that left the Union to form their own national government called the Confederate States of America. p. 491

confederation (kən•fe•də•rā´shən) A loose group of governments working together. p. 65

congress (kän´grəs) A formal meeting of government representatives. p. 303

conquistador (kän•kēs´tə•dôr)) Any of the Spanish conquerors in the Americas during the early 1500s. p. 129

consent (kən•sent´) Agreement. p. 201

consequence (kän´sə•kwens) Something that happens because of an action. p. 431

constitution (kän•stə•tōō´shən) A written plan of government. p. 255

contiguous (kən•ti´gyə•wəs) Next to each other. p. 15

continent (kän´tə•nənt) One of Earth's seven largest land masses. p. 18

contour line (kän´tōōr līn) A line on a drawing or map that connects all points of equal elevation. p. 136

cost (kôst) The effort made to achieve or gain something. p. 114

cotton gin (kä´tən jin) A machine that could quickly remove the seeds from cotton. p. 456

council (koun´sel) A group of leaders who meet to make decisions. p. 74

Counter-Reformation (koun´tər re•fər•mā´shən) A time when the Catholic church banned books and used its courts to punish people who protested Catholic ways. p. 133

cultural region (kul´chə•rəl rē´jən) An area in which people share some ways of life. 60

debtor (de´tər) A person who was put in prison for owing money. p. 256

decade (de´kād) A period of ten years. p. 46

declaration (de•klə•rā´shən) An official statement. p. 325

delegate (de´li•gət) A representative. p. 296

demand (di•mand´) A need or a desire for a good or service by people willing to pay for it. p. 172

democracy (di•mä´krə•sē) A form of government in which the people rule and are free to make choices about their lives and their government. p. 417

dictator (dik´tā•tər) A leader who has complete control of the government. p. 445

dissent (di•sent´) Disagreement. p. 200

diverse economy (də•vûrs´i•kö•nə•mē) An economy that is based on many industries rather than just a few. p. 477

diversity (də•vûr´sə•tē) Differences among people. p. 235

division of labor (də•vi´zhən uv lā´bər) Work that is divided so that it is possible to produce more goods. p. 63

documentary sources (dä•kyə•men´tə•rē sôrs´əz) An item produced by a person after experiencing a historical event. p. 362

drainage basin (drā´nij bā´sən) The land drained by a river system. p. 32

due process of law (doo prä´ses uv lô) The principle that guarantees that people have the right to a fair trial by jury. p. 407

earthwork (ûrth´wərk) A wall made of earth and stone. p. 320

economy (i•kä´nə•mē) The way people of a state, region, or country use resources to meet their needs. p. 84

effect (i•fekt´) The result of an event or action. p. 332

efficiency (i•fi´shən•sē) Using less energy to do the same tasks. p. 45

electoral college (i•lek´tə•rəl kä´lij) A group chosen by citizens to vote for the President. p. 401

elevation (e•lə•vā´shən) The height of land in relation to sea level. p. 37

emancipate (i•man´si•pāt) To free. p. 501

empire (em´pīr) A collection of lands ruled by the nation that won control of them. p. 112

enlist (in•list´) To sign up or to join. p. 347

entrepreneur (än•trə•prə•nûr´) A person who sets up and runs a business. p. 114

environment (en•vī´rən•mənt) The surroundings in which people, plants, and animals live. p. 26

equator (ē•kwā´tər) The imaginary line that divides Earth into the Northern and Southern Hemispheres. p. I16

erosion (i•rō´zhən) The gradual wearing away of the Earth's surface. p. 25

evidence (e´və•dəns) Proof. p. I2

executive branch (ig•ze´kyə•tiv branch) The branch of government that has the power to enforce the laws. p. 401

expedition (ek•spə•di´shən) A trip taken with the goal of exploring. p. 112

expel (ik•spel´) To force to leave. p. 200

export (ek´spôrt) A product that leaves a country. p. 217

fact (fakt) A statement that can be proved or checked. p. 206

fall line (fôl līn) A place where the land drops sharply, causing rivers to form waterfalls or rapids. p. 33

federal system (fe´də•rəl sis´təm) A system of government in which the power to govern is shared by the national and the state governments. p. 390

Federalists (fe´də•rə•list) Citizens who were in favor of ratifying the Constitution. p. 406

ford (fôrd) To cross. p. 447

forty-niner (fôr•tē•nī´nər) A gold seeker who arrived in California in 1849. p. 450

free market (frē mär´kət) An economic system where people are free to choose the goods and services they buy and make. p. 215

free state (frē´ stāt) A state that did not allow slavery before the Civil War. p. 478

freedmen (frēd´mən) Men, women, and children who had been enslaved. p. 520

frontier (frən•tir´) The lands beyond the areas already settled. p. 204

fugitive (fyoo•jə•tiv) Someone who escapes from the law. p. 480

gap (gap) A low place between mountains. p. 427

gold rush (gōld rush) A sudden rush of people to an area where gold has been found. p. 450

grant (grant) A sum of money or other payment given for a particular purpose. p. 129

Great Awakening (grāt ə•wā´kən•ing) A religious movement that began in the Middle Colonies that changed the way many people practiced their religion. p. 236

grid system (grid sis´təm) An arrangement of lines that divide a map into squares. p. I22

grievance (grē´vəns) A complaint. p. 326

gulf (gulf) A large inlet. p. 31

hacienda (ä•sē•en´dä) A large estate or home where cattle and sheep are raised. p. 152

harpoon (här•pōōn´) A long spear with a sharp shell point. p. 82

hemisphere (he´mə•sfir) One half of Earth. p. I17

hogan (hō´gän) A cone-shaped Navajo shelter built by covering a log frame with mud or adobe. p. 78

homesteader (hōm´sted•ər) A person who settled on the land granted by the government. p. 527

human feature (hyōō´mn fē´chər) Something created by people, such as a building or a road, that alters the land. p. 42

igloo (i´glōō) A house made of snow or ice. p. 86

immigrant (i´mi•grənt) A person who comes into a country to make a new life. p. 235

impeach (im•pēch´) To accuse a government official of a crime. p. 401

imperial policy (im•pir´ē•əl pä´lə•sē) Laws and orders issued by the British government. p. 305

import (im´pôrt) A product brought into a country. p. 217

impressment (im•pres´mənt) The taking of workers against their will. p. 437

indentured servant (in•den´chərd sûr´vənt) A person who agreed to work for another person without pay for a certain length of time in exchange for passage to North America. p. 157

independence (in•də•pen´dəns) The freedom to govern on one's own. p. 325

indigo (in´di•gō) A plant from which a blue dye can be produced. p. 269

Industrial Revolution (in•dus´trē•əl re•və•lōō´shən) The period of time during the 1800s when machines took the place of hand tools to manufacture goods. p. 455

industry (in´dəs•trē) All the businesses that make one kind of product or offer one kind of service. p. 216

inflation (in•flā´shən) An economic condition which results in an increase in the price of goods. p. 340

inlet (in´let or in´lət) Any area of water extending into the land from a larger body of water. p. 31

inset map (in´set map) A smaller map within a larger one. p. I20

interchangeable parts (in•tər•chān´jə•bəl parts) Parts that can be made exactly alike by machines. p. 456

interdependence (in•tər•də•pen´dəns) Groups of people who rely on each other. p. 270

intermediate direction (in•tər•mē´dē•it də•rek´shən) One of the in-between directions: northeast, northwest, southeast, southwest. p. I21

interpret (in•tur´prət) To explain. p. I2

irrelevant (i•re´lə•vənt) Something that does not relate to a subject. p. 504

irrigation (ir•ə•gā´shən) The use of canals, ditches, or pipes to move water. p. 44

isthmus (is´məs) A narrow strip of land that connects two larger land areas. p. 123

judicial branch (jōō•di´shəl branch) The court system, which is the branch of government that decides whether laws are working fairly. p. 402

justice (jus´təs) A judge. p. 402

justice (jus´təs) Fairness. p. 229

kayak (kī´ak) A one-person canoe made of waterproof skins stretched over wood or bone. p. 86

labor union (lā´bər yōōn´yən) A workers group that fights for better working conditions and pay. p. 534

land use (land yōōs) How the land is used. p. 42

landform region (land´fôrm rē´jən) A region that has similar landforms throughout. p. 23

legislative branch (le´jəs•lā•tiv branch) The branch of government that makes the laws. p. 400

legislature (le´jəs•lā•chər) The lawmaking branch of a government. p. 157

lines of latitude (līnz uv la´tə•tōōd) Lines on a map or globe that run east and west; also called parallels. p. 20

lines of longitude (līnz uv län´ja•tōōd) Lines on a map or globe that run north and south; also called meridians. p. 20

locator (lō´kā•tər) A small map or picture of a globe that shows where an area on the main map is found in a state, on a continent, or in the world. p. I21

lock (läk) A part of a canal in which the water level can be raised or lowered to bring ships to the level of the next part of the canal. p. 453

locomotive (lō•kə•mō´tiv) A railroad engine. p. 454

lodge (läj) A large round earthen house used by Central Plains Native Americans. p. 72

longhouse (lông´hous) A long wooden building in which several families could live. p. 64

Loyalist (loi´ə•list) A person who remained loyal to the British king. p. 339

majority rule (mə•jôr´ə•tē rōōl) The political idea that the majority of an organized group should have the power to make decisions for the whole group. p. 164

manifest destiny (ma´nə•fest des´tə•nē) Certain future. p. 448

map key (map kee) A part of a map that explains what the symbols on the map stand for. p. I20

map scale (map skāl) A part of a map that compares a distance on the map to a distance in the real world. p. I21

map title (map tī´təl) Words on a map that tell the subject of the map. p. I20

mercenary (mûr´sən•er•ē) A soldier who serves for pay in the military of a foreign nation. p. 347

meridian (mə•ri´dē•ən) A line of longitude that runs from the North Pole to the South Pole. p. 20

Middle Passage (mi´dəl pa´sij) The journey millions of enslaved Africans were forced to travel across the Atlantic Ocean from Africa to the West Indies. p. 218

migration (mī•grā´shən) The movement of people. p. 53

militia (mə•li´shə) A volunteer army p. 238

millennium (mə•le´nē•əm) A period of 1,000 years. p. 46

Minutemen (mi´nət•men) A member of the Massachusetts colony militia who could quickly be ready to fight the British. p. 314

mission (mi´shən) A small religious settlement. p. 151

missionary (mi´shə•ner•ē) A religious teacher sent out by a church to spread its religion. p. 133

modify (mä´də•fī) To change. p. 44

monopoly (mə•no´pə•lē) The complete control of a product or good by one person or group. p. 311

mountain range (moun´tən rānj) A group of connected mountains. p. 25

mutiny (myōō´tə•nē) Rebellion against the leader of one's group. p. 143

N

national anthem (na´shə•nəl an´thəm) The official song of a country. p. 438

nationalism (na´shə•nəl•i•zəm) Pride in one's country. p. 439

natural resource (na´chə•rəl rē´sōrs) Something found in nature, such as soil, plants, water, or minerals that people can use to meet their needs. p. 43

natural vegetation (nach´ə•rəl ve•jə•tā´shən) The plant life that grows naturally in a place. p. 38

naturalization (na•chə•rə•lə•zā´shən) The process of becoming a legal citizen of the United States. p. 418

naval stores (nā´vəl stōrz) Products used to build ships. p. 216

navigation (na•və•gā´shən) The science of planning and following a route. p. 112

negotiate (ni•gō´shē•āt) To try to reach an agreement among different people. p. 351

neutral (nōō´trəl) Not choosing a side in a disagreement. p. 339

nonrenewable resource (nän´ri•nōō´ə•bal rē´sōrs) Resources that cannot be made again by people or nature. p. 43

Northwest Passage (nôrth´west pa´sij) A waterway in North America thought to connect the Atlantic Ocean and the Pacific Ocean. p. 139

olive branch (ä´liv branch) An ancient symbol of peace. p. 322

opinion (ə•pin´yən) A statement that tells what a person feels or believes. p. 206

opportunity cost (ä•pər•tōō´nə•tē kôst) The thing a person gives up in order to get something else. p. 246

ordinance (ôr´dən•əns) A law or set of laws. p. 367

overseer (ō´vər•sē•ər) A hired person who watched enslaved people as they worked. p. 264

palisade (pa•lə•sād´) A wall made of tall wooden poles to protect a village from enemies. p. 64

parallel time lines (pâr´ə•lel tīm līnz) Two or more time lines that show the same period of time. p. 344

parallels (pâr´ə•lelz) A line of latitude. It is called this because parallels are always the same distance from one another. p. 20

Parliament (pär´lə•mənt) The lawmaking branch of the British government. p. 297

Patriot (pā´trē•ət) A colonist who was against British rule and supported the rebel cause in the American colonies. p. 339

petition (pə•ti´shən) A signed request made to an official person or organization. p. 313

petroleum (pə•trō´lē•əm) Oil. p. 533

physical feature (fi´zi•kəl fē´chər) Climate, water, or land forms. p. 41

pilgrim (pil´grəm) A person who makes a journey for religious reasons. p. 163

pioneer (pī•ə•nir´) An early settler of an area. p. 427

plantation (plan•tā´shən) A large farm. p. 150

planter (plan´tar) A plantation owner. p. 264

point of view (point uv vyōō) A person's perspective. p. I4

political party (pə•li´ti•kəl pär´tē) A group that tries to elect officials who will support its policies. p. 408

popular sovereignty (pä´pyə•lər sä´vrən•tē) The idea that government gets its power from the people. p. 417

population (pä•pyə•lā´shən) The number of people who live in an area. p. 18

population density (po•pyə•lā´shən den´sə•tē) The average number of people living in a certain area, usually one square mile or one square kilometer. p. 410

potlatch (pät´lach) A Native American celebration meant to show wealth and divide property among the people. p. 85

prairie (prâr´ē) An area of flat or rolling land covered mostly by grasses. p. 26

preamble (prē´am•bəl) An introduction; first part. p. 326

prejudice (pre´jə•dəs) An unfair feeling of dislike for members of a certain group because of their background, race, or religion. p. 502

presidio (prā•sē´dē•ō) A Spanish fort. p. 151

primary source (prī´mer•ē sôrs) A record or artifact made by a person who saw or took part in an event. p. 160

prime meridian (prīm mə•rid´ē•ən) The imaginary line that divides Earth into the Western Hemisphere and the Eastern Hemisphere. p. I17

principle (prin´sə•pəl) A rule that is used in deciding how to behave. p. 399

proclamation (prä•klə•mā´shən) A public announcement. p. 298

profit (prä´fət) The money left over after all costs have been paid. p. 157

profiteering (prä•fə•tir´ing) Charging an extra-high price for a good or service. p. 340

proprietary colony (prə•prī´ə•ter•ē kä´lə•nē) A colony owned and ruled by one person who was chosen by a king or queen. p. 176

proprietor (prə•prī´ə•tər) An owner. p. 229

prospector (präs´pek•tər) A person who searches for gold, silver, or other mineral resources. p. 525

prosperity (präs•per´ə•tē) Economic success. p. 242

protest (prō´test) To work against, or object to, a certain policy. p. 305

public agenda (pub´lik ə´jen•də) What the people need and want from the government. p. 417

quarter (kwôr´tər) To provide or pay for housing. p. 312

ratify (ra´tə•fī) To approve. p. 405

raw material (rô mə•tir´ē•əl) A resource that can be used to make a product. p. 155

Reconquista (rā•kōn•kēs´tä) The movement to make Spain all Catholic; also called the Reconquest. p. 115

Reconstruction (rē•kən•struk´shən) Rebuilding. p. 515

reform (ri•fôm´) To change. p. 133

Reformation (re•fər•mā´shən) A Christian movement that began in sixteenth-century Europe as an attempt to reform the Catholic Church; resulted in the founding of Protestantism. p. 133

reformer (ri•fôr´mər) A person who tries to improve society. p. 540

refuge (re´fyōōj) A safe place. p. 228

region (rē´jən) An area in which many features are similar. p. 15

relative location (re´lə•tiv lō•kā´shən) The position of one place compared to other places. p. 15

relevant (re´lə•vənt) Something that relates to a subject. p. 504

religious toleration (ri•li´jəs tä•lə•rā´shən) Acceptance of religious differences. p. 236

renewable resource (ri•nōō´ə•bəl rē´sōrs) Resources that can be made again by people or nature. p. 43

repeal (ri•pēl´) To cancel, or undo, a law. p. 304

represent (re•pri•zent´) To speak for. p. 158

representation (re•pri•zen•tā´shən) To have someone speak or act for you. p. 303

republic (ri•pub´lik) A form of government in which people elect representatives to run the government. p. 390

research (ri•sûrch´) To investigate. p. I2

reservation (re•zər•vā´shən) Land set aside by the government for use by Native Americans. p. 528

reserved powers (ri•zûrvd´ pou´ərz) Authority that belongs to the states or to the people. p. 407

resolution (re•zə•lōō´shən) A formal group statement. p. 325

revolution (re•və•lōō´shən) A sudden, complete change, such as the overthrow of an established government. p. 315

river system (ri´vər sis´təm) A river and its tributaries. p. 32

royal colony (roi´əl kä´lə•nē) A colony ruled directly by a monarchy. p. 158

rule of law (rōōl uv lô) The principle that every member of a society, even a ruler, must follow the law. p. 403

scarce (skers) In short supply. p. 73

secede (si•sēd´) To leave. p. 490

secondary source (se´kən•der•ē sôrs) A record of an event made by someone who was not there at the time. p. 160

secret ballot (sē´kret ba´lət) A voting method that does not allow anyone to know how a person has voted. p. 522

sectionalism (sek´shən•ə•li•zəm) Regional loyalty. p. 477

sedition (si•di´shən) Speaking in ways that cause other people to work against a government. p. 201

segregation (se•gri•gā´shən) The practice of keeping people in separate groups based on their race or culture. p. 522

self-government (self•gu´vərn•mənt) A system of government in which people make their own laws. p. 164

separation of powers (se•pə•rā´shən əv pou´ərz) The division of powers among the three branches of the national government. p. 400

settlement house (se´təl•mənt hous) A place that provided food, healthcare, and classes for immigrants. p. 540

sharecropping (sher´kräp•ing) A system of working the land in which the worker was paid by letting them keep a share of the crops they harvested. p. 520

skyscraper (skī´skrā´pər) A very tall steel-framed building. p. 532

slave state (slāv stāt) A state that allowed slavery before the Civil War. p. 478

slavery (slā´və•rē) The practice of holding people against their will and making them work without pay. p. 150

sod (säd) A layer of soil held together by the roots of grasses. p. 72

sound (sound) A long inlet that separates offshore islands from the mainland. p. 31

staple (stā´pəl) Something that is always needed and used. p. 77

states' rights (stāts rīts) The idea that the states, not the national government, should have the final say on all laws. p. 479

stock (stäk) Part ownership in a business. p. 155

strategy (stra´tə•jē) A long-range plan made to reach a goal. p. 499

strike (strīk) The stopping of work to make employers meet worker's demands. p. 534

suffrage (su´frij) The right to vote. p. 417

supply (sə•plī´) An amount of a good that is offered for sale. p. 172

surplus (sûr´plus) An extra amount. p. 77

tariff (tar´əf) A tax on imports. p. 479

technology (tek•nä´lə•jē) The use of scientific knowledge and tools to make or do something. p. 111

tenement (te´nə•mənt) A poorly built apartment building. p. 539

tepee (tē´pē) A cone-shaped tent made from wooden poles and buffalo skins. p. 73

territory (ter´ə•tôr•ē) Land that belongs to a nation but is not a state and is not represented in the national government. p. 367

theory (thē´ə•rē) An idea based on study and research. p. 53

time line (tīm līn) A diagram that shows events the time that events happened. p. 46

time zone (tīm zōn) A region in which a single time is used. p. 534

town meeting (toun mē´ting) An assembly of people in a New England town that made laws and elected leaders. p. 210

trade network (trād net´wərk) A system that allows people to get goods from faraway places. p. 80

trade-off (trād´ôf) The giving up of the chance to buy something in order to buy something else. p. 246

tradition (trə•dish´ən) A way of life or an idea handed down from the past. p. 57

traitor (trā´tər) Someone who acts against his or her own government. p. 359

transcontinental railroad (trans•kän•tə•nen´təl rāl´rōd) The railroad that crossed North America. p. 531

travois (trə•voi´) A device made of two poles fastened to a dog's harness, used to carry goods. p. 73

treason (trē´zən) The act of working against one's own government. p. 303

treaty (trē´tē) An agreement between countries about peace, trade, or other matters. p. 125

trial by jury (trī´əl bī jŏŏr´ē) The right of a person to be tried by a jury, or a group, of citizens to decide if the person is guilty or innocent of committing a crime. p. 229

triangular trade route (trī•ang´gyə•lər trād rŏŏt) Shipping routes that connected England, the English colonies, and Africa. p. 218

tributary (tri´byə•ter•ē) A stream or river that flows into a larger stream or river. p. 32

tundra (tun´drə) A cold, dry region where trees cannot grow. p. 39

turning point (tûr´ning point) An event that causes an important change. p. 349

Underground Railroad (un´dər•ground rāl´rōd) A system of secret escape routes that led enslaved people to free land. p. 485

union (yŏŏn´yən) An alliance that works to reach common goals. p. 414

veteran (ve´tə•rən) A person who has served in the military. p. 341

veto (vē´tō) To reject. p. 401

wampum (wäm´pəm) Beads cut from seashells to make designs that showed important decisions, events, or stories, or traded and exchanged for goods. p. 65

wigwam (wig´wäm) A round, bark-covered shelter. p. 66

GLOSSARY

Index

The Index lets you know where information about important people, places, and events appear in the book. All entries are listed in alphabetical order. For each entry, the page reference indicates where information about that entry can be found in the text. Page references for illustrations are set in italic type. An italic m indicates a map. Page references set in boldface type indicate the pages on which vocabulary terms are defined. Guide words at the top of each page help you identify which words appear on which page.

INDEX

INDEX

INDEX

Frontier, 204. *See also* Western frontier
Frontier Culture Museum (Staunton, Virginia), *251*
Fugitive, 480
Fugitive Slave Act, 480
Fulton, Robert, 454
Fun with Social Studies, 92–93, 180–181, 276–277, 372–373, 460–461, 548–549
Fundamental Orders, 202
Fur trade, 140, 163, 165, 166, 170, 171, 173, 174, *175*, 177, 227

G

Gadsden Purchase, 449
Gage, General Thomas, 312, 314, 320
Gálvez, Bernardo de, 352, 353, *353*
Games, of Native Americans, 62, *62*
Gao, 112
Gap, 427, *m427*
Garment workers, 534, *534*, *535*
Garrison, William Lloyd, 484
Gatherers, 55, 63, 66
Gazetteer, R67–R75
General Assembly (Pennsylvania), 229
General Court (Massachusetts), 210–211
Generalizing, 85, 470–471, 477, 478, 479, 481, 483, 486, 489, 490, 491, 493, 498, 499, 517, 519, 521, 523, 524, 525, 529, 533, 538, 540
Generators, 44
Geography
  of Appalachians, 25
  of Coastal Plain, 24
  of Interior Plains, 26
  of Intermountain Region, 27
  of Pacific Coast Region, 28
Geography Skills, I14–I15. *See also* Map and Globe Skills
Geography Terms, I18–I19
George II, king of England, 256
George III, king of England, 298, 310, 316, 322, *322*, 326, 328, *328*, 329
Georgia, *m255*, 256, 256–257
  agriculture in, 269
  in American Revolution, 358, *m358*
  in Civil War, 509
  in Constitution ratification vote, 406
  Native Americans in, 440
  secession of, 491

German settlers, 235, 257, 258
Germantown, Pennsylvania, 237
Geronimo (Native American chief), 529, *529*
Gerry, Elbridge, 405
Gettysburg, Battle of, 508, *508*, 509, *509*
Gettysburg Address, 508, *508*
Ghost town, 525, *525*
Glacier, 53, *m53*
Goats, *215*
Gold
  colonists' search for, 156
  explorers' search for, 130, 131, 135, 139, 141
  mining for, 524–525, *524*, *525*, 528
  settlers and, 440
  Seven Cities of, 130–131, 135
  on Western frontier, 524–525, *524*, *525*, 528
Gold rush, 450, *450*, 524, 525
Gompers, Samuel, 534–535
Good Night for Freedom, A, 472–473
Government, 56
  branches of, 398–403
  Cabinet in, 408
  checks and balances in, 413, *413*, 414
  of colonies, 151, 156, 157–158, 172, 177, 226–227, 229, 232–233, 253, 254, 255, 316–317, *316*, *317*
  confederation, 65
  constitutional democracy, 412
  corruption of, 521
  creating a plan for, 390–394. *See also* Constitutional Convention (Philadelphia, Pennsylvania)
  executive branch of, 401, *413*. *See also* President
  federal, 412–419, *413*, *419*
  federal system of, 390, 412–419, *413*, *414*, *415*
  formation of, 330–331, *330*, 408–409, *408*, *409*
  judicial branch of, 402–403, *413*, 414. *See also* Supreme Court
  legislative branch of, 157–158, **400**, *413*, 414. *See also* Congress
  local, 416
  of Middle Colonies, 226–227, 229, 232–233, 238
  of Native Americans, 57, 65, 67, 68–69, *68*, 74, 80
  North vs. South on, 479
  of Northwest Territory, 367
  protection of citizens' rights and, 418–419

republic, 390
self-government, **164**, 316, 330
separation of powers in, 400, 413
of Southern Colonies, 253, 254, 255
state, 415, *415*, 416, *416*, 518
state's rights and, 479
Governor, 350, *416*
Grain, *240–241*
Grand Council (Iroquois), 65
Grant, 129
Grant, Ulysses S., 507, 509, 510, *510*, 519
Graph(s)
  bar, *340*, *394*, 544, 545
  circle, 544, 545
  of colonial exports, *242*
  comparing, 544–545
  of free and enslaved population, 1750–1780, *394*
  of imports from Britain, 340
  line, 544, 545
Graphic organizers, 292, 336
Grasse, Francois Joseph Paul, 362–363
Grease, 533
Great Awakening, **236**, *236*, 249
Great Basin, 27, *m61*, 79, 80
Great Britain. *See* Britain
Great Compromise, 392
Great Lakes, 31, *31*, 64, 361
Great Migration, 541, *541*
Great Plains, 26, *26–27*, 527, *527*, 528, *528*. *See also* Plains Indians
Great Salt Lake, 31
Great Salt Lake valley, 447
Great Smoky Mountains, 25
Great Wagon Road, *256–257*, 257, *m257*
Greeley, Horace, 491
Green, Anna, 306, *306*
Greene, General Nathanael, 359
Greenland, 113, 142
Greenville, Treaty of, 368, 369
Grenville, George, 317, *317*
Grievances, 326
Gristmill, 241, *241*
Guadalupe Hidalgo, Treaty of, 449
Guatemala, 57
Guilford Courthouse (North Carolina), 359
Gulf, 31
Gulf of Alaska, 31
Gulf of Mexico, 31, 32, 33, 174, 176, 429, 499
Guns, *130*, 456
Gutenberg, Johannes, 111, *111*

H

Haciendas, 152
Hale, Nathan, 357
Hamilton, Alexander, 392, *392*, 408, 409
Hancock, John, 314, 327, 329
Handicrafts. *See* Crafts
Hannibal, Missouri, 33
Harbors, 225, *310–311*, 311
Harpers Ferry, West Virginia, 490
Harpoons, 82
Harquebus, *130*
Harrison, General William Henry, 438
Hartford, Connecticut, 202
Harvard College, 213, *213*
Hawaii, 15
Hayes, Rutherford B., 523
Hemispheres, *m20*, *mR6–R7*
Henry, Patrick, 303, 309, *309*, 389
Henry, prince of Portugal, 112
Henry VII, king of England, 121
Henry VIII, king of England, 163
Henry Street Settlement (New York City), 540
Heritage, 399, *399*, 442
Hessians, 347, 348
Hiawatha (Iroquois Indian), 65, 68
Hieroglyphs, 57
Highland climate region, 38, *m38*
Highways. *See* Roads
Hispaniola, 123, 153
Historical maps, 300–301, *m301*
Hog(s), *215*
Hogans, 78
Holidays
  Flag Day, 421
  Independence Day, 328
  Thanksgiving, *166*
Holland. *See* Dutch
Holland Land Company, 368
Homestead Act of 1862, 527
Homestead Steel Strike, 534
Homesteaders, 527, *527*
Hooker, Thomas, 202
Hopi Indians, 77, 78, *78*, 148
Hornbook, 212, *212*
Horses, 130, *130*, 152, 215
Hospitals, *239*, 264
House(s)
  adobe, 78
  of Ancient Puebloans, 59, *59*
  hogan, 78
  lodge, 72
  log cabin, *298*
  longhouse, 64, 84, *84–85*
  of Native Americans, 59, *59*, 64, 66, 72, *72–73*, 76–77, 78, 79

INDEX

INDEX

INDEX

INDEX

For permission to reprint copyrighted material, grateful acknowledgment is made to the following sources:

Atheneum Books for Young Readers, an imprint of Simon & Schuster Children's Publishing Division: From *The Courage of Sarah Noble* by Alice Dalgliesh. Text copyright © 1952 by Alice Dalgliesh and Leonard Weisgard; text copyright renewed © 1982 by Margaret B. Evans and Leonard Weisgard.

BookStop Literary Agency, on behalf of Steve Lowe: From *The Log of Christopher Columbus*, selections by Steve Lowe, translated by Robert H. Fuson. Compilation copyright © 1992 by Steve Lowe; translation copyright 1987 by Robert H. Fuson.

HarperCollins Publishers: Illustrations by Charles Santore from *Paul Revere's Ride: The Landlord's Tale* by Henry Wadsworth Longfellow. Illustrations copyright © 2003 by Charles Santore.

Holiday House, Inc.: From *A Good Night for Freedom* by Barbara Olenyik Morrow, illustrated by Leonard Jenkins. Text copyright © 2004 by Barbara Olenyik Morrow; illustrations copyright © 2004 by Leonard Jenkins.

Philomel Books, A Division of Penguin Young Readers Group, A Member of Penguin Group (USA) Inc., 345 Hudson St., New York, NY 10014: Illustrations by Robert Sabuda from *The Log of Christopher Columbus,* selections by Steve Lowe, translated by Robert H. Fuson. Illustrations copyright © 1992 by Robert Sabuda.

G. P. Putnam's Sons, A Division of Penguin Young Readers Group, A Member of Penguin Group (USA) Inc., 345 Hudson St., New York, NY 10014: Illustrations by Wendell Minor from *America the Beautiful* by Katharine Lee Bates. Illustrations copyright © 2003 by Wendell Minor.

Scholastic Inc.: From *If You Were There When They Signed the Constitution* by Elizabeth Levy. Text copyright © 1987 by Elizabeth Levy.

The University of Arizona Press: From "It Has Always Been This Way" in *Sa'anii Dahataal/ The Women Are Singing: Poems and Stories* by Luci Tapahonso. Text copyright © 1993 by Luci Tapahonso.

PHOTO CREDITS

PLACEMENT KEY: (t) top; (b) bottom; (l) left; (c) center; (r) right; (bg) background; (i) inset

COVER:
(bl) Farrell Grehan/Corbis; (cr) Bill Bachmann/Index Stock; (br) Joseph Sohn/Corbis; (bg) PhotoDisc; back cover: (tl) © Peggy and Ronald Barnett/Corbis

TITLE PAGE, END PAGES AND TABLE OF CONTENTS
Title Page: (c) © Peggy and Ronald Barnett/Corbis; (b) Joseph Sohn/Corbis; (bg) PhotoDisc. Front End Pages: (bg) Joseph Sohn/Corbis; (br) Bill Bachmann/Index Stock. Back End Pages: (t) © Peggy and Ronald Barnett/Corbis; (bl) Farrell Grehan/Corbis. iv (bg) Liz Hymans/Corbis; iv (b) Jeremy Woodhouse; v (fg) PlaceStockPhoto.com; vi (bg) Mark Lewis Photography/Mira.com; vi (bc) © Copyright The British Museum; vi (l) SuperStock; vii (l) Dave Bartruff/Corbis; vii (br) Nik Wheeler/Corbis; viii (bg) Michael Sheldon/Art Resource, NY; viii (r) CIGNA Museum & Art Collection; viii (l) Colonial Williamsburg Foundation; ix (bl) The Granger Collection, New York; ix (c) Royal Albert Memorial Museum, Exeter, Devon, UK/Bridgeman Art Library; x (c) The Pierpont Morgan Library/Art Resource, NY; x (l) National Portrait Gallery, London/SuperStock; x (bg) © Massachusetts Historical Society, Boston, MA, USA/Bridgeman Art Library; xi (cl) The Granger Collection, New York; xi (cr) The Granger Collection, New York; xi (l) American Antiquarian Society; xi (r) Museum of Fine Arts, Boston, Massachusetts, USA, Bequest of Winslow Warren/Bridgeman Art Library; xii (bg) Bettmann/Corbis; xii (c) Winterthur Museum, Garden & Library; xii (l) Atwater Kent Museum of Philadelphia, Courtesy of Historical Society of Pennsylvania Collection/Bridgeman Art Library; xii (r) The Granger Collection, New York; xiii (cl) American Numismatic Society; xiii (l) The Granger Collection, New York; xiii (tl) Marilyn "Angel" Wynn/Nativestock.com; xiii (r) Henry Francis Dupont Winterthur Museum, Delaware, USA/Bridgeman Art Library; xiii (c) Private Collection/Bridgeman Art Library; xiv (l) National Portrait Gallery, Smithsonian Institution/Art Resource, NY; xiv (bg) Bettmann/Corbis; xiv (c) Don Troiani/Historical Image Bank; xiv (r) Daniel E. Greene; xv (tr) Royalty-Free/Richard Morris Hunt/Corbis; xv (l) Bettmann/Corbis; xv (r) SuperStock.

INTRODUCTION
I2 (r) Courtesy of APVA Preservation Virginia; I2 (l) John Maier, Jr./The Image Works, Inc.; I2 (c) Social History Division/Smithsonian Institution, National Museum of American History; I3 (tr) Victoria and Albert Museum London/Eileen Tweedy/Art Archive; I3 (br) Joseph Sohm; Visions of America/Corbis; I3 (l) © The Granger Collection, New York; I4 (l) Bettmann/Corbis; I4 (c) Royal Albert Memorial Museum, Exeter, Devon, UK/Bridgeman Art Library; I4 (r) Bettmann/Corbis; I5 (r) David R. Frazier Photolibrary, Inc./Alamy Images; I5 (l) Bettmann/Corbis; I5 (tr) Smithsonian Institution, NNC, Jeff Tinsley; I6 (l) Royalty-Free/Corbis; I6 (br) © Künstler Enterprises; I7 (tl) Marilyn "Angel" Wynn/Nativestock.com; I7 (t) © Archivo Iconografico, S.A./Corbis; I7 (br) © John Slemp/Look South; I7 (l) Museum of the City of New York/Corbis; I14 (tl) Gala/SuperStock; I14 (br) Patrick Eden/Alamy Images; I15 (bc) Mitchell Funk/Image Bank/Getty Images; I15 (tl) Vince Streano/Corbis; I15 (cl) John Lamb/Stone/Getty Images.

UNIT 1
OH 1A (bg) Richard A. Cooke/Corbis; (b) Marilyn Angel Wynn/Nativestock.com; OH 1B (cl) Marilyn Angel Wynn/Nativestock.com; (cr) Paul Gowder; Opener: The Granger Collection, New York; 7 (br) Yoshio Tomii/SuperStock; 12 (bcr) ThinkStock LLC; 12 (bc) Tributary- Connie Ricca/Corbis; 13 (bg) © Ron Watts/CORBIS; 14 (inset) John Mahoney/ Corbis; 16 (l) David Hosking; 16 (b) Carr Clifton; 16 (cr) Scott Lanza; 16 (bcr) Getty Images; 16 (bcl) Copyright © HANLEY, KEVIN & SUZETTE/Animals Animals; 16 (c) Copyright © LEONARD RUE ENTERPRISES/Animals Animals; 16 (br) James Martin; 16 (cl) Phyllis Greenberg/Animals Animals; 16 (tr) Lester Lefkowitz/Corbis; 16 (t) William Ervin/Science Photo Library; 16 (tl) Tom McHugh/Science Photo Library; 17 (t) David R. Frazier; 17 (tr) William Manning; 17 (br) Lynne Siler Photography/Alamy; 17 (bcr) Getty Images; 17 (cl) Getty Images; 17 (bl) Getty Images; 17 (tc) Copyright © STONE, LYNN/Animals Animals; 17 (tcl) Stephen Frink; 17 (bc) Sherwood Hoffman; 17 (cl) Herbert Schwind/Okapia/ Science Photo Library; 17 (c) Royalty-Free/Corbis; 17 (b) Royalty-Free/Corbis; 17 (tc) Picturequest/Tom & Pat Leeson; 18 (tl) Creatas/Fotosearch; 18 (b) Randy Faris; 22 (b) © The Mariners' Museum/CORBIS; 23 (inset) Bettmann; 25 (b) Jeremy Woodhouse; 26 (b) Bob Krist/CORBIS; 28 (b) © Ed Young/CORBIS; 29 (t) Owaki - Kulla; 30 Fotosearch Stock Photography; 34 (tl) Images Etc Ltd/Alamy; 35 Morton Beebe/Corbis; 36 (b) David Hiser; 39 Gary Randall; 41 Panoramic Images; 41 Kraemer Art Co./Library of Congress; 42 James Blair/Corbis; 42 (inset) Frank Whitney; 48 (l) Randy Faris; 48 (r) William Manning; 49 (r) Images Etc Ltd/Alamy; 49 (r) Gary Randall; 50 (bkgd) Jane Faircloth/Transparencies, Inc.; 50 (bl) Archivo Iconografico, S.A./CORBIS; 50 (br) Historical Picture Archive/CORBIS; 50 (bc) Newberry Library/Superstock; 57 (b) Louis Grandadam/Getty Images; 58 (b) © Martin Pate, Newnan, GA. Courtesy Southeast Archeological Center, National Park Service; 59 (t) Richard Sisk/Panoramic Images; 60 © Peter Harholdt/Corbis; 63 (t) © Ian Dagnall/Alamy Images; 66 (t) The Mariners' Museum/Corbis; 67 (tr) The Detroit Institute of Arts, USA; 69 (b) © Myrleen Cate/PhotoEdit; 69 (t) © Myrleen Ferguson Cate/PhotoEdit; 69 (c) Bob Daemmrich/ Stock Boston; 70 © Natural Exposures, Inc.; 71 (inset) © Lowell Georgia/Corbis; 74 (b) Courtesy, National Museum of the American Indian, Smithsonian Institution 01/0617; 75 (t) © Greenwich Workshop Inc.; 78 (b) © PlaceStockPhoto.com; 81 (br) Monty Roessel

Resource, NY; 471 (br) Don Troiani Gallery; 474 (bl) Smithsonian American Art Musuem, Washington, DC/Art Resource, NY; 474 (bc) © Dave G. Houser/CORBIS; 474 (br) Mort Kunstler; 475 (bg) © Minnesota Historical Society; 478 (inset) © New-York Historical Society, New York, USA; 479 (tc) © Bettman/CORBIS; 479 (b) © CORBIS; 481 (b) The Granger Collection, New York; 482 (b) © Missouri Historical Society; 483 (t) The Granger Collection, New York; 484 National Portrait Gallery, Smithsonian Institution/Art Resource, NY; 484 (tl) The Granger Collection, New York; 484 (tc) Library of Congress; 484 (tr) © Bettman/CORBIS; 488 (b) Sophia Smith Collection; Smith College; Northampton, MA; 488 (t) Abolition of Colonial Slavery Meeting, 1830 (letterpress), English School, (19th century)/Private Collection, ;/Bridgeman Art Library; 489 (tl) Mort Kunstler; 489 (tr) Library of Congress; 490 (tc) (c) CORBIS; 490 (tl) Public Domain - The Freeport Wide Awake, Nov. 17, 1860, p.3/http://elections.harpweek.com/1860/cartoons-1860-list.asp?Year=1860; 490 (tr) The Granger Collection, New York; 492 (t) Bettmann/Corbis; 492 (inset) Fort Sumter National Monument, U.S. National Park Service; 494 (tl) National Portrait Gallery; 494 (tr) Library of Congress; 495 (l) National Portrait Gallery, Smithsonian Institution; 496 (bg) Abraham Lincoln Presidential Library and Museum; 496 (inset) Abraham Lincoln Presidential Library and Museum; 497 (tr) Abraham Lincoln Presidential Library and Museum; 497 (tl) Abraham Lincoln Presidential Library and Museum; 497 (tcl) Abraham Lincoln Presidential Library and Museum; 497 (tc) Abraham Lincoln

Presidential Library and Museum; 498 (b) Bettmann/CORBIS; 499 (l) Don Troiani Gallery; 499 (r) Don Troiani Gallery; 500 (b) Don Troiani/Historical Image Bank; 501 The Granger Collection, New York; 502 (bl) The Granger Collection, New York; 502 (bc) National Portrait Gallery, Smithsonian Institution/Art Resource, NY; 502 (br) Eleanor S. Brockenbrough Library, The Museum of the Confederacy, Richmond, VA; 503 (t) The National Guard - Historical Paintings - Heritage Series - Rick Reeves; 503 (tr) Massachusetts Historical Society; 504 (b) Tod Fredericks; 505 (t) © The Granger Collection, New York; 506 (b) Andy Thomas, Maze Creek Studio; 510 (b) Library of Congress; Search; civil war ruins 02660r; 514 (br) Corbis; 514 (bc) (c) CORBIS; 514 (bl) © The Granger Collection, New York; 515 (c) © George H. H. Huey/CORBIS; 516 (b) © CORBIS; 516 (c) Library of Congress; 517 (tc) White House Historical Association; 518 (b) Library of Congress; 519 (tr) © The Granger Collection, New York; 520 (t) The Granger Collection, New York; 520 (tl) The Granger Collection, New York; 521 (b) New York Historical Society; 523 (t) Library of Congress; 523 (tl) © CORBIS; 524 (b) Photo Collection Alexander Alland, Sr./Corbis; 524 (t) National Museum of American History, Smithsonian Institution; 527 Library of Congress/Fred Hulstrand History in Pictures Collection (NDSU, Fargo, N.D.); 528 Mort Kunstler; 529 Christie's Images/Corbis; 529 (bl) The Granger Collection, New York; 530 BuffaloSoldier.net; 532 (bcr) Library of Congress Prints and Photographs Division Washington, D.C. 20540 USA; 532 (tcl) Bettman/Corbis; 532 (tr) CORBIS; 533 (tcr)

Currier & Ives; a catalogue raisonné/compiled by Gale Research. Detroit, MI; Gale Research, c1983, no. 2809; 533 (bl) Bettmann/Corbis; 533 (br) Chicago Historical Society; 535 Brown Brothers; 536 SuperStock; 538 (b) Künstler Enterprises; 538 (t) Getty Images; 539 Library of Congress, Prints & Photographs Division, Detroit Publishing Company Collection, [LC-USZC4-1584]; 540 (inset) Library of Congress; 540 (t) Bettmann/CORBIS; 542 (tl) Jeff Greenberg/Photo Edit; 543 (br) National Portrait Gallery, Smithsonian Institution; 544 Bettmann/CORBIS; 546 Library of Congress/Fred Hulstrand History in Pictures Collection (NDSU, Fargo, N.D.); 547 (tl) BuffaloSoldier.net; 547 (tr) © CORBIS; 549 (bcr) Künstler Enterprises; 550 (tr) Fort Sumter National Monument, U.S. National Park Service; 550 (bc) Bettmann/Corbis;

OH 553A (bg) Roger Bicke/MIRA; (r) The Image Finders; (l) Andrew Sacks/Getty Images; (t) Corbis; OH 553B (l) Glenn Research Center/NASA; (tr) Elyria Chronicle Telegram/AP Images; 576 (b) PhotoEdit, Inc.; 578 (b) PhotoEdit, Inc.; 580 (b) (c) Jose Luis Pelaez, Inc./CORBIS; 581 (t) (c) Royalty-Free/Corbis; 582 (c) © Getty Images; 584 (b) © Reuters/CORBIS; 586 (b) © Lester LefKowitz/CORBIS; 588 Copyright © Jeff Greenberg/Photo Edit -- All rights reserved.; 589 © Svenja-Foto/zefa/Corbis; 590 (b) © Dana White/PhotoEdit; 592 (c) © Getty Images; 593 (t) Andre Jenny/Alamy. R22 London Entertainment/Splash News/Newscom.

All other photos © Houghton Mifflin Harcourt Publishers